Creating Consilience

New Directions in Cognitive Science

Common Sense, Reasoning, and Rationality
Edited by Renée Elio

Reference
Interdisciplinary Perspectives
Jeanette K. Gundel and Nancy Hedberg

Creating Consilience

Integrating the Sciences

and the Humanities

Edited by Edward Slingerland

and

Mark Collard

OXFORD

UNIVERSITY PRESS

OXFORD
UNIVERSITY PRESS

Oxford University Press, Inc., publishes works that further
Oxford University's objective of excellence
in research, scholarship, and education.

Oxford   New York

Auckland   Cape Town   Dar es Salaam   Hong Kong   Karachi
Kuala Lumpur   Madrid   Melbourne   Mexico City   Nairobi
New Delhi   Shanghai   Taipei   Toronto

With offices in

Argentina   Austria   Brazil   Chile   Czech Republic   France   Greece
Guatemala   Hungary   Italy   Japan   Poland   Portugal   Singapore
South Korea   Switzerland   Thailand   Turkey   Ukraine   Vietnam

Published by Oxford University Press, Inc.
198 Madison Avenue, New York, New York 10016

www.oup.com

Oxford is a registered trademark of Oxford University Press

Creating consilience : evolution, cognitive science
and the humanities / edited by Edward Slingerland and Mark Collard.
p. cm.
ISBN 978-0-19-979439-3 (hardcover : alk. paper)
1. Science and the humanities—Congresses.   2. Interdisciplinary approach to knowledge—Congresses.
3. Humanities—Philosophy—Congresses.   4. Science—Philosophy—Congresses.   5. Cognitive
science—Philosophy—Congresses.   I. Slingerland, Edward G. (Edward Gilman)   II. Collard, Mark.
AZ362.C74 2011
001.3—dc22

1 3 5 7 9 8 6 4 2

Printed in the United States of America
on acid-free paper

CONTENTS

ACKNOWLEDGEMENTS

We are extremely grateful to the following units of the University of British Columbia for providing financial support for the "Integrating Science and Humanities" workshop: the Peter Wall Institute for Advanced Studies, the Office of the Dean of Arts, the Brain Research Centre, the Cognitive Systems Programme, the Department of Psychology, the Department of Anthropology, the Department of English, the Department of Classical Near Eastern and Religious Studies, Department of Philosophy, and the Department of Asian Studies. We are also grateful to Steven Heine, Joseph Henrich, Ara Norenzayan, Eva Oberle and Jennifer Lundin Ritchie for helping to organize and run the workshop.

We would like to thank Jeff Pelletier for offering us the opportunity to include this volume in the Oxford University Press "New Directions in Cognitive Science" series, and for being both constantly encouraging and extremely patient during the long process of putting this volume together. Abraham de Jesus put in long hours smoothing out the style and formatting of the various contributions, and Clayton Ashton played an important role assisting Steven Pinker in preparing his chapter. Jan Lermitte did a wonderful job on the index preparation and gave very helpful copyediting advice, and we are grateful for the work of our production editor, Natalie Johnson, copyeditor Dee Josephson, and our project manager Michael Philo Antonie. We also thank the two anonymous reviewers for their many helpful suggestions.

Lastly, we would like to gratefully acknowledge the support we have received in the course of putting together this volume. We have both benefited greatly from the Government of Canada's Canada Research Chair Programme. ES is Canada Research Chair in Chinese Thought and Embodied Cognition and MC is Canada Research Chair in Human Evolutionary Studies. Our work on the volume has also been supported by a SSHRC Standard Research Grant (to ES), the Canada Foundation for Innovation, the British Columbia Knowledge Development Fund, Simon Fraser University and The University of British Columbia.

CONTRIBUTOR NOTES

Adam Arico is a graduate student in philosophy at the University of Arizona. He works at the intersection of philosophy of mind, psychology, and cognitive science. His research focuses on issues surrounding consciousness, folk psychology, and group minds, and their implications for ethics, metaethics, and moral psychology.

Alex Bentley is Professor of Archaeology and Anthropology at the University of Bristol. He has been deputy director of the Leverhulme "Tipping Points" program at Durham University (*www.dur.ac.uk/ihrr/tippingpoints*), a unique interdisciplinary project exploring abrupt change in climate, financial crises, and fashions. His new book with MIT press is called *I'll Have What She's Having: Mapping Human Behavior.*

Pascal Boyer studied philosophy and anthropology at University of Paris and Cambridge, where he did his graduate work with Professor Jack Goody, on the memory constraints on transmission of oral literature. He has done anthropological fieldwork in Cameroon on the transmission of Fang oral epics and on Fang traditional religion. Since then, he has worked mostly on the experimental study of cognitive capacities underlying cultural transmission. The aim is to gather behavioral, developmental, and neurocognitive evidence for domain-specific capacities in human minds. An anthropological application of these results was a series of studies on supernatural concepts and their retention in memory, as well as a more general description of the cognitive processes involved in transmission of religious concepts. After teaching in Cambridge, San Diego, Lyon, and Santa Barbara, Prof. Boyer moved to his present position at Washington University, St. Louis.

Daniel Buchman is a PhD student in the University of British Columbia's Interdisciplinary Studies Graduate Program, focusing on Bioethics and Neuroethics. His research examines ethical issues in addiction and mental health care. Daniel is a Frederick Banting and Charles Best Canada Graduate Scholar from CIHR, and an Ethics Fellow at Providence Healthcare in Vancouver, Canada.

Joseph Carroll is Curators' Professor of English at the University of Missouri, St. Louis. His books include *Evolution and Literary Theory, Literary Darwinism*, and *Reading Human Nature.* He produced an edition of Darwin's *Origin,* co-edited *Evolution, Literature, and Film,* and co-edited the first two volumes of *The Evolutionary Review.*

Mark Collard is Canada Research Chair in Human Evolutionary Studies and Associate Professor of Archaeology in the Department of Archaeology at Simon Fraser University in British Columbia, Canada. He is also the director of the newly established Human Evolutionary Studies Programme, which is an interdisciplinary research and training initiative involving faculty, postdocs and students from several SFU faculties. Dr. Collard's research interests span biological anthropology and archaeological science. Among the topics he has published on are the phylogenetic relationships of the hominins and other primates, the origin and evolution of genus *Homo*, the use of radiocarbon dates to investigate demographic change in the past, and the colonization of the Americas. Details of his publications can be found at the following website: http://www.sfu.ca/~mcollard/Marks_page.htm.

Raymond Corbey took degrees in philosophy, cultural anthropology, and psychology at Radboud University (Nijmegen, the Netherlands). Currently, he is Associate Professor in the Department of Humanities at Tilburg University, and Professor in the Department of Archaeology of Leiden University, both in the Netherlands. His research focuses on conceptual and methodological issues regarding human evolution, human-animal relations, and cultural diversity.

Barbara Dancygier is in the Department of English, University of British Columbia. Dr. Dancygier is a cognitive linguist, working primarily in construction grammar, mental-spaces theory, and blending. She is also interested in the interface between linguistics and literary study. She has published, among others, *Conditionals and Prediction*, *Mental Spaces in Grammar* (with Eve Sweetser), and *The Language of Stories*.

Brian Fiala is a graduate student in philosophy at the University of Arizona. He works in the philosophy of mind and cognitive science, with a special interest in the philosophical problems surrounding consciousness.

Will Gervais is pursuing his doctorate in social psychology at the University of British Columbia. His research targets the causes and consequences of religious (dis)belief.

Herbert Gintis is external professor at the Santa Fe Institute and professor of economics at Central European University (Budapest). He was a member of the Institute for Advanced Study, Princeton in 1973, assistant professor of economics at Harvard University, 1974–1975, and professor of economics at the University of Massachusetts, 1976–2002. He has been a visiting professor at the University of Siena, the University of Paris, Columbia University, New York University, and Harvard University. Professor Gintis is the author of *Game Theory Evolving (2009)* and *The Bounds of Reason (2009)*, and a co-author of *Schooling in Capitalist America (1975)*; *Foundations of Human Sociality (2004)*; *Moral Sentiments and Material Interests (2005)*; and *A Cooperative Species* (forthcoming, 2011).

Jonathan Gottschall teaches English at Washington & Jefferson College. He is the author of *The Rape of Troy: Evolution, Violence, and the World of Homer and Literature, Science, and a New Humanities,* and the co-editor of *The Literary Animal: Evolution and the Nature of Narrative and Evolution, Literature, and Film.*

William Scott Green holds an A.B. in religion from Dartmouth College and a Ph.D. in religion from Brown University. Currently, he is professor of religious studies and senior vice provost and dean of undergraduate education at the University of Miami, Florida. He is also Professor Emeritus of Religion, Philip S. Bernstein Professor Emeritus of Judaic Studies, and Dean Emeritus of the College at the University of Rochester, New York. He has held fellowships from the National Endowment of the Humanities, the American Council of Learned Societies, and the Andrew Mellon Foundation. He writes on ancient Judaism, the theory of religion, and entrepreneurship education.

Geoffrey Galt Harpham is director of the National Humanities Center. A literary scholar, he has become in recent years a prominent historian of, and advocate for, the humanities.

Under his leadership, the National Humanities Center sponsored a multiyear project that engaged humanists and scientists in a conversation on the impact of empirical work on our understanding of the human.

Judy Illes is professor of neurology and Canada Research Chair in Neuroethics at the University of British Columbia. She is director of the National Core for Neuroethics at UBC, and a faculty member in the Brain Research Centre at UBC and the Vancouver Coastal Health Research Institute. She also holds affiliate appointments in the School of Population and Public Health and the School of Journalism at UBC, and in the Department of Computer Science and Engineering at the University of Washington in Seattle, WA, USA. Dr. Illes' research focuses on ethical, legal, social, and policy challenges specifically at the intersection of the neurosciences and biomedical ethics.

Darren Irwin is an associate professor of zoology and member of the Biodiversity Research Centre at the University of British Columbia. His research on speciation in birds of Asia, Europe, and North America has been featured in journals such as *Nature, Science, Evolution,* and *Molecular Ecology.*

John A. Johnson is professor of psychology at the Pennsylvania State University. He spent the 1990–1991 year as visiting professor and Alexander von Humboldt-Stiftung Research Fellow at the University of Bielefeld, Germany. He has published widely on the personality and evolutionary psychology of moral and educational development, career choice, and work performance.

Dennis Krebs is a professor of psychology, a Woodrow Wilson Fellow, and Fellow of the Center for Advanced Study in the Behavioral Sciences. He received his MA and PhD degrees from Harvard University, where he taught for several years before returning to British Columbia to teach at Simon Fraser University. He has won university and national teaching awards, and published several books and more than 90 articles, most of which address issues of morality and altruism. In his latest book, *The Origins of Morality: An Evolutionary Account* (scheduled for publication by Oxford University Press), he presents a biologically based theory of morality that integrates and refines psychological approaches.

Daniel J. Kruger is a research professor at the School of Public Health and Institute for Social Research at the University of Michigan. His research interests include altruism, cooperation, competition, demography, life history, literary Darwinism, mortality patterns, risk taking, and interventions for social and ecological sustainability.

Sofia Lombera has recently completed a Master of Science degree at the London School of Economics and Political Science in Biomedicine, Bioscience and Society. Prior to enrolling in the program she was a Research Manager for the National Core for Neuroethics at the University of British Columbia.

Robert N. McCauley is William Rand Kenan Jr. University Professor of Philosophy and Director of the Center for Mind, Brain, and Culture at Emory University. He is the author of *Why Religion is Natural and Science is Not* and, with Tom Lawson, of *Rethinking Religion* and *Bringing Ritual to Mind.*

Angus Mol is a PhD candidate in the Faculty of Archaeology, Leiden University. His doctoral research, for which he has adopted theories from both the natural and social sciences, is on the form and function of exchange in the Pre-Colonial Caribbean.

Olivier Morin obtained his PhD in philosophy and social science under the supervision of Dan Sperber. His dissertation dealt with cultural transmission. He is currently Allocataire Moniteur Normalien at the Sorbonne University (Paris 4). Next year, he will be a postdoctoral researcher at the Central European University in Budapest.

Shaun Nichols is professor of philosophy at the University of Arizona. He has published widely at the intersection of philosophy and psychology. He is the author of *Sentimental Rules: On the Natural Foundations of Moral Judgment*, and co-author (with Stephen Stich) of *Mindreading: An Integrated Account of Pretense, Self-awareness and Understanding Other Minds*.

Ara Norenzayan is an associate professor of psychology at the University of British Columbia, Vancouver. He received his PhD from the University of Michigan, was a postdoctoral fellow at the Ecole Polytechnique, Paris, and served on the faculty of the University of Illinois, Urbana-Champaign before his appointment at UBC. His most recent work addresses the evolution of religious beliefs and behaviors.

Paul Ormerod is the author of three best-selling books on economics and complexity, *Death of Economics, Butterfly Economics* and *Why Most Things Fail*, a Business Week US Business Book of the Year. He is a visiting professor of anthropology at the University of Durham, UK, and a Fellow of the British Academy.

Steven Pinker is Harvard College Professor and Johnstone Family Professor of Psychology at Harvard University. His research has won awards from the National Academy of Sciences, the Cognitive Neuroscience Society, the Royal Institution of Great Britain, and the American Psychological Association. He is the author of seven books, including *How the Mind Works* and *The Stuff of Thought*.

Peter Schauer obtained his PhD at the Institute of Archaeology, University College London, with a study of the neutral model applied to motifs on Greek figure-painted pottery. He has since been working on a variety of projects, including the practical application of evolutionary theory to social media.

Bradd Shore holds the Goodrich C. White Chair in Anthropology at Emory University. He is the author of three books, including *Culture in Mind: Cognition, Culture and the Problem of Meaning* (Oxford) and many papers spanning both symbolic anthropology and cognitive anthropology. Shore is past president of the Society for Psychological Anthropology.

Richard A. Shweder, a cultural anthropologist, is the William Claude Reavis Distinguished Service Professor in the Department of Comparative Human Development at the University of Chicago. He is a member of the American Academy of Arts and Sciences and past president of the Society for Psychological Anthropology. He has been a Carnegie Scholar and a Guggenheim Fellow. His research is in the areas of cultural psychology and comparative ethics.

Edward Slingerland is Professor of Asian Studies and Canada Research Chair in Chinese Thought and Embodied Cognition at the University of British Columbia. His research specialties and teaching interests include Warring States (5th-3rd c. B.C.E.) Chinese thought, religious studies (comparative religion, cognitive science and evolution of religion), cognitive linguistics (blending and conceptual metaphor theory), ethics (virtue ethics, moral psychology), evolutionary psychology, and the relationship between the humanities and the natural sciences. His publications include *Effortless Action: Wu-wei as Conceptual Metaphor and Spiritual Ideal in Early China* (2003), the *Analects* of Confucius (2003), and *What Science Offers the Humanities: Integrating Body & Culture* (2008).

Stephen Stich is Board of Governors Professor of Philosophy and Cognitive Science at Rutgers University and Honorary Professor of Philosophy at the University of Sheffield. His publications include six books, a dozen anthologies, and over 150 articles. He is a member of the American Academy of Arts and Sciences.

Lawrence S. Sugiyama is an associate professor in the University of Oregon's anthropology department and Institute of Cognitive and Decision Sciences, where he co-directs the Shuar Health and Life History Project. His research addresses questions about the design of the human mind in relation to foraging risk, cooperation, health, parental and alloparental investment, attractiveness assessment, and cultural transmission.

Michelle Scalise Sugiyama is a research associate in the University of Oregon's anthropology department and Institute of Cognitive and Decision Sciences, where she serves as director of the Cognitive Cultural Studies Project. Her work examines narrative and related behaviors vis-a-vis the information demands of ancestral environments and the evolution of childhood.

Kate Tairyan obtained degrees from the State Medical University in Armenia, Armenia's National Institute of Health, and Emory University. Her public health expertise and work experience includes several positions at the Ministry of Health of Armenia and collaborations with international experts on health-policy development and poverty- reduction issues at national and local levels. In 2006 Dr. Tairyan joined Health Sciences Online as content director and moved to work at the University of British Columbia as a postdoctoral fellow. At UBC she is also a member of the National Core for Neuroethics and is spearheading a project to evaluate investigator needs for integrating ethics into neuroscience using imaging as the model. In addition, Dr. Tairyan is a sessional instructor in the Faculty of Health Sciences at Simon Fraser University.

Ranga Venkatachary's research interests include disciplinary subcultures and teaching within the disciplines. As senior curriculum strategist in the Faculty of Arts at the University of British Columbia, she facilitates program level curriculum renewal process and learning-centered pedagogical practice. She belongs to the UBC Leadership Cohort (2010–2011) in the Scholarship of Teaching and Learning.

Harvey Whitehouse is Chair of Social Anthropology and Professorial Fellow of Magdalen College at the University of Oxford. One of the founders of the cognitive science of religion, he has directed several international collaborative projects on the cognitive underpinnings and evolutionary dynamics of religion and ritual. His books include *Inside the Cult* (1995), *Arguments and Icons* (2000) and *Modes of Religiosity* (2004).

David Sloan Wilson is a Distinguished Professor at Binghamton University in New York. He applies evolutionary theory to all aspects of humanity in addition to the rest of life. His latest book is *The Neighborhood Project: Using Evolution to Improve My City, One Block at a Time* (Little, Brown 2011).

Creating Consilience

INTRODUCTION
CREATING CONSILIENCE: TOWARD
A SECOND WAVE

Edward Slingerland and Mark Collard

This volume emerged out of a workshop called "Integrating Science and the Humanities," held at the University of British Columbia in September 2008.[1] The relationship between the sciences and the humanities has long been a fraught one—a tension famously captured by C.P. Snow in the phrase "The Two Cultures" (Snow 1959/1993). The belief that humanists study "texts"—in the broad sense that this term has acquired in recent decades—whereas scientists study "things" is still commonplace in modern universities. The two groups typically perform their work in different parts of the campus, are served by separate funding agencies, and are governed in their work by radically different methodologies and theoretical assumptions. Attempts to bridge the two cultures have often taken the form of hostile takeovers: humanists trying to forcibly bring the work of scientists under the umbrella of arbitrary, interpretable "inscriptions"[2] or scientists arguing for the explanatory irrelevance of human phenomena not amenable to quantification.[3] The purpose of the workshop was to bring together scholars from across the sciences and humanities to explore the potential of an alternative approach—an approach that is referred to as "vertical integration" (Tooby and Cosmides 1992; Slingerland 2008a) or, increasingly commonly, "consilience" (Wilson 1998).

Consilience is often framed in terms of bringing the study of humanistic issues into the same framework as the study of non-human species and non-biotic phenomena (e.g.,Tooby & Cosmides 1992; Wilson 1998; Dennett 2009). However, we think this way

---

1. The workshop was made possible by a grant from the Peter Wall Institute for Advanced Studies. Additional support was provided by the Office of the Dean of Arts, the Brain Research Centre, the Cognitive Systems Programme, and the Departments of Psychology, Anthropology, English, Classical, Near Eastern and Religious Studies, Philosophy, and Asian Studies. For a full list of participants, all of whom contributed to this volume—if only through their questions and comments—see Appendix A. Videos of the workshop presentations and discussion sessions can be watched at http://www.sci-hum.pwias.ubc.ca/.

2. See, e.g., such classic examples of "strong program" science studies as Latour and Woolgar 1979/1986, or more recent calls for the humanities to subsume nature science into its magisterium of interpretation (Menand 2005).

3. For a recent characterization and critique of such "scientism" in the field of religious studies, see Cho and Squier 2008.

of describing the undertaking is not only unhelpful but also inaccurate. It is unhelpful in that it can give the impression that consilience involves the sciences engulfing the humanities—a prospect that is understandably off-putting for humanists. It is inaccurate because it was clear, before the consilience project was initiated, that significant changes would have to be made to the framework used to study non-human species and non-biotic phenomena in order to deal with a number of humanistic issues. Thus, in our view, it is better to think of consilience as an attempt to develop a new, shared framework for the sciences and humanities.

The idea that scholars' work should be informed by engagement with work outside their discipline is uncontroversial, and, indeed, the adjective *interdisciplinary* is bandied about as a term of approval in both the sciences and the humanities. However, the call for consilience, which requires extending interdisciplinarity across the sciences/humanities divide, has, for the most part, been met with by indifference or outright hostility by the majority of humanists. For instance, the work of the person responsible for popularizing the term *consilience* in recent years, E.O. Wilson, has, since the 1970s, inspired a backlash among humanists of such intensity and duration that it begs explanation.[4] Such hostility continues to be the default reaction of humanists to calls for approaches to human behavior informed by scientific theories, as evidenced by the spate of recent pieces in the popular press proclaiming—usually with undisguised glee—the death of evolutionary psychology or of the consilience project in general.[5] Why does the concept of consilience inspire such vociferous resistance among humanists? Are there ways in which the call for consilience could be modified or amended to make it more acceptable to humanists, or must the consilience project simply be abandoned? If consilience can be maintained as an ideal, what would a properly consilient approach to particular humanistic disciplines look like? These were the questions that the "Integrating Science and the Humanities" workshop was designed to explore.

In the remainder of this Introduction, we will outline the structure and content of the volume. We will then discuss a series of issues that the workshop and the contributors to this volume suggest need to be resolved if the consilience project is to advance. Lastly, we will summarize some of the conclusions that emerged concerning what a "second wave" of consilience—one in which humanists and scientists work together as equal partners in constructing a shared framework for inquiry—might look like.

STRUCTURE AND CONTENT OF THE VOLUME

Although by its very nature the workshop primarily attracted scholars with a positive attitude toward consilience, the organizing committee made an effort to include colleagues who are skeptical of consilience as well, and this volume, therefore, includes contributions that express a range of opinions regarding the desirability or possibility of consilience. So, although we will attempt to extract from both the volume contributions and the workshop discussions an integrated vision of how the project of consilience can

4. See Segerstråle 2000 for a helpful account of the reception of consilience in the academy.
5. See, for instance, Begley 2009 or Brooks 2009.

be advanced, we wish to emphasize that not all the contributors to the workshop or the volume are likely to agree with the vision.

The volume is divided into two parts. Part I, consisting of two sections, addresses some of the general theoretical issues raised by consilience. Section 1, "Ontologies for the Human," concerns itself with what emerged at the workshop as the most fundamental of these issues: the question of how we conceive of human beings. Many of the dichotomies that coordinate with the sciences/humanities divide—explanation/interpretation, biology/culture, nature/nurture, determination/freedom—can be boiled down to the intuition that human minds belong to a fundamentally different order of reality than human bodies. The chapters in this section (chapters 1–4), therefore, explore the manner in which body-mind dualism relates to the current divide between the "Two Cultures," as well as the likelihood and desirability of moving beyond this dualism. The four chapters fall roughly into two subsets. In chapters 1 and 2, two leading theorists in the debate surrounding consilience, Steven Pinker and Richard Shweder, respectively defend and critique the argument that human-level realities can and should be studied against a background assumption of physicalist monism, with the human mind and its products being seen as ontologically continuous with the non-human world. Chapters 3 and 4, although ultimately siding with Pinker, attempt to explore the too-often overlooked fact that human beings seem intuitively resistant to such monism, and that innate folk dualism might mean that—at some level of cognition—humans will *always* be resistant to physicalism. Since this particular issue emerged as one of the central concerns of the workshop, we will delay a more detailed discussion of the chapters in this section to the examination of mind-body dualism that occurs later.

Section 2, "Consilience through the Lens of Anthropology," adopts a somewhat more narrow perspective on the problems and prospects of consilience by focusing on the discipline of anthropology. We have singled out anthropology in this way because it uniquely straddles the sciences/humanities divide. Eric Wolf famously described anthropology as the "most scientific of the humanities and the most humanistic of the sciences" (Wolf 1964: 88). This characterization is, however, somewhat misleading. Contrary to what Wolf's aphorism implies, individual anthropologists typically do not engage in both scientific and humanistic research. Rather, anthropology is the most scientific of the humanities and the most humanistic of the sciences because it contains some researchers who are scientists and some who are humanists. Significantly for our purposes, these two groups of researchers have been engaged in a debate about the pros and cons of their respective approaches for more than two decades (e.g., Shanks and Tilley 1987; D'Andrade 1995; Scheper-Hughes 1995; Lewis 1999; Cooper 2006). The disagreements between scientific anthropologists and humanistic anthropologists have occasionally become so heated that departments have reorganized into more or less independent wings or even split into two departments. We, therefore, reasoned that focusing on anthropology should shed particularly intense light on issues that need to be addressed in order to move consilience forward.

The papers in section 2 are by three leading sociocultural anthropologists—Pascal Boyer, Harvey Whitehouse, and Bradd Shore. Boyer (chapter 5) presents a tripartite classification of research within anthropology, and argues that the style of research that currently dominates the humanistic branch of anthropology, which Boyer calls the "relevant connections" approach, is unconvincing and unproductive. Whitehouse (chapter 6) similarly criticizes the current state of humanistic anthropology, and then goes on to offer an explanation of why anthropologists are so resistant to the consilience approach. In the last chapter of the section (chapter 7), Shore warns against adopting an overly simplified conception of consilience on the grounds that it cannot account for the emergent properties of social organization. Many of Shore's criticisms speak to broader humanistic concerns about the dangers and limitations of consilience, and they play an important role in setting up certain problems that any "second wave" of consilience must address.

Our ultimate goal in the workshop was not only to explore the theoretical issues associated with consilience but also to examine how embracing consilience would concretely impact the study of topics in the humanities. Accordingly, Part II of the volume—sections 3–6—consists of case studies in which the consilience approach has been implemented.

The first set of case studies concentrates on culture. Culture is often seen as the main feature of human beings that distinguishes us from "mere" animals. The first contribution to this section, by Irwin (chapter 8), challenges this idea. Perhaps best described as someone looking at the humanities from an avian perspective, Irwin notes that accepted definitions of culture have progressively changed over time in order to protect "culture" as an exclusively human phenomenon.[6] He argues that this human-centric approach to culture is both intellectually indefensible and profoundly unproductive, and that exploring culture in non-human animals can shed important light on the mechanisms of phenomena, such as gene-culture co-evolution, that have important implications for our understanding of humans. In chapter 9, Olivier Morin explores various features of the so-called epidemiological approach to cultural transmission.[7] Morin—like workshop participants Sperber and Boyer—is one of a growing number of sociocultural anthropologists who are trying to take their field beyond Durkheimian "culture as autonomous entity" thinking and identify the processes that give rise to cultural phenomena. They contend that cultural transmission should be viewed instead as a selective process, whereby a large and powerful suite of innate human cognitive biases ensure that certain mental representations are more likely to be entertained and transmitted than others. Morin explores the dynamics of such constraints in more detail, arguing that "the impact of universal human psychology on culture is not everywhere the same" (179), and that the relative importance of innate psychological constraints depends on the length and breadth of the transmission chain. This has important implications for understanding various forms of cultural evolution. The study by Schauer, in chapter 10, gives more flesh to this general model by applying a population-level, quantitative analysis to the development of motifs on figure-painted pottery in ancient Greece. Although Schauer notes that there exists a substantial bias against quantitative methods in the area of artistic cultural history, his study attempts to demonstrate how getting beyond traditional qualitative techniques can reveal hitherto

6. Cf. the work of another workshop speaker, Raymond Corbey, on a similar phenomenon in the history of the conception of the human-ape divide (Corbey 2005).

7. The metaphor of "epidemiology" was originally suggested by the evolutionary psychologists John Tooby and Leda Cosmides (1992), and has since become an important model in consilient approaches to the study of cultural transmission and evolution; see Boyer 1994 and Sperber and Hirschfeld 2004 for good introductions to this approach.

invisible phenomena, requiring an adjustment in the "traditional view of what is important in figure-painted pottery" (202). Bentley and Omerod (chapter 11) also employ quantitative methods in their study of cultural transmission, but take an even more radical step away from conventional humanistic notions of culture. Drawing on work in "social physics," they contend that, in many situations, modeling humans as if they are conscious, rational actors is unnecessary, and that remarkable results can be achieved by simply treating individuals as "zero intelligence" interacting particles. Although such models have enjoyed a considerable amount of empirical success, particularly in identifying "emergent patterns in collective behavior" under situations of complex choice, the fact that they continue to meet with a great deal of resistance among social scientists says much about the difficulties involved in bracketing our intuitive notions of the human.

Religious behavior is the focus of attention of the second set of case studies, which—like the case studies of culture—refuse to grant religious beliefs and practices the sort of autonomy and intuitive realism that they possess in everyday phenomenology. This is, of course, equally true of more traditional work in religious studies: Durkheimian, Marxian or Freudian approaches to religion are resolutely *etic* rather than *emic*,[8] explaining religious beliefs and practices in terms of more basic social, economic, or psychological functions. Evolutionary approaches to religion simply push this process of explanatory reduction one step further, attempting to get at the more basic causality behind the social, economic, and psychological. Chapter 12, by Wilson and Green, lays out the basics of the new field of "Evolutionary Religious Studies," comparing and contrasting it to more traditional approaches in religious studies, as well as describing some large-scale research projects currently under way. The chapter 13, by Norenzayan and Gervais provides an overview of the "evolutionary landscape of religion" (244), focusing on theories concerning the cultural evolution of religious cognition and prosociality. Many contemporary evolutionary theories see religious belief as an evolutionary "spandrel"—that is, an accidental by-product of other evolved cognitive tendencies. The experimental, historical, and ethnographic research reviewed by Norenzayan and Gervais explores an alternative hypothesis: namely, that, although it may have originated as a by-product, religious cognition was exapted by cultural group selection because it increases within-group prosociality. They further argue that it was this cultural-cognitive innovation that allowed human societies to escape the group-size limits imposed by kin selection and reciprocal altruism, facilitating the rise of the sorts of large-scale, agricultural societies that have dominated most regions of the world for the past several thousand years. The last contribution to this section, by Robert McCauley (chapter 14), addresses the more specific phenomenon of religious ritual. Although one of the most salient features of religious ritual is its diversity, McCauley—applying a theory of "religious ritual competence" developed in collaboration with Thomas Lawson (Lawson and McCauley 1990; McCauley and Lawson 2002)—argues that human intuitions about the structure of agency "imposes fundamental, though commonplace, constraints on religious ritual form" and that "attention to these constraints enables us to look beyond the variability of religious rituals' culturally specific details to some of their most general underlying

8. Terms borrowed from anthropology and commonly used in religious studies to distinguish "insider" *(emic)* from "outsider" *(etic)* accounts.

features" (267). In particular, McCauley focuses on the structure of, and some of the tensions associated with, what he and Lawson refer to as "special agent rituals"—rituals in which counterintuitive, supernatural beings are perceived as the primary agents.

The third set of case studies looks at morality from a consilient perspective. The emerging "experimental philosophy" movement described by Stich (chapter 15) is motivated by a desire to get beyond that claim that philosophy—moral or otherwise—is an a priori, autonomous discipline, and aims to "use the data and the methods of experimental psychology, neuroscience, cognitive anthropology, evolutionary biology and... behavioral economics in an attempt to sharpen and resolve traditional issues in moral philosophy" (286). One of Stich's contributions to this project is an argument concerning how moral norms can be viewed as "one kind of socially acquired emotion trigger" (294), a conclusion derived from a growing body of empirical evidence that supports the claim that explicit moral convictions are best viewed as the "rational tail" of the "emotional dog."[9] Chapter 16 by Krebs aims to provide an account of the evolutionary history of the human moral sense—identifying its potential precursors as well as sketching out its cognitive "anatomy"—whereas Gintis (chapter 17) treats human morality as "an emergent property of the evolutionary dynamic that gave rise to our species" (318) and shows how it can be profitably analyzed with the tools of game theory. The contribution of Buchanan et al. (chapter 18) is primarily focused on the more pragmatic institutional and training aspects of consilience, seen through the lens of the emerging field of neuroethics, where the complex nexus of ethical, legal, societal, and policy implications involved requires active collaboration between neuroscientists, clinicians, social scientists, philosophers, and legal scholars. This chapter provides not only a description of the sorts of practical barriers that need to be overcome if consilience is to be advanced, but also some important examples of how "lower-level" disciplines, such as neuroscience, have significant contributions to make to both human moral knowledge and public ethical debates.

The final set of case studies in part II deal with stories in the form of literature and as oral traditions. Chapter 19, the first contribution, by Scalise Sugiyama and Sugiyama, attempts to integrate literary and anthropological perspectives by arguing that oral narratives from foraging cultures can be seen as the records of responses to recurrent problems of the human ecological niche" (352), and thus as informative windows into both past and present fitness challenges faced by human societies. In chapter 20, Corbey and Moll adopt a similar evolutionary perspective in their analysis of *Beowulf*, arguing that approaches informed by costly signaling and kin altruism theory provide a more cogent analysis of the text than "traditional hermeneutic and culturalist understandings" (352)—that is, approaches that consider cultural forms in a manner completely detached from our understanding of the biological world. They do not argue that interpretative approaches are without use but rather that the usefulness of such approaches is maximized when they are "vertically integrated" with our understanding of the biological world. This issue of the value of traditional "culturalist" approaches to literature is also taken up by Carroll et al.

---

9. Haidt 2001; two of our workshop speakers (one, Prinz, not represented in this volume) have played central roles in the modern, empirically driven revival of sentimentalist theories of ethics (see especially Nichols 2004 and Prinz 2007).

(chapter 21), who argue that social constructivist approaches to literature have caused literary studies to become cut off from a large and potentially extremely informative body of empirical knowledge accumulated by the natural sciences. They attempt to bridge this gap between science and the humanities by adopting the methods of data gathering, quantification, and explicit hypotheses testing in their analysis of characters from British novels of the nineteenth century. Their goal is to empirically demonstrate that "major features of literary meaning can be effectively reduced to simple categories grounded in an evolutionary understanding of human nature" (387), as well as to illuminate the manner in which particular forms of literary narrative play an evolutionarily adaptive function in human social life. Like Corbey and Moll, their aim is not to obviate the need for more traditional interpretative approaches, but to see such approaches supplemented and constrained by models of human nature that are integrated with our understanding of the rest of the biological world. In the final contribution to this section, Dancygier (chapter 22) sounds a cautionary note by arguing that the attempt to vertically integrate the discipline of literary studies by directly grounding it in evolutionary psychology—the approach of the three other contributions to the section—is not necessarily the most productive or effective strategy. Emphasizing the importance of such cognitive processes as metaphorical projection and conceptual blending, Dancygier argues that "literary Darwinist" approaches are too often limited by an overly narrow picture of human nature, failing to appreciate the manner in which such cultural artifacts as human language can serve as mediums for cognitive innovation and creativity. She argues that a properly evolutionary approach needs to get beyond the "Pleistocene brain" and take account of human cognitive fluidity, gene-culture coevolution, and purely cultural evolution. "Without an understanding of how language and cognition are jointly responsible for the emergence of literature and other creative forms of expression," she notes, "the evolutionary study of literature will not be able to account for new literary forms and themes and will lack a solid foundation in its work toward the goal—the evolutionary explanation of one of the central manifestations of human creativity" (420).

The volume concludes with an invited Afterword by Geoffrey Harpham, President and Director of the National Center for the Humanities, which—like Dancygier's contribution—draws upon the work of Shakespeare to highlight both the importance and unpredictability of human cultural creativity. In reflecting on the contributions to this volume, Harpham aims to temper our enthusiasm for consilience by giving voice to certain hopes and concerns about its nature and goals—concerns that must be addressed if consilience is to win broader acceptance across the various disciplines of the humanities. We will address the significance of Harpham's reaction to the essays in this volume and provide responses to many of his reservations about the consilience project later in the Introduction.

POINTS OF TENSION

Many of the workshop presentations and resulting discussions circled around a set of recurring tensions, and, not surprisingly, these crop up as points of tension in the contributions to this volume as well. Although there are several ways in which these tensions could be framed, in this section we will organize and discuss them under three rubrics: mind-body dualism, reductionism, and the role of "scientific" methods in humanistic work. It seems clear to us that the tensions revolving around these issues need to be resolved if the consilience project is going to succeed, and, therefore, in addition to characterizing each tension, we also suggest some possibilities for how they might be defused. Subsequently, we explore the productive power of these tensions, sketching out the manner in which responses to them have contributed to a modified, "second wave" of consilience—one likely to be much more appealing to humanities scholars than earlier versions, and, therefore, more likely to remove the remaining barriers to genuinely interdisciplinary collaboration.

Mind-Body Dualism

One of the most fundamental of the concerns aroused by consilience is the question of how we conceive of human beings. As we noted earlier, the first section of this volume is dedicated to this issue, but it also re-emerges in various forms in many of the other contributions. Perhaps the most common way of characterizing the difference between the "two cultures" of the sciences and the humanities—at least from the humanities side of the fence—is to invoke the idea of different modes of knowledge. The humanities are typically characterized as involving a unique mode of apprehension, consciousness studying consciousness, or "understanding" (*Verstehen*), whereas the sciences engage in mechanistic "explanation" (*Erklären*). The latter, on this account, is adequate to deal with the movements of dumb, inert physical objects, but the former is the only way to grasp human meaning.

Although it is rarely explicitly acknowledged today, there is reason to think that the primary rationale behind the distinction between these two modes of knowing—and, therefore, behind the sciences/humanities divide itself—is an intuition that there are two utterly different types of substances in the world that operate according to distinct principles: mind and matter (Corbey 2005, Slingerland 2008a). The humanities study the products of the free and unconstrained spirit or mind—literature, religion, art, etc.—whereas the sciences concern themselves with deterministic laws governing the kingdom of unthinking objects. Many of the other factors involved in the resistance to consilience can be seen as ultimately founded upon mind-body dualism: cries of "reductionism," for instance, are typically inspired by violations of the mind-body distinction, and the concept of human beings as uniquely endowed with mind and its accompanying powers (thought, free will) motivates the idea that there is a fundamental distinction between the human and the non-human, or between the determinism of genes and the free play of culture.

Viewing the sciences/humanities divide from this perspective, the call for consilience can be seen as a plea to move beyond mind-body dualism: to see the realm of the human as coextensive with the realm of nature. This plea, in turn, is motivated by the contention that mind-body dualism—the idea that human bodies are uniquely inhabited by an autonomous "Ghost in the Machine"—is no longer defensible. The mind is the body, the body is the mind, and this mind-body unit is ultimately a physical system produced by evolution, and, therefore, amenable to being studied as a naturalistic system. Daniel Dennett, for instance, sees this collapsing of previously distinct ontological realms as the most profound contribution of Darwinism to modern intellectual life, and a clear warrant for bringing human phenomena under the broad umbrella of the sciences:

In a single stroke, Darwin's theory of evolution by natural selection united the realm of physics and mechanism on the one hand with the realm of meaning and purpose on the other. From a Darwinian perspective the continuity between life-less matter on the one hand and living things and all their activities and products on the other can be glimpsed in outline and explored in detail, not just the striv-ings of animals and the efficient designs of plants, but human meanings and purposes: art and science itself, and even morality. When we can see all of our artifacts as fruits on the tree of life, we have achieved a unification of perspective that permits us to gauge both the similarities and differences between a spider web and the World Wide Web, a beaver dam and the Hoover Dam, a nightingale's nest and "Ode to a Nightingale." (Dennett 2009: 10061)

Our section on "Ontologies for the Human" begins with a similar observation from Steven Pinker (chapter 1), who notes that "the history of modern science has been a his-tory of the unification of supposedly incommensurable metaphysical realms," (46) from Newton's unification of the supralunary and sublunary realms to Darwin's unification of the living and non-living worlds (46). The last remaining ontological chasm is between the cultural and biological, which, in turn, is based on a perceived ontological dualism between mind and body. Pinker argues that the key to bridging the gap between the "two cultures" is to recognize that, although intuitively appealing, such mind-body dualism is no longer plausible in light of what has been discovered about human cognition. The project of consilience is fundamentally premised on the conviction that there is an ontological continuity between the human/mental and the non-human/material, which justifies approaching these two realms of inquiry with a unified explanatory framework.

The converse of this, of course, is that, if one rejects the premise of ontological conti-nuity, then consilience loses its basic rationale. There *are*, in fact, many humanists who reject this premise—who feel that physicalism is not a reasonable ontological stance to adopt because immaterial "mind" or "consciousness" is an irrefutable, bedrock feature of the universe, and, therefore, believe that the sciences/humanities divide is quite reason-able and desirable. Richard Shweder's contribution to this volume (chapter 2) is an impassioned defense of mind-body dualism and the irreducibility of the human, written by a leading cultural anthropologist. It represents a crucial piece of the puzzle when it comes to exploring consilience—a piece often ignored or misunderstood by consilience's proponents. Shweder correctly diagnoses consilience as requiring one to accept "the spectacular and breath-taking (or should we say 'dis-spiriting') counter-intuitive impli-cation of mind/body monism of the materialist variety" (64). This implication is that "mental states (including one's own truth claims about mental states) are epiphenomenal and have nothing to do with the chain of objective events that is the real cause behavior" (65). Like many opponents of physicalist approaches to the human, Shweder feels that the power of the Cartesian *cogito* argument remains undiminished by cognitive science: The ontologically independent nature of consciousness means that there is some irre-ducible "first-person" quality to our experience that can, in principle, never be captured by or reduced to third-person accounts. Since the various disciplines of the humanities study phenomena that are products of this independent human consciousness, they, too, must be viewed as autonomous from the sciences.

Shweder's position is crucial because it represents the dominant view of the sciences/ humanities divide among humanities scholars, and, therefore, needs to be both understood and responded to by those who wish to promote consilience. It is also important because it is not necessarily wrong. Another prominent opponent of consilience, the philosopher Charles Taylor, has long argued that we have no good reason for concluding that human consciousness and intentionality are any less basic than the sorts of physical realities studied by the sciences (Taylor 1989, 2007), especially in light of the fact that current-day neuroscience is still a long way from providing a fully comprehensive physicalist account of what human consciousness might be and how it might arise. Although proponents of consilience are confident that such an account will be developed, Taylor feels that—given our current state of knowledge—declaring physicalism to be the only defensible stance is "a little like selling the skin of the lion before the safari has even left Mombassa."[10] According to Taylor, none but the most dogmatic of physicalists could deny the possibility that the lion might prove indefinitely elusive, or that future discoveries about the human consciousness may verify its irreducibility or ontological independence from the material. There is, therefore, a possibility that the entire consilience movement may one day be viewed as a historical aberration, a misguided intellectual trend inspired by an excessive enthusiasm for the power of the sciences to explain all aspects of the world.

Although we believe this possibility should be acknowledged—and that our attitude as we pursue consilience should be rendered more circumspect as a consequence—our workshop and this volume are premised on the conviction that we should put our money on the lion hunters.[11] The main reason for this conviction is that the physicalist position is consistent with what we already know about the universe, whereas mind-body dualism is not. As far as we can tell, the general structure of the universe is such that higher-level phenomena emerge out of and depend upon lower-level phenomena. For example, molecules form and behave in accordance with more basic principles that govern both inorganic and organic substances. Thus, we have strong reason to expect mind to be a product of lower-level phenomena rather than an ontologically distinct, causally independent force.

The argument in favor of pursuing consilience is also bolstered by what we might call the *ad hominem* argument. Pursued in the contribution by Slingerland (chapter 3), the target *hominus* in this argument is *Homo sapiens*. Slingerland contends that, ironically, physicalist science can provide a good explanation for why human beings are biased against physicalism. His discussion centers on the observation that human beings appear

---

10. Personal communication to Slingerland, August 11, 2009. Of course, this philosophical skepticism concerning the possibility of a physicalist explanation of consciousness has a long history, as discussed in the chapter by Fiala et al. in this volume, going back at least to John Locke's comment that "it is as impossible to conceive that ever bare incogitative Matter should produce a thinking intelligent Being, as that nothing should of itself produce Matter" (Locke 1690/1975: 623).

11. For defenses of the "astonishing hypothesis" (Crick 1994) that consciousness is nothing beyond the firing of neurons, the reader is referred to Crick 1994, Flanagan 2002, Dennett 2003. For resistance to this hypothesis, Chalmers 1996 and Searle 2004 serve as helpful starting points.

to possess an evolved cognitive mechanism—"Theory of Mind" (ToM), the tendency to perceive mental qualities as distinct and causally efficacious forces in the world—that explains why human beings are uniquely vulnerable to the antiphysicalist argument: We simply cannot help seeing both ourselves and the world we live in as pervaded by intentionality and meaning. According to Slingerland, our possession of ToM both explains the continued appeal of mind-body dualism—as well as the sciences/humanities divide that grows out of it—and reduces its empirical plausibility. Descartes' *cogito* argument is so powerful because we are designed by natural selection to find it convincing, not necessarily because it is a good argument.[12]

At the same time, Slingerland argues, the inability of psychologically healthy human beings to ever completely free themselves from mind-body dualism means that human-level truths will always present themselves to us as *truths*, not mere psychological constructions, which means that any program of consilience based upon eliminative reductionism faces an uphill battle. At one point in his piece, Shweder asks rhetorically, "Should the common-sense or folk psychology of everyday life be viewed as little more than error, ignorance and a superstitious faith in the causal powers of an ontological fetish?" (65). Slingerland's response to this is, essentially, yes and no: Humanists pursuing consilience have to adopt a kind of "dual consciousness," acknowledging—and, of course, continuing to experience on a visceral level—the irresistible force of mind-body dualism, while bracketing it when going about their work. The fact that ToM ability is not uniform among humans, and is likely distributed in human populations in a spectrum ranging from autism (deficient) to schizophrenia (excessive) (Crespi and Badcock 2008), may explain, not only why the ability to perform this sort of bracketing varies from person to person, but even why individuals are differentially drawn to the sciences and humanities in the first place.[13]

Fiala et al. (chapter 4) also focus on the perceived "explanatory gap" between physical reality and consciousness that is typically invoked in the defense of mind-body dualism. Philosophical concerns about this gap are, they argue, derived from "a much more pervasive phenomenon—even people without any philosophical training find it bizarre and counterintuitive to think that consciousness is nothing over and above certain processes in the brain" (89). This perceived distinction between consciousness and the physical body is the basis of what Bloom 2004 refers to as "folk" mind-body dualism: the apparently universal intuition that human bodies are inhabited by something separate and

---

12. Cf. the discussion by Fiala et al. concerning possible reasons for being suspicious of the epistemic validity of automatic, low-level systems.

13. See Tanaka (under review) for an argument that such a "spectrum" theory may explain the variety in individuals' levels of acceptance of physicalist, Darwinian models of the mind, as well as Shore's comment in this volume that "differences between the two cultures are also sustained by the fact that the humanistic and scientific camps are populated by individuals with very different mindsets" (152). Also refer to Simonton 2009 for data that demonstrates how scientific disciplines can be clearly ranked in a hierarchical configuration based on a variety of measures, as well as some preliminary, but intriguing, data concerning both how this hierarchy can be extended into the various branches of the humanities and how personality traits and life histories might predict the appeal of various levels of analysis to particular individuals.

autonomous, the "mind" or "soul."[14] With their discussion of "dual process models" of human cognition, Fiala et al. attempt to provide a concrete account of both the intuitive human resistance to consilience, and why this resistance may be misguided. As they explain, adopting the sort of physicalism that undergirds the consilience project involves a conflict between "system 1" (fast, automatic) *agency* cognition, which is firmly dualistic concerning minds and bodies, and "system 2" (slow, effortful) *cognition*, which—for many, at least—is compelled by the weight of empirical evidence to the conclusion that consciousness must have a fully physiological explanation. Although Fiala et al. conclude that conflict between the output of these two systems can be reconciled—through temporarily bracketing the outputs of system 1, something like the sort of "dual consciousness" that Slingerland proposes—the fact that system 1 cannot simply be turned off means that adopting the framework of consilience will likely never be entirely intuitive for human beings.

Reductionism

The central conviction of the consilience project is that human phenomena should not be approached as *sui generis* realities possessing *only* their own internal logic and structure, but rather as objects of inquiry that can also be productively explained by lower-level phenomena—just as, say, organisms' inheritance of traits has been explained in terms of DNA. However, for many humanists, including several of the skeptical contributors to this volume, consilience's commitment to reductionism is problematic. Perhaps the clearest expression of this concern in the volume can be found in Bradd Shore's contribution. As Shore argues,

> While reduction can explain many properties of human life, it cannot explain everything. If the evolution of human life were simple, reduction would go a long way in accounting for its properties. But human life is a complex system of organizations, structured at multiple levels: atomic, chemical, genetic, social, cultural and individual. It seems to me that a serious appreciation of the aims of science and the humanities requires an inter-theoretic discourse, not a reductive one (165).

As this passage illustrates, the skeptics reject consilience because they view it as an attempt to account for all aspects of human life by lower level phenomena, which, in turn, is deemed unacceptable because there are certain aspects of human life that are not amenable to reduction.

---

14. As Fiala et al. observe, there have been recent suggestions concerning how the model of folk dualism originally proposed by Bloom should be modified, particularly concerning the precise relationship between "mind" and "soul," between the "subsouls" present in many religious traditions, or even whether folk divisions are typically dualistic or tripartite (mind-body-soul). Nonetheless, it seems clear that the cultural elaborations of soul-mind distinctions or various subsouls are parasitic on two basic intuitive systems dedicated, respectively, to reasoning about minds and bodies (Slingerland (in preparation)), what Dennett 1987 refers to as the "intentional" vs. the "physical" stance.

While we should acknowledge the dangers of crude or "eliminative" reductionism, we think it equally important to recognize the power and usefulness of reduction. Any truly interesting explanation of a given phenomenon is interesting precisely because it involves reduction of some sort—tracing causation from higher to lower levels or uncovering hidden causal relationships at the same level. Regardless of whether we are scientists or humanists, we are generally not satisfied with explanations unless they answer the "why" question by means of reduction, by linking the *explanandum* to an *explanans*. As Steven Pinker has put it, the difference between reductive and non-reductive explanation is "the difference between stamp collecting and detective work, between slinging around jargon and offering insight, between saying something just is and explaining why it had to be that way as opposed to some other way it could have been" (Pinker 2002: 72). This is why the manner in which even humanists go about their work is, by its very nature, reductionistic. Reduction is at the heart of scholarly activity, and when someone fails to reduce we rightly dismiss their work as trivial, superficial, or uninformative. Thus, if there are aspects of human life that are not amenable to reduction, as the skeptics of consilience contend, they can no more be analyzed within the conventional humanistic framework than they can within the consilience framework.

Another reason for moderating concerns about consilience's commitment to reductionism is that there is considerable evidence that avoiding reduction often results in spurious conclusions being reached. When the deeper principles behind phenomena are poorly understood—that is, when lower levels of causation underlying phenomena we are interested in explaining are not accessible to our prying—we are often forced to invent vague, place-holder entities to stand in for the missing information. Ideally, we are aware of what we are doing. For instance, Mendel could reason about the inheritance of traits without knowing how information about them was physically instantiated or transmitted, and Darwin could similarly map out the implications of natural selection without any clear conception of the substrate of inheritance. In such cases there is an implicit faith that the lower-level entities and processes will eventually be specified; if not, the theory may have to be abandoned. A discipline can find itself in a dead end, however, when it has postulated vague, placeholder entities without realizing that this is what it is doing—when it takes these unspecified and unknowable entities or faculties to have genuine explanatory force because they represent ontologically independent realities.

Richard Shweder's chapter illustrates this problem. At one point in his contribution, Schweder observes that moral intuitions have to do with respect for the human "person" understood to be a subject, not merely a physical object and thereby something that transcends or in some very difficult to understand sense exceeds its physical form, and that such intuitions present themselves to us with inescapable realistic force: "The natural moral order of things is something you discover (or have revealed to you), not something you invent, or at least that is the near universal consensus among the 'natives' of the world" (86). Shweder is no doubt correct in his phenomenological analysis of moral intuitions, but the leap he makes to some form of moral realism is more difficult to defend. His position on the felt sense of dignity inspired in us by other human agents, the distinction that we feel exists between humans and mere objects, and the overwhelming force of the moral law brings to mind Immanuel Kant. Indeed, it is the central intuition behind Kant's claim that morality is an autonomous, a priori field of inquiry, completely independent of any empirical facts about human nature, psychology, or history. However, Kant's position was arguably fatally undermined by Friedrich Nietzsche over a century ago. In response to Kant's analysis of "synthetic a priori judgments"— essentially, moral "truths" that present themselves to the human mind as irrefutably true—Nietzsche observed:

> "How are synthetic judgments *a priori possible*?" Kant asked himself—and what really is his answer? "By virtue of a faculty" (*Vermöge eines Vermögens*)[15]—but unfortunately not in five words, but so circumstantially, venerably, and with such a display of German profundity and curlicues that people simply failed to note the comical *niaiserie allemande* involved in such an answer. (Nietzsche 1886/1966: 18–19)

Nietzsche goes on to compare the "explanation" offered by Kant to the answer of the doctor in Molière's *Tartuffe* to the question of how opium produces sleep: "Because it contains a sleepy faculty, whose nature is to put the senses to sleep." Nietzsche declares that "such replies belong in comedy," and concludes that we need to answer instead the question, "Why is belief in such judgments *necessary*?" (19) —that is, necessary for creatures such as ourselves. This is precisely the question addressed by cognitive scientific and evolutionary approaches to morality—as reflected in our section on this topic—which promise to *explain* the existence, structure, and function of moral intuitions without denying their inescapable phenomenological force.[16]

The need to explain without eliminating brings us to the second aspect of humanistic concern about reductionism: the notion that consilience involves reducing all aspects of human life to some lower-level common-denominator phenomena, such as genes or biological instincts. This notion is incorrect for several reasons. To begin with, there is no single level of explanation that is exclusively privileged within the framework of consilience. Some work within the consilience framework seeks to explain the properties of human life in terms of lower-level phenomena, such as genes, but other work employs higher-level explanatory phenomena, as is illustrated in the case studies in this volume. For example, although Corbey and Moll seek to explain aspects of *Beowulf* with genetic hypotheses, Norenzayan and Gervais argue that religious belief is a culturally selected by-product of evolved psychology, and Dancygier argues that literature cannot be understood without an appreciation of the emergent-level properties of human language, as well as the potential for novel cultural blends that language allows. In these latter cases, cultural-level forces are portrayed as the driving causal entities. The contribution by Alex Bentley and Paul Ormerod demonstrates how completely bracketing our normal view of humans as "cultural, thinking people, in all their complexity and variety" (208) in favor of a model whereby individuals are treated as "zero intelligence" particles can provide us with greatly enhanced predictive power when in comes to modeling certain forms of

---

15. Lit. "By means of a means."

16. In this regard, Nietzsche's demand at the end of this section of *Beyond Good and Evil* that psychology be recognized as "the queen of the sciences" and the "path to fundamental problems" (32) was—as was, of course, much that Nietzsche said—quite prescient.

cultural transmission. The same approach, however, would be of little help in understanding the dynamics at work in a particular work of literature. The contribution by Schauer similarly illustrates the power of a quantitative approach to reveal hitherto invisible patterns in the history of the creation of figure-painted pottery, while still recognizing that more traditional qualitative approaches are needed to decipher "the inner workings of unique objects" (203). Rather than deciding a priori which level of reduction is suitable for human questions in general, consilience argues that the appropriate level of reduction needs to be evaluated on a case-by-case basis, in light of the goals and objects of a particular line of inquiry.

Moreover, there is no reason to believe this sort of methodological diversity will disappear, because the very nature of consilience requires what workshop participant Robert McCauley has referred to as "explanatory pluralism" within its "ontological seamlessness" (McCauley 2008). It should be clear from the history of the sciences not only that reduction is a very effective research strategy, but also that exploring reductive possibilities does not lead to the collapsing of disciplinary boundaries. Biology remains distinct from chemistry, and chemistry from physics, despite the fact that scientists have employed reduction as a research strategy for more than three hundred years. As McCauley observes,

> Reduction has probably been the single most effective research strategy in the history of modern science, engendering more precise accounts of the mechanisms (and their operations) underlying everything from magnetic forces to organisms' inheritance of traits to the visual perception of moving objects... Exploring reductive possibilities opens new avenues for sharing methodological, theoretical, and evidential resources. Successful reductions reliably generate productive programs of research at the analytical levels from which the candidate theories hail, squaring the lower level, mechanical details with the upper level phenomenal patterns and refining our understanding of both in the bargain. (McCauley 2007: 106)

Therefore, it should be recognized that, within the framework of consilience, there is scope for explanations at many levels, including the levels at which humanists typically formulate their explanations. All that consilience demands is that explanations for higher level phenomena—such as ethics, morality, and religion—should take account of any limits that are set by well-established hypotheses concerning lower-level phenomena. Or, to put it another way, all that consilience demands is that humanists be aware of whether their explanations are compatible with the findings of neuroscience, psychology, evolutionary biology, and other relevant sciences, and be motivated to explore and try to resolve any discrepancies.

It is also important to recognize that this exploration can move in either direction along the "vertically integrated" chain of explanation. It is not the case that the sciences simply set limits upon the humanities, but it is also possible that work in the humanities may require reformulations of scientific hypotheses. This phenomenon is illustrated by an interesting case from the history of science that was brought up at the workshop by a skeptic of the consilience project, Alan Richardson. As Richardson observed, the late nineteenth century saw what appeared to be an intractable debate between Charles Darwin and the future Lord Kelvin concerning the age of the Earth. Darwin's theory of evolution required that the Earth be extremely old for there to have been time for evolution to have done its work—roughly ten times older than Kelvin argued was the maximum possible age considering known energy sources and the laws of thermodynamics. Richardson argued that this left Darwin and Kelvin in an intellectual stalemate, and portrayed this as just one example of how there is often a lack of consilience even within the sciences—in this case with evidence from biology fundamentally contradicting evidence from physics. In his concluding comments to the workshop, Slingerland argued that Richardson's Darwin-Kelvin example in fact illustrates quite the opposite point: faced with contradictory evidence, the followers of Darwin and Kelvin did not simply shrug their shoulders and go their own way, declaring biology and physics to be obviously autonomous and incompatible levels of inquiry. The fact that they disagreed profoundly *disturbed* them, and they did not rest until this disagreement was resolved—until consilience between physics and biology was once again restored by the discovery of radioactivity, an energy source of which Kelvin was unaware.

Thus, the Darwin-Kelvin case serves as an important example of causal explanatory force flowing *down* the chain of vertical integration: discoveries at a higher level of explanation—biology—helping to motivate the reorganization of a lower level of explanation—physical geology—breaking the latter field out of a conceptual dead end and sending it off in a new direction. This suggests that, once a two-way communication between humanists and scientists really begins to take hold, contradictions in predictions made by, say, literary scholars and cognitive neuroscientists may force us to revise our cognitive neuroscience rather than the other way around. However, none of this sort of mutual fertilization can even get off the ground until both humanists and scientists begin to feel the same sense of urgency to achieve consilience that motivated the followers of Darwin and Kelvin.

One of the prominent early skeptics of consilience, the late Richard Rorty, responded to E.O. Wilson's call by observing:

> The various things people build and repair with tools are, to be sure, parts of a seamless causal web. But that seems no reason to impugn the plumber-carpenter or the carpenter-electrician distinction. The various vocabularies I use to describe and explain what is going on are all applied to the same seamless web, but why should I strive to bring them all together? (Rorty 1998: 30)

This is to misunderstand the consilience project. Consilience does not demand that we all become plumbers—that literary scholars all drop their books and become quantum physicists. Rather, it asks first that, like plumbers and carpenters, disciplines studying different aspects of reality come together and collaborate when they need each other's help. More importantly, it asks that—again, like plumbers and carpenters—this identification of shared problems and impetus for collaborative work stem from an overall shared conception of the nature of reality and the goals of human knowledge: the only reason that tradespeople can collaborate to build a house is that they share a general sense of both how reality works and what a house is for, and this shared sense constrains in important ways the manner in which they go about their jobs. The call for consilience does not require that humanists or scientists give up or exchange their particular jobs. It merely argues that all academics can do their jobs better, and achieve more satisfactory results, when their efforts are coordinated in a vertically integrated manner.

The Role of Quantification, Hypothesis Testing, Controlled Experiments, and Mathematical Modeling

One of the most striking differences between the sciences and humanities is the rarity of quantification, hypothesis testing, controlled experiments, and mathematical modeling in the latter. In the sciences, it is commonplace to use both qualitative and quantitative data, whereas humanities research is overwhelmingly based on qualitative data. Similarly, hypothesis testing, controlled experiments, and mathematical modeling are widely employed in the sciences, but rarely, if ever, used in the humanities. Based on some of the discussions at the workshop and comments by the more skeptical contributors to this volume, it appears that this difference has played an important role in the failure of consilience to capture the imagination of humanists so far. Or, rather, it appears that a misunderstanding of the *significance* of the difference has played an important role in consilience's failure to capture the imagination of humanists so far. Accordingly, in this section we will try to clarify the nature of quantification, hypothesis testing, controlled experiments, and mathematical modeling, and explain why humanists should embrace them—as at least one tool in their methodological toolbox—alongside reductionism.

The attitude of most humanists toward quantification, hypothesis testing, controlled experiments, and mathematical modeling is one of suspicion. It appears the primary reason for this suspicion is that these methods are viewed as belonging to the "scientific worldview" and the realm of physicalistic, mechanistic explanation. Humanists are likely suspicious of these methods, then, for the same reasons that they are suspicious of physicalism and reductionism. We have already explained why we feel that concerns about physicalism and reductionism are misplaced, but it is also important to recognize that the commonly perceived linkage between these methods and reductionistic physicalism is fundamentally mistaken—the linkages between the two must be disentangled.

Physicalism is an ontological worldview, and, as such, is incompatible at a fundamental level from the (implicitly or explicitly) dualistic worldview that informs much humanistic work. There is nothing, however, that essentially links quantification, hypothesis testing, controlled experiments, and mathematical modeling to physicalism—they are not ontological assumptions, but rather epistemological techniques or devices for obtaining reliable knowledge. Beyond the assumption that there is a reality to learn about, and that some form of more or less reliable knowledge is obtainable, these methods do not involve any particular ontological commitment. Quantification, for example, does not, by its very nature, violate mind-body dualism or the notion that humans are unique. It does not even go against the desire to avoid reductionism, given that much of the work on the phenomenon of emergence is heavily mathematical.[17] Counting products of the human mind neither transforms them into aspects of the body, nor does it challenge their status as humanly produced, nor does it require them to be explained by some lower-level phenomenon. The same is true for hypothesis testing, mathematical modeling, and controlled experiments. Hypothesis testing involves no more than outlining a possible answer to a given question, specifying what the results of an analysis should look like if that answer were correct, and then comparing the actual results with the expected results; controlled experiments and mathematical modeling are also simply ways of evaluating explanations within the hypothesis testing framework. These methods, therefore, involve only a commitment that is shared by scientists and most, if not all, humanists—namely, the idea that it is possible to obtain some sort of relatively stable, relatively reliable knowledge.

These methods are not only ontologically innocuous—and, therefore, nothing to be viewed with suspicion—but also have the potential to be extremely useful to humanists, as we think several of the contributions to this volume illustrate. To begin with quantification, its potential benefits are perhaps best seen in the chapter by Schauer. At the heart of the study, Schauer reports, is a quantitative analysis of the decorations that art historians have recorded on Greek figure-painted pottery from between 650 BC and 300 BC. Although time consuming, the analysis is not complicated. It simply involves calculating frequencies for the motifs in a series of partially overlapping 50-year time periods. Yet despite its simplicity, it has yielded some novel and striking findings. The one Schauer highlights is a major difference between the frequencies of occurrence of Nike compared to Theseus. Prior to 525 BC, both of these mythological figures occur at a low frequency. After 525 BC, the frequency with which Nike is depicted increases dramatically compared to Theseus. This increase peaks between 475 and 425 BC, and then depictions of Nike decline again, although they remain considerably more frequent than depictions of Theseus. As Schauer notes, neither the difference in the popularity of Nike versus Thesus, nor the timing of the increase in popularity of Nike has been identified before, even though the relevant data have been available for decades. Moreover, this pattern presents a significant challenge to traditional ideas of "importance" in motifs on figure-painted pottery. Schauer's chapter demonstrates that quantification is capable of revealing interesting and potentially significant patterns that are difficult, if not impossible, to identify using the qualitative approaches that have been traditionally relied on in the humanities.

Turning to hypothesis testing, its benefits can be traced to the role played by prediction in the process. To reiterate, hypothesis testing involves outlining a possible answer to a given question, specifying what the results of an analysis should look like if that answer were correct, and then comparing the actual results with the expected results. Or, to put it another way, it involves testing explanations by predicting what should be seen at the end of an analysis if an explanation is correct. This method provides several benefits.

17. Indeed, the typical association between mathematical modeling and eliminative reductionism is ironic considering that some of the strongest arguments for the need to take emergence seriously have come out of mathematical modeling work, including that of some of our contributors (see Bentley and Maschner 2003, 2007).

A significant one is that specifying a hypothesis and a prediction ahead of time forces one to pay close attention to both the data one needs to collect and the assumptions involved in the analytical technique that one intends to employ. Most research in the humanities involves these activities, but often they are engaged in *during* data collection and analysis, and as a consequence there is frequent backtracking. Hypothesis testing does not guarantee that there will not be any backtracking, but in our experience it reduces it considerably. As such, hypothesis testing enhances the efficiency of the research process. A second major benefit of having to specify a hypothesis and a predicted set of results, and comparing the actual results with the predicted results is that it is easier to determine whether a researcher has inadvertently biased their results to support the hypothesis. Again, this sort of self-checking is by no means unknown in the humanities, but it is typically pursued in a more ad hoc and cumbersome manner than is the case when hypothesis testing is utilized. A third major benefit of hypothesis testing arises from the final step in the process, the comparison of the actual and predicted results. Being forced to evaluate whether the actual results match the predicted results is a spur to critical thinking and further research. A discrepancy can be the result of four things: (1) a mistake in data collection or analysis, (2) a problematic assumption about the data or an aspect of the analysis, (3) an error in the formulation of the prediction, or (4) an incorrect hypothesis. If, after further analysis, one can exclude possibilities 1–3, then one can conclude that the hypothesis is incorrect and either modify it or begin looking for alternative hypotheses to test.

Several of the case-study contributions to the volume employ the technique of hypothesis testing. Of these, perhaps the most noteworthy is the contribution by Carroll, Gottschall, Johnson, and Kruger, because it applies the technique to what many likely consider the prototypical humanities discipline: literary studies. Carroll et al. report a study in which they used the results of published evolutionary research to formulate hypotheses about aspects of human nature likely to be relevant to readers' responses to literary texts, and then collected survey data to test the predictions of those hypotheses. Their chapter provides an excellent illustration of how specifying a hypothesis and a prediction not only guides data collection and analysis, but also allows potential biases to be straightforwardly evaluated, as the criticisms leveled at the chapter by Dancygier demonstrate. In addition, some of the results of Carroll et al. ran counter to their predictions, and this led them to reconsider their hypothesis and propose a new one (400), which exemplifies the third of the aforementioned benefits of hypothesis testing—its ability to generate a virtuous circle of research.

As mentioned earlier, within the hypothesis-testing framework, controlled experiments and mathematical modeling are two ways of evaluating explanations. As such, they offer all the benefits of hypothesis testing mentioned earlier. What distinguishes controlled experiments and the type of analysis familiar to humanists—the analysis of observational data—is that, in a controlled experiment, researchers try to collect data in such a way that confounding factors are excluded and a "pure" test of the predicted relationship between variables becomes possible. Several techniques fall under the heading "mathematical modeling," including optimization modeling, game theory, and population genetics modeling. As the name suggests, what these approaches have in common is the use of math, specifically algebra, to evaluate relationships that are predicted by hypotheses.

In some mathematical modeling-based studies, predictions are tested entirely in the abstract. In others, modeled results are compared to results obtained from the analysis of observational data.

A number of the case studies in this volume illustrate the utility of controlled experiments. For example, Stich describes the manner in which the new "experimental philosophy" movement has tried to supplement the traditional philosophical methods of armchair speculation and theoretical analysis with the sort of data that can be gleaned from controlled experiments, which, in just a short period of time, have given us a considerable amount of new insight concerning the nature of moral judgments. Several of our contributions also offer case studies that illustrate the usefulness of mathematical modeling. For instance, Gintis's chapter employs game theory to study models of various forms of social cooperation, while Bentley and Ormerod employ a differential equation to assess the relative importance of random copying and purposeful selection in the spread of cultural traits. Obviously, the results yielded by controlled experiments and applications of mathematical modeling are artificial, but—as these and other examples in the volume illustrate—both approaches allow researchers to decisively reject hypotheses more readily than is the case with the analysis of observational data.

A good sense of how methods borrowed from the sciences can benefit the humanities can also be gleaned from the contributions of Wilson and Green and of Norenzayan and Gervais. These scholars are participants in an interlocking set of large, interdisciplinary, international collaborative projects aimed at exploring the hypotheses that religious belief has historically been selected for among human populations because of its role in promoting prosociality.[18] Such hypotheses, of course, have a quite venerable history in the academic study of religion, but they have typically been supported only by ad hoc observation and cherry-picked historical examples. The consilient projects pursued by these scholars are bringing together theorists of religion, philosophers, historians, linguists, anthropologists, psychologists, economists, biologists, and mathematicians in order to generate falsifiable hypotheses concerning the evolutionary origins of religious belief and then test them with a variety of methods, including textual analysis, historical "observation," quantification of historical textual and archaeological data, ethnographic observation, controlled laboratory experiments, and mathematical modeling. Like a team of tradespeople engaged in a large construction project, each specialist takes on only the particular tasks that suit his or her training and aptitudes, but all continuously communicate with one another and work within a consilient framework to pursue a shared set of goals. It is our conviction that the surest way to dispel skepticism about the value of consilience for the humanities is for these sorts of concrete collaborations to produce results that are not only novel and interesting, but that meet the highest standards of both scientific and humanistic inquiry.

---

18. The formation of research groups and planning of grant applications for these projects was one of the concrete results of our exploratory workshop. These efforts have now coalesced into two teams, one based in the United States and Europe and led by Wilson and Whitehouse, the other based in Canada and led by Slingerland, Henrich, Norenzayan, and Collard.

ELEMENTS OF A "SECOND WAVE" OF CONSILIENCE

Having outlined a set of tensions that arose from our workshop proceedings, we will now try to sketch the outlines of a modified consilience project that—responding to these perceived tensions—differs in some significant ways from the project outlined by Tooby and Cosmides (1992) and E.O. Wilson (1998). Borrowing terminology from the feminist movement, we have adopted the term *second wave* to characterize this modified consilience, because it grows out of and includes the earlier wave but pushes it in several new directions.

Perhaps the most common theme that emerged from the workshop discussions themselves—the Q&A after the talks, and the informal interactions over breaks and meals—is that the manner in which consilience has been characterized and presented to humanists has been off-putting and, hitherto, relatively unsuccessful. There was also something of a consensus that this involved both substantive and stylistic factors. More substantively, it was thought that issues such as the relationship between evolved human cognitive architecture and culture, or the status of science in the chain of explanation, needed to be treated in a more sophisticated fashion. More stylistically, many humanists noted that the rhetoric of proponents of consilience (most of them coming from the science side of the sciences/humanities divide) often tended to sound dismissive of the value of traditional humanistic work—needlessly dismissive, because, when pressed, no advocate of consilience would deny the value of such work. By the end of the workshop, a feeling began to develop among the organizers that it might be helpful to draw a line between the sort of consilience initially proposed by, for instance, E.O. Wilson, and the work being pursued by those us in the next generation, many of us coming to consilience from a background in more traditional humanities disciplines, and, therefore, perhaps more sensitized to the aspects of consilience that rub humanists the wrong way.

No actual term for this shift emerged from our discussions. Indeed, it was not until this volume was being assembled that an explicit recognition began to develop among us that a shift was involved, and not until this Introduction was written that a name was concocted to label it. It is probably impossible to speak of being part of a "second wave" of anything without coming off as both smug and ungrateful. This metaphor was chosen in conscious emulation of second-wave feminism, which intended its self-characterization to be an inclusive one, incorporating and acknowledging the achievements of the retroactively designated first wave while also pushing it in new directions. Perhaps the computer metaphor of a "version 1.1" of a program would be a better one,[19] capturing the sense that the sort of consilience that we saw emerging from the workshop is fundamentally the same product as the earlier version, but one modified in various ways in response to bug reports and usability complaints from initial adopters. Responding to the tensions that emerged from the workshop presentations and discussions, summarized earlier, the manner in which this modified "second-wave"

---

19. Especially since it is not at all clear that "third-wave" feminism partakes of this same inclusive and progressive character.

consilience[20] differs from its initial instantiation—in both substantive and stylistic ways—can perhaps be characterized as a desire to transcend three barriers: eliminative reductionism, the nature vs. nurture debate, and entrenched disciplinary chauvinism.

Beyond Eliminative Reductionism: Respecting Emergent Levels of Truth

Having hopefully clarified that reductionism is, when properly done, the central method of intellectual advancement in any field, more has to be said about good and bad forms of reductionism—because, of course, it is really "greedy" or "eliminative" reductionism that most humanists have in mind when they bandy about this charge. If those of us who support consilient approaches to the humanities wish to win broader acceptance among our colleagues, it is incumbent upon us to make it clear that consilience does not entail— as many humanists fear it does—collapsing humanities departments into biology departments or denying the significance of human-level truths. Rather, it merely asks that humanistic work not be treated as disconnected from the world of physical causation. Human-level meaning emerges organically out of the workings of the physical world, and we are being "reductive" in a good and revealing way when we seek to understand how these lower level processes allow the higher-level processes to take place. The argumentative force of defenders of consilience concerning the issue of reductionism is very similar, then, to Nietzsche's point regarding Kant: the humanities have yet to entirely free themselves from "Tartuffery," and continue to rely on impressive-sounding but explanatorily empty entities and faculties.[21] The commonly- cited belief that the humanities deal with sympathetic understanding or "thick" description[22] has traditionally had the effect of systematically denying any possible substantive role to the sorts of "thin" bodily or physical processes studied by the sciences, thereby protecting the work of humanists from the prying eye of science by wrapping it in the mysterious cloud of *Verstehen*. Although this seems more sophisticated than the answer of the doctor in Molière, it is structurally quite similar. Humanists have long recognized the usefulness of reducing human phenomena to more causally basic levels of analysis—whether sociological, economic, psychological, or phonetic—and judging the usefulness of such reduction in terms of its productiveness and revelatory power. Consilience does not ask us to change this, but merely to refrain from drawing an ontological line below which we will not

20. For what we see as some representative examples of this sort of "second-wave" consilience as practiced by workshop participants, the reader is referred to Henrich et al. 2003, the three-volume series on *The Innate Mind* edited by Carruthers, Laurence, and Stich (Carruthers, Laurence, and Stich 2005, Carruthers, Laurence, and Stich 2007, 2008), Schaller and Crandall 2004, Gottschall and Wilson 2005, Slingerland 2008a, Heywood, Garcia, and Wilson 2009, Boyd, Carroll, and Gottschall 2010, and Schaller et al. 2010.

21. See, for instance, Tooby and Cosmides suggestion that terms such as *"learning"* or *"rationality"* as they are currently used in the humanities are as analytically useful as *"protoplasm"* or *"vital force"* was in premodern biology, and are likely to turn out to be blanket terms for what are really a variety of specific, modular, evolved cognitive processes (1992: 122–23).

22. See the classic expression of this attitude in Geertz (Geertz 1973: 6–10), who borrows the distinction between "thick" and "thin" description from the philosopher Gilbert Ryle 1971.

allow such reduction to go. Obviously, this will not satisfy committed ontological dualists such as Shweder, but it should at least respond to the more moderate concerns expressed by Shore.

Worries about levels of explanation and eliminative reductionism arguably also lie behind a charge commonly raised in humanistic circles concerning the ultimate irrelevance of consilience. This issue was raised by one of our workshop attendees, Stefania Burk, an expert on the intersection of poetics and political patronage as manifested in the production of official poetry anthologies in medieval Japan. Burk expressed skepticism concerning the degree that the sort of evolutionary approaches represented by the presentations in the literature session offer her anything of value in her own work. One answer is that adopting a consilient perspective—for instance, learning something about evolutionary psychology and cognitive science and taking it seriously in her work— might very well involve an important shift in her overall interpretative framework. The typical Foucauldian framework that she, like many humanists, learned in graduate school encourages her to see her work as documenting the manner in which aesthetics is primarily driven by politics and power, with "beauty" revealed as no more than culturally specific construction. An evolutionary framework might lead her to focus more on coalition-formation, prosociality, and aesthetic forms as in-group markers—an important advance over Foucault because it would allow her to plug her work into a much broader and more powerful explanatory framework, one that also has the wonderful virtue of being empirically plausible.

However, it is also important to acknowledge that 90 percent of her work is concerned with the specifics of how *this* particular person commissioned *this* particular poetry anthology, and how this historical event influenced some very culturally and linguistically specific forms of poetic expression. Evolutionary theory does not speak directly to these issues. As Dancygier notes in her contribution,

> For the purposes of the humanities, [evolutionary] questions are interesting, but not central to the traditional concerns of the disciplines deeply immersed in cultural concerns. For examples, future answers (if at all possible to provide) might change the underlying assumptions of literary study, but they may do little to affect the core interests of most literary scholars. To put it simply, just knowing that literature is adaptive may not change the way in which most of the historicist or cultural research is done. (410)

It must, therefore, be emphasized that, even if every researcher in the humanities immediately embraced consilience with the sciences, the vast majority of humanistic work would still consist of what we are calling "horizontal analysis": analyzing phenomena by tracing out connections between entities native to emergent levels of explanation. This is of course the case in *any* field of analysis, scientific or otherwise: organic chemists spend most of their time exploring connections that make sense only at the level of organic molecules, and even the most reductive evolutionary approach to poetry will necessarily focus primarily on problematic and modes of analysis native to the phenomenon of poetry. When it comes to humanistic fields, the importance of this sort of horizontal analysis is also heightened when we recognize that even the most trivial of human-level actions and thoughts are not naked facts to be measured by objective instruments but, rather, are embedded in a set of long, complex stories that require the higher-level expertise of anthropologists, novelists, and historians in order to fully unpack. Because humanistic fields tend to concern themselves overwhelmingly with emergent structures and idiosyncratic cultural histories, it is not at all clear that adopting a consilient perspective would have such a global and dramatic effect on the day-to-day work of most humanities scholars. This is particularly the case when one recognizes that many humanists in fact implicitly share many of the assumptions of the consilient approach—such as important commonalities in human nature, universality in certain types of cultural forms, and so on—even if they deny these commonalities in their rhetorical and theoretical posturing.[23]

Here the line between substantive and stylistic changes begins to blur, because it is not necessarily the case that advocates of "first-wave" consilience would disagree with any of this. It *is* the case, however, that respect for emergent-level realities does not come across clearly in their writing, as concerns expressed by many workshop participants attest. An important feature of the sort of consilience we wish to advance is the recognition that, although consilience can provide a crucially important new explanatory framework within which, say, literary studies could operate, it does not necessarily entail radical alterations in the everyday methodology, vocabulary, or focus of interest of the average humanist. Literary scholars, for instance, do not need to stop talking about history and genre, or confine themselves only to terms and concepts drawn from evolutionary psychology.

A final, and more substantive point, concerns what we might call the phenomenological status of human-level truths in a consilient framework. Although no evolutionary psychologist or cognitive scientist would purport to be an eliminative reductionist, and all give at least lip service to the idea that higher levels of explanation can feature emergent qualities not present at the lower levels, there is a common tendency to nonetheless privilege the material level of explanation: we are really just mindless robots or physical systems, no matter how things might appear to us phenomenologically. As we argued in our defense of physicalism earlier, there are some very good reasons for this privileging of lower levels of explanation. It is equally the case, however, that, as we move up the explanatory chain, we witness the emergence of one level of explanation in particular—that of human-level reality, as seen through the filter of Theory of Mind—that must be recognized as possessing such a special, ineradicable hold on the human mind that no third-person description can ever completely dislodge it. In other words, we apparently cannot help but, at some level, see a *Geist* in the machine, which means there will always be something importantly different about the *Geisteswissenschaften* for creatures like us.

This is a substantive point because some advocates of consilience argue that, because intentionality and consciousness are helpful for certain heuristic purposes, but possess no underlying reality, the rigorous study of human affairs will eventually be able to dispense with them entirely.[24] A common analogy drawn by those who feel dualism will soon disappear is the shift in human sensibilities that occurred with the Copernican

---

23. An observation also made by Joseph Carroll 2008.

24. See, for instance, Paul Churchland's description of how we might wean ourselves off mentalistic folk psychology (Churchland 1979: 30–34), or Owen Flanagan's comment that because concepts such as the "soul" or "free will" "do not refer to anything real, we are best off without them" (2002: xiii).

revolution. Copernicanism presented a view of the solar system that contradicted not only Scriptural authority but the evidence of our senses: the Bible states quite clearly that the sun moves around the earth, and this also happens to accord with our everyday sensory experience. Yet an accumulation of empirical evidence eventually resulted in Copernicanism winning the day—trumping both religion and common sense—and nowadays every educated person takes the heliocentric solar system for granted. Dennett (1995), for instance, argues that the physicalism versus dualism controversy explored in our "Ontologies for the Human" section is analogous to the early days of Copernicanism: we are resistant to physicalism because it goes against our religious beliefs and our common sense, but the weight of the empirical evidence is on its side. Eventually—after all of the controversy has played itself out—we will learn to accept the materialist account of the self with as much equanimity as the fact that the Earth goes around the Sun.

A basic problem with Dennett's position, however, is that there is a disanalogy between the Copernican revolution and the revolution represented by physicalist models of the mind. The Ptolemaic model of the solar system falls quite naturally out of the functioning of our built-in perceptual systems, but it is not itself part of that system: we do not appear to possess an innate Ptolemaic solar-system module. Switching to Copernicanism requires us to suspend our common-sense perceptions, but it does not involve a direct violation of any fundamental, innate human ideas. If the claims concerning the innateness and auto-maticity of folk dualism advanced by Slingerland and Fiala et al. are correct, however, physicalism as applied to human minds *does* require such a violation, and this has a very important bearing on how realistic it is to think that we can dispense with mentalistic talk once and for all. The idea of human beings as ultimately mindless robots, blindly designed by a consortium of genes to propagate themselves (Dawkins 1976/2006), has not gained a foothold probably because it dramatically contradicts other firmly entrenched ideas such as the belief in *soul, freedom, choice, responsibility*—in short, all of the qualities that seem to us to distinguish human beings from mere things. The dualism advocated by classic defenders of the autonomy of morality, such as Kant, is not a historical or philosophical accident, but rather a development of an intuition that comes naturally to us, as bearers of Theory of Mind: agents are different from things. Although we are obviously capable of entertaining non-dualist ideas at some abstract level—using our system-2 mechanisms, as Fiala et al. would have it—we seem to have evolved in such a way as to possess system-1 mechanisms that are ultimately invulnerable to the idea of thoroughgoing materialism.

Thus, we may always see meaning in our actions: populating our world with "angry" seas, "welcoming" harbors, and other human beings as unique agents worthy of respect and dignity, and distinct from objects in some way that is hard to explain in the absence of soul-talk, but nonetheless very real for us. Qua physicalists, we can acknowledge that this feeling is, in some sense, an illusion. For better or worse, though, we are apparently designed to be irresistibly vul-nerable to this illusion, at least on some level. In this respect, appearance *is* reality for us.[25]

---

25. This is where, in fact, we see the limits of a thoroughly "scientific" approach to human culture, and need to finesse a bit our understanding of what counts as a "fact" for beings like us. In this respect, humanists and scientists concerned with the issue of levels of explanation and emergent properties have much to learn from the work of Charles Taylor (see especially Taylor 1989). Although Taylor is ultimately opposed to consilience or other forms of naturalism, we believe that his insights on this subject can be drawn upon to formulate a more sophisticated model of vertical integration.

One way of characterizing the attitude of "second-wave" consilience toward this issue is to see it as incorporating the viewpoints of both Kant and Nietzsche. To take moral intuitions as an example, we can follow Nietzsche—somewhat updated and put into the role of an evolutionary psychologist—and see why it is important, unavoidable, and revealing to ask about the adaptive forces that cause us to feel the force of synthetic a priori claims, rather than just experiencing them as unquestioned intuitions. Answering the question of origins—uncovering the lower-level, ultimate explanations for our moral intuitions—has important practical implications, but most of all we just simply want to know. We also need to follow Kant, however, in recognizing that, no matter what the origins of these intuitions, they are the spontaneous product of a powerful, built-in faculty, the output of which seem inescapably right to us. The Nietzschean *Übermensch*, living in accordance only with artificial values freely and consciously created by himself, is psychologically impossible for a cognitively healthy human being—which, of course, Nietzsche was not, at least in his later years. This means that, as empirically responsible humanists, we need to pull off the trick of simultaneously seeing the world as Nietzsche and as Kant, holding *both* perspectives in mind and employing each when appropriate.

So, ironically, proponents of consilience will have to live with a kind of dual consciousness, cultivating the ability to view human beings simultaneously under two descriptions: as physical systems and as persons. On the one hand, we are convinced that Darwinism is the best account we have for explaining the world around us, and, therefore, that human beings are merely physical systems. On the other hand, we cannot help but feel the strong pull of human-level truth. Moreover, those of us who are humanists also earn our keep by studying this emergent level of reality: unlike scientists, we do not necessarily have to withdraw our projections in order to perform our day jobs, which is a nice perk. Conceptualizing the subject of humanist inquiry not as the ineffable workings of some Cartesian *Geist* in the machine, but rather as the wonderfully complex set of emergent realities that constitute the lived human world—in all its cultural and historical diversity—allows us to respect and accommodate the fear, expressed by Shweder, of "completely reducing the 'mental' to the 'material' or 'matterings' to 'matter'" (73) without having to follow him into an empirically implausible form of mind-body dualism. A consilience grounded in McCauley's "explanatory pluralism but ontological seamlessness" provides space for both the appreciation and explanation of the rich world of emergent human meaning.

Beyond the Nature-Nurture Debate: Recognizing the Importance of Gene-Culture Co-evolution

Some of the more recent popular press accounts of the "death of evolutionary psychology" lead one to believe that its potential limitations entirely nullify the value of work done in this field or even invalidate the consilience approach in general.[26] This could not be further from the truth, and these critiques are unhelpful to the extent that

---

26. See, in particular, Begley 2009 and Brooks 2009 on the "death of evolutionary psychology"; for a succinct response to the more extreme critics of evolutionary psychology, see Kenrick 2006.

they have been driven by a fundamental resistance to viewing humans as the potential subject of scientific inquiry. One beneficial effect of such criticisms, however, has been to focus attention on a feature of evolutionary psychology that is open to emendation: its tendency to focus more or less exclusively on the Pleistocene brain and the adaptive environment of our small-band living, hunter-gatherer ancestors. No one at our workshop would deny that the human brain has been shaped by the evolutionary history of our species, nor that the Pleistocene hunter-gatherer lifestyle represents an important and relatively long-lasting period of human cognitive evolution. However, a lot has happened to human beings since the Pleistocene. How to properly deal with human culture and its relationship to innate cognition within an evolutionary framework has been a topic of much concern. In fact, it is as much an issue of contention among proponents of consilience as it is between proponents and skeptics of the approach.

In his contribution to this volume, Shore notes that, although gene-culture co-evolution is often given at least lip service in consilient approaches, the actual treatment of these two aspects of human existence—one of the keys of achieving true consilience—has often been "decisively tilted" (141) toward the genetic. We can see this in E.O. Wilson's perhaps now-infamous metaphor of the human brain as "an exposed negative waiting to be dipped in developer fluid" (1975/2000: 156), which presents culture as a more-or-less direct expression of innate human psychological mechanisms, a mechanically expressed "phenotype" of a fixed human genotype on the order of a termite mound or beehive. The sort of second-wave consilience represented by the contributions to this volume can be seen as a modification of this position because it recognizes that culture and genes exist in a co-evolutionary relationship, and that human culture can play a role in *transforming* human cognition on both individual and evolutionary time scales. Culture on this model is best seen as a semi-autonomous force, with its own process of evolution and selection pressures—*"semi"*-autonomous because it is not some disembodied, Durkheimian superstructure but is necessarily carried by individual human brains and the physical, culturally modified environment. This second-wave approach also adopts a rather broader view of what constitutes the relevant "adaptive environment," which, for humans, has to include the social-cultural world, and the socially and culturally transformed body-mind.[27]

If we wish to frame this as a substantive critique of some advocates of "first-wave" consilience, we might say that the desire to push back against the extreme social constructivism that currently dominates the humanities was taken too far. One unfortunate effect of some recent attempts to bring a robust conception of human nature back to the fore in our study of human culture is the creation—perhaps often unintended—of a false dichotomy between nature and nurture: that the only alternatives are embracing full-blown social constructivism or believing in a single, universal human nature that merely gets "translated"

27. Many representatives of this second wave—including both contributors to this volume (Wilson and Green, and Norenzayan and Gervais) and other workshop participants (Henrich)—also openly embrace a concept that is still too often viewed as a terrible heresy by evolutionary psychologists: multilevel or group selection, which argues that groups of organisms can become vehicles for selection pressure. See especially Wilson 1975 and Wilson 2006 on the "revival" of group selection in both biological and cultural studies.

into various cultures. In fact, a consilient approach to human culture—one fundamentally informed by evolutionary theory and the latest discoveries in cognitive science—can take us beyond such dichotomies. The work of scholars such as Pete Richerson and Rob Boyd (e.g., Richerson and Boyd, 2005) has shown how cultural forms themselves are subject to a kind of evolution, constrained by the structures of human cognition but also exerting their own independent force. In fact, cultural evolution seems to have driven certain aspects of human genetic evolution, favoring our big brains, linguistic skills, and ultrasociality, three of the hallmarks of our species (Henrich and McElreath 2007). Cultural group selection theory gives us a model for how this process of co-evolution may have worked historically among human populations and how its effects can still be observed today.

In addition, tools drawn from cognitive linguistics, such as conceptual metaphor and blending theory,[28] give us very specific models for understanding how universal, innate human cognitive patterns can get projected into new domains or combined to generate entirely novel, emergent structures. Human cognitive fluidity,[29] ratcheted up over time by entrenchment in cultural forms such as language or architecture, can shape human emotions, desires, and perception in quite novel and idiosyncratic ways—from the subtle Japanese aesthetic sentiment of *mono no aware* (lit. "the sorrow of things") to the sort of "cultivated needs" explored in depth by theorists such as Pierre Bourdieu. As Dancygier argues in her contribution:

> Perhaps it is time for literary scholars interested in evolution and the mind to also start looking at language as the tool whereby new meanings can be expressed, and not a set of forms to be acknowledged and then put to one side. Without an understanding of how language and cognition are jointly responsible for the emergence of literature and other creative forms of expression, the evolutionary study of literature will not be able to account for new literary forms and themes and will lack a solid foundation in its work toward the goal—the evolutionary explanation of one of the central manifestations of human creativity. (420)

More of an acknowledgement of how culture can play an active role in reshaping human nature would go a long way toward answering the sort of skepticism voiced by many humanities scholars who remain dubious about the value of the consilience project, and for whom the dazzling variety of various human cultures and the nuances of specific cultural products are the most salient features of human beings.

Beyond Disciplinary Chauvinism: Recognizing that Consilience Is a Two-Way Street

As conference participant Steven Pinker observed, there currently exists a "widespread perception that the humanities are in trouble," which might at least in part be attributed

---

28. On conceptual metaphor theory, see Lakoff and Johnson 1999; on blending theory, see Fauconnier and Turner 2002, or the helpful introduction to blending found in Dancygier 2006.

29. The term *cognitive fluidity* was coined by the archeologist Steven Mithen 1996; for an attempt to sketch out how conceptual blending theory could serve as a powerful tool in both explaining and modeling cognitive fluidity and conceptual innovation, see Slingerland 2008a: Ch. 4.

to the "insularity of the humanities from new ideas and discoveries coming from the sciences" (46). Pushing back against this emphasis on the foundational importance of the sciences, one of our workshop participants, Anne Murphy, made the important point that the empirical rigor of humanists such a herself are not adequately recognized by many scientists, who are sometimes wont to caricature humanistic work as facile storytelling or speculation. Responding to Murphy, we cannot help but observe that although empirical rigor is demanded and delivered when humanists focus on their particular areas of expertise—the development of the novel in nineteenth century England or the details of patron-poet relations in medieval Japan—such rigor is too often thrown out the window when it comes time to locating the significance of this specialized work in the broader framework of human experience. As one of us (Slingerland) put it, Michel Foucault is a profound and careful scholar when wearing his historian hat, producing important insights into, for instance, the history of the perception of homosexuality in the West (Foucault 1978). However, the significance of this empirical work is then undermined by being embedded in a variety of broader theoretical frameworks—for instance, theories concerning the relationship of language to thought, or of social discourse to political power—that betray an ignorance of even the most basic relevant empirical work on the structure of human cognition. Consilience demands that humanists start paying more attention to discoveries about human cognition being provided by cognitive scientists, psychologists, and specialists in non-human animal behavior, which have a constraining function to play in the formulation of broad humanistic theories—calling into question, for instance, such deeply entrenched dogmas as the "blank slate" theory of human nature, strong versions of social constructivism and linguistic determinism, and the ideal of disembodied reason (Pinker 2002, Slingerland 2008a).

However, by the same token, as scientists explore areas traditionally studied by the humanities—the nature of culture, religion, ethics, epistemology, literature, consciousness, emotions, or aesthetics—they need to draw on humanistic expertise if they are to effectively decide what sorts of questions to ask, how to frame these questions, what sorts of stories to tell in interpreting their data, and how to grapple with the ethical and social repercussions of scientific discoveries about complex human phenomena. This two-way dynamic—one of the most prominent themes that emerged from our workshop discussions—has, unfortunately, been too often ignored by earlier proponents of consilience.

To take one example, it was observed that one of the more puzzling features of the modern academy is that philosophy of science is pursued almost exclusively in humanities disciplines, with most working scientists pursuing their research in blithe unawareness of the developments in philosophy of science in the past several decades that has fundamentally questioned old-fashioned, positivistic models of scientific inquiry.[30] For instance, since at least the early 1970s it has become widely recognized that scientific theory and observation are inextricably intertwined, and that the positivistic ideal of a perfectly corroborated theory is a chimera. Too many working scientists today nonetheless continue to evince an overoptimistic faith in the scientific method as an infallible and direct route to "truth," an attitude that can blind them to problematical assumptions or culturally specific elements that may be distorting their results.

---

30. See, for instance, now classic works such as Kuhn 1962/1970 and Feyerabend 1993.

The practical significance of this work can, of course, be exaggerated. When presented with scientific evidence, a common kneejerk reaction among humanists is to declare that such evidence can simply be dismissed, because "after Kuhn" we all know that science is merely one discourse among many—such statements often uttered with the greatest confidence by those who have never read a word of Kuhn.[31] One point of consensus that emerged from the workshop was that the sort of extreme epistemological skepticism that currently permeates many areas of the humanities, and that constitutes one of the primary intellectual barriers to consilience, has outlived its usefulness. A primary benefit of getting beyond mind-body dualism is the ability to move past epistemological problems created by such dualism: both objectivist positivism and its evil skeptical twin are artifacts of an empirically implausible, disembodied, representational model of knowledge (Laudan 1996, Putnam 1999). The commonalities of human embodiment in the world can result in a stable body of shared knowledge, verified (at least provisionally) by evidence based upon common perceptual access. Abandoning strong mind-body dualism—bringing the human mind back into contact with a rich and meaningful world of things—would, therefore, reground the humanities on the foundation of an embodied mind that is always already in touch with the world, as well as a pragmatic model of truth or verification that takes the body and the physical world seriously. At the same time, such an embodied, pragmatic model of truth would also avoid the pitfalls of old-fashioned positivist objectivism, which all the participants also agreed has outlived its usefulness as an epistemological framework (Smith 2006).

Through contact and collaboration with colleagues in the humanities, second-wave "consiliators" coming from a science background can begin to become more aware of potential problems with their basic explanatory categories, and more attuned to the importance of cultural variation. Two examples discussed at the workshop, that of the psychology of religion and cross-cultural psychology, are revealing in this regard. Psychologists interested in the scientific study of religion have tended to be working with a rather unexamined conception of the category of "religion"—the defining of which has been a central, contentious, and extremely fraught issue in the academic study of religion for over a hundred years. This has a potentially significant impact of their work. For example, psychologists wishing to study the effect of "religious" primes on prosocial behavior have to select particular words to serve as their "religious" primes, which can fundamentally skew results when this selection is guided by a very historically unusual and culturally particular form of religiosity—particularly if a proportion of one's subject pool operates according to a very different model of religiosity. Similarly, an entire subfield of cross-cultural psychology is based on a model of East Asian thought as "holistic," as opposed to the "analytic" West (Nisbett 2003, Nisbett et al. 2001). As several workshop participants noted, the empirical data being gathered by these psychologists is extremely interesting, but when it comes to *interpreting* this data—that is, telling a coherent historical narrative that will explain it—they often fall back on unhelpful and essentialistic stereotypes. Eastern "holism," for instance, is traced back to such foundational texts of Chinese thought as the *Classic of Changes*

---

31. Kuhn himself was, of course, rather appalled by the manner in which his work became yoked to a rabid form of epistemological skepticism; see Kuhn 1970.

(*Yi Jing*) or the *Dao De Jing*, but without any clear sense of when or how these texts were composed, how representative they are of "Eastern" thought, or how they have historically been used and interpreted in East Asia.

Researchers in the various branches of the cognitive sciences thus have much to learn from humanists, and the cognitive sciences absolutely require the expertise of anthropologists, literary scholars, and historians if they are to avoid reinventing the wheel or committing egregious interpretative errors. The topic of religion provides another angle on this point. One of our participants and contributors, David Sloan Wilson, has called for scientists interested in studying the evolutionary origins of religion to tap into the rich knowledge base of historians and other more traditional scholars of religion, and for such scholars to seek out the kind of unifying theoretical framework that scientists can provide. One analogy that he has employed to convey this point is the manner in which the rich and detailed, though rather unorganized, data compiled by pre-Darwinian naturalists served as an invaluable resource for post-Darwinian scientists armed with the theory of evolution (Wilson 2002). There is certainly something to this analogy: one could argue that too much of current work in the humanities resembles butterfly collecting—a fundamental limitation of what Boyer refers to as the "erudition mode" in the sciences and humanities is a lack of any sort of guiding theoretical framework to help researchers formulate productive research questions and to make sense of their data. However, as Slingerland pointed out at the workshop, there is an important disanalogy with Darwin and the pre-Darwinian naturalists: when it comes to a phenomena such as "religion," the formulation of the very category itself requires humanistic expertise, and research into the possible evolutionary origins of religion risks going radically awry if not guided by such knowledge. This means that, when it comes to the scientific study of human-level phenomena, scholars with humanities expertise need to be on the ground floor of basic theorizing and experimental design, and not viewed as merely passive providers of cultural and historical data.

Bordering as it does on areas typically studied in core humanities fields, the discipline of psychology provides many examples of puzzling failures on the part of scientists to engage with basic work in the humanities. For example, the vast majority of psychological studies rely upon a subject pool composed exclusively of university undergraduates, and often, more specifically, undergraduate psychology majors. As a recent piece co-authored by some of our workshop participants (Henrich, Heine, and Norenzayan 2010) observes, "broad claims about human psychology and behavior in the world's top journals [are generally] based on samples drawn entirely from Western, Educated, Industrialized, Rich and Democratic (WEIRD) societies":

> Our review of the comparative database from across the behavioral sciences suggests both that there is substantial variability in experimental results across populations and that WEIRD subjects are particularly unusual compared with the rest of the species—frequent outliers. The domains reviewed include visual perception, fairness, cooperation, spatial reasoning, categorization and inferential induction, moral reasoning, reasoning styles, self-concepts and related motivations, and the heritability of IQ. The findings suggest that members of WEIRD societies, including young children, are among the least representative populations one could find for general-

izing about humans…Overall, these empirical patterns suggests that we need to be less cavalier in addressing questions of *human* nature on the basis of data drawn from this particularly thin, and rather unusual, slice of humanity. (61)

This piece has created quite a stir within psychology, and the authors are to be credited for their recognition of this basic problem, their thoroughness in documenting it in a manner likely to be convincing to their colleagues, and their courage in bringing it forward as a topic of debate. However, the response of most humanists, when told that North American university psychology undergraduates might not be representative of universal human nature, can be imagined by anyone with even a modicum of humanistic training. The diversity of human cognition across cultures and through historical time, while only recently a topic of study in psychology, is one of the most basic of truisms in the humanities, and it is a serious possibility that psychologists have wasted a fair amount of time pursuing research agendas that will prove upon reflection to be of only quite parochial cognitive interest.

There are a host of related problems that might be raised in this regard, some broached in the workshop discussions, others that have come up in subsequent collaboration. For instance, there is an often unspoken assumption in what little cross- cultural work that is done in psychology that terms drawn from modern American English can be unproblematically translated into exact equivalents in any language of the world—an assumption viewed as so unproblematic that the actual translations into foreign languages of study questionnaires and similar materials are hardly ever included in the "Methods" appendices of psychology journal articles. This, of course, gives fits to any of us who study languages for a living.

Such examples could be multiplied endlessly, but the take-home message is that analyzing the human mind and its products will often require both humanistic and scientific expertise. The recognition that consilience is a two-way street is not some polite concession to assuage the egos of humanistic scholars, but rather a call for humanists to be willing to collaborate with researchers from the sciences who are interested in traditional humanities issues and stand to profit from their accumulated expertise.

CONCLUSION: MOVING FROM BIVERSITIES TO UNIVERSITIES

It should be clear at this point that "second-wave" consilience calls upon researchers on *both* sides of the sciences/humanities divide to become radically more interdisciplinary. One of the primary questions explored at the workshop was how, practically, to help academics to do this—how to begin transforming Western institutions of higher learning from "biversities" into true universities, where scholars working at different levels of explanation feel comfortable exchanging information and sharing certain very general theoretical and methodological assumptions.[32] Despite their variety and "disunity" (Dupré 1993), the various disciplines of the natural sciences have managed to arrange themselves in a rough explanatory hierarchy, with information and insights flowing both up and down the chain of explanation. The levels of explanation in the natural/social

---

32. See, especially, chapter 18 by Buchman et al.

sciences that most directly border on the humanities—such as social psychology, evolutionary psychology, cognitive science, and animal behavior—have finally advanced to a point that they both need to hear from the humanistic disciplines and have many interesting things to say in return. How do we facilitate this process?

Although a dispiriting panoply of institutional and pragmatic difficulties were identified by workshop participants, there was a general recognition that the primary barrier to such dialogue between the humanities and the sciences is a remaining wall of strong mutual distrust and incomprehension. As Bradd Shore observes concerning the miniature version of the sciences/humanities divide within his own discipline, "Faced with the criticisms and dismissals from the other, each side is convinced of the moral and intellectual rightness of their view of things. Positions harden, mutual respect wanes, and the possibility of dialogue dims" (152). Too many scientists continue to see the humanities as disorganized, "soft" disciplines with little to offer them; too many humanists view the sciences as (at best) irrelevant to their own work, or (at worst) deeply flawed, culturally parochial discourses that threaten human values and dignity.

The invited Afterword to this volume, by Geoffrey Harpham, can be seen as both a plea for dialogue across the sciences/humanities barrier and a paradigmatic example of the sort of mutual incomprehension that allows that barrier to remain standing. Despite his claim that C.P. Snow's caricatured "pure scientists" and "literary intellectuals" are long behind us, their ghosts reappear in Harpham's "sneering" acolyte of scientific methodology (429), who disdains poetry and would banish all meaning from the Academy once and for all, as well as the sensitive students of literature, poetry, and art whose adventurous imaginations are all that lie between mankind and the "profoundly impoverished, gray, savorless, and also terrifying and pathetic" (429) future represented by the triumph of mechanistic science. Like many humanists, Harpham seems sincere in his desire for there to be more dialogue between humanists and scientists, while he remains equally convinced that humanists should continue working within their own particular mode of knowledge, their already quite fertile minds occasionally enriched by an interesting new tool tossed over the wall by the scientists working on the other side. For instance, in the EEG/fMRI study by the literary scholar, Davis, that he cites, the role of brain imaging technology seems limited to serving as a metaphor for something with which humanists are already quite familiar. The "powerful surge on the EEG graph" instigated by an engagement with creative-language use provides us with measurable, "empirical verification" of the existence of conscious self-awareness: the *Geist* in the machine that emerges when the day-to-day, mechanistic functioning of the brain machine is stymied by an encounter with the genius of Shakespeare. This rather sidesteps the deeper question of how we are to conceive of creativity and self-awareness if consciousness *is*, in fact, nothing other than the kind of electrical or blood-flow activity that can be measured by EEG and fMRI—a very profound and troubling question that is currently being explored in an interdisciplinary manner by philosopher-scientists trained on both sides of the wall.[33] Humanists need to have their basic categories fundamentally shaken up, not merely stirred.

33. See, for instance, Flanagan 2002, LeDoux 2002, Wegner 2002, Koch 2004, Searle 2004, Dennett 2005.

At the same time, we also need to resist the dystopic vision that such integration will mean the end of the humanities forever, and transform the university into a monolithic "dried cinder" of a world where poetry is reduced to math, fMRI scanners replace classrooms and books, and human spirit and creativity is suffocated by a dull grey blanket of mechanistic reasoning. As we have argued at some length earlier, the sort of nonreductive vertical integration proposed by "second-wave" consilience not only respects the relative autonomy and heuristic indispensability of human-level concepts and truths, but demands that the flow of explanation and interaction go both ways in the chain. The sciences do not merely provide some basic ontological constraints on humanistic inquiry—although they *should* do that—but also need to be guided by humanistic expertise, as well as being open, when necessary, to restructuring in light of humanistic work. Speaking of his particularly troubled discipline, Shore argues that we need "a genuinely multivocal anthropology that speaks authoritatively in several distinct and irreducible voices about the same material, and whose mode of engagement aims at expansive conversation rather than reductive simplification" (149). It is our conviction that a proper respect for the importance of emergent level truths leads to precisely this sort of genuine multivocality, and a commitment to a unified ontology prevents such multivocality from degenerating into babble. Workshop participant Leslie Heywood and her colleagues, in a discussion of the proper role of evolutionary theory in the study of literature, argue that the framework of evolution provides precisely this sort of space for unified effort combined with multilevel, multidirectional interaction: "Evolution…becomes not the paradigm that can explain everything from a scientific point of view but rather the beginnings of a conversation about lower and upper level questions, and how these questions might inform and enrich each other's research" (Heywood, Garcia, and Wilson 2009: 1).

"Second-wave" consilience contains space for all the disciplines that explore the complexities of human reality, acknowledging that each possesses its own conceptual tools and methods. When interlevel communication is deemed potentially appropriate and productive, it calls for non-eliminative and revealing forms of reduction—reduction that *explains* but does not *erase*. Such consilience is informed by a sophisticated model of scientific inquiry that recognizes the limitations of science without exaggerating them, and understands that the scientific study of human-level truths requires humanistic expertise on the ground floor, not merely as a source of data. It takes us beyond the nature-nurture debate by emphasizing the continuous co-evolution of mind and culture, and acknowledges the phenomenological ineradicability of mind-body dualism without reifying it into a barrier to explanations that cross the perceived mind-body divide. We hope that this volume gives some sense of the potential that such a vision of consilience promises for moving both the humanities and the sciences forward, with the desired effect of profoundly transforming both in the process.

References

Begley, Sharon. 2009. Don't blame the caveman. *Newsweek*, June 29: 42–47.

Bentley, R. A., and H. D. G. Maschner. 2003. *Complex systems and archaeology*. Salt Lake City, UT: University of Utah Press.

———. 2007. "Complexity theory." In *Handbook of archaeological theories*, ed. R. A. Bentley, H. D. G. Maschner, and C. Chippendale. Lanham, MD: AltaMira Press.

Bloom, Paul. 2004. *Descartes' baby: How the science of child development explains what makes us human*. New York: Basic Books.

Boyd, Brian, Joseph Carroll, and Jonathan Gottschall, eds. 2010. *Evolution, literature & film: A reader*. New York: Columbia University Press.

Boyer, Pascal. 1994. "Cognitive constraints on cultural representations: Natural ontologies and religious ideas." In *Mapping the mind: Domain-specificity in culture and cognition*, ed. L. A. Hirschfeld and S. Gelman. New York: Cambridge University Press.

Brooks, David. 2009. Human nature today. *New York Times*, June 25: A25.

Carroll, Joseph. 2008. An evolutionary paradigm for literary study. *Style* 42 (2–3): 103–135.

Carruthers, Peter, Stephen Laurence, and Stephen Stich, eds. 2005. *The innate mind: Structure and contents*. Vol. 1. New York: Oxford University Press.

———, eds. 2007. *The innate mind: Culture and cognition*. Vol. 2. New York: Oxford University Press.

———, eds. 2008. *The innate mind: Foundations and the future*. Vol. 3. New York: Oxford University Press.

Chalmers, David John. 1996. *The conscious mind: In search of a fundamental theory*, *Philosophy of mind series*. Oxford: Oxford University Press.

Cho, Francisca, and Richard Squier. 2008. He blinded me with science: Science chauvinism in the study of religion. *Journal of the American Academy of Religion* 76 (2): 420–448.

Churchland, P.M. 1979. *Scientific realism and the plasticity of mind*. Cambridge: Cambridge University Press.

Cooper, D.E. 2006. "Truthfulness and 'inclusion' in archaeology." In *The ethics of archaeology: Philosophical perspectives on archaeological practice*, ed. C. Scarre and G. Scarre. New York: Cambridge University Press.

Corbey, Raymond. 2005. *The metaphysics of apes: Negotiating the animal-human boundary*. New York: Cambridge University Press.

Crespi, Bernard, and Christopher Badcock. 2008. Psychosis and autism as diametrical disorders of the social brain. *Behavioral and Brain Sciences* 31: 284–320.

Crick, Francis. 1994. *The astonishing hypothesis: The scientific search for the soul*. New York: Simon & Schuster.

D'Andrade, R.G. 1995. Moral models in anthropology. *Current Anthropology* 36: 399–408.

Dancygier, Barbara. 2006. What can blending do for you? *Language and Literature* 15: 5–15.

Dawkins, Richard. 1976/2006. *The selfish gene*. 30th Anniversary Edition ed. Oxford: Oxford Unversity Press.

Dennett, Daniel. 1987. *The intentional stance*. Cambridge, Mass.: MIT Press.

———. 1995. Darwin's dangerous idea: Evolution and the meaning of life. New York: Simon & Schuster.

———. 2003. *Freedom evolves*. New York: Viking.

———. 2005. *Sweet dreams: Philosophical obstacles to a science of consciousness*. Cambridge, MA: MIT Press.

———. 2009. Darwin's "strange inversion of reasoning." *Proceedings of the National Academy of Science* 106(1): 10061–10065.

Dupré, John. 1993. *The disorder of things: Metaphysical foundations of the disunity of science*. Cambridge, MA: Harvard University Press.

Fauconnier, Gilles, and Mark Turner. 2002. *The way we think: Conceptual blending and the mind's hidden complexities*. New York: Basic Books.

Feyerabend, Paul. 1993. *Against method*. 3rd ed. New York: Verso.

Flanagan, Owen. 2002. *The problem of the soul: Two visions of mind and how to reconcile them.* New York: Basic Books.

Foucault, Michel. 1978. *The history of sexuality, vol. 1: An introduction.* Translated by R. Hurley. New York: Random House.

Geertz, Clifford. 1973. *The interpretation of cultures: Selected essays.* New York: Basic Books.

Gottschall, Jonathan, and David Sloan Wilson, eds. 2005. *The literary animal: Evolution and the nature of narrative.* Chicago: Northwestern University Press.

Haidt, Jonathan. 2001. The emotional dog and its rational tail: A social intuitionist approach to moral judgment. *Psychological Review* 108 (4): 814–34.

Henrich, Joseph, and Richard McElreath. 2007. Dual inheritance theory: The evolution of human cultural capacities and cultural evolution. In *Oxford handbook of evolutionary psychology*, eds. R. Dunbar and L. Barrett. Oxford: Oxford University Press.

Henrich, Joseph, Samuel Bowles, Eric. A. Smith, Peyton Young, Robert Boyd, Karl Sigmund, Peter Richerson, and Astrid Hopfensitz. 2003. "The cultural and genetic evolution of human cooperation." In *Genetic and cultural evolution of cooperation*, ed. P. Hammerstein. Cambridge: MIT Press.

Henrich, Joseph, Steven Heine, and Ara Norenzayan. 2010. The weirdest people in the world? *Behavioral & Brain Sciences* 33 (2–3): 61–83.

Heywood, Leslie, Justin Garcia, and David Wilson. 2009. Mind the gap: Appropriate evolutionary perspectives toward the integration of the sciences and humanities. *Science & Education* 19 (4): 505–522.

Kenrick, Douglas. 2006. Evolutionary psychology: Resistance is futile. *Psychological Inquiry* 17: 102–109.

Koch, Christof. 2004. *The quest for consciousness: A neurobiological approach.* New York: Roberts & Co.

Kuhn, Thomas. 1962/1970. *The structure of scientific revolutions.* 2nd ed. Chicago: University of Chicago Press.

———. 1970. Reflections on my critics. In *Criticism and the growth of knowledge*, edited by I. Lakatos and A. Musgrave. Cambridge: Cambridge University Press.

Lakoff, George, and Mark Johnson. 1999. *Philosophy in the flesh: The embodied mind and its challenge to western thought.* New York: Basic Books.

Latour, Bruno, and Steve Woolgar. 1979/1986. *Laboratory life: The construction of scientific facts.* 2nd ed. Princeton: Princeton University Press.

Laudan, Larry. 1996. *Beyond positivism and relativism: Theory, method, and evidence.* Boulder, CO: Westview Press.

Lawson, E.Thomas, and Robert N. McCauley. 1990. *Rethinking religion: Connecting cognition and culture.* Cambridge: Cambridge University Press.

LeDoux, Joseph. 2002. *Synaptic self: How our brains become who we are.* New York: Macmillan.

Lewis, H.S. 1999. The misrepresentation of anthropology and its consequences. *American Anthropologist* 100: 716–731.

Locke, John. 1690/1975. *An essay concerning human understanding.* Oxford: Clarendon.

McCauley, Robert. 2007.: "Reduction: Models of cross-scientific relations and their implications for the psychology-neuroscience interface." In *Handbook of the philosophy of science: Philosophy of psychology and cognitive science*, edited by P. Thagard. Amsterdam: Elsevier.

———. 2008. Respondent, panel on "Cognitive science of religion: What is it and why is it important?." In *American Academy of Religion Annual Meeting, Cognitive Science of Religion Consultation.* Chicago, Il.

McCauley, Robert, and E. Thomas Lawson. 2002. *Bringing ritual to mind*. Cambridge: Cambridge University Press.

Menand, Louis. 2005. Dangers within and without. *Modern Language Association, Profession* (2005): 10–17.

Mithen, Steven J. 1996. *The prehistory of the mind*. London: Thames & Hudson.

Nichols, Shaun. 2004. *Sentimental rules: On the natural foundations of moral judgment*. New York: Oxford University Press.

Nietzsche, Friedrich. 1886/1966. *Beyond good and evil*. Trans.W. Kaufmann. New York: Vintage.

Nisbett, Richard E. 2003. *The geography of thought: How Asians and Westerners think differently . . . And why*. New York: The Free Press.

Nisbett, Richard E., Kaiping Peng, Incheol Choi, and Ara Norenzayan. 2001. Culture and systems of thought: Holistic versus analytic cognition. *Psychological Review* 108 (2):291–310.

Pinker, Steven. 2002. *The blank slate: The modern denial of human nature*. New York: Viking.

Prinz, Jesse. 2007. *The emotional construction of morals*. New York: Oxford University Press.

Putnam, Hilary. 1999. *The threefold cord: Mind, body, and world*. New York: Columbia University Press.

Richerson, Peter, and Robert Boyd. 2005. *Not by genes alone: How culture transformed human evolution*. Chicago, IL: University of Chicago Press.

Rorty, Richard. 1998. Against unity: A review of E.O. Wilson's *Consilience*. *The Wilson Quarterly* 22(1): 28–38.

Ryle, Gilbert. 1971. "The thinking of thoughts: What is "le penseur" doing?" In *Collected papers*. London: Hutchinson and Co.

Schaller, Mark, and Christian Crandall, eds. 2004. *The psychological foundations of culture*. Mahwah, NJ: Lawrence Erlbaum.

Schaller, Mark, Ara Norenzayan, Steven Heine, Toshio Yamagishi, and Tatsuya Kameda, eds. 2010. *Evolution, culture, and the human mind*. New York: Psychology Press.

Scheper-Hughes, N. 1995. The primacy of the ethical: Propositions for a militant anthropology. *Current Anthropology* 36: 409–420.

Searle, John. 2004. *Mind: A brief introduction*. New York: Oxford University Press.

Segerstråle, Ullica. 2000. *Defenders of the truth: The battle for sociobiology and beyond*. New York: Oxford University Press.

Shanks, M., and C. Tilley. 1987. *Reconstructing archaeology*. New York: Cambridge University Press.

Simonton, Dean Keith. 2009. Varieties of (scientific) creativity: A hierarchical model of domain-specific disposition, development, and achievement. *Perspectives on Psychological Science* 4: 441–452.

Slingerland, Edward. 2008a. *What science offers the humanities: Integrating body & culture*. New York: Cambridge University Press.

———. 2008b. Who's afraid of reductionism? The study of religion in the age of cognitive science. *Journal of the American Academy of Religion* 76 (2): 375–411.

———. (in preparation). *Body, mind and religion in early China: Beyond the myth of holism*.

Smith, Barbara Herrnstein. 2006. *Scandalous knowledge: Science, truth and the human*. Durham, NC: Duke University Press.

Snow, C.P. 1959/1993. *The two cultures*. New York: Cambridge University Press.

Sperber, Dan, and Lawrence A. Hirschfeld. 2004. The cognitive foundations of cultural stability and diversity. *Trends in Cognitive Sciences* 8(1): 40–46.

Tanaka, Jiro. (under review). Autism, psychosis, and the two cultures. In *The evolutionary review*, ed. A. Andrews and J. Carroll. Albany, NY: State University of New York Press.

Taylor, Charles. 1989. *Sources of the self: The makings of modern identity*. Cambridge, MA: Harvard University Press.

———. 2007. *A secular age*. Cambridge, MA: Harvard University Press.

Tooby, John, and Leda Cosmides. 1992. "The psychological foundations of culture." In *The adapted mind: Evolutionary psychology and the generation of culture*, eds. J. Barkow, L. Cosmides, and J. Tooby. New York: Oxford University Press.

Wegner, Daniel. 2002. *The illusion of conscious will*. Cambridge, MA: MIT Press.

Wilson, D. S. 1975. Theory of group selection. *Proceedings of the National Academy of Sciences of the United States of America* 72 (1): 143–146.

———. 2002. *Darwin's cathedral: Evolution, religion, and the nature of society*. Chicago: University of Chicago.

———. 2006. "Human groups as adaptive units: Toward a permanent concensus." In *The innate mind: Culture and cognition*, ed. P. Carruthers, S. Laurence, and S. Stich. New York: Oxford University Press.

Wilson, E. O. 1998. *Consilience: The unity of knowledge*. New York: Knopf.

———. 1975/2000. *Sociobiology : The new synthesis 25th Anniversary Edition ed*. Cambridge, MA: Harvard University Press.

Wolf, Eric. 1964. *Anthropology*. Englewood Cliffs, NJ: Prentice Hall.

PART I

Theoretical Issues

SECTION ONE

Ontologies for the Human

1

THE HUMANITIES AND HUMAN NATURE[1]

Steven Pinker

There is a widespread perception that the humanities are in trouble. I have a collection of despondent articles with titles such as "The Decline and Fall of Literature" (Delbanco 1999), "Have the Humanities Disciplines Collapsed?" (Conference at the Stanford University Humanities Center, April 23, 1999), "The Humanities at Twilight" (Steiner 1999), "The Humanities Plight" (Louch 1998), *What Happened to the Humanities?* (Kernan 1997) and so on.

Indeed, some of the signs of the health of the humanities are not good. There has been a decline in enrollment, faculty, and resources, and, most ominously, in interest among high school students. In recent polls only nine percent of high school students express a desire to major in the humanities (Engell and Dangerfield 1998). There is also a widely acknowledged sense of malaise, a resignation about the lack of a progressive agenda in the humanities.

One sign of this desperation was a solution tried by Indiana University a number of years back. The university hired an advertising agency to recruit more students into its humanities programs in a campaign called "Think for a Living." Here are some of the slogans they came up with:

> "Do What You Want When You Graduate or Wait Twenty Years
>   for Your Mid-Life Crisis"
> "Insurance for When the Robots Take Over All The Boring Jobs"
> "Okay Then, Follow Your Dreams in Your Next Life"
> "Yeah, Like Your Parents Are So Happy"

The crisis in the humanities is regrettable, because the humanities are indispensable to a liberal democracy. First of all, our lives are shaped by ideas. Our system of law, government, our economy, our assumptions about education, childrearing, and the relation between the sexes all have a rationale that was first worked out by thinkers in what we now call the humanities. Second, the humanities are touchstones for our private and public discourse. Even within the sciences, one cannot talk about biotechnology or genetic engineering without alluding to the novel *Brave New World*, to take just one example. Third, our lives are affected by the contingencies of our culture and

1. This is an edited transcript of a lecture originally presented to a Dactyl Foundation conference on Poetics and Cognitive Science. Committee for the Scientific Investigation of Claims of the Paranormal Copyright 2006, Gale Group. Used by Permission of the *Skeptical Inquirer* (www.csicop.org).

part of being an engaged citizen in a democracy is having a cosmopolitan appreciation of other times, places, and peoples.

So, given that the humanities are indispensable to an informed citizenry, and that they appear to be in trouble, how can we understand how we got into this state and how we might get out of it?

One diagnosis is that the malaise of the humanities comes in part from its separation from the sciences—the famous "two cultures" of C. P. Snow ([1959]1993)—which has led to an insularity of the humanities, an isolation from the new ideas and discoveries coming from the sciences. For several centuries the sciences have enjoyed a development that was labeled with a lovely word, consilience, by E.O. Wilson (Wilson 1998), although I think the idea has also been expressed by John Tooby and Leda Cosmides, the founders of evolutionary psychology (Tooby and Cosmides 1992). The history of modern science has been a history of the unification of supposedly incommensurable metaphysical realms. Perhaps Newton's greatest accomplishment was to subvert the ancient doctrine that there was a fundamental division in the universe between the supralunary sphere of the moon—supposedly governed by pristine eternal laws—and the grubby, chaotic Earth below. Newton, of course, showed that the same force that brings the apple down to the earth also keeps the moon in orbit around it.

It used to be believed that there is a fundamental division between the formative past, when the planet was shaped and created, and the static present, until Charles Lyell showed that forces that we see around us, such as erosion, climate, volcanoes, and earthquakes, if operating over a sufficient length of time, would have been sufficient to sculpt the landscape as we find it today.

It was once believed that living and non-living matter occupied separate realms: that living things were constituted out of some quivering gel called protoplasm, which is utterly unlike non-living matter. Then Friedrich Wöhler showed that one could synthesize urea out of chemical compounds and, by extension, that the stuff of life was composed of ordinary materials obeying the laws of chemistry.

The integration of the non-living and living worlds was further advanced by Darwin, who showed that the ubiquitous presence of adaptation in the living world could be explained by the natural selection of replicators. Later, the discoveries of Mendel and of Watson and Crick would show that replication itself can be understood as a physical process.

The last remaining chasm in our ontology is between the biological and the cultural, with the sciences on one side and the humanities on the other. The ground for optimism about the humanities is that the process of consilience will continue. We are beginning to see the glimmerings of the unifications of the sciences with the humanities. There are two realms in which this is being carried out.

One is the study of deep history—the use of genetics, linguistics, and archaeology to bridge the end of human biological evolution and the beginning of history, civilization, and culture. Those familiar with Jared Diamond's *Guns, Germs, and Steel* (Diamond 1997), for example, have some exposure to this new science, which bridges biological evolution with the beginning of recorded history. The historian Dan Smail has reciprocated the invitation with his call for historians to incorporate "deep history" into the discipline (Smail 2005).

The other bridge between the sciences and humanities consists of the sciences of human nature, connecting them not in time but in causation. Cognitive neuroscience, evolutionary psychology, and behavioral genetics can play a role in illuminating our culture and giving us a deeper understanding of society.

The key idea is that our culture and society are collective products of human minds. They were not laid out by a committee of Martians but are products of the activity of the brain, which itself is a product of evolution. It is the human faculties of perception, imagination, social cognition, and emotion that artists exploit in order to achieve their effects. Therefore, what we call culture is not a separate realm from the biological or the psychological. These realms emerge from a process of diffusion in which ideas, inventions, and social contracts are shared to the point that they become epidemic in a community, at which point we call them cultures.

The humanities and sciences are already drawing together in several ways. For example, the philosophy of mind nowadays shades into the sciences of cognition and neurobiology: topics such as consciousness, innate ideas, the mind/body problem, imagery, private language, and epistemology are no longer carried out in a hermetically sealed philosophical discourse but incorporate what we know about the incarnation of all of these processes in living brains. The visual arts and the study of visual perception are also beginning to mutually inform one another. An example is evolutionary aesthetics, and the analysis of why certain colors, forms, faces, and landscapes elicit certain affective and cognitive responses.[2] Or consider the cross-fertilization between jurisprudence and moral philosophy on the one hand and moral psychology on the other, this interdisciplinary endeavor suggests that some debates in ethics might be colored by basic intuitions about right and wrong that we may have inherited in the course of human evolution.[3]

Let me mention two examples, not because they represent the best that this approach has to offer but because they are familiar to me: how the studies of language within the humanities can interact with the scientific study of language from psycholinguistics and neurolinguistics and how the analysis of fiction can interact with cognitive and evolutionary psychology.

Let us begin with the fundamental problem in cognitive science, explaining the vast expressive power of language.[4] Just by making noises with my mouth I can cause you to think an unlimited number of ideas, everything from theories of the origin of the universe to the developments in your favorite reality show. How this is possible is the puzzle for language scientists. What is behind our knack of causing each other to think an unlimited range of ideas just by making noises with our mouths?

It turns out that there is not one trick behind this talent, but two. One is the memorized word, whose underlying principle was captured by Ferdinand de Saussure as an arbitrary pairing between a sound and meaning (de Saussure 1960). The word *duck*, for example, does not look like a duck, walk like a duck, or quack like a duck. But I can use it to get you to think of a duck, because all of us at some point in our childhoods have memorized an association between that sound and that idea. That means we have stored in our brain a linkage between that sound and that meaning.

---

2. For a recent review, see Dutton 2009.

3. See Greene 2003 and the chapters in the "Religions and Ethics" section of this volume.

4. The following discussion of language is based on my book *Words and Rules: The Ingredients of Language* (Pinker 1999).

But we do not just blurt out individual words; we combine them into phrases and sentences. And that brings us to the second principle behind language: combinatorial grammar, most famously worked out by the linguist Noam Chomsky, in which we combine words according to a scheme in which the meaning of the phrase or sentence can be computed from the meanings of the individual words and the way they are arranged. The power of combinatorial grammar is that phrases may be composed from symbols that can be recombined in an unlimited number of ways. This allows us to create and understand sentences, rather than memorizing them in the way that we memorize individual words.

A test of the hypothesis that the language faculty has this bipartite architecture is to find some area of language in which the putative word system and the putative rule system express the same ideas but are psychologically and, ultimately, neurobiologically distinguishable. I believe that we do have such a case: regular and irregular forms. In English, and in many other languages, verbs come in two flavors. There are regular verbs, like *walk/walked, jog/jogged*, and *kiss/kissed*, which form the past tense in a predictable way: take the verb and glue the suffix *ed* onto the end.

This is an open-ended class. There are thousands of existing regular verbs in English, and new ones are being added all the time. When you first heard the verb *to spam*, in the sense of sending unwanted e-mail, you did not have to go to the dictionary to look up its past-tense form. Everyone instinctively knows that it is *spammed*. Likewise, *snarf, mosh, flame, diss*, and other neologisms are instantly inflected as *snarfed, moshed, flamed*, and *dissed*, without the benefit of memory for those forms.

Even children do it. If you bring a child into the lab and say, "Here is a man who knows how to wug. He did the same thing yesterday," children will fill in the blank by saying, "wugged," a form that they could not have memorized from their parents. And all children show off this talent when they go through the stage in which they make grammatical errors such as "we holded the baby rabbits" or "the alligator goed kerplunk." They could not have memorized such verb forms from their parents, but must have created them in their minds.

The second flavor of verb is irregular—forms like *bring/brought, go/went, sing/sang, sleep/slept, make/made*, and *fly/flew*. They differ from the regulars in just about every way. In contrast to the monotonous predictability of regular forms, the irregulars are idiosyncratic and quirky: the past of *sink* is *sank*, but the past of *cling* is not *clang*; it is *clung*. The past of *think* is neither *thank* nor *thunk* but *thought*. The past of *blink* is neither *blank* nor *blunk* or *blought* but is regular, *blinked*. And the irregulars form a closed class. There are about 165 irregular verbs in contemporary English and we have not seen any recent new ones.

This leads to a simple theory: irregular forms are words that people memorize in the same way that they memorize *dog* and *duck* and *man*. That is, one memorizes the verb itself, *bring*, and also memorizes its past tense form, *brought*. Each is a separate entry in memory. They are linked, because one of them is the past tense of the other, but in other regards they are simply committed to memory separately. Regular forms, in contrast, do not have to be stored, because they can be generated by a rule whenever they are needed.

If this idea is correct, the brain system for word memory should be tied to irregular forms and the brain system for online grammatical computation should be tied to regular forms.

There is some evidence that this is true. In a study that I did with Jaemin Rhee using magnetoencepholography, which measures the faint magnetic signals emanating from the brain during mental activity, we presented verbs to subjects. They had to pronounce the past tense form while their heads were in the scanner. At each time slice, the apparatus estimated the location of the source of the magnetic field pattern. Initially, in the first quarter of a second after seeing the verb stem, the greatest activity for both regular and irregular verbs is in the same part of the brain, in the temporal lobe where memories are thought to be formed and stored. About a tenth of a second later, with regular forms, we saw a second pattern of activity in more anterior regions of the brain, those that are thought to be responsible for planning and computation in the online assembly of forms. Thus, regular and irregular forms arise from distinct brain systems, tied, respectively, to combination and to memory lookup. Are there any implications of such neurobiological finds for issues studied in the humanities? I believe there are. For one thing, there are implications for explaining the nature and history of languages as we find them today, which are products of human minds accumulated over centuries. If you look at the most frequent verbs in English (Francis and Kucera 1982), as measured by the number of occurrences in a million words of text, you get the following top ten list:

be
have
do
say
make
go
take
come
see
get

Interestingly, all ten are irregular—*be/was, have/had, do/did, say/said, make/made, go/ went*, and so on. Compare them to the least frequent verbs in the language. There cannot be a "bottom-ten" list, because we find a 788-way tie for last place, last place being one in a million which, of course, is the lowest frequency you can measure in a million-word corpus. But here are the first ten of those 788 verbs in alphabetical order:

abate
abbreviate
abhor
ablate
abridge
abrogate
acclimatize
acculturate
admix
adulterate

As you can see, they are all regular: *abate/abated, abbreviate/abbreviated*, and so on. One sees this in most languages—a massive correlation between frequency and irregularity.

Although it might seem perverse, the psychology and neurobiology of language provide a simple explanation. Irregulars depend on memory, because they are idiosyncratic and have to be learned one at a time. Memory depends on frequency: the more often you hear something, the better you remember it. Any word that declines in popularity may reach a point at which it is not heard often enough to be memorized uniformly by a generation of children. If the word is not memorized, children will default to the regular "-ed" form, converting the verb from irregular to regular for their generation and all subsequent generations.

There is some evidence from philology that this is true. Old English and Middle English had more than twice as many irregular verbs as we find today. If Chaucer were here, he would tell you that the past tense of *cleave* is *clove*, likewise that the past of *crow* is *crew*, the past of *chide* is *chid*, the past of *gripe* is *grope*, and so on. The common verbs in Chaucer's time stayed irregular, and the rarer ones defected to the regular side, which is exactly what you would expect based on the properties of human memory.

In addition, the regular rule got first dibs on all of the new entries into the language when English absorbed a massive influx of verbs from French after the Norman Invasion in 1066, and then from Latin during the Renaissance. As with *spam, flame, diss*, and so on, they got sucked into the regular camp, leading to the enormous imbalance favoring the regulars in English today.

You can actually feel this historical force acting today, in your own mind: the remaining infrequent irregulars (the ones that are at the lower end of the frequency range) sound strange to our ears. For example, if I ask you to complete the sequence "I stride. I strode. I have...," you might be tempted to say *stridden*, but there is something unusual about it. Likewise, consider *smite/smote, slay/slew, bid/bade*, and *forsake/forsook*. All have a bookish feel, and one can almost hear them slipping out of the language before our ears. One can predict that, in a few hundred years, they may have the status of *chide/chid* and *gripe/grope*.

This account also has implications for style. Because irregulars are dependent on memory and exposure, they can serve as a shibboleth in a consideration of what is "proper" English, the kind of thing we correct in the term papers or get exercised about when we worry about the decline of the language. Many of the bones of contention are irregular forms. For example, may language mavens maintain that *data* is the plural of *datum*, so one should say "The data are" rather than "The data is." There are also people up in arms over the Disney movie "Honey, I Shrunk the Kids," which they say should have been "Honey, I *Shrank* the Kids." The reason these irregular forms can serve as markers of education and cultural literacy is that no one can deduce them with a general rule. Knowledge of them crucially depends on which people you hung out with at various stages of your life.

Here is another implication for style. Whenever a verb is a doublet, with both regular and irregular forms, poets, novelists, and lyricists tend to prefer the irregular forms, such as *striven, shone, slew, hove, clove*. This is in part because of the euphony of words as opposed to rule products. Irregular forms have the sound of basic words in the language, whereas regular forms sound like agglomerations of a stem and a suffix glued together by a rule. Since irregulars fit the phonological template for a basic word, they are more pleasing to the ear. In contrast, in the product of a concatenation operation, the two units can sometimes be stuck together without any consideration for euphony. In extreme form you get tongue twisters such as *edited* or *sixths* that are perfectly grammatical, but could never have passed muster as ordinary English words.

Also, irregular forms are evocative. Again, because they are memorized, they are tied in connotation and emotion to the circumstances in which they were originally learned. Forms like *smote* and *slew*, for example, place many speakers into the atmosphere of the King James Bible.

Lastly, the organization of words in memory parallels some of the most commonly used poetic devices. The irregular forms are not completely idiosyncratic but tend to fall into families of similar-sounding verbs with similar-sounding past tense forms: *wear/wore, bear/bore, tear/tore, wind/wound, grind/ground, bind/bound; swing/swung, fling/flung, ring/rung.* They also may be grouped by alliteration: *swing/swung, stick/stuck, strike/struck, sneak/snuck.* Sometimes they are grouped by assonance: *feel/felt, dream/dreamt, keep/kept, mean/meant.*

This is puzzling. Why should a list of irregular vocabulary items sound like bad poetry when you read them in sequence? Why would the devices used by poets also characterize the contents of the mental dictionary, just sitting there in no particular order? The basic idea—articulated by Paul Kiparsky (1982), and by Roman Jakobson before him—comes from the fundamental principle of linguistics: that words and phrases are not just linear sequences of sounds but are mentally represented in hierarchical tree structures. Poetic and rhetorical language often repeats one of the basic structures of language: exactly those structures in which words are stored in memory. In the case of words, linguists suggest that the brain represents their sounds by first splitting them into an onset and a rime. When you repeat a rime you get a rhyme. When onsets are repeated, this gives rise to alliteration. Assonance arises from the repetition of the vocalic nucleus, the vowel in the middle. And at higher levels, when what is repeated is a surface or deep syntactic phrase structure, you get the phenomenon known as structural parallelism, which is effective in poetry and rhetoric.

The general moral for consilience is that it is not clear where the science leaves off and the poetics begins. Which part of this investigation belongs in the pile of bricks and mortar at a university called "the humanities," and which part belongs in the pile called "the sciences"?

The other case study that is dear to me is the psychology of fiction.[5] Here the scientific puzzle is that, in all cultures, people lose themselves in stories. They expend time and energy thinking about people and events that do not exist. One might ask, from a Darwinian perspective, why would a mind have evolved that would waste time and energy thinking about nonexistent worlds?

One hypothesis is that fiction does have an adaptive function, similar to the philosophers' thought experiment. In a work of fiction, the author places a character in a hypothetical situation, a world with at least some similarity to our world. The protagonist is given a goal and pursues it in the face of obstacles, and the author plays out the

5. See Pinker 1997, 2007.

consequences for the reader. The reader watches what happens and takes mental notes of the outcomes of the various strategies and tactics in pursuing those goals. Since none of us can actually benefit from the experience of living all the scenarios that we are likely to face in the future, we can benefit vicariously by seeing what would happen in a fictional version of the world.

There is a rich cognitive psychology that is relevant to this process, some of which has been worked out by Lisa Zunshine (Zunshine 2006). First, there is the capacity for metarepresentation: representations of representations, which allow us to entertain a realistic hypothetical world without confusing it with reality. For instance, we may entertain a representation of a person, while knowing that that representation does not refer to a real person in the world—a remarkable ability of the human brain.[6] Second, there is our "theory of mind" or intuitive psychology: the ability to infer beliefs and desires from characters' behavior.[7] As Zunshine has shown, one parameter in fiction is whether the narrator requires the reader to infer thoughts and feelings from a character's behavior or reports the contents of the character's consciousness directly. A third is the use of visual imagery—a recruitment of a cognitive process in fiction that has been explored, for example, by Elaine Scarry (1999). By the use of words, authors can evoke visual images and manipulate the reader's perspective, attention to detail, and vividness of apprehension.

However, fiction is not merely an exercise of our intellectual faculties. It engages our emotions and our social psychology. It has often been noted that the goals of fictitious characters are at least indirectly related to the ultimate goals of evolution: survival and reproduction. This is not just the red-in-tooth-and-claw struggle we are familiar with from the animal world but the contest for survival and reproduction in a species that is intensely cognitive and social—a species that lives by its wits and by its social coalitions.[8]

In his book, *The Thirty-Six Dramatic Situations*, Georges Polti tries to categorize the world's literature and myths into a small number of archetypes (Polti [1921] 1977). About 80 percent of them can be characterized as involving contests between adversaries or tragedies of kinship or love. Examples include "mistaken jealousy," "the vengeance taken by kindred upon kindred," "the discovery of the dishonor of a loved one," and "an enemy loved." All are familiar material in evolutionary psychology.

Yet if literature were nothing more than the playing out of hypothetical scenarios, it would be a dreary affair indeed. Despite claims by Polti and others that there are a finite number of plots, we also know that literature is open-ended, that we will never run out of plots and novels. Although the summaries may be finite, fiction itself is not.

One reason is that the main obstacles to a protagonist's goals are other people in pursuit of their own goals, leading to a combinatorial explosion of possible interactions. The fundamental insight of modern evolutionary psychology—owing to Robert Trivers—is that every kind of social relationship involves both a confluence *and* a

6. It has been suggested that a breakdown of this ability is the main symptom in schizophrenia (Frith, 1992).

7. For a basic introduction to the concept of "theory of mind," see Bloom 2004.

8. For more on this theme, see the contributions in the literature section later in this chapter.

conflict of interests (Trivers 1971 and 1972). These partial conflicts of interest are more cognitively fertile than a near-total overlap of interests (such as one sees in social insects like bees and ants, which make sacrifices for one another that would puzzle a human since they are highly genetically related), or a total conflict of interests, as in a war of all against all. With some overlap and some non-overlap one has a fecund situation for possibilities to play out mentally. Though I have attributed this insight to Trivers and other evolutionary psychologists, the temporal sequence could be argued in reverse: commentators on fiction could have educated evolutionary biologists with this insight long ago.

To take one example, an evolutionary biologist would look at the relationship between two spouses in the following way. The overlap comes from the fact that the Darwinian interests of a pair of spouses are identical under the following idealization: if the spouses are faithful, if they favor their own nuclear family over their blood relatives, and if they can expect to die at the same time, then they are, as far as evolution is concerned, one flesh, and what is good for one is good for the other. One would expect perfect empathy and perfect love.

Needless to say those are not the conditions of any human marriage. Marital conflict is expected to be triggered by infidelity, real or imagined, by in-laws, and by the investment horizon—how long a reproductive career the person can expect. Many works of romance explore how the protagonists stumble into conflict over exactly these areas.

The relationship between a parent and child likewise has some degree of overlap and some degree of non-overlap, as do the relationships between sibling and sibling, man and woman, friend and friend, individual and society. Trivers argued that even the relationship of a person to himself is not one of complete overlap, but gives rise to areas of conflict as well.

It has long been known that partial conflict is a source of the enduring appeal of fiction, but it has been less clear why this should be so. For instance, Aristotle said that a story about two strangers who fight to the death is nowhere near as interesting as a story about two *brothers* who fight to the death. Similarly, Polti's dramatic situations all involve partial conflicts of interest. And in his book *Antigones*, in which George Steiner suggests that *Antigone* may be the best work of fiction ever written (Steiner 1984), he argues "[i]t has, I believe, been given to only one literary text to express all the principal constants of conflict in the condition of man. These constants are fivefold: the confrontation of man and of woman; of age and of youth; of society and of the individual; of the living and of the dead; and of men and gods.... [B]ecause Greek myths encode certain primary biological and social confrontations and self-perceptions in the history of man, they endure as an animate legacy in collective memory and recognition" (Steiner 1984, 300–301).

In sum, I have suggested that the malaise of the humanities is related to their isolation from the sciences, and that we now have an opportunity to extend the consilience enjoyed by the sciences to the social sciences and the humanities. One connection is deep history; another is the sciences of human nature, in particular the sciences of mind, brain, genes, and evolution. I have offered two examples familiar to me from language and literature to give a sense of how such consilience might begin. A danger in this enterprise is that the applications of science to the humanities are bound to consider only a fraction of the richness in a work of art or scholarship. To understand a work of art requires expertise in the particulars of the work and the idiom, and not just generalities of psychology and biology. What we need is, not a hostile takeover of the humanities, but teams of scholars tunneling into a mountain from opposite sides and meeting in the middle. I am confident that there are many opportunities for this to happen, some of them presented in the chapters that follow.

References

Bloom, Paul. 2004. *Descartes' baby: How the science of child development explains what makes us human*. New York: Basic Books.

de Saussure, F. 1960. *Course in general linguistics*. Ed. Charles Bally and Albert Sechehaye. Trans. Wade Baskin. London: Owen.

Delbanco, A. 1999. The decline and fall of literature (English, an embattled profession). *New York Review of Books* 46(17): 32–38.

Diamond, J. 1997. *Guns, germs, and steel: The fates of human societies*. New York: Norton.

Dutton, Denis. 2009. *The art instinct: Beauty, pleasure, and human evolution*. New York: Bloomsbury.

Engell, J. and Dangerfield A. 1998. Humanities in the age of money. *Harvard Magazine* May–June: 48–55, 111.

Francis, N. and Kucera, H. 1982. *Frequency analysis of English usage: Lexicon and grammar*. Boston: Houghton Mifflin.

Frith, C. 1992. *The cognitive neuropsychology of schizophrenia*. New York: Psychology Press.

Greene, J.D. 2003. From neural "is" to moral "ought": What are the moral implications of neuroscientific moral psychology? *Nature Reviews Neuroscience* 4: 847–850.

Kernan, A. ed. 1997. *What's happened to the humanities?* Princeton: Princeton University Press.

Kiparski, P. 1982. Lexical phonology and morphology. In *Linguistics in the morning calm*, ed. I. S. Yang. Seoul: Hansin.

Louch, A. 1998. The humanities' plight. *Philosophy and Literature* 22(1): 231–41.

Pinker, S. 1997. *How the mind works*. New York: W.W. Norton.

———. 1999. *Words and rules: The ingredients of language*. New York: HarperCollins.

———. 2007. Toward a consilient study of literature (review of J. Gottschall and D. Sloan Wilson, "The Literary Animal: Evolution and the Nature of Narrative"). *Philosophy and Literature* 31: 161–177

Polti, G. [1921] 1977. *The thirty-six dramatic situations*. Boston: The Writer.

Scarry, E. 1999. *Dreaming by the book*. New York: Farrar Straus and Giroux.

Smail, D. 2005. In the grip of sacred history. *The American Historical Review* 110: 5. http://www.historycooperative.org/journals/ahr/110.5/smail.html.

Snow, C.P. [1959] 1993. *The two cultures*. New York: Cambridge University Press.

Steiner, G. 1984. *Antigones: How the Antigone legend has endured in Western literature, art, and thought*. New Haven: Yale University Press.

———. 1999. The humanities at twilight. *PN Review* 25: March–April.

Tooby, John and Leda Cosmides. 1992. "The psychological foundations of culture." In *The adapted mind*, ed. J. Barkow, L. Cosmides and J. Tooby. New York: Oxford University Press.

Trivers, Robert L. 1971. The evolution of reciprocal altruism. *The Quarterly Review of Biology* 46: 34–57.

———. 1972. "Parental investment and sexual selection." In *Sexual selection and the descent of man. 1871–1971,* ed. B. G. Campbell. Chicago: Aldine.

Wilson, E.O. 1998. *Consilience: The unity of knowledge.* New York: Alfred A. Knopf.

Zunshine, L. 2006. *Why we read fiction: Theory of mind and the novel.* Columbus: Ohio State University Press.

2

THE METAPHYSICAL REALITIES OF THE UNPHYSICAL SCIENCES: OR WHY VERTICAL INTEGRATION SEEMS UNREALISTIC TO ONTOLOGICAL PLURALISTS[1]

Richard A. Shweder

In the spirit of academic debate I am going to assume the role of the Pyrrhonist with respect to the most distinctive and probably the most provocative (because it is imperialistic sounding) aspect of our conference mission: namely, the invitation to vertically integrate the humanities into the biological and cognitive sciences. My skeptical remarks will revisit (and at times recapitulate) discussions from the distant and not so distant past, including a quip by Woody Allen, parts of an address I delivered 10 years ago evaluating a similar unity of knowledge agenda proposed by the Harvard biologist E.O. Wilson (his so-called consilience program),[2] and including, as well, a pertinent 1868 remark by the English physicist John Tyndall concerning mind-body dualism that I discovered in the notorious (famous and infamous) essay "The Limits of Natural Selection as Applied to Man," written in 1870 by A.R. Wallace, one of the two most significant creators of the theory of evolution by means of natural selection.

Woody Allen asks in one of his books: "Can we actually 'know' the universe?" "My God," he replies, "it is hard enough finding your way around in Chinatown." This conference volume invites us to contemplate a less ambitious but nonetheless vast

1. I wish to thank my friend and colleague, the University of Chicago geophysicist Frank Richter, for the expression "the un-physical sciences" and for raising many searching questions over the years about the distinction within the academy between the physical sciences and the un-physical sciences (including mathematics). Parts of this essay were written while the author was a Rosanna and Charles Jaffin Founders Circle Member of the School of Social Sciences at the Institute for Advanced Study, Princeton, New Jersey.

2. That address was titled "A Polytheistic Conception of the Sciences and the Virtues of Deep Variety" and was delivered at a millennial year conference on the topic of "Consilience" organized by the New York Academy of Sciences and subsequently published in the *Annals of the New York Academy of Sciences* 935, 2001 (and reprinted in R.A. Shweder, *Why Do Men Barbecue? Recipes for Cultural Psychology*, Cambridge, Mass.: Harvard University Press, 2003). Sections of the current paper replay or draw heavily on that address as well as on some of my writings on the foundations of cultural psychology. See for example, R.A. Shweder, "John Searle on a Witch Hunt," *Anthropological Theory* 6 (2006): 89–111.

unification of knowledge proposal, specifically one that views mind/body dualism as an old-fashioned metaphysical belief and hence calls for the integration of the humanities into the biological and cognitive sciences. The original inspiration for the conference was an earnest hope that the humanities might be revitalized (they were judged to have run out of creative intellectual steam) by weaving together the fields of religious studies, normative ethics, literature, aesthetics, the psychology of the emotions, evolutionary biology and the cognitive and brain sciences into a seamless vertically arranged hierarchy of cause and effect explanation.

The phrase "the unity of knowledge," just like the word *consilience* popularized by E.O. Wilson, is an appealing expression, whose phonetic shape and semantic connotations sound an optimistic, even peace loving and ecumenical tone. Nevertheless, the real allure of the intellectual mission it designates, at least for those of our contemporaries who understand the ideal and find it attractive, can be traced to a particular metaphysical program and to a special set of closely related assumptions about the nature of science and the recent history of scientific progress. As I shall suggest later, the intellectual inclusiveness and academic accord sought under the unity of knowledge banner are, in fact, less conciliatory than appearances suggest. Those ideals are neither pluralistic in spirit nor of the live-and-let live variety, and the aspiration to integrate diverse fields of knowledge reaches far beyond the familiar and welcome goals of multidisciplinary or interdisciplinary cooperation. Indeed, one reason I was willing to risk the hazards of playing the part of skeptic at the conference was precisely because I believe that the vertical integration/consilience program is not likely to foster genuine reciprocal cooperation across disciplines, and is tacitly grounded in its own metaphysical viewpoint, one that is inherently hostile to, or at least suspicious of, many of the claims and much of the subject matter of the humanities—including some subjects pretty close to my own scholarly interests, such as morality and religion.

Most of the "consiliators"[3] I know share an ontology or picture of reality that is largely materialist in orientation (ultimate reality, they assume, consists entirely of material things in fields of force) and an epistemology that is largely empiricist in orientation (all genuine knowledge, they assume, must be generated through the application of scientific methods and logical reasoning to sensory perceptions of the world). Many of them are eager to just get on with observing the facts of life and inducing the casual structure of reality. Many share with E.O. Wilson the empiricist's sense of impatience with philosophical disputes and conceptual analysis and tend to view the persisting pluralism or diversity of theoretical languages and intellectual stances or viewpoints in the academy as a failure of some sort or a measure of scientific immaturity.

Notably, most of the consiliators I know are upbeat these days. If they are restive at all it is because they are eager to convince the world that, as a result of recent research in the cognitive and biological sciences (and under the leadership of those sciences),

---

3. The term *consiliators* is coined and used in this essay to refer to researchers, scholars, public intellectuals, patrons, journalists and others who are devoted to the vertical integration/unity of knowledge mission.

the cacophonous, faction prone, paradigm laden Tower of Babel that has been the home for the humanities (and the more humanistic social sciences) has finally entered a progressive stage and is becoming more intellectually unified. Included prominently among those putative recent advances in the cognitive and brain sciences is the supposed empirical demonstration that mind-body dualism is untenable; in the light of such putative advances the consiliators argue that it is no longer reasonable to suggest that there is an inherent disjunction between the languages and methods of the humanists (who study "consciousness" and the life of the mind) and the languages and methods of the biological scientists (who study the workings of the brain). The consiliators in the academy, or at least those who fully understand the implications of their own program, have visions of the day when everything mental and ideational must, can, and will be explainable in physical terms using a theoretical language developed by the biological sciences.

The vertical integration project has also sought ways to incorporate the study of religious and moral consciousness into the cognitive and biological sciences.[4] In that context the project has been an invitation to explain the existence and persistence of religion and morality, either by evaluating the extent to which, and the manner in which, the meanings, motives, and behaviors associated with religious and moral consciousness might make functional sense in the struggle for existence, that is, in terms of the direct contribution of religion to the evolution and survival of human beings, or, alternatively, by arguing that religion is simply an accidentally evolved and nonfunctional or adaptively neutral correlate of some other species typifying functional adaptation.[5] Here the unity of knowledge/vertical integration program begins with the observation that religion and morality are universal (or at least widely prevalent) aspects of human consciousness. The analysis, for example of religious consciousness, then proceeds on the assumption that such distinctive and widely distributed human notions as the idea and experience of the soul, the idea and experience of the sacred, and the idea and experience of supernatural or non-natural forces and processes animating and motivating human beings and helping to make the world go 'round are essentially cognitive illusions or intellectual fictions either directly in the service of reproductive success or highly correlated with something else that is in the direct service of reproductive success. In other words, religious consciousness is re-described and explained (or, as some humanists might complain,

---

4. The distinctions and connections between religious consciousness and moral consciousness (and their relationships to other forms of consciousness such as common sense and scientific consciousness) have been major topics for analysis in the humanities.

5. Evolutionary biologists might describe a member of this taxonomic class as a relatively hairless social biped with a relatively large brain. I have elected to describe the class as "human beings," adopting the language or discourse of the humanists. Humanists have historically conceptualized that particular class as persons, as subjects rather than as objects and have tried to interpret and understand them as such. Thus they have taken a person-centered approach to their subject matter. They have done this largely because of their assumption about the existence of a set of human capacities—for language, self-consciousness, rational thought, morally motivated guilt, religious devotion and (the apparent) exercise of free will - which has inclined many humanists to view human beings as peculiar and special, and to taxonomically locate the species, as Pascal noted, somewhere between the angels and the beasts.

explained away) as a shadow or projection of the human mind whose only potential claim to fame (if such a claim to fame can be advanced at all) is its utilitarian value from an inclusive fitness point of view.[6]

With regard to the study of religion, consilience research is thus founded on the assumption that the intellectual products of the world's religions are themselves without objective or rational foundation, and, if viewed on their own terms, as intellectual claims about the existence and role of souls, the sacred and supernatural forces in human affairs should be judged to be either illusory, even if functional (as Sigmund Freud suggested long ago in his famous book *The Future of an Illusion*), or as delusional (as Richard Dawkins proclaimed more recently in his popular book *The God Delusion*). The basic assumption here is that, although the objects of religious thought do not actually exist, the religious impulse that seems so distinctive of human beings (and has seemed to so many humanists to place human beings somewhere between the angels and the beasts, in part because of the human capacity to forego utilitarian calculations and value things—truth, virtue, and sanctity—for their own sake) can be ultimately tamed, tied down, or hitched to a utilitarian theory about the natural evolution of the human brain.[7]

All this is very neatly suggested in the editors' introduction to this volume. There the main and unflinching contention—the one I referred to earlier as distinctive and provocative—is that the biological and cognitive sciences have now advanced to a point where it is not only feasible to produce a systematic and disciplined scientific account of "human level realities" (morality, religion, literature, emotions, aesthetics) but also (and this is where the provocation begins) to treat those subjects of humanistic scholarship as emergent realities without "ontologically fetishizing" them.

6. When pressed about their metaphysical assumptions, unity of knowledge consiliators who study religious and moral thought (and also care to be consistent in their rejection of mind-body dualism) are likely to hold that human mental states (wishes, wants, beliefs, values, feelings) are little more than shadows, manifestations, or projections of the material forces and processes studied in the biological and brain sciences.

7. It is noteworthy that A.R. Wallace, one of the two major creators of the theory of evolution, was so impressed by the capacities of the human brain to imagine, create, and do things that are complex, elevated and non-utilitarian (and, as he argued, not necessary for the biological survival of the species) that he hypothesized that the development of the human brain could not be accounted for solely by the theory of evolution. He argued, on the basis of his scientific observations, that any naturalistic explanation of the human brain required the invocation of a willful and intelligent process of harnessing natural biological forces for a purpose, a process of planful or intelligently guided biological development of the type we associate with the breeding of animals and the cultivation of new species of plants. He viewed himself as operating strictly within the bounds of scientific observation and reasoning when he suggested that there are "limits to the theory of evolution as applied to man"; and he fully anticipated that his claim that there are things in human nature that don't fit the theory would be scorned or dismissed by other devotees of evolutionary theory. Among the things that Wallace thought did not fit was the capacity and willingness of humans to invest things with a sense of sanctity, sacredness, or virtue and to honor and respect them regardless of the personal biological consequences.

CONCERNING ONTOLOGICAL FETISHES AND THE REALITY OF NON-NATURAL PROPERTIES

Now the verb phrase "to ontologically fetishize" is not a household expression (nor for that matter is the notion of "emergent" realities), but I think I know what the expression means. And I think I can guess how it is going to get applied to one of my main areas of humanistic research, namely, to the study of moral consciousness, with special attention to moral disagreements between members of different cultural communities.[8]

To ontologically fetishize is to treat something as real that is not real.[9] It is to invest something with sanctity or inherent value that, in and of itself, is not deserving of respect. The very use of the expression itself reveals the metaphysical assumption of its user, and carries with it the implication that anyone who actually thinks that un-physical realities exist or subsist as objective features of the world is under the thrall of a superstitious, primitive, and irrational devotion to an outdated dualistic ontology. In making explicit this aim of the vertical integration agenda—the preemptive reduction of human level realities (classified as fetishes) to some level of reality (genetic, hormonal, neurological) viewed as more basic—one discerns how the consilience mission is far less conciliatory than the abstract idea of integrating the science and humanities may suggest.

Now, for the sake of the historical record, one might actually ask: Precisely how outdated is ontological dualism? By ontological dualism I have in mind a belief in the objective existence of both un-physical things (mathematical relationships, logical truths, objective values, abstract ideas, mental states—knowing, feeling, wanting and valuing, etc.) and physical things (neurons, hormones, genes, the particles of particle physics, etc.). I also have in mind the closely related belief that the un-physical realities are things in themselves and not simply or only complex emergences out of physical realities. As far as I can tell, ontological dualism is, and always has been, quite contemporary. Certainly it is the kind of metaphysical devotion that is characteristically embraced by normal, reasonable and morality-sensitive folk in all the cultures with which I am familiar. Indeed, that particular ontological commitment may well be precisely the kind of ontological faith that defines our common sense and makes human beings moral in the first place— the basic idea being that, beyond the physical, there is something more and that something more has value that is deserving of respect.

Dismissing that way of thinking as old-fashioned seems rather hasty and preemptive, given that it is also the way some very reflective and quite modern moral philosophers, for example W. David Ross, who was one of the great moral realists of the twentieth

---

8. These moral disagreements include such matters as polygamy, arranged marriage, physical punishment for children, sexual liberation and sexual modesty, male and female genital modifications, dietary practices and dress codes, a proper burial for the dead, and so forth. See for example, R. A. Shweder, M. Mahapatra, and J. G. Miller, "Culture and Moral Development," In *Cultural Psychology: Essays on Comparative Human Development*, ed. J. Stigler, R.A. Shweder, and G. Herdt (New York: Cambridge University Press, 1990); also R. A. Shweder, N. C. Much, M. Mahapatra, and L. Park, "The Big Three of Morality (Autonomy, Community, Divinity) and the Big Three Explanations of Suffering as Well," In *Why Do Men Barbecue? Recipes for Cultural Psychology*, ed. R. A. Shweder. (Cambridge, Mass.: Harvard University Press, 2003).

9. This is sometimes also called "reification," especially in the social construction of reality literature.

century, reasoned about the moral domain. As noted in Philip Stratton-Lake's brilliant introduction to Ross's classic account of moral intuitionism *The Right and the Good*,[10] Ross "believed that rightness and goodness are objective features of the world in just the way shape, size and mass are." Morality, according to Ross is not an emergent reality, but rather a fundamental and autonomous reality that is not reducible to something mental or something material.

Ross was not only a moral realist; he was a realist in a way that is highly relevant to our conference proceedings. He was a "non-naturalist" realist, which is one way for a humanist to say "not so fast" to the project of vertical integration.[11] Paraphrasing and quoting Stratton-Lake: Non-naturalism in ethics means that Ross thought that moral properties (properties such as good, ought, valuable, duty, or merited) (properties connoting the idea of "something deserving of respect") cannot be understood in wholly non-moral (that is to say, psychological, sociological, or biological evolutionary) terms. The non-moral terms of psychology, sociology, and evolutionary biology, Stratton-Lake notes, are terms such as *desire, approval, society,* or *survival of the fittest.* He goes on to say: "If you define "right" as meaning what is approved of by the community you are putting forward a naturalistic definition. If you define "good" as meaning "such that it *ought* to be desired, you are putting forward a non-naturalistic definition."[12]

To avoid misunderstanding, it is important to note, as Stratton-Lake points out, that so-called

> consequence theories of morality also may be either naturalistic or non-naturalistic. If, as a consequence theorist, you define "right" as "productive of the greatest pleasure," [or "productive of the survival of the group"] you are putting forward a naturalistic definition. If, as a consequence theorist, you define it as "productive of the greatest amount of *good*", you are putting forward a non-naturalistic definition.

(Parenthetically I would remark that, although I have been a critic of many aspects of Lawrence Kohlberg's stage theory of moral development I believe Kohlberg is quite right that a fully developed understanding of the meaning of goodness and rightness by human beings in all cultures requires that goodness and rightness be defined in non-naturalistic terms—as that something more to which one shows respect because it is worthy of respect)[13]

---

10. David Ross, *The Right and the Good*, Oxford University Press, 2003, edited and with an Introduction by Phillip Stratton-Lake.

11. Indeed I would hazard the guess that "non-naturalism" is the characteristic stance in the humanities and humane social sciences, which is one of the several reasons many humanists resist the vertical integration agenda and may even recoil at the dismissive parodies of mind/body dualism that are now commonplace in the biological and cognitive sciences.

12. Phillip Stratton-Lake, Introduction to David Ross, *The Right and the Good*, (Oxford, UK: Oxford University Press, 2003), xi-xii.

13. For a critique of Kohlberg and a discussion of his approach to morality more generally see, for example, R. A. Shweder, M. Mahapatra, and J. G. Miller, "Culture and Moral Development," In *Cultural Psychology: Essays on Comparative Human Development*, ed. J. Stigler, R.A. Shweder and G. Herdt (New York: Cambridge University Press, 1990).

Notice that to seek an emergent account of the human level reality called morality (and to do so without ontologically fetishizing the domain of moral values) is to understand moral properties in wholly non-moral terms—the supposed ontological fetish in this instance being the very idea of objective moral values. This amounts to the substitution of a reductive naturalistic re-definition of what is good (e.g., as any norm that promotes the survival of the group) for the non-natural properties (e.g., objective goodness) characteristic of everyday moral beliefs. It is to interpret everyday moral realism as unreal or at the very least as intellectually absurd. It is basically to advance what Stratton-Lake calls an "error theory" about values and everyday moral judgments, based on a meta-physical presumption that there are no objective value properties in the universe aside from fetishistic human declarations of value; and that, therefore, none of our everyday moral judgments have truth-value. It is to presume the universe is devoid of objective values despite the fact that almost all human beings think that when they make moral judgments they are saying something that is true about the objective world; for example, when they assert that it is good to treat like cases alike and different cases differently.

Everyday human moral judgments are essentially meaningful and interpretable as moral judgments per se (rather than as, for example, aesthetic judgments or as expres-sions of feelings) precisely because they are about a supposed objective and non-natural order of goodness. The analytic generalization can be put this way: A semantic analysis of everyday moral judgments on a worldwide scale suggests that when a Hindu Brahman says "It is wrong for a widow to eat meat and fish" or an American feminist says "It is wrong to deny a women the right to vote" they are not simply or only reporting about the state of their personal feelings or the collective opinion of members of their group or a norm that works to promote genetic fitness. Those who subscribe to an error theory about everyday moral judgments—for example, sociopaths and emotivists in philosophy and psychology—view those everyday moral judgments as a kind of sham. The socio-paths apparently lack any dualistic ontological intuition that could make room for the sense that there exists an objective order of goodness. Most emotivists in philosophy and psychology undoubtedly do have that quite fashionable (because nearly universal) dual-istic intuition, but for theoretical and metaphysical reasons they reflectively subscribe to the belief there are no objective properties "out there" to be represented with such terms as *good* or *bad, divine* or *evil*. According to the writings of the emotivists, moral judg-ments are neither true nor false, but merely expressions of personal or collective choice. Judgments of good and bad, they aver, do no more than express non-moral properties, likes and dislikes, positive and negative feeling states, tastes, and aversions. Moral terms are merely labels for our feelings, they write, although, of course, the emotivists only argue that way when they are wearing their academic hats, because, for the most part, they are not sociopaths. In everyday life they do not act as if they believed that consensus makes logical deductions true, that might makes right, and that non-natural properties (such as goodness or mathematical and logical truths) do not exist except for our saying they do.

In other words the particular type of vertical integration in which human level realities "emerge" by being recast or re-defined in naturalistic terms implies (here again quoting Stratton-Lake) that the kinds of moral disagreements I study in my research (an example of which I will discuss in a moment) "are like disagreements about what color something is in an objectively colorless world."[14] Rendered and interpreted within the framework developed by academic emotivists, moral arguments both within and across societies must be viewed as cognitively empty or intellectually absurd, and analyzed exclusively in emotive terms (for example, as rhetorical political ploys in the contest for power or domination), for if there is no objective moral universe, no transcendental realm of goodness out there, no basis in reason for one's judgments of right and wrong, what precisely is there to reasonably argue about?

HAS BABEL REALLY BEEN UNDONE? OBSERVING PHYSICAL AND UNPHYSICAL SCIENTISTS DISCUSSING BRAINS AND MINDS

Although I confess that I have a place in my heart (and in my mind) for that (perhaps not so) outdated dualistic ontology, it is good and right to be curious about the current intellectual scene in the biological and cognitive sciences, which I have observed to be far less unified than many consiliators suppose. To cite one example, for the past three decades those who have perhaps done the most creative work interpreting the thoughts, feelings, desires, and values of non-human animals are not humanists (philosophers, poets, and creative writers) but rather a group of cognitive ethologists (naturalists, biologists, zoologists, and psychologists) who are convinced that monkeys, apes and other non-human animals are persons too (very much like human beings) and that Renee Descartes was quite wrong when he said that only human beings have a conscience, a mental life, and a soul. They have embraced the languages of consciousness and of the mind rather than the language of a physical system for understanding the behavior of non-human (but, in terms of the humanistic languages of consciousness, person-like) animals. Yet it is quite ironic that the academic field of cognitive ethology has become quite popular in the cognitive and biological sciences at precisely the moment when other cognitive and biological scientists (especially those working on the topics of artificial intelligence and neural networks) have become convinced that our own all-too-human minds can be simulated by a machine and fully understood in the languages of the physical sciences and that, if we could actually experience the way our own brain functions, we wouldn't find a person, a soul, a self, ideas about goodness, or a free will there at all.

In any case one should be curious about recent developments in the cognitive and biological sciences, whether they are consilient or not. So, while residing in Germany a decade or so ago, I attended a major interdisciplinary conference held in Bremen on the subject of "Voluntary Action." It was an illuminating experience that typifies for me the way vertical integration actually works (or more precisely does not work) in practice. The conference featured philosophers, cognitive neuroscientists, psychologists, anthropologists, and legal scholars. All were there ostensibly to explain the apparent fact (or is it just an illusory phenomenal experience? That was the question!) of "voluntary action."[15]

---

14. Stratton-Lake, *The Right and the Good*, see footnote 12.

15. The conference proceedings were published as a book edited by Sabine Massen, Wolfgang Prinz, and Gerhard Roth (Eds.) and published under the title *Voluntary Action: An Issue at the Interface of Nature and Culture* (Oxford: Oxford University Press, 2003). My observations on the conference were published there as well.

"Voluntary action" is a really nice topic for an interdisciplinary meeting aimed at integrating the sciences and the humanities. As the conference organizers (Wolfgang Prinz, Gerhart Roth, and Sabine Maasen) brilliantly pointed out in their invitation, voluntary action

> poses a severe challenge to scientific attempts to form a unitary picture of the working of the human mind and its relation to the working of the body. This is because the notion of mental causation, inherent in the received standard view of voluntary action, is difficult to reconcile with both dualist and monist approaches to the mental and the physical. For dualist accounts, it has to be explained what a causal interaction between mind and matter means and how it is possible at all. Conversely, for monist approaches the question of mental causation does not arise and therefore appears to denote a cognitive illusion [they might have said an "ontological fetish"] at best. Dualist and monist accounts can be found in all the disciplines... [cognitive psychology, neuropsychology, philosophy, ethnology], albeit in different phrasings and/or theoretical frameworks. Moreover, in virtually all disciplines this seemingly insurmountable opposition is [a] subject of ongoing debate.[16]

So "voluntary action" is a challenge for both mind/body monists and mind/body pluralists.[17] At such conferences, the monists always seem to turn up as materialists. Apparently the monistic idealists are either hard to find or are not invited. The monistic idealists are those who argue that the real world does not consist of physical particles in fields of force but rather consists entirely of mental states and that there is no reality aside from human consciousness. That monistic idealist stance is just as counterintuitive to common-sense dualism as the monistic materialist opposite, but why do the idealists hold such a view? I think a typical idealist might say that it is because all sensory or perceptual experiences and all representations of reality (including representations picturing reality as made up exclusively of physical particles in fields of force) are themselves mental states or forms of consciousness. There is no way to transcend your own consciousness they might say, with solipsistic smiles on their faces.

Idealism aside, monism means materialism at these conferences, and if you are a mind/body monist of the materialist variety, then the voluntariness of "voluntary action" must be an illusion—another one of those ontological fetishes. That, of course, is the spectacular and breathtaking (or should we say dis-spiriting) counterintuitive implication of mind/body monism of the materialist variety, namely, the renunciation of all common-

---

16. It is noteworthy that the organizers of the conference do not suggest that dualism is an outmoded or fully discredited ontology and they themselves made note of its enduring presence in several disciplines.

17. Of which mind/body dualism is just one variety; the philosopher Karl Popper for example, argues that the universe encompasses not just two fundamental ontological worlds—the mental and the physical—but three—mathematical and logical truths, for example, would reside in that third world because they are neither physical things nor mental things. See for example, K.R. Popper, and J. C. Eccles, *The Self and Its Brain: An Argument for Interactionism* (Berlin: Springer Verlag, 1977), especially pages 36–50.

sense dualism and the claim (*involuntarily* arrived at and offered, I suppose robotically, at least according to mind/body monists who are materialists) that mental states (including ones own truth claims about mental states) are epiphenomenal and have nothing to do with the chain of objective events that is the real cause of behavior.

You raise your hand in a classroom in a situation where you thought that your intention to signal the teacher was the reason that you deliberately, willfully, or voluntarily raised your hand. In a common-sense sort of way you thought that symbolically communicating your intention to answer her question was what your hand- raising action was all about. "Not so!" says the mind/body monist of the materialist variety. Your hand raising was the end product of material determinants at the neural level, where a human will (and indeed even a human self) cannot be observed, and where ideas qua ideas do not exist and, hence, can play no causal role in the movement of your hand. Given our contemporary received understanding of the nature of the material world that is how mind/body monists think they must talk about so-called voluntary action. They talk of it as an epiphenomenon, an ontological fetish in the extreme.

This leaves the mind/body monists (it's all body, no mind; mind *is* brain) with a whole lot of explaining to do. Why should such a complex epiphenomenal system (amounting to all of human consciousness and its products) exist at all? How could it evolve if it plays no causal role in behavior? Are the humanistic ideas of agency, virtue, value, and human responsibility then incompatible with the teachings of the physical and biological sciences? Should the common-sense or folk psychology of everyday life be viewed as little more than error, ignorance, and a superstitious faith in the causal powers of an ontological fetish, or, at most, as a functional illusion that carries benefits for the survival of the species or the group, as long as one does not abandon the illusion?

Mind/body dualists fare no better when it comes to making sense of voluntary action. As an aside, I would point out that almost all cognitive-neuroscience research programs become tacitly dualist as soon as they treat something mental as an independent variable and something neurological as a dependent variable, or vice versa. In other words, just to carry forward their research agenda, they implicitly, usually un-self-consciously, distinguish thoughts (or ideas) from things (neurons, hormones, blood flows) and differentiate the unphysical things they are going to study (typically thoughts and feelings expressed and interpreted through language or other symbolic forms) from the physical things they are going to study (inferred events in the brain) using ontologically distinct types of criteria.

In any case, if you are a reflective mind/body dualist, you must explain how something that is immaterial (e.g., the mental state associated with choice, planning, free will, and intentionality) can influence or have an effect on something that is physical (the movement of one's hand). So there is a real and deep problem here with our current understanding of voluntary action, and, at Bremen, an interdisciplinary conference was organized to make some progress on resolving it, in the light of recent research in cognitive neuroscience, psychology, and philosophy, with some assistance from the anthropologists and lawyers. Here is the way unification and vertical integration operated in that context.

The philosophers were really good at defining the mind/body problem. Each philosopher was terrific at arguing in favor of just one of the several incompatible solutions (dualistic mind-body interactionism, psychophysical parallelism, eliminative materialism, etc.) that have been contenders, while advancing compelling criticisms against all other solutions. Not much convergence took place among the philosophers, but at least they knew what the mind-body problem was and they tried to address it.

The neuroscientists, on the other hand, came armed with lots of colorful slides, showing this or that brain part lighting up when this or that kind of action took place or sentence got spoken. They named lots of brain parts and they spoke with great confidence and with a sense of pride and excitement about the technological revolution that had taken place on their watch, which had finally made it possible, or so they thought, to *empirically solve* the mind/body problem. After about ten slides, one began to realize that they seemed to think that, because Descartes had committed some grave error, he would be surprised if he were alive today to find out that when thinking occurs something happens simultaneously somewhere in the nervous system. After about 20 slides, one began to realize that they did not really know what the mind/body problem was in the first place and had almost no sense of its intellectual history or even of the history of the brain sciences. However, they had an imagined solution to the problem, which seemed to excite them a great deal. Upon examination this "solution" was simply a form of question-begging in which the very real puzzle of how a non-material thing and a material thing can causally interact at all is "solved" by simply substituting a very thin temporal co-occurrence or correlational notion of causation for the deeper sense of objective causation that makes the mind-body problem a problem in the first place.

If one steps back into the nineteenth century for a moment and reads discussions of this topic, it becomes readily apparent how little progress has been made in solving the mind/body problem and how misguided are the bold claims that ontological dualism has been empirically laid to rest. Consider for example the following remarks made in 1868 by the physicist John Tyndall in his presidential address to the Physical Section at the thirty-eighth meeting of the British Association for the Advancement of Science (and quoted by A.R. Wallace in his essay "The Limits of Natural Selection as Applied to Man"):

> The passage from the physics of the brain to the corresponding facts of consciousness is unthinkable. *Granted that a definite thought, and a definite molecular action in the brain occur simultaneously,* we do not possess the intellectual organ, nor apparently any rudiment of the organ, which would enable us to pass by a process of reasoning from the one phenomenon to the other. *They appear together but we do not know why.* Were our minds and senses so expanded, strengthened and illuminated as to enable us to see and feel the very molecules of the brain, were we capable of following all their motions, all their groupings, all their electric discharges, if such there be, and were we intimately acquainted with the corresponding states of thought and feeling, we should be as far as ever from the solution of the problem. How are these physical processes connected with the facts of consciousness? *The chasm between the two classes of phenomena would still remain intellectually impassable.* [my emphases]

In other words, the neuroscientists at the conference in the year 2000 had solved the mind/body problem by simply begging Descartes' question (of which Professor Tyndall seems quite informed in 1868) because for them mind/body causation amounts to nothing more than the observation that the brain lights up here and there when a person does this or that—an observation that John Tyndall in his own way took as a matter of fact over 150 years ago while also recognizing that such matters of fact do not solve, let alone even address, the issues raised by Descartes and the mind-body problem.[18]

This, of course, is not quite the issue the great philosopher had in his mind, and it is hardly a *theoretical* advance over Descartes or Tyndall; it does not solve the mind/body problem, it simply evades it. But they kept going, slide after slide supposedly demonstrating that the mind/body problem had been empirically solved.

Then there were the psychologists and the anthropologists. They generally presupposed or just took for granted the ontological reality and objective causal powers of mental states and their ideational content (in other words they had not expunged common-sense folk psychology and ontological dualism from their scientific work), and they described the operation of that folk psychology in some detail. One psychologist did present reaction-time evidence, all of it equivocal, trying to prove that mental states are unreal (merely ontological fetishes) and have no causal powers. In the end, the mind/body problem remained unsolved, when acknowledged, or it remained untouched, but it was innocently thought to have been solved by the new technologies for mapping the brain. In the end, the everyday experience and/or reality of voluntary action remained as mysterious and fascinating as ever. I was led by this conference experience to draw the following tentative conclusion.

If one believes, as do all normal human beings, that mental causation is really real, not an ontological fetish, then it would seem to follow that either (1) our current scientific account of the nature of the material world (including the human brain) is incomplete, precisely because we don't know how to explain mental causation within the current terms of our physical and biological sciences; or (2) there is more to reality than just the physical world: for example, Plato's "states of the soul," the realm of mathematical and logical truths, and of values, concepts and ideas—in other words, something like Karl Popper's three-world pluralistic ontology of the real.

Option (1) amounts to a denial of any fundamental division between the physical and the mental (or between the mental and an independent ontological domain of concepts and ideas, including logical and mathematical truths). Those who opt for option (1) will press on trying to revise our current understanding of the physical world so that one day we can move seamlessly within a language for describing matter directly to human consciousness and offer a plausible causal account of how all the things that matter to people at a human level of reality are merely emergent products of physical things at some

---

18. That very thin notion of causation relied on by the neuroscientists is reminiscent of David Hume's radical empiricist claim that the very concept of real causation is itself an ontological fetish or projection of the mind beyond the evidence of the senses, since the senses provide us with nothing more than the perception of events coinciding in time and space. The ontological chasm mentioned by Tyndall is thereby bridged by simply ignoring it. Repeating the same kind of facts about temporal co-occurrence that Tyndall reported in the nineteenth century and that Descartes was aware of as well does not advance the discussion and surely does not refute ontological dualism, as Tyndall clearly notes.

really real (not ontologically fetishized) level "down below" (the vertical metaphor is irresistible).

Those who go for option (1) will surely reject the metaphysical claim that the intellectual objects of our mental states (including mathematical and logical truths) exist in some observer independent realm or "Platonic heaven." They will be inclined to argue that logic and mathematics (and morality and religion) are about nothing other than how people think (rather than about true realities *about which* human beings find themselves *capable* of thinking) and that logic and mathematics (and morality and religion) can be subsumed within the realm of the mental, which will one day be shown to be contained within the realm of the physical.

My own working view is a bit different, for it inclines to option (2), that there is something more, let's call them the unphysical realities, to which one should show respect because they are worthy of it. Here I will try to be self-conscious about some of the ontological assumptions that are philosophical foundations for the type of humanistic anthropology I practice, which also goes by the name romantic pluralism.[19] Basically the romantic pluralist tradition in cultural anthropology seeks to affirm (to the extent such affirmation is reasonably possible) what the philosopher John Gray (writing about Isaiah Berlin) describes as "the reality, validity and human intelligibility of values and forms of life very different from our own."[20] Here is a brief example, with special attention to the practice of caring for the dead, a universal practice, which perhaps as much as any other presupposes a dualistic ontology (the distinction between the self or soul and the body) and gives exquisite expression to the view that there is something more to human nature than just physical reality and it is deserving of our respect.

I am going to briefly describe an encounter of the type I have frequently had in my research in comparative ethics and on moral reasoning in the Hindu temple town of Bhubaneswar in Orissa, India. Warning: the type of account I am about to offer is likely to strike those who choose option (1) and seek an emergent and fully naturalistic account of human level realities as very soft on superstition (ontological fetishism) and all-too-tolerant of alternative pictures of what is real.

"The day after his father's death the first-born son had a haircut and ate chicken." To members of my own interpretive community[21] (and probably yours, too) the conduct described in that sentence is not particularly noteworthy and is certainly not immoral. Yet, in the judgment of men and women in the interpretive community surrounding the Hindu temple where I do research in India, a first-born son having a haircut and eating chicken the day after his father's death is categorized as a "great sin" ("mahapapa"). Being a great sin, the conduct is not only scandalous and a departure from local social norms,

19. See especially the essay titled "John Searle on a Witch Hunt," *Anthropological Theory* 6 (2006): 89–111, from which this discussion is drawn.

20. John Gray, *Isaiah Berlin* (Princeton: Princeton University Press, 1996), 3.

21. By an interpretive community I mean roughly a group of people who share a set of understandings about what is true, good, beautiful, and efficient and participate in a way of life they consider normal, reasonable (in the sense of justified by reference to good reasons) and ethical precisely because it makes manifest, reveals or expresses those understandings. It is what some anthropologists call a "culture."

but it is also perceived as a profound and consequential violation of the natural and objective moral ordering of things (of which the human social order, when properly functioning, is but a part). It is anticipated that the conduct will be profoundly consequential and that bad things will happen to anyone who commits a great sin. The anticipated consequences have nothing to do with secular criminal sanctions (there are none for this type of case) and go well beyond the effects on one's reputation in the local community (although reputation effects can be massive, including, shunning from all forms of exchange, such as marriage arrangements, and, at least in the past, the risk of becoming an outcaste). That particular "transgression"—getting a haircut and eating chicken the day after your father's death—was the single most serious form of misconduct of any investigated in my research, and it was judged to be an even more egregious moral error than the refusal of doctors at a hospital to treat a poor man who was seriously hurt in an accident, but was too poor to pay.

Given what I have just reported, one can easily imagine a typical morally sensitive member of my own interpretive community asking: "What type of moral cretins are those Oriya Hindus?" He or she would be thinking, "Why can't those Oriya Hindus see that there is absolutely nothing wrong with having a haircut and eating chicken the day after your father dies?" (For the sake of this argument I will assume that this imagined member of my own interpretive community is neither a sociopath nor a philosophical or psychological emotivist who believes anything goes and is prepared to be totally nonjudgmental about everyday moral judgments on the grounds that all moral judgments, including ones own, carry no truth value and are nothing more than fetishized personal or collective expressions of taste, and thus hardly worth arguing about).

In what follows I will try, however briefly and inadequately, to step inside this Oriya Hindu form of life with the humanistic aim of giving an intelligible account of its reality and validly—thereby trying to achieve, however inadequately, a form of understanding of the "native point of view" that is neither ethnocentric nor reductive.

Here is my non-reductive (humanistic) explanation for why the conduct in question is a moral fact of a very different sort for Oriya Hindus than for most American observers.

Oriya Hindus, or at least most of those who live in the interpretive community I studied, believe that every person has an immortal reincarnating soul. They believe that when a person dies his or her soul wants to go on its transmigratory journey but is initially trapped in the corpse and held back by the "death pollution" that emanates from the dead body and from its subsequently processed physical remains. As an act of beneficence, care, and reciprocity (all of which are assumed to be objective moral goods) relatives of the deceased (and especially the first-born son, for whom this is a major institutionalized moral obligation in life) undertake the project of assisting the soul of the dead person and enabling it to get free of its ties to the physical form it once occupied. Thus, some of the kinsmen of the dead person turn their own living bodies into what I shall label "death pollution collection sites," and essentially suck up the death pollution associated with the corpse (and its cremation and disposal) into themselves. They believe that the most effective way to do this is by keeping all other types of pollutions away from their living bodies, thus providing maximal space for the personal intake of the death pollution. Among the most commonplace competing types of pollutions that might interfere with their project are sexual activities and the ingestion of "hot foods" (for example, fish and meat—the local classification of all ingested substances on a hot versus cool dimension would need to be spelled out here, but, the relevant social fact is that chicken is a "hot food"). Thus, for 12 days they stay at home fasting (maintaining a very restricted diet of "cool" foods) and abstinent. On the twelfth day they believe the soul of the deceased has been released from its bond to its bygone material form and is free to go on its journey to the world of transmigrating spirits. On that day they cleanse themselves of the death pollution, which they have absorbed into their own bodies and which has accumulated there. They believe that the pollution migrates to the extremities of the body, and is especially concentrated in their hair and under their fingernails. On that twelfth day of abstinence and fasting, the family barber cuts off nearly all their hair and the barber's wife cuts their fingernails. Then they take a ceremonial bath and go back to the workaday world, having fulfilled their moral obligation to the soul of the deceased.

"The day after his father's death the first-born son had a haircut and ate chicken"! To any Oriya Hindu in the temple town that conduct signals a willful and horrifying renunciation of the entire project of assisting the soul of your father and places the father's spiritual transmigration in deep jeopardy. No wonder they are morally distraught at the very idea of such behavior, and judge it more severely than not treating the accident victim at the hospital, who is too poor to pay. Wouldn't you judge things that way too if that was your picture of the natural and moral order of things (including the world of moral values and of social relationships, viewed as part of the natural moral order of things)?

The question immediately arises, of course, whether (within the bounds of what it means for human beings to be rational and moral) a group of human beings might reasonably feel bound by that picture of the natural and moral order of things, to which I would like to suggest the right answer is yes. Here I will simply conclude this illustration of forms of life different from our own by asking, which do you think is the worse transgression: (1) A doctor not treating an accident victim because he is too poor to pay or (2) (I recognize that this example is only a weak analogue of the Oriya Hindu case but I think it makes the point) a son tossing his father's dead body in a trash compacter and holding no funeral service or memorial at all? Would you judge someone a moral cretin or even to be lacking in moral maturity if he or she reacted to the second hypothetical as the more horrifying transgression? Personally I think it is the more horrifying of those two very serious moral transgressions.

I would also hazard the view that the meaning of the idea of a great sin or moral error is not adequately translated when it is theorized and redefined in reductive naturalistic terms by reference to social sanctions, communal consensus or pressures toward conformity. If cultural anthropologists have learned anything from the legacy of Emile Durkheim it is that, from a "native point of view" the social order is thought to be part of the natural moral order of things; and thus when someone says "you have committed a moral error" or "you have sinned" they do not simply mean that some collection of individuals in their interpretive community has decided to define some behavior as wrong. The natural moral order of things is something you discover (or have revealed to you), not something you invent, or at least that is the near universal consensus among the natives of the world.

I can only guess what vertical integrationists and those who define morality and religion as ontological fetishes might say about those death pollution practices of Oriya Hindus. Perhaps something like this: When you are dead you are dead! Souls don't reincarnate! In fact people don't have souls at all. I suppose they do have a "self," but, take my word for it, your "transcendental ego" does not go anywhere when you die and my colleagues in the cognitive neurosciences have not only empirically proved that ontological dualism is untenable but they also promise me that one day very soon they will figure out the answer to the problem that Descartes and Tyndall were unable to solve, precisely how that "ghost in the machine" got into our physical body in the first place. Moreover, the only kind of pollution that exists in the world is not about spiritual purity or the sanctity of one's soul but consists of dirty and nasty physical particles in fields of force and no one in their right mind would want to suck them into their body. Of course, there are many psychological benefits (including a defense against grief, loss, and the fear of death) to imagining that bodies are animated by immortal souls that are thought to already be old souls when they enter our contemporary physical world and survive the demise of their physical form. Wouldn't it be nice and comforting if that were true, but scientific observation has taught us it is not true. And yes, perhaps there are social benefits to endorsing the virtues that bind the generations by enacting the moral drama of turning ones own body into a death pollution collection site. But remember what Nietzsche once said: "Asia is a dreamy place where they do not know how to distinguish between truth and poetry." No one's soul is in jeopardy just because someone gets a haircut and eats chicken! And, by the way, there is no such thing as a sin. If such beliefs are entrenched among human beings it is only because believing such things has worked in a utilitarian way to promote the genetic fitness of our species (or else is highly correlated with something else that promotes our biological survival).

It seems to me there is some kind of chasm there between two very different and not so easily reconciled ways of approaching one's subject matter. Evans-Pritchard, the famous British anthropologist who wrote a seminal ethnographic monograph about what it is like to hunt for a witch in Central Africa once offered the following sage advice to aspiring ethnographers of ways of life different from one's own: "You cannot have a remunerative, even intelligent, conversation with people about something they take as self-evident if you give them the impression you regard their belief as an illusion."[22] It is a good methodological starting point for the type of humanistic anthropology I practice, but it also hints at why the integration of the sciences and the humanities is probably not in the cards and why there are divides in the first place. Reality testing is a metaphysical act, and the metaphysical assumptions characteristic of human level realities and of the humanists who study those realities do not necessarily converge with the metaphysical program of those calling for consilience and a unity of all knowledge.

Hence it seems to me that, if you are a humanist, you ought to opt for option (2) the idea that (ontologically speaking) there is more to reality than the material world, and that those unphysical realities are best comprehended as, in some sense, objective realities worthy of respect and not as "ontological fetishes." That is one of the reasons I find Karl Popper's view congenial when it comes to questions of ontology. Whatever one might think of the practice of humanistic anthropology (or of the very idea of the unphysical sciences), if I were able to spell out the philosophy of the real that informs my own work, I suspect I would end up with some kind of variation on Sir Karl Popper's philosophy of

---

22. E.E. Evans-Pritchard, *Witchcraft, Oracles and Magic Among the Azande* (Oxford: Clarendon Press. 1937). In a postscript "Notes on Method."

the three real worlds: crudely stated, the world of material things, the world of mental states and, finally, quite crucially, the world of meanings, ideas, or concepts—the latter conjectured to be an observer independent realm of intellectual/unphysical objects that human beings are able to discover and grasp by means of their mental powers. In his philosophy of the real, Popper conjectures that besides physical objects and states ("World 1") there are mental states ("World 2") "and that these states are real since they interact with our bodies" (here he is prepared to just assume the reality of mental causation, which always requires a good deal of question begging). Popper also conjectures that the content of our mental states (the ideas or concepts that we think with or about) form part of what he calls World 3. The intellectual objects in World 3 are not themselves mental states, yet are real, in part, because they seem to have something like an observer independent status as objects of discovery (for example, he would argue mathematical truths are neither physical nor mental but they are real), and also, in part, because the ideas or concepts that we are able to grasp by means of our mental powers can ultimately have an effect on our bodies and on the creation of material artifacts.[23]

The details of Popper's three-world philosophy of the real need not concern us here, and there is much in his formulation that I think is problematic and debatable. Nevertheless his three-world metaphysics is a philosophical conjecture about what is real that bears a striking resemblance to the common sense of the diverse peoples of the world studied by anthropologists, which is not a bad starting point when one is trying to develop some analytic tools for making sense of folk mentalities and forms of life different from one's own.

I realize, of course, that by selecting option (2)— there is more reality than just the physical world—one ends up just reaffirming the division between physical matter and other types of real things ("states of the soul," the "soul" itself, transcendent concepts or ideas) without really explaining that division. Nevertheless, when it comes to the mind/body problem, the state of the art has not fundamentally changed since Descartes and Tyndall, and the choices remain the same even in our contemporary decade of the brain: One either denies the ontological difference between mind and body without accounting for consciousness (that's option 1) or one affirms the difference between mind and body without explaining how unphysical things can exist (that's option 2). Despite technological developments in the neurosciences in recent years, I don't think that the state of the art has changed very much since 1913 when Emile Durkheim presented his paper on "The Religious Problem and the Duality of Nature" to the Societe de Philosophie in Paris, summarizing his famous book *The Elementary Forms of the Religious Life*. As noted by Durkheim's intellectual biographer Stephen Lukes, alluding to the apparent dualisms and unconciliatory oppositions that were up for discussion at Durkheim's lecture (dualisms such the physical versus the mental, the body versus the soul, sense experience versus conceptual thought, the profane versus the sacred): "Philosophers had no genuine solution: empiricists, materialists and utilitarians, on the one hand, and absolute idealists on the other, simply denied these antinomies without accounting for them; ontological dualists simply reaffirmed them without explaining them."[24]

23. Popper and Eccles, op cit, see footnote 16.
24. Steven Lukes, *Emile Durkheim, His Life and Work: A Historical and Critical Study*, (New York, Penguin Books, 1973), page 507.

Skepticism has its limits and nothing I have said or implied in this essay should be construed as a critique of innovative interdisciplinary cooperation or of attempts to ask questions about the functional or dysfunctional consequences of human practices and beliefs for either social reproduction or genetic fitness. Rather, my aim has been to examine the announced program of vertically integrating the humanities with the cognitive and biological sciences and the reductive notion that one can fully explain human level realities relying on findings from those sciences. Let me conclude with a small yet provocative antireductive example of what happens when World 3 (the world of meanings available to mentally endowed human beings) enters our nervous system. The example comes from Benjamin Lee Whorf and can be found in his writings on *Language, Thought and Reality*.[25] Whorf is famous for his work on linguistic relativity, but he was fully aware of the existence of some universal human species typifying affective or synesthetic responses to stimuli of various kinds. He notes that the semantically meaningless sound pattern "queep" elicits a universal set of affective or feeling-tone associations when it interacts with the human nervous system. Whether you are in the highlands of New Guinea or in Manhattan, whether you speak English, Guugu Yimidhirr, or Russian, "queep," the nonsense syllable, is judged to be "fast" (rather than "slow"), "sharp" (rather than "dull"), "light" (rather than "dark"), "narrow" (rather than "wide"). Our affective response to "queep" is automatic and may well be preprogramed, a feature of our common biology.

But notice what happens when the world of language and culture-specific semantic meanings (a World 3 unphysical reality) enters the picture. Whorf asks us to consider the sound pattern "deep." As a purely material thing (as a physical pattern of sound) "deep" is very similar to "queep." For speakers of languages in which "deep" is a nonsense syllable (that is most languages of the world) the sound pattern "deep" elicits exactly the same set of affective or feeling-tone associations ("fast," "sharp," "light," and "narrow") as does "queep." However, "deep" is not just a physical entity (or pure sound) for English speakers. It is a word in our language. It has semantic meaning. That meaning totally overrides its impact as pure physical sound (the sound merely becomes the vehicle of the meaning) and completely reverses our nervous- system response. For speakers of English, and only for English speakers, "deep" is judged to be "slow," "dull," "dark," and "wide." That is one of the reasons that so many humanists are prepared to argue for the duality of human nature, of meaning and mind over and above mechanism and body, of the angel over and above the beast. It is what leads them to believe there is something more to our nature than just the material realities that meet the ear (or the eye) plus the nervous system that is more or less common to us all. The challenge for the humanities and for the humanistic social sciences has always been to get ideas and our capacity to be sensitive to what things mean into the picture without completely reducing the mental to the material or "matterings" to "matter." Contemplating a human being as a hairless social biped with a big brain does not quite do the trick. It leaves too much out of its picture of the really real as it tries to descend the vertical hierarchy by interpreting the higher levels as ontological fetishes.

---

25. See B.L. Whorf, *Language, Thought and Reality* (Cambridge, Mass.: The M.I.T. Press, 1964), 257.

3

MIND-BODY DUALISM AND THE
TWO CULTURES

Edward Slingerland

CHARACTERIZING THE "TWO CULTURES"

In order to get a handle on the divide between the intellectual cultures that characterize the humanities and the sciences, it is helpful to turn to one of its classic expressions, the late Clifford Geertz's seminal *The Interpretation of Cultures* (1973), which continues to be required reading in the graduate programs of most core humanities departments. One of the central themes in Geertz's work is the working out of a distinction between two different modes of understanding, derived from the British philosopher Gilbert Ryle. In a passage cited by Geertz, Ryle asks us to consider the following observational situation:

> Two boys fairly swiftly contract the eyelids of their right eyes. In the first boy this is only an involuntary twitch; but the other is winking conspiratorially to an accomplice. At the lowest or the thinnest level of description the two contractions of the eyelids may be exactly alike. From a cinematograph-film of the two faces there might be no telling which contraction, if either, was a wink, or which, if either, were a mere twitch. Yet there remains the *immense but unphotographable difference* between a twitch and a wink. (Ryle 1971, 480—my emphasis)

For Ryle, the difference between the twitch and the wink exemplifies the distinction between "thin" and "thick" description: the former goes no further than the merely material reality of the situation—what could be captured by a video—while the latter encompasses as well the human *meaning* of the physical sequence of events, which stands above and beyond the physical reality. In his gloss of the Ryle quotation, Geertz refers to this additional layer of significance as the "semiotic" meaning of the scene (Geertz 1973, 6), clearly linking the project of "thick" description with the various strands of poststructuralist thought that were just beginning to pervade and transform core humanities disciplines in the early 1970s.

The distinction between "thin" versus "think" description succinctly captures what most humanists today would commonly cite as the difference between the sciences and the humanities: The sciences engage in physical description and mechanistic explanation, whereas the humanities engage in interpretation or "understanding"—the study of what physical realities *mean* for human beings, something that cannot be deduced from the merely physical. Although the metaphysical assumption on which this distinction is based is rarely made explicit, it is nonetheless always at work in the background: Human meaning cannot be captured by physical description because it involves the *mind*, which belongs to an ontological realm separate and independent from the realm of the merely physical or bodily. My experience is that most scholars in the humanities feel uncomfortable if asked to explicitly defend metaphysical mind-body dualism—it has a somewhat archaic and unfashionable ring to a modern secular humanist—but the widely and vociferously defended distinction between humanistic understanding and scientific explanation makes no sense without it.

This link can be seen clearly and unambiguously in German—significant because one can trace a direct line of descent between the structure of German academia in the nineteenth century and the make-up of the modern university. In German the natural sciences are referred to as the *Naturwissenschaften*, or the "structured knowledges" (*Wissenschaften*[1]) of *Natur*, the physical world of nature. They employs a particular mode of knowledge referred to as *Erklären*, or "explanation," which, in this technical sense, refers to the tracing out of the mechanistic chains of cause and effect that characterize dumb, inert objects. The humanities, on the other hand, are referred to as the *Geisteswissenschaften*: the structured knowledges of the *Geist*. This *Geist* is a cognate of the English "ghost," and encompasses a broader range of meanings—including "mind," "spirit," even "wit"—while still retaining the basic sense of a disembodied being. The *Geisteswissenschaften* are thus concerned with the free and mysterious movements of this *Geist*, which—because it is autonomous from the merely physical world—can only be apprehended through the sympathetic understanding of another *Geist*. German also helpfully provides us with another technical term, *Verstehen*, for this particular type of understanding, which corresponds to Geertz's understanding of "thick" description and is a familiar term of art for anyone in the humanities. *Verstehen* is the only manner in which a *Geist* or its products can be grasped, and is moreover an act that only another *Geist* can perform—hence the English rendering "sympathetic understanding," which captures the feeling of like-minded resonance or identification.

Since my graduate school days I have always thought of *Verstehen* as a process very much like the "Vulcan mind-meld" from the TV show *Star Trek*. As viewers of the show will recall, the character Spock was able to touch his fingers to another person's forehead, enter into a sort of trance, and thereby receive a direct impression of their thoughts. The process of *Verstehen* shares the same essential structure. The interpreter comes into contact with the object to be interpreted (a text, a scene, a work of art), "opens" herself to this object in some manner, and thereby "understands" it—a process as mysterious and magical as the Vulcan mind-meld because it cannot be explained in physical terms. Indeed, classic and influential expressions of the process of *Verstehen*, such as that formulated by the German philosophical hermeneut Hans-Georg Gadamer, explicitly portray it as an ecstatic, mystical union, an "event" (*Ereignis*) requiring a "fusion of horizons" (*Horizontverschmeltzung*) that is only possible when the interpreter fully opens himself to the human reality of the interpreted (Gadamer 1975). This is equally the case whether

---

1. *Wissenschaft* is often rendered as "science," but has the much broader meaning of any organized system of knowledge or inquiry.

the thing to be interpreted is the work of a single person or a group of people, since a human culture—the product of a large collection of human minds over historical time—also fundamentally partakes of *Geist*, and, indeed, has typically been viewed by sociologists and anthropologists as a type of *Über-Geist*. Geertz's seminal work, *The Interpretation of Cultures*, has been so influential in the humanities precisely because it succinctly captures what is distinctive about the humanistic method: It applies sympathetic understanding to a phenomenon, human culture, that can only be grasped through this special mode of understanding. This specialness, in turn, has an ultimately metaphysical justification: A culture is a product of the human mind, and the human mind and its products can only be grasped by another human mind.

The humanities-science divide, then, is fundamentally based upon mind-body dualism, and some—though by no means all—of the scholars who are eager to maintain a firewall between the two modes of inquiry are quite explicit about this. Richard Shweder's contribution to this volume is a representative statement from a major theorist in the humanities, one who views with profound suspicion the attempt to reduce "the 'mental' to the 'material,' or 'matterings' to 'matter'" (73), and who sees some form of faith in the actual existence of "un-physical realities" to be a prerequisite for normal, reasonable and morally decent behavior. The intuitive appeal of mind-body dualism is clear, and, in fact, such dualism appears not only to be a universal feature of human folk cognition, but also to play a foundational role in subserving religious and moral cognition.[2] It also possesses an inherent plausibility. Mental causation—apparently grounded in free will, and guided by reasons, goals, and meaning—seems so fundamentally different from the sort of blind, billard-ball causation we see at work in our folk physics universe of inert objects that it seems to require the postulation of a different sort of entity, not subject to the kinds of causation that holds the physical world in an iron, deterministic grip. The Cartesian *cogito* argument is intuitively powerful and seemingly unanswerable. Add to this the fact that we see what we take to be evidence of design all around us in the natural world—eagle eyes designed to spot prey from miles away, human hands admirably designed to grip tools—and it seems that Mind with a capital "M" has to be a fundamental component of the universe. In contrast to the power and easy naturalness of mind-body dualism, physicalist/materialist doctrines claiming that matter is all there is in the universe, advanced as early as Lucretius in ancient Rome, seem to face an insurmountable hurdle. Our inability to believe that mind-like phenomena such as consciousness or design could ever emerge from, as John Locke put it, "dumb, incogitative matter" (Locke [1690] 1975, 623) forms the basis of what Patricia Churchland has called the "boggled skeptic" argument against physicalism (Churchland 1986, 315).[3] Until recently, this boggled skeptic

---

2. For a readable survey of the evidence concerning folk dualism as a human universal, see Bloom 2004. More recent work, such as that by Richert and Harris 2008, Hodge 2008, and Slingerland and Chudek (forthcoming), have problematized some of the details of Bloom's argument, but it seems very likely that an at least "weak"—that is, not rigorously Cartesian—form of mind-body dualism is an innate cognitive universal. For the relationship between such dualism and religious and moral cognition, see Bering 2006 and Norenzayan and Shariff 2008.

3. Cf. Fiala et al.'s discussion of the "explanatory gap" between physicalism and human consciousness in the following chapter.

argument—really more of a feeling than an argument, but no less powerful for that—has proven impossible to defuse.

THE PHYSICALIST REVOLUTION

I say "until recently," because certain developments in the past several decades have, I believe, fundamentally altered the intellectual playing field, transforming physicalism[4] from a bizarre, rather unbelievable notion into the most plausible account of the universe we currently have. To begin with, developments in evolutionary theory have finally and decisively blocked the intuitively powerful argument from design, by both tidying up some lingering theoretical problems in classical Darwinism and providing us with conceptual frameworks that make the logic of evolution crystal clear and inescapable. Richard Dawkins' *The Selfish Gene* ([1976] 2006) is a milestone in this regard, and perhaps the most influential book on evolutionary theory in the past quarter century.[5] Dawkins's seminal book provided a coherent account of how inorganic molecules could conceivably acquire the ability to make copies of themselves, and how this mechanical ability to replicate, combined with limited errors in copying and the forces of natural selection, could give rise to all of the wildly complex forms of life that we currently see around us. Building on existing, but not yet widely appreciated, theoretical work by the likes of William Hamilton (1964), John Maynard Smith (1964; 1974), and Robert Trivers (1971; 1974), he also made a devastatingly effective case for the position that the individual gene is the unit of natural selection—not the group or, as Darwin himself had thought, the individual organism.

The gene-level approach to natural selection solved a variety of theoretical problems that had been plaguing evolutionary theory, from such broad issues as how altruism might have evolved or why sexual reproduction has become so widespread, to smaller but nagging questions such as the presence in organisms of large amounts of "surplus" DNA that does not code for proteins. Perhaps Dawkins's greatest contribution, however, was to create some simple but powerful metaphors for grasping intuitively how something that looks like design could emerge from a purely mechanistic process. Metaphors like the "selfish gene" or the "blind watchmaker" provide us with a framework for comprehending how an utterly mindless, algorithmic process of descent with

---

4. There are various philosophical versions of physicalism, which is usually identified with materialism, the idea that physical material is the only substance that exists in the universe. As Brown and Ladyman note, certain aspects of modern physics appear to make a completely austere form of materialism indefensible; they argue for a slightly modified form of physicalism, which I adopt here: "no new levels...no new theory will be introduced solely to account for mental phenomena; additionally, physicalists may predict that the physics of any new theory or newly reached level will not posit mental or intentional entities" (2009, 30). This physicalism "acknowledges the existence of mental phenomena, but claims there is, and can be, no change at the mental level without there being a corresponding change at the physical level. With the converse relationship denied, the mental is asymmetrically harnessed to the physical" (2009, 34).

5. Grafen and Ridley 2006 present a helpful collection of essays on Dawkin's model of neo-Darwinism and its intellectual impact.

mutation and natural selection can, given enough time, move us from simple, selfish replicators competing for amino acids in the primordial soup to Immanuel Kant's *Critique of Pure Reason*. Like the Reverend William Paley coming across a pocket watch on the heath, we find it extremely difficult to get away from the idea that complex design requires an Intelligence to design it. Darwin's insight was that such an Intelligence was not required, or rather—as the philosopher Daniel Dennett puts it—that "Intelligence could be broken into bits so tiny and stupid that they didn't count as intelligence at all, and then distributed through space and time in a gigantic, connected network of algorithmic process" (1995, 133). Although Darwin himself had provided the basic model for how this process works, and the details of evolutionary theory had been worked out before Dawkins, in an important sense I think that most people did not really *understand* Darwinian evolution until Dawkins provided us with the right metaphors, and it is precisely this kind of visceral understanding that is necessary to overcome the equally visceral "boggled skeptic" position.

A similar sort of revolution in the various branches of the cognitive sciences targeted the other primary barrier to embracing physicalism: the feeling that there is something so special about consciousness that it simply has to constitute an entirely new order of reality. Until recently, a thoroughly physicalist stance toward the person was no more than a notional possibility, perceived dimly by authors such as Dostoevsky and pioneering empiricists such as William James, but patently absurd to most sober thinkers. This was for a very good reason: Conscious beings have powers that seem so genuinely unique that they *must* have their origin in some ontologically distinct substance. This intuition has been undermined in the past few decades by work in cognitive science that has provided a plausible model of how mind and body are integrated, how mindlike powers could arise from a purely physical body-brain system, and how this embodied mind can be seen as much a product of evolution as the spleen. Again, immediately graspable images are crucial to intellectual shifts of this sort. As Daniel Dennett has argued, a crucial and vivid bit of evidence tipping things in favor of the physicalist view of consciousness was the development of Artificial Intelligence, which finally put to rest the "boggled" argument that no amount of physical complexity could produce creative intelligence. We have now built machines that are capable of defeating Grand Masters at chess, passing the Turing Test (i.e., plausibly holding up their end of a free-form conversation), defeating the best humans in the world at complex games of knowledge (Jeopardy), and demonstrating many of the powers that were previously seen as the exclusive province of conscious, intentional agents. Dennett observes that

> the sheer existence of computers has provided an existence proof of undeniable influence: there are mechanisms—brute, unmysterious mechanisms operating according to routinely well-understood physical principles—that have many of the competences heretofore assigned only to minds. (Dennett 2005, 7)

As Hilary Putnam concludes, the overwhelming success of the physicalist model puts the folk model of dualism in an empirically untenable position, despite its intuitive appeal:

We learn the so-called mental predicates by learning to use them in explanatory practices that involve embodied creatures. The idea that they refer to "entities" that might be present or absent independently of what goes on in our bodies and behavior has a long history and a powerful.... appeal. Yet to say that the idea "might be true" is to suppose that a clear possibility has been described, even though no way of using the picture to describe an actual case has really been proposed. (Putnam 1999, 148)

To say that *Geist*-dependent theories "might be true" is thus a little generous; it is more accurate to say that they "appear to be false."

Artificial intelligence (AI) systems are still quite crude, and extraordinarily inept at many tasks that are accomplished with ease by a three-year-old human. Similarly, there is still only a very rudimentary understanding of how the body-brain subserves even quite basic functions as memory, emotion, and self-consciousness. Our current blind spots, however, should not be taken as proof that a useful and empirically rigorous science of human consciousness is a priori impossible. As Owen Flanagan has noted, the current imperfect state of field of the human mind sciences often prompts a jump to what he refers to as "mysterianism," and it is important to see how unnecessary and unjustified this jump is:

Although everyone thinks that cars and bodies obey the principles of causation— that for every event that happens there are causes operating at every junction—no one thinks that it is a deficiency that we don't know, nor can we teach, strict laws of auto-mechanics or anatomy... [so,] when an auto mechanic or a physician says that he just can't figure out what is causing some problem, he never says, "perhaps a miracle occurred." (Flanagan 2002, 65)

We might make a similar observation concerning the unpredictability of human thought and behavior, which is often cited as a sign of human beings' essential ineffability. It is exceedingly likely that, no matter how far the neuroscience of consciousness advances, it will remain impossible—if for no other reason than because of sheer computational intractability—to accurately predict the future behavior of even a single human being, let alone groups of human beings interacting with one another and with a constantly changing physical environment. It is equally likely that, no matter what advances we make in hydrology and meteorology, it will never be possible to pick out a single molecule of H_2O from the ocean inlet outside my window and predict where that molecule will be one year from now. However, we never doubt that that molecule's future movements will be fully determined by the laws of physics. By extension, we have no more reason to believe that the cascades of neural impulses in our brains are any less determined and governed by physical causation than the water molecule.

Contrary to some doctrinaire physicalists, there is nothing about physicalism per se that makes it uniquely scientific. If we had an accumulation of a critical mass of replicable evidence for the existence of some non-physical, causally efficacious, intention-bearing substance, it would unscientific *not* to be a dualist—and, of course, we cannot rule out the possibility that such point will ever be reached.[6] A pragmatic conception of scientific "truth" requires that our ideas of what could count as a viable explanation remain constantly open to revision. It just seems that physicalism is currently our best, most productive stance toward the world. A seeping of this realization of this fact into general educated consciousness—facilitated by the conceptual and scientific innovations discussed earlier—has, I think, something to do with the fact that most humanists will readily and commonly refer to the distinction between "thick" versus "thin" description, or *Verstehen* vs. *Erklären*, when asked to characterize the humanities versus science divide, but tend to be less comfortable with the mind-body dualism on which these two intellectual modes are fundamentally grounded. Shweder's contribution to this volume is an obvious exception, but it seems to me that scholars such as Shweder—unabashedly willing to defend the humanities/science divide on the basis of strong ontological mind-body dualism—are becoming increasingly thin on the ground. And there is a very good reason for this phenomenon: Such mind-body dualism is appearing to be less and less empirically defensible every day.

VERTICAL INTEGRATION AND ITS RECEPTION IN THE ACADEMY

If the humanities/science divide is fundamentally predicated on mind-body dualism, and if such dualism is becoming an increasingly untenable empirical position, then it would appear that the "two cultures" divide is something we need to move beyond. The physicalist position is that consciousness is not a mysterious substance distinct from matter, but rather an emergent property of matter put together in sufficiently complicated way. It would thus seem to follow that the manner in which we engage in the study of consciousness and its products—that is, the traditional domain of the humanities—should be brought into alignment with the manner in which we study less complex (or differently complex) material structures, while never losing sight of the emergent properties that consciousness brings with it. In other words, we need to see the human mind as *part* of the human body, rather than its ghostly occupant, and, therefore, the human person as an integrated body-mind system produced by evolution. This is the sentiment behind the arguments for an explanatory continuum extending equally through the natural and human sciences that have recently and prominently been offered by, for instance, the biologist E.O. Wilson with his call for "consilience" (Wilson 1998), the evolutionary psychologists John Tooby and Leda Cosmides with their argument for the need for "vertical

---

6. I here take issue with John Searle's claim that physicalism functions as a modern religious dogma, accepted "without question" and with "quasi-religious faith" (Searle 2004, 48). No doubt some physicalists are dogmatists as well, but dogmatism is not intrinsic to the position. Searle's assertion that physicalism leaves out "some *essential* mental feature of the universe, which *we know*, independently of our philosophical commitments, *to exist*"—that it denies "the *obvious fact* that we all *intrinsically have* conscious states and intentional states" (Searle 2004, 49—emphases added)— echoes the position defended by Shweder earlier, and seems to me much more faithlike than the claim defended by the likes of Dennett that physicalism just seems to be the best explanation that we have right now.

integration" (Tooby and Cosmides 1992), and the neuroscientist and linguist Steven Pinker with his critique of the humanistic dogma of the "Holy Trinity" (the Blank Slate, the Noble Savage, and the Ghost in the Machine) (Pinker 2002). What all of these approaches have in common is a desire to take the humanities beyond dualistic meta-physics by seeing human-level structures of meaning as grounded in the lower levels of meaning studied by the sciences, rather than as hovering magically above them.

Understood in this way, human-level reality can be seen as eminently *explainable*. Practically speaking, this means that humanists need to start taking seriously discoveries about human cognition being provided by neuroscientists and psychologists, which have a constraining function to play in the formulation of humanistic theories—calling into question, for instance, such deeply entrenched dogmas as the blank-slate theory of human nature, strong versions of social constructivism and linguistic determinism, and the ideal of disembodied reason. Bringing the humanities and the sciences together into a single, integrated chain seems to me the only way to clear up the current miasma of endlessly contingent discourses and representations of representations that currently hampers humanistic inquiry. Of course, the reverse is also true: humanists have a great deal to contribute to scientific research. As discoveries in the biological and cognitive sciences have begun to blur traditional disciplinary boundaries, researchers in these fields have found their work bringing them into contact with the sort of high-level issues that traditionally have been the domain of the core humanities disciplines, and often their lack of formal training in these areas leaves them groping in the dark or attempting to reinvent the wheel. This is where humanist expertise can and should play a crucial role in guiding and interpreting the results of scientific exploration—something that can occur only when scholars on *both* sides of the humanities-science divide are willing to talk to one another.

It is important to acknowledge, however, that this call for vertical integration has, for the most part, been met with hostility among humanists. There are many reasons for this. Some are bad, and stem from the usual panoply of intellectual and personal sins: intellectual inertia, resentment of the relatively greater and growing prestige enjoyed by science in the past few decades, or lazy free-association that connects physicalism and evolution with social Darwinism, Nazism, and the evils of unrestrained capitalism.[7] There is, in addition, however, a constellation of good reasons that need to be addressed. One very good, though empirically indefensible reason—in my opinion at least—is exemplified by Richard Shweder's contribution in this section: there continues to be genuine disagreement about the empirical plausibility of ontological mind-body dualism, and many humanists who clearly grasp the arguments behind vertical integration simply reject them as scientifically unsubstantiated. If it did turn out that we had immaterial mind-souls that operate completely independently from our bodies, this would indeed be a very good reason for rejecting vertical integration.

Beyond disagreement over the ontological status of mind-body dualism, however, there are reasons for being skeptical about the desirability of vertical integration, especially as it has sometimes been practiced in the past. Even among humanists who grasp the physicalist position and are convinced of its empirical plausibility, there are many who have important

7. A classic expression of this sort of intellectual slippage can be found in Rose and Rose 2000, 8–9.

concerns about what a physicalist, consilient approach to the human should look like. Some are worried that many defenders of vertical integration appear to be operating with rather simplistic, and long discredited, conceptions of the nature of scientific inquiry. Since at least Thomas Kuhn's landmark *The Structure of Scientific Revolutions* (Kuhn [1962] 1970), philosophers have documented a host of problems with positivistic models of science. For instance, it is clear that theory and observation are inextricably intertwined; theoretical presuppositions play an unavoidable role in what one perceives (or does not perceive), and the classic ideal of purely objective observer or perfectly corroborated theory is, therefore, unrealizable. Many in the humanities have overreacted to this insight, embracing a kind of extreme epistemological relativism whereby there are no criteria for distinguishing more reliable from less reliable knowledge, and all human knowledge of the world is simply swallowed up in the great maw of *Verstehen*.[8] The underreaction of scientists, however, is equally deplorable. It is an odd feature of the modern Academy that philosophy of science is undertaken and studied almost exclusively in the humanities, while most working scientists—including many defenders of vertical integration—have at best only a dim understanding of the revolutions in philosophy of science that have occurred in the past several decades. This then opens them to the (for humanists) devastating and fatal charge of being "theoretically unsophisticated"—a sufficient justification, in the eyes of many humanists, for simply dismissing or ignoring their work. This is unfair, but nonetheless understandable: it is impossible to defend the vertical integration approach without a robust, theoretically defensible account of why empirical data is preferable to armchair speculation. There are plenty of places to turn for such an account. For instance Larry Laudan 1996, Ian Hacking 1983 and Susan Haack 2003, to name just a few, have developed postpositivist, pragmatic models of science that avoid the skeptical circle by rejecting mind-body dualism, and restore the importance of the empirical by emphasizing our constant contact with and efficacy in the world. Defenders of vertical integration can thus find some extremely helpful allies in the philosophy of science, but they need to recognize the need for such allies, and well as where to look to find them.

Another weakness in certain portrayals of vertical integration—again, often viewed by humanists as immediate grounds for dismissal—is a frequent failure to take into account the foundational role of human culture. Vertical integration rightly targets extreme, dualist conceptions of culture that view it as entirely autonomous from the physical or biological, a *sui generis* reality subject only to its own internal laws and amenable only to *Verstehen*.[9] A common overreaction, however, has been to overemphasize the other extreme of nativism, reducing culture to nothing more than a mechanically expressed phenotypic trait. E.O. Wilson's famous—or infamous—characterization of the human brain as "an exposed negative waiting to be dipped in developer fluid" (Wilson [1975] 2000, 156) is a paradigmatic example. Extreme nativist models can provide no account of how cultural variation—the single most salient feature of the world for most humanists—could arise, and also remains trapped in a kind of culture-nature dualism

---

8. For representative statements on both sides of the so-called science wars, see Marglin and Marglin 1990 and Koertge 1998. Also see Segerstråle 2000 for a short overview of the debate.

9. See, for instance, the critique by Tooby and Cosmides 1992 of the "Standard Social Scientific Model" (SSSM).

that shares all the limitations of mind-body dualism. We need not choose between culture and nature: the recognition that innate human psychology has a very complex and robust structure can coexist with an acknowledgement that this structure can be reshaped and rechanneled by a variety of forces, human cultural forms being the most obvious. Culture clearly functions as a crucial component of the adaptive environment in human mind-culture co-evolution, being carried and filtered by individual minds, but also capable of exerting independent force on them.

A final source of resistance to the project of science-humanities integration is the one most fundamentally tied to mind-body dualism, and the topic with which I would like to conclude this chapter. If human beings are intuitive mind-body dualists, it follows that studying the human as coterminous with the physical—the linchpin of vertical integration—will fundamentally violate our intuitive understanding of the world. This is also the case, of course, when it comes to any counterintuitive system of thought, such as any version of post-Aristotelian physics. The very fact that we have developed modern physics, though, and can train ourselves to think in accordance with it terms, demonstrates that folk intuitions do not have a stranglehold on our minds; when it is deemed appropriate to do so, we are capable of overcoming folk intuitions through sufficient education and conceptual training. However, the violation of mind-body dualism that is required to embrace physicalism—and thus vertical integration—faces at least two unusual hurdles. The first involves the innate[10] nature of mind-body dualism. The Ptolemaic model of the solar system falls quite naturally out of the functioning of our built-in perceptual systems, but it is not itself part of that system: we do not appear to possess an innate Ptolemaic solar system cognitive module. Switching to Copernicanism, at least intellectually, thus requires us to suspend our common sense perceptions, but it does not involve a direct violation of any fundamental, innate human ideas. On the other hand, if it is true that mind-body dualism is an innate, human cognitive universal, then physicalism *does* require such a violation.[11] Moreover, our innate folk dualism appears to be linked in a fundamental manner to human emotional and moral intuitions. Abandoning the Ptolemaic solar system in favor of Copernicus wounds our pride and undermines Scripture, but is something that modern humans appear to accept with equanimity; replacing folk physics with the increasingly stranger models proposed by Newton and Einstein requires specialized training and intellectual acumen, but can apparently be accomplished without meeting with any particular visceral resistance. Seeing people as, in essence, very complicated *things*, however, inspires in us a kind of emotional resistance and even revulsion—a revulsion that obviously lies behind Creationist opposition to the theory of evolution or more strident humanistic critiques of evolutionary psychology,[12] but that must, I would argue, be felt at some level by any thoughtful and psychologically healthy human being.

---

10. I take *innate* in the sense defined by Simpson et al.: "we might take a cognitive mechanism, representation, bias or connection to be innate to the extent that it emerges at some point in the course of normal development but is not the product of learning" (2005, 5).

11. This problem is essentially the same as the disconnect between "System 1" and "System 2" processes discussed by Fiala et al. in the following chapter.

12. See Segerstråle 2000 on the moral dimensions of the debate surrounding evolutionary psychology, as well as Dennett 1995 on the fundamentally "dangerous" nature of "Darwin's idea."

For instance, from the perspective of evolutionary psychology, I can be convinced on an intellectual level that the love that I feel toward my child and my relatives is an emotion installed in me by my genes in accordance with Hamilton's Rule (Hamilton 1964). This does not, however, make my visceral, "on-line" experience of the emotion, nor my sense of its normative reality, any less real to me. At an important and ineradicable level, the idea of my daughter as merely a complex robot carrying my genes into the next generation is both bizarre and repugnant to me. Indeed, this is precisely what one would expect according to evolutionary theory: Gene-level, ultimate causation would not *work* unless we were thoroughly sincere at the proximate level. The whole purpose of the evolution of social emotions is to make sure that these "false" feelings seem inescapably real to us, and this lived reality will never change unless we turn into completely different types of organisms. In a similar way we can say, qua physicalists, that our overactive theory of mind causes us to inevitably project intentionality onto the world—to see our moral emotions and desires writ large in the cosmos, or to see some sort of "meaning" in our lives.[13] It would, moreover, be empirically unjustified to take this projection as "real." Nonetheless, the very inevitability of this projection means that, whatever we may assert as physicalists, we cannot escape from the lived reality of moral space.[14] As neuroscientists, we might believe that the brain is a deterministic, physical system like everything else in the universe, and recognize that the weight of empirical evidence suggests that free will is a cognitive illusion (Wegner 2002). Nonetheless, no cognitively undamaged human being can help *acting* like and at some level really *feeling* that he or she is free. There may well be individuals who lack this sense, and who can quite easily and thoroughly conceive of themselves and other people in purely instrumental, mechanistic terms, but we label such people "psychopaths," and quite rightly try to identify them and put them away somewhere to protect the rest of us (Blair 1995, 2001). The Darwinian model of the origin of human beings and other animals, and its formulation of the ultimate reasons for many of our abilities and behaviors, is thus theoretically powerful and satisfying while appearing alien, and often repugnant, from any sort of normal human perspective.

This has very important, and too-often unrecognized, implications for the limits of vertical integration. The importance of "emergent" realities has long been recognized within the sciences. As one moves up the chain of vertical integration from, for instance, physics to physical chemistry to organic chemistry, new explanatory entities and principles arise that are not predictable from the lower levels, nor fully reducible to them at a heuristic level. This means that it would be foolish to try to replace organic chemistry with physics, or to dismiss the explanatory usefulness of concepts and entities unique to organic chemistry.[15] However, this emergence is clearly understood by everyone involved as merely heuristic: There is nothing going on in organic chemistry that is not ultimately physical, and an organic chemist would never angrily accuse a physical chemist of being

13. On this idea of "hyperactive theory of mind" as the basis for religious belief and morality, see Guthrie 1993, Barrett 2000 and Bering 2006.

14. The Canadian philosopher Charles Taylor 1989 provides an extremely insightful and profound account of the inescapability of human-level truth, although he attributes to this inescapability a degree of ontological significance that I regard as ultimately unjustifiable.

15. For more on levels of explanation and cross-scientific explanation, see McCauley 2007.

"reductionistic" for exploring the physical chemical realities underlying the behavior of organic molecules. The same is simply not true of the human level of explanation. Because of our innate folk dualism, human level realities—beauty, honor, love, freedom—strike us as pertaining to an ontological realm entirely distinct from the blind, deterministic workings of the physical world, and we are always ready to trot out the emotionally fraught charge of "reductionism" whenever the former is explained in terms of the latter. Even if the heuristic autonomy and proximate psychological power of parental love is scrupulously acknowledged, the very idea of considering a parent's love for their child in light of the cold logic of evolution will always seem both "unreal" and "unsavory," to echo Richard Shweder. What this means is that the move from physical explanation to human explanation will always feel different to us than the move from physical chemistry to organic chemistry—though, of course, they are no different in principle. For creatures like us, then, the chain of vertical integration will never be seamless: we will always feel a jolt when we cross from the physical to the mental, from the merely biological to the human, from ultimate evolutionary reasons to proximate psychological mechanisms. Understanding this fact will help us to see why the humanities-science divide continues to prove so difficult to negotiate, as well as why something like this divide will always have some traction in human psychology. This is by no means an insurmountable barrier, but should serve to temper our impatience with those who see vertical integration as a "bargain with the devil" (Menand 2005, 14), as well as to sharpen our sense of the challenges ahead.

References

Barrett, Justin. 2000. Exploring the natural foundations of religion. *Trends in Cognitive Sciences* 4: 29–34.

Bering, J. M. 2006. The folk psychology of souls. *Behavioral and Brain Sciences* 295: 453–498.

Blair, James. 1995. A cognitive developmental approach to morality: Investigating the psychopath. *Cognition* 57: 1–29.

Blair, James. 2001. Neurocognitive models of aggression, the antisocial personality disorders, and psychopathy. *Journal of Neurology, Neurosurgery, and Psychiatry* 71: 727–731.

Bloom, Paul. 2004. *Descartes' baby: How the science of child development explains what makes us human.* New York: Basic Books.

Brown, Robin, and James Ladyman. 2009. Physicalism, supervenience and the fundamental level. *The Philosophical Quarterly* 59 (234): 20–38.

Churchland, Patricia. 1986. *Neurophilosophy: Toward a unified science of the mind-brain.* Cambridge, Mass.: Bradford Books/Massachussetts Institute of Technology Press.

Dawkins, Richard. [1976] 2006. *The selfish gene.* 30th anniversary ed. Oxford: Oxford Unversity Press.

Dennett, Daniel. 1995. *Darwin's dangerous idea: Evolution and the meaning of life.* New York: Simon and Schuster.

Dennett, Daniel. 2005. *Sweet dreams: Philosophical obstacles to a science of consciousness.* Cambridge, Mass.: MIT Press.

Flanagan, Owen. 2002. *The problem of the soul: Two visions of mind and how to reconcile them.* New York: Basic Books.

Gadamer, Hans-Georg. 1975. *Truth and method.* New York: Continuum.

Geertz, Clifford. 1973. *The interpretation of cultures: Selected essays*. New York: Basic Books.

Grafen, Alan, and Matt Ridley, eds. 2006. *Richard Dawkins: How a scientist changed the way we think*. New York: Oxford University Press.

Guthrie, Stuart. 1993. *Faces in the clouds: A new theory of religion*. New York: Oxford University Press.

Haack, Susan. 2003. *Defending science within reason: Between scientism and cynicism*. Amherst, NY: Prometheus Books.

Hacking, Ian. 1983. *Representing and intervening: Introductory topics in the philosophy of natural science*. Cambridge: Cambridge University Press.

Hamilton, William D. 1964. The genetical evolution of social behavior, *Journal of Theoretical Biology* 7: 1–52.

Hodge, K. Mitch. 2008. Descartes' mistake: How afterlife beliefs challenge the assumption that humans are intuitive Cartesian substance dualists. *Journal of Cognition and Culture* 8: 387–415.

Koertge, Noretta, ed. 1998. *A house built on sand: Exposing postmodernist myths about science*. New York: Oxford University Press.

Kuhn, Thomas. [1962] 1970. *The structure of scientific revolutions*. 2nd ed. Chicago: University of Chicago Press.

Laudan, Larry. 1996. *Beyond positivism and relativism: Theory, method, and evidence*. Boulder, Col.: Westview Press.

Locke, John. [1690] 1975. *An essay concerning human understanding*. Oxford: Clarendon.

Marglin, Frederique, and Stephen Marglin, eds. 1990. *Dominating knowledge: Development, culture and resistance*. Oxford: Clarendon.

Maynard Smith, John. 1964. Group selection and kin selection. *Nature* 201: 1145–1147.

Maynard Smith, John. 1974. The theory of games and the evolution of animal conflicts. *Journal of Theoretical Biology* 47: 201–221.

McCauley, Robert. 2007. Reduction: Models of cross-scientific relations and their implications for the psychology-neuroscience interface. In *Handbook of the Philosophy of Science: Philosophy of Psychology and Cognitive Science*, ed. P. Thagard. Amsterdam: Elsevier.

Menand, Louis. 2005. Dangers within and without. *Modern Language Association, Profession* 1: 10–17.

Norenzayan, Ara, and Azim F. Shariff. 2008. The origin and evolution of religious prosociality. *Science* 322 (5898): 58–62.

Pinker, Steven. 2002. *The blank slate: The modern denial of human nature*. New York: Viking.

Putnam, Hilary. 1999. *The threefold cord: Mind, body, and world*. New York: Columbia University Press.

Richert, Rebekah A., and Paul L. Harris. 2008. Dualism revisited: Body vs. mind vs. soul. *Journal of Cognition and Culture* 8: 99–115.

Rose, Hilary, and Steven Rose. 2000. Introduction. In *Alas, poor Darwin! Arguments against evolutionary psychology*, ed. H. Rose and S. Rose. New York: Harmony Books.

Ryle, Gilbert. 1971. The thinking of thoughts: What is "le penseur" doing? In *Collected Papers*. London: Hutchinson and Co.

Searle, John. 2004. *Mind: A brief introduction*. New York: Oxford University Press.

Segerstråle, Ullica. 2000. *Defenders of the truth: The battle for sociobiology and beyond*. New York: Oxford University Press.

Slingerland, Edward and Maciej Chudek. (forthcoming). The prevalence of mind-body dualism in early China. *Cognitive Science*.

Simpson, Tom, Peter Carruthers, Stephen Laurence, and Stephen Stich. 2005. Introduction: Nativism past and present. In *The innate mind: Structure and content*, ed. P. Carruthers, S. Laurence and S. Stich. New York: Oxford University Press.

Taylor, Charles. 1989. *Sources of the self: The makings of modern identity*. Cambridge, Mass.: Harvard University Press.

Tooby, John, and Leda Cosmides. 1992. The psychological foundations of culture. In *The adapted mind: Evolutionary psychology and the generation of culture*, edited by J. Barkow, L. Cosmides and J. Tooby. New York: Oxford University Press.

Trivers, Robert. 1971. The evolution of reciprocal altruism. *Quarterly Review of Biology* 46: 35–57.

Trivers, Robert. 1974. Parent-offspring conflict. *American Zoologist* 14: 249–264.

Wegner, Daniel. 2002. *The illusion of conscious will*. Cambridge, MA: MIT Press.

Wilson, E. O. 1998. *Consilience: The unity of knowledge*. New York: Knopf.

Wilson, E. O. [1975] 2000. *Sociobiology: The new synthesis*. 25th anniversary ed. Cambridge, Mass: Harvard University Press.

4

ON THE PSYCHOLOGICAL ORIGINS
OF DUALISM: DUAL-PROCESS COGNITION
AND THE EXPLANATORY GAP*

Brian Fiala, Adam Arico, Shaun Nichols

1. THE EXPLANATORY GAP

Perhaps the most broad and unassuming philosophical question about consciousness is "What is the relationship between consciousness and the physical world?" It is *prima facie* difficult to see how the pains, itches, and tickles of phenomenal consciousness could fit into a world populated exclusively by particles, fields, forces, and other denizens of fundamental physics. However, this appears to be just what physicalism requires. How could a thinking, experiencing mind be a purely physical thing?

One approach to this problem emphasizes our *epistemic* situation with respect to consciousness, and especially the distinctively *explanatory* situation. Epistemic approaches focus on whether we can acquire knowledge, justified belief, or an adequate explanation of the nature of consciousness. Thomas Huxley famously gestures at this aspect of the problem of consciousness:

> But what consciousness is, we know not; and how it is that anything so remarkable as a state of consciousness comes about as a result of irritating nervous tissue, is just as unaccountable as the appearance of the Djin when Aladdin rubbed his lamp. (Huxley 1866, 193)

Huxley's suggestion is that no account can be given of the relationship between consciousness and the brain, where an "account" amounts to something like an "adequate scientific explanation." Huxley's skepticism about the prospects for a physicalist account of consciousness drives him to *epiphenomenalist dualism*, according to which consciousness is not itself a physical phenomenon and has no causal impact on any physical phenomena (1874/2002).

* Acknowledgements: We have several people to thank for discussion and comments on the manuscript: Sara Bernstein, Mark Collard, Jonathan Cohen, Chris Hitchcock, Terry Horgan, Bryce Huebner, Chris Kahn, Josh Knobe, Uriah Kriegel, Robert Johnson, Alan Love, Edouard Machery, Ron Mallon, Matt McGrath, Nicoletta Orlandi, J. Brendan Ritchie, Philip Robbins, Ted Slingerland, Ernest Sosa, and Josh Weisberg.

Versions of the explanatory worry continue to exercise philosophers. In his encyclopedia article on consciousness, Robert van Gulick describes the "hard problem" of explaining consciousness as providing "an intelligible account that lets us see in an intuitively satisfying way how phenomenal consciousness might arise from physical processes in the brain" (van Gulick 2004). Relatedly, Joseph Levine maintains that brain-based explanations of consciousness inevitably fall short. According to Levine, "psycho-physical identity statements leave a significant *explanatory gap*" (1983). That is, theories that attempt to explain consciousness by identifying it with some physical property or process will inevitably seem to leave out something important about consciousness. What's supposed to be left out is the felt quality of *what it's like* to undergo a conscious experience such as seeing the color red. Since it appears inevitable that purely physical theories will "leave something out," Levine suggests that there is reason to think that such theories will inevitably fail to adequately *explain* consciousness. Levine elaborates on this suggestion by claiming that there is an air of "felt contingency" about the relationship between consciousness and processes in the brain (and indeed, between consciousness and *any* physical process). That is, there seems to be something non-necessary about any purported reductive connections between physical processes and conscious states. However, good explanations are not arbitrary.[1] As a result, it is hard to see how a theory invoking "mere" brain activity could be a complete explanation of consciousness. Levine concludes, echoing Huxley, that the explanatory gap poses a deep challenge to physicalism.

One prominent argumentative strategy at this juncture is to draw on this apparent epistemic obstacle as support for conclusions about the nature of consciousness. For example, one might take the explanatory gap discussed by Huxley and Levine as indicative of a corresponding duality in nature. If no physical theory can fully *explain* consciousness, it seems doubtful that consciousness *is* something physical. For, the argument continues, if something is not fully physically explicable then it is not a completely physical phenomenon. Therefore, consciousness must not be a physical phenomenon. This formulation of the argumentative strategy is overly simple, but it serves to illustrate the strategy of arguing from epistemic premises to conclusions about the nature of consciousness.

Although the explanatory gap is central to contemporary philosophy of mind, it is plausible that the gap gives philosophical expression to a much more pervasive phenomenon; even people without any philosophical training find it bizarre and counterintuitive to think that consciousness is nothing over and above certain processes in the brain. Paul Bloom takes this to be part of a universal inclination toward *folk dualism*. According to Bloom, people are "dualists who have two ways of looking at the world: in terms of bodies and in terms of souls. A direct consequence of this dualism is the idea that bodies and souls are separate" (2004, 191). Folk dualism is associated with a range of beliefs including beliefs about free will and personal identity. The rift between consciousness and the physical world is taken to be one central element of folk dualism:

---

1. Admittedly, this gloss on the issue of modality and reductive explanation crushes many subtleties. We apologize for this injustice. For reasons that will soon become clear, our primary focus in this paper is on the psychological aspects of the problem of consciousness, rather than on the modal aspects.

People universally think of human consciousness as separate from the physical realm. Just about everyone believes, for instance, that when our bodies die, we will survive— perhaps rising to heaven, entering another body, or coming to occupy some spirit world. (Bloom 2006, 211).[2]

What makes brain-consciousness dualism so seductive in both philosophy and ordinary life? Why does the explanatory gap carry so much intuitive weight? We suspect that the answers to these questions have much in common. The common answer we have in mind is *psychological* in nature, and so we turn to the psychological underpinnings of the attribution of consciousness.

2. THE PSYCHOLOGY OF ATTRIBUTING CONSCIOUS STATES

Claims about cognitive architecture figure centrally in our explanation of the capacity to attribute conscious states, and how this capacity figures in dualistic patterns of thought. Specifically we claim that *dual-process* cognitive architecture plays a key role in the psychology underlying explanatory gap intuitions and folk dualism. We thus begin with a brief introduction to dual-process models.

2.1 Dual-Process Models

In recent years, dual-process theories have been proposed for all sorts of cognitive phenomena, including moral judgment (Haidt, 2001), decision-making (Stanovich and West, 2000; Stanovich, 2004), probabilistic reasoning (Sloman, 1996), and social cognition (Chaiken and Trope, 1999). A crude version of dual-process theory holds that mental systems fall into two classes. In one class, system 1, we find processes that are quick, automatic, unconscious, associative, heuristic-based, computationally simple, evolutionarily old, domain-specific and non-inferential. In the other class, system 2, we find processes that are relatively slow, controlled, introspectively accessible, rule-based, analytic, computationally demanding, inferential, domain-general, and voluntary.

Although system 1 and system 2 have different processing characteristics, they sometimes operate over the same domain. Given the processing differences, it's no surprise that a system 1 process and a system 2 process sometimes produce conflicting outputs with respect to the same cognitive task or subject matter. For instance, consider the following argument:

> All unemployed people are poor.
> Rockefsseller is not unemployed.
> Conclusion: Rockefeller is not poor.

2. Experiments by Richert & Harris (2006 & 2008) indicate that, *contra* Bloom (2004), people do not explicitly identify the mind with the soul. Beliefs about the soul are rather messy, but people do largely think that the soul is independent of the body (Richert & Harris 2008). And Richert & Harris seem to agree that people take consciousness to be tied to the soul: "the concepts of identity, consciousness and soul are deeply intertwined in human cognition about other humans" (Richert & Harris 2008, 99–100).

On reading this argument, many people judge incorrectly that the argument is valid. According to dual-process theory, that is because people's belief in the conclusion biases a system 1 reasoning process to the incorrect answer. However, most people can be brought to appreciate that the argument is not valid, and this is because we also have a system 2 reasoning process that has the resources to evaluate the argument in a consciously controlled, reasoned fashion (see, e.g., Evans 2007). Of course, system 1 and system 2 can (and quite often do) arrive at the same verdict. For instance, changing the first premise of the preceding argument to "Only unemployed people are poor" allows both systems to converge on the judgment that the argument is valid.

Although the dual-process paradigm provides a tidy picture of the mind, it is unlikely that all mental processes will divide sharply and cleanly into the two categories, such that either a process has all the characteristic features of system 1 or all of the characteristic features of system 2. It would not be surprising, for instance, to find processes that are fast and computationally simple but not associationistic (cf. Fodor 1983). So if we find that a process has one characteristic system 1 feature, it would be rash to infer that the process has the rest of the characteristic system 1 features. Nonetheless, the dual-process approach is useful so long as one is clear about the particular characteristics of the psychological processes at issue (cf. Samuels, 2009; Stanovich and West, 2000; Stanovich, 2004).

We think the distinction between processes that are automatic and processes that are consciously controlled captures an important difference between cognitive systems in many domains, including the domain of conscious-state attributions. We suggest (1) that there are two cognitive pathways by which we typically arrive at judgments that something has conscious states, and (2) that these pathways correspond to a system 1/system 2 distinction. On the one hand, we propose a "low-road" mechanism for conscious-state attributions that has several characteristic system 1 features: it is fast, domain-specific (i.e., it operates on a restricted range of inputs), and automatic (i.e., the mechanism is not under conscious control).[3] On the other hand, there are judgments about conscious states that we reach through rational deliberation, theory application, or conscious reasoning; call this pathway to attributions of conscious states "the high road."

2.2 Consciousness Attribution: The Low Road

We propose that one path by which we come to attribute conscious states proceeds through the identification of an entity as an AGENT (Arico et al. 2011).[4] This "AGENCY model" charts a low-road path to conscious-state attribution. According to this model, we are disposed to have a gut feeling that an entity has conscious states if and only if we categorize that entity as an AGENT, and typically we are inclined to categorize an entity as an AGENT only when we represent the entity as having certain features. These features

---

3. We remain neutral on whether the mechanism has other features of system 1, like being associationistic, evolutionarily old, and computationally simple.

4. This model was developed in the wake of recent work on the folk psychology of consciousness (Gray et al. 2007, Knobe & Prinz 2008, Sytsma & Machery 2009). As with the other work in the area, our model focuses on attributions of conscious states to others. But it's possible that a quite different mechanism is required to explain attributions of conscious states to oneself.

will be relatively simple, surface- level features, which are members of a restricted set of potential inputs to the low-road process. Previous research has identified three features that reliably produce AGENT categorization: that the entity appears to have eyes, that it appears to behave in a contingently interactive manner, and that it displays distinctive (non-inertial) motion trajectories.[5]

The AGENCY model is a natural extension of work in developmental and social psychology. In their landmark study, Heider and Simmel (1944) showed participants an animation of geometric shapes (triangles, squares, circles) moving in non-inertial trajectories. When participants were asked to describe what was happening on the screen, they tended to use mental-state terms such as "chasing," "wanting," and "trying"—in their descriptions of the animation. This suggests that certain types of distinctive motion trigger us to attribute mentality to an entity, even when the entity is a mere geometric figure.

More recently, developmental psychologists Susan Johnson and colleagues (1998) presented 12-month-olds with various novel items, one of which was a "fuzzy brown object." Johnson and colleagues found that when the fuzzy brown object included eyes, infants were more likely to follow the "gaze" of the fuzzy brown object. They also found that infants displayed the same gaze-following behavior when the fuzzy brown object, controlled remotely, moved around and made noise in apparently contingent response to the infant's behavior. Johnson and colleagues explain these effects by suggesting that when an entity has eyes or exhibits contingent interaction, infants (and adults) will categorize the entity as an agent. Once an entity is categorized as an agent, this generates the disposition to attribute mental states to the entity, which manifests in a variety of ways, including gaze following, imitation, and anticipating goal-directed behavior (see also Johnson 2003, Shimizu & Johnson 2004). Figure 1 depicts the model of mental state attribution suggested by these studies.

We propose that this cognitive process also explains many of our everyday attributions of consciousness. In addition to facilitating imitation, gaze-following, and the attribution of goals and intentions, we suggest that agent-categorization also plays a central role in disposing people to regard entities as capable of having conscious experiences.

This model has empirically testable predictions. For instance, if we assume that the AGENCY model depicts the primary low-road mechanism for attributing conscious states to others, we should expect to find that people will not be immediately intuitively inclined to attribute conscious states to entities that typically lack the triggers for categorizing an object as an AGENT. More specifically, the model predicts that people will not

---

5. There are interesting questions about how and why *these* particular features are important for AGENT categorization. For example, is the connection innate, or acquired? If the connection is acquired, then via what kind(s) of learning? We'll remain neutral on most such questions here. However, it seems beyond doubt that the mechanism is fixed in a certain respect: at a given time, the AGENT mechanism is insensitive to information other than this relatively small set of featural cues. Following McCauley and Henrich (2006), we might say that the AGENT mechanism is *synchronically impenetrable*. It may be that, over time, the AGENT mechanism can acquire a sensitivity to various other kinds of features (perhaps including much more complex features). In other words, it may be that the AGENT mechanism is *diachronically* penetrable. But on this last question, we wish to remain neutral.

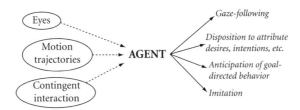

FIGURE 1 Model of AGENT detection (a la Johnson 2003).

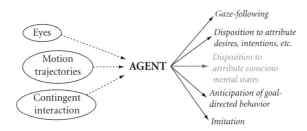

FIGURE 2 The AGENCY model.

have any immediate intuitive inclination to attribute conscious states to things such as trees, clouds, cars, and rivers, since all of them lack eyes, contingently interactive behavior, and the distinctive kinds of motion trajectories investigated by Heider and Simmel.[6] In addition, the model predicts that people *will* be automatically inclined to attribute conscious states to the kinds of entities that have the superficial cues.

This is precisely what we found in a reaction-time experiment (Arico et al. 2011). One characteristic of dual-process models, including ours, is that the low-road system is supposed to be automatic; by contrast the high-road system, which draws on a broader information base, is under deliberate control of the reasoner. In a reaction-time paradigm under speeded conditions, low-road processing should occur automatically (and relatively quickly), with high-road processes lagging behind. Given this standard interpretation of response times, the AGENCY model predicts slower reaction times when participants *deny* conscious state attributions to objects that are typically classified as AGENTS (as compared broadly to non-AGENTS). The idea is that if someone were to overtly respond that entities categorized as AGENTS don't feel pain (e.g., because they lack appropriate neural structures), this would require overcoming the hypothesized low-road disposition to attribute conscious states to those entities, which would take some deliberate reasoning and hence extra time. To test our model, we presented subjects with a sequence of object/attribution pairs (e.g., *ant/feels pain*), and the subjects were asked to respond as quickly as possible (yes or no) whether the object had the attribute.

6. Of course, anthropomorphized cartoon versions of such objects may well induce an immediate inclination to attribute conscious states. On our account, the natural explanation is that cartoons induce consciousness-attribution precisely because they have the right kinds of triggering featural cues.

FIGURE 3 The AGENCY model of the low-road path to attributions of conscious states.

Attributions included properties like "feels happy" and "feels pain," and objects included various mammals, birds, insects, plants, vehicles, and natural objects. We recorded both participants' overt judgments and the time taken to answer each item. We found that participants quickly affirmed attributions of consciousness for those objects that typically possess the relevant features (mammals, birds, insects), while they responded negatively in response to attributions of consciousness to things that typically lack those features (vehicles, inanimate moving objects like clouds and rivers). More importantly, the reaction-time results confirmed the predictions entailed by the AGENCY model of low-road consciousness attributions. Participants responded significantly more slowly when they *denied* conscious states to objects that *do* have the superficial AGENCY cues, namely, insects. This result is neatly explained by our hypothesis that insects automatically activate the low road to consciousness attribution; in order to deny that insects have conscious states, subjects had to "override" the low-road output, which explains why reaction times are slower in such cases.[7]

These experiments provide support for the AGENCY model of low-road consciousness attribution. However, there are numerous ways that this low-road process might be triggered, and many of the details of this process are largely underdetermined by the existing data. Nonetheless, the data corroborate our proposal that low-road attributions of conscious states are generated by an AGENT mechanism that is triggered by a restricted range of inputs. (See Figure 3).

2.3 Consciousness Attribution: The High Road

Thus far, we have focused on one pathway for attributing conscious states. The low-road mechanism is not, however, the only pathway for attributing conscious states. One might instead rely on deliberation and inferential reasoning to conclude that an entity satisfies the criteria laid out by some scientific theory and, thus, judge that it (probably) has conscious states. For instance, if a trusted source tells Uriah that a certain organism has a sophisticated neural system (including nociceptors and dorsolateral prefrontal cortex), and if Uriah relies on a rudimentary theory of pain processing, then he might infer that the organism can probably feel pain. What matters is that one can come to think that an entity has conscious states via a pathway that has features typically associated with system 2—processing that is domain-general, voluntary, and introspectively accessible. The

---

7. Why do people override the low road at all? Why not accept the gut feeling that a spider (for example) can feel pain? People might override because of known facts about arachnid neuroanatomy: for example, that spiders lack nociceptors. Another possibility is that people override because of socially acquired "scripts" about spiders: for example, "*Of course* spiders don't feel pain!"

process is domain general in that the inputs are not restricted— evidence can potentially come from anywhere. The process is voluntary because we can control when reasoning starts and stops. And it is introspectively accessible because the steps of the inferential process are typically available to consciousness. Let us examine these three features in a bit more detail.

First, like much reasoning, high-road attributions of consciousness can potentially draw on an immense supply of information for evidence about an entity's having conscious states. Potential resources include the individual's current perceptual state, background beliefs, memories, and testimony from trusted sources. Second, high-road attributions of consciousness are voluntary actions in the same sense that many conclusions reached via deliberate inferences are voluntary. Like other voluntary inferential processes, we can choose to initiate and sustain the process of reasoning about another entity's consciousness. The high-road attributions are not the result of an automatically triggered process that necessarily runs to completion upon activation. The high-road process is engaged when one deliberately contemplates whether another entity is conscious, which is something that one can decide to do, to continue to do, or to stop doing. Third, because the high road proceeds through deliberate reasoning, the inferential steps from the initial assumption(s) to the conclusion are typically introspectively accessible to the individual. That is, at any point one can take notice of the line of reasoning that the high road is processing and know which inferences are being drawn. Where the low road is hidden from such introspective access, the high road is typically available to introspection.

As another example of a high-road process leading to attributions of conscious states, consider Mill's argument that other humans have sensations and other mental states. Mill writes,

> [B]y what considerations am I led to believe ... that the walking and speaking figures which I see and hear, have sensations and thoughts ...? I conclude that other human beings have feelings like me, because, first, they have bodies like me ... and because, secondly, they exhibit the acts, and other outward signs, which in my own case I know by experience to be caused by feelings. (Mill 1865)

This example exhibits the hallmark features of high road reasoning. Mill draws freely on his observations about the similarity of bodies, as well as beliefs about behavior and its link to experience. At any point, Mill is able to stop or revise the line of reasoning he is pursuing. And not only is he aware of how the reasoning proceeds, he is able to verbalize it for his reader. The high road to consciousness attribution is represented in Figure 4:

FIGURE 4 The high-road path to attributions of conscious states.

We have emphasized the distinctness of the two processes, but of course the two systems both deliver outputs concerning conscious states. Often the outputs will converge. Mill argues on the basis of analogy that others have sensations. This is a paradigmatically high-road affair. But when Mill observed other humans, his low road was, no doubt, also activated. His high-road argument and his low-road reactions converged on the conclusion that other humans have sensations.

Although the two processes will often converge, this won't always be the case. We have already seen one illustration of this. Although insects trigger the low road to attributing conscious states, many people explicitly reject the claim that insects can feel pain on the basis of facts about the limitations of insect neural systems. To take a different sort of example, a philosopher worrying about the problem of other minds might come to reject the arguments that others are conscious. This would be a case in which the high road to attributing conscious states to others resists the conclusion that others are conscious. However, even the skeptic about other minds will still have low-road reactions when humans swirl about him.

3. DUAL-PROCESSING AND EXPLANATORY GAP INTUITIONS

How exactly might our dual-process model explain the intuitive force of the explanatory gap? As sketched earlier, we maintain that third-person mind attribution involves two distinct cognitive processes whose outputs may either comport with or fail to comport with each another. When looking at other people, both of these systems typically produce affirmative outputs: The low road is activated by (at least) one of the other person's surface features, producing a low-level, intuitive attribution of consciousness. At the same time, we can use the high road to reason deliberately about the entity's being conscious. Since the two systems generate the same answer in typical cases, there is typically no resistance to the idea that other people are conscious. However, when we consider the mass of grey matter that composes the human brain (and on which the majority of physicalist reductions of consciousness will focus), the result is altogether different.

Consider Jenny, who is in the grip of physicalism about consciousness. Using high-road reasoning, she could apply the hypothesis that consciousness is identical to a certain kind of brain process, in which case Jenny's high road would produce the output that specific brain processes or brain regions *are* conscious experiences.[8] For example, Jenny might believe that consciousness is identical to populations of neurons firing in synchrony at a rate between 40Hz and 60Hz; on this basis she could infer (using the high road) that specific brain regions that are firing synchronously are conscious experiences. (Crick & Koch, 1990). If Jenny knew that Jimmy's brain had regions that were firing synchronously between 40–60Hz, she could infer (using the high road) that Jimmy's brain states are conscious experiences. However, since this description of Jimmy's brain does not advert to any of the featural cues that trigger AGENCY categorization, Jenny's low road is not

---

8. We use the example of a "type-identity" theory of consciousness for ease of exposition. A similar point could be made using "token-identity" theories, or other sorts of physicalist theories.

activated, and thus remains silent on whether the synchronously firing neurons are conscious.[9]

This example, we think, helps to illuminate why physicalist explanations of consciousness leave us feeling as if something has been left out: our low-level, *low-road* process remains silent when it would normally provide intuitive confirmation of our *high-road* output.[10] In place of the harmony between systems that we typically experience when looking at other people (or any other mammal, for that matter), discussions of neurons, neurotransmitters, and so on create a disparity between the two systems, which, in turn, produces a feeling that the characterization is somehow incomplete.[11] This, we think, is an important part of the explanation for why dualism is so attractive and the explanatory gap is so vexing.[12]

We are suggesting that disparate outputs from the two consciousness-attribution processes produce a sense that something isn't right.[13] To illustrate the idea, consider a

9. By contrast, if Jenny were to view a *picture* of Jimmy (or Jimmy himself), her low road would be activated by the presence of the relevant featural cues, and she would be disposed to attribute conscious states to Jimmy. But saying that Jimmy (the person) activates Jenny's low road is very different from saying that *Jimmy's brain* activates Jenny's low road.

10. Of course, it happens quite often that high-road representations are not accompanied by any corresponding low-road representations. For example, I might use the high road to reason to the conclusion that $e = mc^2$, but there would be no corresponding low-road representations of energy, mass, or the speed of light. (Thanks to Josh Weisberg for the example). Does our theory predict a kind of gap in this case? No. Our theory only predicts these intuitions for cases in which the underlying cognitive architecture is configured for dual processing. In such cases, both high-road and low-road representations play a role in controlling behavior and inference. In cases that only involve system 2 processing, system 2 is free to control inference and behavior unfettered. Thus, it is only in cases involving dual processing that dissonance between system 1 and system 2 can arise. Thus, the case of consciousness is distinct from cases of pure system 2 reasoning, because (we claim) it does involve dual processing.

11. Our view here is anticipated in important ways by Philip Robbins and Tony Jack, who write: "The intuition of a gap concerning phenomenality [i.e., consciousness] stems at least in part from the fact that our brains are configured in such a way as to naturally promote a dualist view of consciousness." (2006, 75) However, Robbins & Jack account for the explanatory gap in terms of *moral capacities.* They write, "At the heart of our account of why consciousness seems to defy physical explanation is the idea that thinking about consciousness is essentially linked to, indeed partly constituted by, the capacity for moral cognition" (2006, 75). In our view, although moral cognition might be associated with conscious attribution, Robbins and Jack get the order of explanation backward. The AGENCY system is primitive and not directly a moral capacity. Yet, we suggest, the AGENCY mechanism provides the primitive basis for consciousness attribution. As a result, our theory allows for the possibility that a person might lack basic moral capacities while retaining the AGENCY mechanism and the associated attributions of conscious states (cf. Robbins & Jack, 76–78).

12. We intend for this explanation to apply specifically to intuitions about the *explanatory gap*, as opposed to other puzzling cases involving consciousness. This is worth mentioning because it is quite common for philosophers to advance *unified* explanations of the explanatory gap, zombie scenarios, the knowledge argument, and so forth. Our ambitions in this paper don't extend that far. We will be well satisfied if we manage to illuminate the source of the explanatory gap.

13. One might object that our account of the explanatory gap cannot be correct, *just because* it makes significant appeal to low-road processing. For example, one might suspect that the explanatory gap is due entirely to our inability to make certain kinds of deliberate inferences about consciousness,

familiar proposal concerning Capgras syndrome, a psychological disorder in which patients think that a loved one has been replaced with a superficially similar duplicate. Davies & Coltheart (2000) describe Capgras as follows:

> Patients who suffer from the Capgras delusion believe that someone close to them, often a close relative, usually their spouse in the first instance, has been replaced by an imposter who looks just like the replaced person…Capgras patients sometimes elaborate their delusion to the extent of invoking some pieces of technology, perhaps robots or, in a biotechnological age, clones (p. 10).

The Capgras delusion is noteworthy both for its bizarre quality and for its relatively circumscribed nature. Typically, the delusion does not "spread out" through the afflicted subject's network of belief at large. For example, Capgras patients tend not to be especially interested in the whereabouts or well-being of their spouse, despite apparently holding the belief that their spouse has gone missing. But the delusion persists nonetheless.

This unusual syndrome demands explanation. On Stone and Young's prominent account, the Capgras delusion arises from an unusual yet persistent subjective experience, in which the purported imposter "looks right," yet does not "feel right" (Stone and Young 1997).[14] The unusual and persistent experience is supposed to give rise to the unusual and persistent delusion. It is hypothesized that, in the typical case, our recognition of faces is supported by at least two distinct cognitive processes. One process identifies the morphology of the face and produces a morphological representation, and another process produces an affective response (e.g., a feeling of familiarity). In Capgras patients, the morphological process is intact and produces normal morphological representations, but the process supporting the affective response is damaged and does not produce any feeling of familiarity. Thus, Capgras patients who undergo the relevant experiences sometimes say things like, "She looks just like my wife, but I don't feel any love for her." It is easy to see how peculiar experiences like this could play a role in generating the delusion, even if they do not fully explain the syndrome. The point is that, on the Stone and Young account, the Capgras delusion results, at least in part, from a breakdown in processing that involves a mismatch between the outputs of distinct processes. Normally, the morphological and affective mechanisms provide harmonious outputs, but in the pathological case, the output of the morphological process is not corroborated by any output from the affective process. Delusion results.

---

and this shortcoming is located entirely in system-2 cognition. As such, the explanatory gap is a *purely* high-road phenomenon, and one can notice this fact simply by reflecting on it. Hence, our dual-process account must be false. This line of criticism is worth more discussion than we can give it here, but here's our glib reply: It's not so easy to tell (by introspection) whether some inferential result is "purely" the product of system 2, thus it's not so easy to tell whether the explanatory gap is exclusively a system-2 phenomenon.

14. Though it is controversial whether this sort of experience provides a *complete* explanation of the Capgras delusion, it is somewhat less controversial that experiences of this sort play a key role in the delusion.

On our view, the explanatory gap works much like the foregoing account of the Capgras delusion. People's natural inclination to judge that broadly physicalist accounts of consciousness "leave something out" depends on a cognitive architecture involving two distinct processes. In typical cases of consciousness attribution, the two processes produce harmonious outputs and lead to unsurprising attributions. However, in the case of the explanatory gap, we claim, one of the relevant cognitive processes fails to produce any output, thus leading to the disharmonious sense that the neural description is fundamentally incomplete as an explanation of consciousness.[15]

4. OBJECTIONS AND REPLIES

Our proposal, although new, has already met with a number of objections. In this section, we deal with what we take to be the most important objections we've encountered thus far.

4.1 Objection: What about Intentionality?

One natural objection is that if our proposed model predicts an explanatory gap for consciousness, then it must also predict an explanatory gap for "about-ness" or *intentionality*. In our view, the activation of AGENT leads to attributions of conscious states like pain, and also to intentional states like goals. Because attributions of conscious states and intentional states are supported by the same mechanisms, we should expect an explanatory gap for intentionality. Our model predicts that completely physicalist explanations of intentionality will fail to trigger AGENT and consequently fail to elicit the normal pattern of gut reactions regarding intentionality-attributions, for reasons analogous to the case of consciousness. However, the objection continues, this prediction is problematic because there is an explanatory gap for consciousness, but no gap for intentionality. Our model predicts a gap where there is none. Whereas consciousness is mysterious and problematic from the standpoint of physicalism, intentionality is relatively easy to locate in the physical world. Or so the objection goes.

  For present purposes, we will simply grant the objector the claim that our model predicts that there should be an explanatory gap for some attributions of intentional states. However, it doesn't follow that *all* attributions of apparently intentional states will give rise to an explanatory gap. People routinely attribute apparently intentional states, such as memory and knowledge, to computers (cf. Robbins & Jack 2006, 78–79). For instance, it's perfectly natural to say that a chess program knows that the queen will be lost if it moves the pawn. More simply, it is familiar to say that that hard disks and flash drives have *memory*. These attributions do not come with any air of explanatory mystery. It's

---

15. A key difference between the Capgras delusion and the explanatory gap involves the nature of the underlying processes. Our model appeals to standard dual-process architecture to explain the gap, whereas in Capgras neither the morphological system nor the affective system is akin to system 2. However, that doesn't diminish the thrust of the analogy. The critical point is that, on both Stone and Young's theory of Capgras and our theory of the explanatory gap, independent systems are involved, and the systems produce disparate outputs about the target domain where harmonious outputs are the norm.

possible that we sometimes apply such computationally domesticated intentional attributions to humans as well. Nonetheless, this hardly excludes the possibility that some intentional attributions do indeed invite an explanatory gap. In fact, in one of the earliest expressions of the explanatory gap, Leibniz seems to articulate an explanatory gap that folds together the intentional and the conscious:

> If we imagine that there is a machine whose structure makes it *think, sense, and have perceptions*, we could conceive it enlarged, keeping the same proportions, so that we could enter into it, as one enters into a mill. Assuming that, when inspecting its interior, we will only find parts that push one another, and we will never find anything to explain a perception. (Leibniz, 1714/1989, sec. 17, emphasis added)

Nor is this view merely a curiosity of the eighteenth century. A number of prominent contemporary philosophers have quite explicitly defended an explanatory gap for intentional states (Cummins 2000, Horgan 2009, McGinn 1988, Rey 2009). Since it is very much a live philosophical question whether there is an explanatory gap for intentionality, we think the intentionality objection is far from decisive.[16]

4.2 Objection: The Proposal Mislocates the Gap, Part 1: Phenomenal Concepts

It might be objected that our account doesn't illuminate the explanatory gap because the gap is really driven by the difference between the first-person properties that are involved in conscious experience, and the third-person properties adverted to by scientific theories of conscious experience.[17] To explain this objection, we first need to review quickly how the apparent alternative goes. A property dualist might maintain that even if mental processes (or events, or things) are identical to physical processes (or events, or things), there still seems to be a distinctive class of mental properties that objective science cannot explain. Specifically, the subjective and qualitative properties of conscious experience seem to resist scientific explanation and reduction to the physical. Relatedly, physicalists (who reject the existence of inexplicable and irreducible subjective properties) may propose something similar at the level of concepts. Such physicalists hypothesize that we possess certain concepts—"phenomenal concepts"—that systematically fail to accord with the concepts deployed in objective physical science.[18] There is considerable disagreement about the precise nature of phenomenal concepts and, hence, about the

---

16. Many have thought that *consciousness* is the feature left out of reductive accounts of belief (e.g., Kriegel 2003, Searle 1991). This is, of course, consistent with the AGENCY model since that model proposes that identifying an entity as an AGENT will incline us to attribute both beliefs and conscious states.

17. In his article (1959), J. J. C. Smart attributes this objection to Max Black. Ned Block explicates and responds to this objection in his chapter in *Phenomenal Concepts and Phenomenal Knowledge* (2006).

18. On many accounts of phenomenal concepts, the failure is supposed to be that no conclusion conceived under exclusively phenomenal concepts can be inferred a priori from any set of premises conceived under exclusively non-phenomenal concepts. The precise nature of the failure (for example, the reason the relevant a priori inferences are supposed to fail) will depend upon the precise nature of phenomenal concepts.

precise way in which phenomenal concepts fail to accord with physical concepts. Some theorists maintain that phenomenal concepts are *recognitional* concepts (Loar 1990; Tye 2003); others maintain that they are *quotational* concepts (Block 2006; Papineau 2006); still others maintain that they are *indexical* concepts (Ismael 1999, Perry 2001). Despite the disagreement about what it is to be a phenomenal concept, all these theorists adopt the basic strategy that the explanatory gap is a direct result of the discord between our phenomenal concepts and our physical concepts. Property dualists sometimes frame their explanation of the gap in terms of phenomenal properties (rather than concepts), but they can, nonetheless, agree with physicalists that explanatory gap arguments are intuitively compelling because they exploit a principled difference between phenomenal concepts and objective concepts. This difference results in a kind of "conceptual gap," which is supposed to be characteristic of the explanatory gap.

Now we can state the objection. Our model attempts to explain the gap without explicitly adverting to "phenomenal concepts. " However, because phenomenal concepts are the real source of the explanatory gap, the AGENCY model does not do any real explanatory work. That is, advocates of the phenomenal concept strategy might object that their theory explains the gap, so our theory is impotent.

There are different ways that the objection might be developed. We focus on what we take to be the most instructive version. Assume that there are phenomenal concepts and also that attributions facilitated by the AGENCY mechanism often involve phenomenal concepts. For example, it may be that the AGENCY mechanism normally triggers the phenomenal-concept PAIN en route to a pain attribution. If all of this holds, we have no particular quarrel with the claim that phenomenal concepts play an important role in generating the explanatory gap. Our proposed model can, in principle, be combined with various accounts of phenomenal concepts, and the two sorts of accounts could potentially be seen as complementary. On this understanding, our model spells out certain conditions under which phenomenal concepts will be deployed, without saying much about the phenomenal concepts themselves. Construed in this way, our model would enrich our understanding of the explanatory gap by enriching our understanding of conditions for the activation of phenomenal concepts.

Alternatively, the AGENCY model itself may be understood as functionally characterizing some phenomenal concept(s). The model specifies the functional dynamics of a distinctive cognitive system that often produces attributions of phenomenal states. So the model could be seen as explaining why a distinctive concept of consciousness plays a very different functional role than the concepts of consciousness deployed in objective science. On this understanding, the model would yield a distinctive account of phenomenal concepts.

Although our account is thus consistent with phenomenal concept approaches, we don't want to commit ourselves to any theses about phenomenal concepts or their role in generating the explanatory gap. For all we've said here, it remains possible that phenomenal concepts do not play any significant role in underwriting the plausibility of explanatory gap arguments.[19] As a result, even if the phenomenal concept strategy fails (despite its present popularity), the AGENCY model can still contribute to a psychological

---

19. For example, phenomenal concepts do not figure in the accounts of materialists such as Dennett (1991) and Rey (1995). However, such accounts seem to be broadly compatible with our AGENCY model.

explanation of the intuitive force of the explanatory gap. Thus, the AGENCY model is consistent with the phenomenal concept strategy, and it might be developed as a version of the strategy. But the AGENCY model is not hostage to the strategy.

4.3 Objection: The Proposal Mislocates the Gap, Part 2: The First-Person Perspective

A related objection is that the source of the gap involves a difference between self-attributions and other-attributions of consciousness. The idea is that I appreciate the qualitative aspect of my pain *in my own case*, and no scientific description can provide a satisfying explanation of *my* pain experience. So, the problem gets off the ground because of something about self-attributions specifically. Since our proposal focuses primarily on other-attributions, it completely misses the problem of the explanatory gap.

Of course, we agree that the explanatory gap can be made salient from the first-person perspective by focusing on one's own experiences. However, it would be somewhat myopic to think that *the* gap essentially involves first-person (or self-attributive) cases. An explanatory gap presents itself even when we restrict our focus to third-person attributions (i.e., other-attributions). People find it quite intuitive to attribute consciousness to many third parties, including dogs, birds, and ants. Setting aside philosophers in their skeptical moods, people rarely look at horses, cats, or humans and think "How could *that thing* be conscious?" On the contrary, it is automatic that we are inclined to attribute conscious states to those organisms. However, just as when we reflect on our own conscious states, a "gappy" intuition surfaces when we turn to *specific kinds* of third-person characterizations of consciousness, namely scientific descriptions. People are happy to credit consciousness to cats, but it is counterintuitive that cat-consciousness is ultimately nothing more than populations of neurons firing synchronously at 40–60Hz. That is where our proposal enters the picture. We claim that the gap arises in part because such scientific descriptions do not trigger the low road to consciousness attribution.

Of course, we find a parallel situation when we focus solely on self-attributions of consciousness. When I compare my own conscious experience with scientific descriptions of my own brain, the neural features do not seem to fully explain my conscious experience; and they certainly don't seem to be my conscious experience. This intuition is generated (we suggest) because the neural description activates the high road but not the low road. By contrast, we don't get a "gappy" intuition when viewing our own image in a mirror. We don't think, "Sure *I'm* conscious, but how can *that thing* in the mirror be conscious?" This, we submit, is because the mirror image *does* suffice to activate the low road to consciousness attribution. So the difference between self-attributions and other-attributions cannot by itself explain our "gappy" intuitions about consciousness. Instead, the explanatory gap emerges at least in part from the contrast between cases in which *there is* intuitive support from the low road, and cases in which there *is not* intuitive support from the low road.

4.4 Objection: The Proposal Is Overly General

We have argued that part of the explanation for the explanatory gap is that our gut-level feelings that an entity has conscious states are driven by a low-road process that is insensitive to the kinds of features that we find elaborated in neuro-functional descriptions of the brain. If that's right, then we should expect to find something similar to the explanatory gap in other domains, because dual-process architecture is supposed to be implicated in many domains. However, the objection goes, these expectations go unsatisfied because the explanatory gap phenomenon is restricted to the domain of conscious experience.

One response to this objection is that, for all we've said here, consciousness might be the only philosophically important domain in which an explanatory gap obtains. It's certainly possible that the cognitive systems underlying other philosophically important domains do not employ the kind of dual-process architecture that we think drives explanatory gap intuitions. It's also possible that such systems *do* have a dual-process architecture, yet never produce "gappy" intuitions because dual-process architecture is not sufficient for generating an explanatory gap. After all, in some cases, the two systems might produce harmonious outputs, rather than the disharmony we find in certain attributions of consciousness. So even if our dual-process account is right for the explanatory gap for consciousness, it might turn out to be singular.

That said, we rather suspect that something like the explanatory gap phenomenon does show up in other cases where we try to reductively analyze intuitive notions. Take causation, for instance. There is good reason to think that we have a low-road process that generates gut-level intuitions about causation. Infancy research suggests that babies are especially sensitive to cues like *contact* (Leslie & Keeble 1987). Seeing a stationary object launch after being contacted by another object generates a powerful and intuitive sense of causation. Work on adults brings this out vividly. In a classic experiment, Schlottman & Shanks (1992) showed adult subjects computer-generated visual scenes with two brightly colored squares, A and B. The participants were told that the computer might be programed so that movement would only occur if there was a color change; participants were told to figure out whether this pattern held. In the critical condition, every movement was indeed preceded immediately by a color change. In half the scenes, there was no "contact" between A and B, but B would change color and then move; in the other half of the scenes, there was contact between A and B just before B changed color and then moved. Importantly, the covariation evidence indicates that color change was necessary for motion. Indeed, the participants' explicit judgments reflected an appreciation of this, but these explicit judgments had no discernable effect on their answers to the questions about *perceived* causation in launching events, viz., "does it really seem as if the first object caused the second one to move? Or does it look more as if the second object moved on its own, independent of the first object's approach" (Schlottman & Shanks 1992, 335). Only when there was contact did people tend to say that it "really seemed" as if the first object caused the second object to move. This gut-level sense of causation seems to be driven by a low-road system that is insensitive to covariation information.

When we turn to reductive philosophical explanations of causation, many such accounts seem intuitively incomplete and unsatisfying. For example, Lewis's counterfactual account has absorbed criticism along these lines (Lewis 1973; cf. Menzies 1996, Schaffer 2001). Very crudely, the account claims that C causes E if and only if E wouldn't have happened if C hadn't happened. It is not just that such accounts are counterintuitive, but that they are counterintuitive in a specific way: counterfactual accounts seem to leave the "oomph" out of causation.[20] Whereas physicalist theories of consciousness seem to be missing *what it's like* to be conscious, counterfactual theories of causation seem to be missing causal *oomph*. It is, we think, an intriguing and promising research question whether this intuitive shortcoming might be illuminated by the considerations we have marshaled here for the explanatory gap. That is, it might be that part of the reason that many reductive explanations of causation are intuitively unsatisfying is the failure of such explanations to trigger the low-road processes that generate the gut-level sense that A caused B.

In light of this work on causation, we take the proposed objection to raise a genuinely interesting possibility for future research. Rather than think of this as an objection to our proposal, we take it to be an invitation to investigate whether the dual process framework can explain the intuitive shortcomings of reductive analyses in other philosophical domains.

5. IMPLICATIONS

We have argued for a partial explanation of the fact that we find physicalist explanations of consciousness deeply counterintuitive: deliberate reasoning about neural and other physical activity does not activate the cognitive systems that generate the gut-level feeling that an entity is conscious. As a result, thinking about neural tissue does not trigger an intuitive sense that the tissue is conscious. If this much is correct, then what are the implications for philosophy? These are treacherous intellectual waters, but we will sketch one way that our account might be used to elaborate an important strand of a physicalist defense against dualist arguments.

As we discussed at the beginning of the paper, a persistent impetus to dualism is the fact that it simply seems bizarre to think that conscious experience is nothing over and above brain activity. The fact that physicalism is counterintuitive, we have suggested, also plays an important role in driving the explanatory gap arguments in philosophy. A standard way of deflating the philosophical import of the counterintuitive aspects of physicalism (including the explanatory gap) is to point out that the view seems counterintuitive because of contingent psychological facts about us. Thus, the fact that we find it difficult to wrap our heads around the idea that conscious states are neural states is not a decisive reason for drawing the metaphysical conclusion that conscious states really are not physical states.

Our present proposal might play a significant role in filling out such an argument by offering a more detailed empirical account of the psychological mechanisms that drive our intuitive resistance to physicalism. To determine how much philosophical weight we should give to our intuitive resistance to physicalism, we would do well to know a good deal about the psychological basis for that resistance. Our proposal is that the resistance is caused partly by the fact that the low-road mechanism will not render a confirmatory gut-feeling to our considered reasons for thinking that conscious states are brain states. A further question is whether we should take that low-road system to carry any epistemic weight, and if so how much weight. Answering this question involves confronting difficult epistemic

---

20. Along similar lines, Lewis uses the term "biff" to describe an intrinsic, non-counterfactual relation in the vicinity of the causal relation (2004).

issues, and we won't presume to do them justice here. However, at a minimum, we think there is reason to take a skeptical stance toward the low road's epistemic credentials.

One line of argument is that we should discount the low-road system simply because it is relatively crude and inflexible. By contrast, our reasoned judgments about consciousness are highly flexible and general, and might be thought to be more trustworthy than the low-road mechanism because they take more information into account.[21] This kind of consideration is clearly not decisive, however, because it's plausible that we are often justified in trusting the outputs of relatively crude and inflexible cognitive systems (low-level vision, for example).

Another possibility is that this particular low-road mechanism is untrustworthy, even if there is little reason to doubt the outputs of low-road mechanisms in general. It is highly plausible that a low-road mechanism for detecting other minds (and other conscious minds) would be subject to a high rate of false positives. Considerations from signal-detection theory and evolutionary psychology support this claim. Consider, for example, the high cost of a false negative. Failing to detect another agent could have potentially disastrous consequences: A rival human or (worse) a hungry predator could easily get the jump on the poor sap whose low-road mechanism outputs a false negative. Since an easy way of producing fewer false negatives is to err on the side of allowing more false positives, this is what we should expect the mechanism to do, and, indeed, it seems plausible that the low-road mechanism does in fact produce many false positives. The Heider-Simmel illusion seems to provide an obvious case in which our intuitive attributions of mentality are misguided; animated cartoons and movies provide a range of similarly clear examples. In these kinds of cases, it is extremely plausible to think that the low-road mechanism has produced inaccurate outputs.

But what about false negatives? False negatives are more directly relevant to the explanatory gap, because (we claim) the gap is a case in which the low-road mechanism is silent. It's worth noting that even mechanisms with a high rate of false positives may sometimes output false negatives. For example, we might expect a snake-detector mechanism to have a high rate of false positives, for reasons similar to those given earlier. However, such a mechanism may occasionally fail to detect a snake: The snake might be camouflaged, or irregularly shaped, or seen from a non-standard vantage point. In such cases, the snake detector would remain silent. Could our proposed low-road mechanism for consciousness attribution be similar to the snake detector in this respect? It is difficult to say, because, in the case of snakes, we can appeal to an independent and relatively uncontroversial standard about which things count as snakes, but in the case of consciousness there is no such independent standard, since there are core philosophical and scientific disputes about the nature and scope of consciousness. So it seems doubtful whether this kind of consideration could yield a decisive reason for saying that the low-road mechanism is untrustworthy in the relevant cases.

Nonetheless, we think there is reason to handle the low-road mechanism's outputs (or lack thereof) with extreme care. Although the low road is routinely triggered by biological organisms, it is rarely or never triggered by the *brains* of those organisms, and

---

21. Greene (2003, 2008) reasons along these lines, for the conclusions that our reasoned moral judgments are more trustworthy than our intuitive moral judgments.

according to some of our best theories, the brain is the part of the organism most crucially responsible for its mind. There is an obvious explanation for this. The low road is, in some fashion, an adaptation to our environment. It might be a domain-specific mechanism that was shaped by evolutionary pressures. Or it might be a developmental adaptation that children achieve through countless interactions with their environment. We take no stand on that issue here. Regardless of which kind of adaptation it is, the AGENCY mechanism was shaped by the environment to which we (or our evolutionary ancestors) were exposed. As a result, it is unsurprising that the mechanism responds to organisms but not to suborganismic bits. We (and our ancestors) interacted most often with entire organisms, not neurons in a petri dish. Once we see the role of the environment in shaping the mechanism, this should lead us to suspect that the low-road mechanism is a relatively shallow and inflexible informant for a theory of consciousness. The mechanism is sensitive only to gross organismic features, but we need not suppose that this is because consciousness *only* attaches to gross organisms. Rather, the reason the low-road mechanism is sensitive to such a restricted set of features is because whole organisms are the parts of the environment that are responsible for shaping the mechanism. Suborganismic features like neuronal firing patterns *never had a chance* to shape the mechanism, because they are hidden away behind skin and bone. So even if these features are crucially important for consciousness, we should still expect our low road mechanism to be insensitive to this fact. As a result, when considering explanations of consciousness, there is reason to doubt that we can assign much evidential weight to the fact that the low road isn't activated by suborganismic features. The fact that the low-road is silent cannot be taken as significant evidence that consciousness is something other than a suborganismic feature.

Even on the supposition that the proposed low-road mechanism is not to be trusted in the relevant cases, we do not claim to have provided a *complete* psychological or epistemological account of the explanatory gap. For example, more must be said about the psychology and epistemology of attributions of particular kinds of conscious states (e.g., reddish visual experience *versus* blueish visual experience), which are sometimes adverted to in illustrations of the explanatory gap. Another possibility is that cognitive systems aimed specifically at processing explanations play an important role in an account of the explanatory gap (see Fiala 2009). A range of additional cognitive mechanisms (e.g., our capacities for imagination and visualization) may also be involved. Nonetheless, we think that our present proposal makes a significant contribution to an account of the explanatory gap. Part of the reason we feel the gap, and part of the reason we are seduced by dualism, is that scientific explanations do not resonate with the basic cognitive systems that generates the intuition that something is conscious.

References

Arico, A., B. Fiala, R. Goldberg, & S. Nichols. (2011). The folk psychology of consciousness. *Mind & Language* 26(3): 327–352.

Block, N. (2006). "Max Black's objection to mind-body identity." In *Phenomenal concepts and phenomenal knowledge*, T. Alter and S. Walter eds. New York: Oxford University Press. 249–306.

Bloom, P. (2004). *Descartes' baby*. New York, NY: Basic Books.

Bloom, P. (2006). My brain made me do it. *Journal of Culture and Cognition* 6: 209–214.

Chaiken, S. and Trope, Y. (eds). (1999). *Dual process theories in social psychology*. New York,: Guilford.

Chalmers, D. (1995). Facing up to the hard problem of consciousness. *Journal of Consciousness Studies* 2(3): 200–219.

Chalmers, D. (2003). "Consciousness and its place in nature." In *Philosophy of mind: Classical and contemporary readings*, ed. D. Chalmers. New York: Oxford University Press. 247–272.

Chalmers, D. (2006). "Phenomenal concepts and the explanatory gap." In *Phenomenal concepts and phenomenal knowledge*, eds. T. Alter and S. Walter. New York: Oxford University Press. 167–194.

Churchland, P. (1988). *Matter and consciousness*. Cambridge, MA: MIT Press.

Crick, F. and C. Koch. (1990). Toward a neurobiological theory of consciousness. *Seminars in the Neurosciences*, 2: 263–275.

Cummins, R. (2000). "'How does it work?' vs. 'what are the laws?' Two conceptions of psychological explanation." In *Explanation and cognition*, eds. F. Keil and R. Wilson. Cambridge, MA: MIT Press. 117–145.

Davies, M. and Coltheart, M. (2000). Introduction: Pathologies of belief. *Mind and Language* 15(1): 1–46.

Dennett, D. (1991). *Consciousness explained*. New York, NY: Little, Brown and Company.

Evans, J. St. B. T. (2007). *Hypothetical thinking: Dual processes in reasoning and judgment*. Hove, UK: Psychology Press.

Fiala, B. (2009). The phenomenology of explanation and the explanation of phenomenology. Manuscript, University of Arizona.

Fodor, J. (1983). *The modularity of mind*. Cambridge, MA: MIT Press.

Graham, G. (1998). *Philosophy of mind: An introduction*. Oxford: Blackwell.

Gray, H., K. Gray, and D. Wegner (2007). Dimensions of mind perception. *Science*, 315: 619.

Greene, J. (2008). "The secret joke of Kant's soul." In W. Sinnott-Armstrong, *Moral psychology*. Cambridge, MA: Cambridge, MA: MIT Press. 35–80.

Greene, J. (2003). From neural "is" to moral "ought": What are the implications of a neuroscientific moral psychology?" *Nature Reviews Neuroscience* 4: 389–400.

Haidt, J. (2000). The emotional dog and its rational tail: a social intuitionist approach to moral judgment. *Psychological Review* 108(4): 814–834.

Heider, F. and M. Simmel. (1944). An experimental study of apparent behavior. *American Journal of Psychology* 57: 243–259.

Horgan, T. (2009). "Materialism, minimal emergentism, and the hard problem of consciousness." In *The waning of materialism*, eds. G. Bealer and R. Koons. New York: Oxford University Press. 309–330.

Huxley, T. H. (1866). *Lessons in elementary physiology 8*. London: MacMillan.

Huxley, T. H. (1874/2002). "On the hypothesis that animals are automata, and its history (excerpt)." In *Philosophy of Mind: Classical and Contemporary Readings*, ed. D. Chalmers. New York: Oxford University Press. Excerpted from *Fortnightly Review* 16: 555–580.

Ismael, J. (1999). Science and the phenomenal. *Philosophy of Science* 66: 351–369.

Jackson, F. (2000). *From metaphysics to ethics: A defence of conceptual analysis*. New York: Oxford University Press.

Johnson, S., V. Slaughter, and S. Carey. (1998). Whose gaze will infants follow? Features that elicit gaze-following in 12-month-olds. *Developmental Science* 1: 233–38.

Johnson, S. (2003). Detecting agents. *Philosophical Transactions of the Royal Society of London* B 358: 549–559

Kim, J. (2000). *Mind in a physical world: An essay on the mind-body problem and mental causation*. Cambridge, MA: MIT Press.

Kim, J. (2007). *Physicalism, or something near enough*. Princeton: Princeton University Press.

Knobe, J. & J. Prinz (2008). Intuitions about consciousness: Experimental studies. *Phenomenology and the Cognitive Sciences* 7(1): 67–83.

Kriegel, U. (2003). Is intentionality dependent upon consciousness? *Philosophical Studies* 116: 271–307.

Kripke, S. (1972). "Naming and necessity." In *Semantics of natural language*, eds. D. Davidson and G. Harman eds. Dordrecht, Holland: Reidel. 253–355.

Leibniz, G. W. (1714/1989). *The Monadology*. In *G. W. Leibniz: Philosophical essays*, eds and trans. R. Ariew and D. Garber. Indianapolis: Hackett Publishing Company.

Leslie, A. and S. Keeble. (1987). Do six-month-old infants perceive causality? *Cognition* 25: 265–288.

Levine, J. (1983). Materialism and qualia: The explanatory gap. *Pacific Philosophical Quarterly* 64: 354–361.

Lewis, D. (1973). Causation. *Journal of Philosophy* 70: 556–567.

Lewis, D. (2004). "Void and object." In *Causation and counterfactuals*, eds. J. Collins, N. Hall, and L. A. Paul. Cambridge, MA: MIT Press. 277–290.

Loar, B. (1990). "Phenomenal states." In *Philosophical perspectives 4: Action theory and philosophy of Mind*, ed. J. Tomberlain. Atascadero, CA: Ridgeview Publishing Company. 81–108. Revised version in *The nature of consciousness*, eds. N. Block and G. Guzeldere. Cambridge, MA: MIT Press. 597–616.

McCauley, R. and J. Henrich. (2006). Susceptibility to the Müller-Lyer illusion, theory-neutral observation, and the Diachronic Penetrability of the visual Input system. *Philosophical Psychology* 19(1): 79–101.

McGinn, C. (1988). Consciousness and content. *Proceedings of the British Academy* 74: 219–239.

Menzies, P. (1996). Probabilistic causation and the pre-emption problem. *Mind* 105(417): 85–117.

Mill, J. S. (1865). *An examination of Sir William Hamilton's philosophy*. London: Longman.

Nagel, T. (1972). What is it like to be a bat? *The Philosophical Review* 83(4): 435–450.

Papineau, D. (2006). "Phenomenal and perceptual concepts." In *Phenomenal Concepts and Phenomenal Knowledge: New Essays on Consciousness and Physicalism*, eds. T. Alter and S. Walter. New York, NY: Oxford University Press. 111–144.

Perry, J. (2001). *Knowledge, possibility, and consciousness*. Cambridge, MA: MIT Press.

Rey, G. (1995). "Toward a projectivist account of conscious experience." In *Conscious experience*, ed. T. Metzinger. Paderborn, Germany: Ferdinand Schoningh, 123–142.

Rey, G. (2009). Philosophy of mind. *WIRES: Cognitive Science* 1(5).

Richert, R. and P. Harris. (2006). The ghost in my body: Children's developing concept of the soul. *Journal of Cognition and Culture* 6: 409–427.

Richert, R. and P. Harris. (2008). Dualism revisited: Body vs. mind vs. soul. *Journal of Cognition and Culture* 8: 99–115.

Robbins, P. and Jack, A. (2006). "The Phenomenal Stance." *Philosophical Studies*, 127(1): 59–85.

Samuels, R. (2009). "The magical number two, plus or minus: Comments on dual systems" In *Two minds: Dual processes and beyond*, eds. J. Evans and K. Frankish, New York: Oxford University Press. 129–148.

Schaffer, J. (2001). Causation, influence, and effluence. *Analysis* 61(1): 11–18.

Schlottmann, A., and D. Shanks. (1992). Evidence for a distance between judged and perceived causality. *Quarterly Journal of Experimental Psychology* 44A: 321–342.

Searle, J. (1991). Consciousness, unconsciousness and intentionality. *Philosophical Issues* 1: 45–66.

Shimizu, Y. and S. Johnson. (2004). Infants' attribution of a goal to a morphologically unfamiliar agent. *Developmental Science* 7: 425–430.

Sloman, S. (1996). The empirical case for two systems of reasoning. *Psychological Bulletin* 119: 3–22.

Smart, J. J. C. (1959). Sensations and brain processes. *Philosophical Review* 68: 141–156.

Stanovich, K. E. (2004). *The robot's rebellion: Finding meaning in the age of Darwin.* Chicago: University of Chicago Press.

Stanovich, K. E. and R. F. West. (2000). Individual differences in reasoning: Implications for the rationality debate? *Behavioral and Brain Sciences* 23(5): 645–665.

Stone, T., and A. W. Young. (1997). Delusions and brain injury: The philosophy and psychology of belief." *Mind and Language* 12: 327–364.

Sytsma, J., and E. Machery (2009). How to study folk intuitions about consciousness. *Philosophical Psychology* 22(1): 21–35.

Tye, M. (2003). "A theory of phenomenal concepts." In *Minds and Persons*, ed. A. O'Hear. Cambridge, UK: Cambridge University Press. 91–106.

Van Gulick, R. (2004). "Consciousness." In *The Stanford Encyclopedia of Philosophy (Winter 2009 Edition)*, E. Zalta (ed.), URL = <http://plato.stanford.edu/archives/win2009/entries/consciousness/>.

Woodward, A. (1998). Infants selectively encode the goal object of an actor's reach. *Cognition* 69: 1–34.

SECTION TWO

Consilience Through the Lens of Anthropology

5

FROM STUDIOUS IRRELEVANCY TO CONSILIENT KNOWLEDGE: MODES OF SCHOLARSHIP AND CULTURAL ANTHROPOLOGY[1]

Pascal Boyer

Why is most cultural anthropology largely irrelevant? The voice of that particular field in broader academic discussions is almost inaudible, its scholars are no longer among the recognizable and important public intellectuals of the day, and its contribution to public debates is close to nonexistent. This last feature is all the more troubling, as the subject matter of cultural anthropology would seem to place it at the center of crucial social debates.

Although I will substantiate this rather harsh diagnosis, the point of this chapter is less to offer a jeremiad than to propose an etiology and perhaps a cure for the current predicament of cultural anthropology. My diagnosis is that this is a largely self-inflected condition. Cultural anthropology has no place in public discourse because most cultural anthropologists have talked and written themselves out of public debate, mostly because they pursued fetishistic interests or advocated methodological postures that are of no possible relevance or interest to culture at large. This is beginning to change. However, that change is to a large degree happening not in the mainstream of cultural anthropology but rather at its margins.

I should start by acknowledging that there *is* a large amount of respectable and, indeed, excellent research conducted in the field—that is hardly the question. What is at stake is that a certain intellectual style, mostly of a rather recent vintage in cultural anthropology but much older in other fields, has stymied the creative energy and social import of cultural anthropology. Equally obviously, not all anthropology is affected by this recent plague of irrelevancy. First of all, the fields of biological anthropology and archaeology seem to be in rude health. I also mention that the traditional concerns of cultural anthropology are currently being given a new lease of life and often a much more lively public relevance by evolutionary biologists and economists, suggesting that there may be such a field as the "science of culture" or at least some incipient moves toward such an integrated discipline.

1. Parts of this essay reprise material from an article published in *Journal of Cognition and Culture* 3(4): 344–358. Thanks to EJ Brill Publishers for permission to reprint these passages.

PUBLIC DECLINE AND A SELF-IMPOSED "MISSION SHRINK"

Consider topics of public debate (e.g., the organization of marriage), family and gender relations, the construction of social trust and norms of cooperation, the consequences of large-scale immigration, the effects of universal cultural contact, the mechanisms of religious persuasion, the relations between religious institutions and civil society, the processes of ethnic conflict. On all these and related questions, a whole variety of disciplines, from economics to neuroscience and from evolutionary biology to history, have a great deal to tell the public—whereas cultural anthropology is, by and large, too busy with obscure academic fads and self inspection.

This is not just an impression. A survey of mentions of cultural anthropologists and cultural anthropological themes in public debates certainly confirms this eclipse of the field. Consider for instance Richard Posner's highly detailed study of *Public Intellectuals*, which comprises a carefully constructed list of individuals with high-profile mentions in public debates (in books, magazines, journals, or newspapers), mostly in the United States in the last 20 years (Posner 2001). Quite remarkably, the list only includes *five* anthropologists out of 416 public intellectuals. More remarkably still, three of those are dead (Margaret Mead, Ruth Benedict, Ernest Gellner) and the other two are elderly (Claude Lévi-Strauss, Lionel Tiger). One might think that the sources used by Posner privilege pundits relative to specialists, as well as politics at the expense of other social concerns, but that is not the case. His list includes such names as Jerome Bruner and Howard Gardner (education and psychology), Steven Pinker (linguistics and psychology), Tzvetan Todorov (literature and moral philosophy), Robert Nozick (philosophy), or Thomas Sowell (economics). Note, incidentally, that the five influential anthropologists (influential, that is, outside academic anthropology) are, apart from Mead, fairly alien to the relativist, "textual" fashions of recent cultural anthropology. Levi-Strauss, Gellner, and Tiger would certainly count among the much-reviled "positivist" ranks, and Tiger, in particular, has consistently argued for the inclusion of biological evidence into anthropological thinking—a position that is anathema to most contemporary cultural anthropologists (Tiger 1969; Tiger and Fox 1971).

For more detailed evidence, consider the occurrence in newspaper articles of the term *anthropologist* compared to the names of other specialists of social and cultural issues. Figure 1 presents the results of a recent Lexis-Nexis search using the terms *racism, marriage, gay marriage, immigration, fundamentalism, and ethnic* (see more detailed results in the Appendix). The figure suggests that, in the context of a discussion of racism, anthropologists are about a third less likely to be quoted or mentioned than either historians or economists. The same goes for immigration, marriage (gay or not), and fundamentalism. Ironically, even the word *ethnic* is associated with *historian six times* more often than with *anthropologist*. Again, this would suggest that, in the discussion of topical social phenomena, the views of cultural anthropologists are no longer really considered at all.

Why this lack of influence? Barring an unlikely conspiracy of media people against cultural anthropologists, the most plausible explanation is that newspapers and magazines do not quote cultural anthropologists because there is nothing much to quote. That is, cultural anthropologists simply do not have a lot to say about such things as gay marriage or immigration—or more specifically they have little to say that actually con-

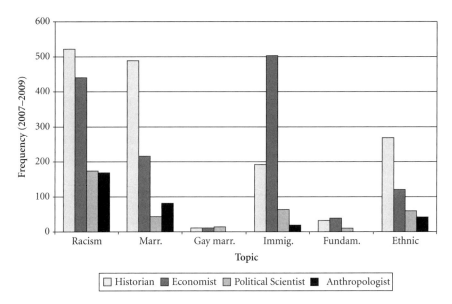

FIGURE 1 Results of Lexis-Nexis search, Source: Major world newspapers from January 1, 2007 to June 30, 2009. Source criteria: joint occurrences (e.g., *racism* and *historian*) within a 50-word neighborhood, roughly a paragraph. See more detailed table in Appendix.

nects with public debates about such issues. Perhaps the strident relativism of cultural anthropology (each culture to its own, values are culture bound, cultural concepts are untranslatable, etc.) seems increasingly irrelevant in a world where people with different norms just have to live together, and, therefore, confront norms and concepts without any respect for the sacred boundaries of each "culture." Perhaps the field's recent addiction to academic fads has made cultural anthropology even less relevant. Disquisitions about culture as text, postcolonialism, or even more arcane issues of reflexivity may not seem of much help to people who wonder how children will be raised in non-traditional families, under what conditions mass immigration can result in peaceful co-existence, what tools we have to resolve entrenched religious hatred, and other such matters for serious public debate.

"Mission creep" is the process, much feared by the military and some politicians, whereby a limited tactical goal turns into an impossibly ambitious political adventure. Cultural anthropology has, in the last 50 years or so suffered from the opposite problem, a quite dramatic form of "mission-shrink." Compared to its original agenda, and even to what is routinely claimed to be its mission in textbooks, cultural anthropology has gradually narrowed its focus to a few obscure problems.

Consider the agenda. Most anthropology textbooks seem to reiterate what has been the official mission of anthropology for the last century: to provide an understanding of human nature through the most challenging and characteristic of the species' features, namely, the production of vastly different norms, concepts, and social structures. The language may have changed a bit, but the overall goal is still expressed in these terms. As a recent textbook puts it:

Anthropologists research, observe, analyze and apply what they learn toward an understanding of the many variations of the human condition. A grounding in past human adaptations, both biological and cultural, contributes to our understanding of adaptations today. (Lenkeit 2007)

The same ambition is expressed at the outset of *Anthropology for Dummies*:

Why isn't everyone the same? Why do people worldwide have differences in skin and hair color and ways of greeting one another? Why doesn't everyone speak the same language? (C. M. Smith 2008)

Now the interesting thing about this agenda is that virtually nobody in cultural anthropology works on such questions—indeed, most cultural anthropologists find this kind of scholarly ambition either quaint or presumptuous. Instead of addressing issues of human nature and cultural diversity, they have more or less renounced the "nature" part of the equation. Rather than address "big" issues, most cultural anthropologists seems content with narrowly circumscribed, often geographically limited, investigations.

This "mission shrink" is all the more deplorable as it happened right at the time when other fields started to provide a wealth of findings and methods that, when combined with cultural anthropological scholarship, could renew our perspective on human cultures. Rather than welcoming these advances, it seems that cultural anthropology has severed links with the other fields that could feed this program, including its sister fields of biological anthropology and archaeology, and it has persistently ignored spectacular developments in psychology, economics, linguistics, and cognitive science.

MODES OF SCHOLARSHIP: SCIENTIFIC AND ERUDITE

Why did this happen? I have a tentative diagnosis for this condition that requires we look into what I call *modes of scholarship*. These are different ways in which particular scholarly contributions are organized, such that they are recognized as valid contributions to a field, and their authors as bona fide members of the "guild." Professional groups maintain specific criteria for entry, and specific criteria for the productions of the guild. This applies equally well to academic disciplines, which are not directly governed by an external market. One's work is academic scholarship to the extent that *other* academics in one's field consider it as such. Each specific community (generally co-extensive with what is called a "field") has shared criteria for who is allowed to join and what counts as a valid contribution. In the same way as a guild, members of a "field" protect their common interest (the reputation of their activity) by restricting entry to those who fulfill certain conditions. In the case at hand, this amounts to: How does the community of cultural anthropologists actually decide that this person could be considered for a position as a cultural anthropologist or decide that their publications count as contributions to cultural anthropology?

To understand the current predicament, the opposition between the humanities versus science, is both too simple and too general. There are, in fact, three distinct modes of scholarship, which I call science, erudition, and salient-connections.

The Science Mode

The science mode should not take too long to describe. This is not because scientific authority and authoritativeness are simple matters—far from it. Philosophy of science is difficult precisely because it is not easy to explain what this particular mode of scholarship consists of and what really makes it different from (and vastly more successful than) all other ways of gathering knowledge (Klee 1999). This does not matter for present purposes, however, because the scientific mode, if difficult to explain, is very easy to recognize. You know it when you see it. Here is a short list of the common "symptoms" by which we recognize a field that employs the science mode of scholarship:

1. There is an agreed corpus of knowledge. What has been achieved so far is taken as given by most practitioners. The common corpus also includes a set of recognized methods, and a list of outstanding questions and puzzles to solve. People also tend to agree on which of these questions are important and which only require some puzzle solving and some tidying up of the theoretical landscape.

2. The fundamentals of the discipline and its results are explained in textbooks and manuals that are all extraordinarily similar, as the essential points and the way to get there are agreed in the discipline.

3. It does not really matter who said what or when. Indeed, many practitioners have a rather hazy picture of the history of their disciplines. Many young biologists would have a hard time explaining what the New Synthesis was, who was involved, and why a synthesis was needed in the first place. Revered figures from the past may be a source of inspiration, demonstrating how to make great discoveries, but they are not a source of truth. Darwin believed in continuous rather than particulate heredity and in some transmission of acquired traits—on both counts we think he was simply wrong, great man though he was (Mayr 1991).

4. People typically publish short contributions. They do not need to establish why the specific problem addressed is a problem or why the methods are appropriate, since that is all part of the agreed background.

5. The typical biographical pattern is that the aspiring member of the guild is intensively trained from an early age in the specialized field and makes important contributions after only a few years of training.

6. There is a large degree of agreement (because of the various features already mentioned) on whether a given person meets the requirements for being a practitioner of the particular field, and there is also a large agreement on how important each individual's contribution is.

Again, let me emphasize that this is by no means a description of *science*, but only of the scientific mode of scholarship, identified here on the basis of fairly superficial but sufficient criteria. By the same token, I am not claiming that all "scientists" work in that way (more on that later) or that "science" only occurs when these features apply. The point of all this is to draw a contrast with other modes of scholarship, where legitimacy and standards are established quite differently.

The Erudition Mode

Another mode of scholarship is erudition, understood as the requirement that specialists of the discipline should have detailed knowledge of a particular domain of facts. Consider, for instance, Byzantine numismatics or the history of Late Renaissance painting. We expect specialists of these fields to have knowledge of the corpus of coins or paintings. We turn to them to identify new findings. The erudition mode was essential to (and still plays a great part in) the development of many scientific fields. For instance biology started as natural history and still includes a large part of it.

The features of erudition are partly similar and partly different from those of science, as we can see by listing some of erudition's key features:

1. There is an agreed corpus of knowledge. There is also a large agreement on what remains to be done. For instance, only a small part of the extant corpus of Mesopotamian tablets has been deciphered. A great number of languages remain to describe. So the remaining tablets or languages are offered to the aspiring specialist as a possible domain of study.
2. A great deal of knowledge is not made explicit in manuals. One picks it up by working under the tutelage of more experienced practitioners and immersing oneself in the material for many years.
3. The history of the field matters and practitioners generally know it. There are some great masters, whose intuitions matter a lot, although they may have been wrong. For instance, to this day classical scholars know their Bachofen or Straus, religious scholars cite Otto or Eliade. But these are not considered infallible sources.
4. People often publish short descriptive contributions, e.g., the first description of a new insect genus or the phonology of a specific language. They also compile monographs that incorporate vast amounts of information about a particular domain (e.g., the comparative morphology of ant species, an encyclopedia of New-Guinean languages, a concordance of Ben Jonson's plays, a catalogue raisonne of Guido Reni).
5. Age is a necessary component of competence. Older experts are generally better, because expertise consists in the accumulation of vast amounts of specific facts, also because an expert needs the kind of intuition that is only shaped by long-lasting familiarity with the material. Only a seasoned Renaissance scholar can tell you that this particular painting is from the Venetian not the Milanese school. A younger scholar may be misled by superficial features.
6. Within a narrow field, people agree on whether a given individual is competent or not, generally based on that person's knowledge of a monograph-sized subfield.

Now, as I said earlier, there is nothing essential about these distinct modes—indeed, as we shall see, they are often found in combination, and this may be an index of "healthy" disciplines. Also, whether a given field uses more or less of one of these modes can change with time. Technical change can have dramatic effects on the mix of modes. Classics used to be strongly based on erudition in the corpus. Knowing obscure (but relevant) textual sources was a *sine qua non*, and the outcome of many years of sustained training, the way it still is for, say scholars of Indian philosophy. Now that the entire Greek and Latin canon is available (and searchable) on CD-ROM, this particular form of knowledge cannot be used as a criterion for admission.

HOW SCIENCE AND ERUDITION COMBINE

The science and erudition modes are frequently found side by side in healthy empirical disciplines. Biology and linguistics are excellent examples.

Molecular biologists these days work mostly in the scientific mode. Evolutionary biologists, in contrast, are supposed to have a "field" (e.g., lekking in antelopes, social coordination in wasps), which means that the erudition mode is required as well as the scientific one. These are not exclusive. Some fields such as ecology often requite both extensive erudite knowledge (e.g., how different species interact, who are the predators and prey of each genus, what minimal density of resources is required, etc.) as well as science-like scholarship (how to run simulations, how to apply optimal foraging models, knowledge of epidemiological techniques, etc.). There is often a fruitful exchange of information between activities belonging to these two modes. Natural history and evolutionary theory feed into each other. To take but one example, one of the most important evolutionary theorists of the century, E.O. Wilson, is also one of the world experts on ant behavior (Hölldobler and Wilson 1990; Wilson 1975). In a similar fashion, linguistics these days combines the two modes in various ways, depending on subfield. Some linguists work purely in the science mode (e.g., asking what formal models can account for regularity in language) and others are more field oriented (e.g., describing Amazonian languages), and many do both. Some scientific models of linguistic evolution, for instance, were inspired by erudite comparisons of creoles and pidgins (e.g., Bickerton, 1990). These overlapping domains of erudition and science modes are illustrated in Figure 2 below.

Although one can find both modes in the same field, even in the same person, they remain distinct in terms of both the purpose of people's activities and the manner in which they are conducted. When they are doing science, biologists or linguists focus on the empirical support that can be given to a particular hypothesis. They also create the relevant domain of data, either by performing experiments or by selecting relevant evidence from a corpus (e.g., testing the hypothesis that all languages have a noun-verb distinction by going through hundreds of grammars). Erudition is not hypothesis- or explanation-driven but description driven. For instance the aspirant specialist is enjoined to catalogue all coins found in a particular Byzantine palace (or all forms of this specific genus of orchid) because collection (or species) in question has not been described before. Obviously, there is no such thing as "pure" or "atheoretical" description. Specific hypotheses about what is and what is not relevant are generally embedded in the agreed descriptive methods of the discipline.

The distinction between modes of scholarship should not be confused with another, and I would argue particularly misleading, distinction between fields that belong to the sciences or the humanities or social sciences. The distinction of modes is actually orthogonal to that institutional distinction. There are many examples of the erudition mode in the sciences and quite a few examples of the scientific mode in the humanities (see Figure 3 for some examples).

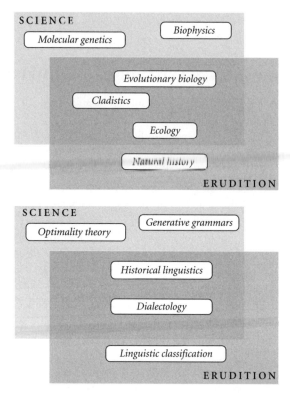

FIGURE 2. The overlap between the "science" and "erudition" modes in two disciplines: linguistics and biology. Various research programs illustrate either one or both of the modes of scholarship.

A THIRD MODE OF SCHOLARSHIP: SALIENT CONNECTIONS

The third mode of scholarship is the most elusive one, as it has not been systematically described, yet it is also most important to our understanding of many modern disciplines, including cultural anthropology. In this mode, people assess new contributions in terms of the connections they establish between facts or ideas which, by themselves, are not necessarily novel or even interesting. Although this way of judging new work has been around for a long time, it has become characteristic of many academic fields of a recent vintage and of the recent evolution of older disciplines. I call this the "salient connections" mode.

Again, I should provide examples before a model, because this is a phenomenon we all know when we see it, even if we do not always reflect on the mechanism at work. For instance, a recent book re-frames the discourse of love in Shakespeare's plays and sonnets as an expression of the colonial outlook. The lover's loving gaze transparently expresses the conqueror's prospect on a recently discovered, clearly gendered, and mythically virginal New World. A student is planning to work on Indian public executions during the Raj as a form of theater, a ritualized performance that constructs colonial power at the same time as it undermines it by exhibiting the gossamer of its dramatic texture. Another colleague has recently finished a study of gay fathers in the Caribbean in the framework

	Science mode	Erudition mode
In the sciences…	• Model of genomic imprinting • Physics of plate tectonics • …	• Comparative morphology of varieties of sea-cucumbers • Geological formations of england • …
In the social sciences…	• Models of cooperation and defence against free-riders • Role of demography in political upheavals • Effect of religion on social cohesion • …	• Compared European nationalisms • Caste systems of South-asia • Diffusion of epic themes across Eurasia • …
In the humanities…	• General organization of narratives • How ecology constrains state formation • Why visual arts only use certain kinds of symmetry • How literacy affects the contents of cultural knowledge • …	• Tempera in late Flemish painting • Byzantine numismatics • Modulation in Couperin's harpsichord pieces • …

FIGURE 3. The science/erudition distinction is orthogonal to the traditional Sciences, Social sciences, and humanities dimensions. Examples of *specific* research projects that instantiate all six cells in the matrix.

of Benjamin's and Bourdieu's accounts of culture, technology, and late capitalism. Steel drums and strong rum prop up the local habitus of globalized self-empowerment.

What is the common thread in these disparate examples? They all seem to offer a new connection between elements that were previously known to everyone in the field and indeed, in many cases, to any educated reader. For instance, all literary scholars presumably know their Shakespeare and educated folk know a little about the conquest of America. But they (supposedly) had never considered Ophelia as American. In the same way, most historians know about the political organization of the Raj and its fondness for state pageantry. They are also cognizant of the "comedian's paradox" from Diderot or some other source. The author's hope is in the fact that the connection between the two—between state ceremonial and precarious theatrical mimesis—is new. In the same way, most cultural anthropologists have some notion of the Caribbean as a place of contrasting influences and original cultural mixes. They also know a little about the various ways in which homosexuality is construed in different places, as well as cultural variation in fathers' duties or roles. The innovative point is to put all these together, creating salient associations, especially by throwing in Bourdieu and Benjamin—two rather dour, bookish, and strait-laced dead Europeans who would seem far removed from your typical Trinidadian gay dad.

One could multiply the examples, but it may be of more help to compare the features of this with the other two modes:

1. In salient-connections fields, there is no agreed corpus of knowledge. Indeed, there is no "knowledge" in the sense of accumulated and organized information, but rather a juxtaposition of different views on different topics.
2. There are no manuals, no agreed techniques or methods. Indeed, each contribution constitutes (ideally) a new paradigm or method, each author is an island.
3. The history of the field, its self-definition, as well as the reframing of past theories, are crucial. A lot of scholarly activity in salient connections-based fields consists in citing various masters, commenting on their texts, finding some connection between what they said and the issue at hand. In cultural anthropological studies, authors like Walter Benjamin or Pierre Bourdieu or the entire Frankfurt school are part of this Pantheon (a very ephemeral one, with a high turnover rate). The masters are generally invoked as validating authority. That is, the particular fact that one is describing (the gay Caribbean father, etc.) is presented as illustrating the general principle laid down by Benjamin or some other luminary. (Incidentally, these authors are *never* shown to have been wrong. Indeed, their work is never discussed as having any connection to empirical fact that could make them right or wrong. Benjamin's or Bourdieu's conceptions of culture are not judged in terms of how much they explain). Also, there is a great deal of emphasis on the self-definition of the field, the ideas various practitioners have about what they do and what they ought to do, compared to what others do. Indeed, most important works are supposed to be not just contributions to the field, but also reflections on the field itself. For instance, a study of German post-Expressionist 1960s cinema will be praised, not just because it tells us a lot that we want to know about that specific genre, but also because it re-frames our views of the connections between cinema or society. A study of recent rock songs is good because it establishes a new approach to popular culture.
4. Books are more important than articles. This, in part, reflects the fact that each contribution should ideally re-frame a field as a whole, introduce a new way of looking at issues, and so on, something that cannot be done in a short article.
5. There is no specific developmental curve. Some authors produce interesting connections in their first piece of work, others are seasoned specialists of the erudition mode who, at some point, decide to let their hair down, as it were, and let salient connections govern their next project.
6. There is no agreement whatsoever on who is a competent performer in this mode, apart from the (generally dead) masters like Bakhtin or Benjamin or Raymond Williams for cultural studies, Derrida or de Man for literary criticism. A consequence is that there are tightly coalitional cliques and exceedingly bitter feuds about who should get what jobs, who is allowed to publish and where, and so on.

In the last three decades or so, some fields have dramatically evolved from almost pure erudition mode to the salient-connections mode. Literary criticism is a case in point. In the past, one could not really expatiate on Shakespeare's plays without thorough knowledge of the First Folio and Quartos and other such recondite source criticism. This kind of erudition is still practiced, but it is not the major criterion of a relevant contribution to Elizabethan studies (Garber 2004). Saying something new about the plays is what matters. One could say that the specialists have (perhaps excessively) taken to heart Forster's dictum. They only connect.

There are various accounts of why this happened to literary studies, whether this is a Good Thing or not, and if not, whether it is all the fault of that awful Leavis or of the dreaded French structuralists (Kermode 1983). I am not enough of an erudite to adjudicate between these normative interpretations of history. I can only comment that polemical narratives generally get in the way of a proper explanation. Neither jeremiad ("No-one knows the Canon anymore!") nor triumphalist epic ("We have overcome! The Canon is dead") is of great help here.

EFFECTS OF SALIENT CONNECTIONS

How does all this work? Outsiders—and disgruntled guardians of the erudite faith, in recently transformed fields like literary studies—will say that *anything goes* in terms of salient connections. Although one can see some merit in this interpretation—a hypothesis that is supported by a great deal of the evidence—it is probably not sufficient. Here, I will not consider the historical and cultural origins of the phenomenon, since that is better left to some serious historian of the social sciences. I can, however, indicate in what way it *cannot* be explained.

Some readers may want to suggest that what I described here as a specific mode of scholarship is, in fact, simply explained as the influence of a particular set of ideas (e.g., readers of early versions of this essay suggested such movements as postmodernism for instance). However, that surely is not the case. First, the mode of scholarship identified here is much more widespread than adherence to this or that particular intellectual fashion (Gellner 1992). Second, and more important, it would be rather strange to assume that what people do (in this case, the way academics legitimize scholarship, recognize new members of the guild, etc.) is sufficiently explained by their own explicit account of why they do it (in this case, a particular intellectual fad). After all, we are supposed to account for fashions, which are no more self-explanatory than any other social dynamics.

Whatever the origins, what matters are the consequences of the salient-connections mode of scholarly activity. These are fairly obvious for all to see. The connections are salient—but only to *some* people, with the proper background. They do not travel well. Try telling a biochemist that Walter Benjamin's essays are a great backdrop to a description of gay fathers in Trinidad. The expected cognitive effects of such connections are, by necessity, confined to a fairly limited market. Indeed, the salient connections are often difficult to use even with apprentices in the field. Ernest Gellner once made fun of those poor Wittgensteinian philosophers trying to spread the Good News that all philosophical problems of epistemology or metaphysics reduced to linguistic issues. They often found themselves teaching students who had never been much bothered by any philosophical problems, epistemological or otherwise, and, therefore, received the news with undisturbed placidity (Gellner 1959). There is a rich comic vein here, also mined by David Lodge, several of whose characters reflect on the difficulty of teaching that the margin is the text or that the Canon is dead to students who do not read much text and had barely noticed that there was a Canon (Lodge 1988).

A more serious problem, obviously, is that such scholarship does not in general solve any questions, contribute to a more precise or accurate description of the world, or even show us the limitations of our knowledge (nor does it aim to do any of these things). Salient connections are a sometime thing, not durable and useable information. They leave the world as they found it, to coin a phrase.

So what is to be done?

INTEGRATED STUDY OF CULTURES:
AN INCIPIENT PROGRAM

A good place to start is with one's most cherished assumptions – those most likely to be wrong and damaging. The field of cultural anthropology suffers from an acute form of the anxiety of influence, in the form of a special fear of *reduction*. In cultural anthropology, intense collaboration with fields that could provide us with useful findings and methods (e.g., demography, economics, psychology, history or genetics) is generally seen as dispensable, and often as downright misguided. It is frequently the case that an argument can be dismissed as "reductionist," as though the epithet required no further elaboration (Ernst 2004). What is meant by this is, in general, that the author has made use of findings or facts that belong to another domain that strictly "social" or "cultural" facts (McCauley and Lawson 1996).

A great many scholars of things cultural remain unaware that causal reduction is omnipresent, is, indeed, the main mode of explanation in all the empirical sciences, from biophysics to geology and from chemistry to neuroscience (Bechtel 1993). The point is so clear that philosophers of science never discuss whether causal reduction is a "good thing," but rather how it works, under what conditions, between what kinds of facts or principles, and so on (Bechtel 1993; McCauley and Bechtel 2001). Practitioners, too, are quite happy with reduction. Psychologists blithely "reduce" mental phenomena to information processing between assemblies of neurons, neuroscientists are happy that neural events "reduce" to organic chemistry, and so on. No successful empirical discipline is based on the strange fantasy of ontological autarky.

This may explain why the most promising developments in understanding human behavior are based on *integrated* scholarship. What I mean by "integrated" models are explanatory models that bypass traditional divisions between "levels" or "domains" of reality (Bechtel 1993), in this case "culture" as opposed to human psychology, genetics, or economics. I also mean models that are resolutely opportunistic in their use of whatever tools do the explanatory work, regardless of particular disciplinary tradition from which they originated.

The prospect of an integrated study of human culture is now much brighter, because of recent and dramatic progress in three crucial domains, namely, human cognition, economic models of behavior, and evolutionary biology. Findings in all three domains are already changing perspectives on the study of culture:

The transmission of cultural representations, concepts, and norms, can be seen as bounded variations within limits set by human cognitive capacities (Sperber and Hirschfeld 2004). Cognitive scientists and evolutionary anthropologists have found that early developed cognitive principles form a background of expectations that make possible the acquisition of particular cultural norms and concepts (Boyer and Barrett 2005) in such domains as folk-biology (Atran 1990, 1998), kinship and ethnic categories (Hirschfeld 1994, 1996), racial categories (Kurzban et al. 2001), religious beliefs (Atran 2002), and social interaction (Cosmides and Tooby 1992; Fiske 1992; Tooby and Cosmides 1996).

Economic theory provides us with the most precise way of describing opportunities and predicting choices, and, of course, extends beyond strictly economic issues (Gintis 2000a). Behavioral and experimental economics in particular have shown how to go beyond strict rationality assumptions (Smith 2003), and how to include in economic models such factors as reputation (Kurzban et al. 2007), punitive feelings (Fehr et al. 2006; Price et al. 2002), and intuitive standards of fairness (McCabe and Smith 2001). These models account for the spread of culturally specific modes of cooperation (Gintis 2000b, this volume).

We cannot provide good accounts of human culture without placing it in its evolutionary context. A persistent misunderstanding in the social sciences is the notion that evolutionary models are about "closed" behavioral programs, inflexibly developed whatever the external circumstances (Tooby and Cosmides 1992). If this were the case, evolution would indeed be irrelevant to any behavior for which there is variation among individuals, including human cultures as well as most behaviors of complex organisms. However, evolution in humans and other species results in highly context-sensitive decision-making systems, such that features of local history fix the parameters for people's preferences. This kind of evolutionary model provides a good account of such disparate cultural phenomena as reproductive strategies, including teen pregnancies (Ellis et al. 2003; Quinlan 2003); different reactions and similar sensitivity to cheating in social exchange, among foragers and industrial societies (Sugiyama et al. 2002); local features of "race" categories (Kurzban et al. 2001; Sidanius and Veniegas 2000); and many more (Buss and Kenrick 1998; Barkow et al. 1992).

BACK TO WHAT REALLY MATTERS

Are the studies cited in the preceding section evidence for a new "paradigm" in the study of human cultures and behavior? It is not certain—nor is it clear that this question is really important. What is clear is that a vast domain is open to cultural anthropological investigation, provided that the practitioners accept substantive re-tooling and discard old fetishes. If slogans are needed, an integrated study of culture should proclaim the great values of *reductionism*, the ambition to understand the causal processes underpinning behaviors; *opportunism*, the use of whatever tools and findings get us closer to that goal; and *revisionism*, a deliberate indifference to disciplinary creeds and traditions.

The integrated view of human culture—what some may call a "vertical integration" in the field—will allow cultural anthropology to return to the highly ambitious set of questions it should have addressed all along. Here is a tentative list:

- Are there natural limits to family arrangements and what are they? Can these limits shift with new reproductive techniques and economic change?
- Can people have an intuitive understanding of large societies? Or are our intuitive understandings of the social and political world limited to the small groups we evolved in?
- Why are despised social categories essentialized? Why is it so easy to construct social stigma?
- What logic drives ethnic violence? Ethnic conflicts are more violent and seem less rational than traditional warfare. They sometimes involve whole populations as victims and perpetrators. What psychological processes fuel this violence?
- Why are there gender differences in politics? What explains women's exclusion from group decision-making in most societies, and their reduced participation in many other societies?
- How are moral concepts acquired? How do locally significant parameters affect general concepts of right and wrong?
- What drives people's economic intuitions? Does participation in market economies create an understanding of market processes?
- What explains individual religious attitudes? Why are some individuals more committed to the existence of supernatural agents than others are? Why is there religious fundamentalism and extremism? Why should people want to oppress or kill others in the name of a supernatural agency?

Obviously, the list is not meant to be exhaustive, but it is indicative, at least, of the potential scope and diversity of a vertically integrated approach to cultural anthropology. The list should also suggest why an integrated program is a Good Thing: because it finally allows cultural anthropology to talk about things that matter. As I argued at the beginning of this chapter, cultural anthropology is simply not heard in the public forum, and the simplest explanation is that it is not talking—or rather, not talking about anything of great importance. This should change soon.

APPENDIX

Table 1. Results of Lexis-Nexis Search. Source: "major world newspapers," over three two-year periods. Source criteria: joint occurrences (e.g., the words *racism* and *historian*) within the same 50-word neighborhood, roughly the size of a newspaper article paragraph. Figures for 2007–2009 include occurences to July 1, 2009 only

		2003–2005	*2005–2007*	*2007–2009*
Racism	Historian	925	909	922
	Economist	384	506	440
	Pol scientist	154	191	174
	Anthropologist	214	232	169
Marriage	Historian	627	595	489
	Economist	299	300	216
	Pol scientist	87	85	43
	Anthropologist	90	94	82
Immigration	Historian	206	263	192
	Economist	467	702	503
	Pol scientist	46	98	64
	Anthropologist	16	25	19
Gay marriage	Historian	24	16	11
	Economist	30	24	11
	Pol scientist	25	27	14
	Anthropologist	2	1	0
Fundamentalism	Historian	41	46	32
	Economist	24	31	39
	Pol scientist	7	16	10
	Anthropologist	4	2	0
Ethnic	Historian	282	324	269
	Economist	111	133	121
	Pol scientist	72	90	60
	Anthropologist	61	69	42

References

Atran, S. A. 1990. *Cognitive foundations of natural history. Towards an anthropology of science.* Cambridge: Cambridge University Press.

Atran, S. A. 1998. Folk biology and the anthropology of science: Cognitive universals and cultural particulars. *Behavioral and Brain Sciences* 21(4): 547–609.

Atran, S. A. 2002. *In gods we trust. The evolutionary landscape of religion.* Oxford: Oxford University Press.

Barkow, J. H., L. Cosmides, and J. Tooby, eds. 1992. *The adapted mind: Evolutionary psychology and the generation of culture.* New York: Oxford University Press.

Bechtel, W. 1993. Integrating sciences by creating new disciplines: The case of cell biology. *Biology and Philosophy* 8(3): 277–300.

Bickerton, D. 1990. *Language and species.* Chicago: University of Chicago Press.

Boyer, P., and H.C. Barrett. 2005. Domain specificity and intuitive ontology. In *The handbook of evolutionary psychology,* ed. D. M. Buss, 96–118. Hoboken: John Wiley and Sons.

Buss, D. M., and D.T. Kenrick. 1998. Evolutionary social psychology. In *The handbook of social psychology, Vol. 2 (4th ed.),* ed. D. T. Gilbert, S. T. Fiske, et al., 982–1026. Boston: Mcgraw-Hill.

Cosmides, L., and J. Tooby. 1992. Cognitive adaptations for social exchange. In *The adapted mind: Evolutionary psychology and the generation of culture,* ed. J. H. Barkow, L. Cosmides, and J. Tooby, 163–228. New York: Oxford University Press.

Ellis, B. J., J.E. Bates, K.A. Dodge, D.M. Fergusson, L.J. Horwood, G.S. Pettit, 2003. Does father absence place daughters at special risk for early sexual activity and teenage pregnancy? *Child Development* 74(3): 801–21.

Ernst, T. 2004. Reductionism and misunderstanding human sociality. *Social Analysis* 48(3): 192–98.

Fehr, E., K.M. Schmidt, S.C. Kolm, and J.M. Ythier. 2006. The economics of fairness, reciprocity and altruism—Experimental evidence and new theories. In *Handbook of the economics of giving, altruism and reciprocity (Vol 1.) Foundations,* ed. Serge-Christophe Kolm, and Jean Mercier Ythier, 615–91. New York: Elsevier Science.

Fiske, A. P. 1992. The four elementary forms of sociality: Framework for a unified theory of social relations. *Psychological Review* 99(4): 689–723.

Garber, M. B. 2004. *Shakespeare after all.* New York: Pantheon Books.

Gellner, E. 1959. *Words and things: A critical account of linguistic philosophy and a study in ideology.* London: Gollancz.

Gellner, E. 1992. *Postmodernism, reason and religion.* London and New York: Routledge.

Gintis, H. 2000a. *Game theory evolving: A problem-centered introduction to modeling strategic behavior.* Princeton: Princeton University Press.

Gintis, H. 2000b. Strong reciprocity and human sociality. *Journal of Theoretical Biology* 206(2): 169–79.

Hirschfeld, L. A. 1994. The acquisition of social categories. In *Mapping the mind: Domain-specificity in culture and cognition,* ed. L. A. Hirschfeld, and S.A Gelman. New York: Cambridge University Press.

Hirschfeld, L. A. 1996. *Race in the making: Cognition, culture and the child's construction of human kinds.* Cambridge: The MIT Press.

Hölldobler, B., and E.O. Wilson. 1990. *The ants.* Cambridge: Belknap Press of Harvard University Press.

Kermode, F. 1983. *The art of telling: Essays on fiction.* Cambridge: Harvard University Press.

Klee, R. 1999. *Scientific inquiry: Readings in the philosophy of science.* New York: Oxford University Press.

Kurzban, R., P. Descioli, and E. O'Brien. 2007. Audience effects on moralistic punishment. *Evolution and Human Behavior* 28(2): 10.

Kurzban, R., J. Tooby, and L. Cosmides. 2001. Can race be erased? Coalitional computation and social categorization. *Proceedings of the National Academy of Sciences of the United States of America* 98(26): 15387–15392.

Lenkeit, R. E. 2007. *Introducing cultural anthropology.* Boston: McGraw-Hill.

Lodge, D. 1988. *Nice work: A novel.* London: Secker and Warburg.

Mayr, E. 1991. *One long argument: Charles Darwin and the genesis of modern evolutionary thought.* Cambridge: Harvard University Press.

McCabe, K. A., and V. L. Smith. 2001. Goodwill accounting and the process of exchange. In *Bounded rationality: The adaptive toolbox,* ed. G. Gigerenzer, and R. Selten, 319–340. Cambridge: MIT Press.

McCauley, R. N., and W. Bechtel. 2001. Explanatory pluralism and heuristic identity theory. *Theory and Psychology* 11(6): 25.

McCauley, R. N., and E.T. Lawson. 1996. Who owns "culture?" *Method and Theory in the Study of Religion* 8: 171–190.

Posner, R. A. 2001. *Public intellectuals: A study of decline.* Cambridge: Harvard University Press.

Price, M. E., L. Cosmides, and J. Tooby. 2002. Punitive sentiment as an anti-free rider psychological device. *Evolution and Human Behavior* 23(3): 203–231.

Quinlan, R. J. 2003. Father absence, parental care, and female reproductive development. *Evolution and Human Behavior* 24(6), 376–390.

Sidanius, J., and R.C. Veniegas. 2000. Gender and race discrimination: The interactive nature of disadvantage. In *Reducing prejudice and discrimination,* ed. S. Oskamp., 47–69. Mahwah, NJ: Lawrence Erlbaum Associates.

Smith, C. M. 2008. *Anthropology for dummies.* Hoboken: Wiley.

Smith, V. L. 2003. Constructivist and ecological rationality in economics. *American Economic Review* 93(3): 465–508.

Sperber, D., and L.A. Hirschfeld. 2004. The cognitive foundations of cultural stability and diversity. *Trends in Cognitive Sciences* 8(1): 40–46.

Sugiyama, L. S., J. Tooby, and L. Cosmides. 2002. Cross-cultural evidence of cognitive adaptations for social exchange among the Shiwiar of Ecuadorian Amazonia. *Proceedings of the National Academy of Sciences of the United States of America* 99(17): 11537–11542.

Tiger, L. 1969. *Men in groups.* London: Nelson.

Tiger, L., and R. Fox. 1971. *The imperial animal,* 1st ed. New York: Holt.

Tooby, J., and L. Cosmides. 1992. The psychological foundations of culture. In *The adapted mind: Evolutionary psychology and the generation of culture,* ed. J. H. Barkow, L. Cosmides and John Tooby, 19–136. New York: Oxford University Press.

Tooby, J., and L. Cosmides. 1996. Friendship and the banker's paradox: Other pathways to the evolution of adaptations for altruism. In *Evolution of social behaviour patterns in primates and man,* ed. W. G. Runciman, J. M. Smith and R.I.M. Dunbar, 119–143. Oxford, England UK: Oxford University Press.

Wilson, E. O. 1975. *Sociobiology: The new synthesis.* Cambridge: Belknap Press of Harvard University Press.

6

WHENCE AND WHITHER SOCIOCULTURAL ANTHROPOLOGY

Harvey Whitehouse

Sociocultural anthropology[1] began by asking big questions about the origins and causes of human nature, society, culture, and history. The intellectual founders of the field (in the ninteenth and early twentiethth centuries) were enchanted by the idea that societies evolve, but they lacked the tools to build up a plausible account of those evolutionary processes and were subsequently castigated by generations of anthropologists for producing theories that were either unverifiable or, if rendered in a testable form, patently false.

The apparent failure of early explanatory ambitions in the field, together with growing anxiety about the association between those ambitions and imperial colonial projects, brought grand theoretical aspirations almost to the brink of extinction. This intellectual retreat *began* with a shift away from *why*-type questions towards *how*-type questions. Instead of asking about causes and origins (Why are societies and cultures the way they are?) anthropologists increasingly restricted themselves to problems of function and structure (How do sociocultural systems fit together?). The French anthropologist, Claude Levi-Strauss, among other great anthropologists of the twentieth century, never entirely reconciled himself to this demotion of the explanatory enterprise. As his British colleague Meyer Fortes once wistfully observed, the "lure of the *pourquois*" remained irresistible for Levi-Strauss—albeit tantalizingly out of reach (Fortes 1980, 198). By the close of the last century, however, even generalizing efforts in the study of structure and function appeared to some anthropologists hopelessly unproductive. Many had by then abandoned theory altogether in favor of exclusively humanist agendas, concerned with interpretation, phenomenology, literary artifice, and postmodern critique.[2]

Almost unobserved, however, some of anthropology's neighbours had been making some startling discoveries. After a long period in the theoretical wilderness, largely under the grip of behaviorism, psychology underwent a dramatic revolution. The invention of computers led, by the middle of the twentieth century, to radically new models of

---

1. For convenience I shall refer to sociocultural anthropology simply as "anthropology" throughout the remainder of this chapter. (Unless otherwise indicated, my comments do not apply to scientific branches of the discipline such as physical, biological, or cognitive anthropology.)

2. See for instance Marcus and Fischer 1986, Norris 1979, Tyler 1986.

information processing which, taken together with advances in evolutionary biology and the neurosciences, opened up a new window on human psychology and its evolutionary history.

A mass of scientific research now points to the naturalness of various features of human thinking and behavior. To qualify as "natural," such features must emerge in a similar fashion in all normal human beings without the need for deliberate instruction or training (barring pathology—itself often a valuable source of insight into natural cognition) (e.g., Farah and Wallace 1992, Hillis and Caramazza 1991). These aspects of human nature shape and constrain sociocultural systems even if, reciprocally, at least some of those features may also be "tuned" by cultural environments (McCauley, 2011). Whereas many social anthropologists today take it as self-evident, for instance, that any psychological differences between *men and women* must be *exclusively* the effects of varying sociocultural, political, or economic institutions, there is increasingly persuasive scientific evidence that some of the contrasting tendencies we observe in male and female psychology are partly rooted in biology (e.g., varying testosterone levels during fetal brain development) (Baron-Cohen 2003). A key question for the anthropological study of gender must now be both whether and how historically constituted sociocultural environments impact the expression of these biologically based sex differences and vice-versa. The nature of human minds is salient also for an understanding of economic behavior, political strategizing, and systems of kinship, marriage, and descent (to take some of anthropology's traditional heartland subject areas), as well as more fashionable areas of research, such as the study of performance, art, and display or of materiality, discourse, and embodiment.

,Although some anthropologists have finally begun to appreciate the need to integrate their findings with those of neighboring human sciences, this remains largely a minority concern. Pascal Boyer has recently argued cogently that anthropology has become preoccupied with the production of "salient connections," at the expense of erudite scholarship and the systematic testing of scientific theories (Boyer, this volume). What counts as an authoritative body of work, or even an individual authority, is hotly contested by anthropologists. There is no agreed method of assessing the relative worth of competing contributions. There are no standard authoritative textbooks. Intellectual factions continually coalesce around fashion-leaders and then disperse. The privileged mode of research dissemination is the meandering monograph or reader rather than short and pithy articles. And the argument of authority (despite the contested nature of that authority) rules supreme—such that merely alluding to a fashion-leader is treated as equivalent to evidential support.

Boyer's bleak diagnosis is hard to contest. Anthropology began with scientific ambitions and it proceeded to build up an impressive corpus of scholarship on comparative ethnography (for instance in the highly specialized study of systems of kinship, marriage, and descent). Nowadays, however, science and erudition have been pushed to the sidelines. The crucial question, which Boyer's chapter does not directly address, is *why*.

Our sorry predicament stems, I will argue, from the limitations of our folk ontological knowledge and the fact that, as a consequence, social science is really hard to do (or at least to do well). Reasoning about sociocultural phenomena does not come naturally. Or to put it more precisely, we humans lack adequate intuitive machinery for reasoning about highly elaborated social morphology. As our societies have grown in size and complexity, we have witnessed the emergence of a vast plethora of specialized offices and corporate groups based on a broad range of sorting principles: kinship, descent, rank, caste, ethnicity, nationality, and so on. Categories of office, coalition, and class are no more than idealized models of how the social world is organized, rather than precise descriptions of how it operates on the ground (Firth 1964; Leach 1954), but they provide robust schemas for individual behavior, establishing behavioral patterns over time that serve to perpetuate those schemas. Nevertheless, many of the highly elaborated schemas required to live in a sprawling, stratified society are a relatively modern and potentially dispensable accretion to human thinking, too recent in our evolutionary history to have led to specialized cognitive skills for reasoning about social complexity. The same cannot be said for patterns of thinking in many other ontological domains.

As part of our evolutionary endowment, we possess dedicated intuitive machinery for reasoning about physical properties (such as solidity and gravity) (McCloskey 1983; Povinelli 2000), biological properties (such as essentialized differences between natural kinds) (Carey 1985; Leslie 1994; Bloom 2000), and psychological properties (such as a capacity to empathize with suffering) (Preston and De Waal 2001). Our intuitive physics, intuitive biology, and intuitive psychology may have to be substantially revised in light of the discoveries of *scientific* physics/biology/psychology, but our intuitions often *also* deliver useful reference points and pedagogic tools. For instance, although our intuitions about the discreteness and stability of natural kinds are inconsistent with the diachronic character of evolutionary processes, nevertheless the taxonomies they produce do provide a convenient on-the-hoof framework within which to conceptualize the plants and animals we encounter.

Problems arise, however, when some of our intuitively grounded ontological commitments also serve as markers of identity. In order to function in that way, such commitments must cause us to differ discernibly from other people so as to become a locus of conflict. If you and I share the intuitively grounded explicit belief that certain features of the natural environment are the outcome of intentional design, then we can live in peace with that delusion. If, however, somebody challenges those beliefs with an alternative account (e.g., that the features in question were caused by some other agent or by no agent at all), we have a basis for conflict, especially where competition for resources, either symbolic or material (or both), depends on who comes down on which side of the debate. In this particular case, some evolutionary biologists and their supporters have been drawn into protracted disputes with young earth creationists and proponents of intelligent design. In scientific circles, however, these kinds of battles tend to be somewhat peripheral to the day-to-day business of formulating hypotheses and gathering data to test them. Any competent biologist who has the slightest sympathy for certain variants of intelligent design, would (despite this oddity) be doing the same kind of science as anybody else in that field. Likewise, the fact that an astrophysicist has theistic commitments need not affect one iota the quality of her scientific research on the origins of the universe. Imagine, by contrast, a domain of scholarly enquiry that based its theories on multiple and conflicting intuitions about the basic nature of the phenomena under study. It would struggle to get off the ground because of interminable turf wars among competing coalitions with widely differing foundational assumptions about the nature and purpose of scholarly enquiry. Unfortunately, we do not have to imagine it. That is exactly the problem, or at least that has been the problem historically, with anthropology.

Since we lack dedicated cognitive machinery for reasoning about social complexity, we are prone to *borrowing* intuitions proper to *alien* ontological domains. Consequently, social scientists at turns reify institutions, biologize social categories, anthropomorphize offices, and mentalize corporate groups. Consider the following examples in scholarly sociologizing.

Instances of *teleological* reasoning about the social are obviously rampant in functionalist and Marxist traditions in the social sciences. For example, the theory of social functions, as elaborated by several generations of British anthropologists since Malinowski (1922) maintained that every social institution serves to bolster some other institution (or cluster of institutions) so as to contribute to the maintenance of stable social systems (e.g., Evans-Pritchard 1940, Radcliffe Brown 1952, Firth 1951). Thus, the ritualized abuse of a monarch in some African kingdom might have the social function of giving public expression to structural tensions running through society (e.g., between commoners in opposition to an exploitative aristocracy and monarchy, or between loyal commoners and the king in opposition to plotting royal heirs, and so on) while publicly affirming in the concluding rites that unification of the kingdom is both necessary and desirable in spite of this (Gluckman 1962). At the core of this mode of social theorizing is the idea that rituals are like tools, with specific functions, and offices (such as the kingship) and social categories (such as commoner clients) are like artifacts that are made and remade through the application of those tools. Marxist scholars have often adopted similar strategies of reasoning, except that the functions of political, legal, and religious institutions are typically said to serve the interests, not of society as a whole, but of a particular sector of society, namely, the ruling class (Bloch 1983).

Just as we are prone to deploy artifact cognition in sociological reasoning, so we are also inclined to treat certain types of persons as natural kinds, based on analogical extension of intuitive knowledge about the biological world. The temptation to biologize the social world grows stronger as societies become larger, more heterogeneous, and the division of labor more elaborate. It is no accident that Emile Durkheim coined the term "organic solidarity" to characterize this type of social morphology. Biologizing the social can lead us also to essentialize institutions, especially where particular offices or membership of social groups and categories are transmittable from parent to offspring. Where that is not the case (for instance, where there is great occupational mobility, where people join and leave clubs and associations at will, where religious affiliations are chosen rather than ascribed, etc.), we may be less likely to essentialize the social. Nevertheless, where people's roles and identities are determined by birth and shared with ancestors, the speciation of social categories is hard to resist.

Despite or perhaps because of the extensive tendency for the man or woman "on the street" to biologize social categories (for instance, in racial stereotyping) this way of reasoning is highly problematic for liberal academics, nowadays at least. The efforts, particularly in the nineteenth century, to carve up humanity into distinct races based on phenotypic characteristics seems to most contemporary social scientists at least as distasteful as it is biologically indefensible (Peers 2007). That is not to say that intuitive biology has ceased to play a role in social theorizing. A particularly widespread, if largely unexamined anthropological practice is (and probably has always been) to talk about cultural traditions as at least implicitly analogous to biological species, especially when threatened with extinction. There are striking continuities for instance between the ways in which some anthropologists reason about the rights of small-scale societies to preserve their traditional beliefs and practices, and the way conservationists campaign for the protection of endangered species. Even though anthropologists have become increasingly sensitive to the contested nature of cultural traditions and their embedding in wider regional and global processes of economic expansion and political struggle, there remains a widespread intuition that *all* traditions should be respected and preserved, that there is no moral high ground beyond the local cultural universe from which we can justly impose reform. From that relativistic perspective, cultural and linguistic diversity comes to be valued by more or less explicit comparison with the taxonomic richness and diversity of the natural world.

Just as we are tempted to borrow from artifact cognition and intuitive biology when reasoning about complex sociocultural phenomena, we are no less inclined to draw on our *intuitive psychology* for similar purposes. For instance, the so-called "culture and personality" school in American anthropology, inspired by the ideas of Franz Boas and Sigmund Freud, was premised on the idea that variable child-rearing practices lead to the predominance of certain personality types at a population level, allowing us to generalize about tribes and nations rather as we might about the character of an old friend.[3] In France, also, the tendency to anthropomorphize social groups and categories has been a recurrent theme, featuring prominently for instance in the ideas of *L'Année Sociologique* whose members talked freely and enthusiastically about such things as "collective memory" (Halbwachs 1950) and "collective conscience" (Durkheim 1964). Some of these ideas have enjoyed a renaissance in recent years—indeed, around the turn of the millennium it was practically impossible to find a major conference in any of the arts, humanities, or social science disciplines that did not in some way emphasize the theme of memory, and, in particular, its putatively collective or social character as understood by social theorists.

The trouble with grounding our ideas about the sociocultural realm in intuitive thinking borrowed from other domains is not merely that we discover these to be, inevitably, inadequate tools for the job. True, social and cultural institutions are not really artifacts with functions, organisms with essences, or minds with collective personalities or memories. If that were the only problem, however, it would be *relatively* easy to surmount (in comparison with the more intractable problem to which we presently turn). After all, mature sciences are accustomed to explaining that our intuitions—for instance about the cosmos or the natural world or the mind—are only going to take us so far, and then we have to abandon them. It is not that those intuitions then disappear. It may still seem to us that the sun moves across the sky (rather than the Earth round the sun) or that some kind of intentional agent is responsible for selecting the characteristics of biological species (rather than effects of random mutation and ecology on the fitness of organisms). Nevertheless, with sufficient education and intelligence, we can realize and remember, when reasoning

---

3. Classic studies include Mead 1928, Benedict 1935, and Wallace 1970.

explicitly, that things are not as they seem. Where it gets tricky is when people's *identities* become wrapped up in a particular intuitive construal of the world. This is how Galileo wound up under house arrest as punishment for his heretical claims about the structure of the solar system. Even today some intuitive forms of Biblical literalism are belligerently espoused by Christian fundamentalists. The problem gets worse—much worse—when the same phenomena attract mutually exclusive and competing intuitive claims, on which professional reputations are pinned.

Every time a new school of thought has emerged in anthropology, anchored in borrowed intuitions, it has eventually provoked a backlash of objections from those inspired by alternative intuitions. Often the arguments are less about the issues at stake and more about whose intuitions should prevail. Ultimately, however, all are losers. Functionalism, for instance, is now considered a dirty word in anthropology whereas it once had been a more or less paradigmatic method of ethnographic enquiry (Goldschmidt 1996). Why? Because although we could trace the functions of real tools and artifacts to the intentions of ancestral (and sometime historical) individuals, nobody could explain how institutions came to have the useful properties that functionalists ascribed to them. Of course, there were other causes of embarrassment too: We found that societies were seldom if ever trapped in a state of functionally integrated equilibrium; looking a little closer we always found a writhing morass of contestation and struggle rather than consensus and harmony; looking a little longer we found upheaval and transformation rather than stability and social reproduction. Although often cited as the reason for functionalism's downfall, however, such considerations are less than compelling. There is no reason tendencies toward functional integration should not be possible to demonstrate in principle, and arguably these have been repeatedly demonstrated in practice. So we return to the real nub of the problem: If institutions really do have functions then this cannot be understandable in terms of intuitive teleology. An alternative possibility is considered presently.

Before we can begin to contemplate solutions to this sorry state of affairs, however, we have to attend to an even deeper tragedy. Disillusioned by all attempts to discover a sociological method grounded in stable intuitions, social theorists in the second half of the last century began to look for ideas with increasing desperation almost *anywhere*. The structure of natural language seemed to many to be a promising starting point, not least because of its systemic character. Claude Levi-Strauss's structuralist paradigm was inspired in no small part by the linguist Ferdinand de Saussure's observation that, not only are most of the sounds of a words discernible only on the basis of arbitrary phonetic differences (*bat* being distinguishable from *mat* by virtue of a small and entirely arbitrary difference between two bilabial consonants), but so, too, are many of the conceptual structures to which those sounds refer (e.g., *river* being distinct from a *stream* in English because the former is larger and wider, while *fleuve* is distinct from *riviere* in French because the former flows into the sea) (Leach 1989). Both the phonetic and semantic properties of words seemed to be determined by arbitrary *systems* of differences, an insight that Levi-Strauss and his followers enthusiastically transferred and extended in the analysis of a wide variety of cultural forms: myths, rituals, kinship, descent, marriage, culinary traditions, and so on. This way of thinking emphasized the relativity of cultural systems, both in terms of directly observable properties (behaviors and artifacts) and interiorized but distributed inner states (meanings and values). Nevertheless, it also greatly exaggerated the importance of binary logic in both language and culture (Boyer 1993). After all, much of the conceptual content entailed by the concept "river" is held in common with the concept "fleuve," and not all variability across languages/cultures may be said to result from arbitrary differences between signs (e.g., the sounds of speech or the concepts they signify).

Levi-Strauss's structuralism founders ultimately on the narrowness of its account of the cognitive foundations of cultural recurrence and variation. Soon, it, too, was abandoned and replaced by ever-more desperate strategies, such as Clifford Geertz's brand of "interpretivism," which sought to detach sociocultural phenomena from mental activity entirely, arguing, with varying degrees of coherence, that culture occupies an ontological domain of its own, and can only be described and interpreted in terms belonging to that domain.[4] These developments, as well as the rise of many varieties of poststructuralist and postmodernist critique, all have something in common: They take sociocultural phenomena to be fundamentally textlike, allowing interpretive flights of fantasy extending far beyond the dull world in which everyday culture is produced and transmitted. Authors rapidly became distracted by the suggestiveness of their own language through the creation of jargon and stylistic innovations, decorating the limited interpretations of informants with vastly more fanciful and appealing interpretations of their own (Gellner 1992). In this runaway inflation of ideas, almost anything goes, as long as it is new and different. Soon the idea of culture as text is not enough, it must be continuously reconceived (Coombe 2008), for instance as something to be experienced (Hastrup and Hervik 1994), embodied (Pedwell 2010), or, as one leading anthropologist has recently suggested, "enwinded" (Ingold, forthcoming).

We can only escape this descent into absurdity by finding a robust and encompassing scientific framework on which to construct our questions and pursue answers. Such a framework exists in the form of evolutionary theory. Since at least the time of Darwin, evolutionary theory has proven to be an exceptionally robust method of explaining the anatomy, appearance, behavior, psychology, history, and development of our species. Despite some false starts and blind alleys, efforts to explain recurrence and diversity of sociocultural traits within this framework, both in humans and other animals, is generating cumulative and, therefore, increasingly sophisticated bodies of theory based on the formulation of precise and testable hypotheses (Henrich and Henrich 2007; Sosis and Alcorta 2003; Boyd and Richerson 2005).

Through the lens of evolutionary theory, we can conceptualize and explain sociocultural phenomena by answering four major kinds of interrelated and complementary questions, what Niko Tinsbergen called the "four whys": a functional why, concerning the adaptive value of the trait in comparison with others; a causal why, concerning the mechanisms required to produce it; a developmental why, concerning the processes by which the trait emerges in the growth and maturation of the individual; and an evolutionary why, concerning the phylogeny of the trait, its appearance via a succession of preceding forms (Tinbergen 1951). These four whys are intimately interrelated. If, for instance, we discover that groups performing certain kinds of rituals tend to absorb or destroy groups that lack such rituals—making the rituals in question a group-level adaptation and possibly also an in-group adaptation if there is variability in the accrual of individual advan-

---

4. For a critical discussion, see Strauss and Quinn 1997.

tages—we can only fully explain the emergence and spread of these functional properties by understanding the psychology required to produce the successful pattern of ritualized behavior, its developmental history, and the constraints on cultural innovation set by prior ritual forms on which the current institution has been modeled. In other words, we need to explore the evolutionary history of the cultural trait.

One may suspect that evolutionary explanations of sociocultural phenomena furtively sneak in old arguments and their problematic intuitive assumptions through the back door. The notion, for instance, that a certain kind of institution might help to reproduce the society in which it occurs (in evolutionary formulations a perfectly respectable hypothesis) may seem to be indistinguishable from the kind of outmoded functionalism that anthropology has largely abandoned, and surely founders on the same errors of intuitive teleological reasoning. Recall, however, that the problem with functionalism was that it failed to specify the mechanism by which socially useful traits came into being. The intuitive solution, based on teleological reasoning, leads hopelessly to notions of intentional design and not to Darwinian evolution (Wilson 2002). It is precisely these intuitive errors that need to be avoided. The same may be said of our accounts of proximate causation. Successful accounts fractionate sociocultural phenomena into component features that are explainable in terms of discrete suites of causes rather than luring us back into familiar traps of reification and anthropomorphism.

By way of illustration, consider the discovery (by anthropologists Alan Fiske and Nick Haslam) that recurrent features of cultural rituals closely resemble the symptoms of obsessive compulsive disorder (or OCD) (Fiske and Haslam 1997), a correspondence that Pascal Boyer and Pierre Lienard have recently sought to explain in terms of the workings of a specialized cognitive system (dysfunctional in OCD patients) concerned with triggering precautionary responses to potential hazards (Boyer and Lienard 2008). Although this new body of research may significantly advance our understanding of some features of ritualized behavior, it certainly does not (and is not intended to) explain in general terms why people perform rituals, why they vary in frequency and emotionality, why they recruit various ideas about the involvement of supernatural agents, and so on. So easily is this point misunderstood, that authors of the hazard-precaution theory of ritual were tempted to forewarn readers that they were offering, not a theory of ritual, but a theory of "XB29" (a random string of letters or numbers chosen to represent the specific aspects of ritualized behavior picked out by their theory). There is little intuitive (or even culturally familiar) about this procedure. Although that may be a problem in communicating the value of this approach to wider audiences, it is also a great strength if we are dealing with phenomena that conflicting intuitions have led us to argue about so unproductively.

Much of anthropology nowadays is "mindblind," but, more generally, the discipline has developed a kind of evolutionary myopia. The future of anthropology lies in the development of much sharper vision in these areas. Anthropology not only needs to be informed by major discoveries in neighboring fields but it can and should be a major a player in making those discoveries. It remains one of the broadest of all the human sciences—and thus a useful representative of the humanities in general—and its emphasis on cross-cultural comparison based on long-term field research makes it also uniquely informed on questions of cross-cultural recurrence and variability. Despite my reservations about some recent trends in the discipline, at the core of anthropology remains an enduring commitment to the production of careful and rigorous ethnography. It is also noteworthy that some of the most important developments in the cognitive science of culture have been spearheaded by scientists with an anthropological background (Sperber 1996; Boyer 2001; Atran 2002). Anthropology has made (and continues to make) valuable contributions that will, if we are wise, be put to increasingly effective use in the scientific study of our species' social and cultural achievements.

References

Atran, Scott. 2002. *In gods we trust*. New York: Oxford University Press.

Baron-Cohen, Simon. 2003. *The essential difference: Male and female brains and the truth about autism*. New York: Basic Books.

Benedict, Ruth. 1935. *Patterns of culture*. London: Routledge and Kegan Paul.

Bloch, Maurice. 1983. *Marxism and anthropology: The history of a relationship*. Oxford: Oxford University Press.

Bloom, Paul. 2000. *How children learn the meanings of words* Cambridge, MA: MIT Press.

Boyd, Robert, and Peter J. Richerson. 2005. *Not by genes alone: How culture transformed human evolution*. Chicago, IL: University of Chicago Press.

Boyer, Pascal. 1993. Cognitive aspects of religious symbolism. In *Cognitive aspects of religious symbolism*, ed. Pascal Boyer. Cambridge: Cambridge University Press.

Boyer, Pascal. 2001. *Religion explained: The evolutionary origins of religious thought*. New York: Basic Books.

Boyer, Pascal. Forthcoming. "From studious irrelevancy to consilient knowledge: Modes of scholarship in anthropology." In *Integrating science and the humanities: Interdisciplinary approaches*, eds. Ted Slingerland, and Mark Collard. Oxford: Oxford University Press.

Boyer, Pascal, and Pierre Lienard. 2006. Why ritualized behavior? Precaution systems and action-parsing in developmental, pathological and cultural rituals. *Behavioral and Brain Sciences* 29: 1–56.

Carey, Susan. 1985. *Conceptual change in childhood*. Cambridge, MA: MIT Press.

Coombe, Rosemary. 2008. Encountering the postmodern: New directions in cultural anthropology. *Canadian Review of Sociology* 282: 188–205.

Durkheim, Emile. 1915/1964. *The elementary forms of the religious life*. London: Allen and Unwin.

Pritchard, E. E. 1940. *The Nuer*. Oxford: Oxford University Press.

Farah M.J., and M.A. Wallace. 1992. Semantically-bounded anomia: Implications for the neural implementation of naming. *Neuropsychologia* 30: 609–621.

Firth, Raymond. 1951. *Elements of social organization*. London: Routledge.

Firth, Raymond. 1964. *Essays on social organization and values*. London: University of London Athlone Press.

Fiske, A. P., and N. Haslam. 1997. Is obsessive-compulsive disorder a pathology of the human disposition to perform socially meaningful rituals? Evidence of similar content. *Journal of Nervous & Mental Disease* 185: 211–222.

Fortes, Meyer. 1980. "Anthropology and the psychological disciplines." In *Soviet and Western anthropology*, ed. Ernest Gellner. London: Duckworth.

Gellner, Ernest. 1992. *Postmodernism, reason and religion*. London: Routledge.

Gluckman, M. 1962. *Order and rebellion in tribal Africa*. London: Cohen and West.

Goldschmidt, Walter. 1996. "Functionalism." In *Encyclopedia of cultural anthropology, vol 2*, eds. David Levinson, and Melvin Ember. New York: Henry Holt.

Halbwachs, Maurice. 1950. *La mémoire collective*. Paris: Presses Universitaires de France.

Hastrup, Kirsten, and Peter Hervik. 1994. *Social experience and anthropological knowledge*. London: Routledge.

Henrich, N., and Joe Henrich. 2007. *Why humans cooperate: A cultural and evolutionary explanation*. Oxford: Oxford University Press.

Hillis, A.E., and A. Caramazza. 1991. Category-specific naming and comprehension impairment: A double dissociation. *Brain* 114: 2081–2094.

Ingold, Tim. 2010. "Walking in the air": On winding paths and the enwindment of the body. In *Making knowledge: Special issue of the journal of the Royal Anthropological Institute*, ed. Trevor Marchand. Oxford: Wiley-Blackwell.

Leach, Edmund. 1954. *Political systems of highland burma: A study of Kachin social structure*. London: University of London Athone Press.

Leach, Edmund. 1989. *Claude Levi-Strauss*. Chicago: University of Chicago Press.

Leslie, Alan M. 1994. Pretending and believing: Issues in the theory of ToMM. *Cognition* 50: 211–238.

Malinowski, Bronislaw. 1922. *Argonauts of the western Pacific, an account of native enterprise and adventure in the archipelagoes of Melanesian New Guinea*. New York: E.P. Dutton and Co.

Marcus, George E., and Michael M. J. Fischer. 1986. *Anthropology as cultural critique: an An experimental moment in the human sciences*. Chicago: University of Chicago Press.

McCauley, Robert N. 2011. *Why religion is natural and science is not*. New York: Oxford University Press.

McCloskey, M. 1983. Intuitive physics. *Scientific American* 248(4): 122–130.

Mead, Margaret. 1928. *Coming of age in Samoa: A psychological study of primitive youth for Western civilisation*. New York: Morrow.

Norris, Christopher. 1979. *Deconstruction: Theory and practice*. New York: Routledge.

Povinelli, Daniel. 2000. *Folk physics for apes*. Oxford: Oxford University Press.

Pedwell, Carolyn 2010 *Feminism, culture and embodied practice: The rhetorics of comparison*. London: Routledge.

Peers, Laura. 2007. "On the social, the biological—and the political: Revisiting Beatrice Blackwood's research and teaching." In *Holistic anthropology: Emergence and convergence*, eds. David Parkin and Stanley Ulijaszek. Oxford: Berghahn Books.

Preston, Stephanie D., and Frans B.M. de Waal. 2001. Empathy: Its ultimate and proximate bases. *Behavioural and Brain Sciences* 251: 1–20.

Radcliffe-Brown, A. R. 1952. *Structure and function in primitive society*. London: Cohen and West.

Sosis, Richard, and C. Alcorta. 2003. Signalling, solidarity, and the sacred: The evolution of religious behavior. *Evolutionary Anthropology* 12: 264–274.

Sperber, Dan. 1996. *Explaining culture: A naturalistic approach*. London: Blackwells.

Strauss, Claudia, and Naomi Quinn. 1997. *A cognitive theory of cultural meaning*. Cambridge: Cambridge University Press.

Tinbergen, N. 1951. *The study of instinct*. Oxford: Clarendon.

Tyler, Stephen. 1986. "Post-modern ethnography: From document of the occult to occult document." In *Writing culture: The poetics and politics of ethnography*, eds. James Clifford, and George E. Marcus. Berkeley: University of California Press.

Wallace, Anthony F. C. 1970. *Culture and personality*, 2nd ed. New York: Random.

Wilson, David Sloan. 2002. *Darwins cathedral: Evolution, religion, and the nature of society*. Chicago: University of Chicago Press.

7

UNCONSILIENCE: RETHINKING THE TWO-CULTURES CONUNDRUM IN ANTHROPOLOGY

Bradd Shore

THE TWO CULTURES, FIFTY YEARS LATER

Half a century ago, in his celebrated Rede Lecture *The Two Cultures and the Scientific Revolution,* C.P. Snow reflected on the apparent irreconcilability of what he called the "cultures" of the scientist and the humanist. "There seems to be," Snow lamented, "no place where the cultures meet" (Snow 1961, 17). It might prove cold comfort to Snow, but I have spent the last 30 years of my life in a setting where the two cultures do indeed meet on a regular basis: an anthropology department. Still one might acknowledge that all too often these meetings are devoted exclusively to departmental "business." The common intellectual commitments that bind us together as a scholarly community are often left unspoken and unclear.

In its classic form, anthropology has been the major academic discipline whose ambitions embrace both the natural sciences and the humanities.[1] Over the years, and throughout the period dominated by the academy's "culture wars," this intellectual environment has helped me to appreciate the gulf separating scientific and humanistic anthropology. However, I have also come to believe that cultivating anthropology's doubleness, including the tensions between its cultures, is vital to a sophisticated and balanced view of human affairs.

The hybridity of anthropology is intrinsic to its claims of being the last holdout of holism in the human sciences.[2] All too often, of course, the breathtaking scope of the discipline has not survived in its practice of the promise for holism set out in our introductory textbooks. C. P. Snow would probably not be edified by observing the state of the union between the two cultures in evidence at most anthropological conferences, where polite mutual disregard contends with smug mutual dismissal by the discipline's scientific and humanistic wings.

THE SEARCH FOR CONSILIENCE

Since the field's traditional claims to holistic explanation are seriously contested in contemporary sociocultural anthropology, it is important to clarify the basis for these

---

1. In fact, anthropology straddles not only the sciences and humanities but also the social sciences. In universities, the discipline is almost always housed in the social sciences understood as a kind of "middle ground" between the sciences and the humanities.

2. On various readings on Anthropological holism, see Shore 1999.

claims.[3] The simplest version of holism is to stress humanity's biocultural nature. Human nature is shaped by "dual inheritance," commonly called gene-culture co-evolution.[4] Though the human capacity for culture is a consequence of brain evolution, the symbolic modeling capacity central to culture was also an important selective force on brain evolution (Geertz 1973a; Donald 1993; Deacon 1997). Since culturally mediated environments exercise a selective pressure on genes, both culture in general and cultures in particular contribute to shaping human adaptation. The relations between genetic and cultural evolution turn out to be reciprocal (Boyd and Richerson 2005a, 2005b).

The co-evolutionary framework would seem to be a sophisticated attempt to reconcile the two cultures, targeting the false dichotomies produced by the nature/nurture opposition. However, co-evolutionary accounts of human evolution are clearly framed in a scientific spirit, not a humanistic one. This approach has many advantages over the traditional opposition between culture and biology, but it also has distinct limitations in accounting for both human nature and human variation.

E.O. Wilson sees co-evolutionary theory as an important advance in the pursuit of what he calls "consilience": a theoretical unification of all the sciences and eventually the reconciliation of scientific and humanistic perspectives. "In order to grasp the human condition," Wilson writes, "both the genes and the culture must be understood, not separately in the traditional manner of science and the humanities, but together, in recognition of the realities of human evolution" (Wilson 1998, 177). If it is a reconciliation of the two cultures, it is one tilted decisively toward one of them: a colonization of the humanities by science. Wilson's hope of the reductive encompassment of the humanities by science is explicit and unapologetic:

> If the world really works in a way so as to encourage the consilience of knowledge, I believe that the enterprise of culture will eventually fall out into science...and the humanities, particularly the creative arts. The social sciences will continue to split within each of its disciplines, a process already rancorously begun, with one part folding into or becoming continuously with biology, the other fusing with the humanities....In the process the humanities, ranging from philosophy, history and moral reasoning, comparative religion and interpretation of the arts, will draw closer to the sciences and partly fuse with them. (Wilson 1998, 12)

Evolutionary science and neuroscience may well eventually illuminate the human capacities for both cultural and genetic evolution and their relations. However, such a project can only make sense of the general "underlying" principles of human co-evolution. What science cannot do is to translate and interpret the particular cultural meanings that are a product of co-evolution. The scientific project is an admirable and powerful enterprise but science can only illuminate the part of "human nature" that is open to scientific inquiry. The proposed solution to the two-cultures conundrum is to develop a scientifically convincing account of the evolution of general human cultural competences and

---

3. For a critical reassessment of anthropology's claim to holism see Segal and Yanagisako (eds.) 2005.

4. On culture/gene co-evolution see Barrett, Frankenhuis and Wilke 2008; Hammerstein 2003; Wilson 1998 (especially Chapter 7); Boyd and Richerson 2005b; McElreath and Henrich 2007.

processes of information transmission. In relation to sociocultural anthropology, its objects of analysis are the general mechanisms of cultural information storage and transmission, not the illumination of local meaning. Depending on the quality of the evidence, co-evolution may or may not be good science, but it bypasses the humanities completely, which is why it has not generally won over the majority of humanists. Something is gained but something important is also lost.

THE PROBLEMATICAL STATUS OF HUMAN VARIABILITY IN THE HISTORY OF WESTERN INTELLECTUAL DISCOURSE

The ultimate goal in this essay is a plea for mutual tolerance from both sides of the cultural divide. Humanists and scientists need each other to make sense of human nature. However, in the following section I want to depart for the moment from my balance beam and argue on behalf of an interpretive cultural anthropology that has, I believe, been unfairly bloodied in recent decades by both the postmodernists (for whom the meaning-making subject and the shared cultural world have both largely disappeared) and the scientists. Humanism in anthropology has not fared well, and I want to suggest why this is not a good thing.

Humanistic anthropology has been my home base in my discipline.[5] Since my graduate training in the early 1970s I have witnessed and participated in both the rise and fall of "interpretive anthropology."[6] Despite the emergence of a vigorous (and vigorously contested) scientific account of co-evolution, the full appreciation of the power and importance of human culture for understanding human nature and human cognition has suffered.

Despite its early success in reshaping the study of culture, Clifford Geertz's potent message about the local nature of human thought is now often understood as a problem rather than an insight, a vision of the field that make scientific generalization all but impossible. Geertz's legacy for sociocultural anthropology once seemed assured, but in

5. My intellectual training has been largely in the humanities. As an undergraduate I studied Renaissance English Literature, and still teach an anthropologically framed class on Shakespeare. My anthropological training at the University of Chicago in the early 1970s focused on what was then called "symbolic anthropology." Under the powerful intellectual sway of Clifford Geertz, David Schneider, and Victor Turner, I was introduced to a compelling vision of cultural interpretation influenced by the hermeneutic turn of mind linked with Schutz, Dilthey, and Weber. My interest in unpacking local cultural meanings was clearly a humanistic project rather than a scientific one. Still, coming to Emory University in the early 1980s, with an anthropology department committed to a biocultural dialogue, and having to contend with putting together a compelling version of Anthropology 101 that brought culture and biology into fruitful connection, gave me an appreciation of the place of the natural sciences in anthropological explanation that has left its mark on my thinking and my work. My struggle to reconcile theoretically and rhetorically the particularistic interpretation of *cultures* with the study of the general implications of the evolution of *culture* resulted in the publication of *Culture in Mind* (Shore 1996).

6. In recent decades the foremost advocate for interpretive anthropology, Clifford Geertz, was largely abandoned by his own discipline while he was being celebrated by historians, literary types, and many others.

recent years it has lost traction. There are many reasons for this, but among the most compelling is a deeply ingrained tradition of understanding human nature in thinning out or otherwise sidelining human difference. The message of classic sociocultural anthropology went, one might say, against the grain. This "grain" is deeply inscribed in Western thinking about human nature and is the result of centuries of speculation on how to reconcile an understanding of the nature of the human species with observations of human variation. The history of the issue—at once theological, philosophical, and scientific—has left us all with a predisposition to view human variation as a kind of problem to be overcome by scientific rigor. Among other consequences, this bias in our thinking is implicated in our long troubled history of race relations. It also significantly shapes public receptivity to different kinds of anthropology. To understand this bias, it is important to trace the early history of Western thinking about the place of human variation in human nature.

Prior to the sixteenth century, Western social thought was grounded in Christian theology. The variations among living things followed from the divine master plan. Genesis was cited as evidence supporting the older Aristotelian assumption of the inherent incommensurability of distinct species. "God..." wrote Paul of Tarsus, in *Corinthians,* "giveth to every seed his own body. All flesh is not the same kind of flesh; but there is one kind of flesh of men, another flesh of beasts, another of fish, and another of birds" (I Corinthians, 15: 38–40).

If categorical multiplicity was the hallmark of all other species, an essential unity defined the nature of humans. This unity of the human reflected the single creator God who had made man in his own image. In the fifth century, St. Augustine defended this orthodox Christian view of what was called *monogenesis,* affirming in *Civitate Dei* that, despite superficial variations in appearance or mental endowment, all humans descend from a single, common creation.

> ...whoever is anywhere born a man, that is a rational, mortal animal, no matter what unusual appearance he presents in color, movement, sound, nor how peculiar he is in some power, part, or quality of his nature, no Christian can doubt that he springs from the one protoplast...if they are human, they are descended from Adam. (Augustine 1871, 19.1)

Augustine's defense of monogenesis was his response to the alternative possibility that the physical and cultural variations among different human communities implied *polygenesis,* multiple acts of creation. This doctrine of plural creation for diverse kinds of humans, parallel to the doctrine of plural creation for distinct species, was heretical to orthodox Christian thinking. However, with Europeans' rapidly expanding knowledge of the human world and its diversity, the idea of multiple creations became harder to resist.

In the eleventh century, the Crusades brought a wide spectrum of Christians in Europe into contact with the cultures of the Near East and North Africa. To Christian thought, observed racial and cultural differences distinguished, not contrasting cultures or races, but rather Christian and infidel. Theologians explained these differences in terms of Biblical history, which traced the dissolution of an original unity of the human species into a plurality of distinct populations. These early reflections on monogenesis and polygenesis focused on language. Language can be invoked as a human universal and a defining feature of human nature. On the other hand, the susceptibility of language to radical local variation makes language a prime exemplar of human diversity. The story of the Tower of Babel gave Christian thinkers a Biblical explanation for the diversity of human language understood as a decline from the unity of human language at creation.

Renaissance thinkers saw a more complex picture in which language represented both the unity and the diversity of human nature. By the thirteenth century, Dante's ideas about language reflected this complex and paradoxical vision of diversity within unity. For Dante, the human was distinguished from both the angel and the animal by the possession of speech. Language is, for Dante, the natural medium of human reason.

> It was...necessary that the human race should have some sign, at once rational and sensible, for the inter-communication of its thoughts, because the sign, having to receive something from the reason of one and to convey it to the reason of another, had to be rational....[7]

Although the possession of *language* defined a common human nature in reason, Dante was quick to note the quite different implications of distinct *languages*. Until the Tower of Babel the original and only language was Hebrew. After the Tower, however:

> ...they were struck by such confusion from heaven that all those who were attending to the work, using one and the same language, left off the work on being estranged by many different languages, and never again came together in the same intercourse. For the same language remained for those who were engaged together in the same kind of work; for instance one language remained to all the architects, another to those rolling blocks of stone, another to those preparing the stone; and so it happened to each group of workers. And the human race was then accordingly divided into as many different languages as there were different branches of the work; and the higher the branch of work the men were engaged in, the ruder and more barbarous was the language they afterward spoke.[8]

So language simultaneously unites and divides *Homo sapiens*. The loss of the original Hebrew tongue was a watershed of human history, replicating linguistically the original fall of humankind. However, for Dante linguistic diversification represents, not simple difference, but a hierarchy of relative decline from Hebrew. The nobler a fallen individual's calling, the greater his fall and the lower the form of language to which he was consigned.

Dante's reflections on the Babel story constitute a version of the orthodox Christian view of language diversity as a sign of man's having fallen away from God. In his *De Vulgari Eloquentia*, written in 1304, Dante speculated that the confusion of tongues brought about at the Tower of Babel resulted in humans being "first scattered through all the climes of the world, and the habitable regions and corners of those climes" (Aligheri

---

7. Aligheri, Dante, cited in Slotkin 1965, 9–10.
8. Aligheri, Dante, cited in Slotkin 1965, 11.

1904, vol. 1, 10). The confusion of tongues produced a fundamental change in human nature. Having lost an original species unity in a direct connection with God, humans became pliant creatures, destined to take on the character of their local habitation. Human variability in language, dress, and manners became the indelible signs of mankind's weakness and fallen state (Aligheri 1904, vol. 1, 19).

By the sixteenth century, travelers' accounts documenting a wide range of variations in the appearances and manners of different groups had posed a significant challenge to the Biblical story of a single creation for humans. The debate between proponents of monogenesis and polygenesis continued into the nineteenth century. The argument took on many forms, but the common underlying problem was the status of human nature. George Stocking put it this way:

> [P]olygenism and monogenism can be regarded as specific expressions of enduring alternative attitudes toward the variety of mankind. Confronted by antipodal man, one could wonder at his fundamental likeness to oneself, or one could gasp at his immediate striking differences. One could regard these differences as of degree or kind, as products of changing environment or immutable heredity, as dynamic or static, as relative or absolute, as inconsequential or hierarchical. (Stocking 1968, 45)

In Renaissance thought this empiricist skepticism about human nature contended with theological orthodoxies about all humans being descended from Adam and sharing a single nature. In his *Essaies* Montaigne struggled to reconcile his belief in a single human creation with his observations of the local diversity of human thinking and behavior. Montaigne's travel writings reveal a distinctly relativist sensibility, emphasizing the power of local custom in shaping human behavior. Although he seems to have shared with his contemporaries a belief in a universal human "reason," Montaigne claimed that local custom had such a powerful influence on the human mind that custom often overcomes human reason. He believed that most humans were essentially prisoners of local custom whose principal effect is

> to seize and grip us so firmly, that we are scarce able to escape from its grasp, and to regain possession of ourselves sufficiently to discuss and reason out its commands....Whence it comes that what is off the hinges of custom we believe to be off the hinges of reason: God knows how unreasonably for the most part. (Stocking 1968, 45)

Paralleling this growing interest in cultural variation, naturalists in the eighteenth century were documenting in detail the great diversity and apparent mutability over time of biological forms, and were struggling to reconcile these observations with Biblical creation. Rather than concluding that variation was a basic organizing principle of all life, both scientists and theologians reconciled the empirical observations of biological and cultural diversity by envisioning nature as a hierarchical order of linked forms.

Georges-Louis LeClerc, Comte de Buffon (1707–1788), Director of Paris's *Jardin du Roi*, (now called the *Jardin des Plantes*), is a case in point. Citing internal anatomical similarities between humans and other animals, Buffon concluded that the major differences among animals were in "the external cover" rather than in their internal structure (Buffon et al. 1791 vol. vi, 3). However, when accounting for the external similarities between apes and humans, Buffon reversed himself and defended the doctrine of special creation. In the case of humans, Buffon argued that external similarities with other creatures were superficial. Humans and apes were to be distinguished by their internal differences. Buffon also went to great lengths to defend monogenesis in human origins. He proposed that the variations among human groups could be explained by a combination of climatic factors, differences in food and, especially, by variations in customs.

Buffon linked his detailed observations of species variations to the medieval notion of a hierarchical cosmology: "All species," he wrote, "are subject to individual differences: But the constant varieties, perpetuated through successive generations, belong not equally to every species. The more dignified the species, its figure is the more fixed, and admits of fewer varieties" (Buffon et al. 1791 vol. viii, 346). In humans, variation was seen as a kind of falling away from an original unity, and was understood by Buffon as a sign of imperfection. Human variability was not a constitutive feature of human nature, but rather its nemesis, a consequence of Adam's Fall.

Nineteenth century thinking about human evolution inverted the Biblical vision of human history. A narrative in which human history represents a falling away from an original perfection becomes a progress narrative of a gradually perfecting species through the application of human reason in science and industry. Like the theological account of history, the evolutionary one translated human diversity into a lower-to-higher gradient of human perfection. The doctrine of survivals understood "primitive" cultures as leftovers from earlier stages of human development. The doctrine of survivals was wedded to notions of race and color, so that early theories of cultural evolution were racist in character. This marriage of race and evolution underwrote a revival of polygenic theories of human origin in the latter half of the nineteenth century, especially among American writers.

Although it is common today to link biologists with an interest in human universals and sociocultural anthropologists with a focus on human diversity, at the turn of the twentieth century it was biological anthropologists who tended to support polygenic theories of human origins while cultural evolutionists favored a common origin of a single human species. The real debate engaged the issue lodged uncomfortably between the phrases "primitive mentality" and "the psychic unity of mankind."[9] Psychic unity, the idea that all humans possessed fundamentally the same capacities for thinking and feeling, was the psychological version of a universal human nature. Psychic unity is an article of faith for modern anthropologists, who fear the racist implications of its rejection. They were anxious to reconcile cultural variability with the doctrine of psychic unity. Herbert Spencer proposed that the human mind operated on the basis of laws that were independent of a particular culture, but that specific cognitive abilities were closely tied to the group's level of social evolution. The mind, unified in its essence, was pluralized in its temporal existence (Spencer 1890 V. II, 607ff.).

9. See Shore 1996, especially Chapter 1, and Shore 2001 for a more detailed version of this history.

How do we draw the line between the fundamental and the purely local? These troublesome issues about psychic unity impelled early anthropological field-workers like Franz Boas and William Rivers to travel to "the field," for a firsthand look at the human mind in diverse settings.

Between 1910 and the publication of *The Mind of Primitive Man* in 1930, Boas gradually moved from a strongly evolutionist position on mind to a vigorous defense of the notion of human psychic unity free of the racist assumptions of much Victorian evolutionism. Differences in thought patterns, he argued, could be accounted for by differences in human institutions, not differences in mental equipment. However, this apparently neat solution to the psychic unity muddle had a serious cost, one that has continued to trouble modern anthropology. A unitary notion of human nature is affirmed without recourse to evolution, but only at the price of disengaging culture from any intimate relation to mind.

With the "fundamental" unity of the mind assured, ethnologists were free to document the variety of cultural traditions that shape a people's "style of thinking" but in no sense reflect any fundamental differences among minds. Culture is treated as purely external and variable whereas mind is treated as purely internal and unitary. In such a vision of culture and cognition, the generally acknowledged plasticity of the human brain is not permitted to affect the assumption of the unity of the human mind. Durkheim and his students reconciled the plurality of mental representations and the unity of mind by characterizing such variations as a distinct order of facts, social rather than psychological. Clifford Geertz borrowed this distinction when he based his well-known claim for the importance of "local knowledge" in cultural models, which were assumed to be social and public in nature rather than private and cognitive.[10] This public (social)-private (psychological) distinction allowed Geertz to reconcile human psychic unity and cultural diversity without clarifying the question of how taking cultural models seriously as a component of cognition affects our conception of both brain and mind.

Anthropology appears to be a deeply divided discipline today, and much of the disagreement (and confusion) stems from the field's inability to come to terms with its own seemingly paradoxical mission: the characterization of human nature in light of human diversity. Sociocultural anthropology is full of proponents of human diversity, but it appears that for many sociocultural anthropologists maintaining this pluralistic vision of the human seems to entail a rejection of evolutionary theory and even of science more generally.

Today, the rift between those who define anthropology as the study of universals and those who focus on the local and contingent properties of human communities has, if anything, widened. The twin offspring of anthropological speculation—human nature and cultural variation—have not been getting along.

RETHINKING HUMAN NATURE IN LIGHT OF HUMAN VARIATION

Gene-culture co-evolution, is a useful approach to conceptualizing human nature that I stress in my Anthropology 101 lectures. The dual-inheritance view of human evolution allows me to bring together in important ways biological and cultural anthropology.

10. Shore 1996, Chap. 1; Geertz 1973b.

In my initial lecture for the course, I define Anthropology as "the study of human nature *through* the study of human physical and cultural variation." At first glance, this definition sounds more or less like a conventional textbook understanding of anthropology. However, in light of the history of Western thinking about human nature and human variation outlined earlier, the radical character of this definition becomes clear. Understanding human nature *in light of* variation suggests a very different solution to the two cultures conundrum than we have been accustomed to.

It implies that human nature is not sufficiently understood by factoring out dimensions of local variation among groups (and individuals) in the interest of exposing the essential human stripped down to the common basics. This point was famously articulated early in his career by Geertz, who sought to place "culture"—extrinsically derived and institutionally grounded patterns of thought and behavior—at the center of any definition of human nature.

> The behavior patterns of lower animals are, at least to a much greater extent, given to them with their physical structure; genetic sources of information order their actions within much narrower ranges of variation, the narrower and more thoroughgoing, the lower the animal. For man, what are innately given are extremely general response capacities, which although they make possible far greater plasticity, complexity, and, on the scattered occasions when everything works as it should, effectiveness of behavior, leave it much less precisely regulated....Undirected by cultural patterns— organized systems of significant symbols—man's behavior would be virtually ungovernable, a mere chaos of pointless acts and exploding emotions, his experience virtually shapeless. Culture, the accumulated totality of such patterns, is not just an ornament of human existence but—the principal basis for its specificity—an essential condition for it. (Geertz 1973b, 45–46)

By minimizing innate human behavioral propensities, Geertz is guilty of strategic overstatement in his characterization of human plasticity. His strategy was eminently successful in its day in drawing attention to the frequently overlooked importance of culture in the evolution of the human nervous system. Nonetheless Geertz's insight remains fundamentally true and significant. It has an important bearing on any attempt to bring together scientific and humanistic approaches to the study of human life.

Obviously neither cultural nor somatic variations constitute a sufficient picture of human nature. Such a claim would clearly violate any reasonable characterization of a species by ignoring shared evolved properties that produce behavioral and physical commonalities among humans. The point is that, in addition to many shared substantive universals, significant human variability and mutability are themselves aspects of human nature.

The appreciation of the depth of such differences and what they have to teach us is of interest to both the scientist and the humanist, but to different ends. The scientist sees in such variations a challenge to uncover the general principles of development and the evolutionary forced underwriting these variations. By contrast, the humanist aims at particular accounts of (rather than accounting for) what Bruner calls the human "effort after meaning" (Bruner 1992). Humanists in anthropology focus on fostering an empathetic understanding of alternative ways of being human. This focus on local meaning encourages an expansion of our repertory of human possibilities, an expansion that challenges and refreshes our understanding of what it means to be human.

Both scientific and humanistic perspectives are important for anthropology, but I do not believe that they are to be reconciled in any simple sense of "consilience," by collapsing legitimate distinctions, by hierarchical subordination of one position to another, or by encompassment. Based on the ideal of reducing one level of explanation to another, an overly simplified conception of consilience cannot account for the important phenomenon of emergent properties of organization (Lewis 1874; Polanyi 1958, 1967, 1968; Bateson 1972; Blitz 1992; Corning 2002). Aristotle anticipated the modern notion of emergence in his *Metaphysics* when he wrote: "[T]he totality is not, as it were, a mere heap, but the whole is something besides the parts..." (Aristotle's *Metaphysics* Book 8.6.1045a). A modern formulation is provided by Goldstein who defines emergence as: "the arising of novel and coherent structures, patterns and properties during the process of self-organization in complex systems" (Goldstein 1999, 49). Although reductionism accounts for phenomena by tracing evolution backward, emergence accounts for the appearance of novelty by tracing evolution forward. The term *emergence* was first proposed in the late nineteenth century by G.H. Lewis. Lewis wrote:

> Every resultant is either a sum or a difference of the cooperant forces; their sum, when their directions are the same—their difference, when their directions are contrary. Further, every resultant is clearly traceable in its components, because these are homogeneous and commensurable...It is otherwise with emergents, when, instead of adding measurable motion to measurable motion, or things of one kind to other individuals of their kind, there is a cooperation of things of unlike kinds...The emergent is unlike its components in so far as these are incommensurable, and it cannot be reduced to their sum or their difference. (Lewis 1874, 413).

Although reduction can explain many properties of human life, it cannot explain everything. If the evolution of human life were simple, reduction would go a long way in accounting for its properties. However, human life is a complex system of organizations, structured at multiple levels: atomic, chemical, genetic, social, cultural, and individual. It seems to me that a serious appreciation of the aims of science and the humanities requires an intertheoretic discourse, not a reductive one. For anthropologists, it suggests a genuinely multivocal anthropology that speaks authoritatively in several distinct and irreducible voices about the same material, and whose mode of engagement aims at expansive conversation rather than reductive simplification.

An appreciation of human variability does not entail ignoring significant human universals, but it does require a crucial reformulation of how we think about the evolution of shared characteristics and their implications for conceptualizing human nature. There is no doubt that human nature includes a long laundry list of evolved psychological and physical characteristics that are shared by all humans.[11] Although it is certainly the case

---

11. Murdock 1945; See Brown 1991 for an influential recent attempt to refute cultural relativism by invoking a long list of human universals.

that geneticists and population biologists have long been interested in biological variability, one would have to acknowledge that there is a distinctive aura of "the scientific" associated with the search for such uniformities. It is hardly surprising that cultural psychology has often made the delineation of such substantive uniformities in human nature its special project, and a useful one at that. Even when empirical variability is encountered and acknowledged, the scientific impulse is to account for it by theorizing generative processes and specifiable causes.

SUBSTANTIVE AND GENERATIVE UNIVERSALS

Human evolution has produced an interesting paradox: a set of species-wide somatic and behavioral characteristics whose impact on human life has been to produce variable outcomes that are not predictable. Genetic evolution appears to rely on such relatively random variability in its dependence on genetic "mistakes," such as mutation, drift, and crossing over. The often-overlooked secret of the theory of natural selection is that apparently orderly adaptations rest on genetic "play," the soft bedrock of mistaken transcription or otherwise faulty reproduction. Mistakes are the engine of adaptation. Living things may share a similar genetic code and its reproductive fallibilities, but shared means do not guarantee shared ends. Elsewhere, I have called these shared evolved human characteristics *generative universals* (Shore 2001). In addition to the dependence on mutations and other forms of genetic play, humans manifest a number of other generative universals that are unquestionably an important part of human nature. Significant examples of such universals for humans include:

- Human language[12]
- Neural plasticity[13]
- The dependence of thought and reasoning on conventional and idiosyncratic mental models[14]
- Developmental retardation and neoteny relative to our closest primate relatives[15]
- A behavioral manifestation of neoteny—the intensification and extension of the child's play impulse into adulthood[16]

Some of these characteristics, like highly evolved language, are uniquely human. Others, like neoteny are also found in other species but have distinctive consequences in the context of human evolution. As a total package, human generative universals

12. The distinctive generative capability of human language codes is discussed in Hockett 1960, Bruner 1972 and Chomsky 1969, 1978.

13. Lerner 1984, Chechik, Gal, Meilijson and Ruppin 1999, Rosenzweig 2007.

14. Johnson-Laird 1983; Gentner and Stevens 1983; D'Andrade and Strauss 1992; Shore 1996; Strauss and Quinn 1997; Magnani and Nersessian 2002.

15. Bolk 1926, Gould 1977, 357, Lerner 1984, The developmental process whereby juvenile characteristics are retained in adults is also called paedomorphosis, a term first used by biologist Walter Garstang (1922).

16. Huizinga 1938, Piaget 1962, Bruner 1972, Shore 1996 (Chapters 3 and 4), Harris and Parks 1983.

are central to the evolution of human cognition and underlie the fact that human nature has evolved in the context of flexible and variable social and cultural adaptations.

This reframing of the status of universals in human evolution is not intended to deny or even minimize those many shared substantive universals that produce similar forms and predictable human behaviors. However, an appreciation of the centrality of generative universals in human evolution helps illuminate the real significance of diversity within our species. Human differences move from the margins of the stage of the human drama to share the spotlight with human similarities. No longer can the particularities of culture be viewed as a mere embellishment to our more basic nature or as noise to be factored out in assessing what makes us "essentially human" or as an index of moral decline. The necessity to manifest our general nature by inventing or taking on the particular character of local worlds must be seen as an intrinsic feature of human nature every bit as central as the delineation of shared species-specific constancies.

SCIENTIFIC AND HUMANISTIC FRAMES OF MIND

I have presented an argument to explain why human variation needs to be treated as a constituent dimension of human nature. What does this focus on human diversity have to do with the two-cultures problem? A simple but somewhat misleading answer is that, within anthropology, there is some inclination to associate scientific approaches to human nature with the discovery of substantive universals. Humanists, in contrast, tend to be drawn to a more pluralistic vision of the human, which focuses on the "thick description" (ethnography) and interpretation of what Geertz famously called "local knowledge" (Geertz 2000). Humanists like endless cultural diversity, whereas most scientists are not so enthusiastic.

This simple answer is not exactly accurate. The elimination of surface diversity in the interest of discovering human universals has never been the sole purpose of scientific anthropology. It is difficult to imagine an anthropology of any flavor that does not acknowledge human diversity. In this context, the difference between scientific and humanistic anthropology is not quite the difference between an interest in diversity and universality. It is, more accurately, the difference between a *comparative* study of cultural variation and a *particularistic* one. In its comparative mode, the aim of scientific anthropology is the reduction of diversity to specifiable principles of variation. By contrast, the aim of a humanistic anthropology is the elaborate description and effective translation of a particular and alien way of experiencing the world. The scientist wants to uncover general laws or principles (even when they account for local variations). The humanist in anthropology seeks to translate and interpret particular experiences. The goals are both valid but quite different.

The scientist aims to simplify an initial misleading complication (apparent random variability) by generalizing principles of orderly variation.[17] As a consequence, the world becomes more ordered and less random than it had initially appeared. By con-

---

17. Wilson (1998, 5) quotes Einstein as having said: "It is a wonderful feeling to recognize the unity of a complex of phenomena that to direct observation appear to be quite separate things."

trast, the humanist aims to complicate an initial misleading simplification (ethnocentrism) by elaborating a description and inferring an interpretation. As a consequence, the world becomes more complex and less predictable than it had initially appeared. The scientific mind makes strict comparison between different forms possible by focusing attention on certain aspects of a plural phenomenon (i.e., specifying variables to be compared). In the process, non-comparable data are treated as noise and factored out of the account. The humanist might well dismiss such an account as "vulgar reductionism": anthropology envisioned as a machine spitting out themes and variations, numbers beyond human experience. However, what is noise for the scientist is often grist for the humanist's mill. In juxtaposing cultures, the humanist will often overlook similarities or predictable variations (treated as banal or obvious) in the interest of highlighting unique differences ("but among the Bongo Bongo."). The scientist might well dismiss such accounts as "mystification" and "exoticism:" anthropology envisioned as a believe-it-or-not pastiche of infinite qualities without number. Faced with the criticisms and dismissals from the other, each side is convinced of the moral and intellectual rightness of their view of things. Positions harden, mutual respect wanes, and the possibility of dialogue dims.

Who is right? The positions outlined earlier define extreme poles of a spectrum. Most anthropologists try to avoid the excesses of the extremes. However, the conflict is in some sense unavoidable. Scientific and humanistic anthropology have produced both excellent and poor scholarship. More to the point, no matter how good the research, each approach will always be subject to legitimate criticisms from the other side. This is because, in order to reveal one important dimension of human life, scholars are inevitably forced to overlook or conceal another. To understand the latent functions of institutions is not to study meaning or experience. Consciousness and intentionality may be false or true or neither, but they are still crucial human phenomena of consequence. This is why, despite the long history of debate about the two cultures, they have neither merged with one another nor disappeared from the scene.

The differences between humanistic and scientific anthropologies have endured, not just because the reality anthropology seeks to reveal is inherently and irreducibly complex, but because of the intellectual predispositions of their practitioners. Despite their differences, talented humanists and scientists share many intellectual tools: careful observation, skilled inference, a passion for detail, and the ability to use both causal and analogical reasoning (Gentner 1983, 1989; Shore 1996; Magnani and Nersessian 2002; Nersessian 2008). However, I am convinced that the differences between the two cultures are also sustained by the fact that the humanistic and scientific camps are populated by individuals with very different mindsets. The extent to which such differences in orientation are temperamental (intrinsic person variables) or simply a function of learning or context (situation variables) is not clear. However, the distinctions between intellectual traditions do appear to emphasize specifiably different ways of looking at the world. The temperament and intellectual skills required to design and carry out a scientific research project to systematically collect and analyze comparable data from a large data set are one thing. The temperament and skills required to enter into an alien life-world, and then to translate this life-world in a detailed and convincing way to the home crowd are another. Rarely are these orientations and skills possessed by the same individual, and rarely are they appreciated by the same individual.

WHAT'S THE USE OF INCLUDING CULTURAL PARTICULARISM IN MODERN ANTHROPOLOGY?

Consilience, the bold idea of reconciling the humanities with the sciences and all the sciences with each other, has great appeal as an ultimate parsimonious explanation. Reductive synthesis in the sense proposed by Wilson is certainly less messy than the dialogic reconciliation of scientific and humanistic anthropology. The humanistic approach to culture emphasizes what Geertz called thick description: detailed accounts of local cultural meanings that make accessible a local life-world that otherwise might go unrecognized or unappreciated (Geertz 1973b).

The spirit of this kind of analysis seems to run in direct opposition to the spirit of generalization and parsimonious explanation of scientific anthropology. So it is fair to ask what is to be gained by keeping interpretive anthropology in dialogue with scientific anthropology. The utility of discovering general principles linking biological and cultural evolution and clarifying the general structures of human thought is obvious. Why muck up the work of science by insisting that we also take seriously local cultural models? As students of human nature, why should we care how others experience the world?[18]

Many humanists will find the answers to such questions to be self-evident, but I believe that taking these questions seriously may help to foster an appreciation of the role of interpretive work in the larger scheme of human studies. To conclude this essay I want to propose five important reasons for keeping anthropology engaged with local meaning.

1. What Bruner has called the human "effort after meaning" is one of the most distinctive characteristics of our species (Bruner 1992). Any version of human nature that does not take seriously both the underlying neurological forms and the particular cultural consequences of fact that human experiences is mediated by cultural models is crucially incomplete and inadequate.
2. Local meanings will never explain all human behavior, but discovering what people think about what they are doing will often make more sense of their behavior than will any outsider's explanation that ignores people's own intentions.[19]

18. In anthropology, the issue of point of view, *ours* and *theirs,* has been understood in terms of the difference between *etic* and *emic* accounts (Pike 1967; Harris 1969, Chapter 20). *Etic* accounts, which appeal to scientists, use a general "scientific" model of classification and explanation to compare and generalize from local cases. By contrast, *emic* accounts attempt to convey via accurate translation the folk-models that communities use to make sense of their world. The difference between the two approaches is not simply different distributions of universal semantic factors (like hue, saturation, and intensity for explaining color differences). Local models may employ heterogeneous semantic factors (like classifying colors by degrees of wetness or dryness) (Conklin 1986). Trying to directly compare models based on such different classificatory dimensions or to reduce one to the other introduces a fundamental distortion into the data.

19. See Shore 1977, 1982 and Levy 1975 for accounts explicitly using local meanings as the basis for explanations of local behavior.

3. Insightful understanding of a wide variety of cultures broadens the palette of human possibilities that we can bring to the study of human life. Close encounters with the variety of human experience enhances intellectual flexibility and the imagination of what Bruner calls "possible worlds," essential to generating novel theoretical insight (Bruner 1987).
4. An understanding of local meanings can generate new theories with explanatory power beyond the local setting from which they originated.

Anthropology is full of such locally derived theoretical constructs. The Indian theory of the Varnas made it possible for Louis Dumont to understand the general differences between egalitarian and hierarchical models of human society (Dumont 1981). Evans-Prichard's insights into the local logic of Nuer social structure produced a generative concept of segmentary lineage structure that has been highly influential in analyzing social conflicts (Evans-Prichard, Edward 1969). Similarly, Gregory Bateson derived his concept of schismogenesis (interaction patterns resulting in cumulative antagonism) initially from his observations of Balinese social interactions. He then applied the concept to a seminal analysis of a New Guinea ritual complex. Eventually the concept of schismogenesis was picked up by others and become an important way to understand the genesis and resolution of human conflicts (Bateson 1936).

Note that these seminal theoretical concepts were initially derived from close analysis and interpretation of local cultural systems, and gradually evolved from culture-specific concepts to more generalized theoretical constructs. Such constructs typically are not simple universals of human behavior but midlevel theoretical constructs that account for patterns of human behavior in a particular type of society. Ethnography is a particularly fruitful source of midlevel theoretical constructs. Just as anthropologists tend to rely on detailed case studies to exemplify theoretical points, particular cases can also produce general theories. Ethnography is a good example of what cognitive scientists call "case-based reasoning" (Schank 1982; Aamodt and Plaza 1994).

CONCLUSION

By viewing all significant aspects of human experience from a common point of view, Wilson's vision of consilience aims at a reduction of perspective. However, the emergence of a model-dependent brain in human evolution introduces a paradox of consequence for Wilson's project. General evolutionary trends are certainly subject to scientific study, but the tougher question is how one incorporates the varied *experiential consequences* of such a brain and its impact on human nature into a unified explanatory framework. How do we explain a general phenomenon without swallowing up its local contours in the process? Human experience can be reduced to a single perspective but only by thinning out the particulars that are a constitutive feature of the human world.

Because of the generative character of so many human universals, many aspects of human nature can only manifest themselves in historically particular forms. This is not a trivial point. It implies that any general account of human subjectivity will necessarily misrepresent its object by simplification and reduction, whatever the power of its general insights.[20] When appropriately framed, such general and reductive accounts are important in the development of the study of human life, but they will always need to be complemented by humanistic studies of specific lived experience—and not just as window dressing. Specific description and interpretation provide the empirical data on which empirically accurate scientific generalizations are based. Moreover, such thickly rendered particulars ultimately keep our accounts honest by reminding us of the actual experience we claim to be explaining.

In rare cases the same individual is gifted with the ability to do both the scientific comparative study and the humanistic particular one. More often, however, this dialogic reconciliation of the two cultures will call on two mutually tolerant communities of scholars, each doing their own thing, but paying careful and respectful attention to each other. In the end, the two cultures will be reconciled, not by the reductive power of consilience, but by the expansive power of intelligent mutual engagement.

References

Aligheri, Dante. 1904. *De vulgari eloquentia, opere.* Edited by E. Moore, trans. A. G. F. Howell. London.

Aamodt, Agnar, and Enric Plaza. 1994. Case-based reasoning: Foundational issues, methodological variations, and system approaches. *Artificial Intelligence Communications* 7(1): 39–52.

Barrett, H. Clark, Willem E. Frankenhuis, and Andreas Wilke. 2008. Adaptation to moving targets: Culture/gene coevolution, not either/or. *Behavioral and Brain Science* 31(5): 511.

Bateson, Geoffrey. 1936. *Naven.* Palo Alto: Stanford University Press.

Bateson, Geoffrey. 1972. *Steps to an ecology of mind: Collected essays in anthropology, psychiatry, evolution, and epistemology.* Chicago: University of Chicago Press.

Blitz, D. 1992. *Emergent evolution: Qualitative novelty and the levels of reality.* Dordrecht: Kluwer Academic Publishers.

Bolk, Louis. 1926. *Der Problem der Menschwerdung.* Jena, Germany: G. Fischer,.

Boyd, Robert, and Peter Richerson. 2005a. *The origin and evolution of culture*s New York: Oxford University Press.

Boyd, Robert, and Peter Richerson. 2005b. *Not by genes alone: How culture transformed human evolution.* Chicago: The University of Chicago Press.

Boyer, Pascal. 2002. *Religion explained.* New York: Basic Books.

Brown, Donald. 1991. *Human universals.* New York: McGraw-Hill.

Bruner, Jerome. 1972. The nature and uses of immaturity. *American Psychologist* 27(8): 1–22.

Bruner, Jerome. 1987. *Actual minds, possible worlds (The Jerusalem-Harvard lectures).* Cambridge: Harvard University Press.

20. A good example of this problem is the development of a robust literature in evolutionary psychology explaining human religion in terms of general and universal cognitive properties of religious thought and practice (Lawson and McCauley 1993; Boyer 2002; Whitehouse 2005; Tremlin 2006). I applaud and admire this development of a science of religious cognition. But it cannot be said (nor do I believe it is intended) to replace detailed evocative interpretive accounts of particular religious thought and experience. Indeed, the general explanation of religion depends on accurate and detailed accounts of religions. The gains in understanding about religious cognition in general are inevitably at the expense of many of the insights gained by accounts of religious experience in particular. So in the end we need them both.

Bruner, Jerome. 1992. Acts of meaning: Four lectures on mind and culture (The Jerusalem-Harvard lectures). Cambridge: Harvard University Press.

Buffon, George 1991. Histoire naturelle, 3rd ed. Trans. W. Smellie. London: Thoemmes Continuum.

Chechik, Gal, Isaac Meilijson, and Eytan Ruppin. 1999. Neuronal regulation: A mechanism for synaptic pruning during brain maturation. Israel: Stanford Journals.

Chomsky, Noam. 1969. Aspects of the theory of syntax. Cambridge: MIT Press.

Chomsky, Noam. 1978. Topics in the theory of generative grammar. The Hague: Mouton de Gruyter.

Conklin, Harold. 1986. Hanunoo color terms. Journal of Anthropological Research. 42(3): 441–446.

Corning, Peter. 2002. The re-emergence of "emergence": A venerable concept in search of a theory. Complexity 7(6): 18–30.

D'Andrade, Roy, and Claudia Strauss, eds. 1992. Human motives and cultural models. Cambridge: Cambridge University Press.

Deacon, Terrence. 1997. The symbolic species: The co-evolution of language and the brain. New York: W.W. Norton.

Donald, Merlin. 1993. The origins of the modern mind: Three stages in the evolution of cognition and culture. Cambridge: Harvard University Press.

Dumont, Louis. 1981. Homo hierarchicus: The caste system and its implications (The nature of human society). Chicago: University of Chicago Press.

Evans-Prichard, Edward E. 1969. The Nuer: A description of the modes of livelihood and political institutions of a Nilotic people. Oxford: Oxford University Press.

Garstang, Walter. 1922. The theory of recapitulation: A critical re-statement of the biogenetic law. Zoological Journal of the Linnean Society 35: 81–101.

Geertz, Clifford. 1973a. The impact of the concept of culture on the concept of man. In The interpretation of cultures: Selected essays, 33–54. New York: Basic Books.

Geertz, Clifford. 1973b. Thick description: Toward an interpretive theory of culture. In The interpretation of cultures: Selected essays, 3–30. New York: Basic Books.

Geertz, Clifford. 2000. Local knowledge: Further essays in interpretive anthropology. New York: Basic Books.

Gentner, Deidre. 1983. Structure-mapping: A theoretic framework for analogy. Cognitive Science 7: 155–170.

Gentner, Deidre. 1989. The mechanisms of analogical learning. In Similarity and analogy in reasoning and learning, ed. S. Vosniadou, and A. Ortony, 199–233. Cambridge: Cambridge University Press.

Gentner, D., and A.L. Stevens, eds. 1983. Mental models. Hillsdale, N.J.: Erlbaum.

Goldstein, Jeffrey. 1999. Emergence as a construct: History and issues. Emergence: Complexity and organization 1(1): 49–72.

Gould, Stephen J. 1977. Ontogeny and phylogeny. Cambridge: Harvard University Press.

Hammerstein, P., ed. 2003. Genetic and cultural evolution of cooperation. Berlin: MIT Press, Berlin: 357–388.

Harris, Carolyn, and Roberta Parks, eds. 1983. Play, games and sports in cultural contexts. Champaign, Il.: Human Kinetic Books.

Harris, Marvin. 1969. The rise of anthropological theory. New York: Routledge and Kegan Paul.

Hockett, C.F. 1960. The origin of speech. Scientific American 203, 89–96

Huizinga, Johan. 1938. Homo ludens: A study of the play element in culture. London: Temple Smith.

Johnson-Laird, P.N. 1983. *Mental models: Toward a cognitive science of language, inference and consciousness.* Cambridge, MA: Harvard University Press.

Kostler, Arthur, and J.R. Smythies, eds. 1969. *Beyond reductionism: New perspectives in the life sciences.* New York: Houghton Mifflin Co.

Lawson, Thomas, and Robert McCauley. 1993. *Rethinking religion: Connecting cognition and culture.* New York: Cambridge University Press.

Lerner, Richard. 1984. *On the nature of human plasticity.* Cambridge and New York: Cambridge University Press.

Levy, Robert. 1975. *Tahitians: Mind and experience in the Society Islands.* Chicago: University of Chicago Press.

Levi-Strauss, Claude. 1968. *The savage mind.* Chicago: University of Chicago Press.

Lewis, G.H. 1877. *Problems of life and mind.* London: Truebner.

Magnani, Lorenzo and Nancy Nersessian, eds. 2002. *Model based reasoning: Science, technology, values.* Berlin: Springer.

McElreath, Richard, and Joseph Henrich..2007. Dual inheritance theory: The evolution of human cultural capacities and cultural evolution. In *Oxford handbook of evolutionary psychology*, eds. R. Dunbar and L. Barrett. Oxford: Oxford Uniersity Press.

Murdock, George P. 1945. The common denominator of cultures. In *The science of man in the world crisis*, ed. Ralph Linton. New York: Columbia.

Nersessian, Nancy. 2008. *Creating scientific concepts.* Cambridge: MIT Press.

Piaget, Jean. 1962. *Play, dreams and imitation.* New York: Norton.

Pike, Kenneth Lee. 1967. *Language in relation to a unified theory of structure of human behavior.* 2nd ed. The Hague: Mouton.

Polanyi, Michael. 1958. *Personal knowledge. Towards a post critical philosophy.* London: Routledge.

Polanyi, Michael. 1967. *The tacit dimension.* New York: Anchor Books.

Polanyi, Michael. 1968. Life's irreducible structure. *Science* 160: 1308–1312.

Rosenzweig, Mark. 2007. Modification of brain circuits through experience. In *Neural plasticity and memory: From genes to brain imaging*, eds. Bermudez-Rattoni, Federico. New York: CRC Press.

St. Augustine. 1871. *De civitate dei.* ed. E. Hoffman. Trans. M. Dodds. New York: The Modern Library.

Schank, Roger. 1982. *Dynamic memory: A theory of learning in computers and people.* New York: Cambridge University Press.

Segal, Daniel, and Sylvia Yanagisako. 2005. *Unwrapping the sacred bundle: Reflections on the disciplining of anthropology.* Durham: Duke University Press.

Shore, Bradd. 1977. *A Samoan theory of action: Social control and social order in a Polynesian paradox.* Ph. D. diss, DepaAnthropology, rtment of University of Chicago.

Shore, Bradd. 1982. *Sala'ilua: A Samoan mystery.* New York: Columbia University Press.

Shore, Bradd. 1996. *Culture in mind: Culture, cognition and the problem of meaning.* New York: Oxford University Press.

Shore, Bradd. 1999. Strange fate of holism. *Anthropology News* 40(9): 4–5.

Shore, Bradd. 2001. Human nature and human variation: The unnatural history of a false dichotomy, In *Being human*, ed. Neil Roughley. Berlin: Walter de Gruyter.

Slotkin, J. S., ed. 1965. *Readings in early anthropology.* Chicago: Aldine Publishing.

Snow, C.P. 1961. *The two cultures and the scientific revolution.* New York: Cambridge University Press.

Spencer, Sir. Herbert. 1890. *The principles of psychology, Vol. II.* New York: D. Appleton and Company.

Stocking, George. 1968. The persistence of polygenist thought in post-Darwinian anthropology. In *Race, culture, and evolution: Essays in the history of anthropology*. New York: The Free Press.

Strauss, Claudia, and Naomi Quinn. 1997. *A cognitive theory of cultural meaning*. New York: Cambridge University Press.

Whitehouse, Harvey, ed. 2005. *Mind and religion: Psychological and cognitive foundations of religion*. New York: Altamira Press.

Tremlin, Todd. 2006. *Minds and gods: The cognitive foundations of religion*. New York: Oxford University Press.

Wilson, Edward O. 1998. *Consilience: The unity of knowledge*. New York: Alfred A. Knopf.

PART II

Case Studies

SECTION THREE

Culture

8

CULTURE IN SONGBIRDS AND ITS CONTRIBUTION TO THE EVOLUTION OF NEW SPECIES

Darren E. Irwin

INTRODUCTION

The human ego has had a two-sided relationship with science. On the one hand, the scientific method has enabled us to understand the natural world in ways previously inconceivable, and to make inventions that would have astounded our ancestors. On the other, the history of science is one of breaking down the ways in which we had previously thought we were special: the Earth is not the center of the universe, our anatomy is similar to that of other primates, our behavior shares many similarities with diverse groups of animals, and some other types of animals have intelligence and emotional awareness that approach our own. Thus the results produced by the scientific method have gradually moved us toward an integration of fields that were previously considered separate: the natural sciences and the humanities. The study of one phenomenon widely considered to be unique to humans, culture, is no exception.

Like other phenomena originally conceived by humans to be unique to humans, culture has experienced a tumultuous definitional history. Originally used in an agricultural sense to refer to the cultivation or improvement of soil, plants, or animals, the term was eventually applied in a similarly value-laden way to human societies (Kroeber et al. 1952). In the eighteenth and nineteenth centuries, the term often was used in a subjective way to refer to the best or ideal traditions that a society can have (Kroeber et al. 1952). Recently, the term has taken on a variety of less value-laden meanings, referring, in general, to socially learned behavior; most dictionaries define *culture* as a property of humans alone:

> "the sum total of ways of living built up by a group of human beings and transmitted from one generation to another." – *Random House Webster's Unabridged Dictionary*, second edition. 1999. Random House: New York.
> "the total set of beliefs, values, customs, and behavior patterns that characterizes a human population; the non-instinctive manner in which humans interact with or manipulate their environment." – *Academic Press Dictionary of Science and Technology*. 1992. Academic Press: San Diego, California.

"the customs, civilization, and achievements of a particular time or people." – *The Oxford Dictionary and Thesaurus, American Edition*. 1996. Oxford University Press: New York.

"the totality of socially transmitted behavior patterns, arts, beliefs, institutions, and all other products of human work and thought." – www.thefreedictionary.com

From a biologist's perspective, the references to a single species in the preceding definitions are somewhat humorous; these definitions seem as absurd as the following:

"Flight: the propelled movement through the air of Townsend's big-eared bats."
"Song: a vocal signal given by yellow-rumped warblers to defend their territories and attract mates."

Defining a phenomenon as existing solely in a single species greatly limits use of the comparative method, a fundamentally important technique in the biological sciences. If we want to understand the origin and evolution of a trait in a single species, we can gain great insight by comparing that trait among multiple species. This approach has allowed us to identify the functions of human genes by studying related genes in fruit flies and mice, and to understand human behavior by studying such behavior in a broad ranges of species and observing common patterns. Thus, defining culture as a feature of humans alone can prevent us from making progress in understanding the origins and evolution of culture.

In fact, there is considerable evidence that cultural phenomena are common in the biological world. Here I define *culture* broadly by simply taking the words *human* or *people* out of the preceding definitions: By *culture* I essentially mean "socially learned behavior that can grow and change through time." By this standard, it is clear that many nonhuman species have culture. This is not to say, however, that the culture of other species approaches human culture in terms of its complexity or richness. Clearly, humans are unusual among species in terms of the extent to which culture has affected our ecology and evolution, as well as our impact on the other species with whom we share our planet.

In this chapter, I first briefly review the evidence for culture in nonhumans and propose birdsong as an excellent system for the study of culture. I then discuss the ways that genetics and learning can be jointly involved in cultural evolution, through a process of gene-culture co-evolution (Feldman and Laland 1996). I consider the role that culture can play in the evolution of new species and propose a model of how sexual selection can drive gene-culture co-evolution along different trajectories in separated populations. I finish with some comments on the lessons of birdsong research for the study of culture in humans and other primates.

Note that I approach the topic of culture as a bit of an outsider: My training is as an evolutionary biologist who uses birds as a model system for the study of how multiple species evolve from one (i.e., the process of speciation). My work on bird song has gradually led toward a general interest in the evolution of learned behaviors. The literature on birdsong commonly refers to birdsong as a form of culture, thus it was surprising to me to read the definitions that limit that term to humans, as well as the arguments among primate biologists about whether other primates have culture.

CULTURE IN NONHUMANS

From my perspective, it is clear that many species have culture. Convincing examples from primates include chimpanzees (Whiten et al. 1999, 2001; Lycett et al. 2007), orangutans (van Schaik et al. 2003), and capuchin monkeys (Perry et al. 2003). Cetaceans also provide clear examples (Rendell and Whitehead 2001) such as songs of humpback whales (Noad et al. 2001), calls of killer whales (Yurk et al. 2002), and tool use of bottlenose dolphins (Krützen et al. 2005).

Culture is especially common in birds. These include feeding methods in such birds as ravens and crows (Marzluff and Angell 2007), and singing behavior in songbirds (Catchpole and Slater 1995). Migratory behavior in some species that migrate in groups is a particularly compelling example: Young geese, ducks, and cranes typically migrate with older individuals, learning the route as they go. Remarkably, humans have used ultralight aircraft to teach young birds a new migratory route to a new wintering area (e.g., with the endangered whooping cranes *Grus americana*; see www.operationmigration.org). This socially learned behavior has then been passed down by experienced birds to younger birds, providing an example of a new socially transmitted tradition. Such cross-species transfers of behavior provide particularly clear examples of the abilities of other species to transmit culture. Singing behavior provides another clear example of socially transmitted behavior (Catchpole and Slater 1995; Price 2008). A role for social learning in the development of an individual's singing behavior has been demonstrated in at least three major groups of birds: oscine passerines (known informally as the "songbirds"), parrots, and hummingbirds.

Examples of culture in animals are not without controversy (reviewed by Laland and Janik 2006). Ironically, though, the amount of skepticism regarding demonstrations of nonhuman culture seems to be highest with regard to that group that is closest to humans, the nonhuman primates, and moderately high with regard to cetaceans as well (Laland and Janik 2006). In contrast, there is wide agreement among ornithologists that bird song, when socially learned, can be viewed as a form of culture (Price 2008). The extreme skepticism encountered by primatologists who claim that nonhuman primates have culture simply has not occurred in relation to similar claims of culture in birds. This reluctance to accept culture in our closest relatives is probably related to the ongoing human desire to keep humans separate from other species (Corbey 2005).

BIRDSONG: A COMBINATION OF GENETICS AND LEARNING

In the vast majority of bird species, vocal signals play a vital role in survival and reproduction (Catchpole and Slater 1995; Collins 2004). Vocal signals can be divided broadly into two categories: calls, which are signals used in a variety of contexts by both sexes throughout the year, and songs, which are sung primarily by males (with some exceptions, notably in the tropics) mainly during the breeding season. Songs are often much longer and more complex than calls, and in many species songs are highly influenced by learning, whereas most calls are not. Songs usually have a role in both mate attraction and territory defense (Collins 2004). In many species, each male defends a small territory—his songs tend to repel other males (unless they decide to challenge his ownership of the territory), while females choose mates partly based on song, often preferring songs that are longer, more complex, or otherwise more elaborate in some way. Songs often differ dramatically between closely related species or even between different populations of the same species, suggesting that they can evolve quickly (Price 2008).

In the literature on culture in humans and other primates, learning and genetics are sometimes viewed as competing or antagonistic influences on traits (i.e., the "nature versus nurture" debate). In primatology, this view is encapsulated in the so-called "ethnographic method" (reviewed by Laland and Janik 2006), which holds that to demonstrate culture, the influence of genetic and ecological variation on the behaviors being studied must be ruled out. In the birdsong literature, a more complex view emerged some time ago: Song is influenced by genes, learning, and environmental characteristics, all of which interact in complex, often synergistic, ways both in the development of an individual's song and in the evolution of song within and between species (reviewed by Marler 2004).

This view is supported by considerable experimental and observational evidence (Marler 2004; Price 2008). In some of the earliest experiments, Thorpe (1961) showed

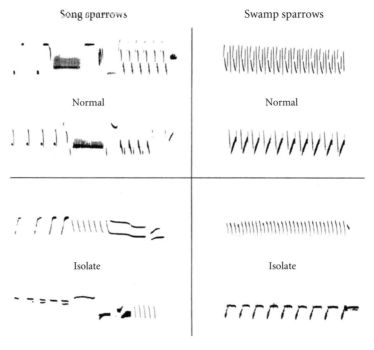

Song sparrows   Swamp sparrows

Normal   Normal

Isolate   Isolate

FIGURE 1 Example song spectrograms of song sparrows (left) and swamp sparrows (right) from wild birds (top) and birds raised in isolation (bottom; in each case, songs of two individuals are shown). Song spectrograms illustrate time along the horizontal axis and frequency along the vertical axis, with the darkness representing amplitude of sound at each frequency and time. Isolate songs are simpler than wild song, illustrating a role for learning in development of wild song. Isolate songs differ between species in a way consistent with wild song, illustrating a genetic difference in instinctive song development. Adapted from Marler (2004), after Marler and Sherman (1983).

that young chaffinches (*Fringilla coelebs*) that were raised in isolation did develop songs, but they sounded very rudimentary compared to wild song. Others were raised while hearing recordings of adult chaffinch songs, and these developed songs similar to those they had heard. Yet others were raised while being exposed only to a variety of artificially created sounds or songs of other species, but these did not learn to produce those sounds. The one exception was the tree pipit (*Anthus trivialis*) song, which has a tonal quality similar to the chaffinch; the chaffinches were able to learn this song perfectly. Thorpe concluded that the young chaffinches have an innate tendency to learn songs that are similar to a crude template, but that to develop the correct wild song they must hear it first. Another good example is provided by Marler and Sherman's (1985) work on song sparrows (*Melospiza melodia*) and swamp sparrows (*Melospiza georgiana*). When reared in isolation, individuals from each species sing rudimentary songs, much simpler and at a slower tempo than wild songs. Yet the songs of isolates differ between species in a way that is similar to the way wild songs differ between species, with song sparrows having a more complex song structure (Fig. 1). This experiment clearly shows that the two species have innate (i.e., genetic) tendencies to sing different songs, yet the full wild song needs to be heard to be learned.

AN EXCELLENT SYSTEM FOR THE STUDY OF CULTURAL EVOLUTION

A number of characteristics of birdsong make it particularly well suited for the study of cultural evolution. Song is an easily recorded behavior; with a portable microphone and recorder, a researcher can record song while having little impact on the subject. Song can be analyzed by converting the recording into song spectrograms; these can be compared visually, and a variety of measurements can be made. Songs of many bird species can be categorized into distinct song-unit types, allowing a quantification of song variability and a comparison of repertoires between individuals (e.g., Lynch and Baker 1993, 1994; Irwin 2000). By recording songs of all individuals in a population, researchers can determine from which of many possible song tutors a young bird learned its song (it is often not the father). These patterns can be compared to patterns of genetic inheritance, when relationships between relatives have been determined (Grant and Grant 1998). Playback experiments can be used to test how birds respond to a variety of recordings; such experiments have been used to test recognition of songs from a different population (e.g., Irwin et al. 2001). Much is known about the neurological and physiological basis of song, providing background knowledge that assists in the understanding of singing behavior (Jarvis 2004). It is relatively easy to sample large numbers of individual birds so that genetic, morphological, and environmental variation can be compared with song variation (e.g., Irwin et al. 2008). Lastly, the large number of songbird species (roughly 4,000) provides a wide variety of research systems that can be studied in a comparative framework.

Evolution, or change in the traits of a population over time, only requires two things: variation and inheritance. Due to random sampling from generation to generation, the frequencies of traits in a population will change stochastically over time, a process known as drift. However, for evolution to be driven in a particular direction, a third factor is required—selection—meaning that variants that differ in some trait have different average survival and reproduction.

Like all cultural phenomena, the evolution of birdsong can be studied from two complementary angles in terms of selection. First, we can consider how variation in singing behavior affects the fitness of individual birds that display that behavior. Using this approach, many experimental and observational studies that have shown that, in most species examined, female birds choose mates partly based on the way that they sing (reviewed by Collins 2004). Studies have also demonstrated that song plays a role in male-male territorial interactions, and that different singing behaviors function better or worse in this context (Collins 2004). These two selective forces on song are both forms of sexual selection: Individuals with some variants of song survive and reproduce more than those with other variants, due to their differential ability to compete for mates. Hence genetic variants that influence singing behavior in favorable ways tend to increase each generation.

Second, rather than focusing on the fitness of organisms that display partially learned behavior, we can examine the fitness of learned behaviors themselves. In other words, we can view a particular learned song as a "meme" (Dawkins 1976; Lynch and Baker 1993) that can be transferred from one individual to another, just as a gene can be passed from parent to offspring. Some memes may be particularly good at being transferred (i.e., they have high fitness), because they transmit well through the environment, are easily learned, or confer greater survival on the individuals that carry them, and, therefore, they get repeated more and are transmitted to more individuals. Because songs of individual birds or populations can often be categorized into distinct song types, it is possible to generate libraries that illustrate the "meme pool" of a population (e.g., Payne 1996). A number of studies have examined song divergence between populations in a "population memetics" framework, using theory originally designed for population genetics. Most applications of this theory so far have looked for evidence of "memetic drift," or the divergence of songs between populations that are not driven by selection. For example, songs of chaffinches on a number of Atlantic Islands show more differentiation from each other than do populations on the mainland, an observation consistent with memetic drift due to population bottlenecks and lower migration rates during the colonization of the islands (Lynch and Baker 1994), although Price (2008) notes these patterns are also consistent with selection on song due to environmental differences on the islands.

GENES AND MEMES: A SINGLE CO-EVOLVING SYSTEM

How do we make sense of these two aspects of the evolution of birdsong—the fitness of genetic variants and the fitness of memetic variants? Biologists have developed two concepts that aid in understanding how these aspects interact.

The first is the concept of gene-culture co-evolution (reviewed by Feldman and Laland 1996). Rather than genes and learning being competing influences on song, the two are, in fact, different components of a single co-evolving system:

> The two transmission systems [genetic inheritance and cultural learning] cannot be treated independently, both because what an individual learns may depend on

its genotype, and also because the selection acting on the genetic system may be generated or modified by the spread of a cultural trait. (Feldman and Laland 1996)

Thus genetic variation influences the types of memes that are preferentially learned by individuals, and memetic variation influences the form of selection on genes.

The second concept is "genetic assimilation" (Waddington 1961; Price 2008). This is the idea that a socially learned behavior can eventually become genetically based. Imagine a newly learned behavior that causes high fitness, such as a new feeding method. Initially, individuals learn the behavior from each other, and it spreads through the population. Those who can learn the behavior most quickly or efficiently benefit most from the new behavior. This exposes to selection any genetic variation that influences how quickly the behavior is learned. Over the generations, individuals become better and better at learning the behavior. Eventually, a few individuals may have so many of the genes for efficient learning of the behavior that they simply exhibit the behavior without having to observe it—they exhibit the behavior without learning. In this way, the learned behavior has become genetically assimilated.

Genetic assimilation is expected to occur with song evolution because a population of birds is under constant selection for efficient learning of its population-specific song. Thus, song may evolve through a process of memetic evolution, but genetic variants that enable efficient learning of that song are constantly favored by selection. In this way, the genetic instinct to learn song of certain characteristics constantly tracks the evolving songs of the population. Although genetic assimilation is constantly occurring, there may still be forces driving song evolution (e.g., sexual selection) and thereby maintaining a benefit of some degree of song learning. Thus cultural evolution and genetic assimilation can occur at the same time.

AN EXAMPLE: THE GREENISH WARBLERS

For a number of years, my colleagues and I have been studying song and other variation in greenish warblers (*Phylloscopus trochiloides*), a group of songbirds that breeds in the temperate forests of Asia (Irwin 2000; Irwin et al. 2001, 2005, 2008). The greenish warblers provide a good illustration of many of the aspects of song research already discussed. Moreover, they provide an example in which cultural evolution may have contributed to the splitting of a single species into two.

Greenish warblers are a rare example of a "ring species," a phenomenon that is particularly illustrative for the study of how two species evolve from one (Wake 2001): Two northern forms, one in west Siberia (known by the subspecies name *Phylloscopus trochiloides viridanus*) and one in east Siberia (*Phylloscopus [trochiloides] plumbeitarsus*), do not interbreed and are genetically distinct where they meet, effectively making them distinct species; yet these forms are connected by a long chain of interbreeding populations encircling the Tibetan Plateau to the south through which genes, body size and shape, plumage patterns, and vocalizations change gradually (Fig. 2; Ticehurst 1938; Irwin 2000; Irwin et al. 2001, 2005, 2008). These patterns have supported the hypothesis that a single ancestral species once occurred in the southern part of the current ring and then

(a)

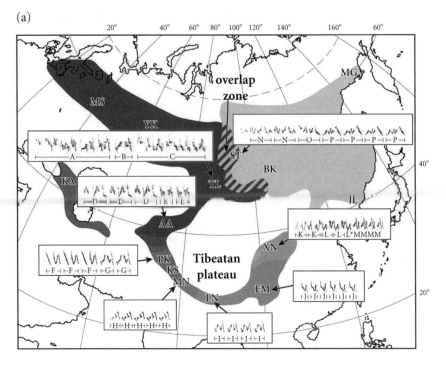

(b)

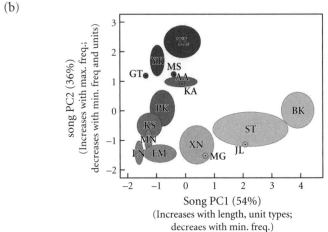

FIGURE 2 Geographic variation in song of greenish warblers, illustrated using (a) spectrograms on a map of Asia and (b) a plot of two composite axes of variation in song, produced using principal components analysis. Research sites are indicated by two-letter codes. On the spectrograms in (a), distinct song units are represented by letters. Various shades of grey represent genetic characteristics of greenish warbler populations, with the grey areas in (a) representing breeding ranges and in (b) representing song variation (population means and standard deviations for two principal components of song variation; small circles with dots indicate sites where only a single bird was recorded and hence no standard deviation can be estimated). West Siberian *viridanus* (dark grey) and east Siberian *plumbeitarsus* (light grey) differ strongly in genetics and song. These traits change gradually between these extremes through a ring of populations to the south. Moving north from the Himalayas (e.g. research site LN, in Langtang, Nepal), songs become longer and more complex, along both western and eastern pathways into Siberia, but in different ways. Adapted from (a) Irwin and Irwin (2004) and (b) Irwin et al. (2008).

expanded northward along two pathways, northwestward and northeastward, into Siberia (Ticehurst 1938). During these expansions, vocalizations, plumage patterns, and genes gradually diverged, such that western and eastern Siberian populations did not interbreed when they finally came into contact in central Siberia.

Geographic variation in song around the ring is especially remarkable. In all locations, songs are constructed out of short "song units" that are highly distinct; each individual has a limited repertoire of song units and constructs songs by joining together song units in various ways (Irwin 2000). However, the characteristics of song units and the rules by which they are joined together into complete songs differ dramatically between populations (Fig. 2). In the south (e.g., in the Himalayas), song units are short and simple, and entire songs are constructed by simply repeating a single unit four to six times. Moving from the western Himalayas northward into western Siberia, song units gradually increase in length and in frequency range, such that each unit becomes more complex. Entire songs are constructed by joining together (usually two to five) different units, resulting in songs that are much longer and more complex than those in the south. By contrast, moving from the eastern Himalayas northward into eastern Siberia, songs again become more complex but in a different way than in the west: Units become only slightly longer, but songs are constructed out of a much larger unit repertoire per bird, unit repetition goes down, and more units are used to construct each song. In both west and east Siberia, songs are much longer and more complex than those in the south. However, the form of complexity differs between the two Siberian forms (Fig. 2b); the birds recognize this difference, as demonstrated by playback experiments (Irwin et al. 2001). Where the two forms meet in the north, their songs are completely different, even though change in songs is gradual around the ring.

To explain this intriguing pattern, we have postulated that the intensity of sexual selection on male song based on female choice has increased during the northward expansions into Siberia (Irwin 2000; Irwin et al. 2008). There is much evidence in a variety of songbird species that females tend to prefer song that is more complex or otherwise more elaborate in some way (Collins 2004). It is likely that the dramatic shifts in various ecological factors (e.g., food abundance, time on the breeding grounds, population density, forest density, day length, temperature at night) have shifted the balance of selective forces on song in a direction that amplifies the impact of female choice for complex song (see Irwin 2000 for some ideas of exactly why this may have occurred). This could have then driven the evolution of long and complex songs during the two expansions into Siberia. This scenario is supported by the parallel increases in a number of characteristics related to the intensity of singing behavior (e.g., time spent singing, repertoire length, song length, and unit switching rate; Irwin 2000).

Assume for the moment that the scenario just described is correct: There has been parallel selection for greater song complexity and length during the two northward expansions. An interesting question arises: By what mechanism has song evolution occurred? What are the relative roles of genetic evolution and memetic evolution? Could this be an example of cultural evolution contributing to the evolution of two species from one? To address these questions, we need to first examine whether there is evidence for learning being involved.

A number of observations support the hypothesis that learning is involved in greenish warbler song. First, greenish warblers are members of the oscine passerine evolutionary group (the "songbirds"), in which song learning is common (Catchpole and Slater 1995; Price 2008). Second, it is difficult to imagine that the pattern of song variation would arise without some role for learning. A bird's entire repertoire consists of a highly complex series of sounds that are organized into discrete units; it is reasonable to think that the detailed structure of each unit was learned from other individuals. Third, there are clear examples of different individuals singing the same unit, except for minor differences. These differences most likely correspond to

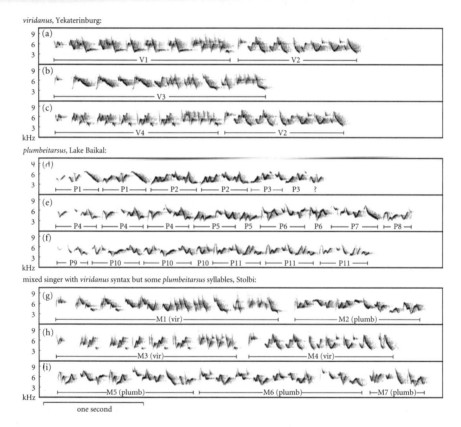

FIGURE 3 Example song spectrograms from (a–c) a single *viridanus* in west Siberia (Yekaterinburg, site YK in Fig. 2), (d–f) a single *plumbeitarsus* in east Siberia (Lake Baikal, site BK), and (g–i) an unusual bird in central Siberia (Stolbi National Park, site ST, recorded in June or July 1998) with songs that combine the syntax of *viridanus* (e.g., long song units, without repetition) with song elements from both *viridanus* and *plumbeitarsus*. For each individual, the three songs shown (one per line) were sung consecutively. Song units are indicated with brackets and names under the spectrograms, and in the case of the mixed singer "vir" and "plumb" indicate the match of the syllables to other *viridanus* or *plumbeitarsus* songs. For example, for *viridanus* song units compare units M1 and V3, units M3 and V4, and M4 to V2. For an example of *plumbeitarsus* parts of song, compare unit M5 with units P6 and P7. Many other parts of the mixed singer's song match units in other recorded *plumbeitarsus* individuals (not shown), but in this mixed singer the short *plumbeitarsus* units are grouped into much longer units, consistent with normal *viridanus* syntax.

cultural mutations. In some cases, there are clear insertions or deletions, in which it appears that an individual simply repeated a syllable or two in the middle of a unit, or conversely that an individual dropped a syllable or two from the unit. In other cases, two units in one individual's song are fused as a single unit in another individual's song. In yet other cases, there are small changes to the detailed structure of a unit in different individuals' songs. Fourth, one unusual individual from central Siberia sings songs that consist of some syllables characteristic of west Siberian *viridanus* and some syllables characteristic of east Siberian *plumbeitarsus* (Fig. 3). This individual had the syntax of a typical *viridanus*, grouping the *plumbeitarsus* syllables into long song units rather than the shorter units typical of *plumbeitarsus*. Unfortunately, we were unable to capture this individual and cannot test its genetic identity, but the singing pattern strongly suggests that it was *viridanus* that learned some elements of *plumbeitarsus* song.

Although the evidence for song learning is strong, it is also likely that genes influence variation in greenish warbler song. Genome-wide genetic signatures differ dramatically around the ring, with *viridanus* and *plumbeitarsus* being at the extremes, suggesting it is quite plausible that many genes that influence the propensity to learn certain kinds of songs vary around the ring. As with many other species (e.g., the song sparrows and swamp sparrows discussed earlier), it is likely that greenish warblers have an innate tendency to learn a particular type of song; this innate template likely differs around the ring. This idea is supported by the unusual *viridanus* that learned some *plumbeitarsus* song but then organized it into a unit length typical of *viridanus* (Fig. 3). It is as if the general acoustic structure of *plumbeitarsus* units was acceptable to this *viridanus*, but the unit length and repetitive structure was not. So it learned the details of the units, but it converted the syntax (the pace and rules by which units are put together into songs) to conform to its own genetically encoded template.

A SIMPLIFIED MODEL OF GENE-CULTURE CO-EVOLUTION DRIVEN BY SEXUAL SELECTION

The preceding observations suggest a model for greenish warbler song evolution: Song units are learned, whereas song syntax is genetically coded. This model, like most, is certainly a great simplification compared to reality and is not intended as a fully precise description of the mechanics of song evolution in greenish warblers. In fact, both units and syntax are likely influenced by both genes and learning, to varying degrees. However, considering this simplified model for the moment may nonetheless allow us to gain real insight into how greenish warbler song evolves. Adopting this model, we see that greenish warbler song evolution can be seen as a form of gene-culture co-evolution (Feldman and Laland 1996): Syntax is controlled by genes, whereas song units are memes. The genes that encode syntax influence the selective environment for memes: The memes that a bird learns (and, therefore, have high fitness) are those that conform best to the bird's genetic template for syntax (i.e., the right length and frequency range). Conversely, memes influence the selective environment for genes: The genes with highest fitness are those that allow efficient learning of memes that convey fitness benefits to individual birds. In this way, genes and memes co-evolve.

Now, we can add sexual selection to the model. We postulate that females prefer males that sing longer and more complex songs, and that the ecological conditions have changed in a way that amplifies the strength of this sexual selection based on female choice or, conversely, relaxes opposing selection against elaborate singing. For example, perhaps a shift toward greater food availability has enabled birds to sing more (Irwin 2000). There are many types of changes in song that would increase length and complexity and, hence, be preferred by females. In terms of memes, longer song units, greater song unit diversity per bird, and song units with more internal complexity may all be favored. In terms of genes, any genetic variation that causes birds to preferentially learn longer or more complex song units, a larger number of song units, and to sing with more complex syntax (e.g., switching more between song units) may be favored. Sexual selection is thus driving both memes and genes to evolve, and changes in memes cause selection on genes, and vice versa. This feedback loop, with memes and genes causing change in each other, enhances the effectiveness of sexual selection in driving evolution of song (Fig. 4).

In this co-evolutionary process, small changes in initial conditions have the potential to cause huge changes in the eventual outcome. To demonstrate this, imagine taking a single population of birds and separating it into two groups, and then applying greater sexual selection for song complexity to each. In one population, the first genetic mutation to become fixed (that is, the first to spread through the population due to selection) may be one that favors the learning of longer song units. This, then, exposes the population of song units to selection for greater length. This, in turn, favors another genetic mutation that favors learning of even longer memes. The population eventually has songs that consist of very long, internally complex song units (such as those of west Siberian *viridanus*).

Imagine that in the second population, the first genetic mutation to become fixed is one that favors the learning of large numbers of song units and using many song units per song. This exposes the population of song units to selection favoring relatively short and easily learned units. This, in turn, causes selection for genetic variants that cause the learning of even larger numbers of song units and perhaps lowering the repetition rate because it is advantageous to display the large song unit repertoire. Eventually, each bird

FIGURE 4 Diagram showing simple model for how sexual selection for more complex song can drive both genetic and memetic evolution. In turn, evolution of genes causes selection on memes, and evolution of memes causes selection on genes. This feedback loop causes the overall path of evolution to depend highly on initial conditions and on random events during evolution, such as mutation. Although we can predict that more complex song will evolve, the form of that complex song is highly unpredictable. Note that the diagram could be made much more complicated, with many more feedback loops, if we were to add the genetics and learning (i.e., sexual imprinting) of female preference for song.

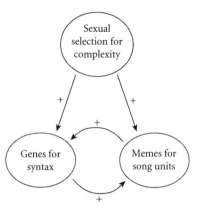

in this population has a large repertoire of song units and sings long songs that consist of many short units that are repeated little (such as those of east Siberian *plumbeitarsus*).

In these two populations, the initial form of sexual selection was identical, but the different initial mutations were magnified by the co-evolutionary interaction of genes and memes, increasing the propensity of the populations to head off on different evolutionary trajectories. Thus, gene-culture co-evolution is a highly stochastic process, because of the strong influence of random events (mutations) on the outcome. The process can quite easily lead to the divergence of two populations, even when the form of selection acting on each is initially the same. Although such divergence can occur in response to parallel selection without gene-culture co-evolution (Price 2008), the influence of memes and genes on each other's selective environment, as well as the high mutation rate of memes, creates especially high potential for divergence.

Now, let us add a bit more complexity to the model: the evolution of female preference. Mate preference, like singing itself, is a behavior that has strong fitness consequences and can, therefore, evolve in response to changing conditions (Price 2008). The co-evolving gene-culture system that shapes the male songs of a population also changes the selective environment for female mate preference; the optimal preference function will depend on the distribution of song types in the population and the association of those song types with other traits that influence male survival and reproduction. Thus, in addition to the feedback interactions that occur between genes and memes in relation to song, there is feedback between male song and female preference for song. Complicating things further, there is much evidence that female mate choice in many species is shaped partially by learning: Females sexually imprint on the songs of their fathers, and generalize from that song when considering potential mates (Irwin and Price 1999). Hence, like song, female song preference can be shaped by both genes and learning. Furthermore, sexual imprinting, like any learning-based behavior, can lead to genetic assimilation: Females initially learn to recognize a novel male song variant through sexual imprinting, but this exposes to natural selection any genetic variation in the ability to learn to recognize that novel variant. In this way, female recognition and preference for song can track the changing male song.

These many co-evolutionary interactions, between memes and genes for song, between male songs and female preferences, and between memes and genes for female preferences, as well as all the higher-order interactions between these factors, clearly lead to a highly complex co-evolutionary system, even in the comparatively simple world of bird song. It is clear that the evolutionary pathway of such a system will be highly contingent on stochastic factors such as mutation, and that two populations with identical starting conditions will rapidly diverge. If the two populations then come back into contact, it is possible that male songs and female preferences have diverged to a degree that the two populations do not interbreed. In this case, the process of gene-culture co-evolution has led to complete speciation: the evolution of two species from one.

Although the preceding model was inspired by the greenish warblers, the essential components of the model are likely quite common. Sexual selection for elaborate signals (e.g., song, mating dances) is common throughout the animal world. Learning of mating signals and/or preferences are also common in many groups of animals. Some genetic control of learning is likely universal (how could it not be?). Thus the central dynamic in this model, of sexual selection driving rapid gene-culture co-evolution, could be quite important in the evolution and diversification of much of life.

LESSONS FROM BIRDSONG FOR THE STUDY OF CULTURE IN OTHER ANIMALS

After this close look at the details of bird-song evolution, we can now take a step back and ask about the lessons from bird song for the study of culture in general. One lesson is that culture is most easily studied in taxonomic groups that are amenable to study through a variety of experimental and observational methods. For reasons already described, birds are especially suitable for such study compared to groups (e.g., nonhuman primates) in which it is more difficult to conduct experiments and observational studies because of various ethical and logistical constraints.

Another important lesson is that culture and genes are not competing or opposing influences on the behavior of a species. Rather, memes and genes together comprise a single co-evolving system; "learning" can be thought of as the process by which genes and memes interact to produce the behavior of an individual. This view contrasts with the view common in the literature on culture of primates, that, to demonstrate that behavioral variation is cultural, one must first exclude any possible influence of genetic variation (or ecological variation) on that behavior (the so-called "ethnographic method" mentioned earlier). This view is flawed in two ways: (1) It ignores the fact that genetic evolution (and ecological shifts) can promote the evolution of culture through gene-meme co-evolution, and (2) absence of genetic variation in a sample of genetic markers does not allow one to rule out a role for genetic variation in causing behavior; there could still be some small part of the genome that causes the behavior in question.

Lastly, we can consider these two points in relation to that most interesting of cultural species, humans. For historical and social reasons, there is sometimes a reluctance to take conclusions from the animal behavioral sciences and apply them in the humanities. In particular, there is a reluctance to accept a role for genetics in the evolution of culture, especially those aspects of culture that seem most intellectual, such as language and arts. However, there is, in fact, clear evidence that gene-culture co-evolution does occur in humans. One of the clearest examples is the interaction between the practice of dairy farming and the genetically encoded ability for adult humans to digest lactose (Holden and Mace, 1997; Hollox 2005; Burger et al. 2007). There is evidence that the genetic variants responsible for this ability have undergone strong natural selection during the last 10,000 years, when dairy farming developed in some societies. Thus, a cultural change (the drinking of milk as adults) caused selection on genetic variants that allow the efficient digestion of lactose. Conversely, it is clear that genes for milk tolerance influence culture: The culture of adult milk drinking has not spread easily to parts of the world where the genes for lactose digestion in adulthood are rare.

It is quite likely that such interactions between culture and genes are not limited to such obvious traits as culinary traditions and genes for digestive enzymes. Any behavior that is jointly influenced by learning and genetics must be influenced to some degree by a process of gene-culture co-evolution. The conditions for gene-culture co-evolution are too simple for this not to be the case. Thus, one area of likely progress in the integration of the sciences and the humanities is the increasing application of gene-culture co-evolutionary theory to the full range of human cultural traits.

ACKNOWLEDGEMENTS

I thank Alan Brelsford, Mark Collard, Carol Irwin, Jessica Irwin, Trevor Price, Dolph Schluter, Edward Slingerland, and David Toews for helpful comments and discussion, and Joe Henrich and Ted Slingerland for the invitation to participate in the conference on "Integrating the Sciences and Humanities." I also thank the many colleagues who have assisted with research on greenish warblers, among these; Trevor Price, Jessica Irwin, and Staffan Bensch played especially important roles.

References

Burger, J., M. Kirchner, B. Bramanti, W. Haak, and M.G Thomas. 2007. Absence of the lactase-persistence-associated allele in early Neolithic Europeans. *Proceedings of the National Academy of Sciences of the USA* 104: 3736–3741.

Catchpole, C.K., and P.J.B. Slater. 1995. *Bird Song: Biological Themes and Variations*. Cambridge, UK: Cambridge University Press.

Collins S. 2004. Vocal fighting and flirting: The functions of birdsong. In *Nature's Music: The Science of Birdsong*, eds. P. Marler, and H. Slabbekoorn, 39–79. London: Elsevier Academic Press.

Corbey, R. 2005. *The Metaphysics of Apes: Negotiating the Animal–Human Boundary*. New York: Cambridge University Press.

Dawkins, R. 1976. *The Selfish Gene*. New York: Oxford University Press.

Feldman, M.W., and K.N. Laland. 1996. Gene-culture co-evolutionary theory. *Trends in Ecology and Evolution* 11: 453–457.

Grant, B.R., and P.R. Grant. 1998. Hybridization and speciation in Darwin's finches. In *Endless Forms: Species and Speciation*, eds. D.J. Howard, and S.H. Berlocher, 404–422. Oxford, UK: Oxford University Press.

Holden, C., and R. Mace. 1997. Phylogenetic analysis of the evolution of lactose digestion in adults. *Human Biology* 69: 605–628.

Hollox, E. 2005. Genetics of lactase persistence – fresh lessons in the history of milk drinking. *European Journal of Human Genetics* 13: 267–269.

Irwin, D.E. 2000. Song variation in an avian ring species. *Evolution* 54: 998–1010.

Irwin, D.E., S. Bensch, J.H. Irwin, and T.D. Price. 2005. Speciation by distance in a ring species. *Science* 307: 414–416.

Irwin, D.E., S. Bensch, and T.D. Price. 2001. Speciation in a ring. *Nature* 409: 333–337.

Irwin, D.E., and J.H. Irwin. 2004. Speciation in a ring: The role of song. In *Nature's Music: The Science of Birdsong*, eds. P. Marler, and H. Slabbekoorn, 204. London: Elsevier Academic Press.

Irwin, D.E., and T. Price. 1999. Sexual imprinting, learning and speciation. *Heredity* 82: 347–354.

Irwin, D.E., M.P. Thimgan, and J.H. Irwin. 2008. Call divergence is correlated with geographic and genetic distance in greenish warblers (*Phylloscopus trochiloides*): A strong role for stochasticity in signal evolution? *Journal of Evolutionary Biology* 21: 435–448.

Jarvis, E.D. 2004. "Brains and birdsong." In *Nature's Music: The Science of Birdsong*, eds. P. Marler, and H. Slabbekoorn, 226–271. London: Elsevier Academic Press.

Kroeber, A.L., C. Kluckhohn, W. Untereiner, and A.G. Meyer. 1952. *Culture: A Critical Review of Concepts and Definitions*. Cambridge, MA: Peabody Museum.

Krützen, M., J. Mann, M.R. Heithaus, R.C. Connor, L. Bejder, and W.B. Sherwin. 2005. Cultural transmission of tool use in bottlenose dolphins. *Proceedings of the National Academy of Sciences of the USA* 102: 8939–8943.

Laland, K.N., and V.M. Janik. 2006. The animal cultures debate. *Trends in Ecology and Evolution* 21: 542–547.

Lynch, A., and A.J. Baker. 1993. A population memetics approach to cultural evolution in chaffinch song: Meme diversity within populations. *The American Naturalist* 141: 597 620.

Lynch, A., and A.J. Baker. 1994. A population memetics approach to cultural evolution in chaffinch song: Differentiation among populations. *Evolution* 48: 351–359.

Lycett, S.J., M. Collard, and W.C. McGrew. 2007. Phylogenetic analyses of behavior support existence of culture among wild chimpanzees. *Proceedings of the National Academy of Sciences of the USA* 104: 17588–17592.

Marler, P. 2004. "Science and birdsong: The good old days." In *Nature's Music: The Science of Birdsong*, eds. P. Marler, and H. Slabbekoorn, 1–38. London: Elsevier Academic Press.

Marler, P., and V. Sherman. 1985. Innate differences in singing behavior of sparrows reared in isolation from adult conspecific song. *Animal Behaviour* 33: 57–71.

Marzluff, J.M., and T. Angell. 2007. *In the Company of Crows and Ravens*. New Haven, CT: Yale University Press.

Noad, M.J., D.H. Cato, M.M. Bryden, M-N. Jenner, and K.C.S. Jenner. 2001. Cultural revolution in whale songs. *Nature* 408: 537.

Payne, R.B. 1996. "Song traditions in indigo buntings: Origin, improvisation, dispersal and extinction in cultural evolution." In *Ecology and Evolution of Acoustic Communication in Birds*, eds. D.E. Kroodsma, and E.H. Miller. 198–220. Ithaca, NY: Cornell University Press.

Perry, S., M. Baker, L. Fedigan, J. Gros-Louis, K. Jack, K.C. MacKinnon, J.H. Manson, M. Panger, K. Pyle, and L. Rose. 2003. Social conventions in wild white-faced capuchin monkeys. *Current Anthropology* 44: 241–268.

Price, T.D. 2008. *Speciation in Birds*. Greenwood Village, CO: Roberts Publishers.

Rendell, L., and H. Whitehead. 2001. Culture in whales and dolphins. *Behavioral and Brain Sciences* 24: 309–324.

Thorpe, W.H. 1961. *Bird-Song: The Biology of Vocal Communication and Expression in Birds*. Cambridge, UK: Cambridge University Press.

Ticehurst, C.B. 1938. *A Systematic Review of the Genus* Phylloscopus. New York: Johnson Reprint.

van Schaik, C.P., M. Ancrenaz, G. Borgen, B. Galdikas, C.D. Knott, I. Singleton, A. Suzuki, S.S. Utami, and M. Merrill. 2003. Orangutan cultures and the evolution of material culture. *Science* 299: 102–105.

Waddington, C.H. 1961. Genetic assimilation. *Advances in Genetics* 10: 257–293.

Wake, D.B. 2001. Speciation in the round. *Nature* 409: 299–300.

Whiten, A., J. Goodall, W.C. McGrew, T. Nishida, V. Reynolds, Y. Sugiyama, C.E.G. Tutin, R.W. Wrangham, and C. Boesch. 1999. Cultures in chimpanzees. *Nature* 399: 682–685.

Whiten, A., J. Goodall, W.C. McGrew, T. Nishida, V. Reynolds, Y. Sugiyama, C.E.G. Tutin, R.W. Wrangham, and C. Boesch. 2001. Charting cultural variation in chimpanzees. *Behaviour* 138: 1481–1516.

Yurk, H., L. Barrett-Lennard, J.K.B. Ford, and C.O. Matkin. 2002. Cultural transmission within maternal lineages: Vocal clans in resident killer whales in southern Alaska. *Animal Behaviour* 63: 1103–1119.

9

WHEN DOES PSYCHOLOGY DRIVE CULTURE?

Olivier Morin

Cultural epidemiologists such as Scott Atran, Pascal Boyer, Lawrence Hirschfeld, and Dan Sperber, have developed an ambitious research program that focuses on the role of universal psychological constraints in the evolution of culture (Atran 2003; Boyer 2000; Sperber and Hirschfeld 2004). One of their main hypotheses is that cultural ideas or practices owe most of their success and stability in time and space to universal mechanisms of the human mind. Psychological constraints orient human minds when they learn, teach, remember, choose, endorse or transform all sorts of culturally transmitted information. As a result, cultural forms that fit these constraints tend to stabilize.

This view of culture seems unconvincing to many, perhaps most, anthropologists or social scientists. They are, after all, specialists of human diversity; they do not necessarily see the point of studying universal features of our psychology, that are, by definition, the same in the vast majority of people. Many also doubt the importance of universal psychological features in the cultural decisions of individuals. This makes some sense. We all know that people often endorse an opinion or belief, choose to learn this or that technique, art, or profession, not on the basis of their intrinsic appeal, but because of social pressure, material incentives, and such like. These local, particular constraints are strong. If general psychological constraints play any part at all, they seem to influence culture in a way that is both uniform and weak. When one is in the business of explaining contrasts between individuals or societies, this makes them twice irrelevant.

In this chapter, I want to argue that the impact of universal human psychology on culture is not everywhere the same. It is quite strong when a chain of cultural transmission is fed by a vast number of different individuals, less strong when fewer people are directly involved in feeding the chain (which happens if the chain is short, or long but fed by a small number of individuals). This impact will vary greatly in strength and scope: It is not uniform. It makes sense to take it into account, not only in the search for human universals, but also when trying to explain contrasts between different forms of cultural transmission.

The chapter begins with a short presentation of cultural epidemiology, and presents three cases in which universal cognitive constraints have been claimed to sustain a tradition: the tradition of etiquette rules in Europe, the representations of *adalo* spirits among the Kwaios, and the tradition of games of contamination ("cooties" in the United States) in children of many different countries. We shall look for the circumstances that make it possible for universal psychological constraints to prevail in these three cases. Then we shall see how the chances of success of universally appealing cultural items can be made to vary, by changing the size and shape of cultural transmission networks. In so doing, we can give universal psychological constraints a variable role in driving culture.

1. CULTURAL EPIDEMIOLOGISTS AT WORK

Human minds shape culture in many ways—sometimes by producing it, sometimes by selectively acquiring certain things but not others, and sometimes by acquiring it, transforming it, and diffusing around them modified versions of what they have learnt. True, cultural learners are not always extremely selective. It has been argued that when we have to choose between cultural variants that are roughly indifferent, such as different first names for children or different dog breeds, we do not seem to show any bias whatsoever, except for choosing the variants we are most likely to be exposed to (Bentley et al. 2004). Still, no one claims that this is true of all things cultural. Even when cultural selection is weak or absent, human minds have other ways of shaping their culture: they produce and transform it in a nonrandom way.

Because of that, cultural epidemiologists think they can use psychological theories to make predictions about the fate of culturally transmitted ideas or practices. I will now give a sketch of the way they use psychological hypotheses, typically very general in scope, to explain cultural phenomena. I will describe three typical hypotheses and try to explain why, and in what conditions, they seem to work. I won't examine these hypotheses in an exhaustive way, nor will I defend them against any possible objection, but I will merely highlight their potential interest and limits.

European Etiquette Norms

In one article on the evolution of social norms, Shaun Nichols (2002) makes a prediction concerning the history of European manners. Many etiquette norms (table manners, norms of posture, ways of behaving in polite society) seem arbitrary or even pointless; still, blind conservatism is not the only reason they are preserved. A sizable fraction of them owe their stability and success to the emotions that are elicited when they are broken, or when one imagines that they could be. Nichols believes, along with many psychologists, that some features of disgust ("core disgust") are well preserved across cultural boundaries. It is a well-established finding in psychology, Nichols remarks, that information eliciting strong emotions (disgust being one of them) is much easier to retrieve, especially on the longer term, than more neutral information. This, he speculates, may boost the long-term survival of disgust-eliciting norms, since a norm that stays longer in individual memories is more likely to be enforced and passed on.

He thus predicts that etiquette norms prohibiting actions that activate "core disgust" are more likely than others to be sustained and enforced, and less likely to be displaced. Inspired by Norbert Elias' work on the evolution of manners in Renaissance Europe (Elias 1939/2000), Nichols examined the rules laid down in Erasmus's widely read guide, *On Good Manners for Boys*, and asked two groups of independent coders to state, for each rule (in several representative sections of the book) whether the conduct it prohibited could elicit "core disgust," as defined by a checklist that was given them (first group of coders), and whether it was still parts of the rules of etiquette they were used to (second group of coders). The study found that most etiquette rules prohibiting some core-disgusting behavior made it to our own time, while most of those that did not failed to stay the course. Although Elias argued that the slow rise of "clean" manners in Europe was due to "an expanding threshold of repugnance" (Elias in Nichols 2002: 20), Nichols claims that the "threshold of repugnance" never moved one bit. Instead, etiquette manners slowly rose above the threshold, because human memory and cultural trans-mission promoted cleaner rules.

Games of Contamination Among Children

Children play games of tag almost everywhere, and in several countries and cultures, this game goes along with reference to some disease or pollution that is supposed to be trans-mitted along with the touch. Most of the time, the contagion takes the name of a disease or parasite, real or imaginary—like the *Bokà* (leprosy) in Madagascar (Sibree 1883), the British *Lurgi* (a fictitious disease) (Opie and Opie 1959) and the American "cooties" (a word also meaning lice and associated by many children with plague or leprosy) (Hirschfeld 1997, Samuelson 1980). I heard from several sources that, in the 1980s, the Paris suburbs saw a dreary epidemic of *chat-sida* ("AIDS-tag.") Typically (but not sys-tematically) the contagion is feared well beyond the limits of the associated game of tag. Superstitions and prophylactic techniques to ward it off flourish. Sometimes (but not always) one or a few ill-fated children are said to concentrate all the pollution into them-selves, and they are shunned accordingly. These features recur over and over again, in a stunning variety of cultures, like India or Japan (Hirschfeld 1997; Haidt 2004).

According to cultural epidemiologist Lawrence Hirschfeld (1997), traditions like "coo-ties" are stable and widespread among children because they recruit the same psychological mechanisms that are responsible for race and caste prejudices in adults. In his view, we are endowed with a specific cognitive device that detects social differences—differences in rank or group membership—and construes them as natural, biological properties of persons. Another hypothesis has been proposed by psychologist Jonathan Haidt (2004). He argues that games of contamination and the associated beliefs and practices appeal to a certain aspect of our faculties for moral reasoning. According to Haidt, moral psy-chology shares certain basic mechanisms with an emotion that first evolved for entirely nonmoral reasons: disgust. According to Rozin, Haidt, and McCauley (2000), the most important adaptive function of disgust is to motivate us to avoid contamination by path-ogens and infectious diseases (a hypothesis that explains several features of disgust, including the association principle,[1] the privileged relation between disgust and meat or bodily excretions, etc.).

---

1. The association principle, as applied to disgust, predicts that people will show a disgust reaction toward any object that is linked with a disgusting object by a material association, however remote the association. For instance, people are disgusted by a glass of water in which one has dipped a three-meter length of thread whose other end is dipped in a glass of urine. The association principle extended to moral disgust explains, for example, why many people would refuse to wear Mussolini's sweater, even if it had been washed a hundred times (Rozin and Nemeroff 1990).

They also found that a fraction of our moral psychology makes heavy use of our disgust faculty. As a result, our intuitions on moral and social matters are often intermingled with judgments of disgust and fears of contamination. Contamination games would appeal to such a mix of preoccupations with both sanitary and social "purity." Hirschfeld's theory and Haidt's are both very tentative, and some of their predictions differ. Yet, the fact that "cooties" traditions are found in many different parts of the world, where they appeared in an apparently independent way, makes it plausible to think that these traditions target some important and widespread cluster of dispositions concerning the fear of social and nonsocial contamination.

Spirit Beliefs Among the Kwaio

Among the Kwaio who live in the mountainous center of Malaita Island (Solomon Islands), almost everyone claims to have interactions with ancestral spirits called *adalo* (Keesing 1982, 33–59). They can be met in dreams or prayed and sacrificed to, and divination yields information about their intentions and ways of action—crucial information, since *adalo* are behind many significant events of daily life. When taro crops are bad, when someone falls ill, one will try and find out which *adalo* caused the trouble, and why, for *adalo* do not harm gratuitously: They use their omniscience to prevent, detect, and punish all sorts of misdemeanors (Keesing 1982, 42). Relations with *adalo* are highly strategic because their intentions, however menacing, are seldom obvious. Aside from the way *adalo* get and use strategic information bearing on human perils and rewards, most Kwaio show very little interest in the properties of *adalo*, their nature, or their place in the universe. Ideas become extremely vague when conversation drifts away from immediate strategic interaction with the spirits.

According to Pascal Boyer's interpretation of Roger Keesing's ethnography (Boyer 2001) belief in *adalo* (as happens with many other ghosts, spirits, and ancestors) owes its stability to a universal human propensity to search for intelligent agency. Detecting intentional agents, the theory goes, is a crucial task for us, and evolution has given us a specific psychological faculty for that purpose. Given the importance and complexity of this task, and the costs of failing to detect intentional agency when it occurs, our intention-detection devices tend to get activated a little too readily. However, when they do, we do not simply dismiss the signal as a false alert. Attributing an event to an intentional agent, real or not, authorizes many interesting inferences on strategic matters, like its dispositions toward us, its overall plans, its future actions, etc. The appeal of strategic information, combined with the ease of inferring it, can easily offset skepticism. Everything else being equal, a belief that allows us to make sense of events in terms of intentional agency will benefit from a favorable prejudice. Boyer signals, in support of his interpretation, the fact that it helps explain the way the Kwaio focus on strategic information, and more generally the lacunar character of representations of ghosts and spirits.

2. WHEN DOES CULTURAL EPIDEMIOLOGY WORK?

These three studies are a fairly representative sample. Each one relies on strong, speculative, and debatable psychological hypotheses. However, my point here is not to discuss in detail the merits of their arguments. Instead, I would like to ask a question. Suppose these authors are right, and cultural things like *adalo*, "cooties," or etiquette rules are successful and stable mostly because they appeal to universal properties of the human mind. Are these cases typical of cultural transmission in general? Or must some special conditions be met if we want cultural items to survive by means of their universal psychological effects? I think that "cooties"-lore, etiquette rules, and *adalo* beliefs are indeed transmitted in special conditions—not weird, not uncommon, but special.

Etiquette Norms

What makes cultural transmission special in the case of European norms of etiquette is indeed quite banal: If Nichols was able to measure the differential survival of Erasmus's prescriptions, that was because enough time had passed for many of them to die out. The fate of cultural habits is not frequently measured at an interval of several centuries. Had Nichols carried out his experiment with European students a few years after Erasmus's book was published, the results would probably have been quite different. In particular, the impact of core disgust might have been harder to detect, as Erasmus's authority would have been weightier. After all, *On Good Manners for Boys* was not just any manners guide. The Renaissance equivalent of a best-seller (130 editions, translated in four languages soon after its publication), it was written by one of Europe's first intellectual superstars. That is a triviality but, I hope to show, one with many consequences: selection in the form of differential survival takes some time. On shorter timescales, the effect of people better remembering and transmitting disgust-related rules may be too noisy to be detectable. It may also be blurred by local accidents, like the influence of Erasmus.

Contamination Games

The traditions around games of contamination also depend on a special network of cultural transmission. Everyone who has written on the topic agrees that "cooties"-lore and other contamination traditions are passed on from child to child, with little or no adult intermediation. They form part of children's very own peer-culture (Hirschfeld 1997; Opie and Opie 1959). Only one out of Sue Samuelson's forty-five informants had not first heard of "cooties" through a peer (Samuelson 1980). Being handed down from child to child is a permanent challenge to the stability of children's peer cultures. Consider a population of children between six and twelve years old—a group of comrades at a primary school for instance. Let us define their peer-culture as including everything that is passed on between the children of the group, while they are between six and twelve years old. In this population, around one sixth of the children will be replaced every year. Every year the eldest children—probably the most knowledgeable about their peer-culture—will leave childhood and be replaced by a contingent of younger children. Six years later, there may not be a single child in the group to remember the group of six years ago.

This rate of population renewal is much higher than that of most human societies. It means that, if a tradition has lasted much longer than 60 years (as have many rhymes and games in children's peer cultures, including "cooties"-lore—Samuelson 1980, Opie and

Opie 1959) then, in our population of children, it has risked complete extinction 10 times at the very least. Ten times, the population has been entirely renewed, with the risk that the new generation might not have come into contact with the tradition. In a regular human society, where people of 50 can teach songs and games to children of 5, a tradition can last 60 years and risk extinction only once. A fifty-year old woman can ensure a song a decent life expectancy by teaching it once to her son; in children's peer cultures that is not possible. If a child manages to transmit a song to her peers, she will buy it only a few years of survival. The vast majority of the participants in the peer culture are beyond her reach: they are not yet born. When these new participants arrive in the culture, current children will not be children anymore. In these conditions, children's peer-transmitted games and rhymes have to be intuitive and attractive: in constantly shifting populations, their hyper-frequent transmission is a matter of survival. One might speculate that this is the reason why the products of children's peer cultures are so catchy: Boring rhymes simply died out.

The comparative analysis of children's and adults' oral traditions by cognitive scientist David Rubin (1995) shows that memorization and transmission in children's peer culture obey particular constraints. I have argued elsewhere (Morin, 2010) that hyper-frequent transmission can explain other unusual properties of children's traditions, including their uniformity and the surprisingly high life expectancy enjoyed by some of them.

Spirit Beliefs

The tradition surrounding *adalo* among the Kwaio is the trickiest case of all, because it is actually not that stable or successful. By Keesing's estimate, belief in ancestor spirits has been alive on Malaita for two millenia at least (Keesing 1982, 217–218). Yet it is no longer dominant. Traditionalist Kwaio are a small minority today; most islanders, many Kwaio included, have embraced Christianity and abandonned their small mountain set-tlements for larger settlements on the coast, dominated by the influence of Christian missionaries. Needless to say, cultural transmission on the coast favors a quite different kind of religion.

On the face of it, the Christian God does not seem more appealing to our intention-detectors than *adalo*. If anything, *adalo* have the upper hand: as we saw, they are almost stripped off of any feature that isn't related to their being intentional agents and ances-tors. The Christian God does share some of the characteristics that make *adalos* inter-esting for an intention-detector, mostly concerned with strategic information. He, too, is an omniscient and vengeful spirit who watches upon us, but some other features of the Christian God that come from a very local and particular tradition are mind-boggling. For example, according to some missionaries, He is three things and one thing at the same time. It is difficult to construe that feature as attractive information for an intention detector to feed on.

However, the missionaries have all means at hand to propagate a complex and occa-sionally puzzling creed. The word they are spreading can afford to be unintuitive in some respects, because its stability does not depend so much on its being extremely easy to teach, store, or recall: Christians have special, standardized institutions and technologies to do the teaching, the storing, and the recalling. They do not have to rely on the mind of the faithful alone. In addition, the missionaries along the coast have spiritual authority over many people, whom they can teach by the hundreds; they can afford to lose some of them.

No such luck for beliefs about *adalo*; their transmission took place in conditions where nothing could make up for a lack of intuitive appeal. They survived the passing of generations for millenia, in a very sparse population, living in tiny, scattered settlements in the most rugged and mountainous sector of Malaita (Keesing 1982, 9–10 and 13). Transmission across space must have been difficult. So must have been transmission across generations. Here, Kwaio culture was confronted with the problem of cultural transmission across population renewals, with an additional complication: demographic scarcity. When groups are so tiny and scattered, some of them at some moments in time will lack entire demographic categories, like middle-aged women or old men (Keesing 1982, 17). As a result, some cultural forms that have to be passed on from one demographic category to another (e.g., elderly grandmother to adolescent daughter), because of some taboo, ritual necessity, or special interest in the other category, cannot be transmitted adequately. A fair proportion of Kwaio religious practices are subject to a transmission restriction of this kind (Keesing 1982, 198–202). The problem is all the more acute because, as Kwaio traditionalists know too well (Keesing 1982, 85 and 90), only a few members of a given demographic category will make good learners: not all youngsters with the appropriate background also happen to have the skill and dedication it takes to master the most complex forms of lore. Many Kwaio cultural practices must have been swallowed by such a demographic glut before they could reach the Kwaio of today. In these conditions, Kwaio traditions have had to travel lightly and efficiently; for things like belief in *adalo*, that means being reduced to their barest and most intuitive components.

Cultural Transmission Chains

What do our examples have in common? Etiquette norms, contamination games, and traditions concerning *adalo* are all passed on through cultural transmission chains: chains linking together different individuals, each of whom received a cultural item from someone else in the chain, and possibly passed it on to someone else.

As cultural transmission chains, they have two special features in common. First, the individuals included in the transmission chain (all individuals reached by the tradition across space, or across time and generations) are numerous, in absolute terms; these chains are *long*. Second, no individual in the chain directly interacts with more than a small number of individuals (I do not mean absolutely small, but small compared to the overall number of individuals in the chain). As a result, no member of the chain can have more than a local impact upon cultural transmission, and the chain has to be fed by many people. Broadcasting is not possible on the scale of the whole chain; these chains are *narrow*.[2]

2. Narrow transmission chains are not social networks with very low connectivity. When long, transmission chains may span many different societies and generations; some of these social groups will have high average connectivity, but not others. A transmission chain is not a society or several connected societies. It is the trajectory of an idea. A chain is narrow when the minimal number of people that one

I think that there is a causal link between the length and narrowness of these chains and the fact that the traditions they carry appeal to universal features of the human mind. This suggests a conjecture: when transmission chains are shorter or broader, what will be passed down the chain depends on the choices of a smaller number of individuals. The smaller their number, the more likely they are to be guided by idiosyncratic or local preferences. But when transmission chains are longer and narrower, many more individuals get to weigh in on the selection of traditions. Idiosyncratic or local preferences, being variable and inconsistent, will tend to cancel one another out, and only universally shared preferences will have a consistent effect on the selection of cultural items.

Therefore, if universal psychological factors exert some pressure over the selection of traditions by individuals, then this pressure varies, depending on the length and narrowness of transmission chains. In what follows, this conjecture will be fleshed out.

4. LONG AND NARROW CHAINS OF CULTURAL TRANSMISSION

Universal psychological features are abstractions; no one is a universal human being. Many of our mental capacities and motivations are peculiar to ourselves: they are idiosyncratic, like my taste for whisky mixed with vinegar. Others, like the admiration many Republicans feel for Sarah Palin, are restricted to the members of a social group. These may be acquired culturally or not: Sarah Palin shares a taste for moose meat with French Canadians, because moose meat is easily accessible in their common environment. All these ideas and motivations can have an important impact on the cultural success of many things, like Balsamic-Whisky cocktails, moose-hunting techniques, or the endorsement of drilling projects in Alaska. I do not intend to downplay the importance of these factors in determining individual cultural behaviors. I actually think that they are typically much stronger—that is to say, much better predictors of an individual's cultural behavior—than universal psychological constraints.

However, they lack two important features that universal psychological factors, however weak, have in common: consistency and reliability. Things like the bias for detecting intentions hypothesized by Pascal Boyer in his explanation of *adalo* beliefs, or the "core disgust" emotional faculty used by Shaun Nichols, are supposed to be present in almost everyone (reliability) and, as far as their effects on cultural transmission are concerned, to weigh in the same direction in almost everyone (consistency). In contrast, one's admiration for Sarah Palin will influence the way one feels about drilling for oil in Alaska, but

has to go through, when one wants to spread an idea far and wide in space and time, is large, because no individual, well-connected though he or she could be, can directly reach most of the population of the chain, not necessarily for a lack of friends, but also because most of the population lives in societies beyond her reach, or in times beyond her own. A chain can be narrow when everyone's connectivity is very high on average, as long as no single individual is so highly connected as to be able to reach most people in the chain directly. If, on the other hand, one single individual can reach everyone in the chain, the chain becomes broad even if average connectivity is very low.

not in a reliable way (not everyone admires Sarah Palin) nor necessarily in a consistent way (Sarah Palin might change her mind about drilling in Alaska, which would probably change the position of her admirers). Without some consistency and reliability, even strong preferences cannot have perceptible effects on the scale of long, narrow chains of cultural transmission. On the contrary, when a factor contributes to the success of a tradition in a consistent and reliable way, its contribution does not need to be strong; it will prevail in long, narrow cultural chains—chains of cultural transmission that include many people, none of these people passing on the tradition to more than a small proportion of other people in the chain.

The local or idiosyncratic factors that weigh upon individual cultural choices can have a huge influence on a cultural transmission chain, if it is short (i.e., if it includes only a small number of individuals[3]). This involves nothing more complicated than the Central Limit theorem of probability theory. If many people make a choice, and there is one reliable factor that consistently influences their choice in a given direction, then the more people you observe, the more chances you have that their cumulated decisions will reflect that factor: noisy factors will average out. On the other hand, when there are few people to observe, noise (that is to say, unreliable factors weighing in inconsistent directions) is more likely to prevail.

When the chain is long, local factors can still have an important effect on it, but then the chain has to be *broad* (as opposed to *narrow*). The chain must allow one or a few individuals to broadcast their cultural preferences to an important proportion of members of the chain. These individuals being so few, their choices can reflect their local preferences as readily as universal ones. Broadness does not erase the influence of universal psychological factors in the choices of receivers, but it can skew it in two ways. First, the item chosen by the broadcasting minority is much more accessible to cultural learners than other (possibly more attractive) items. Second, the prestige and influence of the broadcasting minority can also orient the choices of cultural learners. That is how broadcasting, if carried on at the scale of a long transmission chain, can produce discrepancies between the success of a cultural item and its appeal to human psychology. We saw an example of that with the Kwaio: the cultural transmission chain of Christianity is much longer than that of *adalo* tradition (it includes many more people); still, relatively unintuitive beliefs like the Trinity can stay the course in that chain, because they can be imposed through the use of institutional and technological methods of broadcasting.

Culture is not all about local influences (like the power of prestigious leaders) and idiosyncrasies, nor is it just a matter of following universal psychological tendencies. Obviously, it is both—and it can be more of the first or more of the second, depending

---

3. Long transmission chains are not long relative to the number of people in a given social group. They are long in absolute terms: they include many, many people, from many different times and many different social groups. If a group of 25 people all share the same cultural habit, and nobody else does, then the cultural transmission of that habit does not follow a long chain. It comprises 100 percent of a small group, but it does not extend in time to further or previous generations, and spans no other group. As a result, the cultural habit invented and maintained by these 25 persons are more likely to reflect their local and peculiar preferences than general features of the human mind.

on the type of transmission chain you consider, and the scale at which you consider it. Suppose you want to cause a very long bridge to tumble down. Engineers say that there are two ways of doing so, one of them more cost effective than the other. You can keep hitting the bridge with demolition engines at various points, without planning anything about the direction, location, and pace of the shocks. Or you can apply a series of small shocks that will hit the bridge consistently, in the same direction, at a regular pace, and then wait for a wave of resonance to dislocate the bridge. That, of course, is the cost-effective way of destroying the bridge on all its length. But suppose you are interested merely in tearing down one short segment; in that case, the quick and dirty method of hitting it strongly at random might be just as efficient. It is all a question of scale. Depending on the scale, local influences will be magnified or blunted. Let us see one example of this.

At the end of the seventeenth century, the parish of Warbleton (Sussex, England) was hit by a strange new wave of Christian names (Fisher 1989, 96–97). The local Elizabeths, Marys, and Abigails started to beget children with such names as *Fight-the-Good-Fight-of-Faith White*, *Kill-Sin Pemble*, *Humiliation Scratcher*, or *Mortifie Higgs*. From 1570 to 1630, 43 percent of Warbleton newborns received one of these so-called hortatory names. Needless to say, the fad had religious origins. Hortatory names had long been a Puritan specialty, in Sussex and elsewhere (witness Harvard's Increase Mather). In Warbleton, this tradition was upheld with particular intensity by the local minister, Thomas Hely, whose four children were christened *Much-Mercye*, *Sin-denie*, *Increased*, and *Fear-not* (Caplan 1965). Obedience to religious standards conspired with Hely's authority to make hortatory names a must-have.

However, the Warbleton fad was atypical, even by Sussex standards. In East Anglia, less than four percent of Puritan children were given hortatory names. They were no more successful in Massachussets, Increase Mather notwithstanding. They would probably have been if more Puritans from Sussex had made the trip to New England, but very few did, whereas East Anglians emigrated *en masse*.

There probably were dozens of ministers like Thomas Hely across Puritan England and America, but their influence covered only a tiny portion of a vast cultural transmission chain. Hortatory names could not afford to skip a single step in that chain: they were vulnerable to cultural sampling accidents. Such an accident happened when Sussex Puritans decided to stay in England, while East Anglia opted for emigration. The Thomas Helys of that time also failed because, for every Thomas Hely who rooted for hortatory names, there was another preacher, elsewhere, who could argue against them. The influence of ministers reflected variable religious and onomastic preferences that came and went in their own cycles of fashion. As far as hortatory names were concerned, these preferences pulled the faithful in variable, inconsistent directions. Their cumulated effect on the overall success of hortatory names amounted to little more than noise.

As Fly-Fornication Bull from Sussex discovered, to her discontent, when she was surprised in a compromising position with her neighbor, one Goodman Woodman (Fisher 1989, 97), hortatory names are vulnerable to ridicule. Many, like *Fight-the-Good-Fight-of-Faith*, are unwieldy. Most do not carry information about the sex of their bearer. These are reliable handicaps: they do not depend upon religious fads or the decision of influent preachers. In long chains of cultural transmission, they outweigh such influences quite easily; large scales average out the effect of local preferences and express reliable and consistent factors. Had the chain of cultural transmission been shorter, or had Thomas Hely found a way of influencing many more people, these handicaps could have been suppressed—as they were in Warbleton from 1570 to 1630.

5. HOW LONG AND NARROW CAN CULTURAL TRANSMISSION GET?

These considerations might seem quite trivial. Yet their potential impact on theories of cultural evolution is less trivial. Are humans so fascinated by the prestige of their leaders that they routinely and blindly endorse norms and habits under their influence, even if these fly in the face of basic human motivations (like our desire for survival and the care of our interests)? If so, how does the influence of leaders propagate through time? Are traditions stable enough, and populations varied enough, for the pressure of cognitive constraints to be felt? In order to answer this kind of question, we would need to know a lot about the shape and length of the communication networks that allow culture to spread. How long and narrow, in general, can we expect cultural transmission chains to be? The question is far too general to admit of anything but vague answers, vulnerable to many qualifications. Still, in this last section, I want to take a shot at it. My conclusions will be, first, that we are very bad at assessing the length of transmission chains, and second, that when we can be sure that a transmission chain is long, then, given certain conditions, we can often assume that it is also narrow.

5.1. How Long?

There are unambiguous proofs (from folklore, archeology, prehistory, comparative anthropology, cultural history, etc.) that long chains of cultural transmission exist—and we have seen several examples of this already. Yet, in many cases, the information that we can acquire on the extension in space and time of a given cultural tradition is surprisingly scarce. The very existence of cultural continuities in a society can be hotly debated. Among historians, it has become a commonplace (since Hobsbawm and Ranger 1992) that the traditionality of most traditional practices is a pure invention. This is an exaggeration, but even so, its popularity shows how weak and defenseless claims of cultural continuity can sometimes be in the face of informed criticism. Most of the time, when we claim that something is culturally transmitted, we would be unable to make but the fuzziest estimations concerning its distribution. How long has it been around? Is it shared by everyone in this society? In other societies? If not, who has it? We are often still without reliable means of answering these basic questions.

Today, the public is still persuaded that anthropologists study traditional societies, coherent cultures whose ways have been passed on from generation to generation. However, many anthropologists have all but given up on this hypothesis. For a start, many fieldworkers are simply unable to assess cultural continuity in the societies that they study. As Pascal Boyer (1988, 13) puts it, "ethnographers never observe traditions." Rather, they try and reconstruct them from multiple observations, relying on others to check the extension of the tradition in time and space. In many cases, however, cultural continuity just isn't there to be found. One ethnographer finds that the most highly regarded Big Man on the island does not know the basic rites of a crucial potlach ceremony, and begins to suspect that his own expertise in the local traditions goes well beyond that of his informants (Hocart 1927). Epics taken to epitomize an ancestral tradition turn out to be mostly improvised, with very little in the way of a common pattern (Boyer 1988). Bible students in a Pentecostal Church give stunningly variable accounts of classic tenets of their faith (such as the commandment "Thou shalt not kill" or the Golden Rule—Atran 2001). Such cases can be multiplied. Robert Aunger (1999) draws a convincing list of all the problems that plague claims of cultural consensus for a belief or a practice. The problem is not so much that cultural continuity is often weaker than expected; sometimes, we just don't know how to look for it.

One way of studying cultural transmission in a rigorous, quantitative way seems quite promising. The idea is to provoke chains of cultural transmission artificially, in a lab, with humans or other animals (Mesoudi and Whiten 2008; Whiten and Mesoudi 2008). There is much to learn from these experiments, but the transmission chains that they study are all extremely short (hardly ever more than 100 links). As a result, they tend to exaggerate the impact of transient, local influences on cultural transmission. For example, they overestimate the importance of our tendency to imitate arbitrary behaviors. Many such transmission chain experiments show that functionally indifferent behaviors—for example, opening a box in one way rather than another that is equally efficient—will be reproduced for several cultural generations. A behavior without any intrinsic interest is thus kept alive by arbitrary imitation alone. All these experiments also show that indifferent behaviors disappear very rapidly; very few last more than a dozen transmission episodes. This is true even when conformity is extremely high, with more than 90 percent of individuals imitating the indifferent behavior (Claidière and Sperber, 2010). On the scale of real cultures outside the lab, these effects would be less than weak; they would not be visible at all.

5.2. How Narrow?

There is a link between the extension of a transmission chain in time and space, and its narrowness. Typically, when a chain extends in time and space, most of the individuals the chain includes will drift out of reach of others in the chain. We saw that happen in most of our examples. In the case of *adalo*, demographic scarcity, geographical scattering, and the extension of the chain in time all concur to prevent religious broadcasting. In children's peer cultures, demographic distance is to blame for narrowness; a child does not have access to most other children in the peer-culture, because most of them are not born or are not children anymore.

So, are long cultural chains necessarily narrow? No. Members of long chains are not necessarily inaccessible to one another, because long cultural chains do not necessarily have vast extensions in time or space. Long cultural chains are just chains that include many people. The relation between their length and their extension in time and space is not straightforward. Imagine an archeologist deciphering a secret esoteric prayer written by a priest on the sarcophagus of a Pharaoh; this gives you a cultural transmission chain spanning several millenia, and includes only two individuals. Today, several technologies allow one individual to get direct access to a huge variety of people, scattered in space or time. These chains are long and broad.

Still, the techniques that allow us to communicate across long distances in time (archeological investigations, writing, institutions like libraries, monuments, etc.) and space (regular and extensive travel to densely populated places, institutions for scientific or religious propagation, mass-reproduced writing, TV, etc.) are all quite recent in human evolution, and their influence can be ruled out in many cases. In many societies, there is simply no way for one individual to visit a vast number of people across distances of centuries and hundreds of kilometers. As a result, the proportion of individuals that each person in the chain can reach directly rapidly reaches a ceiling. A quick evolution toward "narrowcasting" is unavoidable when a transmission chain reaches a certain length.

In even more cases, heavy broadcasting will be present, but it will not be sufficient for some individuals to make contact with most participants in the chain. With all his prestige, his connections, and the diffusive power of the printing press, Erasmus's influence on European manners got diluted with time. This puts a limit on models of cultural diffusion that stress the impact of well-connected or prestigious individuals, imitated by their followers, for cultural transmission. Such individuals no doubt exist and, on a short timescale, they are indeed influential. But here is the dilemma: the ideas that these individuals propagate owe their success either to their intrinsic interest or to the prestige of the well connected. If their success is explained by their intrinsic properties, they will no doubt enjoy a competitive advantage, with a little help from their prestigious propagandist, in longer transmission chains. In that case, leader influence can only enhance the success that the idea would have enjoyed anyway, because of its intrinsic interest. On the other hand, if it is entirely arbitrary and explained by leader influence alone, then it will not survive through a long transmission chain, unless that chain is very broad. One might answer that social groups can conserve local arbitrary traditions for quite a long time, for instance as a result of conformism. But long chains of cultural transmission typically span several societies (not only for technologies, but also for major political, legal, and religious innovations). Local conservation of arbitrary traditions, since it is arbitrary, will differ for each society, and hence be averaged out as the chain grows long (if it is also narrow enough for each society to feed the chain).

All in all, the local impact of social influences, spectacular as it may seem when short scales are observed, is not necessarily scalable at the level of long diffusion chains. On other scales, models stressing local social influences may be more appropriate than models based on psychological hypotheses.

6. LONG AND NARROW CHAINS AS WINDOWS TO THE HUMAN MIND

Cultural learners are choosy. They don't learn, adopt, endorse, or produce cultural ideas at random, nor is their choice driven by deference or conformity alone. Among the factors that determine their choices, some are idiosyncratic, some are shared with others, and some are as good as universal. Cultural epidemiologists are interested in the mental mechanisms that consistently orient cultural choices in roughly everyone. However, being cognitively attractive does not, by itself, make a cultural item successful. For that to happen, culture must be able to travel long, narrow chains of cultural transmission.

When such chains can be observed to work, they teach us a lot about the human mind in general. Think of the population of American students tested in an average psychological experiment: so few people, so uniform, so similar from one experiment to the other, so far removed from the rest of humanity in so many respects (Henrich et al. 2009). Now consider all the individuals feeding a long and narrow cultural transmission chain: so many people, from so many times and places, from so many stages of life and situations—so representative of a sample of mankind! When an idea travels through these thousands of different heads, it passes through millions of psychological filters, all different, yet with a small cluster of features in common. Along the chain, idiosyncratic and local features all pull in different, inconsistent directions; their effects will be averaged as the chain grows longer. On the other hand, reliable and consistent features will show clearly through the chain, and idiosyncratic features will be washed out. Culture transmitted in this way will bear the mark of general structures of the human mind: Psychology drives culture, when culture travels long and narrow chains. However, not all cultural things come from such chains, and we cannot treat culture as a mere reflection of the human mind. This is why we need to combine predictions derived from psychology with insights derived from the social sciences and the humanities.

References

Atran, S. 2001. The trouble with memes: Inference versus imitation in cultural creation. *Human Nature* 124: 351–381.

Atran, S. 2003. Théorie cognitive de la culture. Une alternative évolutionniste à la sociobiologie et à la sélection collective. *L'Homme* 166: 107–144.

Aunger, R. 1999. Against idealism/contra consensus. *Current Anthropology* 40: 93–115.

Bentley, R.A., M.W. Hahn, and S.J. Shennan 2004. Random drift and culture change. *Proceedings of the Royal Society B: Biological Sciences* 271: 1443–1450.

Bentley R.A., C.P. Lipo, H.A. Herzog, and M.W. Hahn. 2007. Regular rates of popular culture change reflect random copying. *Evolution and Human Behavior* 28: 151–158.

Boyer, P. 1988. *Barricades Mystérieuses et Pièges à Pensée: Introduction à l'Analyse des épopées Fang*. Paris: Société d'ethnologie.

Boyer, P. 2000. Evolutionary psychology and cultural transmission. *American Behavioral Scientist* 43: 987–1000.

Boyer, P. 2001. *Religion Explained: The Evolutionary Origins of Religious Thought*. New York: Basic Books.

Caplan, N. 1965. Puritan names and the roots of nonconformity. *Transactions of the Congregational Historical Society* 20(1): 19–45.

Claidière, N., and D. Sperber. 2010. Imitation explains the propagation, not the stability of animal culture. *Proceedings of the Royal Society B: Biological Sciences* 277: 651–659.

Elias, N. 1939/2000. *The Civilizing Process, Vol. I. The History of Manners*. Oxford: Blackwell.

Fisher, D.H. 1989. *Albion's Seed: Four British Folkways in America*. Oxford UK: Oxford University Press.

Haidt J. 2004. The emotional dog gets mistaken for a possum. *Review of General Psychology* 84: 283–290.

Henrich, J., S.J. Heine, and A. Norenzayan. 2010. The weirdest people in the world. *Behavioral and Brain Sciences* 33: 61–135.

Hirschfeld, L. 1997. Why don't anthropologists like children? *American Anthropologist* 1042: 611–627.

Hocart, A.M. 1927. Are savages custom-bound? *Man* 27: 220–221.

Hobsbawm, E., and T. Ranger, eds. 1992. *The Invention of Tradition.* Cambridge, UK: Cambridge University Press.

Keesing, R. 1982. *Kwaio Religion: The Living and the Dead in a Solomon Islands Society.* New York: Columbia University Press.

Mesoudi, A., and A. Whiten. 2008. The multiple roles of cultural transmission experiments in understanding human cultural evolution. *Philosophical Transaction of the Royal Society B: Biological Sciences* 363: 3489–3501.

Morin, O. (2010) Pourquoi les enfants ont-ils des traditions? *Terrain* 55, 10–27.

Nichols, S. 2002. On the genealogy of norms: A case for the role of emotion in cultural evolution. *Philosophy of Science* 692: 234–255.

Opie, I., and P. Opie. 1959. *The Lore and Language of Schoolchildren.* Oxford, UK: Oxford University Press.

Rozin P., J. Haidt, and C.R. McCauley. 2000. Disgust. In *Handbook of Emotions,* second edition, eds. M. Lewis, and J. M. Haviland-Jones, 637–653. New York: Guilford Press.

Rozin, P., and C.J. Nemeroff. 1990. The laws of sympathetic magic: A psychological analysis of similarity and contagion. In *Cultural Psychology: Essays on Comparative Human Development,* eds. J. Stigler, G. Herdt, and R.A. Shweder, 205–232. Cambridge, UK: Cambridge University Press.

Rubin, D. 1995. *Memory in Oral Traditions: The Cognitive Psychology of Epics, Ballads and Counting-out Rhymes.* Oxford, UK: Oxford University Press.

Samuelson, S. 1980. The cooties complex. *Western Folklore* 363: 198–210.

Sibree, J. 1883. The oratory, songs, folktales and legend of the Malagasy. *Folk-Lore Journal* 1: 97.

Sperber, D., and L. Hirschfeld. 2004. The cognitive foundations of cultural stability and diversity. *Trends in Cognitive Sciences* 81: 40–46.

Sperber, D. 1996. *Explaining Culture: A Naturalistic Approach.* Oxford, UK: Blackwell.

Whiten A., and A. Mesoudi. 2008. Establishing an experimental science of culture: Animal social diffusion experiments. *Philosophical Transactions of the Royal Society B: Biological Sciences* 363: 3477–3488.

10

QUANTIFYING THE IMPORTANCE OF MOTIFS ON ATTIC FIGURE-PAINTED POTTERY

Peter Schauer

1. INTRODUCTION

Quantitative approaches have never been popular in studies of "artistic" cultural data. Nowhere has this been more true than in Greek figure-painted pottery, produced in Athens from 650 to 300 BC.

In my previous research, I explored whether the frequency and diversity of motifs on figure-painted pottery could be explained as having been the result of unbiased copying. The results of this work showed that, in most cases, the diversity and turnover rate of motifs did not deviate from the predictions of the neutral model for each sample. Although an interesting test of the methodology of applying the neutral model to cultural data, it was difficult to relate these results to previous literature on Athenian figure-painted pottery, due to the terms of reference being very different. This research considered entire samples of motifs on thousands of pots, whereas figure-painted-pottery scholars generally consider single motifs, single pots, or very small groups of pots. The population-level view, which might consider hundreds or thousands of pots in a single analysis, has hitherto been absent.

In the examples that follow, I will demonstrate that by simply quantifying the frequencies of the variants under examination, we can assess existing scholarly claims about the importance of some motifs from a new standpoint as well as make new observations.

2. DATA

This research is based on the works of Beazley, as published in the Attic black-figure vase painters (*ABV*) (Beazley 1956), Attic red-figure vase painters (*ARV*) (Beazley 1963) and *Paralipomena* (Beazley 1971). Beazley's project was to attribute as many Attic vases (produced between 650 and 300 BC) as possible to particular painters or groups of painters. The purpose of this work was to identify lineages and lines of influence between painters, using his own connoisseurial experience as the primary tool. Beazley's works describe "about two-thirds of all known Attic vases" (Stewart 1995: 87). Each description includes key details, including attribution, technique, probable manufacture date, provenance (where known) and description of the figures painted on the surface of the pot. Within these descriptions are named mythological figures, which form the basis of my research.

In 1979, the Beazley archive began to computerize its records of figure-painted pottery. This has been an ongoing process, and has, over time, expanded to include not only Beazley's original works, but also a vast number of additional published pots. At present, the database contains 75,451 entries of the fabric type "Athenian," though around half of these are either fragments or are incomplete, and so have not been included in this analysis.

The remaining data required extensive cleaning and categorization to prepare it for analysis. Due to limitations of space, the procedures will not be described in detail here, but the key steps were to capture data from the online Beazley archive, then clean it to remove any errors introduced by the capture process, then turn the cleaned captured data into consistently spaced fields that could then be entered into a new database. When this stage was complete the data then required extensive cleaning because of internal errors, most of which were the result of the long history of the database, with numerous hands entering data over many years according to different operating guidelines.

The final database contained 41,821 rows of data, with each row describing a single pot. Columns include the following: id (Beazley id number) fabric (always Athenian), technique, sub-technique, shape record, provenance, start date, end date, inscription type, inscription, attribution type, artist, scholar (who made the attribution or description), decorated area and decoration. Using standard SQL syntax, it is possible to build up highly complex queries, such that individual date categories and motifs can be quantified within any defined category.

The present example makes use of date and motif only. Dates are treated as categories rather than as absolute fixed dates, due to the structure of the data source. In the Beazley archive, all dates are presented as overlapping 50-year periods. There are 10 date categories in all, divided into 50-year groupings from 650 BC to 300 BC. The last set, 400 to 300 BC, is a 100-year group rather than 50 years, because this period represents the end of figure-painted pottery production and the dating is less precise. In my database, 39,056 pots fit into one of these ten categories.

Motif is defined as the particular mythological figure present in the decoration on each pot. The identifications of these figures were done by Beazley and other scholars, based on their own research. In some cases, mythological figures can be identified by adjacent painted inscriptions; in other cases, the context of the scene or the attributes of the figure indicate who the painter intended them to be. Because there is no way to check the identifications made in descriptions without personally researching each of the thousands of pots, users of the Beazley data must accept them at face value. From the description field, I produced a list of 2,714 individual descriptive terms, which, through further sorting and research on each term, produced a list of 665 individual mythological figures.

For the present discussion, I will describe the frequency of only a few of these figures. In these discussions, I ask simply whether the popularity of certain motifs is supported by their frequency in the Beazley data. I will also highlight a motif whose popularity is unambiguous in the data but that has yet to receive scholarly attention in this context. The goal of this work is not to undermine existing assumptions about the importance of these motifs, but rather to show how discussions of popularity in the context of motif frequencies are challenged or enhanced through simple quantification.

3. QUANTIFICATION EXAMPLES

Boreas and Pan

The first question addresses whether the appearance of a new motif reported to be significant in the literature can be detected in the data. For this analysis, I will use Webster's discussion of Boreas (Webster 1972: 254–255). Webster states that Boreas was summoned to damage the Persian fleet in 480 BC before the battle of Artemision and that the first appearance of Boreas on figure-painted pottery comes soon after this. Webster goes on to state that there are "no less than 35 Boreas scenes by early classical painters and 6 by classical painters." In the data, appearances of Boreas are distributed as shown in Table 1, for all shapes and all techniques.

The total of 39 is slightly less than the total of 43 given by Webster and the first appearance is in 575 to 525 BC, rather than after 480 BC, but this is only one depiction. Otherwise, the data agree with Webster's description of trends in the popularity of Boreas, but only in terms of absolute numbers and the time of their appearance. When we consider the proportion of all motifs made up by Boreas, then the data are a poorer fit to Webster's statements.

The first problem is that, although there is a rise from 0 to 19 depictions of Boreas between 525–475 and 500–450 BC, a researcher working only from the data might not know that Boreas was a motif worth investigating individually. Boreas is not one of the more popular motifs overall. If all the 665 mythological figures in the study are ranked by their total number of appearances across all periods, techniques and shapes, then Boreas is eightieth, equal with Hektor. In 500–450 BC the 19 appearances of Boreas make up 0.47 percent of the total motifs observed for that period, which places him thirty-ninth for that period, so even his grand appearance is somewhat muted. It is only when we compare all motifs that appeared in 500–450 BC but did not appear in the previous time step, 525–475 BC, that we see that Boreas gains the biggest share of any new motif for that period (table 2 below).

Indeed, as Table 3 shows, when Boreas first appears, his proportion of representations is higher proportion than any new motif since Theseus. However, the proportion made up by Boreas, along with all new entries for the period 500 to 450 BC shown in Table 2, is dwarfed by the shares of Satyrs, Maenads, Warriors, Dionysos, Athletes and Nike, each of which make up more than 5 percent of the total individually.

Table 1. Boreas: Number of Appearances on All Shapes and in All Techniques

Boreas	625–575	600–550	575–525	550–500	525–475	500–450	475–425	450–400	425–375	400–300	Sum of all years
Number	0	0	1	0	0	19	14	2	1	2	39
Proportion	0	0	0.05%	0	0	0.47%	0.36%	0.09%	0.12%	0.08%	0.11%

Table 2. Proportion of All Motifs Made Up by Motifs That First Appeared in 500 to 450 BC

	525–475	500–450	475–425	450–400	425–375	400–300	Sum of all years
Boreas	0	0.47%	0.36%	0.09%	0.12%	0.08%	0.11%
Oreithyia	0	0.39%	0.38%	0.09%	0.12%	0.04%	0.10%
Orpheus	0	0.34%	0.38%	0.33%	0.25%	0	0.12%
Erotes	0	0.15%	0.05%	2.48%	1.73%	3.62%	0.48%
Danae	0	0.12%	0.08%	0.09%	0	0	0.03%
Perithoos	0	0.10%	0.13%	0.19%	0.37%	0	0.06%

Table 3. Highest Proportion Made Up by Motifs That Did Not Appear in the Previous Time Step. 425 –375 BC and 400–300 BC Are Not Shown Because They Contain No New Motifs

	600–550	575–525	550–500	525–475	500–450	475–425	450–400
Motif	Herakles	Theseus	Acontist	Prokrustes	Boreas	Eriphyle	Adonis
Proportion	3.33%	1.47%	0.26%	0.08%	0.47%	0.18%	0.19%

From these results, we see that Webster may have been correct when he correlated the story of the summoning of Boreas in 480 BC with an increase in depictions on figure-painted pottery. Yet without this prior knowledge, we would not have known to look in the data for an increase at this time, given that Boreas is "below the radar" in all measurable aspects.

Pan

Webster makes another connection between the frequency of motifs and the Persian Wars. He proposes that appearances of Pan may have increased after 490 as a result of the story of Pan's help to the Athenians in 490 at Marathon (Webster 1972:254). Table 4 below shows the distribution of depictions of Pan for all shapes and all techniques.

We can see that Pan appeared at very low frequency in 525 to 475 BC but increased in 500 to 450 BC. Both date ranges overlap the battle of Marathon. We are therefore again able to support Webster's correlation. However, the frequencies are again so low that we simply would not have detected this association without prior knowledge. Furthermore, from the frequencies, it appears that the greatest interest in Pan occurred not around 490, but at the end of figure-painted pottery in 400 to 300 BC, when depictions of Pan make up 0.72% percent of all observed motifs. This is still a tiny proportion, but it is a very

Table 4. Pan: Number of Appearances on All Shapes and in All Techniques

Pan	625–575	600–550	575–525	550–500	525–475	500–450	475–425	450–400	425–375	400–300	Sum of all years
Number	0	0	0	0	3	7	7	5	2	19	43
Proportion	0	0	0	0	0.03%	0.17%	0.18%	0.23%	0.25%	0.72%	0.12%

Table 5. Theseus: Number of Appearances on All Shapes and in All Techniques

Theseus	625– 575	600– 550	575– 525	550– 500	525– 475	500– 450	475– 425	450– 400	425– 375	400– 300	Sum of all years
Number	0	0	32	67	81	72	79	38	4	10	383
Proportion	0	0	1.47%	0.78%	0.76%	1.77%	2.02%	1.78%	0.49%	0.38%	1.08%

large increase from the previous time steps, none of which are more than 0.25 percent. If there was a specific event that led to an increase in depictions in 400 to 300 BC, it was far more influential than Pan's involvement in the battle of Marathon.

Theseus

Pan and Boreas are very low frequency motifs whose importance would be undetectable without prior knowledge. I will now contrast their frequencies with Theseus, a higher frequency motif with a substantial body of previous research. Theseus is often identified as the Athenian national hero (Shapiro 1991: 136). The meaning of the myth of Theseus and his relationship with Athens has been well documented (e.g., Walker 1995). Given this importance, we will now examine the correlation between the rise in his popularity generally in the late sixth century and the frequency of his depictions on pottery as shown in the data.

The overall frequencies of depictions of Theseus on all shapes and in all techniques are shown in Table 5.

As can be seen, Theseus appears at a relatively high frequency in 575 to 525 BC. He is one of 62 motifs that appear for the first time in 575 to 525 BC, and he is the most popular of these. It is this increase to which authors refer when they discuss the sudden rise in the popularity of Theseus (Neer 2002: 154, Webster 1972: 82). The biggest increase in depictions of Theseus after his initial appearance comes in 500 to 450 BC (as Table 5 shows, there are actually fewer depictions, but as a proportion of all motifs the percentage is much higher). This increase can be related to the purported recovery of the bones of Theseus in 476/5 BC (Walker 1995: 56). It is tempting but simplistic to also see the steep decline in the popularity of Theseus in 425 to 375 BC and 400 to 300 BC as an outcome of the Peloponnesian war. However, the frequencies of many motifs declined during these periods, so the data alone do not allow us to conclude a political motivation for the decline.

These frequencies show that depictions of Theseus on figure-painted pottery match the accepted story of the popularity of Theseus in Athens in the fifth century BC. However, the frequencies overall are very low. At his height in 475 to 425 BC, he makes up only 2.02 percent of all motifs. As with Boreas and Pan, we would once again have to know in advance that he was of special interest to the Athenians.

Nike

We will now look at motifs whose popularity is obvious and unambiguous: Nike, the winged goddess of victory.

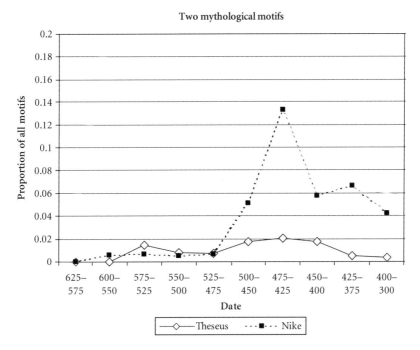

Two mythological motifs

FIGURE 1 Comparison of the proportions of all motifs made up by Theseus and Nike. The small rise in depictions of Theseus between 525–475 and 500–450 is often regarded as a significant increase, whereas the peak in depictions of Nike in 475–425 has not previously been described.

Table 6. Nike: Number of Appearances on All Shapes and in All Techniques

Nike	625–575	600–550	575–525	550–500	525–475	500–450	475–425	450–400	425–375	400–300	Sum of all years
Number	0	2	15	41	69	208	519	123	54	111	1142
Proportion	0	0.56%	0.69%	0.48%	0.64%	5.11%	13.28%	5.76%	6.67%	4.23%	3.23%

The number of appearances and proportions of all motifs for Nike are shown in Table 6. This table clearly shows that Nike was many times more popular than Theseus from 500 to 450 BC onward. On this scale, the "explosion" of Theseus scenes in the sixth century can barely be seen, as Figure 1 clearly shows.

Nike is the eighth most popular motif overall. Only the specific characters Dionysos, Herakles, Athena, and the non-specific/generic characters of satyrs, warriors, maenads, and athletes are more popular. As the personification of victory, Nike resembles the generic figure types more closely than the specific characters of gods and heroes. Like them, Nike can appear multiple times in the same scene (though in our results multiple appearances in one scene count singly), a clear indication that she was not always meant to represent a single specific character, but rather an idea.

It is, however, puzzling that in 475 to 425 BC Nike made up 13.28 percent of all observed motifs in all techniques and across all shapes. In the previous period, 500 to 450 BC, Nike made up 5.11 percent of all motifs, and in the following period, 450 to 400 BC, Nike makes up 5.76 percent. All three figures are very high, but it appears that something happened in 475 to 425 BC, which more than doubled Nike's popularity. This was only temporary, as the figure returns to the previous baseline in the following period.

Nike presents us with a very different problem from Theseus, Boreas, and Pan. In these examples, we have attempted to correlate discussions in the literature with frequencies in the data. In each example, the previous claims of their importance are supported, but the motifs are of such low frequency that it would not be possible for a researcher using the data alone to detect this. Nike, on the other hand, is consistently very popular, yet her appearances are not remarked in the literature of figure-painted pottery. In particular, the striking peak in her appearances in 475 to 425 BC has never before been noted. The most comprehensive extant discussion of Nike as a motif can be found in the entry in the *Lexicon iconographicum mythologiae classicae* (Ackermann and Gisler 1981), which documents appearances of mythological motifs in art of the period, but even this contains no discussion of the motif's relative frequency over time, and therefore makes no comment on the changes in this frequency.

There are several reasons that Nike may have been popular in 475 to 425 BC. First, it is possible that we are dealing with a mistake on the part of the scholars who supplied the information in the Beazley archive. Although many goddesses are virtually indistinguishable from human women, Nike's winged appearance makes her easy to recognize. She can sometimes be confused with Iris (Arafat 1987, Webster 1972: 177). Webster also suggests that the figure identified in the Beazley archive as Nike on loutrophoroi and nuptial lebetes (grouped together as ritual shapes in our study) may in fact be Aurai, as this would make more sense in the context of a wedding scene (Webster 1972: 175). They may also be depictions of Eos. Iris appears 81 times in all (0.23 percent of all observed motifs—about the same as Pan and Boreas combined), while Eos appears 163 times (0.46 percent). It is not hard to imagine a scenario in which nearly all winged females are identified as Nike by default. However, the number of depictions of Nike is so great that it would have to be a very large and consistent error. Even if such an error took place, it is unlikely to have been confined to the single date range shown in the results.

It may be the case that the increase in depictions of Nike correlates with an increase in the manufacture and subsequent survival of shape types on which she was a popular motif. Previous unpublished research into this data set has shown that there was a very large increase in the sample size of lekythoi, on which Nike was a popular motif, in 550 to 500 BC and 525 to 475 BC. This increase can possibly be attributed to the introduction of laws that sought to tone down excessive display through funerary monuments (Osborne 1997: 27), whose function was replaced with figure-painted lekythoi offerings. However, the increase in the sample size of lekythoi does not correlate with the increase in appearances of Nike, so we cannot link the two events.

It is possible but unlikely that the spike in popularity is due to copies being made of a contemporary statue or wall painting. Representations of Nike in sculpture are much more commonly discussed in existing research than representations of her in figure-painted pottery. Webster speculates that early depictions of Nike, which show the winged figure in isolation, are illustrations of a statue by Archermos (Webster 1972: 152), but the many different forms Nike takes by the middle of the fifth century make it unlikely that they were all copies of a particular work or set of works.

It could also be the case that a particular myth associated with Nike became popular at this time; however, Nike has few myths specifically associated with her. She sometimes appears with Zeus as his charioteer (Arafat 1990: 24), but in group scenes it is often unclear whether she is meant to appear as herself, or rather as the personification of the idea she represents (Webster 1972: 177). Previous research has shown that only athletes and warriors come close to being as popular as Nike, and although their popularity helps explain hers, it remains unclear why they both remain relatively stable while representations of Nike increase by 8.17 percent in 475 to 425 BC.

Nike's popularity may be due to her generic nature as a character. As Webster states, the figure of Nike "was pleasing and the purchaser could interpret it as he wished" (Webster 1972: 152). Nike often functions as a comment on the character or actions of figures in scenes in painting, showing others to be victorious, either in themselves or in relation to third parties, in scenes ranging from weddings to combat. This idea would be difficult to portray in vase painting without the use of a figure to embody it. As such, Nike would be at home in scenes with any motifs that were popular in the late fifth century, which include Eros, warriors, maenads, sphinxes, Hermes, Artemis, Charon, Athena, and Aphrodite. It is this plurality that probably contributed to her popularity. Although this would explain her popularity overall, it does not explain the frequencies seen in 475 to 425 BC.

Clearly, the problem of Nike's popularity warrants further investigation. Possible avenues of research should include the co-occurrence of Nike with other motifs, which could be achieved using the existing data set. Comparing these results with scenes of Nike in isolation would show whether her popularity was due to appearance in scenes with other mythological figures, and if one particular scene stands out, correlation could be sought in contemporary texts. Future research should also expand the list of motifs to include more non-mythological figures, in order to determine the degree to which these scenes might increase the overall popularity of the motif. It would also be important to look for correlations in other media, such as sculpture and texts, to determine whether the peak in 475 to 425 BC is isolated to figure-painted pottery. These are but a few possible directions future work might take.

4. DISCUSSION

The preceding examples show both the benefits and limitations of using quantitative approaches in the study of figure-painted motifs. As has been shown, the frequencies of motifs known to be important from other sources, such as Theseus, are dwarfed by more popular motifs such as Nike. This shows that cultural importance cannot be inferred from frequency alone. The examples also show that correlations with contemporary events occur in predicted locations in some motifs, as in the example of Boreas, but in the example of Pan, it was shown that, although an historical correlation exists, a larger increase at a later time has been left unexplained. In the example of Nike, we have seen that a hitherto unseen peak in popularity shows up clearly when the motifs are viewed as frequencies. Although these are starting points, not conclusions, it is remarkable that quantitative research into figure-painted pottery has not previously been attempted on a large scale, given that the data have been available through the Beazley archive for so long.

Much of the opposition to quantitative approaches to figure-painted pottery comes from the idea that we have been left a partial record, and should not infer too much from it. For example, in his study of depictions of Zeus, Arafat states that "because of the partial nature of the evidence, I have preferred not to compile any statistics about the relative frequency of occurrence of Zeus compared with that of other gods" (Arafat 1990: 178).

However, all archaeologists must deal with "partial evidence." All excavated artefacts, including figure-painted pottery, represent a sample of a larger population. The question is how well our sample accurately reflects characteristics of the source population. This has been a source of ongoing debate in the archaeological literature (e.g., Grayson 1970, Hall 1981, Bettinger 1981, Scheps 1982). As Shennan (1997: 51) describes, "the problem is that we do not know how representative the sample is of the population, or how closely the statistic obtained approximates the corresponding unknown parameter, and our goal is to make inferences about various population parameters on the basis of known sample statistics." The solution to this persistent problem is relatively straightforward. As Grayson (1970: 103) describes:

> [Imagine] a large population composed of a high percentage of trait X and a small percentage of trait Y. Since the instances of X greatly outnumber those of Y, the chances of drawing an X on any one sampling trial will be much greater than those of drawing a Y. If a large sample is drawn from this population, then the ratio of X to Y in the sample will approximate that in the population; as the sample size decreases, the poorer this approximation will be, and the more the ratio X/X+Y will tend to overestimate the proportion of X in the population.

In other words, the larger the sample, the more likely it is to accurately reflect the characteristics of the population from which it was drawn. By virtue of its size alone, the sample represented by the Beazley archive is, therefore, more likely to accurately represent the characteristics of Greek figure-painted pottery than any smaller sample drawn from individual excavations or collections. These characteristics include simple proportions, such as the ratio between a given motif and a given shape, as well as more complex statistics, such as whether random copying can be rejected as an explanation for observed variation. As one of the largest collections of data about artifacts of a single type, in fact, the inferences we are able to make from it are likely to be much stronger than those that archaeologists typically have to deal with.

If we then accept that the peak in depictions of Nike in 475 to 425 BC accurately reflects an event in the history of Attic figure-painted pottery, then this presents an interesting challenge to traditional ideas of "importance" in motifs on figure-painted pottery. Theseus may well have been the Athenian national hero, but day-to-day in the late fifth century, people preferred pots depicting winged females, identified as Nike in the Beazley archive. If this is the case, then the traditional view of what is important in figure-painted pottery may need to be adjusted. At present, scholars tend to focus on particular, unique objects and their specific history. Each piece has a narrative, from inspiration to creation to sale, and these narratives are then linked to form a story of an artist's life, or the story of a movement or historical period in time. The perceived importance of the piece to the story dictates the level of detail employed, with more important works receiving more attention and less important works forming a supporting role. The public-facing aspects of art history, such as museums, galleries and auction houses, rely upon these stories to provide context for the artwork they display.

This is a perfectly valid approach to deciphering the inner workings of unique objects. However, it deprecates everyday and unexceptional works, despite these being more numerous and, therefore, by frequency, more representative. Rather than sifting through all known pots for the best examples, we may gain a better understanding of processes that led to the creation of figure-painted pottery by approaching it without preconceptions. This is precisely what a quantitative approach to the material allows us to do. As Osborne states:

> …by ignoring questions of relative quantity, those who study Greek pottery seem to me to have ignored what is potentially a most important source of information about the relationship between the producer and consumer…They have also…ignored a vital tool by which to distinguish the exceptional from the normal, and the only means by which it is possible to sort out what exactly needs explaining in Greek imagery (Osborne 2004:43).

References

Ackermann, H.C., and J.R. Gisler, eds. 1981. *Lexicon iconographicum mythologiae classicae (LIMC)*. Zürich and München: Artemis Verlag.

Arafat, K.W. 1987. Iris or Nike? A divine libation scene on a missing lekythos. *BICS* 33: 127–133.

Arafat, K.W. 1990. Classical Zeus: A study in art and literature. Oxford and New York: Clarendon Press and Oxford University Press.

Beazley, J.D. 1956. *Attic black-figure vase-painters*. Oxford: Clarendon Press.

Beazley, J.D. 1963. *Attic red-figure vase-painters*. Oxford: Clarendon Press.

Beazley, J.D. 1971. *Paralipomena: Additions to Attic black-figure vase-painters and to Attic red-figure vase-painters (second edition)*. Oxford: Clarendon Press.

Bettinger, R.L. 1981. Sampling and statistical inference in Owens Valley. *American Antiquity* 46(3): 656–660.

Grayson, D.K. 1970. Statistical inference and northeastern Adena. *American Antiquity* 35(1): 102–104.

Hall, M.C. 1981. Land-Use Changes in Owens Valley Prehistory: A Matter of Statistical Inference. *American Antiquity* 46: 648–656.

Neer, R.T. 2002. *Style and politics in Athenian vase-painting: The craft of democracy, ca. 530–460 B.C.E.* Cambridge: Cambridge University Press.

Osborne, R. 1997. Law, the democratic citizen and the representation of women in Classical Athens. *Past and Present* 155: 3–33.

Osborne, R. 2004. "Workships and the iconography and distribution of Athenian red-figure pottery: A case study." In *Greek art in view: Essays in honour of Brian Sparkes*, eds. S. Keay, and S. Moser, 78–94. Oxford: Oxbow.

Scheps S. 1982. Statistical Blight. *American Antiquity* 47(4): 836–851.

Shapiro, H.A. 1991. "Theseus: Aspects of the hero in Archaic Greece." In *New perspectives in early Greek art,* ed. D. Buitron-Oliver, 123–139. Washington, D.C.: National Gallery of Art.

Shennan, S.J. 1997. *Quantifying archaeology.* Edinburgh: Edinburgh University Press.

Stewart, A. 1995. "Rape?" In *Pandora: women in classical Greece,* ed. E.D. Reeder, 74–90. Baltimore and Princeton: Walters Art Gallery; Princeton University Press.

Walker, H.J. 1995. *Theseus and Athens.* New York and Oxford: Oxford University Press.

Webster, T.B.L. 1972. *Potter and patron in Classical Athens.* London: Methuen and Co. Ltd.

11

AGENTS, INTELLIGENCE, AND SOCIAL ATOMS

Alex Bentley and Paul Ormerod

Rational models are psychologically unrealistic. . . . the central characteristic of agents is not that they reason poorly, but that they often act intuitively. And the behavior of these agents is not guided by what they are able to compute, but by what they happen to see at a given moment
—Daniel Kahneman, Nobel Economics Lecture, 2003

1. INTRODUCTION

One of the fastest-rising keywords in the physics literature is *social*. Literally thousands of papers in physics are devoted to modeling social systems, and indeed regular sections of leading journals such as *Physica A* and *Physical Review E* are devoted to this topic. The analogy between people and particles has been so consistent that a recent popular review was appropriately titled *The Social Atom* (Buchanan 2007).

In the last 15 years, the science of interacting particles has provided significant insights into modeling collective interactions in social systems, from Internet communities to pedestrian and vehicular traffic, economic markets and even prehistoric human migrations (e.g., Ackland et al. 2007; Barabási 2005; Buchanan 2007; Farkas et al. 2002; Gabaix et al. 2006; Helbing et al. 2000; Newman et al. 2006).

There is, of course, a long history of work in the social science, which effectively applies agent-based modeling and which precedes the modern, computer-aided "complexity science." A good example is Ijiri and Simon (1964). Even earlier, social scientists were discussing the implications of emergent—which Durkheim (1912) called "effervescent"—phenomena resulting from human social interactions. Despite this, awareness of recent work in "social physics" is still low among social scientists themselves. There is a growing list of exceptions to this, such as an increase in the number of complexity science centers, some enthusiastic reviews (Hanson 2004; Valverde 2004; Borgatti et al. 2009), journals such as *Quality and Quantity* and *Journal of Artificial Societies and Social Simulation,* and a few outstanding collaborations (Knappet et al. 2008)

Two major insights have arisen from this work, both from classic studies and the more recent, computer-aided revival. The first is the recognition that human societies are generally open systems, under constant flux, and not the kind of closed system that leads to equilibrium. The second is that many of the emergent, often complex, patterns in society need not require complex behavior on the part of individuals.

As a corollary of the second point, we suggest that the most appropriate null model of individual behavior in larger societies is, in fact, what we term the zero-intelligence model (e.g., Farmer et al. 2005) with its roots in statistical physics, rather than that of the behavioral model from economics of fully rational agents. In other words, decisions are generally taken in circumstances in which the assumption that individuals have no knowledge of the situation is a better approximation to reality than is the assumption that they possess complete information and have the capacity to process this information to make optimal decisions.

Particles, of course, cannot act with purpose and intent, cannot learn, and hence cannot adapt their actions on the basis of the outcomes of previous actions by themselves or by other particles. Social physics is, therefore, quite radical—it posits that we might usefully see how far we can get by modeling human agents *as if* they behaved with "zero intelligence." It is rather literally a "null model"—assuming as little as possible, in order to identify the most general characteristics of collective human behavior.

Economics has of course made some attempt to move in this direction, following the development of the concept of bounded rationality (Akerlof 1970). Individuals may have incomplete information, and the amount of information may vary among individuals. So agents are taking decisions with only a portion of the information assumed to be available to them under the assumption of full rationality. However, agents under bounded rationality are still assumed to make optimal decisions subject to the amount of information they have. So, in general, this concept is closer to that of full rationality than it is to that of zero intelligence.

We expand on these points in the following way. First, we make some remarks on the concept of non-equilibrium. We then set out a rationale underlying the idea that, in general, agents behave as if they had zero, or close to zero, intelligence. We go on in the bulk of the chapter to discuss the various ways in which the zero-intelligence null model may need to be modified in a social-science context, and set out ways in which this has been done, with particular reference to anthropology.

The modifications may appear extensive at first sight, but in any given context only one or two will usually be required in order to develop a satisfactory model rather than the full set. Importantly, these modifications still leave the behavior of agents closer to that of zero intelligence than that of rationality. Finally, we draw some brief conclusions.

2. NON-EQUILIBRIUM

In anthropology, assumptions of equilibrium, optimization and rational cost-benefit analysis by individuals is prominent in optimal foraging theory and human behavioral ecology (Winterhalder and Smith 2000). Such models often assume that human decisions have an optimal value, in the sense of a fitness-enhancing payoff. To fit various case studies, these payoffs can be adjusted to account for behaviors that are highly culturally dependent or individually variable, as within small-scale societies living in similar environments (e.g., Cronk and Gerkey 2007).

Assumptions of optimality and rationality can certainly be useful when payoffs are predictable from one event to the next—hunting and gathering in a consistent environment, for example, or even modern situations in which the complexity of choices is low (Winterhalder and Smith 2000).

Many of these models use differential equations to model "typical" behavior, and often use the assumption of equilibrium to solve them (e.g., Gintis 2007). Equilibrium models often assume that something, such as energy or wealth, is conserved in exchange processes. This is often not the case with human society and economics, which are characterized by open, non-equilibrium systems (Farmer and Geanakoplos 2009).

In modern capitalist economies, for example, "income is most definitely not conserved" (Gallegati et al. 2006, 1). For example, the level of income per head in the United States in 2009, even allowing for inflation, is over six times higher than it was in 1909. Wealth and income both follow highly skewed, non-equilibrium distributions (Pareto 1907), in a vast range of economies. Even in small pastoralist societies, where livestock are the principal form of wealth and transactions (Salzman 1999), wealth is not in equilibrium, because it flows "uphill" rather than "downhill"—that is, the rich get richer through competition (Salzman 1999; Hayden 2001). Even a setback, like major drought, can make the rich richer, as wealthy pastoralists absorb the livestock of smaller holders who are driven out of the pastoral economy (Fratkin 1989, 46; Hayden 2001). As a result, the distributions of wealth in pastoralist societies follow right-skewed distributions, some of which are close to Pareto form (Bentley 2003).

Another aspect of non-equilibrium systems is renewal, that is, a continual flux of entities. In these open systems, new agents are continually added through birth, inauguration, immigration, while others are eliminated through death, modification, and extinction. These agents may be on any human scale, from ideas in the mind to individuals to groups, corporations and so on.

3. THE ZERO INTELLIGENCE AGENT

In addition to its assumption of equilibrium, the standard economic approach ascribes considerable intelligence to agents in the decision making process, both in terms of the information they gather and the rules they use to process it. Even in models in which agents have incomplete information (e.g., Akerlof 1970), the decision making rule is still based on the principle of maximizing (i.e., taking the optimal decision on the basis of the information available).

The most important challenge to this approach comes when decisions do not depend not on omniscient cost-benefit analysis of isolated agents with fixed tastes and preferences, but when the decision of any given agent depends in part directly on what other actors are doing. In such situations, which are probably the norm rather than the exception in social settings, not only do choices involve many options for which costs and benefits would be impossible to calculate (e.g., what friends to keep, what job to pursue, what game to play, etc.), but the preferences of agents themselves evolve over time in the light of what others do.

Complex choices can be fundamentally different from simple two-choice scenarios, such that the problem becomes unpredictable, as has been demonstrated in ecological (Melbourne and Hastings 2009) and human settings (Salganik et al. 2006). Such scenarios are where zero-intelligence models do better at understanding emergent patterns in collective behavior. However, despite their empirical success (e.g., Ball 2004; Buchanan 2007; Newman et al. 2006, 415–551), they have met with resistance among social scientists.

This lack of interest is understandable, given the apparent incongruity between the anthropological focus on cultural, thinking people—in all of their complexity and variety—versus the simple particles of physics. Humans report acting with purpose and intent, and we do not assume that they literally act with zero intelligence, whether as individuals or as part of collective decision-making groups (e.g., kinship groups, economic firms, governments). However, the dimension of the problem that often faces human decision makers, particularly in the modern world, is so large that it is *as if* agents were operating with approximately zero intelligence. In addition, the environment in which agents operate changes frequently, so that it is extremely hard or even impossible for agents to learn systematically and evolve rules of behavior that are in some sense "optimal."

An illustration of the limits to human awareness and social calculation is the well known Prisoner's Dilemma game, invented by Drescher and Flood in 1950. The optimal strategy or "Nash equilibrium" for the one-period game was discovered very quickly. However, as documented in detail by Mirowski (2002), Flood recruited distinguished RAND analysts John Williams and Armen Alchian, a mathematician and economist, respectively, to play 100 repetitions of the game. The Nash equilibrium strategy ought to have been played by completely rational individuals 100 times. It might, of course, have taken a few plays for these high-powered academics to learn the strategy. However, Alchian chose cooperation rather than the Nash strategy of defection 68 times, and Williams no fewer than 78 times. Their recorded comments are fascinating in themselves. Williams, the mathematician, began by expecting both players to cooperate, whereas Alchian, the economist, expected defection, but as the game progressed, cooperation became the dominant choice of both players.

Even now, after almost 60 years of analysis and literally thousands of scientific papers on the subject, when sufficient uncertainty is introduced into the game, the optimal strategy remains unknown. Certainly, some strategies do better than most in many circumstances, but no one has yet discovered the optimal strategy even for a game that is as simple to describe as the Prisoner's Dilemma.

The game of chess offers a further illustration of limits to the ability of agents to process information in an optimal way. Chess has a relatively small number of unequivocal rules, and these rules do not change over any relevant time scale. The agents, the players in this case, have full information about the rules. The position in the game is completely transparent at any point in time, so that a player knows for certain the moves that his or her opponent has already made. In addition, the player knows all the legitimate moves that his/her opponent could make when it is his/her turn to play. So each player has a large amount of precise information about the game.

Yet in most situations in a chess game, there is no known best move. Chess grandmasters such as Gary Kasparov describe how they use their skill and experience to make what they consider to be a reasonable move instead of engaging in a futile search for the best possible move. Computers can now beat the best human chess players, but the fraction of situations in which they can find the optimal move is tiny, and such optimal solutions are believed even by the very strongest players, to be completely beyond the capacity of humans to solve. The information is readily available, but the constraint to finding the best moves is the ability to process it.

The practical limitations on agents' cognitive abilities were in fact discovered almost at the outset of the development of game theory. In addition to the experiment with RAND scientists, Flood carried out a range of practical tests, and, indeed, shortly afterward abandoned game theory altogether because of the disjuncture between how people "ought" to behave and how they actually do behave (Mirowski 2002).

For example, Flood offered RAND secretaries a choice. One of them was given the option of either receiving a fixed sum of money ($10, say), or receiving a total of $15 provided that agreement could be reached with another secretary about how this money was to be divided between them. One Nash solution is that the two split the marginal difference. In other words, they divide the extra $5 between them so that they get $12.50 and $2.50, respectively. In practice most secretaries were not drawn not to the new idea of the Nash equilibrium, but to the concept of fairness: they divided the total amount exactly equally, $7.50 each. The development of experimental and behavioral economics in the past 20 years or so effectively confirms the findings of Flood's initial work (e.g., Smith 2003).

Although some concept of fairness may be as old as humanity itself (Ofek 2001; Hrdy 2009) or even earlier (de Waal 2009), norms of fairness vary among cultures. When the Ultimatum Game (where one player chooses how much of the money pot to share with a second player) has been played in cross-cultural settings— ranging from the Hadza hunter-gatherers of Tanzania to the Machiguenga horticulturalists of the Amazon, to the Lamalera whale hunters of Indonesia—the amount offered varies substantially from culture to culture (Henrich et al. 2005). Societies that survive by more cooperative endeavors, such as whale hunting, generally exhibited more generosity in economic games (> 50 percent) than those based on individual activities (< 50 percent), such as gathering (Henrich et al. 2005).

This further confirms that human decisions are social, with very little "intelligence" in the sense of optimal cost-benefit calculation. There may be a cultural, local logic to these decision tendencies, but even if they were optimally tailored to each particular environment, we see the cost-benefit "calculator" in this case as evolutionary selection over many human generations (O'Brien 1996), rather than on the part of the individual actors (Boone and Smith 1998).

4. ADDING INTELLIGENCE (A LITTLE GOES A LONG WAY)

Consider the extinction of firms in modern economies, which was recently made vivid in the economic crisis of 2008–2009. Two key stylized facts have been established about the extinction patterns of firms. First, the probability of extinction is highest at the start of the firm's existence, but soon becomes more or less invariant to the age of the firm. A second finding—a much more recent one of which most economists are unaware— is that the relationship between the size and frequency of firm extinctions is closely approximated by a power law (Cook and Ormerod 2003 and Di Guilmi et al. 2004). This statistically self-similar relationship is very similar to what exists in the fossil record for the extinction of biological species (Solé et al. 1997; Newman 1996; Newman and Eble 1999).

Economic theory has a great deal to say about many aspects of firm behavior, but offers relatively little on the deaths of firms. Building on previously successful zero-intelligence models (e.g., Amaral et al. 1998; Stanley et al. 1996), Ormerod and Rosewell (2003) developed an evolutionary, agent-based model of firm evolution and extinction, which, following other such evolutionary models (e.g., Sneppen et al. 1995), yielded properties that conform closely to the aforementioned stylized facts.

The base version of the model was a "zero intelligence" version, in that each model firm was unable to acquire knowledge about either the true impact of other firms' strategies on its own fitness or the true impact of changes to its own strategies on its fitness. Specifically, N firms were connected to each other by a matrix of uniformly distributed interconnections $J_{ij} \in [-1, 1]$. The initial connections J_{ij} were drawn at random, and in each step each agent i had one of its J_{ji} updated (i.e., assigned with a new value chosen at random in the interval $[-1,1]$). The fitness $F_i(t)$ of each agent was calculated, where

$$F_i(t) = \sum_{j=1}^{N} J_{ji}(t) \quad (1)$$

If $F_i(t) < 0$ then the agent was deemed extinct. An extinction event of size M is defined as a period in which M agents become extinct.

Despite the fact that agents are acting in a purely random way, the model was nevertheless capable of generating the two stylized facts on firm extinctions: high extinction probability initially and overall power-law distribution of extinction event sizes.

The effect of providing even a small amount of intelligence to the agents was dramatic. Starting with the "zero-intelligence" base, Ormerod and Rosewell then assigned the model firms different amounts of knowledge about the effects of strategy. Even a small amount of knowledge produced a sharp increase in the mean firm age at extinction. However, as both the amount of knowledge available and the number of knowledgeable firms were increased, the extinction patterns of firms departed dramatically from the real-world evidence. Strikingly, as the behavior of firms in the model approached the level of rationality of economic theory, the extinction patterns became completely different from the empirical evidence. Needless to say, this implies that the standard assumption of economic theory that firms act in a rational way—whether full or bounded rationality is wholly incompatible with the empirical evidence on patterns of firm extinction.

5. ADDING COPYING

Ormerod and Rosewell's (2003) study indicates: (1) Economic agents have very limited capacities to acquire knowledge about the true impact of their strategies and (2) if those capabilities were enhanced among firms generally, the effect would be significant even for small increases in knowledge. This suggests that one of the key parameters of a complex interactive system is the degree to which agents are acting upon objective information versus simply responding to neighboring agents or even just copying them.

This question has wide relevance, well beyond the case study of economic firms (e.g., Suroweicki 2004). It is well known, in situations from responding to an emergency to preparing for climate change, that when conditions change rapidly, people do not readily "re-calculate" an optimal response, but rather they often persist in traditional behavior, doing as others do and/or as they are socially expected to do. In fact, in situations in which information is incomplete and/or time to decide is short, copying the behavior of others can be seen as cost-beneficial decision in itself:

> Once some cultural transmission capacities exist, natural selection favors improved learning efficiencies, such as abilities to identify and preferentially copy models who are likely to possess better-than-average information…Copiers thus evolve to provide all sorts of benefits (i.e., "deference") to targeted models in order to induce preferred models to grant greater access and cooperation. (Henrich and Gil-White 2001, 167)

As Henrich and Gil-White (2001, note 2) point out, these benefits are self-serving, in that "as a species' reliance on true imitation increases, the relative benefit from improved copying abilities increases. But, if a species only rarely uses its imitative abilities…the benefits of improved imitation may not exceed the costs."

Assessing independence of behavior from aggregate statistics is a challenge. The paradox is that that the behavior of the majority could arise because that behavior is optimal, and every individual has made the same decision independently, or it could be a rather arbitrary behavior that has spread through the population through copying.

Perhaps the best way to approach this is to assume a continuum: In some cases people make decisions fairly independently, based on the inherent qualities of the choice, whereas in others they are prone to be highly socially influenced. In fact, this distinction can become the subject of empirical testing, rather than an assumption we must put a priori into a model.

The following classic behavioral spread model (e.g., Rogers 1964; Henrich 2001) models the probability of each individual adopting a certain new idea/behavior, at time t as:

$$p(t) = (\mu + qF(t))(1 - F(t)) \quad (2)$$

where the parameters q and μ represent the degree of imitation and individual selection, respectively. Hence by setting the parameters q and μ, this model can represent two evolutionary modes of behavior spread: pure social influence versus purposeful selection.

These different models predict identifiably different patterns in the adoption and subsequent abandonment of ideas or products within a population. The pure social influence (high q, low μ) produces a symmetric pattern through time: What is adopted rapidly in the population does not accumulate, and consequently declines rapidly from peak frequency, whereas what is slower to move to its peak accumulates more, and declines more slowly (Henrich 2001; Berger and Le Mens 2009; Bentley and Ormerod 2009). Deliberate behavioral selection (high μ, low q), in contrast, produces an asymmetric pattern, whereby the decline from the peak is considerably slower than is the rise to the peak, and vice versa.

A modern example is searches on Google of the phrase *swine flu* in late April/early May 2009 (Bentley and Ormerod 2009). We can ask the question, was the interest in swine flu generated from independent selection—perhaps people were genuinely individually scared by the media hype—or was it purely the socially mediated spread of an idea, no different that any other flash news item?

Preceding model (1) can be used to characterize Internet searches for the phrase *swine flu* in a wide range of countries across the world. We find that the phenomenon was somewhere between these extremes, with selection $\mu = 7.4$ percent and imitation $q = 46$ percent. This might seem strongly in favor of social imitation, but the selection parameter was actually much higher for *swine flu* searches than for more solidly socially mediated spread, as with baby names (Hahn and Bentley 2003), where μ might typically be two percent. The selection parameter μ is powerful and just a small increase can lead to a large boost in the rate of popularity increase. Hence, overall, we found that genuine concern (selection) about swine flu was significant in the rise of the mass interest around the world, as opposed to simply the social spread of a panic.

Optimality models would struggle to account for the average degree of social influence in the collective behavior. Of course, our swine-flu study, for example, merely characterizes the parameter values to fit a model to a population, but not the variability in individual for being interested in swine flu among the millions of Googlers. Optimality models are even more insufficient to explain such variability of human behavior (Nettle 2009), and yet the heterogeneity of human behavior is so basic that it may actually have evolved to enable groups to function through specialization and exchange (Ofek 2001; Hrdy 2009).

One of the simplest ways to study the effect of this heterogeneity is to start with a zero-intelligence model and then apply simple *thresholds* to individual behaviors. This can add a rich dimension of realism and complexity to a model. For example, an agent might copy other agents only if the fraction of those agents with a different opinion exceeds a certain discrete threshold.

Watts (2002) did this when incorporating the classic psychological results of Solomon Asch (1955) into a model of information cascades across a network of interconnected agents. The agents were varied according to the fraction of neighbors needed to exhibit a behavior before the agent itself would adopt it. Watts found a rich variety of cascade behavior, based not only on the mean threshold and network structure, but also on the heterogeneity of thresholds among the agents. Ormerod and Colbaugh (2006) extended the model into a dynamic context, in which the topology connecting the agents is not fixed, but evolves over time as agents seek alliances with the aim of increasing their overall fitness.

In general, social science requires some addition to the assumption of purely random interactions between agents (the particles of the social physics models). Our brains are wired to be social (Dunbar and Shultz 2007; Hrdy 2009), which clearly biases the interactions (Henrich and Gil-White 2001). The specific nature of the addition will vary according to the particular circumstances, and we suggest a classification of such potential additions.

6. NETWORKS: STRUCTURED COPYING

Many studies of non-equilibrium social phenomena focus on the origin of long-tail (power-law) distributions (Clauset et al. 2009) as emergent properties. One famous hypothesis for their origin has been the "scale-free network" (Albert and Barabási 2002; Barabási and Bonabeau 2003), which is essentially a zero-intelligence model. In what have become seminal studies of the network of Internet web pages, the number of links to each site was found to be power-law distributed (Huberman et al. 1998; Albert and Barabási 2002). The title of Buchanan's (2007) book does not really capture the explosion of *network* approaches where the "social atoms" are essentially linked to each other and to human collective behavior (e.g., Albert and Barabási 2002; Hufnagel et al. 2006; Newman et al. 2006; Solé et al. 2005).

Despite grandiose claims of re-inventing social science (Barabási 2005), these models as developed in physics often fail to capture essential elements of human behavior. Almost all models of scale-free network growth are ultimately grounded upon the rule of "preferential attachment" (Albert and Barabási 2002), in that new connections continually made within the network are preferentially attached to already well-connected agents.

The Barabási-Albert (1999) model of preferential attachment was hugely influential because it resulted in a power law (or at least long-tailed) degree distribution (connections per network node), a kind of distribution so intriguing to many that the editor of *Wired* magazine wrote an entire book, seven years later, about its significance to modern online economies (Anderson 2006). A variety of preferential attachment models ensued, most in some way modeling the number of connections an agent adds in time $t + 1$ as proportional to the connections it already had at time t and standard deviation σ. With continual growth in the number of agents, this leads to a power-law degree distribution (Adamic and Huberman 2000), as many similar models of cumulative advantage have demonstrated (e.g., Ijiri and Simon 1964; Price 1965; West and Deering 1995; Newman et al. 2006, 335–348). Basically, the larger the variance σ^2 in the growth rate, the more that variance contributes multiplicatively to inequality.

At first glance, preferential attachment may seem to have numerous parallels with anthropology, for example, the classic Big-Man societies of Melanesia (e.g., Sahlins 1963). As a Big-Man's coalition increased in size, so too did his personal prestige, enabling him to attract even more supporters (e.g., Sahlins 1963; Henrich and Gil-White 2001).

As an *explanation* for long-tail phenomena, however, the preferential attachment models are inherently unsatisfying, because preferential attachment is precisely what we would want to explain; with it already built into the model, the long-tail, rich-get-richer result is no surprise. It does not *explain* wealth inequality, for example, to assume the existence of an interest rate (e.g., Bouchaud and Mézard 2000; Burda et al. 2002). Some modelers have produced long-tailed wealth distributions by imposing the interactions onto a power-law network (e.g., Wright 2005), or using a branching "family tree" with inheritance (Coelho et al. 2005), but effectively this presents the same problem of predesigning the long-tailed distribution into the results.

A key problem with preferential attachment models is the constraint on how change occurs over time: In essential form, growth by proportionate advantage means those with less can never overtake those with more. In real cultural arenas, the rising and falling of fortunes is the norm, even where there exists strong positive feedback for success. In the case of cities ranked by population size, which follow a heavily right-skewed distribution, Batty (2006) recently devised "rank clocks" to demonstrate their continual turnover in the rankings, such that, although power-law distributions remain stable in form over time, they nonetheless undergo continual turnover in composition of individual components.

This turnover is part of the essence of an open, non-equilibrium system, but most preferential attachment network models have difficulty accounting for such turnover.

This is due to the restrictiveness of the network analogy for non-network phenomena compared with the majority of real-world cases, in which the idea and the agent are separable. In preferential attachment network models with aging (e.g., Dorogovtsev and Mendes 2000), the probability of the choice itself (node) diminishes with its age. This is inappropriate for the adoption of ideas, because an idea does not go extinct because it is old but because no one uses it anymore. It is more appropriate to model the limited memory of the choosers, rather than the aging of the choices. A recent network model (Hajara and Sen 2006) does, in fact, briefly explore limited memory, but still equates nodes with ideas.

7. RANDOM COPYING WITH INNOVATION

Many of the conceptual problems that arise from social physics approaches, such as preferential attachment, can be overcome by models based on evolutionary principles, in which the agents are still operating much closer to the zero-intelligence null model than they are to the model of full rationality.

These are particularly useful in situations in which each individual has a very large variety of options. A system of agents with many options presents a different category of problem not suited well to either network models or binary decision models. An evolutionary model can generate a wide range of the right-skew distributions observed in cultural, economic, and social situations from different combinations of its very few parameters (Bentley et al. 2011).

Fashions and popular culture—often behaviors that are not essential to survival—are often best considered as "neutral" traits, in that what is chosen has no *inherent* value relative to other options (Gillespie 1998; Hahn and Bentley 2003; Lipo et al. 1997; Shennan & Wilkinson 2001). This has been formalized in a model, akin to the neutral-trait model of population genetics, for popular culture change (e.g., Koerper & Stickel 1980; Neiman 1995; Shennan & Wilkinson 2001; Bentley & Shennan 2003). The model simply allows us to ask, what if everyone simply copied each other, with occasional innovation?

The model assumes that, for example, the decision of whether to choose a pug, a terrier, or a poodle as a pet primarily depends on the relative popularities of the breeds, rather than the inherent properties of the dogs themselves (size, temperament, etc.). As with Watts's (2002) threshold model, there is, therefore, no inherent "fitness" assigned to any of the choices, because actions depend entirely on what *others* are doing. The difference is that the network is never static: Because any agent can copy any other, the "network" of who copied whom changes at every time step of the model.

Derived from evolutionary theory—designed specifically to understand change through time—random drift is a much more powerful analogue than preferential attachment for a range of collective behaviors. As Kimura and Crow (1964) showed decades ago, the simple evolutionary model of random drift produces power-law frequency distributions. This has also been demonstrated analytically (Evans 2007) and through computer simulation (Hahn and Bentley 2003; Bentley et al. 2004). Generally, the more popular a variant is, the more likely it will be copied again. Unlike a predefined rule, this proportionate advantage emerges from the model, and as a general tendency rather than a fixed behavior. As a result, the constituents of the resulting power-law distribution are in continual flux, in just the way that Batty (2006) observed, for the model as well as in ranked lists of pop-culture elements in the real world (Bentley et al. 2007).

The turnover results from a balance of innovation, which introduces new ideas and random drift, by which variation is lost through sampling. New ideas become highly popular by chance alone, and then over time become replaced by others, all through drift. The random-copying model predicts that turnover will increase with the fraction of innovators in the population but (somewhat counterintuitively) not on population size itself. Both these predictions are reflected in real-world data (Bentley et al. 2007).

Hence, without any predefined rules for such effects, random copying can account for (1) power-law distributions and the rich-get-richer effect of the most popular being the most likely to be copied; (2) continual turnover, with any new variant having a finite (if usually small) chance of becoming highly popular and very popular variants eventually falling in popularity; and (3) network dynamics, in that the network is never the same from one time step to the next. With the simple parameters of population size and fraction of innovators, the model can, thus, be used to predict change rates as well as potentially distinguish copying from other forms of collective behavior.

8. THE UNITS OF AGENCY

Because the explanation of what is going on depends critically on the scale of the observation, the units of variation and evolution are a critical variable in evolutionary studies applied to human society (O'Brien and Lyman 2002).

Change through **time** is, of course, the essence of evolution. Human activity and cultural evolution occur on different temporal scales, including *multigenerational* (such as evolving languages, cultures, built environments, or settlement patterns), *intergenerational* (such as wealth inheritance, education, or the migration upon reaching adulthood), *monthly/annual* (such as many economic and political processes), *daily* (e.g., traffic congestion, peak electricity use) and *momentary* (e.g., the spread of a rumor, web-based interactions, or human aggression).

The temporal scale very strongly determines the appropriate rules to assign to agents. For example, particle-like diffusion (random walks) might be appropriate for the spread of migrants across a continent over multi- or intergenerational time scales (e.g., Ackland et al. 2007), but we would not use diffusion to model, say, an individual's deliberate migration to a more desirable community (Boyd and Richerson 2009). Many data now exist to characterize people's movements on these different time scales, from historical/census data to mobile phone records.

Evolution also occurs in our second dimension, **space**, but this does not refer merely to physical space. Sewall Wright (1932) proposed the concept of fitness landscapes, which Kauffman (1995) parlayed into agent-based models of "NK" fitness landscapes, where the space was effectively a medium for interactions. Space may also refer to information, and Daniel Dennett (1996) popularized the concept of a "design space" in which evolution operates. Speaking more specifically of human actions, we can see these taking place in different spatial categories, such as *geographic space* (e.g., commuters, migrants); *network space* (e.g., friendships, hyperlinks, hierarchical relations, telephone calls); *relational space* (to represent non-discrete entities that may overlap); and *abstract space*, for intractable entities without real-world coordinates (e.g., popular ideas in a population).

A third crucial dimension is **demography**. Human interactions are fundamentally dependent on the number of actors and their heterogeneity. Basic scales of difference can include the *neurological* (where multiple intentions may compete within one mind (Daw et al. 2006; Kable et al. 2007); the *isolated individual*, where a "rational" action is selected in the absence of social influence (Gintis 2007); the *small group* (few enough to be known individually (Dunbar and Shultz 2007; Winterhalder and Smith 2000); and the *population*, where there are enough people so that individuals are not recognized (Bentley et al. 2007; Powell et al. 2009, Watts 2002).

In demographic terms, there may even be a crucial "tipping point" in the effect of group size on aggregate behavior. Robin Dunbar (1993) famously proposed that the number of social relations our brains have evolved to handle is on the order of about 150. This number is roughly equal to the typical size of contemporary hunter-gather communities, and so probably reflects the demands of the social environment in which our ancestors evolved. Above this order of magnitude group size, a qualitative transition in social dynamics takes place (e.g., Chagnon 1975; Read *et al.* 2009), such that we can expect societies of many people to behave differently than groups or small communities of a few people.

9. DISCUSSION AND CONCLUSIONS

The preceding material may seem a formidable and extensive list of ways in which the simple null model of zero-intelligence agents may need to be modified in order to be really useful in the social sciences and, specifically, within anthropology. However, as we noted in the introduction, the particular modifications will be context dependent. We are essentially setting out a tool kit from which modelers can select to custom build their model to address a specific problem. None of the potential modifications in themselves are placing the model of behavior closer to that of full rationality rather than that of zero intelligence.

However, it does seem clear that there is much to be gained by making such modifications. Direct analogies between people and particles (or network nodes) often stray too far from reality to justify the convenience for the models. This is not to lament that "people are more complex than particles," but rather to highlight occasions where humans interactions are different. Many physicists would rightfully fear that too much detail compromises the simplifying utility of a *model*—like comedian Stephen Wright's joke about buying an "actual size" map of the United States.

However, the rationale for better collaboration between social physics and anthropology is compelling. On one hand, physicists may characterize a certain category of collective action, but use a flawed assumption about the individual human behavior. On the other hand, anthropologists have such a deep record of individual behavior and its seemingly infinite variability that understanding collective effects can seem impossible.

Aside from refining the basics of human behavior, collaboration with anthropologists would also broaden the new paradigm toward applicability across multiple diverse disciplines, with models based more on real-world human behavior, as opposed to physicists' own academic society—citations, collaborations, and so forth (e.g., Redner 1998;

Newman 2001; Guimera et al. 2005; Wuchty et al. 2007). Unique insight was achieved, for example, when Watts (2002, also Dodds et al. 2005) incorporated the essence of classic psychology of conformity thresholds (Asch 1955) into his network models of information cascades, or when Newman (2002; Newman and Leicht 2007) invoked the sociological concept of assortative mixing into his social-network models.

In return, culture evolution studies could gain substantially from more detailed collaboration with physicists, in at least these three ways:

1. A sophisticated means of dealing with complexity and heterogeneity, without resorting to simplified assumptions of equilibrium or optimality
2. A view of large scale emergent effects (social physics) through individual-scale behavior (anthropology)
3. An insight into "tipping points," or abrupt transitions at the collective level, resulting from nondescript individual interactions

A proper collaboration between social scientists and physicists would use existing social-science data to provide the minimum of behavioral rules necessary to do complexity modeling for real understanding of community issues and policy. The basic action rules for a model must be appropriate to the scale and the dynamics of the problem, yet not be too complex, lest the model's results have little predictive/explanatory meaning.

Bibliography

Ackland, G.J., M. Signitzer, K. Stratford, and M.H. Cohen. 2007. Cultural hitchhiking on the wave of advance of beneficial technologies. *Proceedings of the National Academy of Sciences USA* 104: 8714–8719.

Adamic, A.L., and B.A. Huberman. 2000. The nature of markets on the World Wide Web. *Quarterly Journal of Electronic Commerce* 1: 5–12.

Akerlof, G.A. 1970. The market for lemons: Quality uncertainty and the market mechanism. *Quarterly Journal of Economics* 84: 488–500.

Albert, R., and A.L. Barabási. 2002. Statistical mechanics of complex networks. *Reviews of Modern Physics* 74: 47–97.

Amaral, L.A.N., S.V. Buldyrev, S. Havlin, M.A. Salinger, and H.E. Stanley 1998. Power law scaling for a system of interacting units with complex internal structure. *Physical Review Letters* 80: 1385–1388.

Anderson, P.W. 1972. More is different. *Science* 177: 393–396.

Anderson, C. 2006. *The long tail: Why the future of business is selling less of more.* New York: Hyperion.

Asch, S.E. 1955. Opinions and social pressure. *Scientific American* 193: 31–35.

Ball, P. 2004. *Critical mass: How one thing leads to another.* London: William Heinemann.

Barabási, A.L. 2005. Network theory—the emergence of the creative enterprise. *Science* 308: 639–641.

Barabási A.-L., and R. Albert. 1999. Emergence of scaling in random networks. *Science* 286: 509–512.

Barabási, A.L., and E. Bonabeau. 2003. Scale free networks. *Scientific American* 288: 50–59.

Batty, M. 2006. Rank clocks. *Nature* 444: 592–596.

Bentley, R.A. 2003. Scale-free network growth and social inequality. In *Complex systems and archaeology*, eds. R.A. Bentley, and H.D.G. Maschner, 27–42. Salt Lake City: University of Utah Press.

Bentley, R.A., and P. Ormerod. 2009. Tradition and fashion in consumer choice. *Scottish Journal of Political Economy* 56: 371–381.

Bentley, R.A., P. Ormerod, and M. Batty. 2011. Evolving social influence in large populations. *Behavioral Ecology and Sociobiology* 65: 537–546.

Bentley, R.A, C.P. Lipo, H.A. Herzog, and M.W. Hahn. 2007. Regular rates of popular culture change reflect random copying. *Evolution and Human Behavior* 28: 151–158.

Bentley, R.A., M.W. Hahn, and S.J. Shennan. 2004. Random drift and culture change. *Proceedings of the Royal Society B* 271: 1443–1450.

Bentley, R.A., and S.J. Shennan. 2003. Cultural evolution and stochastic network growth. *American Antiquity* 68: 459–485.

Bentley, R.A., and S.J. Shennan. 2005. Random copying and cultural evolution (Comment). *Science* 309: 877–879.

Bentley, R.A., and H.D.G. Maschner. 2001. Stylistic evolution as a self-organized critical phenomenon? *Journal of Archaeological Method and Theory* 8: 35–66.

Berger, J., and G. Le Mens. 2009. How adoption speed affects the abandonment of cultural tastes. *Proceedings of the National Academy of Sciences USA* 106: 8146–8150.

Boone, J. L., and E. A. Smith. 1998. Is it evolution yet? A critique of evolutionary archaeology. *Current Anthropology* 39: S141–S173.

Borgatti, S.P., A. Mehra, D.J. Brass, and G. Labianca. 2009. Network analysis in the social sciences. *Science* 323: 892–895.

Bouchaud, J.P., and M. Mezard. 2000. Wealth condensation in a simple model of economy. *Physica A* 282: 536–545.

Boyd, R., and P.J. Richerson. 1985. *Culture and the evolutionary process*. Chicago: University of Chicago Press.

Boyd, R., and P.J. Richerson. 2009. Voting with your feet: Payoff biased migration and the evolution of group beneficial behavior. *Journal of Theoretical Biology* 257: 331–339.

Buchanan, M. 2007. *The social atom*. London: Bloomsbury.

Burda, Z., D. Johnston, J. Jurkiewicz, M. Kaminski, M.A. Nowak, G. Papp, and I. Zahed. 2002. Wealth condensation in pareto macroeconomies. *Physical Review E* 65: 02610.

Chagnon, N. 1975. Genealogy, solidarity, and relatedness: Limits to local group size and patterns of fissioning in an expanding population. *Yearbook of Physical Anthropology* 19: 95–110.

Clauset A., C.R. Shalizi, and M.E.J. Newman. 2009. Power-law distributions in empirical data. *SIAM Review* 51: 661-703.

Coelho, R., Z. Neda, J.J. Ramasco, and M.A. Santos. 2005. A family-network model for wealth distribution in societies. *Physica A* 353: 515–528.

Collard, M., S.J. Shennan, and J.J. Tehrani. 2006. Branching, blending and the evolution of cultural similarities and differences among human populations. *Evolution and Human Behavior* 27: 169–184.

Cook, W., and P. Ormerod. 2003. Power law distribution of the frequency of demises of US firms. *Physica A* 324: 207–212

Cronk, L., and A. Gerkey. 2007. "Kinship and descent." In *The Oxford handbook of evolutionary psychology*, eds. R. Dunbar and L. Barrett, 463–478. Oxford, UK: Oxford University Press.

Daw, N.D., J.P. O'Doherty, P. Dayan, B. Seymour, and R.J. Dolan. 2006. Cortical substrates for exploratory decisions in humans. *Nature* 441: 876–879.

Dennett, D. 1996. *Darwin's dangerous idea*. New York: Simon and Schuster.

de Waal, F. 2009. *The age of empathy: Nature's lessons for a kinder society*. New York: Random House.

Di Guilmi, C., M. Gallegati, and P. Ormerod. 2004. Scaling invariant distributions of firms' exit in OECD countries. *Physica A* 334: 267–273.

Dodds, P.S., and D.J. Watts. 2005. A generalized model of social and biological contagion. *Journal of Theoretical Biology* 232: 587–604.

Dorogovtsev, S.N., and J.F.F. Mendes. 2000. Evolution of networks with aging of sites. *Physical Review E* 62: 1842.

Dunbar, R.I.M. 1993. Coevolution of neocortex size, group size, and language in humans. *Behavioral and Brain Sciences* 16: 681–735.

Dunbar, R.I.M., and S. Shultz. 2007. Evolution in the social brain. *Science* 317: 1344–1347.

Dunnell, R.C. 1978. Style and function: A fundamental dichotomy. *American Antiquity* 43: 192–202.

Durkheim, É. 1912. *The elementary forms of the religious life*. New York: Free Press.

Dyson-Hudson, N. 1966. *Karimojong politics*. Oxford: Clarendon Press.

Eerkens, J., and C.P. Lipo. 2005. Cultural transmission, copying errors, and the generation of variation in material culture and the archaeological record. *Journal of Anthropological Archaeology* 24: 316–334.

Evans, T.S. 2007. Exact solutions for network rewiring models. *European Physical Journal B* 56: 65–69.

Farkas, I., D. Helbing, and T. Vicsek. 2002. Mexican waves in an excitable medium. *Nature* 419: 131–132.

Farmer, J. Doyne, and J. Geanakoplos. 2009. The virtues and vices of equilibrium and the future of financial economics. *Complexity* 14: S11–38.

Farmer, J.D., P. Patelli, and I.I. Zovko. 2005. The predictive power of zero intelligence in financial markets. *Proceedings of the National Academy of Sciences USA* 102: 2254–2259.

Fortunato, S. 2005. Damage spreading and opinion dynamics on scale-free networks. *Physica A* 348: 683–690.

Fratkin, E.M. 1989. Household variation and gender inequality in Ariaal Rendille pastoral production: Results of a stratified time allocation survey. *American Anthropologist* 91: 45–55.

Gabaix, X., P. Gopikrishnan, V. Plerou, and H.E. Stanley. 2006. Institutional investors and stock market volatility. *Quarterly Journal of Economics* 121: 461–504.

Gallegati, M., S. Keen, T. Lux, and P. Ormerod. 2006. Worrying trends in econophysics. *Physica A* 370: 1–6.

Gillespie, J.H. 1998. *Population genetics: A concise guide*. Baltimore, MD: Johns Hopkins University Press.

Gintis, H. 2007. A framework for the unification of the behavioral sciences. *Behavioral and Brain Sciences* 30: 1–61.

Guimerà, R., B. Uzzi, J. Spiro, and L.A.N. Amaral. 2005. Team assembly mechanisms determine collaboration network structure and team performance. *Science* 308: 697–702.

Hahn, M.W., and R.A. Bentley. 2003. Drift as a mechanism for cultural change: An example from baby names. *Proceedings of the Royal Society B* 270: S1–S4.

Hajra, B., and P. Sen. 2006. Modelling aging characteristics in citation networks. *Physica A* 368: 575–582.

Hanson, F.A. 2004. The new superorganic. *Current Anthropology* 45: 467–482.

Hayden, B. 2001. The dynamics of wealth and poverty in the transegalitarian societies of Southeast Asia. *Antiquity* 75: 571–581.

Helbing, D., I. Farkas, and T. Vicsek. 2000. Simulating dynamical features of escape panic. *Nature* 407: 487–490.

Henrich, J. 2001. Cultural transmission and the diffusion of innovations. *American Anthropologist* 103: 992–1013.

Henrich, J., R. Boyd, S. Bowles, H. Gintis, E. Fehr, C. Camerer, R. McElreath, M. Gurven, K. Hill, A. Barr, J. Ensminger, D. Tracer, F. Marlow, J. Patton, M. Alvard, F. Gil-White, and N. Henrich. 2005. "Economic man" in cross-cultural perspective: Ethnography and experiments from 15 small-scale societies. *Behavioral and Brain Sciences* 28: 795–855.

Henrich J., and R. Boyd. 2008. Division of labor, economic specialization and the evolution of social stratification. *Current Anthropology* 49: 715–724.

Henrich, J., and F.J. Gil-White. 2001. The evolution of prestige: Freely conferred deference as a mechanism for enhancing the benefits of cultural transmission. *Evolution and Human Behavior* 22: 165–196.

Herzog, H.A., R.A. Bentley, and M.W. Hahn. 2004. Random drift and large shifts in popularity of dog breeds. *Proceedings of the Royal Society B* 271: S353–356.

Hrdy, S. B. 2009. *Mothers and others: The evolutionary origins of mutual understanding.* Cambridge, MA: Harvard University Press.

Huberman, B.A., P.L.T. Pirolli, J.E. Pitkow, and R.M. Lukose. 1998. Strong regularities in World Wide Web surfing. *Science* 280: 95–97.

Hufnagel L., D. Brockmann, and T. Geisel. 2006. The scaling laws of human travel. *Nature* 439. 462–465.

Ijiri, Y., and H. Simon. 1964. Business firm growth and size. *American Economic Review* 54: 77–89.

Kable, J.W., and P.W. Glimcher. 2007. The neural correlates of subjective value during intertemporal choice. *Nature Neuroscience* 10: 1625–1633.

Kauffman, S. 1995. *At home in the universe: The search for laws of self-organization and complexity.* Oxford, UK: Oxford University Press.

Kimura, M., and J. F. Crow. 1964. The number of alleles that can be maintained in a finite population. *Genetics* 49: 725–738.

Knappett, C., T. Evans, and R. Rivers. 2008. Modelling maritime interaction in the Aegean Bronze Age. *Antiquity* 82: 1009–1024.

Koerper, H.C., and E.G. Stickel. 1980. Cultural drift: A primary process of culture change. *Journal of Anthropological Research* 36: 463–469.

Lipo, C.P., M.E. Madsen, R.C. Dunnell, and T. Hunt. 1997. Population structure, cultural transmission and frequency seriation. *Journal of Anthropological Archaeology* 16: 301–333.

Melbourne, B.A., and A. Hastings. 2009. Highly variable spread rates in replicated Biological invasions: Fundamental limits to predictability. *Science* 325: 1536–1539.

Mirowski, P. 2002. *Machine dreams: Economics becomes a cyborg science.* Cambridge, UK: Cambridge University Press.

Neiman, F.D. 1995. Stylistic variation in evolutionary perspective. *American Antiquity* 60: 7–36.

Nettle, D. 2009. Beyond nature versus culture: Cultural variation as an evolved characteristic. *Journal of the Royal Anthropological Institute* 15: 223–240.

Newman, M.E.J. 1996. Self-organized criticality, evolution and the fossil extinction record. *Proceedings of the Royal Society B* 263: 1605–1610.

Newman, M.E.J. 2001. The structure of scientific collaboration networks. *Proceedings of the National Academy of Sciences USA* 98: 404–409.

Newman, M.E.J. 2002. Assortative mixing in networks. *Physical Review Letters* 89: 208701.

Newman, M.E.J., and G.J. Eble. 1999. Power spectra of extinction in the fossil record. *Proceedings of the Royal Society B* 266: 1267–1270.

Newman, M.E.J., A.L. Barabási, and D.J. Watts. 2006. *The structure and dynamics of networks.* Princeton, NJ: Princeton University Press.

Newman, M.E.J., and E. A. Leicht. 2007. Mixture models and exploratory analysis in networks. *Proceedings of the National Academy of Sciences USA* 104: 9564–9569.

O'Brien, M.J., and R.L. Lyman, eds. 1996. *Evolutionary archaeology: Theory and application.* Salt Lake City, UT: University of Utah Press.

O'Brien, M.J., and R.L. Lyman. 2002. The epistemological nature of archaeological units. *Anthropological Theory* 11: 26–36.

Ofek, H. 2001. *Second nature: Economic origins of human evolution.* Cambridge, UK: Cambridge University Press.

Ormerod, P., and R. Colbaugh. 2006. Cascades of failure and extinction in evolving social networks. *Journal of Artificial Societies and Social Simulation* 949: 4.

Ormerod, P., and B. Rosewell. 2003. What can firms know? Plenary talk, *Proc. NAACSOS Conference,* Pittsburgh.

Pareto, V. 1907. *Manuel d'Économie politique.* Paris: Giard et Briére.

Powell, A., S. Shennan, and M.G. Thomas. 2009. Late pleistocene demography and the appearance of modern human behavior. *Science* 324: 1298–1301.

Price, D. de la S. 1965. Networks of scientific papers. *Science* 149: 510–515.

Read, D., D. Lane, and S. van der Leeuw. 2009. The innovation innovation. In *Complexity Perspectives in Innovation and Social Change,* ed. D. Lane. D. Pumain, S.E. van der Leeuw, and G. West, 43-83. Berlin: Springer.

Redner, S. 1998. How popular is your paper? An empirical study of the citation distribution. *The European Physical Journal B* 4: 131–134.

Rogers, E.M. 1962. Diffusion of innovations. New York: Free Press.

Sahlins, M. 1963. Poor man, rich man, big man, chief: Political types in Melanesia and Polynesia. *Comparative Studies in Society and History* 5: 285–303.

Salganik, M.J., P.S. Dodds, and D.J. Watts, 2006. Experimental study of inequality and unpredictability in an artificial cultural market *Science* 311: 854–856.

Salzman, P.C. 1999. Is inequality universal? *Current Anthropology* 40: 31–61.

Shennan, S.J., and J.R. Wilkinson. 2001. Ceramic style change and neutral evolution: A case study from Neolithic Europe. *American Antiquity* 66: 577–594.

Smith, V. 2003. Constructivist and ecological rationality in economics. *American Economic Review* 93: 465–508.

Sneppen, K., P. Bak, H. Flyvbjerg, and M.H. Jensen. 1995. Evolution as a self-organized critical phenomenon. *Proceedings of the National Academy of Sciences USA* 92: 5209–5213.

Solé, R.V., S.C. Manrubia, M. Benton, and P. Bak. 1997. Self-similarity of extinction statistics in the fossil record. *Nature* 388: 764–767.

Solé, R.V., B. Corominas, S. Valverde, and L. Steels. 2005. Language networks: Their structure, function and evolution. *Santa Fe Institute, Working Paper* 05-12-042.

Stanley, M.H.R., L.A.N. Amaral, S.V. Buldyrev, S. Halvin, H. Leschhorn, P. Maass, M.A. Salinger, and H.E. Stanley. 1996. Scaling behaviour in the growth of companies. *Nature* 379: 804–806.

Surowiecki, J. 2004. *The wisdom of crowds: Why the many are smarter than the few.* London: Abacus.

Valverde, Sergi. 2004. A new science for a connected world. *Current Anthropology* 45: 565–566.

Watts, D.J. 2002. A simple model of global cascades on random networks. *Proceedings of the National Academy USA* 99: 5766–5771.

West, B. J., and B. Deering. 1995. *The lure of modern science: Fractal thinking*. Singapore: World Scientific.

Winterhalder, B., and E.A. Smith. 2000 Analyzing adaptive strategies: Human behavioral ecology at twenty-five. *Evolutionary Anthropology* 9: 51–72.

Wright, S. 1932. The roles of mutation, inbreeding, crossbreeding, and selection in evolution. *Proceedings of the Sixth International Congress on Genetics* 1: 355–366.

Wright, I. 2005. The social architecture of capitalism. *Physica A* 346: 589–620.

Wuchty, S., B.F. Jones, and B. Uzzi. 2007. The increasing dominance of teams in production of knowledge. *Science* 316: 1036–1039.

SECTION FOUR

Religion

12

EVOLUTIONARY RELIGIOUS STUDIES:
A BEGINNER'S GUIDE

David Sloan Wilson and William Scott Green[1]

Religion has been studied from a naturalistic perspective for as long as the scholarly study of religion has existed. Early contributors such as Tyler (1871), Frazer (1890), Durkheim (1912), James (1902) and Weber (1930) were trying to explain religion from a *naturalistic perspective*, without invoking the actual existence of supernatural agents or events. Today, there is an enormous body of information on religious phenomena from a naturalistic perspective. Much of it is qualitative, but there is also plenty of quantitative information, gathered and analyzed by the tools of modern science. Some studies are conducted without any theoretical framework in mind, but there are also numerous attempts to understand religion from a particular theoretical perspective, such as Marxism, Freudian psychology, or rational-choice theory.

Against this background, studying religious phenomena from an *evolutionary* perspective is both old and new. Darwin and his colleagues were keenly interested in studying all aspects of humanity from an evolutionary perspective, including religion. However, this inquiry led in directions that can be recognized as false in retrospect. Cultural evolution was envisioned as a linear progression from "savagery" to "civilization," with European societies most advanced (Carniero 2003). Herbert Spencer and others used evolution to justify a hierarchical society ("Social Darwinism") and nonegalitarian social practices such as eugenics (Richards 1987). These views were probably inevitable against the background of Victorian culture, as Janet Browne's (1995, 2002) magnificent two-volume biography of Darwin and his times suggests. Rather than challenging the support that evolutionary theory lent to such views, many scholars and scientists rejected the theory as a useful framework for understanding our species, however insightful it might be for understanding the rest of life. In this fashion, evolutionary theory became restricted to the biological sciences and excluded from most human-related subjects for most of the twentieth century. The controversy surrounding the publication of E.O. Wilson's *Sociobiology* in 1975 illustrates the tenor of the times (Segerstråle 2000).

The modern study of human behavior from an evolutionary perspective represents a fresh start that is based on a much more sophisticated body of theory and knowledge. To

1. This piece was composed in collaboration with the advisory board of the Evolutionary Religious Studies (ERS) project at Binghamton University: Jesse Bering, Lee Cronk, Russell Gray, Dominic Johnson, Michael McCullough, Peter Richerson, and Richard Sosis.

give an idea of how new it is as a field, terms such as *evolutionary psychology* and *evolutionary anthropology* were not even coined until the 1980s and 1990s. Yet the evolutionary perspective is proving so useful and spreading so fast that, in a recent analysis of a premier behavioral science journal (*Behavioral and Brain Sciences*), over 30 percent of the articles were written from an evolutionary perspective during 2000–2004 (Wilson, unpublished data). Evolutionary theory is rapidly becoming a unifying theoretical framework for the study of all human-related subjects, just as it unified the biological sciences during the twentieth century.

The new field of evolutionary religious studies (ERS) is part of this larger trend, although the application of evolutionary theory to the study of religion is still in its infancy. For example, the 2004 meeting of the Society for the Scientific Study of Religion was attended by several hundred participants over a several-day period, yet only a single sparsely attended symposium was devoted to the scientific study of religion from an *evolutionary* perspective. The vast majority of participants were using the tools of science to study religion, but they had never thought about using evolutionary theory as an explanatory framework. In most cases, this was not because they were *hostile* to evolutionary theory but because they had never *encountered* the theory in their disciplinary training, whether they had been trained as psychologists, anthropologists, economists, sociologists, and so on.

This chapter is intended to advance the project of consilience by providing scholars and scientists from all disciplinary backgrounds with an introduction to how religion can be studied from an evolutionary perspective. A remarkably short training period is sufficient to get started. In the aforementioned analysis of the *Behavioral and Brain Sciences*, most of the authors of evolution-related articles received their formal training in other disciplines and acquired their evolutionary expertise on their own initiative. It is, therefore, possible for any scholar or scientist interested in religion to become involved in the emerging field of evolutionary religious studies at the professional level.

SOME PRELIMINARIES

Readers who are newly encountering the field of evolutionary religious studies might come from a variety of backgrounds. Some might be religious believers, others might be primarily scholars and historians of religion, and still others might already employ scientific theories and methods. The following preliminary remarks are intended to get everyone "on the same page" with respect to approaching the subject of religion from an evolutionary perspective.

On the Relationship between Evolutionary Theory and Theological Explanatory Frameworks

Many explanations of religion are theological; that is, they assume the existence of supernatural agents that are capable of intervening in physical processes and human affairs. According to a literal interpretation of the Christian and Hebrew bibles, for example, all living terrestrial animals are descended from ancestors that survived the flood on Noah's Ark. Supernatural explanations such as these are rejected by everyone who adopts a naturalistic perspective, not just evolutionists because they so utterly fail to explain the facts of the world. The geographical distribution of terrestrial animals, for example, cannot be explained as originating from a single geographical location. In addition, the purpose of a theory is to make predictions about measurable properties of the world. Unless we know the will of hypothetical supernatural agents in considerable detail, then we cannot make predictions about their actions. The failure of theology to function as a scientific theory was widely acknowledged before Darwin. For example, Darwin quoted the following passage written by the philosopher and Anglican Priest William Whewell in 1833 on the frontispiece of the first edition of *Origin of Species*: "But with regard to the material world, we can at least go so far as this—we can perceive that events are brought about not by insulated interpositions of Divine power, exerted in each particular case, but by the establishment of general laws." Modern-day creationists and "intelligent-design" proponents have done nothing to alter this assessment (Pennock 1999).

On the Relationship between Evolutionary Theory and Traditional Religious Scholarship

Much traditional religious scholarship, like historical and cultural scholarship in general, is particularistic. The primary effort is to describe and understand a particular religious system (such as early Calvinism), usually in relation to a larger domain of knowledge (such as the Protestant reformation) but not with the goal of explaining religion as a whole on the basis of a general theoretical framework. Mistrust of grand theorizing is understandable, because a succession of grand theories of history, religion, and culture have come and gone. Nevertheless, the fact that evolution is an authentic grand theory for the rest of life on earth suggests that it might also succeed with respect to our own species, even if previous grand theories failed.

On the Relationship between Evolutionary Theory and Other Theoretical Frameworks

When we confine our attention to formal theoretical frameworks, such as Marxism, rational-choice theory, and evolutionary theory, it is important to realize that these are not like alternative scientific hypotheses that invoke different processes, such that one can be right and the other wrong on the basis of empirical observations. Consider rational-choice theory, which assumes that human behavior can be explained in terms of individual utility maximization. When challenged to explain this assumption, most rational-choice theorists would say that utility maximization evolved as a genetic and/or cultural adaptation—those who maximized their utilities survived and reproduced better than their suboptimal competitors. In this fashion, rational-choice theorists assume that their ideas are *consistent* with evolutionary theory, *without requiring much knowledge about* evolutionary theory. This is very different from regarding them as alternative hypotheses, such that one can be right and the other wrong. More generally, when the assumptions of *any* naturalistic explanatory framework are challenged, all roads lead to evolutionary theory.

The case of rational-choice theory is instructive because it has been severely challenged within the field of economics. Many economists have decided that human behavior cannot be explained entirely on the basis of individual utility maximization. In this sense, rational-choice theory is just plain wrong. The field of experimental economics was initiated to empirically discover the actual preferences that drive human behavior in different cultures and environmental situations. This was such an important development that two pioneers, Daniel Kahneman and Vernon Smith, were awarded the Nobel Prize in Economics in 2002. Any experimental research program requires a theoretical framework, however. Where do the human preferences revealed by experimental economics come from? Economists such as Bowles (2003), Fehr and Fischbacher (2003), Gintis (2000), and Hammerstein (2003) are providing a new theoretical foundation for the field of economics that is based explicitly on evolutionary theory. Moreover, their work draws heavily upon anthropologists (such as Boehm 1999) biologists (such as Richerson and Boyd 2005), and psychologists (such as Gigerenzer et al. 2000) in a merging of disciplines that is the hallmark of evolutionary inquiry.

Evolution, Learning, and Culture

A similar story can be told for theories of learning and culture. A common formulation is that biology sets broad limits on human behavior, whereas everything within those limits is determined by learning and culture. According to this formulation, it is true but boring to point out that we like to eat and have sex; much more interesting is our rich cultural diversity, about which evolution has nothing to say. In the same vein, evolution is often equated with genetic determinism, in contrast to the human capacity for change, which is, therefore, imagined as an alternative to evolution.

As with rational-choice theory, this formulation relies upon evolution to justify its own assumptions. The human capacity for short-term change had to come from somewhere, presumably genetic evolution. Less flexible humans existed in the past but were not among our ancestors. The evolutionary account need not rely upon adaptation and natural selection; evolutionists Gould and Lewontin (1979), for example, emphasized chance and developmental constraints in their speculations about human evolution. Either way, those who regard learning and culture as alternatives to biology and evolution are in the precarious position of relying upon the very theory that they reject.

Unsurprisingly in retrospect, the human capacity for fast-paced change is better understood from a sophisticated evolutionary perspective than as an imagined alternative to evolution. Consider an analogy with the immune system: it is a mind-bogglingly complex genetic adaptation for fighting disease organisms, yet its centerpiece is an open-ended process of random antibody formation and selective retention based on their ability to bind to antigens. The immune system is a fast-paced process of antibody evolution, built by the slow-paced process of genetic evolution. Suppose that someone were to argue that the immune system could be understood without recourse to evolution, because it is capable of fast-paced change. This would be deeply wrong for two reasons. First, the immune system could not possibly function without its elaborate, genetically evolved architecture. Second, the immune system's capacity for fast-paced change is itself an evolutionary process. As for the immune system, so also for the human capacity for fast-paced behavioral and cultural change (Wilson 2005).

The immune-system metaphor is highly relevant to the study of religion. One objective of evolutionary religious studies is to explain the genetically evolved psychological architecture that underlies religious belief and practice, such as the propensity for young children to believe in an afterlife (Bering 2006) or the propensity of all people to attribute agency to the events that take place around them (Boyer 2001; Atran 2002). Another objective of evolutionary religious studies is to explain the properties of particular religions in relation to their physical and social environments; for example, why belief in an afterlife features more prominently in Christianity and Islam than in the religion from which they arose, Judaism. These rapid cultural changes—at least compared to genetic evolution, since they can still require decades and centuries to take place—are comparable to antibody formation. Both objectives are integral to the study of religion from an evolutionary perspective.

Is Evolutionary Theory Too General?

The evolutionary perspective is sometimes criticized for being too general. If it includes any kind of human genetic, cultural, or behavioral change, doesn't it explain nothing by explaining everything? To answer this question, consider an analogy with genetic evolution, which is defined as any kind of genetic change, whether by mutation, selection, drift, linkage disequilibrium, and so on. It is important for the definition to include everything to provide a complete accounting system for genetic change. Nevertheless, the definition is not empty because specific categories of genetic change can be determined on a case-by-case basis. Thus, we might decide that guppy spots (and their associated genes) evolve primarily *by selection*, that mitochondrial genes evolve primarily *by drift*, and so on.

The same principle applies when we expand evolutionary theory to include both human genetic evolution and the more fast-paced processes already described. We need to begin with a definition that is sufficiently general to provide a complete accounting system for all kinds of behavioral and cultural change. Then the accounting system needs to include a number of meaningful categories that can be determined on a case-by-case basis; for example, that a given element of religion evolved *by* selection, *or* drift, *or* as a nonadaptive byproduct of another trait, and so on. The generalities that emerge when a large number of cases are assigned to the categories save evolutionary theory from the criticism of being *too* general.

With these general considerations in mind, we can now proceed to the specific subject of religion.

APPLYING BASIC EVOLUTIONARY PRINCIPLES TO THE STUDY OF RELIGION

Six Major Evolutionary Hypotheses

Evolutionists examine a number of major hypotheses for all traits, which, therefore, can be applied to the study of religion, as shown in Table 1.

Table 1 Six Major Evolutionary Hypotheses about Religion, Which Can Apply to Traits That Are Inherited either Culturally or Genetically

Religion As An Adaptation	Religion as Nonadaptive
1. Group-level adaptation (benefits groups, compared to other groups).	4. Adaptive in small groups on related individuals but not in modern social enviroments.
2. Individual-level adaptation (benefits individuals, compared to other individuals within the same group)	5. Byproduct of traits that are adaptive in non-religious context.
3. Cultural parasite (benefits the cultural trait at the expense of human individuals and groups)	6. Neutral traits (drift)

Perhaps the most basic question is whether the trait is an adaptation that evolved by a process of selection. Does a given element of religion exist because it helps an entity (such as an individual or a group) survive and reproduce better than competing entities? If so, then we need to determine the relevant entity. Does the given element of religion increase the fitness of whole groups, compared to other groups (between-group selection), or by increasing the fitness of individuals compared to other individuals within the same group (within-group selection)? With cultural evolution, there is an interesting third possibility. It has been suggested that a cultural trait can spread, not only by benefiting whole groups or individuals within groups, but also by enhancing its own transmission at the expense of human individuals and groups, as if it were a parasitic organism in its own right (Dawkins 2006; Dennett 2006). The concept of religion as a disease is highly novel against the background of traditional religious scholarship.

If a trait it not an adaptation, it can nevertheless persist in the population for a variety of reasons. Perhaps it was adaptive in the past but no longer in the present. For example, our eating habits make excellent sense in a world of food scarcity but have become a major cause of death in modern fast-food environments. Perhaps some elements of religion are like obesity—adaptive in small social groups, but not in the mega-societies of the contemporary West (Alexander 1987).

Alternatively, a trait can be a nonadaptive byproduct of another trait. An architectural example made famous by Gould and Lewontin (1979) is a spandrel, the triangular space that inevitably forms when two arches are placed next to each other. Arches have a function but spandrels do not, although they can acquire a secondary function such as a decorative space. As a biological example, moths use celestial light sources to navigate (an adaptation) but this causes them to spiral inward toward earthly light sources such as a streetlamp or flame—a highly destructive byproduct. Perhaps some elements of religion are like a moth to flame (Dawkins 2006).

Lastly, a trait can have no effect whatsoever on survival and reproduction and simply drift in a population. Many genetic mutations are selectively neutral, enabling them to be used as a molecular "clock" for measuring the amount of time that species have been genetically isolated from each other. Some elements of religion might similarly have no rhyme or reason, other than the vagaries of chance.

These six major hypotheses are summarized in Table 1 and provide an excellent framework for the study of religion. In fact, they can even be used to categorize theories of religion that were formulated without evolution in mind. Consider Durkheim's definition of religion: "[A] unified system of beliefs and practices relative to sacred things…which unite into one single moral community called a Church, all those who adhere to them" ([1912] 1995, 44). Durkheim and the tradition of functionalism that he helped to initiate clearly imagine religion as a system that is adaptive at the level of the group. Nevertheless, it was not classified as "evolutionary" at the time because cultural evolution was associated with other ideas, as outlined earlier. From a modern evolutionary perspective, Durkheim might have been on the right track, but his theory of group-level functionalism requires an explanation in terms of group-level selection.

As a second example, some contemporary sociologists of religion employ rational-choice theory as their theoretical framework. According to Stark and Bainbridge (1987; Stark 1999), the human mind is designed to formulate explanations that are good at obtaining benefits in a nonreligious context. Some benefits cannot be had, such as rain during a drought or everlasting life. That does not prevent us from wanting them, so we invent gods with whom we bargain for that which we cannot have. This is clearly a byproduct theory of religion as something that is not adaptive by itself but connected to something else that is adaptive. Evolutionists such as Pascal Boyer (2001), Scott Atran (2002) and Lee Kirkpatrick (2004) have a different conception of the mind than Stark and Bainbridge, based on evolutionary psychology rather than rational-choice theory, but they also envision the elements of religion as byproducts of mental "modules" that evolved in nonreligious contexts. More generally, it is gratifying that the evolutionary framework can accommodate all naturalistic theories of religion, past and present, without requiring additional major hypotheses. If this seems to make evolutionary theory too general, remember that real progress occurs when we assign particular cases to particular categories— that a given element of religion *is* a byproduct and *not* an adaptation, for example. There are facts that can be agreed upon and hypotheses that can be rejected as just plain wrong, but they need to be organized within a single theoretical framework that acts as an accounting system.

Ultimate and Proximate Causation

All adaptations require two explanations. Why do flowers bloom in spring? The "ultimate" explanation, based on survival and reproduction, is that spring is the best time to bloom. Perhaps flowers that bloomed earlier were nipped by frost, whereas those that bloomed later didn't have time to develop their fruits. The "proximate" explanation is based on the physical mechanisms that actually cause plants to bloom in spring, such as a hormone that is sensitive to day length. Notice that day length by itself has no effect on survival and reproduction. It is merely a signal that reliably causes flowers to bloom at the best time with respect to other environmental factors. In general, the proximate explanation for a trait need bear no relationship whatsoever to the corresponding ultimate explanation, as long as it reliably produces the trait that survives and reproduces better than other traits.

Returning to religion, a belief or practice might exist because it enhances survival and reproduction—for example, by causing the group to function well compared to other groups—but this is only the ultimate explanation. A complementary proximate explanation is required that need bear no relationship to the ultimate explanation, other than to reliably cause the trait to occur. Perhaps a religious believer helps others because she wants to help others, or perhaps because she wants to serve a perfect God who commands her to help others. If these two proximate mechanisms are equally effective at motivating the adaptive behavior, then natural selection will be indifferent about which one evolves. If wanting to serve a perfect God is more powerfully motivating than directly wanting to help others, then it is likely to evolve as the proximate mechanism, even though it is less obviously related to the behavior that it produces and requires belief in an agent for which there is no tangible proof.

The ultimate/proximate distinction bears an intriguing resemblance to a distinction that is often made between the "vertical" and "horizontal" dimensions of religion, as in the following definition of the word *Islam*:

> A noun derived from the verb aslama ("to submit or surrender [to God]"), designates the act by which an individual recognizes his or her relationship to the divine and, at the same time, the community of all those who respond in submission. It describes, therefore, both the singular *vertical* relationship between the human being and God and the collective, *horizontal* relationship of all who join together in common faith and practice. (Eliade 1987, v 7, 119, italics ours)

This passage suggests that the psychological religious experience can exist on a very different plane than the behaviors typically associated with religion. Yet, they are also tightly yoked to each other. The same idea is expressed in a more homespun fashion by the bluegrass lyric "If you don't love your neighbor then you don't love God." The two-dimensional nature of religious belief and practice is exactly what is expected on the basis of the ultimate/proximate distinction.

Often, a *single* adaptive trait can be implemented by *numerous* proximate mechanisms. Not all plants that bloom in spring are sensitive to day length; some species are sensitive to temperature, others to internal biological clocks, and so on. The same one-to-many relationship can potentially explain important differences among religions. For example, belief in a glorious afterlife appears to be central in some religions but peripheral and even absent in others. This makes sense as soon as we regard belief in a glorious afterlife as one of numerous proximate mechanisms capable of motivating adaptive behavior. In general, the ultimate/proximate distinction plays a fundamental role in ERS, along with the six major evolutionary hypotheses.

Niko Tinbergen (1963), who received the Nobel Prize in 1973 for his pioneering research on animal behavior, famously divided evolutionary inquiry into four questions, which he termed "survival value," "causation," "ontogeny," and "evolution." In modern terms, "survival value" corresponds to what we have already described as ultimate causation. "Causation" and "ontogeny" together comprise what we have described as proximate causation, but distinguishes between the final proximate mechanism (causation) and their development over the lifetime of the organism (ontogeny). "Evolution" refers to the phylogeny of a given trait; how it is derived from the traits in ancestral species. Tinbergen's four questions are still much cited today as a description of fully rounded evolutionary inquiry.[2] His emphasis on development and phylogeny certainly needs to be included in

---

2. The journal *Animal Biology* (2005, volume 55, issue 4) includes a reprint of the original paper and a number of articles discussing its relevance to modern research.

the study of religion, along with the distinction that we have already made between ulti-mate and proximate causation.

EXAMPLES OF RESEARCH PROGRAMS WITHIN THE FIELD OF EVOLUTIONARY RELIGIOUS STUDIES

This chapter will conclude with a sample of specific research programs that comprise the emerging field of ERS. They are diverse in their specific aims but unified by the basic principles outlined earlier. There is plenty of disagreement within the field: Some regard religion as primarily a by-product, others as a group-level adaptation, others as a cultural parasite, and so on. What is new and important is that these debates are taking place within an overarching theoretical framework that enables a convergence of views on the basis of empirical information.

The Afterlife Project

Belief in an afterlife is one of the most characteristic elements of religion that sets it apart from most other belief systems. Yet, religious conceptions of the afterlife are also highly diverse. The Afterlife Project[3] is an ambitious effort to understand this diversity in terms of basic evolutionary principles. It is also intended as a model research program that can be used to study other elements of religion.

The goal of the Afterlife Project is to gather information on a large sample of specific conceptions of the afterlife, providing a database for evaluating evolutionary hypotheses on a case-by-case basis. The project is coordinated by the co-authors of this chapter, David Sloan Wilson (an evolutionist) and William Scott Green (a religious scholar). During phase one of the project, a team of evolutionists representing diverse views within the field (Jesse Bering, Lee Cronk, Russell Gray, Dominic Johnson, Peter Richerson, and Richard Sosis) met to agree upon the information that would be required to test the relevant hypotheses. This team then met with a group of religious scholars (Douglas R. Brooks, Dexter Callender, John T. Fitzgerald, Th. Emil Homerin, David Kling, and Michelle Gonzalez Maldonado, with evolutionist Michael McCullough joining the project at this point) to develop a survey for obtaining the information in a standardized fashion for specific conceptions in the afterlife, as they originated and spread at particular times and places in world history. The survey consists of 22 questions that are answered in a narrative format with supporting references, and 76 questions that are answered on a numerical scale for quantitative analysis. During phase two of the project (in progress) the survey is being sent to religious scholars who are best qualified to provide the information. The responses will be posted on the evolutionary religious studies web site in a format that allows discussion and modification by other qualified individuals. In this fashion, comparable information will be gathered for conceptions of the afterlife, for the religions of indigenous societies in addition to the major religious traditions.

---

3. Funded by the Templeton Foundation and administered through the Metanexus Institute.

This project illustrates the central role that traditional religious scholarship can play in the field of evolutionary religious studies. Evolution is fundamentally about the relationship between organisms and their environment. In the case of religion, it is about the relationship between religious groups and their environments, conceived broadly to include physical, economic, and social factors. Traditional religious scholarship provides this kind of information, comprising a fossil record of cultural evolution that is often so detailed that it puts the biological fossil record to shame. The Afterlife Project provides a model for gathering and quantifying this kind of information to test evolutionary hypotheses, for many elements of religion in addition to conceptions of the afterlife.

The Psychological Development of Conceptions of the Afterlife

Are conceptions of the afterlife purely a social construction, or are they more deeply embedded in the psychological architecture of the human mind? Developmental psychologist Jesse Bering (2006) is attempting to answer this question by studying conceptions of the afterlife in young children. In one experiment, children aged 4–12 viewed a puppet show in which an alligator eats a mouse and then answered questions about the mouse. Now that it has died, does it miss its Mom? Is it still hungry? Can it still taste the grass that it ate before it died? Curiously, the younger the children, the more likely they were to attribute mental states to the recently deceased mouse. This is the opposite of what one might expect if the mind begins as a blank slate and all beliefs about the afterlife are culturally acquired.

In another set of experiments, children were told that a friendly invisible magic princess named Alice might tell them when they make the wrong choice in a guessing game. The room was rigged so that a picture fell off the wall or a light flashed on and off after the children made their initial choice. In this case, it was the *older* children (age seven) and not the younger (age four), who treated the mysterious event as a message from Alice to switch their choice. This is probably because the younger children had not yet developed the higher-order reasoning required to infer that "Alice knows that I don't know where the ball is."

These and other experiments, which are conducted in the spirit of Tinbergen's development question, turn conventional wisdom on its head. To an adult nonbeliever, it might seem that belief in an afterlife is weird because it has no basis in observable reality, and, therefore, must be taught. The experiments suggest that children begin life with a default belief in an afterlife and learn to become nonbelievers, or at least to believe less in the afterlife. Why should this be so? Perhaps because the human mind is innately adapted to think of people and other animals as active agents; continuing to regard them in this way after death might be a nonadaptive by-product of genetic evolution.

Even if this hypothesis turns out to be correct, the status of adult beliefs in the afterlife remains an open question. Evolution has been aptly described as a tinkerer, building new structures out of old parts (Jacob 1977). Genetic evolution has resulted in an innate psychological architecture that provides the "parts" for subsequent cultural evolution. It is possible that an innate nonadaptive propensity to believe in an afterlife was elaborated by cultural evolution into highly adaptive specific beliefs about the afterlife. On the other hand, it is also possible that culturally derived adult beliefs in the afterlife are also nonadaptive. Only empirical research can settle these issues. Bering's studies on child development and the Afterlife Project illustrate how very different research programs can be productively related to each other within the framework of evolutionary theory.

Religion as an Adaptation for Promoting Cooperation and Altruism

Taken at face value, many religious beliefs and practices appear designed to promote cooperation and altruism, at least among members of the religion and often more widely. Evolutionary theory offers a comprehensive explanation of how cooperative and altruistic traits can evolve, despite their vulnerability to exploitation by self-serving individuals, which can be brought to bear on the study of religion.

Human cooperation and altruism are strongly dependent upon social control mechanisms, including the ability of group members to monitor each other and effectively punish transgressions at small cost to themselves. Remarkably, the watchful presence of others has such a powerful effect on human behavior that even the presence of disc-shaped objects resembling eyes increases the amount of cooperation in controlled laboratory experiments (Haley and Fessler 2005). Belief in supernatural agents that are always present and motivated to punish transgressions can have a similar effect (Johnson and Bering 2006). In one test of this hypothesis, college students who were casually told that the ghost of a dead graduate student has been spotted in their private testing room were less willing to cheat on a computerized spatial reasoning task than those told nothing (Bering, McLeod and Shackelford 2005). In another test, subjects first performed a scrambled-sentence task and then played the Dictator game, which involved being given ten dollars and deciding how much to keep for oneself and how much to give to an anonymous second person. One version of the scrambled sentence task included religious words such as *spirit*, *divine*, *God*, *sacred*, and *prophet*, whereas another version included words that were unrelated to religion. Subjects who were implicitly primed with religious words in the scrambled sentence task gave an average of $4.22 to the second person, compared to only $1.84 for subjects who were not primed with religious words. Self-reported atheists were as susceptible to religious primes as self-reported believers (Shariff and Norenzayan 2007).

Another mechanism for ensuring cooperation within a group is by requiring commitments that are hard to fake, often because they are so costly that the only way to recoup the cost is by remaining in the group as a cooperator (Irons 2001, Sosis 2004). Numerous elements of religion that appear bizarre and dysfunctional to outsiders make sense in terms of costly signaling theory. For example, in a historical study of nineteenth-century communal societies, Sosis and Bressler (2003) found that religious communes demanded more of their members than their secular counterparts, such as celibacy, relinquishing all material possessions, and vegetarianism. This cost had a collective benefit, however, since religious communes survived longer than their secular counterparts. Among religious communes, those that demanded the greatest cost survived longest, but this relationship did *not* exist for secular communes. Thus, there appears to be something about religious belief per se that makes costly signaling effective.

As an additional test of costly-signaling theory, Sosis and Ruffle (2003, 2004) conducted experiments on cooperative behavior in ongoing secular and religious Israeli kibbutzim (Sosis and Ruffle 2003, 2004; Ruffle and Sosis 2007). Controlling for effects such as the age of the kibbutz, privatization, size of the kibbutz, and numerous other variables, religious kibbutzniks exhibited much higher levels of intra-group cooperation than secular kibbutzniks. Furthermore, religious males were more cooperative than religious females, whereas a sex difference did not exist among the secular kibbutzniks. This pattern makes sense, based on the fact that Jewish ritual requirements are largely publicly oriented toward men and privately oriented toward women.

In a third test of costly signaling theory, Sosis, Kress, and Bressler collected data from 60 geographically dispersed societies on the cost of religious practices, intensity of cooperative food production and consumption, warfare frequency, and a number of other control variables (Sosis et al 2007). Warfare frequency—a strong indicator of the *need* for cooperation—was the strongest predictor of the costliness of a society's male rites. Moreover, Sosis et al. discovered a relationship between the kind of warfare present within a society and the type of religious practice adopted as a commitment signal. Societies with a high degree of external warfare (against other cultural groups) adopted signals of group identity that resulted in permanent badges such as tattoos or scars. Permanent badges were avoided in societies marked by a high degree of internal warfare (within the same cultural grouping), since one's enemy on one occasion might become one's ally on another.

Religion as an Adaptation for War—and Peace

As we have just seen, between-group conflict has been a recurrent event in human history, probably all the way back to our pre-human ancestors. Nevertheless, between-group conflict is not inevitable; instead, it is part of the full range of relationships that can exist among groups. An analogy with biological species is instructive. Ecological relationships among species include predation, competition, parasitism, mutualism, and co-existing without interacting. The particular relationship between any two species depends upon the underlying environmental circumstances. Some species of ants, for example, forage for food and defend their colonies without aggressively attacking other colonies. Other species of ants aggressively attack other colonies to take their resources, territory, and even the ants themselves, which are made into slaves. Both species are highly adapted to their respective ecological niches. The reason nonaggressive species persist is that aggression is not the most adaptive strategy in many environmental situations. Also, calling aggression adaptive (in some environmental situations) does not mean that it is benign or morally acceptable when exhibited in our species. Adaptations frequently result in long-term negative effects, such as the ability to harvest food leading to the depletion of resources. The relationship between adaptation and morality is complex and certainly not direct. Understanding the concept of morality from an evolutionary perspective is an emerging field in its own right, which is developing in parallel with evolutionary religious studies.[4]

---

4. See, e.g., Joyce 2006 and Haidt 2007, and the essays in the "Ethics" section of this volume.

Cultural evolution differs from genetic evolution in many of its details, but it similarly results in a diversity of forms that are adaptive in their respective environments. This is obviously the case for subsistence technologies, such as the ability to make boats in maritime cultures but not desert cultures, but it can be equally true for the ability to make war.

As soon as we start employing the ecological/evolutionary paradigm for cultural evolution in general, two common claims about religion emerge as highly unlikely. First, it is unlikely that religion categorically disposes people toward universal brotherhood. Second, it is equally unlikely that religion categorically disposes people toward between-group conflict. Both of these claims, which are easy to understand as expressions of fondness or hatred toward religion, make little sense as hypotheses from an evolutionary perspective. Instead, to the extent that religions adapts human groups to their environments at all, they should adapt groups to the full range of environmental situations; war *and* peace, not war *or* peace.

An essay titled "The Disarmament of God" by Jack Miles (2003), who won the Pulitzer Prize for his book *God: A Biography*, shows how these ideas can be applied to a specific case such as early Christianity. According to Miles, the Hebrew God was essentially a warrior who commanded his people to fight and promised them victory in the future, no matter how many defeats they had endured in the past. The Christian God reflected the reality that military victory was no longer possible and the only strategy for survival involved a more peaceful co-existence. The Christian God could be said to be a different God entirely from the Hebrew God, as some scholars have noted. Cultural evolution seldom involves such radical discontinuities, however, so Christians imagined their God as continuous with the past. In any case, "turn the other cheek" can be a successful non-militaristic strategy, as the spread of early Christianity amply confirms. Once Christians became politically powerful, cultural evolution promoted the resumption of militaristic strategies, as in the Crusades.

More generally, every major religious tradition has the flexibility to tailor prescribed behaviors to environmental circumstances. This very basic statement follows directly from evolutionary theory, but it is not always obvious from other perspectives. When we take it seriously, it becomes clear that the way to eliminate between-group conflict is not to foster religion (if you love it) or eliminate religion (if you hate it), but to manage the social environment so that war is not an adaptive strategy.

Individual Benefits of Religion

The behavioral consequences of religion include but also go beyond cooperation and altruism. Numerous studies show that religious beliefs and practices increase individual health and other aspects of well-being (e.g., Post 2007). Although these are certainly individual benefits of religion, they are not necessarily individual-level adaptations in the evolutionary sense of the term. If the individual benefits are provided by the activities of other individuals or by the culture as a whole, then they are manifestations of group-level adaptations.

Other elements of religion might be individually advantageous in the less benign sense of increasing the welfare of some individuals (often the leaders) at the expense of other members of the same religious group (Cronk 1994). The Catholic practice of selling indulgences prior to the Protestant Reformation was clearly a form of exploitation that enriched the elites at the expense of lay members of the religion. This kind of behavior, which benefits individuals *compared to other individuals within the same group*, is found to some extent in all social groups, and, therefore, in all religious groups. The degree to which it occurs is a question that must be answered empirically on a case-by-case basis. At one extreme, a religious system might be so well designed to promote cooperation that within-group exploitation becomes a rarity and is conceptualized as a corruption of the religion when it occurs. Alternatively, the entire religion could be designed as a tool of exploitation, like a well-planned sting operation. As yet another possibility, a given religious system—like any cultural system—could be a largely dysfunctional by-product of individual striving within the system. It is so easy to think about culture in functional terms that the following passage by anthropologist Lee Cronk (1995, 187–188) is worth keeping in mind as an antidote:

> As part of my continuing effort to find an improved metaphor for the role of culture in human affairs, I place tongue in cheek and offer the following: Culture is to human social interaction as mud is to mud-wrestling. The metaphor of wrestling conveys the idea that social interaction is in many ways a contest or struggle between people with competing goals. But wrestling of the nonmuddy variety does not do the metaphorical job. The mud is needed to stand for culture in order that the analogy may more fully convey the nature of human social interactions as they take place in cultural contexts. Just as mud drastically changes the nature of the contest when it is introduced into a wrestling match, so does culture drastically change the nature of social interaction in humans compared to nonhumans. Just as mud-wrestlers are coated in mud, people are coated in culture: It shapes who they are and how they interact with others in profound ways, which of course is an old lesson to anthropologists. Like mud, culture can get in your eyes, leading you to do things that may not be in your own best interests. Just as mud-wrestlers may use the mud itself in their contest— flinging it, wallowing in it, using it to blind their opponents—so do people use culture as a tool in social interaction. Just as one wrestler covered in mud is likely to muddy others in the ring, so do culture traits cling to people and move from one to another through social contact. The mud-wrestling analogy also inspires some interesting questions about culture. For instance, how deep is the mud? That is, to what extent does culture limit and guide human actions? Are we up to our necks in mud, able to move only in culturally prescribed ways, or is the mud down around our ankles, causing us to slip now and then but not influencing our basic strategies in meaningful ways? Or is it somewhere in between? As apt as the mud-culture metaphor may be, the wrestling part of the metaphor needs some modification because it makes it appear that all social interaction consists of contests in which only one person may win. That of course, is not the case. A better image might be an n-person mud melee, in which cooperation and coalitions (tag teams?) are possible.

One insight that emerges from thinking about cooperation and exploitation from an evolutionary perspective is that they can actually be arranged in a temporal sequence.

In a remarkable book titled *War and Peace and War*, Peter Turchin (2005) outlines an ambitious theory of human history as a process of multilevel cultural evolution. Geographical zones of extreme between-group conflict act as a crucible for extremely cooperative cultures, which spread at the expense of less cooperative cultures. Their success is their undoing, however, as exploitation, free riding, and factionalism spread by cultural evolution *within* the society—the rise and fall of empires. Turchin's theory applies to all cultural systems, religious or otherwise. If we confine our attention to religious systems, we can observe the same cycle of cooperation, corruption, and renewal (Wilson 2002, 182–187).

Religion on a Moment-by-Moment Basis

The psychologist Mihaly Csikszentmihalyi pioneered the Experience Sampling Method (ESM) which involves signaling people at random times during the day, prompting them to record where they are, what they are doing, who they are with, and a checklist of cognitive and emotional states on a numerical scale. The method has been used on large numbers of people, enabling the effects of religion to be studied on a moment-by-moment basis. In one sample of American high school students, religious believers were more prosocial than nonbelievers, felt better about themselves, used their time more constructively, and engaged in long-term planning rather than gratifying their impulsive desires. On a moment-by-moment basis, they reported being more happy, active, sociable, involved, and excited. Some of these differences remained even when religious believers and nonbelievers were matched for their degree of prosociality (Wilson and Csikszentmihalyi 2007).

In addition to comparing religious believers vs. nonbelievers, the ESM can be used to make even finer comparisons between religious denominations. Using the same sample of American high school students, Storm and Wilson (2009) demonstrated substantial differences between members of liberal versus conservative Protestant denominations. For example, conservatives spent less time alone and their psychological mood quickly started to deteriorate when they were alone. Liberals appear to have internalized their value system so that they were less dependent upon the physical presence of others. In general, the differences between varieties of religion (such as conservative vs. liberal) can be as great as the differences between religions and cultural systems that are classified as nonreligious.

But What about Religion Per Se?

One issue that is sometimes raised about ERS is that the basic principles are so general that they apply to all cultural systems. If the same principles can be used to explain religious systems, political systems, military systems, and business systems, then what does evolutionary theory tell us about religion per se? We think that the generality of evolutionary theory is a strength rather than a weakness when it comes to explaining a particular phenomenon such as religion. Religion is decidedly a fuzzy set. Any particular feature that seems to be part of the essence of religion can be found in cultural systems that are conventionally regarded as nonreligious. Moreover, religious systems compete with nonreligious systems in the real world of cultural evolution. The best theoretical framework for understanding religion is one that can situate the big picture of religion within the even bigger picture of all human cultural systems.

SUMMARY

Our sample of specific research programs shows how diversity of methods, drawn from virtually every human-related academic discipline, can be integrated within a single theoretical framework for the study of religion. The fact that evolutionary theory *integrates* disciplines rather than *excluding* them means that virtually any scholar with a serious interest in religion can join the emerging field of ERS with a manageable amount of initial training. In addition to this beginners guide, a web site has been established to make evolutionary religious studies the theoretical framework of choice for all scientists and scholars interested in the study of religion.[5]

ACKNOWLEDGEMENTS

The project that gave rise to this essay is supported by a TARP (Templeton Advanced Research Program) grant provided by the John Templeton Foundation (http://www. templeton.org/) and administered through the Metanexus Institute (http://www .metanexus.net/).

References

Alexander, R. D. 1987. *The biology of moral systems*. New York: Aldine de Gruyter.

Atran, S. 2002. *In gods we trust: The evolutionary landscape of religion*. Oxford: Oxford University Press.

Bering, J. M. 2006. The cognitive psychology of belief in the supernatural. *American Scientist* 94: 142–149.

Bering, J. M., K. McLeod, and T. Shackelford. 2005b. Reasoning about dead agents reveals possible adaptive trends. *Human Nature* 16: 360–381.

Boehm, C. 1999. *Hierarchy in the forest: Egalitarianism and the evolution of human altruism*. Cambridge, MA: Harvard University Press.

Bowles, S. 2003. *Microeconomics: Behavior, institutions, and evolution*. Princeton: Princeton University Press.

Browne, J. 1995. *Charles Darwin: Voyaging*. New York: Knopf.

Browne, J. 2002. *Charles Darwin: The power of place*. New York: Knopf.

Boyer, P. 2001. *Religion explained*. New York: Basic Books.

Carniero, R. 2003. *Evolution in cultural anthropology: A critical history*. Boulder, CO: Westview Press.

Cronk, L. 1994. Evolutionary theories of morality and the manipulative use of signals. *Journal of Religion and Science* 29(1): 81–101.

Cronk, L. 1995. Is there a role for culture in human behavioral ecology? *Ethology and Sociobiology* 16: 181–205.

5. Please consult the web site http://evolution.binghamton.edu/religion/for a directory of researchers and research programs, some of which invite your participation.

Dawkins, R. 2006. *The god delusion*. Boston: Houghton Mifflin.

Dennett, D. C. 2006. *Breaking the spell: Religion as a natural phenomenon*. New York: Viking.

Durkheim, E. 1912/1995. *The elementary forms of religious life*. New York: The Free Press.

Eliade, M., ed. 1987. *The encylopedia of religion*. New York: MacMillan.

Fehr, E., and U. Fischbacher. 2003. The nature of human altruism. *Nature* 425: 785–791.

Frazer, J. G. 1890. *The golden bough*. London and New York: MacMillan.

Gigerenzer, G., P. M. Todd, and A. R. Group, eds. 2000. *Simple heuristics that make us smart*. Oxford: Oxford University Press.

Gintis, H. 2000. *Game theory evolving*. Princeton, NJ: Princeton University Press.

Gould, S. J., and R. C. Lewontin. 1979. The spandrels of San Marco and the panglossian paradigm: A critique of the adaptationist program. *Proceedings of the Royal Society of London* B205: 581–598.

Haidt, J. 2007. The new synthesis in moral psychology. *Science* 316: 998–1002.

Haley, K. J., and D. M. T. Fessler. 2005. Nobody's watching? Subtle cues affect generosity in an anonymous economic game. *Evolution and Human Behavior* 26: 245–256.

Hammerstein, P., ed. 2003. *Genetic and cultural evolution of cooperation*. Cambridge, MA: MIT press.

Irons, W. 2001. "Religion as a hard-to-fake sign of commitment." In *Evolution and the capacity for commitment*, ed. R. Nesse, 292–309. New York: Russell Sage Foundation.

Jacob, F. 1977. Evolution and tinkering. *Science* 196: 1161–1166.

James, W. 1902. *The varieties of religious experience*. New York: Longmans, Green.

Johnson, D. D. P., and J. M. Bering. 2006. "Hand of God, mind of man: Punishment and cognition in the evolution of cooperation." In *The believing primate: Scientific, philosophical, and theological reflections on the origin of religion*, ed. J. Schloss and M. Murray, 26–43. New York; Oxford University Press.

Joyce, R. 2006. *The evolution of morality*. Cambridge, MA: MIT Press.

Kirkpatrick, L. A. 2004. *Attachment, evolution, and the psychology of religion*. New York: Guilford Press.

Miles, J. 1996. *God: A biography*. New York: Vintage.

Miles, S. (2003). The self-disarmament of God as evolutionary preadaptation. *Midwest Studies in Philosophy* 27(1): 153–165.

Pennock, R. 1999. *Tower of Babel: Evidence against the new creationism*. Cambridge, MA: MIT Press.

Post, S. G., ed. 2007. Altruism and health: Perspectives from empirical research. Oxford: Oxford University Press.

Richerson, P. J., and R. Boyd. 2005. *Not by genes alone: How culture transformed human evolution*. Chicago: University of Chicago Press.

Richards, R. J. 1987. *Darwin and the emergence of evolutionary theories of mind and behavior*. Chicago: University of Chicago Press.

Ruffle, B. J., and R. Sosis. 2007. *Does it pay to pray? Costly ritual and cooperation. The B.E Journal of Economic Analysis and Policy* 7: 1–35.

Segerstråle, Ullica. 2000. *Defenders of the truth: The battle for sociobiology and beyond*. New York: Oxford University Press.

Shariff, A. F., and A. Norenzayan. 2007. God is watching you: Supernatural agent concepts increase prosocial behavior in an anonymous economic game. *Psychological Science* 18: 803–809.

Sosis, R. 2004. The adaptive value of religious ritual. *American Scientist* 92: 166–172.

Sosis, R., and E. R. Bressler. 2003. Cooperation and commune longevity: A test of the costly signaling theory of religion. *Cross-cultural research* 37: 211–239.

Sosis, R., H. Kress, and E. R. Bressler. 2007. The scars of war: Evaluating alternative signaling explanations or cross-cultural variation in ritual costs. *Evolution and Human Behavior*, 28: 234–247.

Sosis, R., and B. J. Ruffle. 2003. Religious ritual and cooperation: Testing for a relationship on Israeli religious and secular kibbutzim. *Current Anthropology* 44: 713–722.

Sosis, R., and B. J. Ruffle. 2004. Ideology, religion, and the evolution of cooperation: Field experiments on Israeli Kibbutzim. *Research in Economic Anthropology* 23: 89–117.

Stark, R. 1999. Micro foundations of religion: A revised theory. *Sociological Theory* 17: 264–289.

Stark, R., and W. S. Bainbridge. 1987. *A theory of religion*. New Brunswick, NJ: Rutgers University Press.

Storm, I., and D.S. Wilson. 2009. Liberal and Conservative Protestant Denominations as Different Socio-Ecological Strategies. *Human Nature* 20: 1–24.

Tinbergen, N. 1963. On aims and methods of ethology. *Zeitschrift für Tierpsychologie* 20: 410–433.

Turchin, P. 2005. *War and peace and war*. Upper Saddle River, NJ: Pi Press.

Tyler, E. B. 1871. *Primitive culture*. New York: Brantano's.

Weber, M. 1930/1992. *Protestant ethic and the spirit of capitalism*. London: Routledge.

Wilson, D. S. 2002. *Darwin's cathedral: Evolution, religion, and the nature of society*. Chicago: University of Chicago Press.

Wilson, D. S. 2005. Evolutionary social constructivism. In *The literary animal: Evolution and the nature of narrative*, eds. J. Gottschall, and D. S. Wilson, 20–37. Evanston: Northwestern University Press.

Wilson, D. S., and M. Csikszentmihalyi. 2007. Health and the ecology of altruism. In *The Science of Altruism and Health*, ed. S. G. Post, 314–331. Oxford: Oxford University Press.

13

THE CULTURAL EVOLUTION OF RELIGION

Ara Norenzayan and Will M. Gervais

After almost a century of dwelling in two "non-overlapping magisteria," as Steven Jay Gould once put it, scientific interest in religion is on the rise again. Long the exclusive province of the humanities and left outside of the mainstream of psychology and the cognitive and behavioral sciences, religion is gaining scientific attention at a rapid pace. The dismantling of the taboos that have kept religion out of the scientific spotlight will take time (Dennett 2006). Nevertheless, these are exciting times 123, and we can now safely say that religion—to paraphrase Chomsky about language—has been upgraded from scientific mystery to scientific puzzle (Boyer 2001). This growing scientific interest promises to offer a naturalistic account for a deeply affecting aspect of human lives that is widespread in all known cultures in the world.

In this chapter we explain the relation between religion and prosocial behaviors within an evolutionary perspective. In putting together this synthesis, we cover a large amount of territory from evolutionary biology, sociology, history, evolutionary and cultural anthropology, game theory, neuroscience, behavioral economics, and our home field, social psychology. We show how different findings from these diverse fields can be fruitfully integrated under a unifying theoretical framework that is grounded in an evolutionary perspective that gives center stage to human cultural evolution, and thus is compatible with cultural variability in religious thought and behavior across societies and throughout history (for discussions, see Richerson and Boyd 2005; Henrich and Henrich 2007). No doubt, this synthesis is in its infancy, and many important details and assumptions continue to be actively debated and elaborated. In this regard, we also highlight a number of unresolved questions for future research, such as the relation between religion and moral psychology, how modern secular societies sustain cooperation and trust without religion, and—as any theory of religion worth its salt must attempt—we offer theoretical speculations to explain the widespread existence of atheism as a psychological and cultural phenomenon.

The debate on religion's role in prosocial behavior has been polemical. In recent years, two new developments have altered this picture. First, explanations for the evolutionary origins of religion have gained focus and empirical plausibility, bolstered by a small but growing empirical base that unites several academic disciplines (Boyer 2001; Barrett 2004; Atran and Norenzayan 2004; Sosis and Alcorta 2003; McNamara 2006). Second, evolutionary explanations for the origins of human prosociality have been developed that model the interaction of innate tendencies with cultural learning (Henrich and Henrich

2007; Richerson and Boyd 2005). These two developments can now be fruitfully synthesized to explain two fundamental, interrelated aspects of human social life: (1) the key role of religion in the rise of large, cooperative societies in the last 15,000 years; and (2) the cultural spread and persistence of prosocial religious beliefs on a worldwide scale.

Religious prosociality is the idea that religions facilitate acts that benefit others at a personal cost (Norenzayan and Shariff 2008). All major world religions explicitly encourage prosociality in their adherents (Batson, Schoenrade, and Ventis 1993). This is an influential idea with a long history (for early discussions of religion and social cohesion that emphasizes ritual, see Durkheim, 1912/1995; for recent evolutionary treatments, see Irons 1991; Johnson and Kruger 2004; Sosis and Alcorta 2003; Wilson 2002; Bering 2011). Our thesis has many similarities with these approaches, but also departs from previous ones in that we argue for the central role of belief in supernatural agents (in addition to religious ritual), and emphasize the importance of culturally evolutionary processes in religious prosociality (in addition to and interacting with genetic evolution).

THE EVOLUTIONARY LANDSCAPE OF RELIGION

There is growing agreement that the suite of psychological tendencies that support and give rise to religious beliefs have been shaped by the evolutionary forces that have constrained ordinary human social life throughout history. However, to date there is no scientific consensus among evolutionary researchers as to whether religious belief itself was naturally selected in the human lineage. One view is that at least some religious beliefs and behaviors are biological adaptations for cooperative group-living that have maximized genetic fitness at the individual level (Johnson and Bering 2006; Bering 2011; Sosis and Alcorta 2003); another is that religion is a biological adaptation for group living that evolved by multilevel selection (Wilson 2002).

Two additional accounts view religion as a cultural by-product of evolved psychology, and invoke cultural evolutionary processes to explain religion's wide reach. One of these accounts proposes that religious content itself is a cultural by-product of a suite of psychological tendencies evolved in the Pleistocene for other purposes, in particular detecting and inferring the content of other minds and sensitivity to one's prosocial reputation in the group (Atran and Norenzayan 2004; Boyer 2001). Religious beliefs that were compatible with these psychological tendencies culturally spread through social learning mechanisms and could solve social or psychological problems—especially, but not exclusively, the problem of cooperation in large groups. The other cultural by-product account maintains that competition among social groups may have favored the spread of fitness-enhancing, socially transmitted cultural beliefs that gave rise to religious prosociality (Boyd and Richerson 2002; Henrich and Henrich 2007; Wilson 2002). These various evolutionary theories of religion have much in common, and all predict that religious beliefs and behaviors have facilitated human prosocial tendencies, but there is disagreement about exactly how this might have occurred. In this chapter, we outline an evolutionary scenario that is compatible with either of the two cultural evolutionary perspectives; toward the end we return to these different theoretical accounts in light of the evidence presented, but first, we start with a brief account of the psychological capacities that were evolutionary by-products of human cognitive architecture that, once in place, could give rise to belief in supernatural agents (gods, ghosts, ancestor spirits).

Religious beliefs draw on several core cognitive features that are reliably developing, and regularly reoccur across cultures and historical periods (Atran and Norenzayan 2004; Barrett 2004; Boyer 2001; Lawson and McCauley 1990). One such feature is derived from a mentalizing or "Theory of Mind" faculty, which allows people to detect and infer the content of other minds. This in turn supplies the cognitive basis for the dualistic intuition that "mind stuff" is distinct from "physical stuff" (Bloom 2007) and may give rise to the pervasive belief in disembodied supernatural agents, such as gods and spirits, who are believed to possess humanlike beliefs and desires (Guthrie, 1993; Barrett and Keil 1996). Consistent with this reasoning, thinking about God activates brain regions associated with theory of mind (Kapogiannis, et al. 2009; Schjoedt, Stodkilde-Jorgensen, Geerts, & Roepstorff 2009). Furthermore, the autistic spectrum—which involves deficits in theory of mind—is associated with lower belief in God, and individual differences in mentalizing ability mediate this relationship (Norenzayan, Gervais, & Trzesniewski 2011). Finally, it appears that mentalizing may also explain why women tend to be more religious than men: women, who are generally superior mentalizers, find it easier to mentally represent supernatural agents, and, therefore, are more likely to believe in them (Norenzayan et al 2011).

The relationship between mentalizing and belief in supernatural agents rests on the important distinction between the "proper" domain of a mental faculty, and its "cultural" domain (Sperber 1996. The mentalizing faculty, that is applicable to human agents (its proper domain), is also partially triggered by supernatural agent beliefs (one of its cultural domains that overlaps with the proper domain). This explains how a genetically evolved mental faculty (mentalizing), that was naturally selected because of a pre-existing proper domain (human agents), can produce culturally diverse mental representations (various supernatural agent beliefs) that nevertheless are activated by it. Once supernatural agent beliefs were cognitively in place, their content could be subjected to cultural selection. Despite being anthropomorphized (Barrett and Keil 1996), supernatural agents, unlike their earthly counterparts, are believed to transcend physical, biological, and psychological limitations, some more than others (Atran and Norenzayan 2004; Boyer 2001). Furthermore, some cultural versions gave rise to belief in morally concerned policing agents who use these supernatural powers to observe, punish, and reward human social interactions. Hard-to-fake religious behavior, such as fasts, food taboos, and costly ritual performance, in turn may have reliably signaled the presence of devotion to these agents and galvanized greater group commitment, reinforcing ingroup cooperative norms. Religious prosociality thus softened the genetic constraints inherent in kinship-based and (direct or indirect) reciprocity-based altruism that otherwise severely limit group size. In this way, religious prosociality facilitated the rise of stable, large, cooperative moral communities of genetically unrelated individuals (Norenzayan and Shariff 2008; Roes & Raymond 2003).

A second core psychological feature that religions exploit is the acute human sensitivity to prosocial reputation (Fehr and Fischbacher 2003), a psychological mechanism originally unrelated to religion, which evolved to facilitate various strategies of reciprocal cooperation among interacting humans (Nowak and Sigmund 2005; Gintis, Bowles,

Boyd, and Fehr 2003). In an intensely social, gossiping species, reputational concern likely contributed to the evolutionary stability of strong cooperation between strangers. Individuals known to be selfish could be detected and subsequently excluded from future interaction, and under some conditions punished even at personal cost (Gintis, et al. 2003; Henrich, et al. 2006). The threat of being found out, therefore, became a potent motivator for good behavior. Highlighting the importance of reputational mechanisms in the evolution of prosocial behavior, studies have shown that people are more prosocial in economic games when the situation is not anonymous (Hoffman, McCabe, Shachat, and Smith 1994), and when they expect repeated future interactions than if future interactions are absent (Fehr and Gachter 2002. Even subtle exposure to schematic drawings resembling human eyes increase prosocial behavior in anonymous economic games (Haley and Fessler 2005) and decrease cheating in naturalistic settings (Bateson, Nettle, and Roberts 2006). The cognitive awareness of morally concerned Gods is likely to heighten prosocial reputational concerns among believers, just as the cognitive awareness of human watchers do among believers and non-believers alike. Omniscient, morally concerned supernatural watchers, to the degree that they are genuinely believed and cognitively salient, offer the powerful advantage that cooperative interactions can be monitored even in the absence of humans (for distinct but related arguments, see Johnson and Bering 2006; Johsnon 2009; Bering 2011).

The line of reasoning just outlined accounts for a wide range of empirical evidence linking religion to prosocial tendencies, and predicts that this relationship ought to be context sensitive, with clear boundary conditions. First, religious devotion is expected to be associated with greater prosocial reputational concern. Second, religious situations would automatically activate thoughts of moralizing divine agents and habitually facilitate prosocial behavior. It follows that experimentally inducing awareness of morally concerned supernatural agents would also increase prosociality even when no one is watching—that is, even when the situation is objectively anonymous. However, this should be the case only to the extent that thoughts of supernatural agents are cognitively accessible in the moment when prosocial decisions are called for. Third, religious behavior that signals genuine devotion would be expected to induce greater cooperation and trust. Fourth, large societies that have successfully stabilized high levels of cooperative norms would be more likely than smaller ones to espouse belief in morally concerned Gods who actively monitor human interactions. In the remainder of this chapter, we critically examine the available empirical evidence in light of these four predictions.

RELIGION AND PROSOCIAL BEHAVIOR: DOING GOOD VS. LOOKING GOOD

If religions centered around moralizing Gods promote prosociality, it would be expected that individuals who report stronger belief in such Gods have stronger altruistic tendencies. Sociological surveys suggest this is the case. Those who frequently pray and attend religious services reliably report more prosocial behavior, such as charitable donations and volunteerism (Brooks 2006). This "charity gap" is consistent across surveys, and remains after controlling for income disparities, political orientation, marital status, education level, age, and gender. These findings have been much publicized as evidence that religious people are more prosocial than the non-religious (Brooks 2006). However, it remains unresolved whether this charity gap persists beyond the in-group boundaries of the religious groups (Monsma 2007). More importantly, these surveys are entirely based on self-reports of prosocial behavior. Psychologists have long known that self-reports of socially desirable behaviors (such as charitability) may not be accurate and may instead reflect impression management or self-deception (Paulhus 1984). If, as we hypothesize, religious individuals are more motivated to maintain a prosocial reputation than the non-religious, then the former may be more likely to engage in prosocial reputation management. Supporting this hypothesis, psychological research summarizing many studies has found that measures of religiosity are positively associated with tests of socially desirable responding, a common human tendency to project a positive image of oneself in evaluative contexts (Trimble 1997). This latter association raises questions not only about the nature of the prosocial tendencies found in the sociological surveys, but about the behavioral reality of the differences as well. To address the methodological limitations inherent in self-reports, experiments with behavioral outcomes must be consulted.

In several behavioral studies, researchers failed to find any reliable association between religiosity and prosocial tendencies. In the classic "Good Samaritan" experiment, for example, researchers staged an anonymous situation modeled after the Biblical parable—a man was lying on a sidewalk appearing sick and in need of assistance. Participants were students at the Princeton Theological Seminary who were generally religious, but nevertheless scored differently on several distinct dimensions of religiosity. They were led to pass by this victim (actually a research confederate) on their way to complete their participation in a study. Their likelihood of offering help to the victim was unobtrusively recorded. Results showed no relationship between dimension or degree of religiosity and helping in this anonymous context (Darley and Batson 1973). Only a situational variable—whether participants were told to rush or take their time—led to reliable differences in helping rates.

Other behavioral studies, however, have found reliable associations between religiosity and prosociality, albeit under limited conditions. In one study, participants played a public-goods game, which allowed researchers to compare levels of cooperation between secular and religious kibbutzim in Israel (Sosis and Ruffle 2003). In this game that assesses cooperation and/or coordination, two members of the same kibbutz who remained anonymous to each other were given access to a "public good"—an envelope with a certain amount of money. Each participant simultaneously decided how much money to withdraw from the envelope and keep for themselves. If the sum of the withdrawals was equal or below the total amount in the envelope, players got to keep the money they requested. If the sum of the withdrawals exceeded this total, the players received nothing. The results showed that, controlling for relevant predictors, systematically less money was withdrawn in the religious kibbutzim than in the secular ones.

Thus, unlike studies such as the "Good Samaritan," there were greater levels of contributions to the public good in religious rather than secular kibbutzim. One key difference is that reminders of God are likely to be chronically present in religious kibbutz, where religious prayer and attendance are a daily part of life. Another is that prosociality in the religious kibbutz clearly benefited in-group members. In the kibbutzim study, highly religious men, who engaged in daily and communal prayer, took the least amount of money from the common pool, thereby showing the greatest amount of in-group coop-eration. It is also possible that regular, communal prayer involves public ritual participa-tion, which, independent of devotion to a morally concerned deity, might also encourage more prosociality (Sosis and Ruffle 2003).

In another ambitious investigation spanning 14 small-scale societies of pastoralists and horticulturalists, Henrich and colleagues (2009) measured the association between reli-gious belief and prosocial behavior in three well-known economic games. In the Dictator Game, two anonymous players are allotted a sum of real money in a one-shot interaction. Player 1 must decide how to divide this sum between himself and Player 2. Player 2 then receives the allocation from Player 1, and the game ends. Player 1's allocation (the offer) to Player 2 provides a measure of generosity or fairness in this context. The Ultimatum Game is identical to the Dictator Game, except that Player 2 can accept or reject the offer. If Player 2 specifies that he would accept the amount of the actual offer, then he receives the amount of the offer and Player 1 receives the rest. If Player 2 specifies that he would reject the amount offered, both players receive zero. Player 1's offer measures a combination of intrinsic motivation toward fairness in this context and an assessment of the likelihood of rejection. In the Third-Party Punishment Game two players are again allotted a sum of money, Player 1 must decide how much of this sum to give to Player 2, but now a third player also receives the equivalent of one-half the sum and has the opportunity to punish Player 1 for any given offer by paying a certain cost. Player 1's offer measures a combination of intrinsic motivation toward fairness and an assessment of the punishment threat.

Henrich and colleagues found that, controlling for a variety of sociodemographic var-iables, those who believed in the moralizing Abrahamic God (as opposed to those who believed in the local deities who are not as morally concerned) made larger offers in the Dictator Game and the Ultimatum Game. However, belief in God did not reliably predict offers in the Third-Party Punishment Game. One possible explanation for this pattern of findings is that belief in a morally involved supernatural watcher is most likely to matter when the situation contains no threat of third-party punishment. In other words, the credible threat of punishment might have crowded out the motivation to act fairly that is induced by fear of supernatural punishment.

Another approach to clarifying the nature and boundary conditions of religious proso-ciality is to investigate the altruistic or egoistic motivation underlying the prosocial act. One possibility holds that the greater prosociality of the religious is driven by an empathic motive to ameliorate the condition of others. Alternatively, prosocial behavior could be driven by egoistic motives, such as projecting a positive image or avoiding guilt (failing to live up to one's prosocial self-image). The preponderance of the evidence supports the latter explanation. Studies repeatedly indicate that the association between conventional religiosity and prosociality occurs primarily when a reputation-related egoistic motiva-tion has been activated (Batson et al. 1993). In one experiment, for example, participants were given the option of volunteering to raise money for a sick child who could not pay his medical bills (Batson et al. 1993). In one condition, participants were led to believe that they would certainly be called upon if they volunteered. In another, participants could volunteer while told that they were unlikely to be called upon. In the latter condition, participants could reap the social benefits of feeling (or appearing) helpful without the cost of the actual altruistic act. Only in this latter situation was a link between religiosity and prosociality evident. Several studies conducted by Batson and his colleagues have corroborated that religiosity predicts prosocial behavior primarily when the prosocial act could promote a positive image for the participant, either in their own eyes or in the eyes of observers (Batson et al. 1993).

As insightful as these behavioral studies are, however, causal inference has been limited by their reliance on correlational designs. If religiosity is related to prosocial behavior under some contexts, it is possible that having a prosocial disposition causes one to be religious, or that a third variable (such as dispositional empathy or guilt-proneness) causes both prosocial and religious tendencies. Recent controlled experiments have addressed this issue by experimentally inducing thoughts of supernatural agents and then measuring prosocial behavior.

WHEN BIG EYE IN THE SKY IS WATCHING

If religious belief has a causal effect on prosocial tendencies, then experimentally induced thoughts of morally involved supernatural agents should increase prosocial behavior in controlled conditions. In one such experimental study, children were explicitly instructed not to look inside a box, and then left alone in the room with it (Bering 2006). Those who were previously told that a fictional supernatural agent, Princess Alice, was watching were significantly less likely to peek inside the forbidden box. Another study (Johnson and Bering, 2006) found a similar effect among university students. Participants who were randomly assigned to a condition in which they were casually told that the ghost of a dead student had been spotted in the experimental room cheated less on a rigged computer task. In these two studies, however, it is unclear whether the supernatural constructs being activated were perceived to be morally concerned. In a different study, temporary and subliminal activation of God concepts led to lower rates of cheating in an anonymous context (Randolph-Seng and Nielsen 2007). In the control condition of this study, religiosity as an individual difference measure did not predict levels of cheating.

We have proposed that the concept of moralizing Gods stabilized cooperation levels in large groups of anonymous individuals, where reputational and reciprocity incentives are insufficient. If so, then reminders of God may not only reduce cheating, but also curb selfish behavior and increase generosity toward strangers. This hypothesis was tested and confirmed in two anonymous Dictator Game experiments, one with a sample of university students, and another with non-student adults (Shariff and Norenzayan 2007). In one experiment, adult nonstudent participants were randomly assigned to three groups. Participants in the religious prime group unscrambled sentences that contained words such as *God, divine*, and *spirit*. The neutral control group played the same word game, but with nonreligious content. The secular prime group played the game with words such as *civic, jury*, and *police*—thereby priming them with thoughts of secular moral authority. This well-established implicit priming procedure activates a particular concept without any conscious awareness (Bargh and Chartrand 1999). Each participant subsequently played the anonymous Dictator Game. Nearly double the money was offered by the givers with God on their minds. Furthermore, the results showed not only a quantitative increase in generosity, but also a qualitative shift in social norms. In the control group, the modal response was purely selfish: Most players pocketed all ten dollars. In the God group, the mode shifted to fairness: A plurality of participant split the money evenly. The group that was primed with secular institutions of morality also showed greater generosity than the control group—in fact, as much as was found in the God group—this important finding suggests that religious belief is only one of several sources of prosociality—an idea to which we will return later. This finding has been replicated with a Chilean Catholic sample, showing similar religious priming effects on generosity in the Dictator Game and on cooperation levels in the Prisoner's Dilemma Game (Ahmed and Salas 2008). Another set of studies demonstrated that religious primes increased (1) the accessibility of prosocial thoughts, and (2) charitable behavioral intentions (Pichon, et al. 2007).

What are the psychological processes that might explain this link between God primes and prosociality? Two accounts suggest themselves, and both gain plausibility given two distinct but well-supported empirical literatures. The *behavioral priming* or *ideomotor* account is supported by considerable evidence showing that prosocial behavior can be facilitated by activating non-conscious altruistic thoughts (e.g., Bargh et al. 2001). Thoughts of God are associated with notions of benevolence and charity, and, therefore, activating these thoughts may activate prosocial behavior. The *supernatural watcher* account is supported by extensive evidence that heightened reputational concerns increase prosociality (e.g., Fehr and Fischbacher 2003). Thoughts of God may have increased the feeling of being watched by a morally concerned observer, thus removing the purported anonymity of the situation. This, in turn, is known to increase prosocial behavior. These two mechanisms are not mutually exclusive, and may even reinforce each other in everyday life.

This raises a crucial question: What evidence can distinguish the supernatural watcher account from behavioral-priming processes? First, if the priming effects of God concepts are weaker or nonexistent for nonbelievers, then the effect could not be solely due to ideomotor processes, which are typically impervious to prior explicit beliefs or attitudes. Second, if God primes make religious participants attribute actions to an external source of agency, these effects could not be explained by ideomotor processes, as such manipulations disambiguate the felt presence of supernatural watchers from their alleged prosocial consequences. Lastly, if the supernatural watcher explanation is at play, religious primes should arouse social evaluation of the self. Moreover, such reputational awareness should moderate the magnitude of the prime's effect on prosocial behavior.

Currently, evidence on the first point is mixed, with some experiments showing religious priming effects irrespective of participants' prior religious conviction, whereas others demonstrating effects specific to believers only (Norenzayan, Shariff, and Gervais 2010). However, close examination of the findings betrays a revealing pattern. All but one of the relevant studies recruited student samples, which can be problematic because beliefs, attitudes, and social identity among students can be unstable, raising questions about the reliability of chronic individual-difference measures of religious belief and identity measures for students who are still in transition to adulthood (Sears 1986; Henrich et al. 2010). Thus, student atheists might be at best "soft atheists." In the only religious priming experiment we are aware of that recruited a nonstudent adult sample (Shariff and Norenzayan 2007, Study 2), the effect of the prime emerged again for theists, but disappeared for these "hard" atheists.

Regarding the second question, one experiment clearly separates the felt presence of a supernatural agent from prosocial outcomes. Dijksterhuis et al. (2008) found that after being subliminally primed with the word *God*, believers (but not atheists) were more likely to ascribe an outcome to an external source of agency, rather than their own actions. In addition, religious belief positively correlates with greater concern with social evaluation of the self (Trimble, 1997), and recent experimental evidence points to this being a causal relationship. Gervais and Norenzayan (2009) found that priming God concepts increased public self-awareness (Govern and Marsch 2001)—a measure that taps into feelings of being the target of social evaluation. In contrast, and as predicted, the prime had no effect on private self-awareness. All the evidence points to the prediction that prosocial effects of religious primes are moderated by measures of evaluative concern, which is a key expectation of the supernatural watcher hypothesis and incompatible with a purely ideomotor account.

IN GODS WE TRUST

In the absence of reputational information about a stranger's prosocial inclinations, outward evidence of sincere belief in the same or similar morally concerned Gods may serve as a reliable cooperative signal. Evidence from attitudinal surveys shows religious individuals to be considered more trustworthy and more cooperative than non-believers, and not just by the religious (Edgell, Gerteis, and Hartmann 2006). Extensive ethnographic evidence also suggests that in historical and social contexts lacking reliable social monitoring institutions, membership in religious communities who adhere to the same Gods may have lowered monitoring costs and thereby facilitated trade relations across geographical boundaries and even ethnically diverse communities that heavily depend on trust. The spread of Islam in Africa, which preceded the flourishing of wide-scale trade among Muslim converts (Ensminger 1997), and the trade networks of Medieval Jewish Maghrebi merchants (Greif 1993) are two examples consistent with the idea that costly commitment to the same supernatural deity can foster intense cooperation in communities otherwise highly vulnerable to defection. These ethnographic data provide rich case studies. However, they are open to other interpretations, for example that religious conversions led to greater access to pre-established trade networks along these religious lines, or that some other feature correlated with religiosity elicited greater trust. Therefore, further controlled studies are needed to address these limitations.

The few laboratory studies that have examined religion's role in trusting behavior support this conclusion as well. Trust can be defined as a costly investment in a person or entity, with the future expectation of return. In one well-researched laboratory game of trust (Berg, Dickhaut, McCabe 1995), participants were randomly assigned to be a proposer (truster) or a responder (trustee). In the first step, the proposer decides how much money to forward to the responder, knowing that any transferred amount gets multiplied. In the second step, the responder decides how much money, if any, to send back to the proposer. By transferring money to the responder, the proposer stands to gain, but only if the responder can be trusted to reciprocate. In a variation of this trust experiment, researchers measured individual differences in the religiosity of the proposer and the responder. In addition, in some trials, proposers knew about the level of religiosity of the responder. Results indicated that more money was forwarded to responders when they were perceived to be religious, and this was particularly true for religious proposers (Tan and Vogel 2008). Furthermore, religious responders were more likely to reciprocate the proposer's offer than less religious responders. However, if sincere belief in a morally concerned deity serves as a reliable signal that elicits cooperation, where does religious trust end and distrust begin? How do believers approach believers of other faiths, and especially those who do not believe at all? In other words, what are the limits of religious prosociality?

RELIGIOUS DISTRUST AND THE LIMITS
OF RELIGIOUS PROSOCIALITY

The literature reviewed thus far suggests that beliefs in supernatural agents capable of monitoring human behavior are potent motivators of prosocial behavior and trust. How far does this trust extend? For example, do religious believers preferentially trust members of other, perhaps competing, faiths? If so, are there any groups of people who are systematically excluded from the reach of religious prosociality?

People should be most trusting of those who worship the same deities as themselves. However, the logic of religious prosociality predicts that trust can be extended beyond the immediate religious community as long as these outsiders adhere to some kind of supernatural sanctioning that constrains their behavior. Thus Muslims might be able to trust Christians, who at least in principle believe in the same all-powerful, morally involved God. Christians might trust Hindus who believe in an entire pantheon of supernatural monitors. Trust can be extended to potential cooperation partners if the latter adhere to some kind of supernatural monitoring that induces greater cooperativeness.

The claim that members of one religious group will also trust members of other religious groups is admittedly speculative, but it does receive some support. Sosis (2005) argues that religious signals of trustworthiness can be co-opted by members of other religious groups. He notes, for example, that Mormons are viewed as particularly trustworthy nannies by non-Mormon New Yorkers (Frank 1988), and Sikhs are viewed by non-Sikhs as trustworthy economic partners (Paxson 2004). In at least some situations, observers appear to use commitment to even rival gods as signals of trustworthiness.

Matters are different for atheists, however. If belief in gods is perceived to be a reliable signal of trustworthiness, it follows that those who explicitly deny the existence of God are sending the wrong signal: They are perceived to be noncooperators by the religious. A key consequence of religious prosociality, therefore, is distrust of atheists. History is rife with distrust of atheists. Even as major a figure of the Enlightenment as John Locke thought that atheists undermine the moral fabric of society: "...those are not at all to be tolerated who deny the being of a God. Promises, covenants, and oaths, which are the bonds of human society, can have no hold upon an atheist. The taking away of God, though but even in thought, dissolves all." Ironically, this quote comes from his 1689 "Letter Concerning Toleration"! (Locke [1983] 1689).

At first glance, anti-atheist distrust and prejudice is puzzling. Atheists are not a particularly large, visible, or powerful group in religious societies. Yet there is abundant evidence that atheists are the least trusted group in cultures that have religious majorities. Polls leading up to the 2008 presidential election in the United States vividly illustrate this selective exclusion of atheists. In a February, 2007 Gallup poll, for instance, 95 percent of respondents stated that they would vote for a Catholic candidate, 92 percent for a Jewish candidate, and 72 percent for a Mormon Candidate. However, fewer than half (45 percent) said they would vote for an atheist. In fact, atheists were the only group included in the poll (including twice-divorced candidates, elderly candidates, and homosexual candidates) that could not recruit a majority vote. Relative to other minority groups, antipathy toward atheists as measured in this sort of poll has remained remarkably stable over the last 50 years in the United States, decades that saw increasing acceptance of most other groups (Edgell, Gerteis, and Hartmann 2006). This pattern of findings is consistent with the idea that religious distrust is not merely a reflection of a general distrust of out-group members. People following other religions are as much outsiders, and often more so, than atheists. Yet atheists who are ethnically similar are trusted less than even members of out- groups who are religiously, linguistically, and ethnically different.

Anti-atheist prejudice extends to a wide range of moral domains. In a widely discussed paper, Edgell and colleagues (2006) found that respondents rated atheists as the group that least shares their own vision of America, and rated an atheist as the individual that they would most disapprove of as a marriage partner for their child. This pattern is striking. As these authors note:

> Americans are less accepting of atheists than of any of the other groups we asked about, and by a wide margin. The next-closest category on both measures is Muslims. We expected Muslims to be a lightning-rod group, and they clearly were. This makes the response to atheists all the more striking. For many, Muslims represent a large and mostly external threat, dramatized by the loss of life in the World Trade Center attacks and the war in Iraq. By contrast, atheists are a small and largely silent internal minority. (217–218)

Indeed, in the context of recent conflicts in the world that involve Americans, it is surprising that atheists were liked less than Muslims. However, in the context of religious prosociality, the logic underlying anti-atheist prejudice becomes clear. Atheists, who do not believe in punishing supernatural agents and who do not adopt conspicuous signals of religious commitment, should be viewed as untrustworthy rather than "merely" unpleasant. This prediction stands apart from a long tradition in social psychology that takes a one-size-fits-all approach to prejudice, viewing it as a generalized feeling of dislike toward out-groups. Although there is some tangential evidence that distrust is central to anti-atheist prejudice—for instance, most Americans report that morality is impossible without belief in God (Pew Research Center 2002)—the hypothesis has only recently received rigorous empirical attention.

Gervais, Shariff, and Norenzayan (2009) derived a number of specific predictions about the psychological underpinnings of potential atheist distrust (rather than atheist dislike).

First, and most obviously, they predicted belief in God would be more strongly related to specific distrust of atheists rather than general dislike of atheists. As expected, belief in God was more strongly related to distrust of atheists than to dislike of atheists, based on a computer task that measures implicit associations (based on reaction times when an atheist target was paired with distrust words like "lying" and "dishonest," as opposed to dislike words like "hostile" and "hate").

Second, they predicted that exclusion of atheists would be most pronounced when trust is a particularly valued characteristic. To explore this possibility, they had participants state whether they would prefer to hire an atheist or a religious candidate for either a high-trust job (a day-care worker) or a low-trust job (a waitress) that were matched for other characteristics such as friendliness and intelligence. As expected, participants significantly excluded the atheist when hiring a day-care worker, and showed no such preference when hiring a waitress.

Lastly, Gervais and colleagues predicted that participants would rate an atheist as less trustworthy, though no less pleasant or intelligent, than a religious believer. In addition, they sought to compare anti-atheist prejudice to ethnic prejudice, which is a benchmark comparison in the study of prejudice. To do so, they gave participants two fictional targets to rate on a number of attributes. They rigged the experiment so that one target would always be an atheist of the participant's own ethnicity and the other target would always be religious, but of a different ethnicity. Overall, participants did not report that they felt more warmly toward either target. Nor did they differentiate between the targets based on intelligence or pleasantness. However, they rated the atheist as significantly less trustworthy than the religious target.

These studies reveal consistent distrust of atheists, even within the relatively secularized context of a liberal university in Vancouver, Canada. Atheist distrust should be even more potent in more strongly religious societies, in which atheists would be viewed as even more deviant. At the same time, distrust of atheists among religious believers might be reduced in countries with more atheists. Though seemingly intuitive, this prediction runs counter to decades of research demonstrating that prejudice increases in concert with relative outgroup size (e.g., Fossett and Kiecolt 1989; Giles and Evans 1986; Pettigrew 1959). Gervais (in press) explored the relationship between atheist prevalence and distrust of atheists in a series of three studies. In an archival analysis of anti-atheist prejudice among more than 40,000 believers from 54 countries, anti-atheist prejudice was reduced where atheists are more common, controlling for individual differences in age, sex, educational attainment, income, liberalism/conservativism, and church attendance, as well as international differences in socioeconomic development and individualism/collectivism. In another study, a more focused follow-up study using a university sample, perceptions of how common atheists are were associated with reduced anti-atheist prejudice, especially among the *most* deeply religious participants. Lastly, it was found that experimentally induced reminders of how common atheists are statistically eliminated anti-atheist prejudice. Across all these studies, anti-atheist prejudice was reduced where atheists are common, further setting anti-atheist prejudice apart from other forms of prejudice that are less influenced by religious prosociality. Combined, these studies support the notion that anti-atheist prejudice is based on distrust and is distinct from other types of prejudice, as an understanding of religious prosociality predicts.

HOW TO GALVANIZE GROUP SOLIDARITY: THE EVOLUTION OF COSTLY RELIGIOUS DISPLAYS

One of the most striking aspects of many religious groups is the prevalence of costly religious displays. Costly ritual performances—such as rites of terror, various restrictions on behavior (sex, material belongings), diet (fasts and food taboos), and lifestyle (strict marriage rules, dress codes)—consume effort, time, and resources, are emotionally loaded, and appear irrational to outsiders. However, just as the irrationality of falling in love communicates commitment to a relationship (Gonzaga and Haselton 2008), religious fervour may have its logic too: it communicates a hard-to-fake commitment to the beliefs of the religious group.

However, the exact mechanisms by which these behaviors achieve evolutionary stability are currently debated. One prominent view is ritual signaling. Grounded in the behavioral ecology perspective, this view argues that the tendency for costly religious displays is a reliable signal of group commitment that was a naturally selected adaptation for life in cooperative groups (Sosis and Alcorta 2003). We have seen that religious thoughts increase prosocial behavior, religious faith evokes trust, and lack of belief leads to social exclusion. In this view, a signal is reliable only to the extent that it is costlier to fake by potential freeloaders than for cooperators. If religious groups are cooperative groups, what would prevent selfish imposters from faking belief, receiving cooperative benefits without reciprocating? Because mere professions of religious belief can be easily faked, evolutionary pressures have favored costly religious displays that are not subject to rational calculations of cost-benefit analysis (Irons 2001; Sosis and Alcorta 2003). Thus, costly religious behaviors are seen as honest signals that reliably advertise the unobservable trait of religious belief and/or group commitment.

However, this reasoning has been challenged on several grounds (Henrich 2009). For example, it is unclear why it is more costly for non-believers to perform the costly acts than for believers, since beliefs are culturally transmitted, and are quite unlike possessing a genetically fixed physical attribute (such as physical stamina or height). It seems that explaining costly religious displays presupposes cultural transmission of beliefs underlying these behaviors. Another distinct hypothesis, then, derives from a cultural evolutionary perspective, and holds that costly religious behaviors are credibility-enhancing displays (CREDs), which are reliably associated with genuine belief in counterintuitive gods and can be used to infer sincere commitment to them (Henrich 2009). Costly religious displays are often seen in successful religious leaders. For instance, Henrich discusses how early Christian saints, by their willing martyrdom, became potent cultural models and encouraged the cultural spread of Christian beliefs. When religious leaders' actions credibly signal their underlying belief, this, in turn, helps their beliefs to spread. If, on the other hand, they are not willing to make a significant sacrifice for their belief, then observers—even children—withhold their own commitment. Once people believe, they are more likely to perform similar displays themselves, which offers another explanation about why potentially costly behaviors spread in religious groups. Potentially costly displays often come in the form of altruism toward other ingroup members, further ratcheting-up the level of in-group cooperation and benefiting such groups. One key difference between these two frameworks, then, is in regard to whether costly displays cause greater commitment to religious beliefs. The CRED framework predicts that costly religious displays *cause* greater commitment to the religious beliefs of the group as a result of cultural contagion, whereas the ritual signaling framework sees costly displays merely as reliable signals that elicits cooperation without causal effects on levels of group commitment.

Regardless of the theoretical debates and the precise mechanisms that are at play, there is mounting evidence that costly religious displays emerge and contribute to group solidarity, further cementing religious prosociality in groups with moralizing gods. Sociological analyses are consistent with the idea that groups that impose more costly requirements have members who are more committed (Iannacone 1994). Controlling for relevant socio-demographic variables, "strict" Protestant and Jewish denominations (Mormons, Orthodox) show higher levels of church and synagogue attendance and more monetary contributions to their religious communities (despite *lower* average income levels) than less strict ones (Methodist, Reform) (Iannacone 1992). However, these findings do not demonstrate that strictness predicts community survival and growth. In another investigation, religious and secular communes in ninteenth century America, which had to solve the collection-action problems to survive, were examined. Religious communes were found to outlast those motivated by secular ideologies such as socialism (Sosis and Alcorta 2003). In a further quantitative analysis of 83 of these religious and secular communes (Sosis and Bressler 2003) for which more detailed records are available, it was found that religious communes imposed more than twice as many costly requirements (including food taboos and fasts, constraints on material possessions, marriage, sex, and communication with the outside world) than secular ones, and this difference emerged for each of the 22 categories of costly requirements examined. Moreover, religious communes were about three times less likely than secular ones to dissolve at any given year as a result of internal conflict or economic hardship. Importantly for costly religious signaling, the number of costly requirements predicted religious commune longevity ($R^2 = .38$) after controlling for population size and income, and year the commune was founded; contrary to expectations, the number of costly requirements did not predict longevity for secular communes. Religious ideology was not a predictor of commune longevity once the number of costly requirements was statistically controlled, suggesting that the survival advantage of religious communes was due to the greater cost commitment of their members. Although these findings are revealing, more research is clearly needed, including further experimental studies and alternative mathematical models of costly religious behavior (either as a stable strategy characteristic of individuals, or as a stable strategy that takes into account intergroup social competition), before firm conclusions can be reached. The evidence, however, is suggestive of the possibility that religious belief, to the extent that it can be advertised with sincerity, may enhance within-group interpersonal trust and commitment, further reinforcing intragroup prosocial tendencies. This resolves a key puzzle about religion that has long baffled observers—why many religious behaviors and rituals demand sacrifice of time, effort, and resources.

HOW BIG WATCHFUL DEITIES HELPED CONSTRUCT BIG GROUPS

It appears, then, that belief in moralizing Gods, supported by costly religious displays, enhance within-group interpersonal trust and group solidarity, and thus stabilize prosocial norms even in the absence of social monitoring mechanisms. This being the case, religious prosociality would be expected to expand the reach of cooperative norms, facilitating the emergence of larger cooperative communities that otherwise would be vulnerable to collapse. We examine this hypothesized association between moralizing Gods and large group size next.

From large village settlements at the dawn of agriculture to modern metropolises, human beings are capable of living in extraordinarily large cooperative groups. However, extrapolating from cross-species comparisons of neocortex size, it has been estimated that human group sizes cannot exceed 150 individuals before groups divide or collapse (Dunbar 2003). Although this specific number can be debated, it is apparent today that, since the end of the Pleistocene, the size of human groups has often far exceeded the limitations that kin-based and reciprocity-based altruism placed on group size.

It has been hypothesized that cultural evolution, driven by between-group competition for resources and habitats, has favored large groups (Alexander 1987). There is evidence supporting this hypothesis: in the 186 societies of the standard cross-cultural sample (SCCS), prevalence of conflict among societies, resource-rich environments, and group size are positively intercorrelated (Roes and Raymond 2003); in fact, it has been argued that these were the antecedent conditions that gave rise to politically centralized states (see Carneiro 1970). However, as groups expand in size, situations become more anonymous, and prosocial norms are harder to stabilize. Therefore, large groups, which until recently lacked social monitoring mechanisms, are vulnerable to collapse due to high rates of freeloading (Gintis et al. 2003). If unwavering and pervasive belief in moralizing Gods buffered against such freeloading, then belief in such Gods should be more likely in larger human groups where the threat of freeloading is most acute. In a cross-cultural analysis using again the SCCS, group size was indeed a strong predictor of belief in moralizing Gods. The larger the group size, the more likely the group culturally sanctioned omniscient, all-powerful, morally concerned deities who directly observe, reward, and punish social behavior (Roes and Raymond 2003). This finding held controlling for the cultural diffusion of moralizing Gods via Christian and Muslim missionary activity, as well as for indicators of population density and societal inequality. Similarly, controlling for a number of factors, moralizing Gods are more likely in societies with high water scarcity, where the need to minimize freeloading is also pronounced (Snarey 1996). Thus, moralizing Gods appear to be culturally selected for when freeloading is more prevalent or particularly detrimental to group stability.

HOW BIG WATCHFUL DEITIES CAME TO BE: ALTERNATIVE EVOLUTIONARY SCENARIOS

We have argued (Norenzayan and Shariff 2008; Norenzayan, 2010; Shariff et al. 2010) that integrating cognitive by-product theories of religion and cultural evolutionary explanations for cooperation yields a cogent explanation for the rise and persistence of religious beliefs. Once belief in supernatural agency emerged as a by-product of mundane cognitive processes, cultural evolution favored the spread of a special type of supernatural agent—moralizing high Gods. Growing evidence is converging on the conclusion that belief in these omniscient supernatural watchers facilitated cooperation and trust among strangers (Norenzayan and Shariff 2008). Not surprisingly, this cultural spread coincided with the expansion of human cooperation into ever- larger groups over the last 15 millennia (Cauvin 2000).

An alternative evolutionary account (e.g., Bering et al. 2005; Johnson and Bering 2006; Johnson, 2009) is that belief in morally concerned Gods was selected by maximizing the genetic fitness of group-living individuals. In particular, it is argued that such belief reduced the fitness costs associated with noncooperation in an intensely social, gossiping species such as ours, in which individual survival heavily depends on group living. There is considerable agreement between this view and ours, and it may be premature to reach firm conclusions. Nevertheless, we can offer some preliminary speculations toward the goal of ultimately distinguishing these possible scenarios and testing their plausibility against the growing amount of evidence.

The cultural evolutionary scenario we have outlined here has the virtue of explaining a feature of religious prosociality that would be baffling if it arose as a genetic adaptation—namely, the systematic cultural co-variation between the prevalence of moralizing Gods and group size (e.g., Roes and Raymond 2003). The deities of most small-scale societies tend to be neither fully omniscient nor morally concerned. This is puzzling for adaptationist arguments, since these groups more closely approximate ancestral conditions, and they should be most likely to reveal such a genetic adaptation. However, we gain appreciation for why this is so when we realize that, in small hunter-gatherer bands, relationships typically are among kin or reciprocating partners, and, although people may encounter strangers occasionally, especially outside of group boundaries, situations calling for cooperation are rarely anonymous. In these intimate, transparent groups, reputations can be monitored with ease and social transgressions are difficult to hide. As a result, supernatural policing is unnecessary and relationships with spirits and gods in these groups tend not to have a moral dimension (Wright 2009). In contrast, in evolutionarily recent anonymous social groups interactions among strangers is a regular aspect of daily life. It is these large modern societies, facing the breakdown of reputational and kin selection mechanisms for cooperation, which most strongly espouse belief in such Gods. This cross-cultural pattern—increased moral involvement of Gods as groups gain in size—can be elegantly explained by the cultural evolutionary scenario. It also speaks against the genetic adaptation account, unless we assume that a genetic adaptation for belief in moralizing Gods arose independently, multiple times in multiple societies, in the last 15 thousand years. Although this latter possibility cannot be conclusively ruled out, it is an unlikely scenario.

Second, a genetic adaptation account at the level of individuals faces another theoretical challenge: mathematical modeling of cooperative behavior shows that reputation management as a strategy does not achieve evolutionary stability beyond dyadic relationships (Henrich and Henrich 2007). To the extent that this is the case, widespread belief in God concepts cannot be explained by reputational sensitivity at the individual level. To account for this, another variant of the cultural evolutionary account would invoke cultural group selection, such that ancestral societies that learned to uphold moralizing God concepts would have outcompeted those without, given the cooperative advantage of believing groups (Wilson 2002). Unlike genetic group selectionist accounts of altruistic behavior in humans, which face a number of well-known theoretical and empirical challenges (e.g., Atran 2002), cultural group selection, although a minority view among researchers, is more plausible theoretically and better substantiated empirically (see Henrich and Henrich 2007).

Lastly, a purely genetic adaptation account makes a surprising prediction, which remains to be examined, namely, if belief in moralizing Gods is innate, then real atheists should not exist in any great numbers. In fact, atheists are the fourth largest "religious" group in the world, trailing only Christians, Muslims, and Hindus; people who do not believe in any gods are 58 times more numerous than Mormons, 41 times more numerous than Jews, and twice as numerous as Buddhists (Zuckerman 2007). One argument is that "explicit atheism" masks a universal "implicit theism." A number of authors have argued for such a scenario and have doubted the long-term plausibility of atheism (e.g., Barrett 2004; Boyer 2008; Bloom 2007; Slingerland 2008). This possibility should be taken seriously—after all, explicit belief can be unhinged from implicit belief, as people often have little or no introspective access into their own mental states that operate outside of conscious awareness (e.g., Nisbett and Wilson 1977). Nevertheless, the claim that explicit atheism masks implicit theism has remained untested. Furthermore, there is preliminary evidence that, in at least some cases (as already discussed), self-proclaimed atheists, unlike believers, are uninfluenced by even implicit and subliminal reminders of God (Dijksterhuis et al. 2008; Shariff and Norenzayan 2007). Barrett (2004) noted that we must explain, not only why it is that most people believe, but also why some don't. It is presently unknown how a genetic adaptationist explanation for belief explains why anyone—let alone hundreds of millions of people—could fail to believe in gods. In contrast, a cultural evolutionary account can more easily accommodate the viability of non-belief, even at a large scale. Even if humans are equipped with deeply rooted, reliably developing cognitive dispositions that make belief in supernatural agents "easy to think," cultural variability in the availability of religious models in one's environment may interact with these tendencies, and give rise to different levels of religious conviction in adulthood, including non-belief. However, given that we know next to nothing about the psychological antecedents of atheism, we do not yet understand what aspects of one's social environment, if any, or socialization period predicts the likelihood of non-belief in adulthood.

CONCLUSIONS

Voltaire said, "if there were no God, it would be necessary to invent him." We have argued, with Voltaire, that the idea of morally involved, omniscient Gods was a remarkable cultural innovation that solved the problem of cooperation in the large anonymous communities of recent human history. As groups grow in size, social situations become more anonymous, and prosocial tendencies are hard to sustain. However, if "watched people are nice people," as extensive research in social psychology and behavioral economics shows, then "supernatural watchers" who can observe social interactions and threaten to punish selfish acts and reward prosocial ones, encourage cooperative behavior and trust, even when no one is watching. Because religious groups are communities of co-operators based on trust, they are vulnerable to collapse unless free-riders are detected and excluded. Therefore, evolutionary pressures must have selected for costly religious behaviors (such as fasts and some forms of costly ritual participation) that are hard to fake and are reliable indicators of honest commitment.

Religious prosociality is a complex co-evolutionary phenomenon that draws jointly on genetic and cultural processes. The human psychological repertoire honed by natural selection gave rise to hypervigilence in detecting intentional agents and their mental states, and active management of prosocial reputations. These tendencies facilitated the cultural transmission of belief in moralizing Gods, which, in turn, caused greater levels of prosocial tendencies, ultimately leading to larger and more stable cooperative groups. Costly religious commitment further buffered religious groups from freeloaders by serving as a reliable signal that advertised a hard-to-fake cooperative intention toward in-group members.

Many religious traditions around the world explicitly encourage the faithful to be unconditionally prosocial (Batson et al. 1993; Monsma 2007), yet theoretical considerations and empirical evidence indicate that religiously socialized individuals should be, and are, much more discriminate in their prosociality. Although empathy and compassion as social-bonding emotions do exist and may play a role in prosocial acts some of the time (Keltner and Haidt 2001), there is little direct evidence we are aware of that such emotions are implicated in religious prosociality. We await more research to shed light on any possible links between religious prosociality and the prosocial emotions such as empathy, compassion, guilt, and shame.

The preponderance of the evidence points to religious prosociality being a bounded phenomenon. Religion's influence on prosociality is most evident when the situation calls for maintaining a favorable social reputation within the in-group. When thoughts of morally concerned deities are cognitively salient, an objectively anonymous situation becomes nonanonymous and, therefore, reputationally relevant. This could occur either when such thoughts are induced experimentally, or in religious situations, such as when people attend religious services or engage in ritual performance. This explains why the religious situation is more important than the religious disposition in predicting prosocial behavior.

Morally concerned deities, combined with costly religious signaling, were, until recently, the primary stabilizers of large cooperative social groups. However, the spread of secular institutions—such as courts, policing authorities, and effective contract-enforcing mechanisms in some modern societies—raise the specter of large scale prosociality without religion. Religions continue to be powerful facilitators of prosociality, but they may no longer be the only ones. Although this is a complex question that cannot be resolved with the current available evidence, there are some indications that secular societies may have passed a threshold, no longer needing religion to sustain large-scale prosociality. For example, active members of secular organizations are at least as likely to report donating to charity as active members of religious ones (Putnam 2000). Supporting this conclusion, experimentally induced reminders of secular moral authority had as much effect on generous behavior in an economic game as reminders of God (Shariff and Norenzayan

2007), and there are many examples of modern large, cooperative societies with a great degree of intragroup trust that are not very religious (Hermann, Thöni, and Gächter 2008). In fact, some of the most cooperative and trusting societies on earth, such as those in Scandinavia, are also the least religious in the world (Zuckerman 2008). People have found ways to be nice to strangers without God.

Is the future of the world toward secularization, or toward more religious fervor? Worldwide sociological evidence shows that societies, as they experience economic growth and greater conditions of existential security, move toward more secularization; yet, because religiosity has a net positive effect on fertility rates, even after controlling for socioeconomic status (Blume 2009), secular societies are shrinking while religious ones are expanding. As a result, a larger proportion of the world's population remains religious, and the world has more religious people than ever before (Norris and Inglehart 2004).

Despite the scientific progress in explaining the effects of religion on prosociality, open and important questions remain. In recent years, moral psychology has received a great deal of scientific attention (Haidt 2007), and although most of the studies already reviewed concern behavioral outcomes, the relation between religious prosociality and moral intuitions and reasoning is ripe for further investigation. The finding that religiosity evokes greater trust also calls for more experimental and theoretical research, including mathematical modeling to establish the specific conditions under which costly religious commitment could evolve as a stable individual strategy, and whether multi-level selection models are needed. Finally, as we have seen, religious prosociality is not extended indiscriminately: The dark side of within-group cooperation is between-group competition and conflict (Choi and Bowles 2007). The same mechanisms involved in in-group altruism may also facilitate out-group antagonism. This is an area of no small debate, but scientific attention is needed to examine precisely how individuals and groups determine who are the beneficiaries of religious prosociality, and who are its victims.

References

Ahmed, A. M., and O. Salas. 2008. In the back of your mind: Subliminal influences of religious concepts on prosocial behavior. *Working Papers in Economics* 331:

Alexander, R. D. 1987. *The biology of moral systems.* New York: Aldine de Gruyter.

Atran, S., and A. Norenzayan. 2004. Religion's evolutionary landscape: Counterintuition, commitment, compassion, communion. *Behavioral and Brain Sciences* 27: 713–770.

Atran, S. 2002. *In gods we trust: The evolutionary landscape of religion.* Oxford, UK: Oxford University Press.

Bargh, J. A., and T. L. Chartrand. 1999. The unbearable automaticity of being. *American Psychologist* 54: 462–479.

Bargh, J. A., P. M. Gollwitzer, A. Lee-Chai, K. Barndollar, and R. Troetschel. 2001. Automating the will: Nonconscious activation and pursuit of behavioral goals. *Journal of Personality and Social Psychology* 81: 1014–1027.

Barrett, J. L. 2004. *Why would anyone believe in God?* Lanham, MD: AltaMira Press.

Barrett, J. L., and F. C. Keil. 1996. Anthropomorphism and God concepts: Conceptualizing a non-natural entity. *Cognitive Psychology* 31: 219–247.

Bateson, M., D. Nettle, and G. Roberts. 2006. Cues of being watched enhance cooperation in a real-world setting. *Biology Letters* 2: 412–414.

Batson, C. D., P. Schoenrade, and W. L. Ventis. 1993. *Religion and the individual: A social-psychological perspective.* New York: Oxford University Press.

Berg, J., J. Dickhaut, and K. McCabe. 1995. Trust, reciprocity, and social history. *Games and Economic Behavior* 10: 122–142.

Bering, J. 2011. *The belief instinct: The psychology of souls, destiny, and the meaning of life.* New York: W. W. Norton.

Bering, J. M. 2006. The folk psychology of souls. *Behavioral and Brain Sciences* 29: 453–498.

Bering, J. M., K. McLeod, and T. K. Shackelford. 2005. Reasoning about dead agents reveals possible adaptive trends. *Human Nature* 16: 360–381.

Bloom, P. 2007. Religion is natural. *Developmental Science* 10: 147–151.

Blume, M. 2009. "The reproductive benefits of religious affiliation." In *The biological evolution of religious mind and behavior,* eds. E. Voland, and W. Schiefenhövel, 117–126. Berlin: Springer-Verlag.

Boyd, R., and P. J. Richerson. 2002. Group beneficial norms spread rapidly in a structured population. *Journal of Theoretical Biology* 215: 287–296.

Boyer, P. 2001. *Religion explained: The evolutionary origins of religious thought.* New York: Basic Books.

Boyer, P. 2008. Religion: Bound to believe? *Nature* 455: 1038–1039.

Brooks, A. C. 2006. *Who really cares: The surprising truth about compassionate conservatism.* New York: Basic Books.

Carneiro, R. L. 1970. A theory of the origin of the state. *Science* 169. 733–738.

Cauvin, J. 1999. *The birth of the gods and the origins of agriculture.* Trans. T. Watkins. Cambridge, UK: Cambridge University Press.

Choi, J. K., and S. Bowles. 2007. The coevolution of parochial altruism and war. *Science* 318: 636–640.

Darley, J. M., and C. D. Batson. 1973. "From Jerusalem to Jericho": A study of situational and dispositional variables in helping behavior. *Journal of Personality and Social Psychology* 27: 100–108.

Dennett, D. C. 2006. *Breaking the spell.* New York: Viking.

Dijksterhuis, A., J. Preston, D. M. Wegner, and H. Aarts. 2008. Effects of subliminal priming of self and God on self-attribution of authorship for events. *Journal of Experimental Social Psychology* 44: 2–9.

Dunbar, R. I. M. 2003. The social brain: Mind, language, and society in evolutionary perspective. *Annual Review of Anthropology* 32: 163–181.

Durkheim, E. 1915/1995. *The elementary forms of the religious life.* New York: Free Press.

Edgell, P., J. Gerteis, J., and D. Hartmann. 2006. Atheists as "other": Moral boundaries and cultural membership in American society. *American Sociological Review* 71: 211–234.

Ensminger. J. 1997. Transaction costs and Islam: Explaining conversion in Africa. *Journal for the Institute of Theoretical Economics* 153: 4–29.

Fehr, E., and S. Gächter. 2002. Altruistic punishment in humans. *Nature* 415: 137–140.

Fehr, E., and U. Fischbacher. 2003. The nature of human altruism. *Nature* 425: 785–791.

Fosset, M. A., and K. J. Kiecolt. 1989. The relative size of minority population and White racial attitudes. *Social Science Quarterly* 70: 820–835.

Frank, R. H. 1988. *Passions within reason: The strategic role of the emotions.* New York: W. W. Norton.

Gervais, W. M. (in press). Finding the faithless: Perceived atheist prevalence reduces anti-atheist prejudice. *Personality and Social Psychology Bulletin.*

Gervais, W. M., and A. Norenzayan. 2009b. Like a camera in the sky? *Thinking about God makes believers feel watched*. Unpublished manuscript, University of British Columbia.

Gervais, W. M., A. F. Shariff, and A. Norenzayan. 2009. Do you believe in atheists? Distrust is central to anti-atheist prejudice. Unpublished manuscript, University of British Columbia.

Giles, M. W., and A. Evans. 1986. The power approach to intergroup hostility. *The Journal of Conflict Resolution* 30: 469–486.

Gintis, H., S. Bowles, R. Boyd, and E. Fehr. 2003. Explaining altruistic behavior in humans, *Evolution and Human Behavior* 24: 153–172.

Gonzaga, G., and M. G. Haselton. 2008. The evolution of love and long-term bonds. In *Social relationships: Cognitive, affective, and motivational processes*, eds. J. P. Forgas, and J. Fitness, 39–54. New York: Psychology Press.

Govern, J. M., and L. A. Marsch. 2001. Development and validation of the Situational Self-Awareness Scale. *Consciousness and Cognition* 10: 366–378.

Greif, A. 1993. Contract enforceability and economic institutions in early trade: The Maghribi trader's coalition. *The American Economic Review* 83: 525–548.

Guthrie, S. G. 1993. *Faces in the clouds: A new theory of religion*. Oxford: University Press.

Haidt, J. 2007. The new synthesis in moral psychology. *Science* 316: 998–1002.

Haley, K. J., and D. M. T. Fessler. 2005. Nobody's watching? Subtle cues affect generosity in an anonymous economic game. *Evolution and Human Behavior* 26: 245–256.

Henrich, J. 2009. The evolution of costly displays, cooperation, and religion: Credibility enhancing displays and their implications for cultural evolution. *Evolution and Human Behavior* 30: 244–260.

Henrich, N. S., and J. Henrich. 2007. *Why humans cooperate: A cultural and evolutionary explanation*. Oxford, UK: Oxford University Press.

Henrich, J. et al. 2006. Costly punishment across human societies. *Science* 312: 1767–1770.

Henrich, J. et al. 2010. Market, religion, community size and the evolution of fairness and punishment. *Science* 327: 1480–84.

Henrich, J., S. J. Heine, and A. Norenzayan. 2010. The weirdest people in the world? *Behavioral and Brain Sciences* 33: 61–135.

Hermann, B., C. Thöni, and S. Gächter. 2008. Antisocial punishment across societies. *Science* 319: 1362–1367.

Hoffman, E., K. McCabe, K. Shachat, and V. Smith. 1994. Preferences, property rights and anonymity in bargaining games. *Games and Economic Behavior* 7: 346–380.

Iannacone, L. R. 1992. Sacrifice and stigma: Reducing free-riding in cults, communes, and other collectives. *The Journal of Political Economy* 100: 271–291.

Iannacone, L. R. 1994. Why strict churches are strong. *American Journal of Sociology* 99: 1180–1211.

Irons, W. 2001. "Religion as a hard-to-fake sign of commitment." In *Evolution and the capacity for commitment*, ed. R. Nesse, 292–309. New York: Russell Sage Foundation.

Johnson, D. D. P. 2009. "The error of God: Error management theory, religion, and the evolution of cooperation." In *Games, groups, and the global good*, ed. S. A. Levin, 169–180. Berlin: Springer-Verlag.

Johnson, D. D. P., and J. M. Bering. 2006. Hand of God, mind of man: Punishment and cognition in the evolution of cooperation. *Evolutionary Psychology* 4: 219–233.

Johnson, D. D. P., and Kruger, O. 2004. The Good of Wrath: Supernatural Punishment and the Evolution of Cooperation. *Political Theology* 5(2): 159–176.

Keltner, D., and J. Haidt. 2001. "Social functions of emotions." In *Emotions: Current issues and future directions*, eds. T. Mayne, and G. A. Bonanno, 192–213. New York: Guilford.

Kapogiannis, D., A. K. Barbey, M. Su, G. Zamboni, F. Krueger, and J. Grafman. 2009. Cognitive and neural foundations of religious belief. *Proceedings of the National Academy of Sciences* 106: 4876–4881.

Lawson, E. T., and R. N. McCauley. 1990. *Rethinking religion: Connecting cognition and culture.* Cambridge: Cambridge University Press.

Locke, J. 1689/1983. *A letter concerning toleration.* Indianapolis, IN: Hackett.

McNamara, P. 2006. *Where god and science meet: How brain and evolutionary studies alter our understanding of religion*, Vols. 1–3. Westpor, CTt: Greenwood Press-Praeger.

Monsma, S. V. 2007. Religion and philanthropic giving and volunteering: Building blocks for civic responsibility, *Interdisciplinary Journal of Research on Religion* 3: 1–27.

Nisbett, R. E., and T. Wilson. 1977. Telling more than we can know: Verbal reports on mental processes. *Psychological Review* 84: 231–259.

Norenzayan, A. (2010). Why we believe: Religion as a human universal. In *Human morality and sociality: Evolutionary and comparative perspectives*, ed. H. Hogh-Oleson, 58–71. New York: Palgrave Macmillan.

Norenzayan, A., A. F. Shariff, and W. M. Gervais 2010 . The evolution of religious misbelief. *Behavioral and Brain Sciences* 32: 531–532.

Norenzayan, A., W. M. Gervais. 2009, & K. Trzesniewski 2011. *Autism and atheism: Mentalizing constrains belief in God.* Unpublished manuscript, University of British Columbia, Vancouver.

Norenzayan, A. and A. F. Shariff. 2008. The origin and evolution of religious prosociality. *Science* 322: 58–62.

Norris, P., and R. Inglehart. 2004. *Sacred and secular: Religion and politics worldwide.* Cambridge, UK: Cambridge University Press.

Nowak, M. A., and K. Sigmund. 2005. Indirect reciprocity. *Nature* 437: 1291–1298.

Paulhus, D. L. 1984. Two-component models of socially desirable responding. *Journal of Personality and Social Psychology* 46: 598–609.

Paxson, N. 2004. The entrepreneurial ethics of the Sikhs: Religious signaling and the importance of social capital for trust and exchange. Unpublished manuscript.

Pettigrew, T. F. 1959. Regional variation in anti-negro prejudice. *Journal of Abnormal and Social Psychology* 59: 28–36.

Pew Research Center. 2002. Americans struggle with religion's role at home and abroad. *The Pew Research Center for the People and The Press*, Washington, D. C.

Pichon, I., G. Boccato, and V. Saroglou. 2007. Nonconscious influences of religion on prosociality: A priming study. *European Journal of Social Psychology* 37: 1032–1045.

Putnam, R. D. 2000. *Bowling alone: The collapse and revival of American community.* New York: Simon and Schuster.

Randolph-Seng, B., and M. E. Nielsen. 2007. Honesty: One effect of primed religious representations. *The International Journal for the Psychology of Religion* 17: 303–315.

Richerson, P., and R. Boyd. 2005. *Not by genes alone: How culture transformed human evolution.* Chicago: University of Chicago Press.

Roes, F. L., and M. Raymond. 2003. Belief in moralizing gods. *Evolution and Human Behavior* 24: 126–135.

Schjoedt, U., H. Stodkilde-Jorgensen, A. W. Geerts, & A. Roepstorff 2009. Highly religious participants recruit areas of social cognition in personal prayer. *SCAN* 4: 199–207.

Sears, D. 1986. College sophomores in the laboratory: Influences of a narrow data base on social psychology's view of human nature. *Journal of Personality and Social Psychology* 51: 515–530.

Shariff, A. F., and A. Norenzayan. 2007. God is watching you: Priming God concepts increases prosocial behavior in an anonymous economic game. *Psychological Science* 18: 803–809.

Shariff, A. F., A. Norenzayan, and J. Henrich. 2010. "The birth of high gods." In *Evolution, culture, and the human mind*, eds. M. Schaller, A. Norenzayan, S. J., Heine, T. Yamagishi, and T. Kameda. New York: Psychology Press-Taylor and Francis.

Slingerland. E. 2008. *What science offers the humanities: Integrating body and mind*. Cambridge, U. K.: Cambridge University Press.

Snarey, J. 1996. The natural environment's impact upon religious ethics: A cross-cultural study. *Journal for the Scientific Study of Religion* 80: 85–96.

Sosis, R. 2005. Does religion promote trust? The role of signaling, reputation, and punishment. *Interdisciplinary Journal of Research on Religion* 1: 1–30.

Sosis, R., and C. Alcorta. 2003. Signaling, solidarity, and the sacred: The evolution of religious behavior. *Evolutionary Anthropology* 12: 264–274.

Sosis, R., and E. Bressler. 2003. Cooperation and commune longevity: A test of the costly signaling Theory of Religion. *Cross-Cultural Research* 37: 211–239.

Sosis, R., and B. J. Ruffle. 2003. Religious ritual and cooperation: Testing for a relationship on Israeli religious and secular kibbutzim. *Current Anthropology* 44: 713–722.

Sperber, D. 1996. *Explaining culture: A naturalistic approach*. Malden: Blackwell.

Tan, J. H. W., and C. Vogel. 2008. Religion and trust: An experimental study. *The Journal of Economic Psychology* 29: 832–848.

Trimble, D. E. 1997. The religious orientation scale: Review and meta-analysis of social desirability effects. *Educational and Psychological Measurement* 57: 970–986.

Wilson, D. S. 2002. *Darwin's cathedral*. Chicago: Chicago University Press.

Wright, R. 2009. *The evolution of God*. New York: Little, Brown.

Zuckerman, P. 2007. "Atheism: Contemporary numbers and patterns." In *The Cambridge companion to atheism*, ed. M. Martin, 47–65. Cambridge, UK: Cambridge University Press.

Zuckerman, P. 2008. *Society without God: What the least religious nations can tell us about contentment*. New York: New York University Press.

14

THE IMPORTANCE OF BEING "ERNEST"

Robert N. McCauley

1. INTRODUCTION

In a scene in "The Importance of Being Earnest" Oscar Wilde pinpoints an array of properties of religious ritual systems that cognitive theorizing about religious rituals, viz. the theory of religious ritual competence, has subsequently systematized (Lawson and McCauley 1990; McCauley and Lawson 2002). To the amusement of hundreds of audiences, Wilde's play also identifies a conundrum for religious ritual systems. Cognitive theory about religious ritual suggests that the solutions to that conundrum may bear directly on the comparative advantages of religious systems in competitive religious markets. After briefly sketching some connections between cognition and religious ritual that constitute the foundations of my and Tom Lawson's theory of religious ritual competence in section 2, section 3 summarizes the theory's account of a set of systematic relations that arise in all religious ritual systems as a result of cognitive constraints on rituals' representation. Section 4 explores how increasing the frequency with which some religious rituals are performed purchases for a religious system some selective advantages but how realizing that pattern of ritual practices would require overcoming some formidable empirical and logical challenges. Wilde's handling of these matters in one of the scenes of his famous drawing room comedy is the subject of section 5. Section 6 discusses the relative promise of three ritual arrangements that offer hope of circumventing the conundrum, which this scene from "The Importance of Being Earnest" highlights. Section 7 shows that Wilde's treatment encapsulates the tell-tale features, save one (which is the source of the humor), that, according to the theory of religious ritual competence, would arise under such circumstances.

2. RELIGIOUS RITUALS AND THEORY OF MIND

Religious rituals always involve presumptions about some very special agents. Simply construing them as "agents" with whom humans can interact is every bit as important for grasping the structure and character of religious ritual systems as is anything about those agents' counterintuitive properties. Religious ritual systems allow transactions with such agents that have import for participants' quasi-social relationships with them. Participants' understandings of their religious rituals rely on standard cognitive equipment for the representation of agents and their actions. These components of theory of mind furnish the basic framework for explicating the logic behind participants' ritual interactions with the gods, and they are ones that even children understand (Richert 2006).

In a world populated with both predators and nefarious characters, it is not difficult to see how vital to humans' survival it is that they quickly learn to distinguish agents from other things in the world and actions from other events. Many animals can detect predators and prey, but the detection of the bad guys among conspecifics requires more (Tomasello 1999, 74). That depends on an ability to discern others' intentional states. Developing a sophisticated version of theory of mind that comprises, among other things, the capacity to read disreputable characters' intentional states establishes someone as qualified to participate readily in human society—but not just in human society. They are qualified to interact with *any* intentional agents. Armed with an ability to surmise others' intentional states, we recognize a subset of agents with whom we can interact in complicated ways and whose aid we might be able to recruit. Religions introduce agents possessing counterintuitive properties (CI-agents, hereafter) to the membership of that subset, and religious rituals are the principal means by which humans interact with those agents.

Religious rituals cue humans' cognitive systems for representing actions, which leads people to infer that something is getting done. In religious rituals humans move their heads, limbs, and bodies in coordinated ways or they move around in the kinds of paths that suggest that their movements are both goal directed and intentional. They bow their heads, kneel, and lift their hands; they pile stones, circle designated spaces, lift objects, lay out food, pour liquids, and, especially, wash and clean people and things. People also emit formulaic utterances.

Pascal Boyer and Pierre Lienard have advanced insightful proposals about "ritualized behaviors" in our species (Lienard and Boyer 2006; Boyer and Lienard 2006). They argue that various cultural arrangements' "cognitive capture" of evolved dispositions of the human mind is responsible for everything about religious rituals from the fact that they must be carried out just right each and every time, to the fact that, at each step, they require concentration on the particular components of the action at hand, to their focus on a comparatively small set of recurrent themes. Those themes have to do with such things as managing problems of contamination, hence the focus on cleaning and washing, and creating and maintaining order and boundaries.

This paper takes up but one example of such capture of maturationally natural mental systems by religious ritual, though arguably it is the most basic example. That is the ability of religious rituals to mimic enough features of everyday intentional action to cue the operation of humans' mental equipment for its representation as action carried out by intentional agents. The motions and the utterances that people execute in religious rituals give the appearance that things are being done by intentional agents. In our theory of religious ritual competence Lawson and I have argued that this activation of the human cognitive system for the representation of action imposes fundamental, though commonplace, constraints on religious ritual form (Lawson and McCauley 1990; McCauley and Lawson 2002). Attention to these constraints enables us to look beyond the variability of religious rituals' culturally specific details to some of their most general underlying features. Religious rituals, despite what often seem to be their bizarre, inexplicable qualities, are conceived as intentional actions too, and human beings bring the same representational apparatus to bear on them as they do on all other actions.

Religious rituals have various counterintuitive properties. The fact that in many religious rituals participants interact with perpetually undetectable CI-agents is only the beginning. Unlike their everyday actions, the ritual actions religious participants undertake also have no transparent instrumental aim. Why, for example, must some persons be cleaned, when what *is* transparent is that they have already gone to great lengths to cleanse themselves? Why must people be kneeling when they drink from a cup? Why must initiates be put through excruciating tortures? The repetitions with which religious rituals are replete only magnify their lack of instrumentality. Why must pilgrims climb a mountain seven times? Why must a priest walk around an altar three times, especially since no matter how many times he does so he ends up where he started?

Harvey Whitehouse observes that, in this respect, rituals resemble works in the performing arts. Rituals, like theater, dance, and concertizing, have no "technical motivation" (Whitehouse 2004, 166). This is one of the reasons that both ritual and artistic performances can often be repeated time and time again, where the idea at least at one level of description is precisely that the *same* act is carried out each time.

Rituals are like works in the performing arts in a second respect. The connections between people's intentional states and their actions in rituals and plays are indirect at best. Caroline Humphrey and James Laidlaw (1994) have stressed that many features of people's actions in these settings take the forms that they do not as a *direct* result of the ritual participants' (or the actors') current states of mind but because they follow a prescribed script. Whitehouse's observation that this intentional indirection in rituals poses unending interpretive problems for our mind-reading machinery is, no doubt, true (Whitehouse 2004, 166). The disconnect in religious rituals between agents' actions and their current intentional states, however, occurs at another point as well. Not only can ritual participants be thinking about something else entirely, *it does not matter if they are.* That, at least, is what Lawson and I have argued for a set of rituals that stand at the core of each religious ritual system (McCauley and Lawson 2002, 13–16). These religious rituals are effective, not because of human participants' states of mind but, putatively, because of their *forms*, which CI-agents have specified. The prescribed scripts for these rituals disclose the gods' wishes about how they and humans are to interact. Thus, properly qualified participants cannot fake those core religious rituals. If a properly qualified ritual practitioner carries out one of these rituals on an appropriate ritual patient, the ritual has been performed, regardless of what the practitioner or the patient might have been thinking.

The theory of religious ritual competence maintains that even minimal assumptions about humans' representation of actions, as opposed to their representations of other events, disclose avenues for understanding recurrent properties of religious rituals and religious ritual systems *across cultures* (Malley and Barrett 2003). Anthropologists and scholars of religion have identified various patterns in religious ritual systems (e.g., Van Gennep 1960), but it has only been an appeal to underlying cognitive considerations that has yielded a theory that organizes and explains those patterns. Assuming no more than that humans can readily distinguish agents from other things and actions from other events and that their representations of actions will include slots (1) for agents, (2) for the acts that those agents carry out (including the instruments they employ), (3) for the patients of those actions, and (4) for properties that distinguish these various items provides a framework for organizing, explaining, and predicting features of religious rituals. No matter how extraordinary religious rituals may appear, they call for no unique representational apparatus. They enlist the same maturationally natural cognitive capacities that children use in the representation of actions, whether real *or pretend*. They do incorporate representations of agents with some modestly counterintuitive properties, but in that respect, they countenance nothing more than what is at stake in the comprehension of folk tales and fantasy—and a good deal *less* than what the representation of most scientific theories demands (McCauley 2000 and in press).

Agents do things to other things, including other agents. Since all the actions that constitute a religious system's core rituals involve agents acting upon patients, the cognitive representation of a religious ritual will contain three ordered slots. These slots represent the three fundamental roles, that is, they represent, first, the ritual's agent; second, the act that is carried out (with instruments optional); and, third, its patient. All of a religious ritual's critical details fall within the purviews of one or the other of these three roles. Accommodating the rest of the details about the ritual's form, then, amounts to nothing more than elaborations on the entries for these three slots. My and Lawson's claim that all *core* religious rituals are represented as actions in which an agent does something to a patient departs from widespread, less restrictive assumptions about what may count as religious rituals. Priests baptize babies, ritual participants burn offerings, and pilgrims circle shrines, but people also carry out religious actions that have no patients. For example, they pray, sing, chant, and kneel. Even though such activities may accompany core religious rituals, such activities, in and of themselves, do not qualify as core religious rituals. Religious rituals—in this narrower sense—involve CI-agents doing things to ritual patients or participants doing things to or for those CI-agents. What I am here calling "core" religious rituals are concerned with transactions between participants and CI-agents. These rituals are inevitably connected sooner or later with actions in which CI-agents play a role and that bring about some change in the religious world, whose recognition is available to some public or other.

Many other actions in religious contexts constitute ritualized behaviors in Boyer and Lienard' sense, but the distinction Lawson and I draw is not arbitrary. A variety of theoretically independent considerations triangulate on the same set of religious actions as a religious system's core rituals. For example, these core religious rituals *cannot be faked*. People can pretend to pray, but a priest in good standing cannot just go through the motions when baptizing an eligible patient. If those motions are gone through by a duly ordained priest, then the patient is baptized, regardless of people's intentions. This feature is a function of core rituals' public availability. The consequences of carrying out these core rituals are inter-subjectively available to at least some participants, though usually to the public at large as well. Under the appropriate publicly observable conditions, participants who are privy to performances of these rituals can know what has been accomplished. Therefore, these core religious rituals, unlike other religious acts and ritualized behaviors, bring about recognized changes in the religious world (temporary in some cases, permanent in others). This is by virtue of the fact that these rituals involve transactions with CI-agents. *How people act subsequently and the categories they employ change* as a result of the alterations in someone or something's religious status that these core rituals achieve. In particular, they sometimes bring about *changes in participants' eligibility to participate in additional core rituals.* Although participating in anything other than entry-level religious rituals turns unwaveringly on having performed earlier religious rituals, carrying out other sorts of ritualized behaviors and religious actions does not. So, for example, a Jew must have gone through his bar mitzvah in order for him to qualify to become a rabbi, but that ritual accomplishment is not a necessary condition for him to pray.

To repeat, it is not any special transformations of the operations or the structures of the outputs of the human action representation system that sets religious rituals apart. Their distinctiveness, instead, turns exclusively on introducing CI-agents into at least one of the slots of their action representations (see Figure 1). It is the insertion of agents possessing counterintuitive properties into the slots of religious rituals' action structures that is both distinctive and determinative. It distinguishes the subset of those events receiving action representations that qualify as core religious rituals, and it determines what type of core religious ritual is at stake and, thus, what properties it will exhibit. What Lawson and I call the Principle of Superhuman Agency (PSA in Figure 1) holds, in effect, that the role a CI-agent is accorded in a religious ritual's action structure is the key consideration for predicting a number of that ritual's features (Barrett and Lawson 2001; Sorensen et al. 2006). The role that an agent with counterintuitive properties assumes in the action representation of a religious ritual may arise on the basis of that CI-agent's direct participation in the ritual or through the direct participation of the CI-agent's ritually established intermediary, typically some religious specialist such as a priest (Stark and Bainbridge 1996, 89–104).

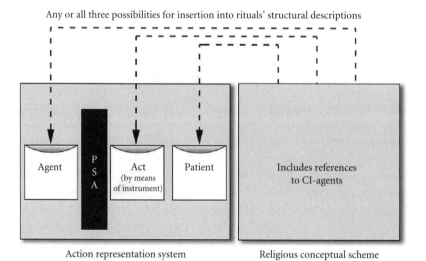

Any or all three possibilities for insertion into rituals' structural descriptions

| Agent | P S A | Act (by means of instrument) | Patient | Includes references to CI-agents |

Action representation system   Religious conceptual scheme

FIGURE 1 Possibilities for inserting representations of CI-agents into representations of religious ritual actions.

3. TYPES OF CORE RELIGIOUS RITUALS

In rituals in which representations of these CI-agents arise first in connection with the agent-slot of a ritual representation (e.g., in Christian baptism, where the priest as intermediary baptizes the ritual patient), the ritual in question will normally be performed on each individual patient *only once*. Lawson and I have dubbed these "special agent rituals" (McCauley and Lawson 2002, 26–33). The idea here is that when the CI-agents do something—even through their intermediaries—it is done once and for all. The gods do not have to do things to the same patient over and over. This is the sense in which we have described these rituals as non-repeated—even though the ritual is repeated with different patients. Since the CI-agents act in special agent rituals (rites of passage such as baptisms, confirmations, and bar mitzvahs as well as weddings, ordinations, consecrations, investitures, etc.), the consequences of these rituals are what Lawson and I have dubbed "super-permanent" (McCauley and Lawson 1990, 134, fn. 8). Their effects can extend beyond or can even occur completely outside of the time when the ritual patient exists.

Under most circumstances, people readily comprehend that these special agent rituals are supposed to effect lasting changes in ritual patients. One danger, however, is that the ritual patients themselves might notice that little, if anything, has been done. Consequently, these special agent rituals need to incorporate features that will convince patients that something remarkable has transpired. This is why successful religious ritual systems evolve in a direction that insures that these rituals contain comparatively high levels of sensory pageantry aimed at seizing the patient's attention and arousing his or her emotions. What counts as "high levels of sensory pageantry" in any particular community is relative to local standards, but special agent rituals are more likely to engage more means and more extreme means for producing sensory stimulation than other types of religious rituals. In many religious systems, these rituals will routinely be accompanied by special food and drink, clothing, music, dance, flowers, oils, incense, and more. "Sensory pageantry" is intended to be inclusive. The means for eliciting appropriately receptive states of mind are not confined to arousal through sensory stimulation.[1] Some religions administer psychotropic substances to ritual participants. Nor do special agent rituals always employ appealing forms of sensory stimulation. Deprivations and torture are just as effective at seizing attention and arousing emotion, and, generally, they are cheaper (Whitehouse 1996; Atran 2002, 175).

Ritual patients in states of emotional or other psychic arousal are more likely to affirm that something important is happening to them in those rituals (Richert et al. 2005). They are, after all, directly experiencing those rituals' effects. In such fraught circumstances, if someone is convinced that something profound has happened, human minds, infiltrated with mythological narratives, leap to the conclusion that *someone* must be responsible.

These special agent rituals evolve to manipulate precisely the variables that research in experimental psychology has suggested are pivotal in generating particularly salient memory for specific events (McCauley 1999). Emotional arousal can intimate that some

---

1. For particularly intriguing possibilities, see Persinger and Healey 2002.

event may be noteworthy in the life of an individual. By itself, though, this is not enough. We regularly forget events of high emotion, if, for example, they turn out to be false alarms or if we have no reason or occasion to rehearse or recall them subsequently. If, however, the event produces emotional or cognitive arousal (Whitehouse 2004, 113–115), *and* the individual directly participates in the event, *and* the individual has occasions to rehearse the event in memory or to describe the event to others, *and* social companions acknowledge over the long term the event's import, not only for the individual but also for the community as a whole, then the event is likely to stand as a benchmark in that individual's life story (McCauley and Lawson 2002, chapter 2). These are just the conditions that special agent rituals produce.

Other core religious rituals secure their recollection differently. When a representation of a CI-agent first arises in connection either with that ritual's instrument or with its patient, it occasions a contrasting constellation of properties. These "special instrument" and "special patient" rituals, unlike their special agent counterparts, are capable of repetition with the same participants and can even involve what can, sometimes, seem like incessant repetition. For example, Christians may bless themselves repeatedly or partake of the Eucharist weekly, even though they are typically baptized only once. Special instrument and special patient rituals are ones that participants perform so frequently that they feel habitual. Ritual performance often becomes the exercise of a well-rehearsed skill like any other, such as riding a bicycle. Within religious communities, the levels of sensory pageantry associated with these rituals are less than those with special agent rituals.

In these rituals, people either do things to or for the CI-agents (in special patient rituals such as sacrifices) or they do things with the help of artifacts, including verbal artifacts, associated with CI-agents (in special instrument rituals such as blessings). These rituals are repeatable, because their effects are temporary only. They do not have super-permanent consequences. Humans are always in need of further help—another blessing never hurts. Or, in the case of special patient rituals, the appetites of the gods are insatiable— the gods *never* cease to want their share of material wealth (Diamond 1998, chapter 14). Therefore, participants typically perform these rituals over and over. Obligations to repeat these rituals can consume considerable time and resources. Consequently, religious ritual systems are more likely to permit a wider range of substitutions in rituals of these forms. For example, when times are tough, it will be acceptable for a Nuer to sacrifice a wild cucumber as a substitute for an ox (Firth 1963).

Performance frequency, levels of sensory pageantry, and participants' cognitive representations of religious rituals' *forms* are psychologically influential variables that can define an abstract three-dimensional space of possible ritual arrangements. This space contains two attractors (see Figure 2). Most religious rituals fall at one or the other of these two attractor positions. These two attractors make sense of the paradoxical associations most of us have about religious rituals

The first attractor, at the bottom right in the front, depicts our notion that rituals are routine actions that are performed so frequently that participants are often said to do them "mindlessly." Special instrument and special patient rituals typically rely on the sheer frequency with which they are performed to ensure that participants recall them. For reasons both psychological and economic, they usually do not enlist high levels of sensory pageantry.

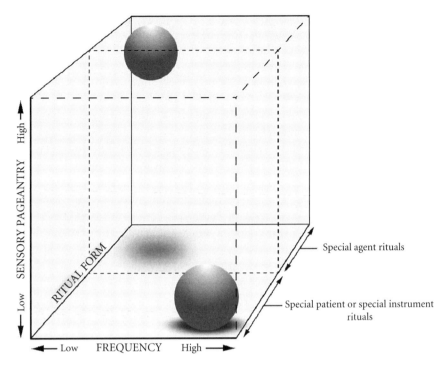

FIGURE 2 Two attractors in an abstract 3D space pf possible ritual arrangements.

People, however, also think of religious rituals as highly stimulating events that mark some of the most important and memorable moments of their lives. Those rituals cluster at the second attractor at the top left in the back. So, although special agent rituals are infrequently performed (typically only once), they characteristically recruit high levels of sensory pageantry, which help establish both prominent episodic memories and a conviction that the patient has been touched by the gods. Serving as the patient of such rituals is likely to manufacture salient memories that contribute fundamentally to participants' understandings of themselves (Hinde 1999, 110). These rituals and the culturally available narratives that surround their performance become integral to participants' identities.

Whether through seemingly endless repetition in the case of special instrument and special patient rituals or through signaling culturally momentous events in the case of special agent rituals, the inherent mnemonic advantages of rituals at these two attractors increase the probabilities that participants will transmit both these rituals and the religious systems in which they are embedded. Memory for rituals that is sufficient to secure a collective sense of continuity is vital for transmission. People cannot transmit what they cannot remember. People will not transmit rituals that they regard as spurious (Barth 1987). Religious rituals cluster at these attractors, then, because the conditions they represent are virtually guaranteed to enhance memory for these rituals, because they cohere with participants' cognitive representations of the actions in question, and, in the case of special agent rituals especially, because they enhance participants' commitment to the religious system and increase the probabilities of their transmitting it.

4. SELECTION PRESSURE FOR REPEATING SPECIAL AGENT RITUALS WITH THE SAME PATIENTS

That enhancing memory, conviction, and motivation to transmit a religious system is a good thing for the perpetuation of that system, especially in competitive religious markets, suggests that a religion would enjoy a distinct advantage over its competitors by increasing the number of special agent rituals that a ritual participant undergoes. A variety of possibilities are available.

One way to achieve that end is simply to invent more special agent rituals. Fredrik Barth's *Ritual and Knowledge Among the Baktaman* (1975) describes the initiatory rites for males in a small-scale society in highland New Guinea. The Baktaman have seven degrees of initiation. Collectively, the performances of these various rituals span approximately 20 years in initiates' lives. Some of these rites involve excruciating treatment. A cohort of youngsters begins this series of initiations every few years and goes through each of the rituals together as a group. The demand for secrecy among the initiates concerning these rites (in a non-literate culture) signifies that the contents of the initiations may be less important than the fact that they go through them together. Their joint experiences establish a bond among these young men that continues throughout their lives. In a society as small as that of the Baktaman (which numbered fewer than 200 people when Barth did his fieldwork), such bonds are a major thread in the social fabric. In groups that are thousands or tens of thousands of times larger than Baktaman society, however, such a system is less practical, less intimate, and less likely to be permissible legally.

A second way to increase the number of special agent rituals that participants undergo would be to find a way to repeat special agent rituals with the same ritual patients. Perhaps the most obvious example is introducing the possibility for multiple marriages (whether in various small-scale societies, in Islam, or in the Church of Jesus Christ of the Latter Day Saints). The problem here, of course, is that for a host of reasons—social, political, and economic—such opportunities are confined to small numbers of participants, usually, only powerful, wealthy males. Since so few people qualify to participate in these repeated rites, they are unlikely to have much impact on the transmission of the religious system overall.

The widespread repetition of special agent rituals with the same patients is not as easy as it may first appear. Empirical and logical considerations constrain their repetition. Psychological, biological, and material constraints restrict the increasing levels of sensory pageantry that are necessary when high-arousal special agent rituals occur with increasing frequency with the same patients. The principal psychological problem is participants' progressive habituation to increasing levels of sensory stimulation (McCauley and Lawson 2002, 184–189). Ritual patients can become habituated to the sensory pageantry when high pageantry rituals occur frequently enough. Participants will require increasingly higher "doses" of that sensory stimulation in order to achieve the same levels of engagement, arousal, and inspiration.

Two sorts of considerations, however, regulate how much sensory pageantry a ritual should incorporate. At the individual level, the human organism's biological limits check how much sensory stimulation a person can endure before it induces unconscious states such as sleep, coma, or death. There are also material limits on how much sensory pageantry a community can produce (e.g., how much food is available for feasts). The human and material resources that are necessary to produce ever-increasing amounts of sensory pageantry for the patients of special agent rituals can be substantial. With repeated performances those costs can easily become prohibitive.

The repetition of special agent rituals with the same patients also generates a conundrum. In these rituals, CI-agents do things to participants, and there is no need for them to do them again. Individuals normally serve as the patients of special agent rituals only once. Baktaman boys go through each initiation only once, just as Jewish males have only one bar mitzvah, and Christians (usually) get baptized only once. The gods do not need to repeat themselves ritually, so religions must circumvent a formidable conceptual roadblock if they are to obtain the advantages that result from repeating special agent rituals.

5. EARNEST EXPLOITATION

Oscar Wilde's "The Importance of Being Earnest" (1996) exploits these distinctive features of special agent rituals to comic ends. Two young women, Gwendolen Fairfax and Cecily Cardew, who both entertain exalted romantic ideals, also both profess their preference to marry a man named "Ernest." That mutual inclination is motivated by their mistaken beliefs that their respective suitors are both named "Ernest." Their suitors, Jack Worthing and Algernon Moncrieff, have each led his beloved into believing that his name *is* Ernest. In order to bring reality into conformity with their deceptions, Jack and Algy independently hit upon the idea of being christened "Ernest" by the local vicar, Dr. Chasuable. Once they learn about one another's plans, they debate their relative suitability for that rite:

> ALGY: ...I have just made arrangements with Dr. Chasuable to be christened at a quarter to six under the name of Ernest.
> JACK: My dear fellow, the sooner you give up that nonsense the better. I made arrangements this morning with Dr. Chasuable to be christened myself at 5:30, and I naturally will take the name of Ernest....I have a perfect right to be christened if I like. There is no evidence at all that I have ever been christened by anybody....It is entirely different in your case. You have been christened already.
> ALGY: Yes, but I have not been christened for years.
> JACK: Yes, but you have been christened. That is the important thing.
> ALGY: Quite so. So I know my constitution can stand it. If you are not quite sure about your ever having been christened, I must say that I think it rather dangerous your venturing on it now. It might make you very unwell. (Wilde 1996, 351)

The humor in this exchange turns on the fact that some religious rituals, including christenings, not only do not need to be repeated with the same ritual patient, but, in fact, should not be. Once christened, a person should not be christened again. Wilde understood that this fact is obvious to anyone who has the most elementary knowledge of Christianity. (The exchange also discloses Wilde's recognition of some far less obvious points about religious ritual systems, viz. that it is just the kind of rituals in question that can be physically and psychologically taxing but that repeating some of these rituals carries some attractions, nonetheless.[2])

Implicitly appealing to the principle that having undergone some rituals (e.g., christening) as their patient renders a participant ineligible to undergo them again, Jack argues that his and Algy's cases fundamentally differ. Jack has never been christened, whereas Algy has been christened already. Jack's unstated conclusion is that, unlike Algy, he is eligible to be christened "Ernest." As evidenced by both his forceful assertion of his own suitability for this rite and his observation that Algy has already been christened, Jack signals that Algy is obligated to supply a rationale for any second christening. The fact that Algy immediately offers an explanation signals that Algy also understands that it is he who bears the burden of proof. Algy concedes that he has been christened, but he goes on to point out that he has "not been christened for years." Algy's pretext is a guaranteed laugh-line. Audience members recognize that Algy owes an explanation of a particular sort to justify a second christening. What Algy must show is that his situation constitutes a circumstance in which a special agent ritual can justifiably be repeated.

The humor of Algy's rationalization for his hastily scheduled christening, viz. that he has not been christened for years, lurks in his utterly ignoring the distinctive feature of special agent rituals that provokes his need to provide an excuse for his second christening in the first place. Algy's response thoroughly disregards the ritual's most conspicuous consequence, viz. its super-permanent effect on the patient's religious status. In more than a century of productions, directors and actors know intuitively how and why this scene works. They know how to play it. They know how audiences who possess even the most rudimentary knowledge of Christianity will respond.

The operative principle is that *special agent rituals should only be performed once with each ritual patient.* Under normal circumstances to re-perform some special agent ritual with the same patient violates participants' understandings of *any* religious ritual system. Additional performances will demand a rationale that points to some extraordinary circumstance justifying the ritual's repetition. Both the contents and the readiness of Algy's response indicate that Wilde understood all of this, so I dub the italicized rule in the first sentence of this paragraph the Oscar Wilde Principle. The next section inventories the unusual circumstances that supply means for evading the Wilde Principle and assesses their prospects.

6. AN INVENTORY OF RITUALLY RELEVANT, EXTRAORDINARY CIRCUMSTANCES

At least three circumstances, reversibility, failure, and substitution, promise paths around the Oscar Wilde Principle.

Because their consequences are temporary, there is no reason to reverse special instrument and special patient rituals. By contrast, all special agent rituals are reversible in principle, if not in fact. Reversing a special agent ritual's consequences permits its re-performance with the same patient.

2. See McCauley and Lawson 2002, 42–44 and 183–201.

Divorce is the best known example of reversing the consequences of a special agent ritual, but there are plenty of other examples. These include excommunication and defrocking, as well as deconsecration, that is, reversing the religious status of consecrated buildings and objects. Although many of these reversals of special agent rituals are accomplished by juridical (rather than ritual) means, for example, in Roman Catholicism, innovative ritual reversals do pop up in religious communities (Sibley 1994).

By whatever means they are accomplished, though, reversals of most special agent rituals are comparatively rare; even in the case of divorce, divorces occur far less often than weddings. None of this should be too surprising, for plentiful, religiously sanctioned reversals of special agent rituals generate problems of their own. The obvious practical problems may be the least of it. Indiscriminate reversals risk portraying the gods as fickle—an arrangement that seems less likely to ground a stable religious system, especially if that fickleness extends to matters that are as integral to human groups as pair bonding. Whether the perception that the proliferation of serial divorces or of priests being defrocked so that they may marry will undermine a culture's religious and moral foundations is accurate or not, the fact remains that religiously sanctioned ritual reversals are infrequent, relative to the number of performances of the special agent rituals that they undo. For *any* religious system, widespread, religiously sanctioned, reversals of special agent rituals will be destabilizing.

The second path around the Wilde Principle is a declaration of ritual failure. This has two advantages over reversals. First, whereas the reversal of a special agent ritual's consequences only renders its repetition possible, the failure of a special agent ritual can create a sense of urgency about its re-performance. For some unknown reason, the gods have refused to carry out the religious transformation of the patients that they were to accomplish. Participants must ascertain the reason for the gods' refusal, address it, and then enlist them again in a repetition of the special agent ritual. Its second advantage is that ritual failure can justify the repetition of special agent rituals with large numbers of ritual patients. Failure can apply to all of the uninitiated (as opposed to the few participants who have undergone reversals). Still, for different reasons, this second path for eluding the Wilde Principle proves even more perilous than the first.

Whitehouse (1995) documents the rise and fall of a splinter group among participants in the Pomio Kivung cargo cult on East New Britain Island in the late 1980s and provides a glimpse of the consequences of repeated failures to perform a special agent ritual. The members of the splinter group repeatedly performed a new special agent, ring ritual that was to mark the ancestors' arrival with vast amounts of cargo and transform the participants' religious status that very night. Repeated failures to bring about this new millennium over six weeks provoked both daily ruminations about the reasons for the failures and recurring habituation among the participants. Each subsequent performance required increasing levels of sensory pageantry to sustain participants' interest. Numerous re-performances of the unsuccessful ring ritual consumed the community's resources at a break-neck pace. After six weeks of increasingly stimulating performances on what was nearly a nightly basis, the splinter group crashed from, among other things, want of resources. They had slaughtered all their pigs, eaten all their crops, and neglected all their gardens. The moral of the story seems to be that without firm interpretive control of the outcomes of ritual performances, declarations of failure quickly run up against the psychological, biological, and material perils (outlined in section 4) that are associated with the frequent repetition of high pageantry, special agent rituals.

Other problems arise, even when a religious system can manage the interpretation of a ritual failure, for none of the obvious interpretations are particularly palatable, especially in the case of *repeated* failures. A failure suggests any or all of (a) *iniquity* on the part of the participants, (b) *incompetence* on the part of the practitioners, or (c) *indifference* or *impotence* on the part of the gods. The first option is probably the most popular, but none of them can wear terribly well in the long run. A further liability of declarations of ritual failure is that they are only made retrospectively in an ad hoc fashion. Failures do not offer systematic grounds for repetition.

The third means for eluding the Wilde Principle is ritual substitution. It offers the greatest promise for meeting what is, in effect, a selection pressure on religious systems to repeat these rituals with the same patients. If participants who have already served as the patients of special agent rituals can serve repeatedly as substitutes for other patients, this would permit their periodic inspiration without acquiring the liabilities that attach to reversals and failures.

Ritual substitution is not burdened by the drawbacks that plague reversals. Reversals can only justify a single repetition with small numbers of ritual patients, and if reversals become widespread, they inspire unflattering views of the gods. By contrast, ritual substitution faces no intrinsic limits on either the number of times a special agent ritual can be repeated with the same ritual patients or the number of ritual patients, who are eligible to participate in those repeated performances. Nor does ritual substitution impugn the reputations of the CI-agents involved.

Ritual substitution also avoids the problems that come with declarations of ritual failures. Even with full conceptual control, such declarations typically require an unflattering view of some ritual participants, whether it is the gods, the practitioners, or the patients. Ritual substitution does not. Moreover, unlike ritual failure, substitution is capable of supplying a motivation for repeating special agent rituals with the same ritual patients that is both systematic and prospective. Large groups of participants have religious approval for anticipating periodic repetition of special agent rituals in which they will serve as ritual patients. They will be the targets of the accompanying sensory pageantry, which will likely enhance their commitment to the religious system and their motivation to transmit it.

That, at least, holds for one prominent example among one of the world's fastest growing religions, viz. the ritual of the baptism of the dead in the Church of Jesus Christ of the Latter Day Saints (LDS hereafter). (Note that if I am right about the advantages of periodically repeating special agent rituals with the same patients, then it is among fast growing religions that it makes sense to search.) The LDS church has become famous as a repository of genealogical information. This is not some idle pastime. The aim is to identify ancestors of LDS members (and others) in order that they may be individually baptized as members of the LDS church. Since the deceased are not available to attend their own baptisms, a subset of the current members of the LDS church, who obtain official documentation of their faithfulness (known as a "temple recommend"), serve periodically as substitutes in the ritual of the baptism of the dead. These LDS members periodically undergo baptisms in ornate baptismal fonts at LDS temples. They serve as substitute patients in a special agent ritual in which they are the targets of the ritual's accompanying sensory pageantry. That they do this periodically in multiple baptisms with other faithful LDS members only increases their sense of the event's significance and of their commitment to their religious community.

By many measures, the LDS church is one of the world's fastest growing religions. Rodney Stark (1984; 2005) argues that we live in a period that is comparatively rare in human history, since we are witnessing what will prove to be the birth of a new world religion. Stark argues that, across its first two centuries, the LDS church has grown at least as fast and probably faster than the early Christian church did,[3] which is to say at a rate of about 40 percent per decade (2005, 22–23). Stark acknowledges the pitfalls of straight-line projections of any trend but argues that there are no obvious reasons to expect any diminution of LDS growth, especially in the light of its facility for flourishing in modern, secular environments (Stark 2005, chapters 5 and 7). Stark (1984) offered projections of LDS church growth, using official LDS church figures and projecting a growth rate of 30 percent per decade as his low estimate and 50 percent per decade as his high estimate. Stark emphasizes, though, that in 2003, nineteen years after his initial projections, the LDS church's growth had exceeded his high estimate (2005, 140–146). By the year 2080 the LDS church would number nearly 64 million on the low estimate and more than 267 million on the high estimate. Stark's point is that either number would qualify the LDS church as a major world faith.

Though it is, by no means, the only mechanism contributing to the LDS church's explosive growth, the line of analysis that I have offered suggests that there is ample reason to hold that the repetition of special agent rituals with the same ritual patients is a contributing factor. It is close to an ideal ritual mechanism, since it obtains all of the benefits (enhanced arousal, memory, commitment, and probability of transmission) of repeating a high pageantry, special agent ritual with large numbers of ritual patients while circumventing the problems presented by habituation and the Oscar Wilde Principle.

7. SPECIAL AGENTS IN THE FIELD

As Algy's comments indicate, repeating special agent rituals with the same patients requires a rationale. To be convincing that rationale will involve an account that appeals to one of three ritually relevant circumstances scouted in the previous section. First, the perceived need for such a rationale and, second, the penchant to offer a rationale in terms of either reversal, failure or substitution both arise as a direct result of the constraints that garden variety cognitive machinery for representing actions imposes on *all* religious ritual systems once CI-agents are implicated.

That point is critical for attempts to apply the theory of religious ritual competence in the field. This pair of features marks special agent rituals uniquely. Eliciting responses along these lines from informants even to hypothetical questions about ritual practices (e.g., "Can this action be repeated with exactly the same persons serving in exactly the same roles?") suffices to distinguish special agent rituals from special instrument and

3. ... a topic about which Stark also has considerable expertise – see Stark 1997.

special patient rituals in a way that is clear and relatively uncontaminated theoretically. The query involves little or no theoretical contamination, because neither fieldworkers nor informants need to know anything about the theory of religious ritual competence either to pose the question or to respond to it. The criterion should also be fairly clear, since, across *all* religious systems, the answer to the preceding question for special instrument and special patient rituals should be "yes" and the answer for special agent rituals should be either "no" or "no, unless…" followed by references to either ritual reversals, failures, or substitutions.

It is the last of these that is the most intriguing theoretically. Algy finds himself in just this fix. He meets the formal demand for a rationale, but his substantive response is absurd in the light of the ground for his needing to offer the rationale in the first place. This constitutes evidence of Wilde's wry appreciation in "The Importance of Being Earnest" not only of the importance of being earnest but of the importance of being "Ernest."[4]

Bibliography

Atran, S. 2002. *In gods we trust.* Oxford, UK: Oxford University Press.

Barrett, J. L., and E. T. Lawson. 2001. Ritual intuitions: Cognitive contributions to judgments of ritual efficacy. *Journal of Cognition and Culture* 1, 183–201.

Barth, F. 1975. *Ritual and knowledge among the Baktaman of New Guinea.* New Haven, CT: Yale University Press.

Barth, F. 1987. *Cosmologies in the making: A generative approach to cultural variation in Inner New Guinea.* Cambridge, UK: Cambridge University Press.

Boyer, P., and P. Lienard. 2006. Why ritualized behavior? Precaution systems and action parsing in developmental, pathological, and cultural rituals. *Behavioral and Brain Sciences* 29: 595–612.

Diamond, J. 1998. *Guns, germs, and steel: The fates of human societies.* New York: Norton.

Firth, R. 1963. Offering and sacrifice: Problems of organization. *Journal of the Royal Anthropological Institute* 93: 12–24.

Hinde, R. 1999. *Why gods persist.* New York: Routledge.

Humphrey, C., and J. Laidlaw. 1994. *The archetypal actions of ritual: A theory of ritual illustrated by the Jain rite of worship.* Oxford, UK: Oxford University Press.

Lawson, E. T., and R. N. McCauley. 1990. *Rethinking religion: Connecting cognition and culture.* Cambridge, UK: Cambridge University Press.

Lienard, P., and P. Boyer. 2006. Whence collective rituals? A cultural selection model of ritualized behavior. *American Anthropologist* 108: 814–828.

Malley, B., and J. Barrett. 2003. Can ritual form be predicted from religious belief? A test of the Lawson-McCauley Hypotheses. *Journal of Ritual Studies* 17: 1–14.

McCauley, R. N. 1999. "Bringing ritual to mind." In *Ecological approaches to cognition: Essays in honor of Ulric Neisser,* eds. E. Winograd, R. Fivush, and W. Hirst, 285–312. Hillsdale, NJ: Erlbaum.

McCauley, R. N. 2000. "The naturalness of religion and the unnaturalness of science." In *Explanation and cognition,* eds. F. Keil, and R. Wilson, 61–85. Cambridge, MA: MIT Press.

4. I wish to express my gratitude to Ted Slingerland and Mark Collard for their helpful comments on an earlier version of this chapter.

McCauley, R. N. (2011). *Why religion is natural and science is not.* New York: Oxford University Press.

McCauley, R. N., and E. T. Lawson. 2002. *Bringing ritual to mind: Psychological foundations of cultural forms.* Cambridge, UK: Cambridge University Press.

Persinger, M. A., and F. Healey. 2002. Experimental facilitation of the sensed presences: Possible intercalation between the hemispheres induced by complex magnetic fields. *Journal of Nervous and Mental Disease* 190: 533–541.

Richert, R. A. 2006. The ability to distinguish ritual actions in children. *Method and Theory in the Study of Religion* 18: 144–165.

Richert, R. A., H. Whitehouse, and E. Stewart. 2005. "Memory and analogical thinking in high arousal rituals." In *Mind and religion: Psychological and cognitive foundations of religiosity,* eds. H. Whitehouse and R. N. McCauley, 127–145. Lanham, MD: AltaMira Press.

Sibley, C. 1994. Bless this divorce. *Atlanta Journal Constitution* September 16, 1994: A1.

Sørensen, J., P. Lienard, and C. Feeny. 2006. Agent and instrument in judgements of ritual efficacy. *Journal of Cognition and Culture* 6: 463–482.

Stark, R. 1984. The rise of a new world faith. *Review of Religious Research* 26: 18–27.

Stark, R. 1997. *The rise of Christianity: How the obscure, marginal Jesus movement became the dominant religious force in the Western World in a few centuries.* San Francisco: HarperCollins.

Stark, R. 2005. *The rise of Mormonism.* Ed. R. Neilson. New York: Columbia University Press.

Stark, R., and W. S. Bainbridge. 1996. *A theory of religion.* New Brunswick, NJ: Rutgers University Press.

Tomasello, M. 1999. *The cultural origins of human cognition.* Cambridge: Harvard University Press.

Van Gennep, A. 1960. *The rites of passage.* Chicago: The University of Chicago Press.

Whitehouse, H. 1995. *Inside the cult: Religious innovation and transmission in Papua New Guinea.* Oxford, UK: Clarendon Press.

Whitehouse, H. 1996. Rites of terror: Emotion, metaphor, and memory in Melanesian initiation cults. *Journal of the Royal Anthropological Institute* 24: 703–715.

Whitehouse, H. 2004. *Modes of religiosity: A cognitive theory of religious transmission.* Lanham, MD: AltaMira Press.

Wilde, O. 1996. *The complete Oscar Wilde.* New York: Quality Paperback Book Club.

SECTION FIVE

Morality

15

WE'RE ALL CONNECTED: SCIENCE, ETHICS, AND THE LAW

Stephen Stich

INTRODUCTION

From Plato and Aristotle to the present, empirical hypotheses have played an important role in moral philosophy. Moral theorists have made claims about a long list of broadly empirical issues including the role of character in fostering moral behavior, the role of reason and emotion in moral judgment, the nature of moral motivation, the sources of moral disagreement, the extent to which moral beliefs are innate, the extent to which genuinely altruistic behavior is possible, and a host of others. In support of these claims, the great moral theorists of the past used the only sources of evidence available to them: introspection, careful observation of human behavior, and human history. Perhaps not surprisingly, these sources of evidence were not adequate to establish or refute the empirical claims moral philosophers made, and thus most of the debates over issues in moral psychology remained unresolved.

In the late nineteenth and early twentieth century, psychology became an experimental science, and by the last decade of the twentieth century, experimental psychology and the various branches of neuroscience had developed quite sophisticated techniques for testing hypotheses about the mind. But, as late as 1990, neither neuroscience nor experimental psychology had made a significant impact on moral theory. The reasons for this are many and complex. One important factor was the behaviorist orientation that prevailed in much of experimental psychology until the early 1970s. Since talk about mental states was taboo in behaviorist psychology, philosophers could find little in this literature that addressed the questions they were interested in. A second factor that played a role was the lamentable fact that many philosophers (and many others in the humanities) were taken in by the claptrap of psychoanalysis. A third factor was the influence of arguments and claims variously attributed to Kant, Frege, G.E. Moore, the logical positivism, and even Hume, which suggested that moral theory, or philosophy more generally, is (or should be) an a priori discipline that is independent of the sciences.[1] It was also the case that some of the prominent scientists who wrote about morality had only the most superficial understanding of the philosophical issues about which they were writing. So it is hardly surprising that moral philosophers who dipped into that literature decided it could safely be ignored.

---

1. For an insightful critical discussion of these arguments, see Rachels (2000).

All this began to change in the 1990s when a small, but growing group of psychologically sophisticated philosophers and philosophically sophisticated psychologists began to use the data and the methods of experimental psychology, neuroscience, cognitive anthropology, evolutionary biology and, more recently, behavioral economics in an attempt to sharpen and resolve traditional issues in moral philosophy.[2] In this paper I will survey some of this work with the goal of making the case that scientific research can and does advance and transform traditional philosophical debates. However, in order to participate productively in conversations in the humanities, scientists must understand the issues being discussed and how they are connected. Since I am one of the "designated humanists" in this section of this volume, I will begin by attempting to explain and clarify some of the philosophical issues to which the sciences have lately been contributing.

SOME ISSUES IN MORAL THEORY
The Definition of Morality

In the first sentence of an article called "What Morality Is Not," first published in 1957, the eminent moral philosopher, Alasdair MacIntyre, observed that "the central task to which contemporary moral philosophers have addressed themselves is that of listing the distinctive characteristics of moral utterances" (MacIntyre 1957). Figure 1 will help to clarify what this "central task" is. The large rectangle represents the class of all judgments (or beliefs or rules). The circle represents the subset of these that are *moral* judgments (or beliefs or rules). I will explain the oval within the circle in the section that follows. Philosophers who pursue the project that MacIntyre has in mind are trying to determine what distinguishes the moral judgments from the nonmoral judgments. Of course, that latter class is itself very heterogeneous. As indicated in Figure 1, it includes scientific judgments, religious judgments, prudential judgments, etiquette judgments, aesthetic judgments and, no doubt, various other sorts of judgments as well. In 1970, MacIntyre's article was reprinted in an anthology, called *The Definition of Morality*, that also reprinted a dozen other papers by such leading figures as Elizabeth Anscombe, Kurt Baier, Philippa Foot, William Frankena, and Peter Strawson (Wallace and Walker 1970). In one way or another, all these papers tackled the question of how "morality" or "moral judgment" is best defined. As one might expect from this distinguished list of authors, many of the arguments to be found in that book are careful and sophisticated. And as one might expect, in just about any group of 13 philosophers, no consensus was reached.

It is clear that the question of how to define terms like "morality," "moral judgment," and "moral rule" is one that philosophers think is important. But in my experience, nonphilosophers are often puzzled by the debate. "Why," they ask, "does it *matter* how terms like 'morality' or 'moral judgment' are defined? So long as they are clear about it, why can't each theorist define them as he or she sees fit?" Since this puzzlement may be shared by many readers, let me illustrate why the issue is important beyond the confines

---

2. Many of these scientists and scholars are associated with the Moral Psychology Research Group whose web site (http://moralpsychology.net/group/) is an excellent resource for those interested in learning more about empirically informed moral psychology.

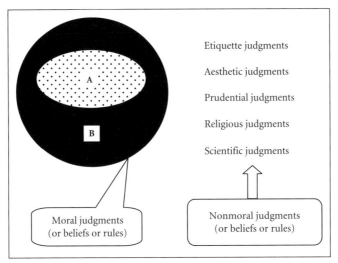

The Set of All Judgments (or Beliefs or Rules)

FIGURE 1 Moral and Nonmoral Judgments (or Beliefs or Rules)

of philosophy. One clear example of the importance of the debate can be found in Richard Joyce's widely discussed book, *The Evolution of Morality* (2006). Joyce notes that one cannot address the evolution of morality seriously unless one has some account of what morality *is*. He then goes on to argue that most of the extensive literature that purports to address the evolution of morality is simply irrelevant, because it is aimed at explaining the evolution of biological or psychological *altruism*, and altruism is neither necessary nor sufficient for morality. What Joyce is claiming is not that altruism is neither necessary nor sufficient for morality *as he chooses to define it*. Rather, he is making the much more interesting and important claim that altruism is neither necessary nor sufficient for morality *correctly defined*. Obviously, this critique of the existing literature makes little sense unless there is a correct definition of morality—a definition that tells us what morality really is.

Another illustration of the importance of the issue can be found in some recent work by Jonathan Haidt and his collaborators who have accused other researchers in the field of moral psychology of "inappropriately narrowing the moral domain." According to Haidt,

> the psychological study of morality, like psychology itself . . . has been dominated by politically liberal researchers. . . . The lack of moral and political diversity among researchers has led to an inappropriate narrowing of the moral domain to issues of harm/care and fairness/reciprocity/justice. Morality in most cultures (and for social conservatives in Western cultures), is in fact much broader, including issues of ingroup / loyalty, authority / respect, and purity / sanctity. . . . (Haidt and Joseph 2007, 367)

The paper from which this quote is drawn is about "how morality might be partially innate," and in that paper Haidt and Joseph "begin by arguing for a broader conception of morality and suggesting that most of the discussion of innateness to date has not been about morality per se; it has been about whether the psychology of *harm* and *fairness* is innate" (Haidt and Joseph 2007, 367). To make their case for a broader conception of morality, Haidt and Joseph offer a brief overview of norms that prevail in other cultures, which include "rules about clothing, gender roles, food, and forms of address" and a host of other matters as well (Haidt and Joseph 2007, 371). They emphasize that people in these cultures care deeply about whether others follow these rules. This is, however, an odd way to proceed. For surely Haidt and Joseph do not think that the "politically liberal researchers" responsible for the "inappropriate narrowing" of the moral domain are unaware that rules governing these matters are widespread in other cultures. They are not accusing those they criticize of being anthropologically illiterate. The issue in dispute is not whether rules like these exist in many cultures or whether people care about them. What is in dispute is whether these rules are moral rules. And to resolve that dispute we need to have a correct account of what it is for a rule to be a moral rule—an account that will enable us to draw the distinction depicted in Figure 1 in a principled way.

Moral Realism, Moral Relativism, and Moral Skepticism

Once we have some idea about which judgments are moral judgments, an obvious question to ask is: Which moral judgments are correct and which are incorrect? Philosophers who embrace the view called "moral realism" have no qualms about this question. They maintain that most moral judgments are correct or incorrect—true or false—in roughly the same way that judgments in mathematics or science or history are correct or incorrect.[3] Moral realists would have no objection to labeling oval A in Figure 1 "correct moral judgments" and labeling B "incorrect moral judgments." However, other philosophers would strenuously object to that picture. Moral relativists maintain that in an important respect moral judgments are like legal judgments, which can be true in one jurisdiction and false in another. So, for example, "Gay marriage is legal" is true in Canada but it is false in Florida. According to moral relativists, it might also be the case that "Gay sex is morally permissible" is true in one cultural setting and false in another. So moral relativists would be willing to replace "A" and "B" in Figure 1 with "correct in our culture" and "incorrect in our culture," but they would insist that different ovals would be required to represent the moral judgments that were correct in ancient Athens, or in Aztec society, or in Yanamomö society.[4]

Moral realism and moral relativism do not exhaust the range of options in this area. Moral skeptics, who disagree with both moral realists and moral relativists, maintain that no moral judgments are either true or false, even when relativized to a culture. Moral judgments, the skeptics argue, just are not in that line of work. So, although moral skeptics have no qualms about the project of characterizing the judgments that are in the circle in Figure 1, they would reject any suggestion that some of those judgments are correct in a

---

3. For a useful collection of essays defending and criticizing moral realism, see Sayre-McCord (1988).

4. For a sophisticated defense of moral relativism and an equally sophisticated critique, see Harman and Thomson (1996).

society, or correct without qualifications. For moral skeptics, there should be no light oval at all in Figure 1.[5] One influential group of moral skeptics, the emotivists, maintain that moral judgments are expressions of emotion, like smiles or shouts of joy or winces of embarrassment. If a Yankees fan leaps from her seat and shouts "Way to go!" when the Yankees score a run, it would be misguided to ask whether what she said is true or false, and equally misguided to ask whether it is true in the Bronx and false in Boston. Much the same, the emotivists insist, is true about moral judgments. No moral judgment is true in New York and false in rural India, because no moral judgment is true or false at all.[6]

Moral realism is compatible with lots of disagreement about moral matters, just as scientific realism is compatible with lots of disagreement on scientific matters. Indeed, moral realists recognize that scientific disagreement and other sorts of factual disagreement is a major source of moral disagreement. For example, if George and Al have a factual disagreement about the causes of global warming, this might lead Al to believe that the United States *should* sign the Kyoto Treaty, and it might lead George to believe that the United States *should not* sign the Kyoto Treaty, but the disagreement might well dissolve if they came to agree on the factual issues in dispute. Since moral realists think that moral judgments are correct or incorrect in roughly the same way that judgments in math and science are, most of them maintain that moral disputes are in principle resolvable.[7] For example, Richard Boyd, who played an influential role in the development of contemporary moral realism, claims that "careful philosophical examination will reveal…that agreement on nonmoral issues would eliminate almost all disagreement about the sorts of issues which arise in ordinary moral practice" (Boyd 1988, 213). David Brink, another well-known moral realist, insists that "it is incumbent on the moral realist…to claim that *most* moral disputes are resolvable at least in principle" (Brink 1989, 200).

HOW SCIENCE CAN JOIN THE CONVERSATION ON THE DEFINITION OF MORAL

There is, of course, much more to be said about the debates sketched in the previous section. However, it is time to turn to our central concern and ask how work in the sciences can contribute to these ongoing conversations in philosophy. I will begin with the definition of morality.

What we saw earlier is that getting the definition of morality right is important both within philosophy and beyond. But how are we to know whether a proposed definition is correct or incorrect? And, to ask an even more basic question, what counts as getting a definition right; what are the facts that a proposed definition is trying to capture? When philosophers or ordinary folks disagree about the definition of a term, it is often the case that the right answer is determined by how reflective speakers actually use the term. So, for example, when philosophers debate the merits of the venerable view that "knowledge"

---

5. For an excellent discussion, see Sinnott-Armstrong (2006).

6. For a classic statement of emotivism, see Stevenson (1944).

7. Most, but not all. There are some moral realists who argue that moral realism would not be challenged if many moral disputes are not in principle resolvable. For discussion of these "divergentist" realists, see Doris and Plakias (2008).

can be defined as "justified true belief," what is usually at issue is whether reflective speakers would say that a person knows that *p* if and only if that person has a justified true belief that *p*. However, when the term whose definition is in dispute is what philosophers and semanticists call a natural kind term, ordinary usage can be overruled by scientific discoveries about the nature of the kind that the term picks out. The word *fish* is the standard example. At one time, reflective common-sense usage applied the term *fish* to whales. However, biologists discovered that whales and fish are members of very different natural kinds. And since *fish* is a natural kind term, the correct definition of *fish* excludes whales, even though speakers who are not biologists may be unaware of this. So perhaps science could make a similar discovery about moral judgments or moral rules. Perhaps psychology could discover that moral judgments and rules are a psychological natural kind, in which case it would be the nature of the kind, uncovered by scientific research, rather than ordinary usage, that determines the correct definition.

Is it the case that moral judgments or moral rules are psychological natural kinds? Some philosophers and psychologists have interpreted Elliot Turiel's influential work on the moral/conventional distinction as providing a positive answer to this question (Turiel 1983; Turiel et al. 1987; Nucci 2001). Beginning in the 1970s, Turiel and his associates developed an experimental paradigm that has become known as the moral/conventional task. In this task, participants are presented with examples of transgressions of prototypical moral rules and prototypical conventional rules, and are asked a series of questions in order to determine how the participants think about the behavior in question. Standard versions of the moral/conventional task are designed to explore the following issues:

1. Do the participants consider the action to be wrong, and if so, how serious it is?
2. Do the participants think that the wrongness of the action is "authority dependent"? To determine this, a participant who has said that a specific rule-violating act is wrong might be asked: "What if [some appropriate authority figure—for example the teacher, if the transgression occurred in a classroom] said there is no rule in this school about that sort of behavior. Would it be wrong to do it then?" If the participant says that it would *not* be wrong under those circumstances, then she thinks that the wrongness of the action *is* authority dependent. However, if she says that the action would still be wrong, despite what the teacher said, then she thinks that the wrongness of the action is authority *in*dependent.
3. Do the participants think the rule is general in scope: is it applicable to everyone, everywhere, or just to a limited range of people, in a restricted set of circumstances?
4. How do the participants justify the rule; do they invoke harm (or justice or rights), or do they invoke other factors?

What Turiel and his associates found was that, when asked about prototypical moral transgressions, like one child hitting another or one child pushing another child off a swing, and prototypical conventional transgressions, like a child talking in class when she has not been called on by the teacher or a boy wearing a dress to school, participants' responses differed systematically. Transgressions of prototypical moral rules (almost always involving a victim who has clearly been harmed) were judged to be wrong and to be more serious than transgressions of prototypical conventional rules; the wrongness of the transgression was judged to be authority independent; the violated rule was judged to be general in scope; and judgments were justified by appeal to harm. By contrast, transgressions of prototypical conventional rules were judged to be wrong but usually less serious; the wrongness of the transgression was judged to be authority dependent; the violated rule was judged not to be general in scope; and judgments were not justified by appeal to harm.

During the last 30 years, this pattern of results has been found in an impressively diverse array of participants, including people of different ages, ranging from preschool and grade school children to adults, people of different nationalities and cultures, including Americans, Chinese, Koreans, Israelis, Indians, Brazilians, and Nigerians, and people with a number of different religious affiliations.[8] On the basis of these findings, some have concluded that moral rules are indeed a natural kind, and that the essential properties that characterize the kind are those revealed in typical moral/conventional task experiments. Moral rules are judged to have objective, prescriptive force—they are not authority dependent; people believe that they hold generally, not just locally; they are justified by invoking harm (or justice or rights); and violations of moral rules are typically more serious than violations of conventional rules. The conclusion that moral rules are a natural kind plausibly follows from the fact that they are a class of rules that exhibit a "homeostatic cluster" of properties and there is an important lawlike generalization about members of the class—transgressions of moral rules always involve harm (or injustice or the violation of someone's rights).[9] It is not surprising that work in the Turiel tradition has had a profound influence on many naturalistically inclined philosophers and on many philosophically astute psychologists as well. For the conclusion that moral rules are a natural kind is a profoundly important one. But, alas, it may not be true.

In addition to the studies by Turiel and his associates, the literature also includes a substantial number of studies by Shweder, Haidt, Nisan, Nichols, and others who report that in many societies, including our own, some transgressions that do not involve harm (or justice or rights) do not evoke the conventional response pattern. Rather, these transgressions evoke one or more component of the signature moral response pattern (Shweder et al. 1987; Haidt et al. 1993; Nisan 1987; Nichols 2002). Perhaps the most famous of these is a study by Haidt and colleagues (1993) using a colorful range of non-harm transgressions including eating the remains of the family dog who had been accidentally killed in a traffic accident, cleaning the toilet bowl with an old and unwanted national flag, and having sex with a dead chicken that has been purchased at the market, then cooking the chicken and eating it for dinner. Haidt found that low socioeconomic status participants in both Brazil and the United States judged all of these nonharm transgressions to be both authority independent and generally applicable, despite the fact that these judgments are central components in the moral response pattern. More recently, Kelly et al. (2007) explored people's reactions to a range of transgressions that clearly involve harm but that do not take place in the schoolyard settings that are typically invoked in Turiel's studies. They found that for many participants these transgressions do not evoke the full "moral transgression" profile. In some cases, participants judged

---

8. For reviews, see Smetana (1993), Tisak (1995) and Nucci (2001).
9. For more on homeostatic clusters and natural kinds, see Boyd (1991).

that the wrongness of the harmful transgressions was authority dependent. In other cases, they judged that the harmful actions would not be wrong in other countries or at other times in history. These findings, along with the findings of Haidt and others pose a *prima facie* challenge to the argument that purports to show that moral rules are a natural kind, since they suggest that the "homeostatic clustering" of responses, on which that argument was based, comes apart in a variety of ways.

This is not the place for an extended debate about whether Turiel and his colleagues have shown that moral rules and moral judgments are a natural kind.[10] What is important for present purposes is that, no matter how that debate is resolved, it is clear that experimental work on the moral/conventional task has become an important component in the philosophical conversation about the definition of morality. And the project of constructing and defending that definition, it will be recalled, was described by MacIntyre as "the central task to which contemporary moral philosophers have addressed themselves."

HOW SCIENCE CAN JOIN THE CONVERSATION ON REALISM AND DISAGREEMENT

There has been much discussion, in the last few years, about the emergence of a new field called "experimental philosophy" (Appiah 2007; Shea 2008; Knobe and Nichols 2008), and from time to time I am described as a pioneer of the experimental philosophy movement, or more ominously as "the Godfather." However, an excellent case could be made that the real pioneer of contemporary experimental philosophy was the late Richard Brandt who taught for many years at the University of Michigan. Brandt was deeply interested in the phenomenon of moral disagreement, and he was familiar with the rich anthropological literature, going back to Westermark (1906), documenting radically divergent moral outlooks in different cultures. But he found that traditional ethnography gives little guidance about what people's moral attitudes would be under "idealized" circumstances in which relevant factual disagreement has been eliminated. So, in the 1950s, Brandt launched a study of the moral views of the Hopi Indians in the American southwest, with the goal of doing the sort of ethnography that would be useful to philosophers. In his book, *Hopi Ethics* (1954), Brandt recounts a number of moral differences between the Hopis and white Americans that he could not trace to nonmoral disagreement. Perhaps the best-known example deals with the treatment of animals. The Hopi, Brandt observed, had no moral qualms about allowing children to "play" with small animals in a way that caused them great pain, broke their bones and ultimately killed them. Brandt looked for evidence that the difference between the Hopis' moral view and the view of contemporary white Americans was based on some nonmoral disagreement, but he found none. Among the possibilities he explored were that the Hopi might believe that the animals subjected to harsh treatment by children do not feel pain, or they might believe that the animals are rewarded for martyrdom in the afterlife, but the Hopi assured him that neither of these was the case. Nor could Brandt find any other nonmoral belief or failure of imagination that could account for the moral disagreement between the

10. For further discussion, see Sousa, Holbrook, and Piazza (2009) and Stich, Fessler and Kelly (2009).

Hopis and white Americans of the time. He concluded that these moral disagreements are fundamental: they reflect a "basic difference of attitude" that would not disappear under idealized circumstances—like those specified by the moral realists—in which factual disagreement had been eliminated.

A much more recent project that sheds light on the nature of moral disagreement is the study by Joseph Henrich and his collaborators of decisions made by people in fifteen small scale societies who were offered the opportunity to play a number of standard economic games including the Ultimatum Game, the Dictator Game, and the Public-Goods Game (Henrich et al. 2004). All these games have been extensively investigated in a number of industrialized western societies. However, Henrich and his collaborators found much more diversity in small-scale societies than had been found in the West. They also showed that the cross-cultural diversity in behavior in these economic games cannot be entirely explained by strategic considerations or culturally variable risk aversion. Rather, the data seem to indicate that people in these fifteen small-scale societies distribute windfall gains differently because they hold different culturally transmitted views about fairness. More specifically, they appear to have different views about what counts as a fair or morally acceptable distribution of windfall gains. It is unlikely that these culturally transmitted differences in what people take to be a fair distribution depend on disagreements in nonmoral beliefs. If that's true, it would pose a significant problem for moral realists like Richard Boyd who maintain that most moral disagreement depends on nonmoral disagreement.

Though they are very suggestive, the studies by Brandt, by Henrich et al. and other studies that point in the same direction are not enough to convince those philosophers who think that most moral disputes are in principle resolvable. These philosophers have raised a variety of objections, some focusing on the details of the studies and others pointing to possible factual disagreements that might underlie the moral disagreements but that have not been ruled out. One way to address these concerns is to do further studies that explore whether the proposed factual disagreements really exist. But, of course, the number of possible factual disagreements is open ended, and only a limited number of them can be investigated in any one study. So to move the debate forward, I believe that what is needed is an empirically supported theory of the psychological mechanisms underlying the acquisition and utilization of moral norms. As it happens, Chandra Sripada and I have recently published just such a theory (Sripada and Stich 2006). Figure 2 depicts the mechanisms posited by our account. The theory claims that moral judgments are largely determined by rules stored in a norm "database," and that those rules are acquired by an acquisition mechanism that is heavily influenced by the norms that prevail in the individual's social environment. If this model is on the right track, people who grow up in social environments in which different norms prevail would often make different moral judgments, even under ideal conditions where there are no relevant factual disagreements.

In our paper, Sripada and I survey a substantial body of empirical evidence that, we maintain, is consistent with the model in Figure 2. But since the editors of this volume have steadfastly rejected my request for another twenty pages, I want to focus on just one strand of that evidence. According to our model, emotions play a central role in generating moral judgments. Indeed, a moral norm, on our model, can be viewed as one kind

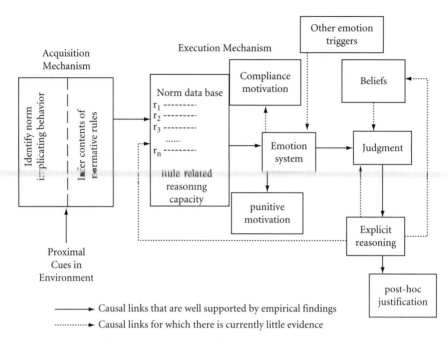

FIGURE 2 The Sripada and Stich Model of the Psychological Mechanisms Underlying Moral Norms.

of socially acquired emotion trigger. In recent work, Daniel Kelly (forthcoming) has argued that at least one pre-existing component of the emotion system—the component that subserves the human emotion of disgust—was co-opted by the moral judgment system when that latter system evolved. Prior to that, the human disgust system had itself been cobbled together from a pair of pre-existing systems, one designed to foster the avoidance of poisonous foods, the other designed for the avoidance of parasites and pathogens. Homologues of each of these systems exist in many other animals, but only in humans have they fused together.

Because the disgust system has its own complicated evolutionary history and an array of adaptive functions, it can be triggered in lots of ways that have nothing to do with norms. A number of important and disquieting studies have shown that even when it is activated by these nonmoral triggers, the disgust system can have a dramatic and persistent influence on a person's judgments about moral issues. In one study, Wheatley and Haidt (2005) used hypnosis to induce participants to feel a brief pang of disgust when they encounter the word *often*. Participants were then presented with very similar vignettes describing some morally problematic behavior. The only difference between paired descriptions was that some of them said that an agent engaged in the problematic behavior "often" while others said that the agent engaged in the activity "frequently." When asked to make moral judgments about the agent's behavior, the judgments of those who had heard the description containing the word *often* were significantly more severe. Even more unsettling was the finding that participants made negative moral judgments about behavior that control subjects found to be completely unproblematic. Here is a scenario that Wheatley and Haidt used:

> Dan is a student council representative at his school. This semester he is in charge of scheduling discussions about academic issues. He often picks topics that appeal to both professors and students in order to stimulate discussion.

Many participants who had been hypnotized to feel disgust when they heard the word *often* insisted that Dan was doing something wrong—though not surprisingly they were hard pressed to give any plausible reason for their judgment.

In another study, Schnall and her colleagues (2008) compared the moral judgments that participants made when seated in a neat and clean office with those of another group of participants who judged the same scenarios in an office arranged to evoke mild feelings of disgust. There were greasy pizza boxes in the trash, the desk chair was sticky, there was a dried up smoothie on the desk, and to record their judgments, participants were given a chewed up ball point pen. The judgments that were made in the mildly disgusting setting were significantly more severe.[11] In a later study, exploring what has become known as "the Lady Macbeth Effect," Schnall and her colleagues (2008) compared judgments about moral severity in two groups of participants. One group had just used an alcohol-based cleansing gel on their hands; the other group had used an ordinary, non-cleansing hand cream. Strikingly, the moral judgments of those using the cleansing gel were significantly less severe.

Each of these studies can plausibly be interpreted as supporting two hypotheses that are built into the Sripada and Stich model. The first is that disgust plays a significant role in generating some moral judgments; the second is that moral psychology co-opted a pre-existing emotion system that could be triggered by factors that have nothing to do with moral norms. As François Jacob (1977) famously observed, natural selection is like "a tinkerer who uses everything at his disposal to produce some kind of workable object." And in the case of moral psychology, what the tinker came up with is a kludge.[12]

SCIENCE, ETHICS, AND THE LAW: KLUDGE MEETS KASS

In this final section, I want to illustrate how experimental findings in moral psychology can play a role in conversations about issues in political philosophy and the law. The findings I will focus on are those sketched at the end of the previous section, which suggest that moral psychology is kludge, and the conversation I will target is one in which the eminent, politically conservative, bioethicist, Leon Kass, has played a central role. Kass was appointed to the President's Council on Bioethics by George W. Bush and served as chairman from 2001 until 2005. In a widely reprinted article that first appeared in *The New Republic*, Kass argues that "in crucial cases...repugnance is the emotional

---

11. Though my focus in this paper is on theoretical issues, it's worth noting that findings like this have important practical implications as well. You don't want to be tried by a jury that deliberates in a filthy room!

12. Though there is some dispute about the exact meaning of this slang term that is widely used by computer programers, my favorite definition is: "An ill-assorted collection of poorly matching parts, forming a distressing whole." Better still is the backronym (or post hoc acronym) **k**lumsy, **l**ame, **u**gly, **d**umb, but **g**ood **e**nough.

expression of deep wisdom, beyond reason's power fully to articulate it." "In this age," Kass tells us, "in which everything is held to be permissible so long as it is freely done, and in which our bodies are regarded as mere instruments of our autonomous rational will, repugnance may be the only voice left that speaks up to defend the core of our humanity. Shallow are the souls that have forgotten how to shudder." (Kass, 1997) These ideas play a central role in Kass' critique of human cloning, and other writers have adopted them to argue against abortion, pornography, and same-sex marriage. All these activities apparently evoke repugnance—disgust—in the deep souls of Kass and other social conservatives who have not forgotten how to shudder. Some philosophers, most notably Martha Nussbaum (2004), have challenged Kass. Borrowing an idea from Paul Rozin (Rozin et al. 1999), Nussbaum argues that disgust should be discounted in moral and legal deliberation because it reminds us of our animal origins. I am more than a bit dubious about this idea, and I think that the empirical work I have been discussing offers a far more plausible and powerful critique of Kass. There is no reason to think that there is wisdom in repugnance or in the moral judgments that disgust can engender. Disgust is a kludge, and the psychological system that bases moral judgments on disgust is a kludge twice over. The covert effects of greasy pizza boxes and antiseptic cleansing gels serve as a stark warning of how unwise the effects of repugnance can be.

A final word: All the empirical claims I have presented in this chapter should be taken with a big grain of salt. It is early days in the scientific study of moral judgment; there is much more to learn, and it is inevitable that some of the findings and theories that I have discussed will turn out to be misleading or mistaken. My primary objective in this chapter is not to defend any specific claim about moral psychology but to make the case that moral theorists, political philosophers, and legal scholars must include empirical investigators in their conversations. I will be well satisfied if I have convinced you that the rapidly developing scientific study of moral psychology has a crucial role to play in advancing and transforming some of the most important debates in the humanities.

References

Appiah, A. 2007. The new new philosophy. *New York Times Magazine*, December 9, Available online at http://www.nytimes.com/2007/12/09/magazine/09wwln-idealab-t.html

Boyd, R. 1988. "How to be a moral realist." In *Essays on moral realism*, ed. G. Sayre-McCord, 181–228. Ithaca, NY: Cornell University Press.

Boyd, R. 1991. Realism, anti-foundationalism and the enthusiasm for natural kinds. *Philosophical Studies* 61(1 and 2): 127–148.

Brandt, R. 1954. *Hopi ethics: A theoretical analysis*. Chicago: The University of Chicago Press.

Brink, D. 1989. *Moral realism and the foundations of ethics*. Cambridge: Cambridge University Press.

Doris, J., and A. Plakias. 2008. "How to argue about disagreement: Evaluative diversity and moral realism." In *Moral psychology, volume 2: The cognitive science of morality: Intuition and diversity*, ed. Walter Sinnott-Armstrong, 303–331. Cambridge, MA: MIT Press.

Haidt, J., and C. Joseph, C. 2007. "The moral mind: How five sets of innate moral intuitions guide the development of many culture-specific virtues, and perhaps even modules." In *Innateness and the structure of the mind, volume III, foundations and the future*, eds. P. Carruthers, S. Laurence, and S. Stich, 367–391. New York: Oxford University Press.

Haidt, J., S. Koller, and M. Dias. 1993. Affect, culture and morality, or is it wrong to eat your dog? *Journal of Personality and Social Psychology* 65: 613–628.

Harman, G., and J. Thomson. 1996. *Moral relativism and moral objectivity*. Oxford: Blackwell.

Henrich, J., R. Boyd, S. Bowles, H. Gintis, E. Fehr, and C. Camerer, eds. 2004. *Foundations of human sociality: Economic experiments and ethnographic evidence from fifteen small-scale societies*. Oxford: Oxford University Press.

Jacob, F. 1977. Evolution and tinkering. *Science* 196: 1161–1166.

Joyce, R. 2006. *The evolution of morality*. Cambridge, MA: Bradford/MIT Press.

Kass, L. 1997. The wisdom of repugnance. *New Republic*: June 2, 216(22): 17–26.

Kelly, D., S. P. Stich, K. Haley, S. Eng, and D. Fessler. 2007. Harm, affect and the moral/conventional distinction. *Mind and Language* 22: 117–131.

Kelly, D. forthcoming. *Yuck! The Nature and Moral Significance of Disgust*. Cambridge, MA: MIT Press.

Knobe, J., and S. Nichols. 2008. *Experimental philosophy*. Oxford: Oxford University Press.

MacIntyre, A. 1957. What morality is not. *Philosophy* 32: 325–335.

Nichols, S. 2002. Norms with feeling: Toward a psychological account of moral judgment. *Cognition* 84: 223–236.

Nisan, M. 1987. Moral norms and social conventions: A cross-cultural comparison. *Developmental Psychology* 23: 719–725.

Nucci, L. 2001. *Education in the moral domain*. Cambridge: Cambridge University Press.

Nussbaum, M. 2004. *Hiding from humanity: Disgust, shame, and the law*. Princeton, NJ: Princeton University Press.

Rachels, J. 2000. "Naturalism." In *The Blackwell guide to ethical theory*, ed. H. LaFollette, 74–91. Oxford: Blackwell Publishing.

Rozin, P., J. Haidt, and C. McCauley. 1999. "Disgust: The body and soul emotion." In *Handbook of cognition and emotion*, eds. T. Dalgleish, and M. Power. Chichester: John Wiley.

Sayre-McCord, G., ed. 1988. *Essays on moral realism*. Ithaca, NY: Cornell University Press.

Schnall, S., J. Benton, and S. Harvey. 2008. With a clean conscience: Cleanliness reduces the severity of moral judgments. *Psychological Science* 19: 1219–1222.

Schnall, S., J. Haidt, G. L. Clore, and A. H. Jordan. 2008. Disgust as embodied moral judgment. *Personality and Social Psychology Bulletin* 34: 1096–1109.

Shea, C. 2008. Against intuition: Experimental philosophers emerge from the shadows, but skeptics still ask: Is this philosophy? *Chronicle of Higher Education* October 3, 55(6): B8–B12. Available online at: http://chronicle.com/free/v55/i06/06b00901.htm.

Shweder, R., M. Mahapatra, and J. Miller. 1987. "Culture and moral development." In *The emergence of morality in young children*, eds. J. Kagan, and S. Lamb, 1–83. Chicago: University of Chicago Press.

Sinnott-Armstrong, W. 2006. *Moral skepticisms*. Oxford: Oxford University Press.

Smetana, J. 1993. "Understanding of social rules." In *The development of social cognition: The child as psychologist*, ed. M. Bennett, 111–141. New York: Guilford Press.

Sousa, P., C. Holbrook, and J. Piazza. 2009. The morality of harm. *Cognition* 113: 80–92.

Sripada, C., and S. Stich. 2006. "A framework for the psychology of norms." In *The innate mind: Culture and cognition*, eds. P. Carruthers, S. Laurence, and S. Stich, 280–301. New York: Oxford University Press.

Stevenson, C. 1944. *Ethics and language*. New Haven: Yale University Press.

Stich, S., D. Fessler, and D. Kelly. 2009. On the morality of harm: A response to Sousa, Holbrook, and Piazza. *Cognition* 113: 93–97.

Tisak, M. 1995. "Domains of social reasoning and beyond." In *Annals of child development vol.* 11, ed. R. Vasta, 95–130. London: Jessica Kingsley.

Turiel, E. 1983. *The development of social knowledge.* Cambridge: Cambridge University Press.

Turiel, E., M. Killen, and C. Helwig. 1987. "Morality: It's structure, functions, and vagaries." In *The emergence of morality in young children*, eds. J. Kagan, and S. Lamb, 155–243. Chicago: The University of Chicago Press.

Wallace, G., and A. Walker. 1970. *The definition of morality.* London: Methuen.

Westermark, E. 1906. *Origin and development of the moral ideas, vol.* 2. New York: MacMillian.

Wheatley, T., and J. Haidt. 2005. Hypnotic disgust makes moral judgments more severe. *Psychological Science* 16(10): 780–784.

16

THE EVOLUTION OF A SENSE OF MORALITY

Dennis L. Krebs

INTRODUCTION

One of the oldest issues considered by scholars from the humanities and sciences pertains to the origin of a sense of morality. In this chapter, I ask, and attempt to answer, six questions. I begin by asking what a sense of morality is, then suggest that it consists of a set of distinct psychological experiences that share a common function, namely, to support forms of conduct and social norms that enable individuals to foster their interests in cooperative ways. Second, I ask what kinds of mental processes produce a sense of morality, and suggest that moral sentiments may stem from several sources, including structures of moral reasoning, moral heuristics, emotional reactions, moral intuitions, and internalized beliefs. Third, I argue that, to answer the question, "Why do people possess a sense of morality?" we must identify the functions that the mental mechanisms that produce this sense evolved to serve. Fourth, I ask what these precursors of a sense of morality were, and suggest that moral sentiments arose from the emotional and motivational experiences produced by the mental mechanisms that regulate prosocial behaviors and strategic interactions among members of groups. With respect to the origin of a sense of morality, I argue that these experiences assumed a moral flavor when they became embedded in ideas about how people are obligated to behave in order to uphold the social orders of their groups. I end by suggesting that the mental mechanisms that give rise to a sense of morality became refined when early humans acquired cognitive and linguistic abilities that enabled them to use increasingly sophisticated moral judgments and forms of moral reasoning as tools in strategic social interactions, and that contemporary children's sense of morality becomes refined through the same process as they develop.

THEORY AND RESEARCH ON THE EVOLUTION OF MORALITY

Most theory and research on the evolution of morality has focused on the problem that apparent acts of altruism appeared to present for Darwin's theory. This problem has been solved by modern evolutionary theorists, who have identified at least five ways in which altruistic behaviors can evolve: (1) through the return benefits produced by reciprocity and other forms of cooperation (Alexander 1987; Trivers, 2006); (2) through kin selection (Burnstein 2005; Hamilton 1964); (3) through sexual selection (Miller 2007); (4) through cultural group selection (Gintis, Bowles,

Boyd, and Fehr 2005; Richerson and Boyd 2005); and (5) as by-products of mental mechanisms that regulate social learning and moral reasoning (Simon 1990; Bloom 2004).

Accounting for the evolution of altruism and cooperation does not, however, equate to accounting for the evolution of morality. Although evolutionary theorists have explained how mental mechanisms that dispose humans to behave in ways that they consider moral originated, they have not explained how the mental mechanisms that produce these considerations evolved. They have not, in Darwin's (1874) words, accounted for the evolution of the "moral sense."

WHAT IS A SENSE OF MORALITY?

The first challenge faced by anyone who seeks to explain how humans acquired a sense of morality is to explain what this phenomenon is. Although, by definition, all aspects of a sense of morality pertain to morality, people experience different aspects in different ways. Some aspects are experienced as "hot" feelings, which may be positive or negative in nature, and other aspects are experienced as "colder" ideas. Some aspects emerge quickly and automatically; others emerge more slowly, after deliberation. Some aspects give rise to strong, compelling motives and are closely linked to behavior; others give rise to more purely intellectual judgments (see Haidt 2001; Krebs 2005, 2008a, 2011; and Sinnott-Armstrong 2008, for reviews of studies supporting these claims).

The main aspects of the moral sense can be classified in a 2x2x2x2 matrix (see Figure 1). In terms of this classification, (1) moral sentiments about oneself differ from moral sentiments about others, (2) positive sentiments about moral acts differ from negative sentiments about immoral acts, (3) a priori judgments about how people ought to behave differ from post hoc judgments about how people have behaved, and (4) feelings differ from ideas (though each may affect the other).

Missing from, but implied in, this matrix, is a sense of fairness, or justice. This aspect of a sense of morality consists of ideas about how the rights and duties of members of groups (self and others) and the benefits and burdens of cooperative living should be balanced—what people owe to others, and what they deserve. As expressed by Rest:

> [The philosopher] Frankena (1970) and others regard morality...as standards or guidelines that govern human cooperation—in particular how rights, duties, and benefits are to be allocated. Given that people live together and that their activities affect each other, morality provides guidelines and rationales for how each person's activities should affect the others' welfare. The guidelines are not fashioned to serve any one person's interests, but are constructed with consideration for each individual's intrinsic value...morality, at least in principle, deals with sharable values because moralities are proposals for a system of mutual coordination of activities and cooperation among people. (Rest 1983, 558)

Self / Others	Right / Wrong	Prescriptive / Prohibitive / Judgmental	Hot / Cold
			Hot (a sense of duty)
		Prescriptive	
	Right		Cold ("I should" deontic judgments and justifications)
			Hot (a sense of self-approbation and pride)
Self		Judgmental	
			Cold ("I did right" judgments and justifications)
			Hot (resisting temptation, showing restraint)
		Prohibitive	
	Wrong		Cold ("I should not" deontic judgments and justifications)
			Hot (a sense of guilt, remorse, self-contempt, shame)
		Judgmental	
			Cold ("I did wrong" judgments and justifications)
			Hot (attributions of moral obligation)
		Prescriptive	
	Right		Cold ("You/he/she/they should" deontic judgments and justifications)
			Hot (feelings of moral approval)
Others		Judgmental	
			Cold ("You/he/she/they did right" judgments and justifications)
			Hot (a sense of prohibition)
		Prohibitive	
	Wrong		Cold ("You/he/she/they should not" judgments and justifications)
			Hot (a sense of moral disapproval, blame, righteous indignation)
		Judgmental	
			Cold ("You/he/she/they did wrong" judgments and justifications)

FIGURE 1 Anatomy of a Sense of Morality.

WHAT KINDS OF MENTAL PROCESSES PRODUCE A SENSE OF MORALITY?

Cognitive-developmental psychologists such as Kohlberg (1987) and many philosophers of ethics have argued that the only valid sources of moral judgments are structures of moral reasoning; judgments that stem from any other source do not qualify as moral. To assess people's level of moral development, Kohlberg and his colleagues ask people to deduce solutions to hypothetical moral dilemmas and to justify their prescriptive moral judgments, or deontic choices, in rational ways.

Clearly, people can, and sometimes do, derive moral judgments from structures of moral reasoning in deliberate, logical, and impartial ways. However, structures of moral reasoning are not the only, or even the most prominent, source of moral judgments (Haidt 2001; Krebs and Denton 2005; Prinz 2007). People also derive moral judgments from mental mechanisms that produce less rational, more automatic, and more emotional experiences, such as those that give rise to moral heuristics, moral intuitions, moral emotions, and beliefs in moral norms. In the past, the nature of these mechanisms was inferred mainly from their products. Recently, neuroscientists have begun to identify the areas of the brain that are activated when they operate (Moll et al. 2008).

Processes That Produce Moral Heuristics

Researchers have demonstrated that people often make moral judgments in fast, frugal, and irrational ways, by invoking a variety of moral heuristics. Research on moral heuristics has demonstrated that people tend to judge acts of commission, such as killing someone, more harshly than they judge acts of omission, such as passively permitting someone to die. People tend to feel that punishment should be proportionate to the outrageousness of an act, and they tend to consider directly harmful acts more immoral than indirectly harmful acts, even though the two types of acts produce the same consequences (see Hauser 2006, and Sunstein 2005, for reviews of this literature).

The role played by moral heuristics in people's sense of morality has been demonstrated in research on "trolley dilemmas" (Hauser 2006; Greene 2008). People tend to believe that pushing a heavy person off a footbridge to stop a train that is headed toward five people walking on the tracks is more immoral than pulling a switch to divert the train onto a sidetrack containing five people. The question is, what is the source of this difference?

Although philosophers of ethics have invested a great deal of effort attempting to find a rational ethical basis for the differences in such judgments, I think that they are barking up the wrong tree. Most people are unable to offer rational ethical justifications for why aspects of moral problems such as omission-commission, directness-indirectness, personal-impersonal affect their moral judgments; indeed, they are usually unaware that these variables are affecting their judgments (Greene 2008). Even when participants (including professional philosophers) are able to offer moral justifications for the effect of such variables, the justifications may constitute post hoc rationalizations of judgments engendered in irrational ways (Haidt 2001).

Processes That Produce Moral Intuitions

Haidt has proposed that people may derive moral judgments from two qualitatively different types of mental mechanisms: those that produce moral intuitions and those that produce moral reasoning. Haidt defines moral intuitions as "the sudden appearance in consciousness of a moral judgment, including an affective valence (good-bad, like-dislike), without any conscious awareness of having gone through steps of searching, weighing evidence, or inferring a conclusion" (Haidt 2001, 818). Moral intuitions are like "gut feelings in the mind."

To evaluate this proposition, Haidt and his colleagues have given people scenarios such as those involving a brother and sister making love, cleaning a toilet with one's country's flag, or eating one's dog after it died. They have found that virtually all participants in their studies viewed the behaviors in question as wrong—often very wrong—but had difficulty explaining why. When pressed to justify their reactions, participants tended to give invalid reasons that were inconsistent with the assumptions in the scenarios, such as those that stipulated that the sister could not get pregnant and that the brother and sister would not feel bad. When the invalidity of participants' reasons was pointed out, they became lost for words, saying things like, "I can't explain it, I just know it's wrong" (Haidt 2001, 814). Haidt has dubbed this phenomenon "moral dumbfounding" (Haidt 2001, 814).

Processes That Produce Moral Emotions

Several theorists have argued that the primary source of people's sense of morality is emotional experiences such as guilt, gratitude, and righteous indignation, which are evoked in particular contexts, are produced by specific brain circuits, and dispose people to behave in particular ways. Consider feelings of guilt and gratitude, for example. Moll and his colleagues have suggested that feelings of guilt are evoked when people feel responsible for causing those to whom they feel attached to experience negative outcomes, especially as a result of behaviors that violate social norms. These researchers report that "recent neuroimaging data showed the involvement of the anterior PFC, the anterior temporal cortex, the insula, the anterior cingulated cortex, and the STS [superior temporal sulcus] regions in guilt experience" (Moll et al. 2008, 13). With respect to gratitude, Moll and his colleagues assert that, "[Gratitude] is elicited by (1) detecting a good outcome to oneself, attributed to (2) the agency of another person, (3) who acted in an intentional manner to achieve the outcome. (4) Gratitude is associated with a feeling of attachment to the other agent and often promotes the reciprocation of favors. … Activated brain regions include the ventral striatum, the OFC, and the anterior cingulate cortex.…" (Moll et al. 2008, 16).

Processes That Mediate the Internalization of Moral Beliefs

I have asked hundreds of students how they acquired a sense of morality. By far the most frequent answer is that they learned the difference between right and wrong from their parents and other members of their societies. Learning theorists (e.g., Aronfreed 1968), social learning theorists (e.g., Bandura 1989), psychoanalyists and many other theorists (e.g., Campbell 1978) embrace the assumption that children are born fundamentally amoral, but acquire a sense of morality when adults teach them the moral norms of their cultures. According to these theories, the primary sources of a sense of morality are social learning mechanisms that induce individuals to copy the ideas of others, to conform to moral norms, and to believe that it is right to behave in ways that evoke approval from members of their groups. Evolutionary theorists such as Alexander (1987) and Richerson and Boyd (2005) do not deny the impact of social learning on the acquisition of morality. However, they argue that to fully understand this impact, we must understand how social learning mechanisms evolved and are activated in modern environments (see Krebs and Janicki, 2004, for a discussion of the role of social learning in the acquisition of morality).

Summary

Several evolved mental mechanisms contribute to people's sense of morality—mechanisms that house structures of moral reasoning and moral heuristics, mechanisms that produce moral intuitions and moral emotions, and mechanisms that mediate social learning. Questions raised by an evolutionary analysis of the moral sense include: How did these mechanisms originate, and why? Which mechanisms evolved first? What activates them, and when more than one is activated, how do they interact?

WHY DID A SENSE OF MORALITY ORIGINATE?

If we accept that a sense of morality originated in the humans species because individuals who inherited mental mechanisms that produced it propagated their genes more successfully than individuals who did not, an important task is to identify the adaptive problems that these mental mechanisms helped early humans solve, which entails explaining what functions a sense of morality evolved to serve: What it was for? (Tooby and Cosmides 2005).

With other evolutionary theorists (e.g., Alexander 1987; Gintis et al., 2005; Richerson and Boyd 2005) I believe that a sense of morality evolved in early humans to solve the adaptive social problems that arose when they formed increasingly large groups to advance their interests. Moral obligations pertain to shared standards, norms, and rules about how members of groups should behave in order to uphold their social orders and promote their common welfare, which are usually supported by sanctions. On this line of thought, all aspects of a sense of morality (Figure 1) should be designed to induce members of groups to behave in ways that advance their biological interests by upholding the social orders of their groups, with different aspects of this sense contributing to this function in different ways. Some aspects of this sense should dispose people to behave in prosocial ways (e.g., aspects designed to engender feelings of moral obligation, and aspects designed to make people regret behaving in antisocial ways), and other aspects should be aimed at inducing others to behave in prosocial ways (e.g., aspects that induce people to make positive judgments about others when they cooperate and behave altruistically, feel vengeful toward those who cheat them and their relatives, and feel indignant when they observe members of their groups behaving unfairly).

WHAT WERE THE PRECURSORS OF A SENSE OF MORALITY?

The mental mechanisms that produce a sense of morality did not appear full blown one sunny morning in the Pleistocene era. They grew out of previously evolved mechanisms that humans share with other animals. With other theorists, I believe that the overriding trend in the evolution of a sense of morality was for emerging higher-order cognitive processes to refine more primitive affective reactions. Consider, for example, positions advance by de Waal (2006) and Moll et al. (2008).

In an account of the evolution of empathy, de Waal wrote:

> Empathy covers all the ways in which one individual's emotional state affects another's, with simple mechanisms at its core and more complex mechanisms and perspective-taking abilities at its outer layers. Because of the layered nature of the capacities involved, we speak of the Russian doll model, in which higher cognitive levels of empathy build upon a firm, hard-wired basis.... The claim is not that [this basis] by itself explains [all forms of empathy], but that it under-pins...cognitively more advanced forms..., and serves to motivate behavioral outcomes (de Waal 2006, 11).

More broadly, Moll et al. have asserted that "what is experienced as a moral emotion is probably the result of the blending of elementary subjective emotional experiences, which are ubiquitous in mammals, with emotional and cognitive mechanisms that are typically human" (Moll 2008, 4). They go on to suggest that,

> Moral emotions might prove to be a key venue for understanding how phylogeneti-cally old neural systems, such as the limbic system, were integrated with brain regions more recently shaped by evolution, such as the anterior PFC [prefrontal cortex], to produce moral judgment, moral reasoning, and behavior. (Moll et al. 008, 17)

Accounting for the evolution of the moral senses in this manner involves identifying the precursors to a sense of moral obligation, evaluative moral judgments about one-self, conscience, evaluative moral judgments about others, abstract ideas about morality, and a sense of justice, then explaining how these precursors became refined in the course of human evolution to produce moral judgments. I will consider each of these precursors in turn.

Precursors of a Sense of Moral Obligation

Many laypeople and scholars assume that moral beliefs and moral reasoning precede, and give rise to, prosocial behaviors. However, phylogenetically, the order in which the mechanisms that produce these products evolved was surely the reverse. Many animals behave in prosocial ways, but only humans make moral judgments, and the brain mech-anisms that mediate prosocial behaviors evolved before the brain mechanisms that mediate higher order reasoning abilities and language (see Darwin 1874; Moll et al. 2008). The mechanisms that gave rise to prosocial behaviors evolved before the mechanisms that gave rise to moral beliefs and moral reasoning, even if the latter possessed the ability to activate the former.

In his early work on the evolution of the moral sense, Darwin suggested that the activation of (pro)social instincts may engender a rudimentary sense of duty: "The imperious word ought seems merely to imply the consciousness of the existence of a rule of conduct, however it may have originated" (Darwin 1874, 112). However, "consciousness of the existence of a rule of conduct" does not constitute a sense of *moral* obligation. As demonstrated by researchers such as Turiel (1998), people may be conscious of rules of conduct such as "don't call your teacher by her first name," "avoid hot objects" and "eat nutritious foods," yet not consider them moral. To account for the origin of a sense of *moral* obligation, we must explain how hominins came to distinguish between moral and nonmoral obligations, and why they came to feel differently about each type.

Precursors of a Sense of Moral Self-Evaluation

Prosocial behaviors usually evoke positive reactions from others (which helped mediate the evolution of the mechanisms that produce them). Positive consequences tend to activate pleasurable psychological states in people, which induce them to feel that the prosocial behaviors they emitted were "good" and "right"; whereas negative reactions tend to induce people to feel that the antisocial behaviors they emit are "bad" and "wrong." Such states constitute primitive forms of self-evaluation: "I did right"; "I did wrong." However, again, the sense that one made a good practical choice or a bad practical mistake is different from the sense that the choice was morally good or bad, right or wrong. Some of the most difficult choices people make are between behaving in ways that they consider right, but will cost them dearly, and behaving in ways that they consider wrong, but will reap physical and material rewards.

It is telling that prescriptive and evaluative words such as "should," "right," "wrong," "good," and "bad" may allude to nonmoral and moral judgments. On the one hand, people say things like "I should be more careful," and "I should not have eaten so much," when they prescribe prudentially correct courses of action, and people say things like, "I was right" or "I was wrong" to convey judgments about the validity of facts. On the other hand, people say things like, "I should have kept my promise" and "I should not have lied," to refer to moral prescriptions and prohibitions, and they say things like, "It is right to help others, and it is wrong to lie" to make moral judgments.

Precursors of Conscience

As Darwin pointed out, humans and other social animals inevitably experience conflicts between satisfying their needs at the expense of members of their groups or suppressing their desires for the good of others. In Darwin's terms, individuals face conflicts between selfish instincts and social instincts. Noting that social instincts are significantly more enduring than selfish instincts, such as hunger, which dissipate after they are satisfied, Darwin suggested that if a person "gratif[ies his] own desires at the expense of other men... past and weaker impressions [of his selfish behaviors will be] judged by the ever-enduring social instinct, and by his deep regard for the good opinion of his fellows... [As a consequence], retribution will surely come. He will feel remorse, repentance, regret, or shame … [and] resolve to act differently" (Darwin 1874, 110). Although Darwin suggested that this process gives rise to conscience, it does not seem sufficient. Choosing to satisfy a pressing but transient personal need that leaves a more enduring social need unsatisfied may induce people to feel that they made the wrong (prudential) choice; however, it need not necessarily induce them to feel that the choice was immoral.

I suspect that people's "deep regard for the good opinion of [their] fellows" played a more significant role in the evolution of conscience than the enduring nature of the social instincts did. Learning theorists have demonstrated that social conditioning is instrumental to children's acquisition of conscience (Aronfreed 1968). Parents and other people show approval when children behave in prosocial ways, and disapproval when they behave in antisocial ways, and these reactions are often followed by physical and material rewards and punishments. Through conditioning, children come to feel good when they behave in ways that have evoked approval, and to feel bad when they behave in ways that have evoked disapproval. Children experience the psychological states associated with anticipating approval and disapproval as a primitive sense that it is right to behave in prosocial ways and wrong to behave in antisocial ways—that one should behave prosocially, and that one should not behave antisocially (see Bugental and Goodnow 1998, and Kochanska and Thompson, 1998 for reviews of research supporting these claims). As Darwin(1874) realized, there is nothing inconsistent with evolutionary theory in acknowledging the role of learning and social learning in the acquisition of conscience.

Precursors of Moral Sentiments about Others

In addition to the moral sentiments people experience about themselves, they also experience moral sentiments about others (Figure 1). Some of the evaluative feelings people experience about the behavior of others, such as moral indignation, are qualitatively different from the evaluative feelings they experience about themselves, such as guilt and shame. What were the precursors of moral sentiments about others?

Early hominins would have been inclined to react positively when others treated them and their kin in prosocial (inclusive fitness-enhancing) ways, and negatively when others treated them and their kin in antisocial ways. Positive emotional reactions to being treated in prosocial ways would have evoked a primitive sense that the prosocial behaviors were right, and that those who emitted them were good; and negative emotional reactions to being treated in antisocial ways would have evoked a primitive sense that the antisocial behaviors were wrong, and that those who emitted them were bad. Note that such affective reactions are directed at the people who evoke them, not just at their behavior, and, as such, they constitute trait attributions. We tend to approve of those who treat us right and to disapprove of those who wrong us.

Such aspects of people as their status, physical appearance, accomplishments, and cleanliness also may affect the ways in which observers react to them. As irrational as it may be, emotional reactions evoked by such features may affect observers' moral judgments. For example, in one study, investigators found that people who were in a filthy, messy, room made harsher moral judgments than people who were in a tidy, clean room (Schnall, Haidt, and Clore 2005).

Rozin, Haidt, and McCauley (1993) have found that phenomena associated with the risk of harm due to germs, such as bodily fluids, dead animals, garbage, and rancid smells, evoke disgust, which people experience in moral terms. As these researchers have pointed out, sexual acts involve the exchange of bodily fluids, and many sexual prohibitions are structured by concepts associated with pollution and disgust—prohibitions such as those associated with menstruation, anal sex, and bestiality. Rozin et al. have argued that in some cultures emotional reactions to physical impurity (and purity) help structure ideas about spiritual impurity (and purity): acts that contaminate people's spirit are viewed as immoral, and pureness of spirit is viewed as moral.

The adaptive function of moral disgust is similar to the adaptive function of other forms of disgust—it motivates people to withdraw from, and reject, noxious stimuli, whether physical or social in nature. People tend to steer clear of those who behave in morally impure ways (Schaller, Park, and Faulkner 2003).

Precursors of Abstract Ideas about Morality

The positive and negative feelings early hominins experienced about their own prosocial and antisocial behaviors would have converged with the positive and negative feelings they experienced about others' prosocial and antisocial behaviors to contribute to a more general sense that prosocial forms of conduct are right, that antisocial forms of conduct are wrong, and that those who behave in prosocial ways are good, and that those who behave in antisocial ways are bad. People from all cultures consider altruistic and cooperative forms of conduct right, and selfish, antisocial forms of conduct wrong, even though there are significant differences between and within cultures in how these forms of conduct are defined (Krebs, 2011). Although people from all cultures believe that it is right to help others and to conform to social norms, the range of others whom people believe it is right to help and the content of the norms they believe it is right to obey may differ greatly across cultures. For example, although there are food prohibitions in all cultures, people from some cultures believe it is wrong to eat pork; whereas people from other cultures believe it is wrong to eat beef, or lobster, or meat from dogs.

Precursors of a Sense of Justice

The thoughts and feelings produced by the mental mechanisms that evolved to uphold fitness-enhancing systems of cooperation were precursors of a sense of justice. Feelings of appreciation, gratitude, and indebtedness engender the sense that we should reciprocate the favors that others have bestowed on us. Feelings of anger, indignation, and vindictiveness make people want to get even with those who have cheated them and others. Feelings of guilt induce people to make amends. In all cases, the effect of the behaviors in question is to even up, or balance, the scales. Feelings of forgiveness and mercy induce individuals to restore disrupted cooperative relationships with those on whom their fitness is dependent (McCullough 2008). Each of these emotional states stems from a different brain circuit (Moll et al. 2008).

The emotions that dispose people to uphold systems of cooperation have been called "moral emotions" (e.g., Moll et al. 2008). However, these emotional states do not necessarily contain feelings of right and wrong. People can feel gratitude without feeling that they have a moral obligation to repay, and they can experience feelings of indignation without feeling that others have committed a moral infraction. People sometimes feel guilty about behaving in ways that they do not consider morally wrong, and people may forgive others whom they do not believe deserve to be forgiven.

To summarize, I have argued that different aspects of a sense of morality emerged in the human species from emotional reactions that dispose social animals to behave in prosocial ways and uphold systems of cooperation. Although these emotional reactions constitute precursors to a sense of morality, they are not sufficient to engender moral sentiments. To explain how moral sentiments originated, we must attend to the cognitive mechanisms that induce people to construe them in moral ways.

HOW DID A SENSE OF MORALITY ORIGINATE?

Systems of cooperation pay off because they enable individuals to advance their interests through gains in trade, and because groups replete with cooperators tend to fare better than groups replete with selfish individualists. However, within cooperative groups, all individuals encounter opportunities to maximize their gains by behaving selfishly, cheating, and free-riding—giving less than their share, and taking more. Modern humans consider the dilemmas created by these aspects of cooperation moral dilemmas. I believe that the function—or at least a central function—of a sense of morality is to induce members of groups (self and others) to resolve such dilemmas in prosocial ways—to resist the temptation to foster their short-term interests in ways that threaten the long-term benefits they and others can obtain by upholding the systems of cooperation in their groups. As suggested by Haidt (2001), the central difference between moral sentiments and other kinds of sentiments is that moral sentiments are associated with the welfare or interests of people and groups, and are usually linked to behaviors that conform to or violate moral norms.

People experience emotions in moral terms when these emotions are embedded in ideas about the rights and duties of individuals participating in systems of cooperative exchange, and accompanying conceptions of fairness. Feelings of gratitude, guilt, and indignation become moral emotions when they are embedded in conceptions of rights and duties, equity and fairness. People experience the sense that they should repay those who have helped them as a moral obligation when they feel that failing to repay them would be unfair. Guilt and indignation assume a moral flavor when they are embedded in the sense that people have violated the norms that uphold the social orders of their groups, treated others unfairly, or failed to do their share.

In 1985, Trivers suggested that "a sense of fairness has evolved in the human species as the standard against which to measure the behavior of other people, so as to guard against cheating in reciprocal relationships" (388). In 2006, he argued that being cheated evokes strong emotional reactions, "because unfair arrangements, repeated often, may exact a very strong cost in inclusive fitness" (77). In a similar vein, de Waal and Brosnan suggested that, "the squaring of accounts in the negative domain…may represent a precursor to human justice, since justice can be viewed as a transformation of the urge for revenge, euphemized as retribution, in order to control and regulate behavior" (2006,

88). On the positive side of fairness, Trivers and de Waal argue that receiving goods and services from others evokes positive reactions such as feelings of gratitude, which dispose people to reciprocate.

In his classic article on the evolution of reciprocal altruism, Trivers (1971) distinguished between gross cheating and subtle cheating, and discussed the implications of this distinction for the design of the mental mechanisms that regulate cooperative exchanges. Early hominins who possessed the cognitive sophistication to reckon the value of the goods and services they received from others and use these calculations to guide their decisions about how much they owed in return would have fared better than those who were unable to perform such calculations. The increasingly finely tuned cognitive mechanisms that enabled our ancestors to evaluate social exchanges in terms of standards of equity gave rise to an increasingly refined sense of justice.

The precursors to a sense of justice discussed by Trivers and de Waal stem primarily from the cognitive and emotional reactions of animals to the ways in which they are treated by members of their groups. There is, however, more to humans' sense of justice than the sense that one has been treated fairly or unfairly. Humans also react to the ways in which third parties are treated—a phenomenon dubbed "strong reciprocity" by Gintis and his colleagues (Gintis, Bowles, Boyd, and Fehr 2005). As expressed by Wilson, "our sense of justice...involves a desire to punish wrongdoers, even when we are not the victims, and that sense is a 'spontaneous' and 'natural' sentiment" (1993, 40). Summarizing the findings from several studies employing economic games, Gächter and Hermann conclude:

> Overall, the results suggest that free riding causes negative emotions...[that are] consistent with the hypothesis that emotions trigger punishment....the majority of punishments are executed by above-average contributors and imposed on below-average contributors...punishment increases with the deviation of the free rider from other members' average contribution...evidence from neuroscientific experiments supports the interpretation that emotions trigger punishment. (2006, 297)

In addition to reacting to injustices perpetrated against themselves and others, people react to the injustices they perpetrate against others, but not, perhaps, in the same way. From an evolutionary perspective, we would not expect people to be naturally inclined to pass judgment on themselves and others in impartial ways, or to be unconditionally motivated to behave fairly. If the original function of moral sentiments were to help people maximize their benefits from strategic interactions, we would expect them to be susceptible to self-serving biases. As expressed by Trivers, "an attachment to fairness or justice is self-interested and we repeatedly see in life...that victims of injustice feel the pain more strongly than do disinterested bystanders and far more than do the perpetrators" (2006, 77) In support of the idea that moral sentiments suffer from self-serving biases, studies have found that people are more inclined to feel that others should sacrifice their interests for their sake than the reverse, to hold others to higher moral standards than those they apply to themselves, to overestimate how much they deserve (their rights) and underestimate how much they owe (their duties), while underestimating how much others deserve, and overestimating how much others owe (Chaiken, Giner-Sorolla, and

Chen 1996; Krebs and Denton 2005; Krebs 2008a,c; Kunda 2000; Lerner and Miller 1978; Pyszczynski and Greenberg 1987).

However, there is another side to this story. Researchers have found that people tend to feel worse when they fail to repay their friends than they do when their friends fail to repay them, and that people feel bad when they treat their friends unfairly (Janicki, 2004). In a study on real-life moral decisions about how to divide resources, brain researchers concluded that "the emotional response to [treating others unfairly] pushes people from extreme inequity and drives them to be fair … [indicating that] our basic impulse to be fair isn't a complicated thing that we learn" (Ming, Cedric, and Quartz 2008, 5879).

So, to summarize, I have argued that the emotional precursors to morality apparent in primates other than humans assumed a moral flavor in hominins when they became embedded in ideas about how members of cooperative groups should treat one another, and why they should uphold social norms that fostered their interests.

HOW WAS A SENSE OF MORALITY REFINED IN THE HUMAN SPECIES?

To account for the evolution of a sense of morality, we must identify the factors responsible for the refinement of the mental mechanisms that produce it. I believe that these mechanisms were refined during the evolution of the human species through strategic social interactions among members of increasingly large and complex groups, and that they continue to be refined and calibrated in children and adults through the same process as they develop in contemporary environments. Strategic interactions are like games with offensive and defensive moves. Individuals invoke strategies to induce others to behave in ways that improve their welfare, while resisting attempts by others to induce them to behave in ways that diminish their welfare. As mental mechanisms that housed "offensive" strategies improved in quality through natural selection, they created a selective pressure for improved "defensive" mechanisms, and so on, leading to an arms-race escalation of the refinement of the brain structures housing the strategies. The capacities that children inherit in each generation are refined, calibrated, and adapted as they develop.

Two prominent ways in which members of groups attempt to manipulate others are by offering incentives and by imposing sanctions. Before early hominins acquired language, they probably used tactics similar to those used by chimpanzees and other apes, such as issuing threats, administering physical and material rewards and punishments, and signaling their approval and disapproval through facial expressions, body language, and auditory signals that conveyed respect, gratitude, anger, disgust, and so on (de Waal 1991). However, the dynamics of strategic interaction would have changed dramatically when early hominins acquired the capacity to transmit ideas symbolically through language. As suggested by Williams, "the unparalleled human capability for symbolic communication has an incidental consequence of special importance for ethics. In biological usage, communication is nearly synonymous with attempted manipulation. It is a low-cost way of getting someone else to behave in a way favorable to oneself" (1989, 211).

As Darwin(1874) suggested, the capacity for language was instrumental in the refine-ment of the moral senses. Ironically, moral judgments and moral reasoning probably originated in the hominin lineage as tools of social influence and tactics in strategic interaction. The capacity for symbolic speech enabled early hominins to express their approval of prosocial behaviors and their disapproval of antisocial behaviors with words like *good* and *bad*, and to buttress these judgments with reasons, explanations, and justi-fications designed to increase their persuasive power. Because moral judgments pertain to forms of social conduct that affect people's welfare, and because they are associated with positive and negative social sanctions, they tend to evoke stronger affective reactions than other kinds of judgment do (Kagan 1984). Language also would have improved early hominins' ability to hold members of their groups accountable for their moral and immoral behaviors by enabling them to enhance or diminish others' reputations through gossip (Alexander 1987; Dunbar 1996).

THE ADAPTIVE VALUE OF MORAL REASONING

Moral reasoning is a powerful tool in strategic social interactions. People use it to activate one another's moral intuitions and prosocial emotions (Haidt 2001; Saltzstein and Kasachkoff 2004), and to buttress their moral judgments with arguments designed to increase their persuasive power (Haidt 2001; Krebs and Denton 2005).

If the original function of moral reasoning were to exert social influence on others, and if people use it for this purpose in their everyday lives, we would not expect the types of moral reasoning that people display in response to the hypothetical moral dilemmas that many psychologists employ to assess moral development to correspond to the types that they invoke in their everyday lives (Krebs and Denton 2005). To understand the types of moral reasoning that people invoke, we need to attend to the goals that people are using it to achieve. If you give people complex hypothetical moral dilemmas in academic con-texts, and ask them to resolve them, you can expect them to engage in high-level moral reasoning. However, when people are faced with moral dilemmas in the real world that have significant implications for their welfare, especially in highly charged situations in which decisions must be made quickly or under constraint, they rarely invoke the sophis-ticated forms of moral reasoning they employ to solve hypothetical dilemmas (Krebs and Denton 2005).

CONSTRAINTS ON SELF-SERVING BIASES IN MORAL JUDGMENT

Even though real-life moral reasoning is susceptible to self-serving biases, we would expect antidotes to these biases to emerge naturally during the process of strategic interaction. To begin with, manipulating others into advancing one's personal interests may diminish one's genetic and biological interests, because personal interests may not correspond to genetic and biological interests (Krebs 2008b). Second, we would not expect unconstrained self-serving judgments and arguments to constitute effective tactics in strategic interac-tions. Biased forms of moral manipulation face the same evolutionary obstacles in real life as selfish tactics do in Prisoner's Dilemma games: It is not in the interest of individuals to permit others to exploit them, and, if both parties invoke selfish strategies, they end up doing each other in. Although we would expect individuals to be evolved to exhort others to perform more altruistic and self-sacrificial acts than others are inclined to perform, we would not expect blatantly biased exhortations such as, "you should always sacrifice your interests for me" to have much persuasive impact. We would expect natural selection and developmental experiences to hone receiving mechanisms in ways that reduce their receptiveness to fitness-diminishing forms of moral judgment and moral reasoning.

Inasmuch as early humans were able to gain more by coordinating their efforts with the efforts of others and engaging in mutually beneficial social exchanges than they were by attempting to exploit others, we would expect mechanisms that dispose and enable people to find common ground to have evolved and to become refined as children develop. In support of this expectation, my colleagues and I have found that people often attempt to resolve real-life moral conflicts through negotiation, and that, during this process, they tend to adapt their moral judgments to the moral orientations they impute to others. For example, couples who were engaged in real-life moral conflicts tended to tailor their moral judgments to the kinds of judgments made by their partners (Krebs et al. 2002). More generally, studies have found that people tend to modify their attitudes to fit with those of people with whom they are interacting in cooperative ways (Chen and Chaiken 1999). Indeed, there is evidence that when two people engage in a social interaction, they coordinate their mannerisms and body language—a phenomenon dubbed the "chameleon effect" by Chartrand and Bargh (1999).

When people use reason and logical consistency as weapons in moral arguments, they often end up hoisting themselves on their own petards. The process of justifying moral judgments tends to induce people to believe that they are valid. People persuade themselves in the process of persuading others (Festinger 1964). Believing the prescriptive judgments one makes to others may reap adaptive benefits by increasing their persuasive power (Trivers 2000). In addition, people may be inclined to accept moral judgments and standards generated during moral negotiations because they are supported by good arguments, because they are supported by others, because the parties involved actively participated in generating them, and because they enable people to resolve their differences in optimal ways. Several theorists have suggested that moral dialogues are equipped to generate emergent preferences (Elster 2000; Habermas 1993).

EXPANDING THE CIRCLE

Prosocial dispositions that evolved through kin selection and reciprocity tend to be activated by a relatively small circle of in-group members. However, as Darwin observed, during the course of evolution, our "sympathies became more tender and widely diffused, so as to extend to men of all races...and [even] to the lower animals" (1874, 121). Like Darwin, the philosopher, Singer, attributed the expansion of the circle of those equipped to activate moral judgments to reason, especially as invoked in moral argumentation:

> Ethical reasoning, once begun, pushes against our initially limited ethical horizons, leading us always toward a more universal point of view.... If I claim that what I do

is right, while what you do is wrong, I must give some reason other than the fact that my action benefits me (or my kin, or my village) while your action benefits you (or your kin or your village." (1981, 118–119)

It is worth noting, however, that reason is not the only process equipped to expand the circle of those people treat in prosocial ways. Kin-selected altruistic dispositions may be activated by nonkin (Burnstein 2005); people may identify with groups to which they have been assigned on an arbitrary basis (Tajfel and Turner 1985); and small groups may unite to pursue a common cause (Richerson and Boyd 2005).

CONCLUSION

In this chapter, I asked, and attempted to answer, six questions: (1) What is a sense of morality? (2) What kinds of mental processes produce a sense of morality? (3) Why do people possess a sense of morality? (4) What are the precursors of a sense of morality? (5) How did a sense of morality originate? and (6) How did this sense become refined in the human species?

I concluded that the mental states that people experience in moral terms stem from a set of qualitatively distinct mental mechanisms, some of which run hot and others of which run cold. Although other animals possess precursors of these mechanisms, they are not sufficient to produce a sense of morality. A sense of morality emerged in the human species when hominins acquired the cognitive sophistication to interpret their emotional states in terms of rights and duties, and the linguistic sophistication to communicate their ideas to others. The moral sense became refined during the course of human evolution through strategic social interactions, in essentially the same way that this sense becomes refined in children as they develop in contemporary environments. To understand this phenomenon, we must attend to the function it evolved to serve, which I have argued is to induce individuals to resist the temptation to advance their interests unfairly, at the expense of members of their groups, and to uphold the rules and norms that prescribe forms of conduct that enabled our human ancestors to maximize their gains from cooperative exchanges.

References

Alexander, R.D. 1987. *The biology of moral systems.* New York: Aldine de Gruyter.

Aronfreed, J. 1968. *Conduct and conscience.* New York: Academic Press.

Bandura, A. 1989. Social cognitive theory. *Annals of Child Development* 6: 1–60.

Bloom, P. 2004. *Descartes' baby: How the science of child development explains what makes us human.* New York: Basic Books.

Bugental, D. B., and J. J. Goodnow. 1998. "Socialization." In *Handbook of child psychology vol. 3, 5th ed.*, eds. W. Damon, and N. Eisenberg, 389–462. New York: Wiley.

Burnstein, E. 2005. "Altruism and genetic relatedness." In *The handbook of evolutionary psychology*, ed. D. Buss, 528–551. Hoboken, NJ: John Wiley & Sons.

Campbell, D. 1978. "On the genetics of altruism and the counterhedonic components in human culture." In *Altruism, sympathy, and helping: Psychological and sociological principles*, ed. L. Wispe. New York: Academic Press.

Chaiken, S., R. Giner-Sorolla, and S. Chen. 1996. "Beyond accuracy: Defense and impression motives in heuristic and systematic information processing." In *The psychology of action: Linking cognition and motivation to behavior*, eds. P.M. Gollwitzer, and J.A. Bargh, 553–578. New York: Guilford Press.

Chartrand, T. L., and J. A. Bargh. 1999. The chameleon effect: The perception-behavior link and social interaction. *Journal of Personality and Social Psychology* 76: 893–910.

Chen, S., and S. Chaiken. 1999. "The heuristic-systematic model in its broader context." In *Dual process theories in social psychology*, eds. S. Chaiken, and Y. Trope. New York: Guilford Press.

Darwin, C. 1874. *The descent of man and selection in relation to sex*. New York: Rand, McNally and Company.

de Waal, F.B.M. 1991. The chimpanzee's sense of social regularity and its relation to the human sense of justice. *American Behavioral Scientist* 34: 335–349.

de Waal, F. B. 2006. *Primates and philosophers: How morality evolved*. Princeton N.J.: Princeton University Press.

de Waal, F. B., and S. F. Brosnan. 2006. "Simple and complex reciprocity in animals." In *Cooperation in primates and humans*, eds. P. M. Kapeler, and C. P. van Schaik, 85–105. New York: Springer-Verlag.

Dunbar, R.I.M. 1996. "Determinants of group size in primates: A general model." In *Evolution of social behavior patterns in primates and man*, eds. G. Runciman, J. Maynard Smith, and R.I.M. Dunbar, 33–58. Oxford, United Kingdom: Oxford University Press.

Elster, J. 2000. *Ulysses unbound: Studies in rationality, precommitment, and constraints*. Cambridge, UK: Cambridge University Press.

Festinger, L. 1964. *Conflict, decision, and dissonance*. Stanford, CA: Stanford University Press.

Gächter, S., and B. Herrmann. 2006. "Human cooperation from an economic perspective." In *Cooperation in primates and humans*, eds. P. M. Kapeler, and C. P. van Schaik, 275–302. New York: Springer-Verlag.

Gintis, H., S. Bowles, R. Boyd, and E. Fehr. 2005. *Moral sentiments and material interests: On the foundations of cooperation in economic life*. Cambridge, MA: MIT Press.

Greene, J. 2008. "The secret joke of Kant's soul." In *Moral psychology vol 3: The neuroscience of morality: Emotion, brain disorders, and development*, ed. W. Sinnott-Armstrong, 35–80. Cambridge MA: MIT Press.

Habermas, J. 1993. *Justification and application*. Cambridge, MA: MIT Press.

Haidt, J. 2001. The emotional dog and its rational tail: A social intuitionist approach to moral judgment. *Psychological Review* 108: 814–834.

Hamilton, W. D. 1964. The evolution of social behavior. *Journal of Theoretical Biology* 7: 1–52.

Hauser, M.D. 2006. *Moral minds: How nature designed our universal sense of right and wrong*. New York: Harper Collins.

Janicki M. (2004). Beyond sociobiology: A kinder and gentler evolutionary view of human nature. In C. Crawford & C. Salmon (Eds.), *Evolutionary psychology: Public policy and personal decisions* (pp. 51–72). Mahwah, NJ: Erlbaum.

Kagan, J. 1984. *The nature of the child*. New York: Basic Books.

Kochanska, G., and R. A. Thompson. 1998. "The emergence of conscience in toddlerhood and early childhood." In *Parenting and children's internalization of values: A handbook of contemporary theory*, eds. J. E. Grusec, and L. Kuczynski, 53–77. New York: Wiley.

Kohlberg, L. 1984. *Essays in moral development: The psychology of moral development vol. 2*. New York: Harper and Row.

Krebs, D. L. 2005. "The evolution of morality." In *The handbook of evolutionary psychology*, ed. D. Buss, 747–771. Hoboken, NJ: John Wiley and Sons.

Krebs, D. L. 2008a. Morality: An evolutionary account. *Perspectives on Psychological Science* 3: 149–172.

Krebs, D. L. 2008b. "How selfish by nature?" In *Foundations of evolutionary psychology*, eds. C. Crawford, and D. L. Krebs, 293–312. London: Taylor Francis.

Krebs, D. L. 2008c. "The evolution of a sense of justice." In *Evolutionary forensic psychology*, eds. J. Duntley, and T. K. Shackelford. New York: Oxford University Press.

Krebs, D. L. 2011. *The origins of morality: An evolutionary account.* New York: Oxford University Press.

Krebs, D.L., and K. Denton. 2005. Toward a more pragmatic approach to morality: A critical evaluation of Kohlberg's model. *Psychological Review* 112: 629–649.

Krebs, D. L., K. Denton, G. Wark, R. Couch, T. P. Racine, and D. L. Krebs. 2002. Interpersonal moral conflicts between couples: Effects of type of dilemma, role, and partner's judgments on level of moral reasoning and probability of resolution. *Journal of Adult Development* 9: 307–316.

Krebs, D. L., and M. Janicki. 2004. "Biological foundations of moral norms." In *Psychological foundations of culture*, eds. M. Schaller, and C. Crandall, 125–148. Mahwah, NJ: Erlbaum.

Kunda, Z. 2000. *Social cognition: Making sense of people.* Cambridge, MA: MIT Press.

Lerner, M.J., and D. T. Miller. 1978. Just world research and the attribution process: Looking back and ahead. *Psychological Bulletin* 85: 1030–1051.

McCullough, M.E. 2008. *Beyond revenge: The evolution of the forgiveness instinct.* San Francisco: Jossey-Bass

Miller, G. F. 2007. The sexual selection of moral virtues. *The Quarterly Review of Biology* 82: 97–125.

Ming, H., A. Cedric, and S. R. Quartz. 2008. The right and the good: Distributive justice and neural encoding of equity and efficiency. *Science* 320 (5879): 1092–1095.

Moll, J., R. di Oliveira-Sourza, R. Zahn, and J. Grafman. 2008. "The cognitive neuroscience of moral emotions." In *Moral psychology: The neuroscience of morality: Emotion, brain disorders, and development*, ed. Sinnott-Armstrong, 1–18. Cambridge, MA: MIT Press.

Prinz, J. 2007. *The emotional construction of morals.* New York: Oxford University Press.

Pyszczynski, T., and J. Greenberg. 1987. Toward an integration of cognitive and motivational perspectives on social inference: A biased hypothesis-testing model. *Advances in Experimental Social Psychology* 20: 297–340.

Rest, J. F. (1983). Morality. In J. H. Flavell & E. M. Markman (Eds.), *Handbook of child psychology (Vol. 3): Cognitive development* (4th ed.) (pp. 556-629). New York: Wiley.

Richerson, P. J., and R. Boyd. 2005. *Not by genes alone: How culture transformed human evolution.* Chicago: University of Chicago Press.

Rozin, P., J. Haidt, and C. McCauley. 1993. "Disgust." In *Handbook of emotions*, eds. M. Lewis, and J. Haviland, 575–594. New York: Guilford Press.

Saltzstein, H. D., and T. Kasachkoff. 2004. Haidt's moral intuitionist theory: A psychological and philosophical critique. *Review of General Psychology* 8: 273–282.

Schaller, M., J. H. Park, and J. Faulkner. 2003. Prehistoric dangers and contemporary prejudices. *European Review of Social Psychology* 14: 105–137.

Schnall, S., J. Haidt, and G. L. Clore. 2005. Disgust as embodied moral judgment. Unpublished manuscript, Department of Psychology, Charlottesville, Virginia: University of Virginia.

Simon, H. 1990. A mechanism for social selection of successful altruism. *Science* 250: 1665–1668.

Singer, P. 1981. *The expanding circle: Ethics and sociobiology.* New York: Farrar, Straus, and Giroux.

Sinnott-Armstrong, W. (Ed.) (2008). *Moral psychology*. Cambridge MA: MIT Press.

Sunstein, C. R. 2005. Moral heuristics. *Behavioral and Brain Sciences* 28: 531–573.

Tajfel, H., and J. C. Turner. 1985. "The social identity theory of intergroup behavior." In *Psychology of intergroup relations*, eds. S. Worchel, and W.G. Austin, 7–24. Chicago: Nelson-Hall.

Tooby, J., and L. Cosmides. 2005. "Conceptual foundations of evolutionary psychology." In *The handbook of evolutionary psychology*, ed. D. Buss, 5–67. Hoboken, NJ: John Wiley and Sons.

Turiel, E. 1998. "The development of morality." In *Handbook of child psychology*, ed. W. Damon, 863–932. New York: Wiley Press.

Trivers, R.L. 1971. The evolution of reciprocal altruism. *Quarterly Review of Biology* 46: 35–57.

Trivers, R. 1985. *Social evolution*. Menlo Park, CA: Benjamin Cummings.

Trivers, R. 2000. "The elements of a scientific theory of self-deception." In *Evolutionary perspectives on human reproductive behavior*, eds. D. LeCroy, and P. Moller, 114–131. New York: New York Academy of Sciences.

Trivers, R. 2006. "Reciprocal altruism: 30 years later." In *Cooperation in primates and humans*, eds. P. M. Kapeler, and C. P. van Schaik, 67–84. New York: Springer-Verlag.

Williams, G.C. 1989. "A sociobiological expansion of 'evolution and ethics'." In *Evolution and ethics*, eds. J. Paradis, and G.C. Williams, 179–214. Princeton, NJ: Princeton University Press.

Wilson, J.Q. 1993. *The moral sense*. New York: Free Press.

17

BEHAVIORAL ETHICS

Herbert Gintis

1. BEHAVIORAL ETHICS AND THE RATIONAL ACTOR MODEL

Philosophical views about morality have traditionally been supported by abstract reasoning and introspection, with, at best, passing reference to actual human behavior. Behavioral ethics develops models of human morality based upon the fact that morality is an emergent property of the evolutionary dynamic that gave rise to our species. Propositions concerning moral behavior are framed and tested using the methods of game theory, using subjects from a variety of social backgrounds and cultures. In this paper I will outline some major themes in behavioral ethics, and suggest how they relate to philosophical ethics.

Homo sapiens is one of many social species, but alone is the product of an evolutionary dynamic known as *gene-culture co-evolution*. Like language and the social emotions (shame, pride, contempt, empathy), morality is an emergent human universal.

Individual fitness in humans depends on the structure of social life. Because culture is limited by and facilitated by human genetic propensities, human cognitive, affective, and moral capacities are the product of an evolutionary dynamic involving the interaction of genes and culture (Cavalli-Sforza and Feldman 1982; Boyd and Richerson 1985; Dunbar 1993; Richerson and Boyd 2004). This co-evolutionary process has endowed us with preferences that go beyond the self-regarding concerns emphasized in traditional economic and biological theory. Gene-culture co-evolution explains why we have a social epistemology facilitating the sharing of intentionality across minds, as well as why we have such non-self-regarding values as a taste for cooperation, fairness, and retribution, the capacity to empathize, and the ability to value character virtues (e.g., honesty, loyalty, trustworthiness).

In behavioral ethics, we recognize that people consider moral statements to have truth values, but we consider these values as being valid only for the specific social group involved, rather than having universal scope. We thus treat ethics in a manner similar to linguistics, in which grammaticality and correct usage are important and analytically tractable yet highly specific to a particular society of speakers. As it turns out, there are a host of human values that are universal in that they are present in virtually every known society (Brown 1991). We account for this universality in terms of the general requirements for social living of our species.

Moral behavior is often held to be incompatible with rational choice. This is incorrect. The rational actor model of economic theory presupposes that people have consistent preferences, but does not require that preferences be self-regarding or materialistic. We can just as easily chart how people value honesty or loyalty in the same way that we can chart how they value fried chicken or cashmere sweaters.

Some caveats are in order, however, in interpreting the rational actor model. First, individuals do not consciously maximize "utility" or anything else. As long as people have consistent preferences, we can represent their choices as the solution to a maximization problem. This is analytically useful and gives accurate predictions, but it does not mean that individuals really maximize. This analytical ploy is similar to the physicist predicting the path followed by a light wave by assuming the light minimizes path length traveled. This works, but of course light waves do not really minimize anything.

Second, individual choices, even if they are self-regarding (e.g., personal consumption) are not necessarily welfare enhancing. In the sense of the rational actor model, it may thus be rational to smoke, have unsafe sex, and even cross the street without looking. Third, individual preferences are not fixed, but rather are a function of an individual's current state (e.g., state of hunger or sexual arousal). Fourth, the fact that we model individuals as rational decision makers does not imply that we are methodological individualists. In particular, we may adopt the rational actor model yet assert that it is not possible to derive either social norms or moral values from individual rationality. In fact, it is quite possible that both social norms and the moral realm are emergent properties of human evolution that cannot be derived from the aggregation of individual rational choice.

Beliefs are the Achilles' heel of the rational actor model. The standard model of rational choice treats beliefs as purely subjective (the so-called "subjective priors"), whereas individual beliefs are in fact a part of a social network of interdependent socially constructed beliefs. The rational actor model is really a lower-dimensional projection of a general model of human action, which includes an interpretive and a deliberative dimension as well. Full human reason operates in this larger action framework.

Because the use of the word *rational* in the rational actor model is so circumscribed compared with the general usage of the word, we often call the rational actor model the "beliefs, preferences, and constraints" model (BPC), because this captures the notion of consistent preference, the centrality of beliefs, and the notion of making trade-offs subject to informational and material constraints.

In the BPC model, choices give rise to probability distributions over outcomes, the expected values of which are the payoffs to the choice from which they arose. Game theory extends this analysis to cases in which there are multiple decision makers. In the language of game theory, players are endowed with strategies and have certain information, and for each array of choices by the players, the game specifies a distribution of payoffs to the players. Game theory predicts the behavior of the players by assuming each is rational; in other words, each maximizes a preference function subject to beliefs as well as to informational and material constraints.

The following experiments are all based on using game theory to set up the choices available to subjects, the knowledge they have on which their choices are based, and the payoffs to each subject as a function of their joint strategy choices. We assume the subjects are rational (i.e., consistent) decision makers, so that their choices reflect their subjective trade-offs among heterogeneous payoffs—some material and some moral and/or regarding others.

2. EXPERIMENTAL FINDINGS ON THE RATIONALITY OF ALTRUISTIC BEHAVIOR

There is nothing irrational about caring for others, but do preferences for altruistic acts entail transitive preferences as required by the notion of rationality in decision theory? Andreoni and Miller (2002) showed that, in the case of the Dictator Game, they do. Moreover, there are no known counterexamples.

In the Dictator Game, the experimenter gives a subject, called the dictator, a certain amount of money and instructs him to give any portion of it he desires to a second, anonymous subject, called the receiver. The dictator keeps whatever he does not choose to give to the receiver. Obviously, a self-regarding dictator will give nothing to the receiver. Suppose the experimenter gives the dictator m points (exchangeable at the end of the session for real money) and tells him that the price of giving some of these points to the receiver is p, meaning that each point the receiver gets costs the giver p points. For instance, if $p = 4$, then it costs the dictator four points for each point that he transfers to the receiver. The dictator's choices must then satisfy the budget constraint $\pi_s + p\pi_o = m$, where π_s is the amount the dictator keeps and π_o is the amount the receiver gets. The question, then, is simply, is there a preference function $u(\pi_s, \pi_o)$ that the dictator maximizes subject to the budget constraint $\pi_s + p\pi_o = m$? If so, then it is just as rational, from a behavioral standpoint, to care about giving to the receiver as it is to care about consuming marketed commodities.

Varian (1982) developed a generalized axiom of revealed preference (GARP) that ensures that individuals are rational as in the sense of traditional consumer demand theory. Andreoni and Miller (2002) worked with 176 students in an elementary economics class and had them play the Dictator Game multiple times each, with the price p taking on the values $p = 0.25$, 0.33, 0.5, 1, 2, 3, and 4, with amounts of tokens equaling $m = 40, 60, 75, 80$, and 100. They found that only 18 of the 176 subjects violated GARP at least once and that of these violations, only 4 were at all significant. By contrast, if choices were randomly generated, we would expect that between 78 percent and 95 percent of subjects would have violated GARP.

As for the degree of altruistic giving in this experiment, Andreoni and Miller found that 22.7 percent of subjects were perfectly selfish, 14.2 percent were perfectly egalitarian at all prices, and 6.2 percent always allocated all the money so as to maximize the total amount won (i.e., when $p > 1$, they kept all the money, and when $p < 1$, they gave all the money to the receiver).

We conclude from this study that, at least in some cases, and perhaps in all, we can treat altruistic preferences in a manner perfectly parallel to the way we treat money and private goods in individual preference functions. We use this approach in the rest of the problems in this chapter.

2.1. Conditional Altruistic Cooperation

A social dilemma is a situation in which a number of people can gain by cooperating, but cooperating is costly, so each individual does better personally by not cooperating, no matter what the others do. For instance, suppose that, if a member of a group of size $n \geq 2$

pays the cost $c > 0$, he benefits each of the others by an amount $b > 0$. If $b(n-1) > c$, we have a social dilemma. At cost c, an individual can help the group by the amount $(n-1)b > c$, but a selfish individual will not do so. If all cooperate, each will earn $b-c > 0$, but in a group of self-regarding individuals, each will earn zero.

Conditional altruistic cooperation is a predisposition to cooperate in a social dilemma as long as the other players also cooperate. Consider the preceding social dilemma, with $n = 2$, called the Prisoner's Dilemma. In this game, let CC stand for "both players cooperate," let DD stand for "both players defect," let CD stand for "Player 1 cooperates but his partner defects," and let DC stand for "Player 1 defects and his partner cooperates." A self-regarding player 1 will prefer DC to CC, will prefer CC to DD, and will prefer DD to CD, whereas an altruistic cooperator will prefer CC to DC, will prefer DC to DD, and will prefer DD to CD; that is, the self-regarding individual prefers to defect no matter what his partner does, whereas the conditional altruistic cooperator prefers to cooperate so long as his partner cooperates.

Kiyonari et al. (2000) ran an experiment based on this game with real monetary payoffs using 149 Japanese university students. The experimenters ran three distinct treatments, with about equal numbers of subjects in each treatment. The first treatment was a standard simultaneous Prisoner's Dilemma, the second was a second-player situation in which the subject was told that the first player in the Prisoner's Dilemma had already chosen to cooperate, and the third was a first-player treatment in which the subject was told that his decision to cooperate or defect would be made known to the second player before the latter made his own choice. The experimenters found that 38 percent of the subjects cooperated in the simultaneous treatment, 62 percent cooperated in the second-player treatment, and 59 percent cooperated in the first-player treatment. The decision to cooperate in each treatment cost the subject about $5 (600 yen). This shows unambiguously that a majority of subjects were conditional altruistic cooperators (62 percent). Almost as many were not only cooperators, but were also willing to bet that their partners would be (59 percent), provided the latter were assured of not being defected from, although, under standard conditions, without this assurance only 38 percent would in fact cooperate.

2.2. Altruistic Punishment

"Strong reciprocity" is an altruistic behavioral propensity often exhibited in daily life and in the laboratory as well. A strong reciprocator is a conditional altruistic cooperator who is willing to punish non-cooperators even when this is personally costly and is unlikely to be compensated by higher material returns in the future. The simplest game exhibiting the altruistic punishment of the strong reciprocator is the Ultimatum Game (Güth et al. 1982). Under conditions of anonymity, two players are shown a sum of money, say $10. One of the players, called the proposer, is instructed to offer any number of dollars, from $1 to $10, to the second player, who is called the responder. The proposer can make only one offer and the responder can either accept or reject this offer. If the responder accepts the offer, the money is shared accordingly. If the responder rejects the offer, both players receive nothing. The two players do not face each other again.

There is only *one* responder strategy that is a best response for a self-regarding individual: accept anything you are offered. Knowing this, a self-regarding proposer who believes he faces a self-regarding responder offers the minimum possible amount, $1, and this is accepted.

However, when actually played, the self-regarding outcome is almost never attained or even approximated. In fact, as many replications of this experiment have documented, under varying conditions and with varying amounts of money, proposers routinely offer responders very substantial amounts (50 percent of the total generally being the modal offer) and responders frequently reject offers below 30 percent (Güth and Tietz 1990, Camerer and Thaler 1995). Are these results culturally dependent? Do they have a strong genetic component or do all successful cultures transmit similar values of reciprocity to individuals? Roth et al. (1991) conducted the Ultimatum Game in four different countries (United States, Yugoslavia, Japan, and Israel) and found that, although the level of offers differed a small but significant amount in different countries, the probability of an offer being rejected did not. This indicates that both proposers and responders share the same notion of what is considered fair in that society and that proposers adjust their offers to reflect this common notion. The differences in level of offers across countries, by the way, were relatively small. When a much greater degree of cultural diversity is studied, however, large differences in behavior are found, reflecting different standards of what it means to be fair in different types of societies (Henrich et al. 2004).

Behavior in the Ultimatum Game thus conforms to the strong reciprocity model: fair behavior in the Ultimatum Game for college students is a 50–50 split. Responders reject offers under 40 percent as a form of altruistic punishment of the norm-violating proposer. Proposers offer 50 percent because they are altruistic cooperators, or 40 percent because they fear rejection. To support this interpretation, we note that, if the offers in an Ultimatum Game are generated by a computer rather than by the proposer, and if responders know this, low offers are rarely rejected (Blount 1995). This suggests that players are motivated by *reciprocity*, reacting to a violation of behavioral norms (Greenberg and Frisch 1972). Moreover, in a variant of the game in which a responder rejection leads to the responder getting nothing but allows the proposer to keep the share he suggested for himself, responders never reject offers, and proposers make considerably smaller (but still positive) offers (Bolton and Zwick 1995). As a final indication that strong reciprocity motives are operative in this game, after the game is over, when asked why they offered more than the lowest possible amount, proposers commonly said that they were afraid that responders would consider low offers unfair and reject them. When responders rejected offers, they usually claimed they want to punish unfair behavior. In all of the foregoing experiments a significant fraction of subjects (about a quarter, typically) conformed to self-regarding preferences.

We should note that, although strong reciprocity is a form of moral behavior, a high level of moral cognition does not generally back it. Rather, individuals cooperate because it pleases them to do so, and they punish non-cooperators out of anger or pique, not because it is a moral duty to do so. Thus, Sanfey et al. (2003) subjected players of the Ultimatum Game to fMRI brain scans, and found that when responders rejected unfair offers, they exhibited activity in the anterior insula, which is usually associated with emotional responses.

2.3. Strong Reciprocity in the Labor Market

Fehr et al. (1997) (see also Fehr and Gächter 1998) performed an experiment to validate what is known as a gift-exchange model of the labor market. The experimenters divided a group of 141 subjects into employers and employees. The rules of the game are as follows: If an employer hires an employee who provides effort e and receives a wage w, his profit is $\pi = 100e-w$. The wage must be between 1 and 100, and the effort is between 0.1 and 1. The payoff to the employee is then $u = w-c(e)$, where $c(e)$ a cost of effort function such that $c(0.1) = 0, c(1.0) = 20$. All payoffs involve real money that the subjects are paid at the end of the experimental session. We call this the Experimental Labor Market Game.

The sequence of actions is as follows: The employer first offers a "contract" specifying a wage w and a desired amount of effort e^*. A contract is made with the first employee who agrees to these terms. An employer can make a contract (w,e^*) with at most one employee. The employee who agrees to these terms receives the wage w and supplies an effort level e that *need not equal the contracted effort* e^*. In effect, there is no penalty if the employee does not keep his promise, so the employee can choose any effort level, $e \in [0.1,1]$, with impunity. Although subjects may play this game several times with different partners, each employer-employee interaction is a one-shot (non-repeated) event. Moreover, the identity of the interacting partners is never revealed.

If employees are self-regarding, they will choose the zero-cost effort level, $e=0.1$, no matter what wage is offered them. Knowing this, employers will never pay more than the minimum necessary to get the employee to accept a contract, which is 1 (assuming only integer wage offers are permitted). The employee will accept this offer and will set $e=0.1$. Because $c(0.1)=0$, the employee's payoff is $u=1$. The employer's payoff is $\pi=0.1100-1=9$.

In fact, however, this self-regarding outcome rarely occurred in this experiment. The average net payoff to employees was $u=35$, and the more generous the employer's wage offer to the employee, the higher the effort provided. In effect, employers presumed the strong reciprocity predispositions of the employees, making quite generous wage offers and receiving higher effort, as a means to increase both their own and the employee's payoff, as depicted in Figure 1. Similar results have been observed in Fehr, Kirchsteiger, and Riedl (1993, 1998).

Figure 1 also shows that, though most employees are strong reciprocators, at any wage rate there still is a significant gap between the amount of effort agreed upon and the amount actually delivered. This is not because there are a few bad apples among the set of employees but because only 26 percent of the employees delivered the level of effort they promised! We conclude that strong reciprocators are inclined to compromise their morality to some extent.

To see if employers are also strong reciprocators, the authors extended the game by allowing the employers to respond reciprocally to the *actual effort choices* of their workers. At a cost of 1, an employer could *increase* or *decrease* his employee's payoff by 2.5. If employers were self-regarding, they would, of course, do neither because they would not (knowingly) interact with the same worker a second time. However, 68 percent of the

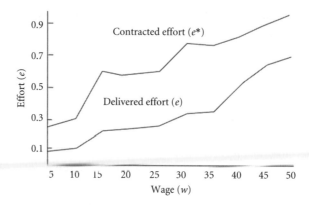

FIGURE 1 Relation of contracted and delivered effort to worker wage (141 subjects). (Fehr, Gächter, and Kirchsteiger (1997).

time, employers punished employees who did not fulfill their contracts, and 70 percent of the time, employers rewarded employees who overfulfilled their contracts. Employers rewarded 41 percent of employees who *exactly* fulfilled their contracts. Moreover, employees *expected* this behavior on the part of their employers, as shown by the fact that their effort levels *increased significantly* when their bosses gained the power to punish and reward them. Underfulfilling contracts dropped from 71 percent to 26 percent of the exchanges, and overfulfilled contracts rose from 3 percent to 38 percent of the total. Finally, allowing employers to reward and punish led to a 40 percent increase in the net payoffs to all subjects, even when the payoff reductions resulting from employer punishment of employees are taken into account.

We conclude from this study that subjects who assume the role of employee conform to internalized standards of reciprocity even when they are certain there are no material repercussions from behaving in a self-regarding manner. Moreover, subjects who assume the role of employer expect this behavior and are rewarded for acting accordingly. Finally, employers reward good behavior and punish bad behavior when they are allowed, and employees expect this behavior and adjust their own effort levels accordingly. In general, then, subjects follow an internalized norm not because it is prudent or useful to do so, or because they will suffer some material loss if they do not, but rather because they desire to do this *for its own sake*.

2.4. Altruism and Cooperation in Groups

The Public Goods Game, an *n*-person social dilemma, captures many areas of altruistic cooperation in social life, including voluntary contributions to team and community goals. Researchers (Ledyard 1995; Yamagishi 1986; Ostrom et al. 1992; Gächter and Fehr 1999) uniformly find that groups exhibit a much higher rate of cooperation than can be expected, assuming the standard model of the self-regarding actor.

A typical Public Goods Game consists of a number of rounds, say ten. In each round, each subject is grouped with several other subjects—say three others. Each subject is then given a certain number of points, say 20, redeemable at the end of the experimental session for real money. Each subject then places some fraction of his points in a common account and the remainder in the subject's private account. The experimenter then tells the subjects how many points were contributed to the common account and adds to the private account of *each* subject some fraction, say 40 percent, of the total amount in the common account. So, if a subject contributes his whole twenty points to the common account, each of the four group members will receive eight points at the end of the round. In effect, by putting the whole endowment into the common account, a player loses 12 points but the other three group members gain in total 24 (8 x 3) points. The players keep whatever is in their private accounts at the end of the round.

A self-regarding player contributes nothing to the common account. However, most of the subjects do not, in fact, conform to the self-regarding model. Subjects begin by contributing on average about half of their endowments to the public account. The level of contributions decays over the course of the ten rounds until, in the final rounds, most players are behaving in a self-regarding manner. This is, of course, exactly what is predicted by the strong reciprocity model. Because they are altruistic contributors, strong reciprocators start out by contributing to the common pool, but in response to the norm violation of the self-regarding types, they begin to refrain from contributing themselves.

How do we know that the decay of cooperation in the Public Goods Game is due to cooperators punishing free riders by refusing to contribute themselves? Subjects often report this behavior retrospectively. More compelling, however, is the fact that when subjects are given a more constructive way of punishing defectors, they use it in a way that helps sustain cooperation (Orbell, Dawes, and Van de Kragt 1986; Sato 1987; Yamagishi 1988a, 1988b, 1992).

Fehr and Gächter (2000), for instance, used 6- and 10-round Public Goods Games with groups of 4, and with costly punishment allowed at the end of each round, employing 3 different methods of assigning members to groups. There were sufficient subjects to run between 10 and 18 groups simultaneously. Under the partner treatment, the four subjects remained in the same group for all 10 periods. Under the stranger treatment, the subjects were randomly reassigned after each round. Finally, under the perfect-stranger treatment, the subjects were randomly reassigned but assured that they would never meet the same subject more than once.

Fehr and Gächter (2000) performed their experiment for 10 rounds with punishment and 10 rounds without. Their results are illustrated in Figure 2. We see that when costly punishment is permitted, cooperation does not deteriorate, and in the partner game, despite strict anonymity, cooperation increases almost to full cooperation even in the final round. When punishment is not permitted, however, the same subjects experienced the deterioration of cooperation found in previous Public Goods Games. The contrast in cooperation rates between the partner treatment and the two stranger treatments is worth noting because the strength of punishment is roughly the same across all treatments. This suggests that the credibility of the punishment threat is greater in the partner treatment because, in this treatment, the punished subjects are certain that, once they have been punished in previous rounds, the punishing subjects are in their group. The prosociality impact of strong reciprocity on cooperation is thus more strongly manifested, the more coherent and permanent the group in question.

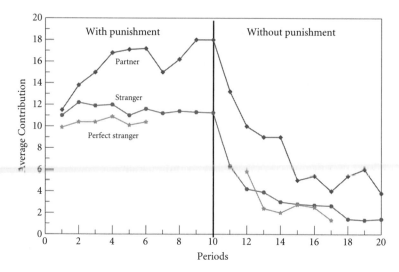

FIGURE 2 Average contributions over time in the Partner, Stranger, and Perfect Stranger Treatments when the punishment condition is played first (Fehr and Gächter 2000).

2.5. Character Virtues

Character virtues are ethically desirable behavioral regularities that individuals value for their own sake, while having the property of facilitating cooperation and enhancing social efficiency. Character virtues include honesty, loyalty, trustworthiness, promise keeping, and fairness. Unlike such other-regarding preferences as strong reciprocity and empathy, these character virtues operate without concern for the individuals with whom one interacts. An individual is honest in his transactions because this is a desired state of being, not because he has any particular regard for those with whom he transacts. Of course, the sociopath *Homo economicus* is honest only when it serves his material interests to be so, whereas the rest of us are, at times, honest, even when it is costly to be so and even when no one but us could possibly detect a breach.

Common sense, as well as the experiments described later, indicate that honesty, fairness, and promise-keeping are not absolutes. If the cost of virtue is sufficiently high, and the probability of detection of a breach of virtue is sufficiently small, many individuals will behave dishonestly. When one is aware that others are unvirtuous in a particular region of their lives (e.g., marriage, tax paying, obeying traffic rules, accepting bribes), one is more likely to allow one's own virtue to lapse. Finally, the more easily one can delude oneself into inaccurately classifying an unvirtuous act as virtuous, the more likely one is to allow oneself to carry out such an act.

One might be tempted to model honesty and other character virtues as "self-constituted constraints" on one's set of available actions in a game, but a more fruitful approach is to include the state of being virtuous in a certain way as an argument in one's preference function, to be traded off against other valuable objects of desire and personal goals. In this respect, character virtues are in the same category as ethical and religious preferences and are often considered subcategories of the latter.

Numerous experiments indicate that most subjects are willing to sacrifice material rewards to maintain a virtuous character even under conditions of anonymity. Sally (1995) undertook a meta-analysis of 137 experimental treatments, finding that face-to-face communication, in which subjects are capable of making verbal agreements and promises, was the strongest predictor of cooperation. Of course, face-to-face interaction violates anonymity and has other effects besides the ability to make promises. However, both Bochet et al. (2006) and Brosig et al. (2003) report that only the ability to exchange verbal information accounts for the increased cooperation.

A particularly clear example of such behavior is reported by Gneezy (2005), who studied 450 undergraduate participants paired off to play three games of the following form, all payoffs of which were of the form (b, a), where player 1, Bob, receives b and player 2, Alice, receives a. In all games, Bob was shown two pairs of payoffs, $A:(x,y)$ and $B:(z,w)$, where x, y, z, and w are amounts of money with $x < z$ and $y > w$, so, in all cases, B is better for Bob and A is better for Alice. Bob could then say to Alice, who could not see the amounts of money, either "Option A will earn you more money than option B," or "Option B will earn you more money than option A." The first game was $A:(5,6)$ versus $B:(6,5)$ so Bob could gain one by lying and being believed while imposing a cost of 1 on Alice. The second game was $A:(5,15)$ versus $B:(6,5)$, so Bob could gain 1 by lying and being believed, while still imposing a cost of 10 on Alice. The third game was $A:(5,15)$ versus $B:(15,5)$, so Bob could gain ten by lying and being believed, while imposing a cost of 10 on Alice.

Before starting play, Gneezy asked the various Bobs whether they expected their advice to be followed. He induced honest responses by promising to reward subjects whose guesses were correct. He found that 82 percent of Bobs expected their advice to be followed (the actual number was 78 percent). It follows from the Bobs' expectations that, if they were self-regarding, they would always lie and recommend B to Alice.

The experimenters found that, in game 2, in which lying was very costly to Alice and the gain from lying was small for Bob, only 17 percent of Bobs lied. In game 1, in which the cost of lying to Alice was only 1 but the gain to Bob was the same as in game two, 36 percent of Bobs lied. In other words, Bobs were loathe to lie but considerably more so when it was costly to Alices. In game 3, in which the gain from lying was large for Bob and equal to the loss to Alice, fully 52 percent of Bobs lied. This shows that many subjects are willing to sacrifice material gain to avoid lying in a one-shot anonymous interaction, their willingness to lie increasing with an increased cost to them of truth telling, and decreasing with an increased cost to their partners of being deceived. Similar results were found by Boles et al. (2000) and Charness and Dufwenberg (2007). Gunnthorsdottir et al. (2002) and Burks et al. (2003) have shown that a sociopsychological measure of Machiavellianism predicts which subjects are likely to be trustworthy and trusting.

2.6. Norms of Cooperation: Cross-Cultural Variation

Experimental results in the laboratory would not be very interesting if they did not aid us in understanding and modeling real-life behavior. There are strong and consistent indications that the external validity of experimental results is high. In one very important study, Herrmann et al. (2008) had subjects play the Public Goods Game with punishment with 16 subject pools in 15 different countries with highly varying social characteristics (one country,

Switzerland, was represented by two subject pools, one in Zurich and one in St. Gallen). To minimize the social diversity among subject pools, they used university students in each country. The phenomenon they aimed to study was "antisocial punishment."

The phenomenon itself was first noted by Cinyabuguma et al. (2006), who found that some free riders, when punished, responded not by increasing their contributions, but rather by punishing the high contributors! The ostensible explanation of this perverse behavior is that some free riders believe it is their personal right to free-ride if they so desire, and they respond to the "bullies" who punish them in a strongly reciprocal manner—they retaliate against their persecutors. The result, of course, is a sharp decline in the level of cooperation for the whole group.

This behavior was later reported by Denant-Boemont et al. (2007) and Nikiforakis (2008), but because of its breadth, the Herrmann, Thöni, and Gächter study is distinctive for its implications for social theory. They found that, in some countries, antisocial punishment was very rare, whereas in others it was quite common. As can be seen in Figure 3, there is a strong negative correlation between the amount of antipunishment exhibited and the World Democracy Audit's assessment of the level of democratic development of the society involved.

Figure 4 shows that a high level of antisocial punishment in a group translates into a low level of overall cooperation. The researchers first ran 10 rounds of the Public Goods Game without punishment (the N condition), and then another 10 rounds with

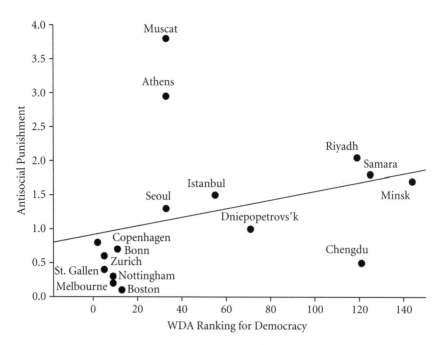

FIGURE 3 Countries judged highly democratic (political rights, civil liberties, press freedom, low corruption) by the World Democracy Audit engage in very little antisocial punishment, and conversely. (Statistics from Herrmann, Thöni, and Gächter, 2008.)

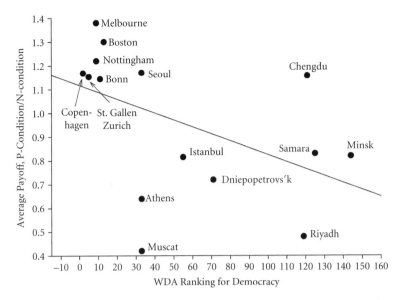

FIGURE 4 Antisocial punishment leads to low payoffs (Statistics from Herrmann, Thöni, and Gächter, Online Supplementary Material, 2008).

punishment (the *P* condition). The figures show clearly that the more democratic countries enjoy a higher average payoff from payoffs in the Public Goods Game.

How might we explain this highly contrasting social behavior in university students in democratic societies with advanced market economies on the one hand, and more traditional societies based on authoritarian and parochial social institutions on the other? The success of democratic market societies may depend critically on moral virtues as well as material interests, so the depiction of economic actors as *Homo economicus* is as incorrect in real life as it is in the laboratory. These results indicate that individuals in modern democratic capitalist societies have a deep reservoir of public sentiment that can be exhibited even in the most impersonal interactions with unrelated others. This reservoir of moral predispositions is based on an innate prosociality that is a product of our evolution as a species, as well as the uniquely human capacity to internalize norms of social behavior. Both forces predispose individuals to behave morally, even when this conflicts with their material interests, and to react to public disapprobation for free-riding with shame and penitence rather than antisocial self-aggrandizement.

More pertinent to the purposes of behavioral game theory, this experiment shows that laboratory games can be deployed to shed light on real-life social regularities that cannot be explained by participant observation or cross-country statistical analysis alone.

3. CONCLUSION

The problems behavioral ethics poses for moral philosophy include the finding that individuals tend to treat morality the same way they treat a standard consumer good: The higher the price of behaving morally, the less likely they are to do so. Moreover, subjects exhibit forms of moral behavior, including strong reciprocity, which are not considered moral by most contemporary ethical theories. It can be argued that popular views of ethics are no more relevant to modern moral philosophy than popular accounts of physical phenomena are to modern physics. If, for instance, we discover that cannibalism is morally prohibited, the fact that humans have practiced cannibalism for tens of thousands of years is no more a problem than our believing the big bang theory of the origins of the universe, despite the fact this theory does not correspond to the origins story of any known society. On these grounds, universalist moral theories, including utilitarian and deontological theories, can simply ignore popular morality as a source of insight, and can reject the notion that observed human behavior is the ultimate arbiter among ethical theories.

Although I believe physicists are correct in rejecting folk physics as a basis for adjudicating among alternative approaches to the laws of physics, the same cannot be said of philosophers who reject behavioral ethics. Although physicists have a proven track record of developing ever more powerful models of physical reality, philosophers have only a long history of alternative models of morality, none of which explains anything about the material world, and none of which is embraced by more than a few experts in the field. Aristotle and St. Thomas Aquinas are read today not just as historical *reliquia*, but as living documents from which new insights can be drawn. Even within a contemporary philosophical tradition, it is rare for two philosophers to agree on all major issues. Moral philosophy is, thus, more like art or literature in creatively illuminating the human condition without generating the sort of demonstrable truths that would be needed to justify ignoring actual human moral behavior.

If morality is identified with moral behavior, the most salient and immediate implication is that moral truths are relative to particular cultures: individuals can disagree on the content of morality in a manner that cannot be adjudicated through a careful examination of the evidence or because the individuals differ concerning matters of fact that, if resolved, would lead their moral differences to evaporate. Moral relativism of the sort suggested by behavioral ethics is widely rejected by moral philosophers because moral relativism appears not to leave a role for a reasoned investigation of morality at all. *De gustibus*, as the saying goes, *non est disputandum*. More important, if we relinquish the notion of a universal morality, then must we not accept a situation in which there is no real right or wrong, but only differences in what people believe to be right or wrong? Does it not follow from this that, because our moral beliefs have no status privileged by our superior expertise, education, or scholarly dedication, are we not obliged to tolerate moral beliefs and practices that we consider vile, abhorrent, and disgusting?

The answer philosopher David Wong gives to these questions in *Nature Moralities* (2006) is in the negative. Wong's alternative to universality, which he calls pluralistic relativism, holds that "there is no single true morality. However, it recognizes significant limits on what can count as a true morality" (p. xii). The reason for these limitations is that morality is the product of the evolutionary history of our species, serving the role of social cohesion by endowing all, or at least most, members of a group whose survival depends on cooperation with a set of common commitments, expectations, and conventions that promote group solidarity. Wong's explanation is clearly dependent upon the facts of human existence, and is far from the sort of empirical blindness that is favored by many philosophers.

I suspect there will be a bright future for pluralistic relativism in meta-ethics. The sort of virtue theory first proposed by Aristotle and revived in recent years by G. E. M Anscombe, Philippa Foot, Martha Nussbaum, and Amartya Sen interacts fruitfully with pluralistic relativism, and, thus, also complements the scientific findings of behavioral ethics.

Bibliography

Andreoni, James, and John H. Miller. 2002. Giving according to GARP: An experimental test of the consistency of preferences for altruism. *Econometrica* 702: 737–753.

Blount, Sally. 1995. When social outcomes aren't fair: The effect of causal attributions on preferences. *Organizational Behavior Human Decision Processes* 632: 131–144.

Bochet, Olivier, Talbot Page, and Louis Putterman. 2006. Communication and punishment in voluntary contribution experiments. *Journal of Economic Behavior and Organization* 601: 11–26.

Boles, Terry L., Rachel T. A. Croson, and J. Keith Murnighan. 2000. Deception and retribution in repeated ultimatum bargaining. *Organizational Behavior and Human Decision Processes* 832: 235–259.

Bolton, Gary E., and Rami Zwick. 1995. Anonymity versus punishment in ultimatum games. *Games and Economic Behavior* 10: 95–121.

Boyd, Robert, and Peter J. Richerson. 1985. *Culture and the evolutionary process.* Chicago: University of Chicago Press.

Brosig, J., A. Ockenfels, and J. Weimann. 2003. The effect of communication media on cooperation. *German Economic Review* 4: 217–242.

Brown, Donald E. 1991. *Human universals.* New York: McGraw-Hill.

Burks, Stephen V., Jeffrey P. Carpenter, and Eric Verhoogen. 2003. Playing both roles in the trust game. *Journal of Economic Behavior and Organization* 51: 195–216.

Camerer, Colin, and Richard Thaler. 1995. Ultimatums, dictators, and manners. *Journal of Economic Perspectives* 92: 209–219.

Cavalli-Sforza, Luca L., and Marcus W. Feldman. 1982. Theory and observation in cultural transmission. *Science* 218: 19–27.

Charness, Gary, and Martin Dufwenberg. 2007. Broken Promises: An Experiment. November 5. Available at Social Science Research Network, http://ssrn.com/abstract=1114404.

Cinyabuguma, Matthias, Talbott Page, and Louis Putterman. 2006. Can second-order punishment deter perverse punishment? *Experimental Economics* 9: 265–279.

Denant-Boemont, Laurent, David Masclet, and Charles Noussair. 2007. Punishment, counter-punishment and sanction enforcement in a social dilemma experiment. *Economic Theory* 31: 145–167.

Dunbar, R. I. M. 1993. Coevolution of neocortical size, group size and language in humans. *Behavioral and Brain Sciences* 164: 681–735.

Fehr, Ernst, and Simon Gächter. 1998. "How effective are trust and reciprocity-based incentives?" In *Economics, values and organizations*, eds. Louis Putterman, and Avner Ben-Ner, 337–363. New York: Cambridge University Press.

Fehr, Ernst, and Simon Gächter. 2000. Cooperation and punishment. *American Economic Review* 904: 980–994.

Fehr, Ernst, Georg Kirchsteiger, and Arno Riedl. 1993. Does fairness prevent market clearing? *Quarterly Journal of Economics* 1082: 437–459.

Fehr, Ernst, Georg Kirchsteiger, and Arno Riedl. 1998. Gift exchange and reciprocity in competitive experimental markets. *European Economic Review* 421: 1–34.

Fehr, Ernst, Simon Gächter, and Georg Kirchsteiger. 1997. Reciprocity as a contract enforcement device: Experimental evidence. *Econometrica* 654: 833–860.

Gächter, Simon, and Ernst Fehr. 1999. Collective action as a social exchange. *Journal of Economic Behavior and Organization* 39(4): 341–369.

Gneezy, Uri. 2005. Deception: The role of consequences. *American Economic Review* 951: 384–394.

Greenberg, M. S., and D. M. Frisch. 1972. Effect of intentionality on willingness to reciprocate a favor. *Journal of Experimental Social Psychology* 8. 99–111.

Gunnthorsdottir, Anna, Kevin McCabe, and Vernon Smith. 2002. Using the Machiavellianism instrument to predict trustworthiness in a bargaining game. *Journal of Economic Psychology* 23: 49–66.

Guth, Werner, and Reinhard Tietz. 1990. Ultimatum bargaining behavior: A survey and comparison of experimental results. *Journal of Economic Psychology* 11: 417–449.

Guth, Werner, R. Schmittberger, and B. Schwarze. 1982. An experimental analysis of ultimatum bargaining. *Journal of Economic Behavior and Organization* 3: 367–388.

Henrich, Joseph, Robert Boyd, Samuel Bowles, Colin Camerer, Ernst Fehr, and Herbert Gintis. 2004. *Foundations of human sociality: Economic experiments and ethnographic evidence from fifteen small-scale societies.* Oxford, UK: Oxford University Press.

Herrmann, Benedikt, Christian Thöni, and Simon Gächter. 2008. Anti-social punishment across societies. *Science* 319: 1362–1367.

Kiyonari, Toko, Shigehito Tanida, and Toshio Yamagishi. 2000. Social exchange and reciprocity: Confusion or a heuristic? *Evolution and Human Behavior* 21: 411–427.

Ledyard, J. O. 1995. "Public goods: A survey of experimental research." In *The handbook of experimental economics*, eds. John H. Kagel, and Alvin E. Roth, 111–194. Princeton, NJ: Princeton University Press.

Nikiforakis, Nikos S. 2008. Punishment and counter-punishment in public goods games: Can we still govern ourselves? *Journal of Public Economics* 921(2): 91–112.

Orbell, John M., Robyn M. Dawes, and J. C. Van de Kragt. 1986. Organizing groups for collective action. *American Political Science Review* 80: 1171–1185.

Ostrom, Elinor, James Walker, and Roy Gardner. 1992. Covenants with and without a sword: Self-governance is possible. *American Political Science Review* 862: 404–417.

Richerson, Peter J., and Robert Boyd. 2004. *Not by genes alone.* Chicago: University of Chicago Press.

Roth, Alvin E., Vesna Prasnikar, Masahiro Okuno-Fujiwara, and Shmuel Zamir. 1991. Bargaining and market behavior in Jerusalem, Ljubljana, Pittsburgh, and Tokyo: An experimental study. *American Economic Review* 815: 1068–1095.

Sally, David. 1995. Conversation and cooperation in social dilemmas. *Rationality and Society* 71: 58–92.

Sanfey, Alan G., James K. Rilling, Jessica A. Aronson, Leigh E. Nystrom, and Jonathan D. Cohen. 2003. The neural basis of economic decision-making in the ultimatum game. *Science* 300: 1755–1758.

Sato, Kaori. 1987. Distribution and the cost of maintaining common property resources. *Journal of Experimental Social Psychology* 23: 19–31.

Varian, Hal R. 1982. The nonparametric approach to demand analysis. *Econometrica* 50: 945–972.

Wong, David B. 2006. *Natural moralities: A defense of pluralistic relativism*. Oxford, UK: Oxford University Press.

Yamagishi, Toshio. 1986. The provision of a sanctioning system as a public good. *Journal of Personality and Social Psychology* 51: 110–116.

Yamagishi, Toshio. 1988. The provision of a sanctioning system in the United States and Japan. *Social Psychology Quarterly* 513: 265–271.

Yamagishi, Toshio. 1988. Seriousness of social dilemmas and the provision of a sanctioning system. *Social Psychology Quarterly* 511: 32–42.

Yamagishi, Toshio. 1992. "Group size and the provision of a sanctioning system in a social dilemma." In *Social dilemmas: Theoretical issues and research findings*, eds. W. B. G. Liebrand, David M. Messick, and H. A. M. Wilke, 267–287. Oxford, UK: Pergamon Press.

18

INTERDISCIPLINARY EDUCATION
AND KNOWLEDGE TRANSLATION
PROGRAMS IN NEUROETHICS

Daniel Buchman, Sofia Lombera, Ranga Venkatachary,
Kate Tairyan, Judy Illes*

The human condition is the most important frontier of the natural sciences. Conversely, the material world exposed by the natural sciences is the most important frontier of the social sciences and humanities. The consilience argument can be distilled as follows: The two frontiers are the same.
—E. O. Wilson (1998, 267)

INTRODUCTION

E. O. Wilson's thesis that the natural and social sciences (including humanities) have the same ultimate goal is a powerful motivator for interdisciplinary collaboration and education. In this chapter, we explore approaches to education programs in the brain health sciences that integrate teaching material from both the sciences and humanities. Inclusive, interdisciplinary educational programs that share learner-centered curricula and inquiry-based learning are the defining characteristics of our focus. The value of learner-centered education lies in fostering critical and creative thinking in a knowledge community. In the sciences, considering the human, social, ethical, and legal aspects of basic and clinical research and intervention has gained importance, as the academy along with funding agencies and policy makers increasingly require that research and training programs pay attention to these issues. The specific domain of *neuroethics,* on which we focus our efforts, covers topics ranging from bio-, medical, research, and public health ethics for brain science to neuro- and moral philosophy. In this context, we describe: (1) how neuroethics research brings basic clinical and social scientists together to foster interdisciplinary collaboration; (2) the importance of education and training and the move toward integration of science and humanities; and (3) our approach to developing interdisciplinary neuroethics education. To achieve the third goal specifically, we present three case studies. The first case is a multi-modal training program in knowledge translation (KT) for building capacity in

* Equal lead authors in alphabetical order

dementia care.[1] The second case is a participatory learning design for a dialogue-based course in Clinical Neuroethics for residents in the clinical neurosciences. Both of these examples illustrate our beliefs about the nature of learning, learners, and inquiry into an emerging field of interdisciplinary research. The third case is about Web-based education as a platform for integrating science and humanities through openness and outreach. Our specific example draws on Health Science Online (HSO) "a portal where health professionals in training and practice can access free comprehensive, high quality, current courses, references, and other learning resources to improve global health." Each is at the core of our interdisciplinary educational endeavors.

Relationships Between Neuroscience and Ethics: Neuroethics

Neuroethics lies at the intersection of novel developments in neuroscience and the implications of those developments for society. Issues relevant to neuroethics emerge in a wide array of settings such as the laboratory, the home, the clinic, the courthouse, and the classroom, among others. Scholars in neuroethics study the ethical, legal, social, cultural, clinical, and policy challenges associated with new ways to think about, manipulate, and evaluate brain function.

Topics in neuroethics research can be generally categorized into four areas:

1. **Self and mental states**: Neurobiology of moral responsibility, decision making, and free will.
2. **Social policy**: Legal or policy challenges including privacy, legal consequences of behavior, access to innovation, and health care disparities.
3. **Clinical practice**: Research and medical ethics challenges associated with moving advances along the trajectory from research to translation.
4. **Education and engagement**: Neuroscience literacy, public engagement, training, and science reporting. (adapted from Marcus, 2002)

There has been an explosion of neuroethics activity in the past decade exemplified by growth in neuroethics-related peer-reviewed publications by scholars from around the world (Lombera and Illes 2008); and the creation of dedicated, high-impact factor neuroethics journals, and the founding of a professional society (The Neuroethics Society; neuroethicssociety.org).

Though many questions related to the nature of the mind, brain, and the self have been discussed by great thinkers such as Aristotle, Plato, and Descartes (Zoloth 2006, 61), new neurotechnology has begun to provide deeper insights into the human brain, the "seat of our very humanity" (Leshner 2005). Indeed, Patricia Churchland believes that "as neuroscience uncovers more about the organization and dynamics of the brain, it becomes increasingly evident that theories about our nature must be informed by neuroscientific data" (1998, 304). Churchland and others support an integrated and interdisciplinary approach to both neuroscience and philosophy that involves bridging the gap, not only

---

1. The CIHR Canadian Dementia Knowledge Translation Network (CDKTN) is a national consortium spearheaded by Dalhousie University, Canada.

between scientists trained in different specialties (e.g., behavioral and cellular neuroscience), but also between scientists and scholars in the social sciences and humanities. The emergence of hybrid subspecialties such as neuroeconomics, neurophilosophy, neuromarketing, and neurolaw, are evidence that scholars are taking the first steps toward these forms of collaboration.

Neuroethics Education as a New Model for Interdisciplinary Collaboration

C.P. Snow's characterization of the science and the humanities in his 1956 *New Statesman* article "The Two Cultures" produced, and continues to generate, heated debate. In particular, scholars have focused on his assertion that there exists a "gulf of mutual incomprehension—sometimes (particularly among the young) hostility and dislike but most of all lack of understanding" between literary intellectuals and scientists (Snow 1956). Attitudes among natural and social scientists have changed since Snow's analysis, in part thanks to the emphasis on interdisciplinary teams by sponsors of research (Eddy 2005). Policy makers and funding bodies have begun to seek and lay down criteria for impact in concrete, social terms, rather than according to historically pure academic inquiry limited to one discipline. The fields of medicine and healthcare have responded by strengthening the ties between evidence-based practice and the capacity of professionals through innovative approaches to continuing professional development. Such approaches underscore how knowledge is created in a dynamic way from research laboratories to the clinic through the interconnectedness of researchers, clinical practitioners, allied healthcare professionals, and patients. The value of research and education is seen in terms of the extrinsic rewards it can bring to people and communities (Tetroe 2008). For instance, approaches that fall under the umbrella of Community Based Research[2] (CBR) focus on bringing about social change or action as a direct result of investigations (Reid, Brief, and Ledrew 2009). This in turn justifies the investment made in pursuing the goals of creating and acquiring new knowledge (Graham and Tetroe 2007a, 2007b).

Various models have been proposed to bridge the gulf that Snow identified. Integrating knowledge produced by different approaches to a particular question by promoting dialogue and exchange is only one method. E.O. Wilson, borrowing from William Whewell, proposed consilience as the "jumping together" of knowledge by linking of facts and fact-based theory across disciplines to create a common groundwork of explanation" (Wilson 1998, 8). This requires not only open dialogue but also the willingness to re-visit definitions and models established within certain disciplinary traditions. Neuroscience and cognitive science (Slingerland 2008) have been proposed as good staring points for consilience or integration since "[t]here has never been a better time for collaboration between scientists and philosophers, especially where they meet in the borderlands between biology, the social science and humanities" (Wilson 1998, 11). Given the very nature

---

2. CBR is "conducted by, with, and for communities...[and] has its roots in participatory action research traditions and includes action research, participatory research, participatory evaluation, and other schools of participative inquiry" (Reid, Brief and LeDrew 2009, 12).

of neuroethics and the broad topics characterized, this is exactly where the interests and purpose of scholars in the field lie.

Studies on neuroscientists' attitudes toward neuroethics show that despite significant interest, there are limited training opportunities (Lombera et al., 2010; Tairyan et al. 2009). Interviews with neuroscience program directors reveal that time constraints and lack of expertise are barriers to integrating neuroethics into training curricula, although doing so is considered an important goal. In response to these and other data showing lack of ethics education in the clinical setting for residents in clinical neuroscience (Schuh and Burdette 2004), we have developed a series of education programs ranging from regular discussion groups and knowledge translation initiatives to online reference resources. These training programs have the dual purpose of educating people working in the brain sciences about ethical, legal, societal, and policy implications of their work, as well as serving as a forum for active dialogue between scientists and clinicians on the one hand, and ethicists and social scientists on the other.

It is often suggested that relationships and face-to-face contact are more important to effective research utilization than the quality, methods, content of a research study (Kothari et al. 2005). For this reason, knowledge dissemination in the sciences is most effective when it embraces the methodological frameworks of humanistic traditions of knowledge, placing person-centered, experiential knowledge and situational analysis on par with factual findings. Ethics is about the way people live with and relate to each other. Understanding the dynamics of interpersonal connections and decision-making, therefore, must be at the center of curriculum and methods of instruction. When this is achieved, the learning transforms both what one knows and what one does in practice simultaneously. Like Gagne, who believed that "the central point of education is to teach people to think, to use their rational powers and to become better problem solvers" (1980, 85), our conceptual framework for neuroethics education reflects communication, responsiveness, and non-hierarchical relationships between the constituencies of researchers, clinical practitioners, and ultimately the translators of the products of these relationships to health and public policy (See Figure 1).

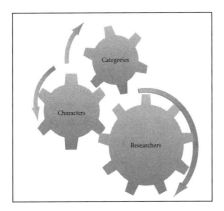 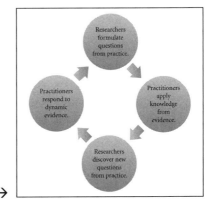

FIGURE 1 A Conceptual framework for knowledge translation in dementia care.

Knowledge structures within disciplines are characterized by the ways of scholarship that characterize them (Ausubel 1968; Anderson et al. 1978). Each discipline thus demonstrates distinct attributes in the way knowledge is generated and codified. The questions of interest in the context of education have focused on discipline-specific preferences with regard to the content and organization of curricula, methods of teaching, and modes of assessing learning. Traditions of science education have had strong roots in the transmission model of teaching with the belief that content should be learned in its authorized form and the process of learning is additive (Pratt et al. 1998, 1999; Nesbit 1998). Vygotsky (1978) argued that education is a matter of engaging the learners within their zone of proximal development, the space that falls between what they can do on their own and what they can do with expert guidance. In alignment with this interpretation of knowledge as a social construct, the humanities have embraced a developmental approach to education under the premise that learning is a personal search for meaning. In such a developmental approach, the teachers and programs support the learners in a quest through dialogue and questioning.[3]

Education has a powerful influence in shaping and changing our understanding of ourselves in the world we inhabit. Education is also not value neutral: what is learned is of value to oneself and to the professional community to which one belongs. What we describe and discuss in the rest of this chapter stems from our response to these imperatives for education. Over the last two years we have developed two major interdisciplinary initiatives to foster inquiry into the ethical and clinical issues around brain research: a professional development program for knowledge translation specifically in dementia, and an educational program in Clinical Neuroethics. Our approach to and rationale for developing these programs is highlighted in the sections that follow. It is important to note that these education initiatives are new and evolve as we write. This sets the tone and is the context for the descriptive nature of our discussion.

There are several unifying features behind the development of our education programs. First, there is value in introducing physicians to the foundations of bio-, medical, public health and neuro-ethics. Second, our education initiatives focus on the process of addressing ethics challenges in neuroscience by promoting dialogue and reflection. This approach to ethics training has been used before and is usually referred to as the hidden curriculum (Hafferty and Franks 1994; Fryer-Edwards 2002). The motivation for designing the initiatives as we have done are based on our duty, as researchers and stakeholders, to:

- Inform best medical practice by providing accurate medical and clinical neuroethics education and information.
- Maximize federal and private investment in biomedical research by facilitating the translation of science knowledge from bench to bedside and to society.
- Make findings publicly and widely accessible via centralization of resources.
- Foster the development of communities of practice (see Figure 1) in brain science and related humanities.

---

3. [Editors' note: on a related theme of "different modes of scholarship," see Boyer's contribution to this volume.]

There is skepticism that a logical positivist view of knowledge as the mainstay of all physical, natural, and medical sciences is not conducive to the learner-centered orientation to education (White and Fredrickson 1998; Pratt et al. 2001) that we support. This challenge is also at the heart of the difficulty in coalescing the traditions of the sciences and the humanities.

NEUROETHICS EDUCATION INITIATIVES—FROM THEORY TO PRACTICE

Although we realize that both students and lecturers are often plagued with already challenging schedules, we propose that as standard good practice, academic departments should ensure that mechanisms are in place for teaching neuroethics.
Sahakian and Morein-Zamir (2009, 147)

Building Communities of Practice through Knowledge Translation

Clinical disciplines such as medicine and nursing have viewed training in research and practice as two layers in a vertical structure: researchers create and disseminate knowledge; practitioners modify, change, and improve their approaches based on the quality and the relevance of that knowledge. Research utilization and knowledge dissemination have been the currency for over three decades (Weiss 1979; Green and Johnson 1996) and certainly precede the constructs of knowledge exchange and knowledge translation. Knowledge translation is the exchange, synthesis, and ethically sound application of knowledge—within a complex system of interactions among researchers and users—to accelerate the capture of the benefits of research for citizens through improved health, more effective services and products, and a strengthened health care system (Canadian Institutes of Health Research [CIHR] 2006). This implies a fundamental shift in the relationship between research and practice—placing both on a continuum, rather than viewing them as a hierarchy. For example, psychological research has contributed to bioethics and neuroethics, not only at the level of ethical norms of work but also at the level of improvement of care (Suhler and Churchland 2009). This, in turn, has a significant impact on how evidence-based medicine and the ethical framework surrounding it are both interpreted and practiced.

The human, moral, and ethical aspects of knowledge translation discourse are well articulated by interdisciplinary work groups such as the National Initiative for the Care of Elderly in Canada (Farkas and Guse 2008). In acknowledgement of this state of the environment and learners, competencies in the areas of collaboration, communication, problem solving, and critical and creative thinking, which are the hallmarks of a high-functioning professional community, are an integral part of the curriculum. Our approach to program design, development, implementation, and evaluation takes the learners on board in a partnership role. Phenomenographic research and practice traditions in clinical disciplines scaffold this approach as they are particularly successful at illuminating how students contend with structure and meaning when their experiences become an integral part of the curricula, learning contexts, and goals. The theoretical background to this approach is drawn from the research on deep and surface learning. In deep learning, the learner looks for meaning in a holistic way, preserving the intended discourse structure and personal meaning. In contrast, the surface approach is evident when learners focus on key words and process the text in an atomistic way (Marton and Saljo 1976; Ramsden 1988, 1992, 1998; Biggs 1999).

To build intellectual, clinical, and human capacity in Canada in dementia research and clinical practice, our approach has three specific aims: (1) to argue that knowledge in clinical disciplinary context is a complex entity, consisting of research-based findings as well as practical wisdom from contexts, people, and processes, which situate the application of knowledge; (2) to consider the value of training and education in process competencies on the function of researchers and knowledge users; (3) to establish closer links between what people know and how they enact their knowledge in situations because competency in knowledge translation empowers a knowledge user to perform better in interaction, problem solving, communication, and persuasion. The stakeholders are our informants, partners, and target audience at once.

In an environment scan conducted in early 2009 by our collaborators (Harris & Lusk 2009), a small group of academics, health administrators, and policy makers evaluated the status, challenges, and priorities in knowledge translation in dementia research and clinical practice. They raised concerns about access to experiential knowledge and physical distance as major barriers to the effort, and further articulated challenges related to institutional support and linkages to the community. A new, larger scale study of beliefs and practices is now underway is further elucidate those preliminary results. Taken together, the findings will lead to a robust, multi-tiered training curriculum. Remaining true to the goal of building a community of practice, the final product will bridge experiential knowledge from personal narratives with strategies for managing ethical dilemmas, including those that involve loss of autonomy and the burden of decision making on caregivers of patients with degenerating brain disorders.

CLINICAL NEUROETHICS FOR MEDICAL RESIDENTS IN THE CLINICAL NEUROSCIENCES

In the seminal work by Jonsen, Siegler, and Winslade entitled *Clinical Ethics*, the authors define clinical ethics as "a practical discipline that provides a structured approach for identifying, analyzing, and resolving ethical issues in clinical medicine" (1998, 1). The authors note that medicine—and by extension all healthcare—is a process of engagement and exchange between human beings and thus resides within a moral context. Clinical ethics emerged as a branch of applied biomedical ethics in the early 1970s to proactively address complex ethical issues that arise in health-care settings. Clinical *neuroethics*, then, is the pragmatic application of clinical ethics of brain science and practice. In effect, clinical neuroethics represents an integration of the sciences (clinical neuroscience subspecialties of medicine[4]) and humanities (philosophy and ethics), to discover,

---

4. Clinical neuroscience includes neurosurgery, neurology, and specialty subfields such as neuropathology, neuropsychiatry, neuroradiology, and neurophysiology.

examine, and work toward solutions. Scholarly engagement in neuroethics, like bioethics, is not an innate skill and requires specialized training. Singer, Pellegrino, and Siegler state that, "ethics is an inherent and inseparable part of good clinical medicine" (2001, p.1), hence the process of *being ethical* may be conceived as applying a series of professional skills. Learning and developing professional skills and traits reflect agent-based virtue ethics that place the integrity of the clinician, trust, benevolence, and compassion, at the core of clinical medicine (Lakhan, Hamlet, Mcnamee, Laird 2009; Pellegrino 2002). The notion of practical wisdom is reflected in the Aristotelian virtue of *phronesis*. To possess phronesis is to develop capacity to consider the method and action to promote change, particularly in improving quality of life (Aristotle 1999). Phronesis includes both the ability to determine how to reach a particular end and to reflect upon that end. As Frank states, "phronesis can only be a process of perpetually ongoing attainment; it is a commitment to a form of life, not a fixed quality of competence" (2004, 356). Indeed, competency in ethics is associated with increased quality of patient care (Rubin and Zoloth 2004). In that light, ethical competency entails practical wisdom (Skinner, Russell, and Buchman 2008). Despite consensus for the recognized need of ethics training for medical residents (Goold and Stern 2006), concrete recommendations concerning content and methods are not well described, particularly the clinical neurosciences. A deeper engagement with ethics teaching and texts is required given the duty of care and frequency of ethical issues arising even in new clinical careers. In this section, we briefly describe the philosophical, theoretical, and scientific foundations of an applied clinical neuroethics program for medical residents in neurology, psychiatry, radiology, and neurosurgery.[5]

A Pragmatic Approach to Clinical Neuroethics

The primary goal of engaging medical residents in clinical neuroethics education is to improve their ability to care for patients and families through thoughtful reflection of the ethical underpinnings of their work. Clinicians require a skill set that will aid their ability to recognize the ethical issue at hand, analyze the issue using the appropriate tools, apply relevant knowledge, determine action, implement action, and finally reflect upon the outcome. Training that addresses ethical issues in a pragmatic and applied manner, therefore, is a useful method to achieve the goal of better clinical care.

The approach of *clinical pragmatism* seeks results to challenging clinical ethics issues that are feasible in real-world settings. Drawing from the philosophical traditions of John Dewey and naturalistic philosophy, the aim of clinical pragmatism is to reach consensus among all stakeholders involved in a particular clinical case. To achieve real, workable solutions, the methodological process must support inquiry, discussion, negotiation, and reflection (Fins, Bacchetta and Miller 2003). A pragmatic approach in teaching clinical neuroethics is beneficial because the ethics challenges in health care largely depend on the many contextual variables at play in any particular case (e.g., religious views of the patient, family structure, socioeconomic status, legal parameters of the jurisdiction). The

5. The site of this program is the University of British Columbia in Vancouver, Canada, in collaboration with the Vancouver Coastal Health Research Institute (VCHRI).

pragmatic approach to ethics education employs a loose principle-based framework to guide or facilitate thinking in diverse scenarios as opposed to adherence to fixed ethical principles. In developing an ethics education program for neurologists at the American Academy of Neurology, Fryer-Edwards (2009) suggests four pragmatic objectives:

1. Foster trainee professional development
2. Provide knowledge, skills, attitudes that will lead to improved patient care
3. Integrate multidisciplinarity with relevance to clinical practice
4. Pursue rigorous standards and clear expectations and benchmarks for achievements.

The foundations of the clinical neuroethics program described here build upon and integrate all the aims.

The Clinical Neuroethics Program

The clinical neuroethics program at VCHRI is designed to explore the intersection of cutting edge neuroscience research with ethics knowledge and to expand the resident's critical thinking skills with regard to clinical ethics. This approach not only fosters an awareness of some of the potential ethical challenges of clinical neuroscience, but also encourages residents to identify opportunities for ethical reflection and evaluation in their practice, resulting in improved patient and family care.

Formal ethics education can provide residents with a foundation of knowledge, skills, and perspectives regarding ethical conduct in the clinical setting. Residents have a diverse background with regard to knowledge and experience with clinical ethics and moral philosophy, and this background has a significant impact on how ethics concepts, principles, and approaches are embodied. Consider, for example, different views on answers to questions such as: What ought a resident in neurosurgery consider when obtaining consent from an individual for deep brain stimulation when all other treatment efforts for depression have failed? Will advances in neuroscience shed light on issues of decision-making capacity in individuals who experience symptoms of psychosis? How will psychiatry use this knowledge to respond to issues of autonomy and shared medical decision-making? What discussions are needed with families who, through the exuberance of the media, hear of hopeful treatment for conditions such as minimal states consciousness but for which research is not ready to be applied clinically? What are the obligations for the ethical management and allocation of medical resources for brain diseases for which there are no cures in a public health system?

To establish a baseline of substantive ethics content, we provide a primer in biomedical ethics during initial sessions based largely on the four principles: respect for autonomy, beneficence, non-maleficence, and justice (Beauchamp and Childress 2001). Given our pragmatic approach, however, our ethics education model moves beyond consideration of these principles and instead focuses on resident-generated tough-case discussions.

The clinical neuroethics program places an emphasis on didactic teaching where the residents inform the pedagogical output upstream. The focus of the program is on the educational motivations and interests of the residents (Reimschisel 2009). For instance, during initial brainstorming sessions, residents in neurosurgery indicated that they were interested in learning about the current state of the bioethics literature with regard to deep brain stimulation to treat symptoms of Parkinson's disease and treatment-resistant depression. To meet the need, we provided a journal club based on a case study of a patient who revoked consent during awake craniotomy for the implantation of deep brain stimulation electrodes (Ford et al. 2007). This case stimulated considerable discussion on issues of capacity, consent, safety, and autonomy, and it prompted an evaluation of a risk-benefit calculus for this type of procedure as compared to other less non-invasive neurosurgical operations. Several neurosurgery residents discussed the possibility that the patient may have incurred more harm by demanding that the procedure be stopped. Others suggested that the patient's expressed wishes at the time of the surgery must be honored in consideration of autonomy, irrespective of any possible future benefit that the surgeons believed might result from the intervention. By contrast, one resident challenged the autonomy position altogether, arguing that the patient lacked capacity to make a decision as serious as to revoke consent.

We also developed a tough-case template in which residents can document challenging ethics-related cases, real or fictional. The purpose of the template is to inform content of future interactive sessions. The design and structure of the template has undergone several iterations informed by feedback from the residents themselves, culminating in a format that primarily accommodates narrative descriptions about the details and concerns of a case. The template has inspired significant documentation of tough clinical cases, and requests have been made from various departments for electronic access so that all can benefit from its configuration.

Training in ethics that has both historical roots in bioethics and is up to date with clinical neuroscience will positively impact the quality of care at the bedside. Education is more than an informative process of knowledge acquisition, skills, and attitudes. In this way, our approach to ethics—to borrow the term from Frank (2004)—is a process of continual learning. Still, competency in ethics, or rather practical wisdom, takes time to mature. It requires an examination of the particular situation at hand, a space for dialogue, adequate time to reflect on decisions made and those in progress, and opportunity for collaboration with others. We are moving vigorously now to implement benchmarks of impact and achievement.

NEUROETHICS EDUCATION FOR THE TWENTY-FIRST CENTURY: INTEGRATED, INTERDISCIPLINARY, INTERACTIVE, AND INTERNET-BASED

Research developments in the neurosciences have led to an enhanced understanding of neurological conditions such as minimally conscious states and Alzheimer's disease and have resulted in improved therapeutic options for many diseases of the central nervous system. For example, recent imaging studies suggest that individuals in minimally conscious states may possess the capacity to perceive pain (Boly et al. 2008), and some individuals in the persistent vegetative state may retain some neural capacity for awareness (Owen et al. 2006). Research of this kind challenges current understandings and best practices in the clinical neurosciences, and have fueled discourse on both philosophical and clinically relevant ethical issues such as consciousness, personhood, quality end-of-life care, and advance-care planning. It is important to attend to these challenges as knowledge is accumulating rapidly, and thus demands further education, training, and integration of ethics thinking into practice. A particular challenge for the integration of neuroethics education into neuroscience and medical programs around the world is the limited number of scholars currently involved in the field. This is partially due to the novelty of neuroethics as a specialized area of study. While the discipline builds capacity, an effective parallel route to address this challenge is to capitalize on the capabilities of information technologies and enable virtual learning.

Harnessing the Internet to Deliver Integrated Educational Resources

In the past decade, the rapid development of digital technologies combined with the growth of the Internet has revolutionized traditional methods of research and teaching and led to a proliferation of digital material. The amount of health-related material generated in digital format has also increased tremendously over a short period of time (Blanoit and Connor 1999). The Internet already offers a convenient and cost-effective solution for delivering and enhancing professional education. The emergence of the Internet has introduced new ways for users to access information resources and has shaped user behaviour.

Making educational resources widely and freely available via the Internet is particularly relevant in a field in which human resources for teaching are a limiting factor. Given how young neuroethics is as field, embracing new pedagogical models such as Internet-based training can address some of the current gaps in information dissemination. Successful models of Internet-based neuroethics educations and resources exist (e.g., Columbia University's Neuroethics: Implication of Advances in Neuroscience course available at: http://ccnmtl.columbia.edu/projects/neuroethics/index.html).

To provide neuroethics training content for an international audience, we partnered with Health Sciences Online (HSO; www.hso.info), a rich Web-based resource of health-related materials for physicians. We developed a reading list of landmark papers in neuroethics the Neuroethics Resources and References (NRR) (Lombera and Illes 2009) based on existing neuroethics syllabi available online and other materials that draw on our in-house expertise and that of an international advisory group. The content was designed with special attention to key emerging topics in neuroethics, priority areas for the international community identified in the peer-reviewed literature, and to the neurologic and mental health challenges facing the developing world. The material is updated regularly to ensure the readings and topics are up to date. Similarly, like the UBC KT Dementia and Clinical Neuroethics programs, the NRR is responsive to the interest of its users by soliciting and integrating suggestions for content both via e-mail as well as by other traditional forms of correspondence.

CONCLUSIONS

Although the sciences and humanities seem foreign to one another at first blush, they are not mutually exclusive: they share the fundamental goals of learning, and share the means to those ends. Interdisciplinary bodies of knowledge, such as neuroethics and flexible, learner-centered educational programs, are products that integrate the sciences and humanities. Such is the phenomenon of convergence, "the merger of initially independent lines of inquiry" (Bunge 2003, xi).

As we reflect upon our guiding principles, program imperatives, and initial experiences in the context of the examples we described in this chapter, the following two observations summarize our approach to shaping neuroethics and our educational programs:

(1) We believe that learning is a search for meaning through association, influenced by prior knowledge. In our research, we inquire and learn from the field, our partners, and our target audience as we move toward a community of practice. We start with the learner's point of view, ask more questions than we provide answers, challenge our established ways of understanding, and use experiential bridges between the learner's experience and ways of knowing.

(2) As we spearhead an emerging interdisciplinary domain, we understand that it is our responsibility to help construct identities for those with whom we engage from established professional cultures of practice and research. At all levels of engagement—as researchers, scholars and educators—we strive to model and demonstrate skillful and tailored ways of working in interdisciplinary arenas. Both the professional development program in KT and the clinical neuroethics program illustrate this principle in that they (1) identify the learner's zone of development as a first step, (2) use authentic and relevant problems drawn from their experience as the base for discussion and learning, and (3) uphold the standards of the profession or community—both as they are and as they emerge.

The rapid advancement of neuroscience research and the impact it has on society raise complex ethical questions. Engagement in these debates warrants fair participation from researchers, practitioners, and the general public. Interdisciplinary discourse is evident in education and training and serves both as a repository of new and emerging knowledge and a vehicle for translating it to those communities of practice who, in turn, transform it through their own experience.

As E.H. Carr (1961) observes, human knowledge does not go beyond human experience. However, both historians and neuroscientists study causation—the former as a logical chain of events explaining the past and predicting the future, and the latter as a means to make sense of phenomena. Thus, on both the frontiers, human experience informs and generates new knowledge that constitutes the basis for academic and professional practice and learning.

ACKNOWLEDGMENTS

Supported by the Canadian Institutes for Health Research-Institutes for Neuroscience, Mental Health and Addiction (CIHR-INMHA) CNE #85117, CIHR #200711DIP, the British Columbia Knowledge Development Fund (BCKDF), the Canadian Foundation for Innovation (CFI), NIH/NIMH 9RO1MH84282-04A1, Michael Smith Foundation for Health Research, Vancouver Coastal Health Research Institute.

References

Anderson, R. C, R. J. Sprio, and M. C. Anderson. 1978. Schemata as scaffolding for the representation of information in connected discourse. *American Educational Research Journal* 15(3): 433–440.

Aristotle. 1999. *Nicomachean ethics*. Trans. T.H. Irwin. Indianapolis: Hackett Publishing Company.

Ausubel, D. P. 1978. *Educational psychology: A cognitive view*. New York: Holt, Rinehart, and Winston.

Beauchamp, T.L., and J. F. Childress. 2001. *Principles of biomedical ethics* (5th ed.). New York: Oxford University Press.

Biggs, J. 1999. *Teaching for quality learning at university assessing for learning quality: II. Practice, teaching for quality learning at university*, 165–203. Buckingham, U.K.: SRHE and Open University Press.

Blansit, B.D., and E. Connor. 1999. Making sense of the electronic resource marketplace: Trends in health related electronic resources. *Bulletin of the Medical Library Association*, 87(3): 243–250.

Boly, M., M. F. Faymonville, C. Schnakers, P. Peigneux, B. Lambermont, C. Phillips, P. Lancellotti, A. Luxen, M Lamy, G. Moonen, P. Maquet, S. Laureys S. 2008. Perception of pain in the minimally conscious state with PET activation: An observational study. *Lancet Neurology* 7: 1013–1020.

Bunge, M. 2003. *Emergence and convergence: Qualitative novelty and the unity of knowledge*. Toronto: University of Toronto Press.

Canadian Institutes of Health Research (CIHR). 2006. Knowledge translation—Your health research dollars at work, 2006–2007. http://www.cihr-irsc.gc.ca/e/35195.html

Carr, E.H. 1961. *What is history?* New York: Vintage Books.

Churchland, P.S. 1988. The significance of neuroscience for philosophy. *Trends in Neuroscience* 11(7): 304–307.

Eddy, S.R. 2005. "Antedisciplinary" science. PLoS Computational Biology, 1(1), e6. doi:10.1371/journal.pcbi.0010006.

Farkas, T., and L. Guse. 2008. Recommendations for interprofessional core competencies for care of older adults, NICE. http://www.nicenet.ca/files/NICECompetenciesDraft.pdf Accessed: July 3, 2009.

Fins, J.J., M.D. Bacchetta, and F.G. Miller. 2003. "Clinical pragmatism: A method of moral problem solving." In *Pragmatic Bioethics* 2nd Ed, ed. G. McGee, 39–44. Boston: MIT Press.

Ford, P.J., N.M. Boulis, E.B. Montgomery, and A.R. Rezai. 2007. A patient revoking consent during awake craniotomy: An ethical challenge. *Neuromodulation* 10(4): 329–332.

Frank, A.W. 2004. Ethics as process and practice. *Internal Medicine Journal* 34: 355–357.

Fryer-Edwards, K. 2009. "Why teach ethics? Education colloquium: Ethics and education." In *education colloquium: Ethics and education*, ed. L. Schuh, 12–19. Seattle, WA: American Academy of Neurology 61st Annual Meeting.

Gagne, R.M. 1980. *The conditions of learning*. New York: Holt, Rinehart, and Winston.

Goold, S., and D. Stern. 2006. Ethics and professionalism: What does a resident need to learn? *American Journal of Bioethics* 6(4): 9–17.

Graham, I.D., and J. Tetroe. 2007a. How to translate health research knowledge into effective healthcare action., *Healthcare Quarterly* 10(3): 20–22.

Graham, I.D., and J. Tetroe. 2007b. Some theoretical underpinnings of knowledge translation. *Academic Emergency Medicine* 14(11): 936–941.

Green, L.W, and J.L. Johnson. 1996. Dissemination and utilization of health promotion and disease prevention knowledge: Theory, research and experience. *Canadian Journal of Public Health.* 87(2): S11–17.

Hafferty, F.W, and Franks R. 1994 . The hidden curriculum, ethics teaching, and the structure of medical education. *Acad Med.* Nov; 69(11): 861–71.

Harris, M., and E. Lusk. 2009. The road ahead, knowledge bank progress report, March 2009. Available at: www.KTEknowledgebank.ca.

Jonsen, A.R., M. Siegler, and W.J. Winslade. 1998. *Clinical ethics: A practical approach to ethical decisions in clinical medicine* 4th ed. New York: McGraw-Hill.

Kolb, A.Y, and D.A. Kolb. 2005. Learning styles and learning spaces: Enhancing experiential learning in higher education. *Academy of Management Learning and Education* 4(2): 193–212.

Kothari, A, S. Birch, and C. Charles. 2005. "Interaction" and research utilisation in health policies and programs: Does it work? *Health Policy* 71: 117–125.

Lave, J., and E. Wenger. 1991. *Situated learning: Legitimate peripheral participation.* Cambridge: Cambridge University Press.

Lakhan, S., E. Hamlet, T. Mcnamee, and C. Laird. 2009. Time for a unified approach to medical ethics. *Philosophy, Ethics, and Humanities in Medicine* 4(13): Accessed at http://www .peh-med.com/content/4/1/13.

Leshner, A. 2005. It's time to go public with neuroethics. *The American Journal of Bioethics*, 5(2): 1–2.

Lombera, S., and J. Illes. 2008. The international dimensions of neuroethics. *Developing World Bioethics*, 9(2): 57–66.

Lombera, S., and J. Illes. 2009. *Health Sciences Online neuroethics references and resources.* Available at: http://www.hso.info.

Lombera, S., A. Fine, R. Grunau, and J. Illes. 2010. *Ethics in neuroscience graduate training programs: Views and models from Canada. Mind, Brain and Education.* 4(1): 20–32.

Lomas, J. 2000. Connecting research and practice. *ISUMA: Canadian Journal of Policy Research* 1(1): 140–144.

Marcus, S., ed. 2002. *Neuroethics: Mapping the field conference proceedings.* New York: The Dana Foundation.

Marton, F., and R. Saljo. 1976. On qualitative differences in learning I: Outcomes and process, *British Journal of Educational Technology* 46: 4–11.

Nesbit, T. 1998. Teaching in adult education: Opening the black box. *Adult Education Quarterly* 48(3): 157–170.

Owen, A. M., and M. R. Coleman. 2008. Functional neuroimaging of the vegetative state. *Nature Reviews Neuroscience* 9(3): 235–243.

Pellegrino, E.D. 2002. Professionalism, profession and the virtues of the good physician. *Mount Sinai Journal of Medicine* 69(6): 378–384.

Pratt, D. D. 1998. "Alternative frames of understanding: Introduction to five perspectives." In *Five perspectives on teaching in adult and higher education*, ed. D. D. Pratt and Associates. Malabar: Krieger.

Pratt, D. D., M. Kelly, and W.S.S. Wong. 1999. Chinese conceptions of "effective teaching" in Hong Kong: Towards culturally sensitive evaluation of teaching. *International Journal of Lifelong Education* 18(4): 241–258.

Pratt, D.D, R. Arsneau, and J. B. Collins. 2001. Reconsidering "good teaching" across the continuum of Medical Education. *The Journal of Continuing Education in the Health Professions* 21: 70–81.

Ramsden, P., ed. 1988. *Improving learning: New perspectives.* London: Kogan.

Ramsden, P. 1992. *Learning to teach in higher education.* London: Routledge.

Ramsden, P. 1998. *Learning to lead in higher education.* London: Routledge.

Reid, C., E. Brief, and R. LeDrew. 2009. *Our common ground: Cultivating women's health through community based research.* Vancouver: Women's Health Research Network.

Reimschisel, T. 2009. "Is it ethically permissible to teach ethics without a curriculum? The basics." In *Education colloquium: Ethics and education,* ed. L. Schuh, 2–19. Seattle, WA: American Academy of Neurology 61st Annual Meeting.

Rubin, S. B., and L. Zoloth. 2004. Clinical ethics and the road less taken: Mapping the future by tracking the past. *Journal of Law, Medicine and Ethics* 32: 218–225.

Sahakian, B.J., and S. Morein-Zamir. 2009. Neuroscientists need neuroethics teaching. *Science* 325(5937): 147.

Schmidt, H.G, and J.H. Moust. 1995. What makes a tutor effective? A structural-equations modeling approach to learning in problem based curricula. *Academic Medicine* 70: 708–714.

Schuh, L. A., and D.E. Burdette. 2004. Initiation of an effective neurology resident ethics curriculum. *Neurology* 62(10): 1897–1898.

Singer, P.A., E.D. Pellegrino, and M. Siegler. 2001. Clinical ethics revisited. *BMC Medical Ethics,* 2(1). Available at: http://www.biomedcentral.com/1472-6939/2/1.

Skinner, W., B. Russell, and D. Buchman. 2008. *The essentials of…ethics and professionalism.* The Canadian Centre on Substance Abuse. Available at: http://www.cnsaap.ca/SiteCollectionDocuments/PT-Essentials%20of%20Ethics-20081017-e.pdf

Slingerland, E. 2008. *What science offers the humanities: Integrating body and culture.* New York: Cambridge University Press.

Snow, C.P. 1956. The two cultures. *The New Statesman & Nation.* October 6, 413–414.

Suhler, Christopher, and Patricia Churchland. 2009. Psychology and medical decision-making, *American Journal of Bioethics* 9: 6–7.

Tairyan, K., C. Federico, G.H. Glover, and J. Illes. 2009. Internal and external ethics motivators in neuroscience: A large-scale survey. Chicago, IL: Society for Neuroscience 39th annual meeting.

Tetroe, J, I.D. Graham, R. Foy, N. Robinson, M. P. Eccles, M. Wensing, P. Durieux, F. Légaré, C. P. Nielson, A. Adily, J. E. Ward, C. Porter, B. Shea B, J. M. Grimshaw. 2008. Health funding agencies' support and promotion of knowledge translation: An international study. *The Milbank Quarterly* 86(1): 125–155.

Weiss, C. H. 1979. The many meanings of research utilization. *Public Administration Review* 39(5): 426–431.

White, B., and J. Frederickson. 1998. Inquiry, modeling and meta cognition: Making science accessible to all students. *Cognition and Instruction* 16(1): 97–118.

Wilson, E.O. 1998. *Consilience: The unity of knowledge.* New York: Alfred A. Knopf.

Vygotsky, L.S. 1978. *Mind in society: The development of higher psychological processes.* Cambridge, MA: Harvard University Press.

Zoloth, L. 2006. Being in the world: Neuroscience and the ethical agent. In *Neuroethics: Defining the issues in theory, practice and policy,* ed. J. Illes, 61–73. New York: Oxford University Press.

SECTION SIX

Literature and Oral Traditions

19

"ONCE THE CHILD IS LOST HE DIES": MONSTER STORIES VIS-A-VIS THE PROBLEM OF ERRANT CHILDREN

Michelle Scalise Sugiyama and Lawrence S. Sugiyama

I. THEORETICAL FOUNDATIONS

When did humans begin telling stories? This type of inquiry is not normally pursued by literary scholars, nor is it part of their training, yet it is the logical starting point for any theory of narrative function: If we want to understand why storytelling emerged, we need to understand the conditions under which it developed. Multiple lines of evidence indicate that storytelling emerged tens of thousands of years ago—before the development of agriculture, permanent settlements, and writing (Scalise Sugiyama 2005). Thus, our understanding of narrative can be enriched through study of the challenges presented by a foraging lifestyle and the role that oral traditions play in meeting them. On this view, the study of narrative function is, in part, the study of anthropology. However, inquiry regarding the origins and function of storytelling does not typically fall within the parameters of anthropology either. This omission is striking, especially given our species' highly developed ability to generate and exchange information (Tooby and DeVore 1987; Flinn 1997), and the pan-human use of narrative as a medium of cultural transmission. In short, narrative theorists have an interest in illuminating the function of storytelling, and anthropologists have an interest in illuminating the function of cultural transmission. We believe that these interests meet in, and can be well-served by study of, the oral traditions of foraging peoples.

Making a living as a forager requires extensive, specialized knowledge (Laughlin 1968; Blurton Jones and Konner 1976; Tonkinson 1978; Lee 1984), and ethnographic evidence indicates that much of this knowledge is acquired from others (Hewlett and Cavalli-Sforza 1986; Ohmagari and Berkes 1997). Moreover, comparison of human and non-human primate cognitive abilities indicates that human minds are better equipped for social learning than those of other primates (Byrne 1995). This is due, in part, to a suite of uniquely human capacities, called *joint attention*, that include the ability to follow another's gaze, direct another's attention (e.g., by pointing), and check to see whether the other person is looking where one has indicated (Scaife and Bruner 1975; Butterworth and Cochran 1980; Tomasello 1995, 1999; Carpenter et al. 1998). These capacities emerge predictably at the end of the first year of life, and are soon followed by language. Thus, by the end of infancy, humans are wired for information exchange.

The development of joint attention and language so early in human ontogeny is a powerful indication that the ability to exchange information conveys a critical fitness advantage. This advantage is summarized by Dawkins as follows:

> More than any other species, we survive by the accumulated experience of previous generations, and that experience needs to be passed on to children for their protection and well-being. Theoretically, children might learn from personal experience not to go too near a cliff edge, not to eat untried red berries, not to swim in crocodile-infested waters. But, to say the least, there will be a selective advantage to child brains that possess the rule of thumb: believe, without question, whatever your grown-ups tell you. (2006: 203)

A study of children's fears lends credence to the existence of a disposition on the part of juveniles to believe what adults tell them. Field et al. (2001) presented children between the ages of seven and nine with either positive or negative information about previously unencountered monsters. Subjects' fear beliefs, regarding the monster about whom they received negative information, significantly increased when the information was provided by an adult. However, when a peer provided the negative information, fear beliefs did not change significantly. Field et al.'s study also suggests that, for some kinds of information, narrative may be a more effective medium than direct observation. Information about the monsters was presented in one of two formats: video (observational) and narrative (verbal). Subjects who received negative information in narrative format reported a greater increase in fear beliefs than subjects who received negative information in video format.

One of the things that grown-ups tell children is stories, which are verbal representations of the experiences of actual or imagined agents. Be they fact or fiction, these representations can provide knowledge that is applicable in real-world situations. In this respect, narrative can serve as a means of passing on accumulated knowledge to subsequent generations. This claim is supported by evidence that pretend play—the ability to participate in fictional worlds with others—begins to appear between 18 and 24 months (Leslie 1994; Baron-Cohen 1995), and that the understanding of pretense is present at 15 months (Onishi et al. 2007). As with joint attention and language, the relatively early emergence of pretense in human development indicates that this faculty is instrumental to survival in the human ecological niche.

The claim that narrative provides useful real-world information is also supported by cross-cultural evidence that forager folklore themes reference recurrent problems of the human ecological niche, such as manipulating and being manipulated by others, subsistence, predator avoidance, cheating, foraging risk, and way finding (Scalise Sugiyama 1996, 2001a,b, 2006, 2008; Scalise Sugiyama and Sugiyama 2009, under revision). Although folklore obviously contains fantasy elements, many social scientists posit a link between recurrent themes in oral traditions and real-world problems. A case in point is Hill and Hurtado's observation that "[f]loods have apparently killed enough Ache in the distant past that they figure importantly in Ache mythology" (1996, 152). They further note that dangers such as jaguar attack and snakebite "place important constraints on the lives of Ache foragers, and they permeate Ache mythology" (1996, 153).

Similarly, in their discussion of the Cinderella motif, Daly and Wilson argue that the cross-cultural themes of malevolent stepmothers and abused stepchildren "cannot be arbitrary or chance inventions. The characters and their conflicts are too consistent" (1998, 4).

These predictable patterns in forager folklore content—and in world folklore content overall (Thompson 1957; Kluckhohn 1959)—are the basis for our claim that oral traditions are cognitive artifacts (Scalise Sugiyama and Sugiyama 2009. Because these traditions are transmitted orally and stored in the minds of storytellers and their audiences, their content is constrained by the bounds of memory—that is, by the kinds of information the mind is designed to attend to, store, and recall. Information that engages our attention may be said to interest us, and interest, like all emotions, is not random. A given stimulus attracts our interest because, in ancestral environments, fitness benefits accrued to individuals who paid attention to the cues associated with it (Tooby and Cosmides 1990, 2001). Thus, narratives that persist in collective memory do so because their content triggers motivational mechanisms designed to respond to the cues associated with the agents, objects, activities, and/or phenomena represented within them. Collectively, then, forager oral traditions may be seen as a subset of information that is important to fitness and that humans are motivated to exchange with each other in foraging contexts. Although modern forager groups are not directly comparable to ancestral human populations, their oral traditions may nevertheless point to recurrent, cross-cultural information demands of past foraging environments.

It is in this context that we examine the cross-cultural theme of monsters. At first glance, this theme may seem puzzling: anthropomorphic agents that prey on humans obviously were not a recurrent feature of past environments. Although sympatric hominin species might be considered anthropomorphic agents, the only evidence of interspecies predation among hominins—the recent finding of an allegedly cannibalized Neanderthal jawbone at a *H. sapiens* site (Rozzi et al. 2009)—indicates that *H. sapiens* was the predator, not the prey. Thus, one might conclude, as do Field et al., that the monster figure "has no evolutionary significance" because "it isn't real" (2001, 1266). In contrast to this view, we see the monster figure as a hybrid stimulus that combines two selection pressures: animal and human attack (e.g., raiding, warfare). As such, these figures could theoretically provide information about the *modus operandi* of either or both types of predator. However, this explanation raises the question, How is the audience to determine which of the monster's habits and characteristics accurately reflect the habits and characteristics of its constituent real-world animal and human predators? A hybrid creature might be more confusing than illuminating in this respect. Moreover, forager folklore is replete with stories about dangerous animals (Scalise Sugiyama 2004, 2006) and warfare (Scalise Sugiyama and Sugiyama, in preparation), which suggests that humans track these problems separately (see Barrett 2005 on adaptations specific to non-human predators, and Duntley 2005 on adaptations specific to human predation). For these reasons, we believe that instead of being used to transmit information about animal and human predators per se, monster stories are used to strategically frighten children. Like dragons, which combine salient characteristics of three major primate predators (raptors, snakes, and felines; Jones 2000), monsters are superstimuli, simultaneously referencing two recurrent threats to human life: animal and human predators. The monster figure is, therefore, likely to trigger multiple threat-detection and threat-response modules, making it particularly wellsuited to provoking fear in children.

Why would parents want to frighten their children? The answer, in a word, is discipline: Informants and observers frequently comment that these stories are told to children to make them behave. Juvenile infractions can be divided into two general categories: violating cultural norms and engaging in life-threatening behaviors. An example of the former is seen in a Kolyma tale about a lazy young man who is captured by a cannibal woman. When he pleads with her to let him return to his parents, she refuses: "'I shall not let you go. In former times, whenever your parents sent you for water and for wood, or tried to urge you to go hunting, you were too indolent to follow their advice'" (Bogoras 1918, 97). Thus, for refusing to fulfill his cultural role as hunter and provider, the young man is threatened with becoming food for others. Because Scalise Sugiyama has discussed the use of storytelling to inculcate cultural norms elsewhere, we will focus here on the second type of infraction: life-threatening behavior (Scalise Sugiyama 2008). Anecdotal evidence indicates that the behaviors parents target with monster stories are chiefly crying and wandering away from camp. Significantly, both of these behaviors increase vulnerability to human and animal predation. Wandering removes an individual from the safety of the group, and crying exposes an individual's location—and that of his/her companions—to potential assailants. Wandering also carries the risk of getting lost and dying of thirst, hunger, exposure, or injury. In this paper, then, we argue that one reason foragers tell stories about voracious monsters is to strategically frighten children into staying close to their adult protectors. In support of this claim, we present evidence that: (1) errant children are a potential problem in a range of foraging environments; (2) errant children are vulnerable to injury and death; (3) forager parents take precautions to prevent their children from wandering; (4) parents tell monster stories to children to frighten them into obedience; and (5) monster stories underscore the dangers of wandering away from the group.

II. THE PROBLEM OF ERRANT CHILDREN: ACCIDENTAL DEATH

The problem posed by a lost child is neatly spelled out by Hill and Hurtado: "In theory parents can lower offspring mortality by locating their children in environments that contain fewer potential environmental and biological health insults. Conversely, they can actively eliminate health hazards in small areas or eliminate contact with such hazards" (1996, 295). Preventing young children from wandering off is one way of "eliminating contact with"—or, more accurately, reducing children's chances of coming into contact with—environmental hazards. Although close contact between mother and infant "results in an attachment which prevents the newly mobile toddler from getting lost" (Konner 1976, 244), this attachment tends to wear off as the child gets older: fear of strangers emerges at around seven months and lasts until sometime between 18 and 24 months (Heerwagen and Orians 2002, 39). Like attachment behavior, infants' preference for playing with small objects may have "evolved in part because it reduces their tendency to wander" (Heerwagen and Orians 2002, 37), but this preference also wanes by 24 months. Animal phobias, in contrast, emerge rather late, tending to appear between age seven and nine

(Öst 1987; Field and Davey 2001). Thus, as any parent knows, there is a phase of development, beginning in the toddler years and ending in early childhood, when a child's ambulatory abilities and curiosity far exceed its appreciation and knowledge of the life-threatening opportunities afforded by its environment. It is also during this period that the costs of taking a child on foraging excursions begin to outweigh the benefits: the child has too little endurance to walk long distances on its own, yet is too heavy (i.e., calorically expensive) to carry. In response to this problem, many forager women opt to leave their young children in camp under the care of older children or aged relatives. However, this system offers no guarantee that the child will not slip away when its caretaker is not looking.

Evidence suggests that the degree to which errant children are a problem varies with the intensity of warfare (see Section III) and ecological risk. For example, the Paraguayan forest inhabited by the Ache is rife with environmental hazards, and accidents—including drowning, snakebite, and getting lost—are one of the main causes of death among children between the ages of 4 and 14. Simply crossing a river or falling behind the group can be fatal. In their discussion of causes of mortality among the Ache, Hill and Hurtado report that one girl was swept away when she fell off a log bridge into a river, and several adolescent boys wandered off from the adults while hunting and were "either never seen again or found dead several days later" (1996, 162). Exposure is another hazard: Temperatures can fall below freezing, and the combination of cold and rain can kill a person who happens to get lost without fire (Hill and Hurtado 1996). Due to this high level of environmental risk, Ache children between the ages of 3 and 4 are supervised continuously, and spend nearly all of their daylight hours less than one meter from their mother (Hurtado et al. 1992; Hill and Hurtado 1996). Indeed, the environmental risk to which Ache children are exposed is so great that Kaplan and Dove (1987) believe it might account for their pronounced delay in motor development. Ache children do not walk independently until between 21 to 23 months, which is 9 months later than American children and a year later than !Kung children. Kaplan and Dove suggest that this delay might be due to parents discouraging and/or children curbing their environmental exploration until they are older and less vulnerable.

The vulnerability of Ache children reaches a crisis point at age 5 or 6, when they become too heavy to carry and thus must walk on their own when adults forage or when camp is moved. The difficulties and discomforts of traveling through thick jungle make this an arduous task, and children use a variety of tactics to encourage their parents to carry them, including refusing to walk. Adults respond by leaving the child behind, which

> leads to a dangerous game of "chicken" in which parents and children both hope the other will give in before the child is too far behind and may become lost. We observed one small boy to be lost for about half an hour during a parent-child transportation conflict. When the boy was finally located it was unclear whether he or his parents were more frightened. A small child cannot survive long in the Paraguayan forest, and if not found within one day is unlikely to survive. (Hill and Hurtado 1996, 222)

For a young child in the Paraguayan forest, getting lost means almost certain death. Tellingly, one of the most important skills Ache children learn is how to read the signs that adults leave when they walk through an area (e.g., bent leaves and twigs). The ability to follow these "trails" is acquired by approximately age 8, and "enables children to navigate between camps without always being within sight of adults, and it allows boys to begin small hunting forays without getting lost" (Hill and Hurtado 1996, 223).

Like the Ache, the !Kung occupy an environment that is hazardous to small children. In their comparative study of !Kung and Hadza children's foraging, Blurton Jones et al. (1994) interviewed !Kung adults in several villages (six women and three men), ranging in age from forty to eighty. These informants reported that children were discouraged from foraging alone in the bush, and were expressly warned about the dangers this presented. When informants were asked whether these dangers were real or just something adults said to make children obey, informants said they were afraid that children would get lost if they left camp, and that getting lost is very dangerous for children. Informants were then asked what adults fear will happen to children if they leave camp: "'Getting lost. They think that if the children are alone together they will get lost. Once the child is lost he dies'" (Blurton Jones et al. 1994, 201). When asked what lost children die from, informants reported, "'Hunger, thirst and cold'" (Blurton Jones et al. 1994, 201). Informants were then asked if they knew of any children who had gotten lost. Eight cases were reported (age range 5–10), in which two children died. According to the authors, the informants did not seem to think that predators were a serious threat to children; however, in one out of the two deaths the child was killed by a predator (a leopard at a water-hole). Moreover, the !Kung claim that lions, leopards, and wild dogs will all take children who wander off unattended and (Blurton-Jones and Konner 1976), on account of this danger, !Kung women are reported to carry children as old as 6 when they go foraging in the bush (Low 1998).

!Kung fear of children wandering off is very intense: according to Blurton Jones et al., "It is impossible to overstate the degree of panic expressed by !Kung on these occasions" (Blurton Jones et al. 1994, 204). Draper gives a detailed account of one such incident:

> The women are especially mindful of the 5- and 6-year-olds who are old enough to wander but too immature to keep oriented in the bush. One hot afternoon…I was sitting with five women and a few infants….It was almost too hot to talk; we all sat listlessly, waiting for the sudden lifting of the heat which came everyday at about 5:30 PM. Suddenly one woman jerked herself to a sitting position, neck arched, eyes darting to all directions. "Listen…listen!" she whispered. "Where are the children?" All the women leapt to their feet, looking about and calling to other people sitting farther off in the village. About that time we heard a child's voice calling in the distance and looking in that direction we saw the missing children…who were walking through the bush toward the camp. The wave of alarm which had galvanized the women, raised them from torpor, and scattered them twelve or more meters in a few seconds, subsided immediately. (Draper 1976, 207)

As the authors conclude, the "risks to children who do get lost are extremely high (two deaths out of eight cases), and thus worth the adults' efforts to ensure that the children do not get lost" (Blurton Jones et al. 1994, 203). One step that !Kung parents take is to indoctrinate their children with the fear of getting lost if they leave camp. Although Blurton Jones et al. (1994) do not mention the use of storytelling to accomplish this, telling stories about monsters that will attack you when you are alone is certainly one way of indoctrinating children. Significantly, Khoisan peoples are reported to tell stories about monsters, such as ogres and cannibals (Biesele 1993, 36).

Although they did not conduct similar interviews among the Hadza, Blurton Jones et al. (1994) report that Hadza adults evince no fear when children are out of camp, out of sight, or at an unknown location. According to Blurton Jones, "Hadza children are neither supervised nor confined to camp while the women are out gathering" (1993, 316), and may spend several hours a day away from camp. Blurton Jones et al. attribute this parenting style to specific features of the Hadza environment: ample shade, "expansive vistas" with salient landmarks, and "many small dry season water sources dotted over the hills" (1994, 197). The varied, hilly terrain, with views of a mountain, a lake, and the rift valley escarpment, makes it easy for a forager to see where she is headed and where she has been, greatly reducing the chances of becoming lost. The ready availability of shade and water reduces the danger of heat exhaustion. In contrast, water holes in !Kung territory are few and far between, shade is nonexistent, visibility is limited by the flat terrain and thick brush, and orientation is difficult due to a lack of salient topological features. In short, due to differences in their respective habitats, Hadza children are less likely than !Kung children to get lost and suffer from heat exhaustion if they wander away from camp. This does not mean, however, that Hadza children forage alone or that they wander far afield. Although they may spend hours away from camp, they typically play in "sizable mixed-sex groups" (Blurton Jones 1993, 316), and "mostly forage within a quarter mile of camp and usually much closer, within sight, or at least within earshot" (Blurton Jones et al. 1994, 204). Moreover, although lost children do not appear to be a problem, adults nevertheless take precautions that reduce the likelihood of children being taken by predators. Hadza women take their infants with them on foraging trips until the age of weaning (between two and three years of age), and after weaning leave them in camp under the care of the older children they are playing with (Crittenden and Marlowe 2008). However, "it is still necessary that some adult be in camp within earshot, otherwise lions, leopards, and hyenas would eventually lose their fear of camps during the day and these children would become easy prey. Toddlers are never left in camp without an adult there" (Marlowe 2005, 188)

Like the Hadza, the Martu of the Western Australian occupy an environment that is conducive to children's foraging. Yuka Napanankga, a Martu woman, describes her childhood foraging experiences as follows:

> Mothers and fathers gone out hunting and leave us kids in camp. When we got hungry we go hunting for little lizard, get him and cook it and eat him up. Me little bit big now, I go hunting myself, tracking goanna and kill him....Soon as mother leave him, little ones go hunting, kill animals, blue tongue, mountain devil, take them home before mother and father come back, cook and eat it. (Napanangka 1995, 143)

Martu children appear to minimize the risk of heat exhaustion by going on short (average length 48 ± 7 minutes) forays close to camp (average distance 1.8 km), and concentrating their foraging efforts on areas of higher prey density (Bird and Bliege Bird 2005).

The area of the Congo Basin inhabited by the Mbuti also appears to be conducive to children's foraging. It is described by Turnbull as "a cool, green wonderland where you can walk with ease, comfort, and safety. The leafy canopy high overhead protects you from the heat and glare of direct sunlight, and the leaves and twigs underfoot protect you against snakes and any predators that might be sleeping nearby, warning them well in advance of your approach.... Just about the only animal that might attack unprovoked is the forest buffalo, and even it will not attack if there is too much noise" (1983, 26–27). From the age of three onward, children spend much of their day playing in the *bopi*, "a tiny camp perhaps a hundred yards from the main camp, often on the edge of a stream" (Turnbull 1983, 41). Baka Pygmy children play at *ngbusu* (going on a safari with a dog) and building huts in the forest, apparently without incident (Kamei 2005).

To the best of our knowledge, Blurton Jones et al. (1994) and Hill and Hurtado (1996) are the only studies of contemporary foragers that document the number of lost children. However, some studies make indirect reference to the dangers that newly weaned, mobile children can get into if not adequately supervised. For example, in his time-allocation study of child care among the Ye'kwana, Hames recorded the percentage of time children under the age of 41 months spent outside the village while their caretakers were engaged in economic tasks. He was interested in this measure because it "gives one an idea of the constraints that children place on caregivers in locations up to 6 kilometers away (i.e., forest, garden, or river) from the village where high-quality care or monitoring in necessary because of the elevated risk of environmental trauma" (Hames 1988, 243). Interestingly, of all children under 41 months, children between the ages of 27 and 40 months spent the least amount of time outside the village. Hames attributes this to children of this age having been weaned, which means they can be left in the village under the care of someone other than their mother. From a mother's perspective, there are many reasons for wanting to forage unencumbered by child care; Hames' comment on the increased risk of environmental trauma suggests that the problem of children wandering off while mother is foraging might be among those reasons.

The picture that emerges from these studies is that environments vary in the degree of danger they pose to a lost child, and that—this variation notwithstanding—a lost child can be vulnerable to death from a variety of sources, including exposure, thirst, hunger, injury, and/or animal attack. Thus, regardless of environment, a variety of circumstances that are potentially fatal to a child can be avoided simply by preventing that child from wandering off. Unfortunately, the dearth of empirical data on frequencies with which children get lost makes it impossible to determine the extent to which errant children are a problem for forager parents. Clearly, the tendency of young children to wander was not sufficiently costly in ancestral environments for selection to have eliminated it. On balance, the benefits of exploratory forays (e.g., learning resource locations, observing animal behavior, building way-finding skills, developing strength and stamina) must have outweighed the risks of being injured or killed while engaging in them. However, these studies also show that, in some environments, the risks associated with wandering are sufficiently high that parents take measures to reduce them (e.g., !Kung parents indoctrinating their children with the fear of getting lost). We propose that monster stories are one of these measures. These stories may activate threat-detection modules specific to the dangers of human and non-human predation. Periodic re-telling of such stories would recurrently activate these modules, bombarding them with the message that the threats of human and non-human predation loom large in their surroundings. This, in turn, might provoke re-calibration of mechanisms that gage environmental danger levels, boosting assessments of threat and, consequently, increasing aversion to exploratory behavior.

III. THE PROBLEM OF ERRANT CHILDREN: WARFARE

Compared with life as a citizen of the modern industrialized state, life as a hunter-gatherer involves relatively frequent contact with animals that can bite, crush, gore, kick, scratch, and/or sting. Children are particularly vulnerable to animal attack due to their small size, slow speed, and lack of experience. In modern environments, tragic accidents periodically remind us of the vulnerability of young children to predation: in February 2009, the remains of a missing 5-year-old boy were found inside a crocodile in North Australia (www.dailymail.co.uk/news/worldnews/article-1148502/Pictured-The-boy-5-eaten-alive-crocodile-brother.html). The animal grabbed the unsupervised boy, who was accompanied only by his 7-year-old brother, when he followed his puppy into a mangrove swamp behind his house. Because Scalise Sugiyama (2004, 2006) has previously discussed the theme of animal predation in folklore, we will focus here on the second adaptive problem evoked by the monster figure: human predation.

Attachment behavior in infants is believed to be an evolved defense against not only animal (Bowlby 1972) but also human predation (Dickemann 1984; van Schaik and Dunbar 1990; Hrdy 1999). Sadly, humans can and do maim, torture, rape, enslave, kill, and even eat other humans. Many of these behaviors occur in the context of feuding and warfare, and primatological (Goodall 1986; Nishida et al. 1985; Wrangham 1999), archaeological (Martin and Frayer 1997), and ethnographic evidence (Chagnon 1997; Chagnon and Hames 1979; Ember and Ember 1997; Wadley 2003a, b) indicate that coalitional aggression may have been a recurrent feature of ancestral human environments. The practice of trophy-taking (the taking of body parts in the course of battle) is widespread across cultures (including foraging peoples) (Chacon and Dye 2007), and evidence of cannibalism is widespread as well (e.g., Villa 1992; White 1992; Turner 1993; Askenasy 1994; Turner and Turner 1995; Aguadé and Lory 1997; Arsuaga et al. 1997; Defleur et al. 1999; Kantner 1999; Petrinovich 2000).

In forager and other small-scale societies, the surprise attack is favored (LeBlanc and Register 2003). A common tactic is to attack at dawn when people are still asleep or when they leave camp to relieve themselves (e.g., Burch 1974; Chagnon 1997). Significantly (with regard to the problem of errant children), another method is to attack people when they are alone or in small groups away from the comparative safety of camp. The Dusun of North Borneo are a case in point: "After the first raid and counterraid full-scale fighting between large war parties becomes difficult because of the preparations on both sides for defense. Attacks then tend to be made by war parties on older women gathering food alone in the jungle, a solitary hunter, or children playing at the edge of a village" (Rhys Williams 1965, 67).

As this last example indicates, children are not necessarily spared in these conflicts, and may be abducted, enslaved, tortured, or killed. Chagnon describes a raid in which a

Yanomamö headman was killed and his 10-year-old son abducted. The boy was later shot by a man who couldn't stand to see the boy persecuted and tormented by the other children (1997, 189). Biocca's account of a Yanomamö raid describes the systematic killing of child captives: "Then the men began to kill the children; little ones, bigger ones, they killed many of them. They tried to run away, but they caught them, and threw them on the ground, and stuck them with bows, which went through their bodies and rooted them to the ground. Taking the smallest by the feet, they beat them against the trees and rocks" (Biocca 1970, 35). According to Burch (1974), Inuit groups sought to annihilate their enemies, including women and children. Among the forest-dwelling Ache, "Dozens of men, women and children were shot by Paraguayans who raided their camps to capture slaves or in retaliation for the theft of a cow or horse" (Hill and Hurtado 1996, 165). In all Ache age groups except unweaned children, most deaths (including individuals who were captured and never seen again) were caused by raids and warfare: "Only one of the individuals captured alive was over fifteen years of age, and very few of those captured are known to have survived. Among infants and children, being captured accounted for about one-fourth of all 'deaths' to both sexes. Individuals in all age-sex categories were shot and killed by non-Ache enemies" (Hill and Hurtado 1996, 163). Among the Dusun of Borneo, raiders took women and children captive and also took heads and hands as trophies. An analysis of 35 trophy skulls at the village of Sensuron indicated that "much recent head-hunting warfare was directed against the aged, adolescents, and females; at least half of the skulls were female, the majority being either young or very old, while some 10 percent of the remainder were adolescent boys" (Rhys Williams 1965, 67). The present-day Mikea of Madagascar are the descendants of people who, over the last four centuries, escaped into the forest "to resist tribute demands and threats of slavery and livestock loss" or "to avoid interpersonal disputes and accusations of witchcraft" or "as an alternative to French colonial policies of forced relocation, taxation, and mandatory labor" (Tucker and Young 2005, 152). Tellingly, Mikea children fear "encounters with *olo raty*, 'bad people,' including cattle thieves, evil sorcerers, brain stealers, and *vazaha*, a term referring collectively to foreigners, white people, policemen, military, gendarmes, and other representatives of authority" (Tucker and Young 2005, 164). Mikea children also fear encounters with monsters, but whether this fear is related to their fear of thieves and outsiders, Tucker and Young do not say.

The archaeological and historical records also attest to the vulnerability of children in warfare. For example, in a survey of Anasazi (AD 700–1700) skeletal remains exhibiting severe perimortem trauma, the remains of children were present at 21 out of 29 (72 percent) sites, and the remains of adolescents were present at nineteen out of 29 (66 percent) sites (Kantner 1999). At the Saunaktuk site (AD 1370±57) in the Mackenzie River Delta, archaeologists have found the remains of women and children who appear to have been massacred, dismembered, and eaten (Walker 1990; Melbye and Fairgrieve 1994). Historical accounts attribute these actions to Athapaskan Indians, who attacked the village while the men were away. Hints of this and other conflicts can be seen in the oral traditions of the inheritors of these enmities. For example, the story of "Kumagdlat and Asalok" describes an attack that, according to Rink, is rooted in historical fact, referring to "conflicts and meetings of the Eskimo with the Indians, which in recent times have still taken place on the banks of the Mackenzie and Coppermine Rivers" (1875/1997, 109). In this story, three Inuit cousins (Kumagdlat, Asalok, and Merak) attack a settlement of Indians who are rumored to be rich and have knives in abundance. After killing all the adults, the cousins dispatch the children (whom they kill by piercing them through the ears), sparing only one boy and one girl, and then proceed to loot the camp (Rink 1875/1997, 114). Farther south, along the Pacific Northwest Coast, slavery was practiced by several tribes; these slaves were largely war captives, and both adults and children were taken (McDowell 1997). Tribes of the American Southeast also killed children in warfare. In an address to the Choctaw and in talks with other tribes, Shawnee chief Tecumseh declared that "the Indian custom of killing women and children in war" should be abandoned (Halbert and Ball 1969, 44).

Although entire camps or villages might be massacred, as at the Saunaktuk site, the Crow Creek site on the upper Missouri, and the Cave 7 site in southeastern Utah (LeBlanc and Register 2003), children were sometimes able to save themselves. For example, Rink recorded an Inuit war story about two brothers who elude their attackers by hiding. In this tale, which "seems to have its origin in historical facts" (Rink 1875/1997, 132), two orphaned brothers are fetching water by moonlight when they see a premonition. The older brother, Kunuk, looks into the water and sees a group of armed men advancing toward them. The boys run back to camp to warn the people, but no one believes them, so they hide their little sister in a pile of chips next to the window, and hide themselves in the rafters beneath the roof of the house-passage: "they were keeping hold of one beam with their hands, and supported their feet against the next, and thus lay at full length, with their faces turned downwards" (Rink 1875/1997, 133). The boys thus witness the entire massacre:

> Presently a large man with a spear made his way through the entrance; after him another one appeared; and all told, they counted seven, who came rushing into the house. But as soon as they got inside a fearful cry was heard from those who were put to death by them. While they were still lingering inside Kunuk's brother was losing strength and was nearly giving way, when the aggressors came storming out, fighting about, right and left, and flinging their spears everywhere, and likewise into the heap of chips, where their little sister was lying. When the last of them had disappeared the younger boy fell to the ground, and Kunuk after him.... on entering the house the floor was all covered with blood, every one of the inmates having been killed, besides one of the assailants. (Rink 1875/1997, 133–134)

Although their sister is killed, the boys survive. After the attack, they set about making themselves into more formidable opponents: They begin boxing and lifting large stones to build their fighting skill and strength, eventually becoming so accomplished that they can kill a bear with their bare hands. The boys are later adopted by an older couple who encourage them "never to forget their enemies, but always to be exercising themselves in order to strengthen their limbs" (Rink 1875/1997, 135). The moral of the story is clear: Be prepared. As we will see in the next section, stories about monsters might serve as a means of encouraging children to exercise vigilance and caution.

IV. MONSTER STORIES

According to Turnbull, the Mbuti use stories about monsters to dissuade their neighbors from venturing into their territory: "It was an almost universal belief among all villagers…that the forest was filled with dangerous and malevolent spirits, to whom the Mbuti were closely allied. As a matter of fact, it was the Mbuti themselves who were largely responsible for these beliefs, always telling the villagers about the grotesque monsters that even they had to contend with in the forest. It was one of their many techniques for making sure that the villagers stayed outside the forest world" (Turnbull 1983, 31). In a similar vein, a Yanomamö headman used the specter of *rahuras* (water monsters) to try to talk Chagnon out of visiting a rival village (Chagnon 1997). In this section, we present ethnographic evidence that parents use monster stories to discourage children from wandering off, and that monster stories underscore the dangers of wandering away from camp.

Although the evidence that parents tell monster stories to children to frighten them into obedience is anecdotal, it has been reported by numerous anthropologists and folklorists from a variety of small-scale societies occupying a range of habitats. In some cases, informants report only that adults tell these stories in order to make children "behave," without reference to specific infractions. For example, Smith reports that the Aboriginal story of the Yara-ma-yha-who was "one of the stories told to naughty children to teach them that if they do not behave the Yara-ma-yha-who will come and take them and make them become one of themselves" (1930, 342). This creature is described as a little man about four feet tall, with a huge head, mouth, throat, and stomach. He has no teeth, so he swallows humans whole. First, however, he drains their blood until there is just enough left to keep them alive "while he walks around and gets an appetite" (1930, 343). Similarly, the Bimin-Kuskusmin of Papua New Guinea tell of animal-man monsters who "are said to eat their firstborn children at whim and even to gnaw on their own limbs.…Unwary travelers who fall prey to their lust for blood and flesh may be eaten alive, for they are known to delight in torture" (Poole 1983, 12). These monsters are "portrayed largely in tales that are told at night around the flickering hearth fires to frighten unruly children" (Poole 1983, 12).

When specific reference is made to the desired end of these stories, it is typically to prevent children from wandering off. For example, the Yiwara tell of *mamus*—cannibalistic spirits (ghosts) that attack humans in the night. They can only be seen by dogs and sorcerers. Their presence is indicated by a low whistling sound in the bush. According to Gould (1969), adults use fear of *mamus* to keep children away from sacred areas and to keep them from wandering away from camp at night. With their predilection for attacking "unwary travelers" (Poole 1983, 12), the Bimin-Kuskusmin cannibal monsters, too, reference the dangers of leaving the village. Among the Ahtna, "Unruly children were threatened by the Owl, by huge monsters…underground or in deep lakes, by Bush Indians who kidnap those who stray, or by…an abductor of naughty children" (de Laguna and McClellan 1981, 657). Rhys Williams reports that, among the Dusun, children are considered to be "incurable wanderers" (1965, 87), and "are threatened constantly by parents with being eaten alive, carried off, injured, or damaged by disease givers, souls of the dead, or animals of the jungle" (1965, 88). Although Rhys Williams does not mention the use of narrative in this context, he argues that these threats are reflected in the lullabies sung to babies, of which he provides two examples. The first references human predation in the form of "souls of the dead," who are human beings condemned to "an eternity of wandering and cannibalism because of evil deeds [done] while alive" (1965, 18):

> Sleep, sleep, baby,
> There comes the *rAgun* (soul of the dead)
> He carries a big stick,
> He carries a big knife,
> Sleep, Sleep, baby,
> He comes to beat you! (1965, 88)

The second references animal predation:

> Bounce, Bounce, baby
> There is a hawk,
> Flying, looking for prey!
> There is the hawk, looking for his prey!
> He searches for something to snatch up in his claws,
> Come here, hawk, and snatch up this baby! (1965, 88)

The dangers referenced in these songs appear to be rooted in genuine parental fears: Dusun mothers typically take their youngest children with them when they go to work in the field or garden, and leave their older children at home in the care of an adolescent or elderly relative. Significantly, when no babysitter is available, "it is not uncommon for a mother to lock her young children in the household while she spends the day at work" (1965, 81).

Silencing crying children is also mentioned as a motive for telling monster stories. For example, among the White Mountain Apache (who tell stories about a cannibal figure named Big Owl), "'Owl will carry you off' is a common threat to silence crying children" (Goodwin 1939, 15). The Iglulik, Greenland, and Netsilik Inuit tell of an ogress who attacks humans and puts them in her huge parka, from which none can escape without help. In some versions, she specifically targets children: in a Netsilik variant, for example, she is described as a "giant woman who steals children" (Rasmussen 1931, 248; see also Rasmussen 1930, 110). This ogress is so feared that the "naughtiest children *can be made to stop crying* at the mere mention of her name" (Rasmussen 1929, 212, emphasis added). Like wandering away from camp, crying increases vulnerability to predation, particularly if one is trying to hide from attackers (as in the story of the two orphan boys cited previously).

Because peasants often live at the periphery of woods, mountains, or jungles, their children are vulnerable to many of the same threats that forager children are: getting lost, exposure, injury, accident, and predation. Tellingly, peasant folklore is replete with monsters and other agents that prey on lone wanderers (Scalise Sugiyama 2004). A classic example is the *nøkk* or water sprite (also called *grim*), which appears throughout Scandinavian folklore, and lives in waterfalls, rivers, and lakes. The *nøkk* takes the shape of a horse in order to lure people, especially children, to a watery death by tempting them to ride it and then jumping into a lake (Christiansen 1964, xxxii; Kvideland and Sehmsdorf 1988, 252 and 257). Another common motif in Scandinavian folklore is being "taken into the mountain" by the *huldre* (invisible) folk, which refers to getting lost in the mountains or woods. Tellingly, this expression is also used to refer to a sudden psychological change in a person caused by "a traumatic experience such as getting lost on a mountain or in a forest" (Kvideland and Sehmsdorf 1988, 212). Presumably, if getting lost did not have potentially dangerous consequences, it would not be considered a traumatic experience.

Tellingly, one message that reverberates through monster stories is that there is safety in numbers: people are more likely to be attacked when they are away from camp, and a camp is more likely to be attacked when a large subset of its members—especially the adult males—is away. For example, the Bella Bella tell of Cannibal-of-the-North-End-of-the-World, who eats three brothers and their dogs as they are hunting in the mountains (Boas 1932, 155). In a similar vein, the Salishan tell a story about a cannibal who uses an elk decoy to lure his victims into arrow range; while the hunter is stalking the elk, the cannibal shoots and eats him (Teit 1917, 9). The Caribou Eskimo tell of the *kukilialuit*, trolls with sharp claws: "When they come upon human beings, they fall upon them and eat them up, picking the meat off their bones with their sharp claws. Many people who have disappeared and been carried off have been attacked and eaten up by these trolls with the long claws" (Rasmussen 1930, 114). The Pueblo peoples of Taos tell of a hairy giant that attacks and eats the people, one or two at a time:

> Long ago, when the pueblos were first where they are now, everything was wild. They were always on the lookout, they never made fire at night, they did all their cooking in the daytime. They went out in the daytime for firewood. Someone noticed that some people were missing, one or two every day. They wondered why. They did not know what became of them. The old men kept watch to see if it was enemies hiding. (Parsons 1940, 13)

The Kiowa tell a similar tale about the *k'ozapot'o* or mountain ogres that may reflect the same threat. In this story, Sendeh "was going along anywhere. Some people began to run after him.... They were the *k'ozapot'o*, mountain *zapot'o* (ogres).... They were hairy all over. They had big eyes and big mouths.... They were cannibals" (Parsons 1929, 40).

V. DISCUSSION

In this essay we have discussed one possible factor contributing to the ubiquity of the monster story. In arguing that the monster figure evokes the adaptive problems of human and non-human animal predation, we are not suggesting that it has no other resonances or referents, or that it is only used to frighten children. Nor do we deny that specific monster characters or types (e.g., Big Owl, the Cyclops, Grendel) embody the historic, worldview, and regional particularities of their parent cultures. Narrative is inherently polysemous: Its ability to transmit many messages simultaneously may account for its mass appeal and accessibility, both within and across cultures.

The argument that adults use monster stories to frighten children into obedience does not preclude the possibility that (at least some) adults believe in the existence of monsters themselves. Cross-culturally, adult humans believe in a variety of supernatural and/ or hybrid agents (Boyer 2001). It is also true, however, that there is a lot of variation in credulity both across and within cultures. Western society is a case in point. Some people believe in ghosts, guardian angels, and/or extraterrestrials; others do not. Some forager parents may truly believe in the monsters they describe to their children, whereas others may simply participate in a fiction that serves their interests. This brings us back to our original question: Given that there is no exact real-world correlate of the monster, what is the impetus for this concept? Fear of monsters cannot be exploited unless at least some people accept the possibility of their existence.

Asking what would cause people to believe in the existence of part-human, part-animal predators is similar to asking what would cause people to believe in the existence of a talking tree (part human, part plant) or a weeping stone (part sentient being, part inanimate object). Boyer (2001) argues that supernatural entities are conceptually compelling because they violate one (or a few) of the assumptions of their ontological domain, while conforming to the rest. In other words, aside from one or two anomalous features, supernatural entities are representations of real-world agents, objects or phenomena. Monsters follow this formula in that they tend to have one or two anomalous, animal-like characteristics, but an otherwise human anatomy and psychology. These conceptual hybrids beg the question of why people believe that such violations of ontological domain can occur. These concepts ultimately must be rooted in conclusions (however farfetched) drawn from real-world observations. What real-world phenomenon would cause people to believe in the existence of humans with animal characteristics?

We believe that one likely source of the monster concept is warfare and its concomitant horrors: torture, trophy taking, corpse mutilation, and cannibalism. Cannibalism appears to have occurred in a number of forager and other small-scale societies (Oswalt 1967; Melbye and Fairgrieve 1994; Hearne 1958; Burch 2005), and torture is known to have been practiced by the Northern Iroquoian tribes (Williamson 2007) and Inuit (Burch 2005). Trophy-taking occurred in a wide range of cultures, from the sub-Arctic and Arctic (Maschner and Reedy-Maschner 2007), to the American Plains and Southwest (Parsons 1939; LeBlanc 1999; Owsley et al. 2007; Schaafsma 2007), the American Southeast (Jacobi 2007), the Amazon Basin (Chacon 2007), and coastal Peru (LeBlanc 2003). Mutilation of enemy corpses was practiced from the Arctic (Burch 2005) to the Plains (Quaife 1950) and the Southwest (LeBlanc 2003). Kantner (1999) argues that cannibalism was used strategically by some groups to inspire terror in their enemies. Torture, trophy taking, and corpse mutilation are likely to have had the same effect. Consider the following description of techniques used by the Crow and other Plains peoples:

> Eyes torn out and laid on rocks; noses cut off; ears cut off; chins hewn off; teeth chopped out; joints of fingers; brains taken out…hands cut off; feet cut off; arms taken out of sockets…eyes, ears, mouth, and arms pierced with spearheads, sticks, and arrows; ribs slashed to separation with knives; skulls severed in every form from chin to crown. (Quaife 1950: 335)

The same practices are evident in prehistoric Arctic and sub-Arctic North America, where raiding was a regular feature of life (Oswalt 1967; Hearne 1958; Burch 2005; Maschner and Reedy-Maschner 2007). Nowhere and no one was safe: Men were attacked when they went out on hunting trips (Hearne 1958), and villages were attacked while the men were away (Burch 2005). For example, in the course of hostilities between the Kaŋiġmiut of the Buckland River valley and the Kiitaaġmiut of the lower Selawik River valley, the Kaŋiġmiut avenged the gang-rape and torture of one of their women by killing two elderly Kiitaaġmiut women: "According to the Buckland version…they cut the bodies into strips, and hung them on a drying rack, like so many pieces of fish or caribou meat. According to the Selawik version, they inserted a spear into each of their rectums, elevated their bodies over a fire, and roasted them to death" (Burch 2005, 113).

It is easy to see how stories about monsters could grow out of such practices. Regardless of whether a group engaged in such practices itself, these behaviors would have appeared "monstrous" when performed by its enemies: extreme in viciousness, excessive in appetite, and terrifying in force. It would not be illogical to attribute the strength and ferocity of powerful beasts (e.g., bears, jaguars, wolves) to people capable of committing such acts, or to conclude that they were part animal. Ethnographic evidence suggests that at least some foraging peoples characterize their enemies or potential enemies in this manner. According to Tonkinson, for example, the Mardudjara traditionally divided their social world in to three general categories—kin, strangers, and "distant people"— the latter of whom are people who "are never encountered and who are thought to possess many less than human characteristics and behaviors, such as long teeth, cannibalistic habits, huge sexual organs, and depravities to match" (1978, 44).

Between-group aggression is probably not the only source of the monster concept, but it is a plausible one, and goes a long way toward explaining the ubiquity of this motif. What we hope to have shown here is that, as evidence of the thoughts and worries elicited by occupation of the foraging niche, and of the kinds of information hunter-gatherers share with each other, patterns in the content of forager folklore can help illuminate the design and uses of cultural transmission. The oral traditions of foraging peoples are the Laetoli footprints of narrative theory. It is up to us to trace their logical implications.

References

Aguadé, C., and J. Lory. 1997. "Evidence for human sacrifice, bone modification and cannibalism in ancient México." In *Troubled times: Violence and warfare in the past*, eds. D. Martin, and D. Frayer. Amsterdam: Gordon and Breach.

Arsuaga, J. L., I. Martinez, A. Gracia, J.M. Carretero, C. Lorenzo, N. Garcia, and A. I. Ortega. 1997. Sima de los Huesos (Sierra de Atapuerca, Spain). The Site. *Journal of Human Evolution* 33: 109–127.

Askenasy, Hans. 1994. *Cannibalism: From sacrifice to survival*. Amherst, NY: Prometheus Books.

Baron-Cohen, S. 1995. *Mindblindness*. Cambridge, MA: MIT Press.

Barrett, H. Clark. 2005. "Adaptations to predators and prey." In *Handbook of evolutionary psychology*, ed. D. Buss, 200–223. New York: John Wiley and Sons.

Biesele, M. 1993. *Women like meat*. Bloomington: Indiana University Press.

Biocca, E. 1970. *Yanoáma: The narrative of a white girl kidnapped by Amazonian Indians.* New York: Dutton.

Bird, D., and R. Bliege Bird. 2005. "Martu children's hunting strategies in the Western Desert, Australia." In *Hunter-gatherer childhoods*, eds. B. Hewlett, and M. Lamb. Piscataway, NJ: Aldine Transaction.

Blurton Jones, N., and M. Konner, eds. 1976. *Kalahari hunter-gatherers.* Cambridge, MA: Harvard University Press.

Blurton Jones, N. 1993. "The lives of hunter-gatherer children: Effects of parental behavior and parental reproductive strategy." In *Juvenile Pprimates: Life history, development, and behavior*, eds. M. Pereira, and L. Fairbanks. New York: Oxford University Press.

Blurton-Jones, N., K. Hawkes, and P. Draper. 1994. "Differences between Hadza and !Kung children's work: Original affluence or practical reason?" In *Key issues in hunter-gatherer research*, ed. E. S. Burch. Oxford: Berg.

Boas, Franz. 1932. *Bella Bella tales.* New York: American Folk-Lore Society.

Bogoras, Waldemar. 1918. "Tales of Yukaghir, Lamut, and Russianized natives of eastern Siberia." In *Anthropological papers of the American Museum of Natural History, Vol. XX*, ed. Clark Wissler. New York: American Museum Press.

Bowlby, John. 1972. *Attachment. Attachment and loss, vol. 1.* London: Hogarth Press.

Boyer, Pascal. 2001. *Religion explained.* New York: Basic Books.

Burch, E. S. 1974. Eskimo warfare in northwest Alaska. *Anthropological Papers of the University of Alaska* 16: 1–14.

Burch, E. S. 2005. *Alliance and conflict: The world system of the In piak Eskimos.* Lincoln: University of Nebraska Press.

Butterworth, G. E., and E. C. Cochran. 1980. Towards a mechanism of joint attention in human infancy. *International Journal of Behavioural Development* 3: 253–272.

Byrne, Richard. 1995. *The thinking ape.* Oxford: Oxford University Press.

Carpenter, M., K. Nagell, and M. Tomasello. 1998. Social cognition, joint attention, and communicative competence from 9 to 15 months of age. *Monographs of the Society for Research in Child Development* 63.

Chacon, R., and D. Dye. eds. 2007. *The taking and displaying of human body parts as trophies by Amerindians.* New York: Springer.

Chacon, R. 2007. "Seeking the headhunter's power: The quest for arutam among the Achuar of the Ecuadorian Amazon and the development of ranked societies." In *The taking and displaying of human body parts as trophies by Amerindians*, eds. R. Chacon, and D. Dye. New York: Springer.

Chagnon, Napoleon. 1997. *Yanomamo*, 5th ed. New York: Harcourt.

Chagnon, N., and R. Hames. 1979. Protein deficiency and tribal warfare in Amazonia: New data. *Science* 203: 10–15.

Christiansen, Reidar, ed. 1964. *Folktales of Norway.* Chicago: University of Chicago Press.

Crittenden, A., and F. Marlowe. 2008. Allomaternal care among the Hadza of Tanzania. *Human Nature* 19: 249–262.

Daly, M., and M. Wilson. 1998. *The truth about Cinderella.* New Haven: Yale University Press.

Dawkins, R. 2006. *The God delusion.* Boston: Houghton Mifflin.

Defleur, A., T. White, P. Valensi, L. Slima, and É Crégut-Bonnoure. 1999. Neanderthal cannibalisim at Moula-Guercy, Ardèche, France. *Science* 286: 128–131.

de Laguna, Frederica, and Catherine McClellan. 1981. In *Ahtna. Handbook of North American Indians, Vol. 6*, ed. June Helm. Washington, D.C.: Smithsonian.

Dickemann, Mildred. 1984. "Concepts and classification in the study of human infanticide: Sectional introduction and some cautionary notes." In *Infanticide: Comparative and evolutionary perspectives*, eds. G. Hausfater, and S. Blaffer. Hawthorne, NY: Aldine.

Draper, P. 1976. "Social and economic constraints on child life." In *Kalahari hunter-gatherers*, eds. R. B. Lee, and I. DeVore. Cambridge, MA: Harvard University Press.

Duntley, Joshua. 2005. "Adaptations to dangers from humans." In *Handbook of evolutionary psychology*, ed. D. Buss. New York: John Wiley and Sons.

Ember, Carol, and Melvin Ember. 1997. "Violence in the ethnographic record: Results of cross-cultural research on war and aggression. In *Troubled times: Violence and warfare in the past*, eds. D. Martin, and D. Frayer. Amsterdam: Gordon and Breach.

Field, A. P., N. G. Argyris, and K. A. Knowles. 2001. Who's afraid of the big bad wolf: A prospective paradigm to test Rachman's indirect pathways in children. *Behaviour Research and Therapy* 39: 1259–1276.

Field, A. P., and G. C. L. Davey. 2001. "Conditioning models of childhood anxiety." In *Anxiety disorders in children and adolescents: Research, assessment, and intervention*, eds. W. K. Silverman, and P. A. Treffers. Cambridge: Cambridge University Press.

Flinn, M. 1997. Culture and the evolution of social learning. *Evolution and Human Behavior* 18: 23–67.

Goodall, Jane. 1986. *The chimpanzees of Gombe: Patterns of behavior*. Cambridge, MA: Harvard University Press.

Goodwin, G. 1939. "Myths and tales of the White Mountain Apache." *Memoirs of the American Folk-Lore Society*, Vol. XXXIII. New York: J. J. Augustin.

Gould, R. A. 1969. *Yiwara: Foragers of the Western Desert*. New York: Scribner.

Halbert, H., and T. Ball. 1969. *The Creek War of 1813 and 1814*. Southern Historical Publications No. 15. University: University of Alabama Press.

Hames, R. 1988. "The allocation of parental care among the Ye'kwana." In *Human reproductive behavior*, eds. L. Betzig, M. Borgerhoff Mulder, and P. Turke. Cambridge: Cambridge University Press.

Hearne, S. 1958. *A journey from Prince of Wales's Fort in Hudson's Bay to the Northern Ocean, 1769–1772*, ed. R. Glover. Toronto: McMillan.

Heerwagen, J. H., and G. H. Orians. 2002. "The ecological world of children." In *Children and nature: Psychological, sociocultural, and evolutionary investigations*, eds. P. H. Kahn, and S. R. Kellert. Cambridge: MIT Press.

Hewlett, B., and L. Cavalli-Sforza. 1986. Cultural transmission among Aka Pygmies. *American Anthropologist* 88: 922–934.

Hewlett, Barry, J. M. H. van de Koppel, and M. van de Koppel. 1986. "Causes of death among Aka pygmies of the Central African Republic." In *African Pygmies*, ed. L. Cavalli-Sforza. Orlando, FL: Academic Press.

Hill, K., and M. Hurtado. 1996. *Ache life history: The ecology and demography of a foraging people*. Hawthorne, NY: Aldine de Gruyter.

Hrdy, Sarah Blaffer. 1999. *Mother nature: A history of mothers, infants, and natural selection*. New York: Pantheon Books.

Hurtado, M., K. Hill, H. Kaplan, and I. Hurtado. 1992. Trade-offs between female food acquisition and child care among Hiwi and Ache foragers. *Human Nature* 3: 185–216.

Jacobi, K. 2007. "Disabling the dead: Human trophy-taking in the prehistoric Southeast." In *The taking and displaying of human body parts as trophies by Amerindians*, eds. R. Chacon, and D. Dye. New York: Springer.

Jones, David E. 2000. *An instinct for dragons*. New York: Routledge.

Kamei, Nobutaka. 2005. "Play among Baka children in Cameroon." In *Hunter-Gatherer Childhoods: Evolutionary and Developmental Perspectives*, ed. B. Hewlett and M. Lamb, 343–359. New Brunswick, NJ: Transaction Publishers.

Kantner, J. 1999. Survival cannibalism or sociopolitical intimidation? Explaining perimortem mutilation in the American Southwest. *Human Nature* 10: 1–50.

Kaplan, H., and H. Dove. 1987. Infant development among the Ache of Paraguay. *Developmental Psychology* 23: 190–198.

Kluckhohn, C. 1959. Recurrent themes in myth and mythmaking. *Daedalus* 88: 268–279.

Konner, Melvin J. 1976. "Maternal care, infant behavior and development among the !Kung." In *Kalahari hunter-gatherers*, eds. R. B. Lee, and I. DeVore. Cambridge: Harvard University Press.

Kvideland, Reimund, and Henning K.Sehmsdorf, eds. 1988. *Scandinavian folk belief and legend*. Minneapolis: University of Minnesota Press.

Laughlin, W. 1968. "Hunting: An integrating biobehavior system and its evolutionary importance." In *Man the hunter*, eds. R. B. Lee, and I. DeVore. New York: Aldine.

LeBlanc, Steven. 1999. *Prehistoric warfare in the American Southwest*. Salt Lake City: University of Utah Press.

LeBlanc, Steven, and Katherine Register. 2003. *Constant battles: The myth of the peaceful, noble savage*. New York: St. Martin's Press.

Lee, Richard B. 1984. *The Dobe !Kung*. New York: Holt, Rinehart and Winston.

Leslie, A. M. 1994. "ToMM, ToBy, and agency: Core architecture and domain specificity." In *Mapping the mind: Domain specificity in cognition and culture*, eds. L. Hirschfeld, and S. Gelman. Cambridge: Cambridge University Press.

Low, Bobbi S. 1998. "The evolution of human life histories." In *Handbook of evolutionary psychology: Ideas, issues, and applications*, eds. C. Crawford, and D. L. Krebs. Mahwah, NJ: Lawrence Erlbaum Associates.

Marlowe, Frank. 2005. Who tends Hadza children? In *Hunter-gatherer childhoods*, eds. B. S. Hewlett, and M. E. Lamb. Piscataway, NJ: Aldine Transaction.

Martin, D., and D. Frayer. eds. 1997. *Troubled times: Violence and warfare in the past*. Amsterdam: Gordon and Breach.

Maschner, H., and K. Reedy-Maschner. 2007. "Heads, women, and the baubles of prestige: Trophies of war in the Arctic and Subarctic." In *The taking and displaying of human body parts as trophies by Amerindians*, eds. R. Chacon, and D. Dye. New York: Springer.

McDowell, J. 1997. *Hamatsa: The enigma of cannibalism on the Pacific Northwest coast*. Vancouver: Ronsdale Press.

Melbye, J., and S. Fairgrieve. 1994. A massacre and possible cannibalism in the Canadian Arctic: New evidence from the Saunaktuk site (NgTn-1). *Arctic Anthropology* 31: 57–77.

Napanangka, Y. 1995. "Kid left behind in camp." In *Footprints across our land*, ed. J. Crugnale. Broome, Western Australia: Magabala.

Nishida, T., M. Hiraiwa-Hasegawa, T. Hasegawa, and Y. Takahata. 1985. Group extinction and female transfer in wild chimpanzees in the Mahale National Park, Tanzania. *Z. Tierpsychol* 67: 284–301.

Ohmagari, K., and F. Berkes. 1997. Transmission of indigenous knowledge and bush skills among the Western James Bay Cree women of Subactic Canada. *Human Ecology* 25: 197–222.

Onishi, K., R. Baillargeon, and A. Leslie. 2007. 15-month-old infants detect violations in pretend scenarios. *Acta Psychologica* 124: 106–128.

Öst, L.G. 1987. Age of onset in different phobias. *Journal of Abnormal Psychology* 96: 223–229.

Oswalt, W. 1967. *Alaskan Eskimos*. San Francisco: Chandler.

Owsley, D. W., K. S. Bruwelheide, L. E. Burgess, and W. T. Billeck. 2007. "Human finger and hand bone necklaces from the Plains and Great Basin." In *The taking and displaying of human body parts as trophies by Amerindians*, eds. R. Chacon, and D. Dye. New York: Springer.

Parsons, Elsie Clews. 1929. *Kiowa tales. Memoirs of the American Folklore Society, vol. XXII*. New York: American Folk-Lore Society.

Parsons, Elsie Clews. 1939. *Pueblo Indian Religion*, 2 vols. Chicago: Chicago University Press.

Parsons, Elsie Clews. 1940. *Taos tales. Memoirs of the American Folklore Society, Vol. XXXIV.* New York: J. J. Augustin.

Petrinovich, Lewis. 2000. *The cannibal within*, New York Aldine de Gruyter.

Poole, Fitz John Porter. 1983. "Cannibals, tricksters, and witches: Anthropophagic images among Bimin-Kuskusmin." In *The ethnography of cannibalism*, eds. P. Brown, and D. Tuzin, 6–32. Washington, D. C.: Society for Psychological Anthropology.

Quaife, Milo. 1950. *Absaroka, home of the Crows*. Chicago: Lakeside Press.

Rasmussen, Knud. 1929. *Intellectual culture of the Iglulik Eskimos. Report of the 5th Thule Expedition 1921–24, vol. VII, no. 1*. Copenhagen: Gyldendalske Boghandel, Nordisk Forlag.

Rasmussen, Knud. 1930. *Observations on the intellectual culture of the Caribou Eskimos. Report of the 5th Thule Expedition 1921–24, vol. VII, no. 2*. Copenhagen: Gyldendalske Boghandel, Nordisk Forlag.

Rasmussen, Knud. 1931. *The Netsilik Eskimos: Social life and spiritual culture. Report of the 5th Thule Expedition 1921–24, vol. VIII, no. 1–2*. Copenhagen: Gyldendalske Boghandel, Nordisk Forlag.

Rink, Hinrich. 1875. *Tales and traditions of the Eskimo*. London: Blackwood and Sons. Republished in 1997 by Dover Publications: Mineola, NY.

Rhys Williams, Thomas. 1965. *The Dusun: A north Borneo society*. New York: Holt, Rinehart and Winston.

Rozzi, F., F. d'Errico, M. Vanhaeren, P. Grootes, B. Kerautret, and V. Dujardin. 2009. Cutmarked human remains bearing Neanderthal features and modern human remains associated with the Aurignacian at Les Rois. *Journal of Anthropological Sciences* 87: 153–185.

Scaife, M. and J. Bruner. 1975. The capacity for joint visual attention in the infant. *Nature* 253: 265–266.

Scalise Sugiyama, Michelle. 1996. On the origins of narrative: Storyteller bias as a fitness-enhancing strategy. *Human Nature* 7: 403–425.

Scalise Sugiyama, Michelle. 2001. Food, foragers, and folklore: The role of narrative in human subsistence. *Evolution and Human Behavior* 22: 221–240.

Scalise Sugiyama, Michelle. 2004. Predation, narration, and adaptation: "Little Red Riding Hood" revisited. *Interdisciplinary Literary Studies* 5: 108–127.

Scalise Sugiyama, Michelle. 2005. "Reverse-engineering narrative: Evidence of special design." In *The literary animal*, eds. J. Gottschall and D. S. Wilson. Evanston, IL: Northwestern University Press.

Scalise Sugiyama, Michelle. 2006. "Lions and tigers and bears: Predators as a folklore universal." In *Anthropology and social history: Heuristics in the study of literature*, eds. H. Friedrich, F. Jannidis, U. Klein, K. Mellmann, S. Metzger, and M. Willems. Paderborn: Mentis.

Scalise Sugiyama, Michelle. 2008. Narrative as social mapping—Case study: The trickster genre and the free rider problem. *Ometeca* 12: 24–42.

Scalise Sugiyama, Michelle, and Lawrence Sugiyama. 2009. "A frugal (re)past: Use of oral tradition to buffer foraging risk." *Studies in the literary imagination* 42: 15–41.

Scalise Sugiyama, Michelle, and Lawrence Sugiyama. Under revision. Humanized topography: Storytelling as a wayfinding strategy. *American Anthropologist*.

Scalise Sugiyama, Michelle, and Lawrence Sugiyama. In preparation. "War stories: A survey of warfare methods and tactics described in forager oral traditions."

Schaafsma, Polly. 2007. "Head trophies and scalping: Images in Southwest rock art." In *The taking and displaying of human body parts as trophies by Amerindians*, eds. R. Chacon, and D. Dye, 90–123. New York: Springer.

Smith, William Ramsay. 1930. *Aborigine myths and legends.* London: George G. Harrap.

Teit, James A. 1917. *Folk-tales of Salishan and Sahaptin Tribes.* Lancaster, PA: American Folk-lore Society.

Thompson, S. 1957. *Motif index of folk literature.* Bloomington: Indiana University Press.

Tomasello, M. 1995. "Joint attention as social cognition." In *Joint attention: Its origins and role in development*, eds. C. Moore, and P. Dunham. Hillsdale, NJ: Erlbaum.

Tomasello, M. 1999. *Cultural origins of human cognition.* Harvard: Harvard University Press.

Tonkinson, R. 1978. *The Mardudjara Aborigines: Living the dream in Australia's desert.* New York: Holt, Rinehart and Winston.

Tooby, John, and Leda Cosmides. 1990. The past explains the present: Emotional adaptations and the structure of ancestral environments. *Ethology and Sociobiology* 11: 375–424.

Tooby, John, and Leda Cosmides. 1992. "The psychological foundations of culture." In *The adapted mind*, eds. J. Barkow, L. Cosmides, and J. Tooby. New York: Oxford University Press.

Tooby, John, and Leda Cosmides. 2001. Does beauty build adapted minds? Toward an evolutionary theory of aesthetics, fiction and the arts. *Substance* 94/95: 6–27.

Tooby, J., and I. DeVore, I. 1987. "The reconstruction of hominid behavioral evolution through strategic modeling." In *The evolution of human behavior: Primate models*, ed. W. G. Kinzey. Albany: SUNY Press.

Tucker, B., and A. Young. 2005. "Growing up Mikea: Children's time allocation and tuber foraging in southwestern Madagascar." In *Hunter-gatherer childhoods*, eds. B. Hewlett, and M. Lamb. Piscataway, NJ: Aldine Transaction.

Turnbull, Colin. 1983. *The Mbuti Pygmies: Change and adaptation.* New York: Holt, Rinehart and Winston.

Turner, Christy. 1993. Cannibalism in Chaco Canyon: The charnel pit excavated in 1926 at Small House Ruin by Frank H. H. Roberts, Jr. *American Journal of Physical Anthropology* 91: 421–439.

Turner, C., and J. Turner. 1995. Cannibalism in the prehistoric American Southwest: Occurrence, taphonomy, explanation, and suggestions for standardized world definition. *Anthropological Science* 103: 1–22.

van Schaik, Carel, and Robin Dunbar. 1990. The evolution of monogamy in large primates: A new hypothesis and some crucial tests. *Behaviour* 115: 30–62.

Villa, Paola. 1992. Cannibalism in prehistoric Europe. *Evolutionary Anthropology* 1: 93–104.

Wadley, Reed. 2003a. Lethal treachery and the imbalance of power in warfare and feuding. *Journal of Anthropological Research* 59: 531–554.

Wadley, Reed. 2003b. Treachery and deceit: Parallels in tribal and terrorist warfare? *Studies in Conflict and Terrorism* 26: 331–345.

Walker, Phillip. 1990. *Appendix 5: Tool marks on human bone from Saunaktuk.* Yellowknife: Prince of Wales Northern Heritage Center.

White, Tim D. 1992. *Prehistoric cannibalism at Mancos.* Princeton: Princeton University Press.

Williamson, Roy. 2007. "Otinontsiskiaj ondaon (The House of Cut-Off Heads): The history and archaeology of Northern Iroquoian trophy taking." In *The taking and displaying of human body parts as trophies by Amerindians*, eds. R. Chacon, and D. Dye. New York: Springer.

Wrangham, R. 1999. Evolution of coalitionary killing. *American Journal of Physical Anthropology* 110: 1–30.

20

"BY WEAPONS MADE WORTHY":
A DARWINIAN PERSPECTIVE
ON *BEOWULF*

Raymond Corbey and Angus Mol

Beowulf is one of the highlights of English literature. Line 3,182 of the eleventh-century manuscript, kept at the British Museum, recount events that purportedly occurred in pre-Christian Scandinavia a few centuries earlier—a world of clan- and alliance-based chiefdoms centered on courts, of gifting and feasting, of raids and feuds. Although a work of lore, historians and archaeologists use the epic chronicle as a major resource for the study of the Anglo-Saxons. The poem has been proposed as a key to, among other things, the interpretation of early medieval grave contents, warrior accoutrements, long ships, and the spatial layout of castles and courts. The lavish, seventh century ship burial of Sutton Hoo (Suffolk, England), for example, shows great similarity to the four burials that, together with various battles, punctuate the plot (Owen-Crocker 2000).

The story develops as follows. A cannibalistic monster terrorizes the court of Hrotgar, King of the Danes, for twelve years. The Geatish retainer Beowulf arrives, defeats the monster and, subsequently, its revengeful mother in two epic battles. He is lavishly honored and rewarded by Hrotgar. Beowulf returns to the land of the Geats laden with Danish gifts, which he again presents to his uncle, the king of the Geats. Later Beowulf becomes a king himself and rules wisely for 50 years. Then a servant steals from the den of a dragon, which attacks. Old Beowulf defeats this monster, too, but dies from his wounds. The story ends with his magnificent burial, in a ship in a mound.

"Never have I seen a mightier noble, a larger man," King Hrothgar's coast guard exclaims upon seeing Beowulf come ashore, "than that one among you, a warrior in armor. That's no mere retainer, so honored in weapons; may that noble bearing never belie him!" (lines 244ff. All *Beowulf* translations are taken from Chickering 2006. Hereafter cited as [*Beowulf*, line number]). Another plausible and often-used translation of the phrase *waepnum geweorðad*—"honored in weapons"—is "by weapons made worthy." It refers to how, in the plot, and among Anglo-Saxon elites at large, the personal identity and prestige of a king's followers—his *sibbengedryht*—changes and builds up through reciprocal exchanges between follower and liege, as will be analyzed in some detail in what follows. Weapons and valuables figure as prominently in this context as, archaeologically less visible, honors and loyalty.

In this chapter, we are more interested in the *Beowulf* as a source for and key to aspects of early medieval culture and society, and less than the other contributions to this section in the text as creative fiction (see Dancygier, this section) or the responses of listeners/readers (Carroll et al., this section). Consequently we will focus not so much on the value of evolutionary approaches to literary studies but on their bearing on mainstream ethnology. We will specifically examine and criticize two ethnological readings of reciprocal exchange in *Beowulf* from the perspective of costly signaling theory and altruism theory. We will show how these adaptationist approaches crucially add to traditional hermeneutic and culturalist understandings of basic aspects of the plot to do with the constitution of personal identity through lord-retainer exchanges. The wider relevance of this type of analysis for the way in which ethnologists usually study the germane role of exchange in sociality and identity will be discussed in terms of the distinction between ultimate and proximate explanations in biology.

ETHNOLOGICAL APPROACHES

Although the *Beowulf* plot is extremely rich ethnographically, only a few score from among the almost 3,000 scholarly publications now available on the poem deal with such matters as law, feud, boasting, riches, drinking, hoarding, kinship, the symbolism of weapons, kingship, and so on, from an ethnological perspective. The overwhelming majority is textual criticism—hermeneutic, philological, stylistic, character-oriented, structural, poststructuralist, feminist, psychological, psychoanalytical, Lacanian, and so on. Both authors whose ethnographic interpretations we will examine in the following, Jos Bazelmans and John Hill, have expressed their regret that systematic and thorough attempts at ethnographic analysis were not available to them. Matters ethnographical, such as the ones just listed, Hill laments, "have usually been discussed in relative isolation from each other, rather than receiving an ethnologically integrated viewing that would allow us to see *Beowulf* as a world that works rather than, in effect, as a partly misunderstood assortment of customs, values, and relationships the poet busily transcends" (Hill 1997, 255). Both Bazelmans, an archaeologist-ethnologist, and Hill, an ethnologically oriented *Beowulf* scholar, aim to make up for this by approaching the dense social and cultural reality the text imaginatively depicts "as an integrated world rather than seen piecemeal or as a congeries of customs, values, and institutions" (Hill 1997, 264).

In *By Weapons Made Worthy: Lords, Retainers and their Relationship in Beowulf*, Bazelmans—carefully weighing, and working his way through, several centuries of partly Christian reception history—interprets the goings-on in and around Anglo-Saxon courts in terms of traditional ideas and values (1999). He shows how these regulate the exchange of valuables and services that are constitutive for the development of the identities of those involved, knitting together society as a whole as primarily a moral, not so much a politico-economic, order.

Bazelmans' strongly holistic, structuralist, and idealist approach follows on from Marcel Mauss's *Essay on the Gift*, especially as interpreted by Louis Dumont and his school. *Idées-valeurs*, widely shared, traded from generation to generation, impose themselves on social relations. They determine how exchanges during life-cycle rituals cause such constituents as "body," "life," "image" and "soul"—Dumontian terminology for which Bazelmans does provide rough but no precise Anglo-Saxon equivalents—to merge into the person of warrior-follower or king (Bazelmans 1999, 156ff.). Following Dumont, Bazelmans rejects approaches that see individuals as strategically striving for "increases of economic, socio-political or symbolic capital and enhanced authority" (Bazelmans 2000, 370) as erroneously reading modern preoccupations into nonmodern societies. Weapons for him are less related to power struggles and bloodshed than they are to the outward expression of honor and worth and, in typical Dumontian idiom, "commensurable" with persons.

Bazelmans models his sophisticated, fine-grained analysis of the constitution of Anglo-Saxon identity and sociality in *Beowulf* after a body of mainly Austronesian ethnography by the Dumont school who see every-day exchanges in villages as governed by a value-orientated matrix. This matrix, constantly renewed and reaffirmed, the Dumontians hold, is "constitutive for the persons involved, including the dead and the spirits" (Barraud et al. 1994, 105). It causes "subjects and objects [to] intertwine ceaselessly in a tissue of relations which make of exchanges the permanent locus where these societies reaffirm, again and again, their highest values" (ibid., 105). Analogously the commensurability of valuables and persons "is the most important principle that is constitutive of social order," of early medieval "society as a whole" (Bazelmans 1999: 227–228).

John Hill in his 1995 volume *The Cultural World in Beowulf* and various other publications also employs ethnographic analysis but opts for an approach that is more functionalist, transactionalist, and individualist, and, thus, closer to the sort of biological explanations we will discuss later. Hill, too, draws upon Marcel Mauss: "[the] giving of gifts is at the heart of ethical life, of lawful and right behavior in the hall, and of continuing alliance and reciprocity among men" (Hill 1995, 86), and "[the] crucial imperative is the settling of feuds and the continuation of fruitful exchange" (Hill 1997, 265). However, he is less monotheoretical than Bazelmans, seeing "the economy of honor and gift giving as open to social complexity, competitiveness, and possibilities for manipulation" (Hill 1997, 259). Hill works bottom-up, starting with individuals, while Bazelmans interprets top-down, starting with cosmological ideas and values. For Hill "the social world depicted *in* the poem" (Hill 1995, 18; his italics) is one in which a revenge ethic, feuding, and violence loom as large as loyalty and peace making. For Bazelmans, who, more explicitly than Hill, is interested in the poem as a key to historical reality, Beowulf's world is a quite harmonious one, despite the conflict-ridden plot. It is, with a phrase he uses time and again, "society as a whole," which comes to the fore in the totality of exchanges.

Bazelmans in particular, and less emphatically Hill, interpret what happens in terms of ideas and the values the characters act by. In this sense their approach is hermeneutical or interpretive, and, as such, comparable to most of the extensive nonethnological secondary literature on *Beowulf*. Their culturalist stance, emphasizing the importance of culture in determining individual behavior and the way in which society functions, is typical of contemporary ethnography. Both the European Durkheimian/Maussian tradition and the American Boasian tradition see humans as moral subjects, as having entered a different order of existence: the intellectually, spiritually, and morally superior world of society, language, and culture (Carrithers 1996; Corbey 2005). We will now offer a different, adaptationist reading of exchange and identity in the world of *Beowulf*.

SHOWING OFF

Biological approaches to human social and cultural behavior are based on the presupposition that the behavior of all species, including the human one, are to be studied in the same manner: in the light of evolution, analyzing how individuals maximize their reproductive success and inclusive fitness in the context of optimal foraging, dispersal patterns, mating tactics, life history strategies, and the like. This presupposition is diametrically opposed to that of many, if not most, present-day ethnographers, in particular the two aforementioned traditions.

"Ethnological observations can increase the depth of our understanding and illuminate the social and dramatic coherence of the poem" (Hill 1995, 20), John Hill holds, speaking for Bazelmans as well. We think that just as ethnology adds to literary criticism, evolutionary biology can, analogously, add to both ethnology and literary criticism. It can deepen our understanding not just, specifically, of Anglo-Saxon sociality and identity in *Beowulf*, but also, more generally, of reciprocity and exchange as studied in by ethnologists. Both authors analyze how the "distribution, sharing, and bestowal of [...] treasures" in *Beowulf* creates "a social economy of honor, worth, status and loyalties" (Hill 1997: 106). In line with recent work under the heading of "biopoetics" (Cooke & Turner 1999) or "literary Darwinism" by, among others, Brian Boyd, Joseph Carroll, and Jonathan Gotschall (see their contributions to this volume) we will now try and show how that economy of honor connects to costly signalling and altruism as studied by biologists.

The term "costly signaling" was coined by Michael Spence (1973), an economist. It is also known as the "handicap principle" (Zahavi and Zahavi 1997; Grafen 1990a, 1990b). Costly signaling theory was inspired by an explanation for "conspicuous consumption" by the sociologist Thorstein Veblen, published in 1899 (Veblen 2007). "Costly signaling" refers to traits that, all else being equal, would lower the relative fitness of the bearer, but, at first sight paradoxically, continue to be selected for—because expending in an ostensibly superfluous manner makes qualities visible, which would otherwise be difficult to observe. Such behaviors convey information about underlying fitness.

An example of a costly trait is the long, brightly colored feathers of certain bird of paradise species that make them easier to catch for predators but also signal to potential mates that their genes are so good that they can get away with it. Evolutionary anthropologists have explained human big-game hunting, which is pursued even though it would be more efficient to gather plant resources and hunt small game, as a costly behavior, a "hunting handicap" (Alden Smith et al. 2003; Bliege Bird et al. 2000; Hildebrandt and McGuire 2002). The key idea here is that a costly signal is an honest indicator of an individual's quality because a lower-quality individual would be unable to perform the signal.

Beowulf's arrival on Danish shores and, subsequently, at the court of Danish King Hrotgar figures prominently in Bazelmans's and Hill's readings (Hill 2008). When Beowulf arrives with his Geatish followers, unsolicited and unannounced, he is fully armed. Although Geats and Danes are on good terms, in appearance the troop of Geats does not look very differently from a raiding party, so a warm welcome is not obvious. Hrotgar's coast warden is suspicious and starts to question the Geats. However, when his eye falls on Beowulf, his tone changes considerably. Although Beowulf has not yet explained who he is and what he wants, his weapons already signal his worthiness. He states his intent—aiding Hrotgar against the monster—and the warden allows passage to Heorot, the golden-roofed "mead hall" where King Hrotgar holds court.

As Beowulf and his followers enter the outer perimeter of the mead-hall, their physical appearance is highlighted once more: "Bright their war-mail, hardened, hand-linked; glistening iron rings sang in their battle-shirts as they came marching straight to that hall, fearful in war-gear [...] That iron-fast troop was honored in weapons" (*Beowulf*, 321ff.). At the doorstep Beowulf and his men are stopped and questioned once more, this time by the "haughty" Wulfgar, doorkeeper and advisor to the king. Wulfgar, too, even before Beowulf can reply, reacts favorably upon seeing the visitors' "gold-trimmed shields," "iron-gray corselets," and "grim mask-helmets." "I expect in pride, scarcely in exile, out of high courage you have come to Hrotgar," he speaks to the guests, and counsels his king to "choose among answers, but give no refusal, [...for] in battle-dress, weapons, they appear worthy of nobles' esteem" (ibid., 321ff.). Hrotgar, who already knows Beowulf's background, then allows him and his troop of Geats access to the mead hall, the sociopolitical heart of his kingdom.

We agree with Bazelmans and Hill that warrior accoutrements are a central means of displaying status in early medieval Anglo-Saxon society, but see this pattern of behavior as not just an expression of local ideas and values, but also of an underlying biological mechanism that is at play in all human societies, and other species, too. When Geatish individuals, Beowulf in particular, flaunt their lavishly adorned weapons and armor they are expending in an ostensibly superfluous manner. They advertise qualities to do with their fitness that would be difficult to observe otherwise. If Beowulf has been "honored in weapons" by his Geatish king, this shows that he has borne the cost of fitness inhibiting acts—such as risking injury and death for his king—in the past and that he will very probably be able to do so in the future.

Both in terms of functionality and in terms of costliness, the intricately decorated weapons in *Beowulf*, similar to those found by archaeologists on scores of sites from this period, not least in graves, are analogous to stag antlers. Although antlers do not have a perfect shape for inflicting injury, they are functional when used in battles between males in the mating season. At the same time, as large and conspicuous as they are, they constitute a liability, limiting mobility in dense forests and requiring a large investment of energy to grow (Zahavi and Zahavi 1997, 87–88). Similarly, the heavy weapons of elites in the uncertain so-called Migration Period demanded physically strong and adroit individuals to be functional in battle. Their elaborate and refined appearance required a large investment in terms of production costs.

Beowulf, in front of Hrotgar on his throne, has to convince the king that he is able to take control of the mead hall and to engage Grendel. Although Beowulf's appearance bodes well, Hrotgar doubts whether Beowulf will succeed where others have failed. In the course of all those years, many of his own men have boasted that they could handle the problem but have lost their lives in the attempt, leaving him with ever-fewer followers. He sees an uninvited, relative stranger before him to whom he would have to temporarily surrender control of the court. Adding to the effects of his appearance, Beowulf then announces that, if he is allowed to give it a try, he will kill Grendel on his own and with his bare hands. Hrotgar postpones reacting to this boast, and orders that a feast be prepared for the Geatish guests. During the feast Beowulf is challenged by Unferth, another advisor to the king (on Unferth's position at the court, see Orchard 2003, 247–250).

Unferth argues against Beowulf's plan, claiming that this visitor is not all that he claims to be and has a penchant for bluffing. He brings up a boast Beowulf has made in the past but was unable to fulfill: to win a swimming match against Breca of the tribe of the Heathoreamas. This poses a serious threat for Beowulf, because it puts his present ostentation in an unfavorable light. He adroitly averts damage by Unferth's slur by recounting what actually happened during the swimming contest. Breca only won because Beowulf was attacked by a throng of sea-monsters, all of which he killed, a much more heroic accomplishment than winning a swimming match. Beowulf adds that Unferth is in a poor position to pass judgment since he was responsible for his own brother's death. "Never would Grendel have done so much harm," Beowulf adds to this successful rebuttal of Unferth's provocation, if the "heart and intention" of Hrotgar's retainers "were as sharp as [their] words" (**Beowulf**, 593–559).

From the perspective of costly signaling theory, the Danes are faced with the problem of whether Beowulf's signals are honest. Do they truly represent his capacities and underlying fitness, or is he pretending to be something he is not? Unferth, who may feel his position threatened by Beowulf, is further assessing his fitness and is ready to punish cheaters, which would add a costly signal on Unferth's behalf to the benefit of himself. Beowulf may indeed be a "freerider" who tries to gain from the cooperation of others. He might be keen on taking over throne treasures, possibly with violence, not an unusual happening in those days as the text itself hints at and even describes in detail—witness the Finnsburh episode (*Beowulf*, 1068ff.; see also Orchard 2003, 174–178). Even temporary control of the highly prestigious mead hall, of great symbolic value, and temporary quasi-kingly status would bring enormous benefits.

Interactions such as this confrontation have been proposed as a foundational element of social behavior in humans (Flesch 2007; Gintis et al. 2005; Henrich and Boyd 2001). In social interaction, it is difficult to be sure of another's disposition to either cooperate or defect, because free riders will always try to defect and take advantage of those who choose to cooperate. Individuals who test and "altruistically" punish free riders safeguard group cooperation at a possible cost to themselves, thus, arguably, giving off a costly signal.

Unfortunately for Unferth, Beowulf defends himself well against the claim that he is a free rider and a dishonest signaler. In a reversal of fortune Beowulf uses Unferth's own ploy against him and exposes Unferth as a cheater who is responsible for the death of a sibling and is all dishonest words but no honest deeds. Hrotgar, who has, of course, closely followed these interactions, agrees with Beowulf and decides to let him take on the monster. Beowulf's ensuing battle with Grendel and his mother is successful, but also conspicuously risky, even more so because he declines to use weapons or armor against Grendel. Together with the valuables and honors he receives afterward, this adds substantially to his reputation.

Culturalist approaches leave in the dark why Beowulf would boast in the first place. That costly signaling theory can deepen Bazelmans' and Hill's rich but exclusively ethnologically informed interpretations of the Migration Period warrior ethic is also clear from the confusion around *oferhygd*, roughly translatable as "immoderation," "arrogance" or "overconfidence," which the text emphatically ascribes to its hero. The way Beowulf combines brave exploits and noble intentions with boasts and acts of derring-do have left many a reader with uncomfortable feelings of ambivalence toward the protagonist. The most common reaction to this conundrum is to stress one and ignore the other aspect, thus either vilifying or idealizing him. Is he either an ethical person, whose actions are steered by what is morally just, or just a self-aggrandizing, arrogant, reckless individual striving for glory? Scott Gwara, for example, recently devoted a whole monograph to Beowulf's *oferhygd*. In a convoluted argument he struggles to make sense of the protagonist's ambiguity in terms of his identity as a foreign fighter who learns more prudence while he seeks glory abroad (Gwara 2008).

However, within the framework of costly signaling theory it makes perfect sense that king Beowulf, as the last lines of the poem have it, was at the same time *mannum mildust*, "kindest to his men" and *lof-geornost*, "most eager for fame." We suggest that, as the foregoing analysis of the constitution of warrior identity clearly implies, *oferhygd* is costly signaling behavior and does not detract from but is a logical concomitant to a man's worth. Thus, we do not agree with Howell Chickering that "[whether] Beowulf is an ideal king or flawed by his heroic quest for fame remains a question that disturbs every full interpretation of the poem's philosophy" (Chickering 2006, 269). We also do not agree with Bazelmans when he criticizes several interpretations for stressing the provocative, boastful stance Beowulf takes in his first interaction with King Hrotgar. From his structuralist position, he argues that provocative, competitive exchanges would not be possible between a young warrior and a mighty king, for they are "individuals [...] in structurally different positions" (Bazelmans 1999, 225, cf. 227). Here again Bazelmans underplays conflict and exaggerates contractual aspects of the complex conflict/contract dynamic the poem describes. From a costly signaling viewpoint, however, Beowulf's arrogance is perfectly understandable.

"SIBBENGEDRYHT"

After a prosperous 50-year reign as king, Beowulf is faced with a monster once more. The lands of the Geats are ravaged by a fearsome dragon, its fury awakened by the theft of a golden cup from its hoard. Although Beowulf could field the whole Geatish army against the dragon, he opts to engage the dragon himself with the support of only twelve trusted warriors. In all likelihood, these followers are key members of his *sibbengedryht*. In Old English, *sibbe* means "kinship," "relationship," "amity," and *gedryht* means "troop." The phenomenon closely resembles the Germanic *comitatus* as described in some detail by Tacitus in his *Germania* (Benario 1999): a strongly reciprocal relationship between a chief and his retainers whose loyalty and military efforts he rewards with gifts and honors. Although there is a gap of several centuries between the worlds depicted in *Germania* and in *Beowulf*, we find this concept clearly elucidated in the opening passage of *Beowulf*: "So ought a [young] man, in his father's household, treasure up the future, by his goods and goodness, by splendid bestowals, so that later in life his chosen men stand by him in turn, his retainers serve him when war comes" (*Beowulf*, 20ff.). Beowulf has collected men around him whose worthiness he has enhanced with lavish gifts made during public feasts, similar to those thrown in his own honor after his victory over Grendel and

Grendel's mother. These men are honor-bound to defend him in this moment of danger.

The monster turns out to be a fearsome opponent. Although Beowulf claims to forego boasting, he insists that his men keep back to await the outcome of the clash. When he announces his intention to fight the dragon alone he is probably acting out of a sense of duty and concern for his men, but also, our biological heuristic suggests, showing off. Perhaps some of his followers are kin, in which case he may be altruistically motivated. However, he is not able to wound the dragon and, instead, incurs horrible injuries himself. At this point the men who have followed him into this fight are faced with a difficult decision: should they come to the aid of their liege and risk being killed, or should they avoid the fight and survive, but then face shame and dishonor? The majority of the warriors opt for the latter alternative, their decision somewhat eased by the fact that Beowulf has ordered them to stand back.

Of course, the specific goings-on the poem describes so beautifully may be partly or even entirely fictitious, but it is not so much the historical details of one particular event as the type of social interaction that shows how an adaptationist approach can complement or deepen ethnological analysis. In such relationships between chief and follower reciprocal altruism looms large, next to loyalty to kin and solidarity with group members. Reciprocal altruism is a *quid pro quo* one between non-relatives in the sense this concept has been used in a substantial body of literature inaugurated by the groundbreaking article by Trivers (1971).

However, the followers do not hold up to their part of the exchange, and they defect. They let their interests as individuals outweigh their loyalty to liege and group, maximizing their own inclusive fitness, and thereby forsake the possibility of showing off. Faced with a classic dilemma between egoistic and altruistic courses of action, they behave as free riders. Altruistic punishment theory (Flesch 2007, West et al. 2007) predicts harsh repercussions for such behavior, and the defectors are indeed ostracized in the aftermath of the battle. However, they survive. The only follower who does not flee is Beowulf's young and inexperienced nephew Wiglaf. When, during the fight, the tables turn in favor of the dragon, Wiglaf urges the other warriors to help Beowulf. They refuse, and Wiglaf charges into battle to help his uncle, in accordance with "kin selection" theory (Hamilton 1964a,1964b), which shows how helping relatives indirectly serves one's own genes (partly shared with relatives) and fitness.

In Wiglaf's case, kinship forges even stronger bonds and altruistic motivation than two other forms of altruism do in the case of the defecting followers, who are probably not or less closely related to Beowulf. Instead, reciprocal altruism, in principle between non-kin, and group altruism characterize their relation to Beowulf. In addition, Wiglaf's heroic behavior may constitute yet another costly signal. For the other retainers, the costs of reciprocating are too high, but "[nothing] can ever hold back kinship in a right-thinking man" (*Beowulf*, 2600ff.), as the poem underlines repeatedly. Beowulf and Wiglaf together manage to defeat the dragon, but Beowulf is mortally wounded. After Beowulf's death and magnificent burial, Wiglaf becomes the leader of the Geats.

In an exclusively culturalist perspective on reciprocity in the context of *sibbengedryht*, it remains unclear what prompts the inexperienced Wiglaf, who is not even honored by gifts from his king yet, to risk his own life by helping Beowulf. Although such actions at first sight would seem to be disinterestedly heroic and noble, basically, from an adaptationist perspective, Wiglaf is defending his own kin. Or is he driven by youthful recklessness and poor judgment? Again, we will never know exactly. In the present context, we do not so much aim at a definitive, precise interpretation of the behaviors under consideration as at the general point that evolutionary perspectives crucially add to the Maussian analysis of the constitution of social order and cultural identity through reciprocal exchanges.

DISCUSSION: BEYOND POWER?

"Evidence for the relationship between kinship ties and *sibbengedryht* ties and how they affect feud and exchange needs to be evaluated in some analytical way," Hill writes, adding that "[at] present our understanding of these matters is vague, rather than particular and focused" (Hill 1995, 15). This point is well taken, and we have shown that, although it may not entirely be what Hill had in mind, an evolutionary perspective can be of considerable help here, deepening textual criticism and ethnologically informed interpretation. To philology and textual criticism, Hill and Bazelmans add comparative ethnology; to intercultural comparative ethnology we add comparative behavioral biology. The latter sort of analysis can easily be extended to, for example, the so-called Finnsburh digression, the obstruction by queen Wealtheow of Beowulf's adoption by Hrotgar, or, more generally, the role of women and patterns of violence and vengeance in the poem.

Bazelmans presented the gist of the argument of his monograph *By Weapons Made Worthy* again in a book chapter entitled "Beyond Power: Ceremonial Exchanges in Beowulf" (Bazelmans 2000). It is ironic that, under these two headings, he hardly deals with real weapons and real power plays in the conflict-ridden Anglo-Saxon world the poem describes. Our plea is not to do away with culturalist, interpretive analysis in terms of meanings and values but rather to "vertically integrate" (Tooby and Cosmides 1992; Slingerland 2008) such interpretations by supplementing them with analyses in terms of utility and power. In terms of a distinction germane to evolutionary biology (Tinbergen 1963) but not heeded by Bazelmans, Hill, or, indeed, most ethnographers: Although proximally men may fight because of Dumontian, cultural *idées/valeurs* and immediate, perceived benefits, ultimately, from a biological perspective, they fight because of genes. When early medieval Anglo-Saxon elite males negotiated and articulated their status in terms of exchanged and displayed swords, helmets, and other warrior accoutrements, this ultimately was an evolutionary strategy.

On this deeper, causally more fundamental, level the harmony that looms so large in Bazelmans' holistic and idealist reconstruction of the world of Beowulf would seem to be an overstatement of historical reality. Honor, loyalty, and reciprocity are inextricably intertwined with free riding, egoism, and violence, and altruism is, ultimately, self-serving. Because culturalist interpretations operate with culturally specific native meanings and values, they fail to identify much of the ultimate causality that reaches beyond and below culturally specific life-world categories and even beyond the human species. In the end, the latter type of causality has explanatory priority.

It should not be forgotten that Marcel Mauss, upon whom Bazelmans and Hill build, himself saw reciprocal exchange as a *fait social total*, a *phénome de totalité* with many interconnected aspects—normative, economic, legal, biological, religious, and so on (Mauss 1990, 4). We "hardly ever find man divided into several faculties," he wrote in 1924 in his *Essai sur le don*; we "always come across the whole human body and mentality, given totally and at the same time, and basically, body, soul, society, everything is entangled here" (Mauss, 1995, 303). Mauss did not live up to this heuristic himself entirely, though, because of his dualistic view of humans.

"Societies have progressed," he argues in connection with exchange, "in so far as they themselves, their subgroups, and, lastly, the individuals in them, have succeeded in stabilizing relationships, giving, receiving, and finally, giving in return. To trade, the first condition was to be able to lay aside the spear. From then onward, they succeeded in exchanging goods and persons [...] Only then did people learn how to create mutual interests, giving mutual satisfaction, and, in the end, to defend themselves without having to resort to arms" (Mauss 1990, 82). In this way, by "opposing reason to emotion," a Hobbesian "natural state" (*état naturel*) of "war, isolation and stagnation" gives way to sociality as seen by Bazelmans and other Dumontians: a moral order of "alliances, gift and commerce" (Mauss 1990, 65).

Exchange pacifies, the Hobbesian war of all against all gives way to Maussian exchange of all with all, or, at least, many with many. This is a basic theme in Mauss' essay on the gift (Corbey 2006). Unfortunately, this sort of dualistic thinking is not just typical for an influential French and British, Maussian/neo-Durkheimian conception of the disciplinary identity of ethnology, but also for much of American cultural anthropology. A major intellectual root in both cases, explaining their convergence in this respect and contributing to the present humanities/science gap (Slingerland 2008), is nineteenth-century French and German neo-Kantianism, emphatically dualist and antinaturalist, and close to universally human folk perceptions (see Slingerland, this volume).

A culturalist *locus classicus* of the North-American Boasian *homo symbolicus* spirit, as antifunctionalist and as much of French *ethnologie*, is Sahlins's critique of (socio) biological approaches to human culture: "[While] the human world depends on [...] organic characteristics supplied by biological evolution...its freedom from biology consists in just the capacity to give these their own sense. [...] In the symbolic event, a radical discontinuity is introduced between culture and nature. [...] The symbolic system of culture is not just an expression of human nature, but [...] an invention in nature" (Sahlins 1976; in the same spirit, Sahlins 2008). Cases in point are the well-known controversies around, for example, the research of Margaret Mead in Samoa and Napoleon Chagnon in Amazonia, as well as discussions on the traditional "four fields" of anthropology since the early 1990s (Corbey 2005).

The intellectual background of Bazelmans is brought out clearly by the mission statement implied by the title of the *Revue du M.A.U.S.S.* of the French Maussians: "Revue du Mouvement Anti-Utilitariste en Sciences Sociales" (since 1981). In 2008, in line with this program, this periodical came up with a special entitled *Contr'Hobbes*, criticizing the "identification of life and nature with utility and functionality," deploring "the narrow rhetorics of suspicion which characterizes the gaze of science and of utilitarian dogmatism" and arguing for "the irreducibility of [...] sympathy or empathy to self-interest" (*Revue du Mauss* 2008, Introduction: 12, 26ff.).

CONCLUSION

We are well aware that what we engage in the foregoing tends toward what many biologists would frown upon as not very rigorous, "adaptationist storytelling," based on scarce and ambiguous, even fictitious, data. In most cases alternative or complementary explanations are possible. We probably analyze too readily and too broadly as if individuals would optimize their fitness continuously in all settings, including highly idiosyncratic ones, which is obviously not the level that evolutionary theory aims at. We also concede that we have left understudied adaptational aspects of the cultural traditions steering the behaviors we have looked at.

Yet we feel the point we aim at is germane: interpretive approaches to sociality and identity in *Beowulf* and, in particular, the real cultural world reflected by the poem are much too dualist and thus unrealistic, and can profit considerably from complementary evolutionary readings. This goes in particular for the ethnological analysis, in a Maussian vein, of how all sorts of exchanges are constitutive of social order and personal identity, in the Anglo-Saxon world and beyond. There is a deep irony in the fact that there are two longstanding, sophisticated, bodies of theory regarding cooperation and reciprocity—one Maussian, the other Darwinian—with so little mutual interaction, or even knowledge of the basics of the other angle.

In this chapter, we have updated Mauss's programmatic heuristic of *l'homme total* and exchange as "total social fact," taking this heuristic more seriously than the master himself and, in particular, his followers. The "fundamental motives for human action: emulation between individuals of the same sex, that <basic imperialism of human beings>" (Mauss 1990, 65), we have argued against Mauss, are *not* transcended to make sociality feasible as a presumedly harmonious moral order, beyond conflicts and tensions. The view of sociality, morality, and identity presented here is a much more Darwinian and, therefore, much more Hobbesian one. Beyond power? No!

ACKNOWLEDGMENTS

For their feedback we would like to thank, among many others, Claire El Mouden, Adam Jagich, and Michelle Scalise Sugiyama.

References

Alden Smith, Eric, Rebecca Bliege Bird, and Douglas W. Bird. 2003. The benefits of costly signaling: Meriam turtle hunters. *Behavioral Ecology* 14 (1): 116–126.

Barraud, Cécile, Daniel de Coppet, André Iteanu, and Raymond Jamous. 1994. *Of relations and the dead: Four societies viewed from the angle of their exchanges*. Oxford and Providence, RI: Berg.

Bazelmans, J. 1999. *By weapons made worthy: Lords, retainers and their relationship in beowulf*. Amsterdam: Amsterdam University Press.

Bazelmans, J. 2000. Beyond power. Ceremonial exchanges in Beowulf. In *Rituals of power from late antiquity tot the early middle ages*, ed. F. Theuws, and J. L. Nelson. Leiden: Brill.

Benario, Herbert W. 1999. *Tacitus: The Germany*. Warminster: Aris & Phillips.

Bliege Bird, Rebecca, Eric Alden Smith, and Douglas W. Bird. 2000. The hunting handicap: Costly signaling in human foraging strategies. *Behavioral Ecology and Sociobiology* 50: 9–19.

Borofsky, Robert. 2005. *Yanomami: The fierce controversy and what we can learn from it* Berkeley, CA: University of California Press .

Carrithers, Michael. 1996. Nature and culture. In *Encyclopedia of social and cultural anthropology*, eds. A. Barnard, and J. Spencer. London and New York: Routledge.

Chickering, Howell D. Jr. 2006. Beowulf: *A dual-language edition*. New York: Anchor Books.

Cooke, Brett, and Frederick Turner, eds. 1999. *Biopoetics: Evolutionary explorations in the arts*. Bridgeport, CT: ICUS.

Corbey, Raymond. 2005. *The metaphysics of apes: Negotiating the animal-human boundary*. Cambridge and New York: Cambridge University Press.

Corbey, Raymond. 2006. Laying aside the spear: Hobbesian war and the Maussian gift. In *Warfare and society: Archaeological and social anthropological perspectives*, ed. T. Otto, H. Thrane & H. Vandkilde, pp. 29–36. Aarhus: Aarhus University Press.

Flesch, William. 2007. *Comeuppance: Costly signalling, altruistic punishment and other biological components of fiction*. Cambridge, MA and London: Harvard University Press.

Gintis, Herbert, Samuel Bowles, Robert Boyd, and Ernst Fehr, eds. 2005. *Moral sentiments and material interests: The foundations of cooperation in economic life*. Cambridge, MA: MIT Press.

Grafen, Alan. 1990. Biological signals as handicaps. *Journal of Theoretical Biology* 144 (4): 517–546.

Grafen, Alan. 1990. Sexual selection unhandicapped by the fisher process. *Journal of Theoretical Biology* 144(4): 473–516.

Gwara, Scott. 2008. *Heroic identity in the world of* Beowulf. Vol. 2, *Medieval and Renaissance Authors and Texts*. Leiden: Brill.

Hamilton, William D. 1964. The genetical evolution of social behaviour: I, ii. *Journal of Theoretical Biology* 7: 1–16 and 17–52.

Henrich, Joseph, and Robert Boyd. 2001. Why people punish defectors: Weak conformist transmission can stabilize costly enforcement of norms in cooperative dilemmas. *Journal of Theoretical Biology* 208 (1): 79–89.

Hildebrandt, William R., and Kelly R. McGuire. 2002. The ascendance of hunting during the California middle archaic: An evolutionary perspective. *American Antiquity* 67 (2): 231–256.

Hill, John M. 1995. *The cultural world in* Beowulf. Toronto: University of Toronto Press.

Hill, John M. 1997. The social milieu in *Beowulf*. In *A* Beowulf *handbook*, ed. R. E. Bjork, and J. D. Niles. Lincoln: University of Nebraska Press.

Hill, John M. 2007. Current general trends in Beowulf studies. *Literature Compass* 4 (1): 66–88.

Hill, John M. 2008. *The narrative pulse of* Beowulf: *Arrivals and departures*. Toronto, Buffalo, and London: The University of Toronto Press.

Mauss, Marcel. 1995. *Sociologie et anthropologie*. Paris: PUF.

Mauss, Marcel. 1990. *The gift: The form and reason for exchange in archaic societies*. Transl. W. D. Halls. London and New York: Routledge.

Orchard, Andy. 2003. *A critical companion to* Beowulf. Woodbridge, UK: D.S. Brewer.

Owen-Crocker, Gale R. 2000. *The four funerals in* Beowulf: *And the structure of the poem*. Manchester, UK: Manchester University Press.

Sahlins, Marshall. 1976. *The use and abuse of biology: An anthropological critique of sociobiology.* Ann Arbor, MI: University of Michigan Press.

Sahlins, Marshall. 2008. *The western illusion of human nature.* Chicago: Prickly Paradigm Press.

Slingerland, Edward. 2008. *What science offers the humanities: Integrating body and culture.* Cambridge, UK: Cambridge University Press.

Spence, Michael. 1973. Job market signaling. *The Quarterly Journal of Economics* 97 (3): 355–374.

Tinbergen, Nikolaas. 1963. On aims and methods of ethology. *Zeitschrift für Tierpsychologie* 20: 410–433.

Tooby, John, and Leda Cosmides. 1992. The psychological foundations of culture. In *The adapted mind: Evolutionary psychology and the generation of culture*, ed. J. H. Barkow, L. Cosmides, and J. Tooby. New York, NY: Oxford University Press.

Trivers, Robert L. 1971. The evolution of reciprocal altruism. *The Quarterly Review of Biology* 46(1): 35.

Veblen, Thorstein. 2007. *The theory of the leisure class.* Oxford, UK: Oxford University Press.

West, S. A., A. S. Griffin, and A. Gardner. 2007. Social semantics: Altruism, cooperation, mutualism, strong reciprocity and group selection. *Journal of Evolutionary Biology* 20(2): 415–432.

Zahavi, Amotz, and Avishag Zahavi. 1997. *The handicap principle: A missing piece of Darwin's puzzle.* New York and Oxford, UK: Oxford University Press.

21

PALAEOLITHIC POLITICS IN BRITISH NOVELS OF THE NINETEENTH CENTURY

Joseph Carroll, Jonathan Gottschall,
John A. Johnson, and Daniel Kruger

MOVING PAST THE TWO CULTURES

Scientists typically operate by formulating testable hypotheses and producing data to test the hypotheses. Students of literature, in contrast, usually proceed by way of argument and rhetoric. In their most scholarly guise, they aim at producing objective textual and historical information, but all such information must ultimately be interpreted within some larger order of ideas. During the first two-thirds of the twentieth century, the most prominent theoretical systems taken from outside the humanities and used for literary study were Marxist social theory, Freudian and Jungian psychology, and structuralist linguistics. Even in their own fields, these systems were only quasi-scientific, more speculative than empirical, and in literary study, they served chiefly as sources for imaginative stimulation. Most critics operated as eclectic free agents, gleaning materials from every region of knowledge—from philosophy, the sciences, history, the arts, and especially from literature itself. Though using selected bits of information from the sciences, students of literature commonly regarded their own kind of knowledge—imaginative, subjective, and qualitative—as an autonomous order of discourse incommensurate with the quantitative reductions of science.

Over the past three decades or so, these older forms of literary criticism have been superseded by a new theoretical paradigm designated variously as poststructuralism or postmodernism. The new paradigm incorporates psychoanalysis and Marxism in their Lacanian and Althusserian forms, but poststructuralists explicitly reject the idea that scientific methods secure the highest standard of epistemic validity. Instead, they include science itself within the rhetorical domain formerly set aside as the province of the humanities. As Stanley Aronowitz puts it, science "is no more, but certainly no less, than any other discourse. It is one story among many stories" (Aronowitz 1996, 192). Within the postmodern frame of thinking, it is not permissible to say that a given scientific idea is "true" or that it "corresponds" closely to a "reality" that exists independently of the human mind. Consider, for instance, Gowan Dawson's commentary on efforts to integrate evolutionary psychology with studies in the humanities. As Dawson rightly observes, by adopting a "realist" or "objectivist" approach to science, literary Darwinism "undermines the entire premise of recent literature and science studies" (Dawson 2006, 306).

In his own work and that of his postmodern colleagues, Dawson explains, formulations implying that science constitutes an "intellectually authoritative mode of knowledge" have "long been proscribed" (Dawson 2006, 306, 308).[1]

As literary culture has been moving steadily further away from the canons of empirical inquiry, the sciences have been approaching ever closer to a commanding and detailed knowledge of the subjects most germane to literary culture: human motives, human feelings, and the operations of the human mind (See Barrett, Dunbar, and Lycett 2002; Buss 2005; Buss 2007; Carroll 2008, 111–115; Carroll 2005; Dunbar and Barrett 2007; Gangestad and Simpson 2007). Evolutionary psychology and affective neuroscience have been penetrating the inner sanctum of the "qualitative" and making it accessible to precise empirical knowledge (see Damasio 1994; Davidson, Scherer, and Goldsmith 2003; Ekman 2003; Lewis and Haviland-Jones 2000; McEwan 2005; Panksepp 1998; Plutchik 2003; Tanaka 2010). Since the early 1990s, some few literary scholars have been assimilating the insights of evolutionary social science and envisioning radical changes in the conceptual foundations of literary study. These "literary Darwinists" have produced numerous theoretical and interpretive essays.[2] Until recently, though, most literary Darwinists have remained within the methodological boundaries of traditional humanistic scholarship. Their work has been speculative, discursive, and rhetorical. They have drawn on empirical research but have not, for the most part, adopted empirical methods. Instead, they have used Darwinian theory as a source of theoretical and interpretive concepts. With respect to method, then, their work is similar to that of old-fashioned Marxist and Freudian literary scholars.[3]

In the project we describe here, we aimed at moving past the barrier that separates the methods of the humanities from the methods of the social sciences. Building on research in evolutionary social science, we aimed to (1) construct a model of human nature—of motives, emotions, features of personality, and preferences in marital partners; (2) use that model to analyze some specific body of literary texts and the responses of readers to those texts, and (3) produce data that could be quantified and used to test specific hypotheses about those texts.

PROJECT DESIGN

We created an online questionnaire and listed approximately 2,000 characters from 201 canonical British novels of the nineteenth and early twentieth centuries (Austen to Forster). Using e-mail, we asked hundreds of scholars specializing in the novel to participate in the

1. For other postmodern commentaries on science, see Feyerabend 1987; Latour 1979; Levine 1987; Peterfreund 1990; Rorty 1982; Smith 2006; Woolgar 1988. For critiques of postmodern conceptions of science, see Boghossian 2006; J. Brown 2001; Gross and Levitt 1994; Gross, Levitt, and Lewis 1997; Koertge 1998; Sokal and Bricmont 1998; Weinberg 2001; E. Wilson 1998.

2. See for instance Boyd 2009; Boyd, Carroll, and Gottschall 2010; Carroll 2004; Cooke 2002; Gottschall and Wilson 2005; Fromm 2009; Nordlund 2007. For surveys of this work, see Carroll 2008; Carroll 2010b.

3. For arguments on using empirical methods to renovate literary study, see Gottschall 2008. For examples of evolutionary literary study by both humanists and scientists, see Andrews and Carroll 2010; Boyd, Carroll, and Gottschall 2010; Gottschall and Wilson 2005.

study. We also solicited participation from members of Web-based organizations devoted to nineteenth century literature (Victorian Literature on the Web, The Dickens Society, The Brontë Society, etc.). The pool of potential respondents thus consisted of people particularly interested in canonical British novels of the nineteenth century. We invited these potential respondents to visit our web site and fill out as many questionnaires as they liked. Each questionnaire ("protocol") was devoted to a single character. Respondents selected a character from the list and answered a series of questions about that character. Approximately 519 respondents completed a total of 1,470 protocols on 435 separate characters.[4]

The questionnaire contains three sets of categories. One set comprises elements of personal identity: age, attractiveness, motives, the criteria of mate selection, and personality. (The sex of the characters was a given.) The second has to do with readers' emotional responses to characters. We listed 10 possible emotional responses and asked readers to rate the intensity of their response on each of the ten emotions. The third set focuses on four "agonistic" role assignments: (1) protagonists, (2) friends and associates of protagonists, (3) antagonists, and (4) friends and associates of antagonists. Dividing the agonistic characters into males and females produced a total of eight character sets. We conducted statistical tests to determine which scores on various categories differed significantly among the character sets. The patterned contrast between protagonists and antagonists is a contrast between desirable and undesirable traits in characters—a contrast we reference as "agonistic structure." We also calculated degrees of correlation among the various categories of analysis: motives, criteria for selecting mates, personality factors, and the emotional responses of readers.[5]

TESTING A HYPOTHESIS

The questionnaire we used to collect data is couched in everyday language and pitched at the level of everyday understanding, but it is also formulated within the framework of an evolutionary model of human nature. The questions we pose are thus situated at the point at which the evolutionary model converges with the everyday understanding. The questions register the everyday understanding, quantify it, and locate it within the context of empirical social science. Quantification enables us to give an objective, formal analysis of everyday understanding and to assess statistically the structural relations among its conceptual elements. A major goal of our study was simply to demonstrate that major features of literary meaning can be effectively reduced to simple categories grounded in an evolutionary understanding of human nature.

Generating empirical knowledge in this way has an intrinsic value, but empirical findings clearly gain in value when they are brought to bear as evidence for specific hypotheses about important problems. Perhaps the most important problem in evolutionary literary study concerns the adaptive functions of literature and other arts—whether there are any adaptive functions, and if so, what they might be. Steven Pinker has suggested that

4. A copy of the questionnaire used in the study can be accessed at http://www-personal.umich.edu/~kruger/carroll-survey.html.

5. For more technical statistical details on the project, and more background bibliography, see Johnson, Carroll, Gottschall, and Kruger 2008; Johnson, Carroll, Gottschall, and Kruger 2011.

aesthetic responsiveness is merely a side effect of cognitive powers that evolved to fulfill more practical functions (Pinker 1997, 524–43), but Pinker also suggests that narratives can provide information for adaptively relevant problems—an idea also championed by Michelle Scalise Sugiyama (2005). Geoffrey Miller (2000) argues that artistic productions serve as forms of sexual display. Brian Boyd (2009) argues that the arts are forms of cognitive "play" that enhance pattern recognition. Boyd and Ellen Dissanayake also argue that the arts provide means of creating shared social identity. In company with Dissanayake (2000), E. O. Wilson (1998), Tooby and Cosmides (2001), Salmon and Symons (2004), Carroll (2008), and Dutton (2009) all argue that the arts create "meaning." They provide imaginative structures that give emotionally and aesthetically modulated form to the relations among all the features of our lives—natural, supernatural, individual, and social. The hypothesis of "meaning" subsumes the ideas that the arts provide adaptively relevant information, enable us to consider alternative behavioral scenarios, enhance pattern recognition, and serve as means for creating shared social identity. And of course, the arts can be used for sexual display. In that respect, the arts are like most other human products—clothing, jewelry, shelter, means of transportation, etc. The hypothesis that the arts create meaning is not incompatible with the hypothesis of sexual display, but it subordinates sexual display to a more primary adaptive function.

In this current study, our central hypothesis was that protagonists and their associates would form communities of cooperative endeavor and that antagonists would exemplify dominance behavior. If this hypothesis proved correct, the ethos reflected in the agonistic structure of the novels would replicate the egalitarian ethos of hunter-gatherers, who stigmatize and suppress status seeking in potentially dominant individuals (Boehm 1999). Hunter-gatherers use spoken language to enforce an egalitarian ethos. Written narratives are, of course, merely a cultural technology extending the usages of spoken language. In hunter-gatherer cultures, language as a medium for articulating a social ethos is restricted to face-to-face interactions. In a literate culture, authors and readers who have never met can form communities of shared values through the medium of written narratives. We hypothesized that, on the average, protagonists, in their motives and personality traits, would reflect values the authors approve and that they expect their readers to approve. Antagonists would reflect values authors and their readers do not approve. Approval and disapproval would be registered in the emotional responses of our respondents.

A basic working hypothesis in our study was that the novels do, in fact, form a medium of shared values. The validity of this hypothesis could be assessed through the degree to which respondents converged in identifying the traits of characters and responding to those traits in emotionally negative or positive ways. Our respondents produced an extremely high level of "intercoder reliability." That is, they converged to a high degree in assigning scores to characters, in assigning characters to agonistic roles, and in rating their emotional responses to the characters. (For characters who received dozens of codings—for instance, Elizabeth Bennett of *Pride and Prejudice* and the eponymous Jane Eyre—"alpha" reliability scores registered in the high 90s.)

Twelve motives, five personality traits, seven criteria for selecting mates, and ten basic emotions produced a vast number of possible combinations. Focusing on the contrast between protagonists and antagonists made it possible to determine whether this array of potential value structures could be understood as an opposition between "good" and "bad" characteristics.[6]

How does all this bear on the question of the adaptive function of literature and the other arts? Our results converge on one chief adaptive characteristic: the evolved human disposition for suppressing dominance and enforcing an egalitarian, communitarian ethos. If suppressing dominance in hunter-gatherers fulfills an adaptive social function—facilitating cooperative social action—and if agonistic structure in the novels engages the same social dispositions that animate hunter-gatherers, the novels would, as a literate cultural technology, fulfill the same adaptive function that is fulfilled through face-to-face interaction in nonliterate cultures.

Assuming we can make the case that agonistic structure in the novels displays an ethos stigmatizing dominance behavior and promoting cooperative, prosocial behavior, how far can we generalize from that finding to all literature, in every period and every culture? Logically, it is possible that no other literary texts anywhere in the world display highly polarized differences between protagonists and antagonists or fulfill any adaptive function at all. Hypothetically possible, but not very likely. If our arguments hold good for this body of texts, they demonstrate that at least one important body of fictional narratives fulfills at least one adaptive function. It seems unlikely that, in this important respect, this body of novels is wholly anomalous.

In arguing that agonistic structure in these novels fulfills an adaptive social function, we do not suppose that we have isolated the sole adaptive function of all literature and its oral antecedents. Quite the contrary. Along with other evolutionary literary theorists, we strongly suspect that literature and its oral antecedents fulfill other functions. We argue that the social dynamics animating these novels derive from ancient, basic features of human nature. Such features would in all likelihood appear in some fictional narratives in most or all cultures. We would, of course, be interested to know whether the kind of agonistic structure we identify in these novels is in fact a human universal. If it is a human universal, we would also be interested to know how it varies in form in different cultural ecologies. (Marriage is a human universal but varies in form from culture to culture. We might expect agonistic structure, like marriage, to vary in form.) These questions would make good topics of research for other studies. Until those studies are conducted, though, the topics are only a matter for theoretical speculation. For this current study, we can positively affirm only the conclusions we think our data allow us to draw. Hence, the limiting terms in our title: paleolithic politics in British novels of the nineteenth century.

HUMAN LIFE HISTORY

All species have a life history, a species-typical pattern for birth, growth, reproduction, social relations (if the species is social), and death (Hill 2007; Kaplan et al. 2000; Low 2000). For each species, the pattern of life history forms a reproductive cycle. In the case of humans, that cycle centers on parents, children, and the social group. Successful parental care produces children capable, when grown, of forming adult pair bonds,

---

6. On the universality of polarized emotional responses, see Saucier, Georgiades, Tsaousis, and Goldberg 2005; Saucier and Goldberg 2001.

becoming functioning members of a community, and caring for children of their own. "Human nature" is the set of species-typical characteristics that form the human reproductive cycle.

The four main categories of analysis in this study are all conceived as elements in an evolutionary understanding of human life history. Attributes of characters include three of the categories: motives, the criteria for selecting mates, and the five factors of personality. Emotional responses are the fourth, and in this study are used to register the correlations between character attributes and the responses of readers. Motives are the basis for action in human life. Selecting a sexual or marital partner drives reproductive success and evokes, accordingly, exceptionally strong feelings. In the majority of the novels in this study, selecting a marital partner is the central concern of the plot. Marriage in these novels takes forms specific to the period and culture, of course, but some form of marriage is recognized in every known culture (D. Brown 1991; Symons 1979). Even a quick glance over collections of tales and stories from every period and every culture will confirm that stories involving problems of mating bulk large in every culture. Given the centrality of marriage to problems of human reproduction, that is hardly surprising. Nor is it surprising that evolutionary literary studies of works from widely diverse cultures have given concentrated attention to problems of selecting mates.[7] Selecting a mate is a primary plot concern in these novels, as it is in narratives from other cultures, but selecting mates is only one of several specific motives about which we ask questions. We ask questions, also, about motives oriented to survival, parenting, engaging in social life, gaining an education, and pursuing a vocation. All choices that humans make with regard to motives reflect their individual personalities. And indeed, personality traits can be trenchantly defined as dispositions to act on motives. These dispositions are themselves human universals, but individuals vary considerably in their scores on specific traits—on pleasure seeking, for instance, or sensitivity to pain (Nettle 2007). Personality traits are primary constituents of individual identity. They are more basic and more comprehensive than the factors of social identity that shape "identity politics." Emotions are the proximal mechanisms that activate motives and guide our social judgments, including our judgments of imaginary people (Ekman 2003; Plutchik 2003).

GETTING MOTIVATED

For the purposes of this study, we reduced human life history to a set of 12 basic motives—that is, goal-oriented behaviors regulated by the reproductive cycle. For survival, we included two motives: survival itself (fending off immediate threats to life) and performing routine work to earn a living. We also asked questions about the importance of acquiring wealth, power, and prestige. We asked respondents to rate characters on how important acquiring a mate was to them in both the short term and the long term. In the

---

7. Cultures studied by literary Darwinists and giving concentrated attention to problems of mating include ancient Greece (Boyd 2009; Gottschall 2008; Scalise Sugiyama 2001), medieval Japan (Thiessen and Umezawa 1998), Elizabethan England (Carroll 2010a; Nordlund 2007; Scalise Sugiyama 2003), America in the nineteenth century (Love 2003), America in the early twentieth century (Saunders 2009), and Soviet Russia (Cooke 2002).

context of these novels, short-term would mean flirtation or illicit sexual activity; long-term would mean seeking a marital partner. (For the great bulk of the novels in this period, illicit sexual activity is not a main subject. In this summation of main results, we do not display results for short-term mating.) Taking account of "reproduction" in its wider significance of replicating genes one shares with kin ("inclusive fitness"), we asked about the importance of helping offspring and other kin. For motives oriented to positive social relations beyond one's own kin, we included a question on "acquiring friends and making alliances" and another on "helping non-kin." To capture the uniquely human dispositions for acquiring culture, we included "seeking education or culture" and "building, creating, or discovering something."

"Factor analysis" is a statistical process in which variables that correlate with one another are grouped together to form a smaller number of metavariables designated "factors." When we submitted scores on the 12 separate motives to factor analysis, five main factors emerged. We refer to these as Social Dominance, Constructive Effort, Romance, Subsistence, and Nurture. Seeking wealth, power, and prestige all have strong positive loadings on Social Dominance, and helping nonkin has a moderate negative loading. (That is, helping nonkin is inversely related to seeking wealth, power, and prestige.) Two cultural and two prosocial motives load on Constructive Effort: seeking education or culture; creating, discovering, or building something; making friends and alliances; and helping nonkin. Short-term and long-term mating load on Romance. Survival and performing routine tasks to gain a livelihood load on Subsistence. Nurturing/fostering offspring or other kin loads most heavily on Nurture, and that motive correlates negatively with short-term mating. Helping nonkin also loads moderately on this factor, bringing affiliative kin-related behavior into association with generally affiliative social behavior.

Male and female antagonists both display a pronounced preoccupation with Social Dominance (Figure 1). Male protagonists score higher than any other character set on Constructive Effort and on Subsistence. Female protagonists score higher than any other character set on Romance, but their positive motives are fairly evenly balanced among Constructive Effort, Romance, and Nurture. In these novels, female protagonists are largely restricted to the reproductive age range. That restriction corresponds with a pronounced emphasis on Romance as a motive.

The opposition between dominance and affiliation in the novels is consistent with a robust and often replicated finding in psychological studies of motives and personality. Summarizing research into basic motives, Buss observes that, in cross-cultural studies, the two most important dimensions of interpersonal behavior are power and love (Buss 1995, 21). Surveying the same field and citing still other antecedents, Paulhus and John (1998) observe that in debates about "the number of important human values," there are two, above all, that are "never overlooked" (1039). They designate these values "agency and communion" and associate them with contrasting needs: the need for "power and status" on the one side and for "approval" on the other (1045).

Paulhus and John link the contrasting needs for power and approval with contrasting forms of bias in self-perception. "Egoistic" bias attributes exaggerated "prominence and status" to oneself, and "moralistic" bias gives an exaggerated picture of oneself as a "'nice person'" and "'a good citizen'" (1045–1046). Adopting these terms, we can say that the novels in this study, taken collectively, have a moralistic bias. In protagonists,

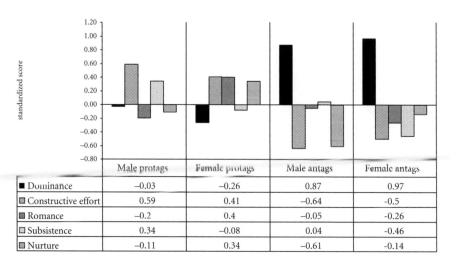

standardized score	Male protags	Female protags	Male antags	Female antags
■ Dominance	−0.03	−0.26	0.87	0.97
▨ Constructive effort	0.59	0.41	−0.64	-0.5
■ Romance	−0.2	0.4	−0.05	-0.26
▢ Subsistence	0.34	−0.08	0.04	-0.46
▣ Nurture	−0.11	0.34	−0.61	-0.14

FIGURE 1 Motive Factors in Protagonists and Antagonists.

striving for personal predominance is strongly subordinated to communitarian values. Protagonists and their friends typically form communities of affiliative and cooperative behavior, and antagonists are typically envisioned as a force of social domination that threatens the very principle of community.

Most of the novels included in this study are "classics." It seems likely that one reason novels become classics is that they gain access to the deepest levels of human nature—not necessarily because they produce in every case mimetically accurate representations of human nature, but because they evoke elemental human passions and deploy elemental forms of imaginative organization. The novels contain a vast fund of realistic social depiction and profound psychological analysis. In their larger imaginative structures, though, the novels evidently do not just represent human nature; they embody the impulses of human nature. Those impulses include a need to derogate dominance in others and to affirm one's identity as a member of a social group. Our evidence strongly suggests that those needs provide the emotional and imaginative force that shapes agonistic structure in the novels.

The novels create a virtual imaginative world designed to give concentrated emotional force to the opposition between dominance and affiliation. That imaginative virtual world provides a medium in which readers participate in a shared social ethos. The social ethos shapes agonistic structure, and agonistic structure, in turn, feeds back into the social ethos, affirming it, reinforcing it, integrating it with the changing circumstances of material and social life, and illuminating it with the aesthetic, intellectual, and moral powers of individual artists. If Boehm and others are correct that human social life is structured at a basic level by an interplay between dominance and affiliation, images of dominant and prosocial individuals would form part of the imaginative repertory common to the human species. Depictions of dominant and prosocial individuals in narratives expand the range, force, and particularity of such images available to readers. Even in a highly mobile, modern culture, the number of individuals with which any one person can interact on a regular basis is fairly restricted.

Narratives vastly increase the number and quality of social images available to every reader. In these novels, the features of characters have evidently been selected and organized in such a way that they make dominance and affiliation salient factors. Moreover, the characters are presented with all the vividness and power of the novelists' imagination. Almost by definition, a novelist's ability to imagine the mental and emotional life of characters is more vivid and more penetrating than that of the average person. Because of their exceptional talent and skill, novelists can make a profession out of depicting the personalities and the emotional lives of their characters. By reading the novels in this study, readers thus receive highly concentrated, condensed images of dominance and affiliation. Those images form an active part of the total cultural ethos shared by the community of authors and readers.

CHOOSING A PARTNER

Most of the novels in this study are love stories. Plots usually involve individuals choosing a marital partner. Along with questions about motives, we asked questions about the criteria characters used in selecting mates. Evolutionary psychologists have identified mating preferences that males and females share and also preferences in which they differ (Geary 1998; Kruger, Fisher, and Jobling 2003). Males and females both value kindness, intelligence, and reliability in mates (Buss 2003). Males preferentially value physical attractiveness, and females preferentially value wealth, prestige, and power (Buss, 2003; Gangestad 2007; Geary 1998; Schmitt 2005; Symons 1979). These sex-specific preferences are rooted in the logic of reproduction. Physical attractiveness in females correlates with youth and health in a woman, hence with reproductive potential. Wealth, power, and prestige enable a male to provide for a mate and her offspring. We anticipated that scores for mate selection would correspond to the differences between males and females found in studies of mate selection in the real world. We also anticipated that protagonists would give stronger preference to intelligence, kindness, and reliability than antagonists would.

In the results of the factor analyses for mate selection, the loadings divide with the sharpest possible clarity into three distinct factors. We call these Extrinsic Attributes (a desire for wealth, power, and prestige in a mate), Intrinsic Qualities (a desire for kindness, reliability, and intelligence in a mate), and Physical Attractiveness (that one criterion by itself).

Female protagonists and antagonists both give a stronger preference to Extrinsic Attributes—wealth, power, and prestige—than male protagonists or antagonists, but female antagonists exaggerate the female tendency toward preferring Extrinsic Attributes (Figure 2). The emphasis female antagonists give to Extrinsic Attributes parallels their single-minded pursuit of Social Dominance. Female protagonists give a more marked preference to Intrinsic Qualities—intelligence, kindness, and reliability—than male protagonists.

We did not anticipate that male protagonists would be so strongly preoccupied with Physical Attractiveness relative to other qualities, nor did we anticipate that male antagonists would be so relatively indifferent to Physical Attractiveness. The inference we draw from these findings is that the male desire for physical beauty in mates is part of the ethos the novels. Male sexuality is not demonized or stigmatized. Male antagonists' relative

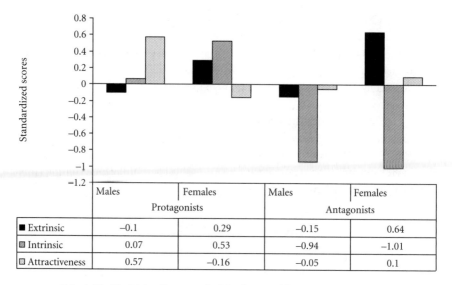

	Males	Females	Males	Females
		Protagonists		Antagonists
■ Extrinsic	−0.1	0.29	−0.15	0.64
▨ Intrinsic	0.07	0.53	−0.94	−1.01
▨ Attractiveness	0.57	−0.16	−0.05	0.1

FIGURE 2 Criteria Used by Major Characters for Selecting Martial Partners.

Indifference to Physical Attractiveness seems part of their general indifference to the quality of their personal relations.

If one were to look only at the motive factors, one might conclude that male antagonists correspond more closely to their gender norms than female antagonists do. Male antagonists are personifications of male dominance striving. The relative indifference male antagonists feel toward any differentiating features in mates might then look like an exaggeration of the male tendency toward interpersonal insensitivity (Baron-Cohen 2004; Blum 1997; Geary 1998; Moir and Jessel 1991). Conceived in this way, male antagonists would appear to be ultramale, and female antagonists, in contrast, would seem to cross a gender divide. Their reduction to dominance striving would be symptomatic of a certain masculinization of motive and temperament. They would be, in an important sense, de-sexed. Plausible as this line of interpretation might seem, it will not bear up under the weight of the evidence about male antagonists' relative indifference to Physical Attractiveness in a mate. Like female antagonistic dominance striving, that, also, is a form of de-sexing. Dominance striving devoid of all affiliative disposition constitutes a reduction to sex-neutral egoism. The essential character of male and female antagonists is thus not a tendency toward masculinization. Antagonists are sexually neutered egos isolated from all social bonds.

COMPARING MALE AND FEMALE CHARACTERS BY MALE AND FEMALE AUTHORS

In the total set of 435 characters, characters by male authors outnumber characters by female authors by nearly two to one (281 vs. 154). Nonetheless, because a greater percentage of characters by female authors are major females (protagonists or antagonists), 47 percent of the major females in the whole data set are from novels by female authors (45 percent of female protagonists and 52 percent of female antagonists). Female authors contribute close to half of all major females (47 percent), of all good females (protagonists and their associates, 47 percent), and of all minor females (associates of both protagonists and antagonists, 45 percent).

In order to determine whether the sex of the author significantly influenced the depiction of sex-specific features in the characters, we compared the depiction of male and female characters by male and female authors. Male and female authors converge in most of the ways they describe similarities and differences between male and female characters. (We found one statistically significant difference in criteria for selecting a partner for short-term mating.) However, they also display biases. Though falling short of statistical significance, those biases tend in a clearly discernible direction. Both male and female authors tend to mute differences between their male and female characters. Male and female characters by male authors tend to resemble one another, and male and female characters by female authors tend to resemble one another. Male characters by female authors tend to look more like females. Female characters by male authors tend to look more like males. Male and female authors concur more closely in the depictions of motives in female characters than in the depictions of motives in male characters. That is, male characters by female authors look more like female characters than female characters by male authors look like male characters.

When we compare male and female characters by male and female authors in the major character sets (protagonists and antagonists), three features reach statistical significance. Male protagonists by female authors score significantly lower on valuing Extrinsic Attributes in a mate (wealth, power, and prestige). Male protagonists by female authors score significantly higher on Nurture. Female protagonists by female authors score significantly higher on Constructive Effort.

With respect to seeking Extrinsic Attributes in a long-term mate, male protagonists by female authors are less demanding than male protagonists by male authors. This result is a specific instance of a general tendency: compared to authors of the other sex, authors of each sex tend to depict characters of the sex different from the author as less demanding in selecting mates.

In novels by female novelists, male protagonists are more domestic (more nurturing), and female protagonists occupy a more prominent place in the public sphere to which Constructive Effort gives access. In novels by female authors, then, the difference in male and female sociosexual roles—relative to the difference in novels by male authors—is diminished from both directions: by differences in male motives and by differences in female motives.

The constituent elements of Constructive Effort are seeking education or culture; creating, building, or discovering something; making friends and forming alliances; and helping nonkin. Female protagonists by female authors score higher than female protagonists by male authors on making friends, seeking education, and helping nonkin. Out of all 12 motives that enter into the motive factors, the one motive with the largest difference for female protagonists by male and female authors is seeking "prestige." Across the whole set of 435 characters, prestige loads very strongly on the motive factor Social Dominance, where it clusters with seeking wealth and power. For female protagonists by female authors, in contrast, prestige separates out from the pursuit of wealth and power and clusters instead with the elements of Constructive Effort.

Characters with motivational profiles like those of female protagonists by female authors would scarcely be contented with purely domestic social roles. They want more education, a more active life in the public sphere, and greater public standing. In the advanced industrial nations, the social roles of women have, of course, changed dramatically in the past one hundred years. The depictions of female protagonists by female authors give evidence of the undercurrents that ultimately helped to produce these changes. Male authors also contribute to this movement—female protagonists by male authors score moderately high on Constructive Effort—but female authors clearly take the lead.

Despite differences in cross-sexed depictions—male characters by female authors and female characters by male authors—male and female authors fundamentally concur on the motivational tendencies that distinguish male and female characters. In novels by both male and female authors, male characters score higher than female characters on Constructive Effort and Subsistence, and they score lower than female characters on Nurture. In novels by both male and female authors, male characters choosing long-term mates score higher than female characters on preferring Physical Attractiveness, and they score lower than female characters on preferring Intrinsic Qualities and Extrinsic Attributes. In all these factors, it is only the magnitude of the differences that vary in male and female characters by male and female authors, and the magnitude of that difference reaches statistical significance in none of the factors.

Besides motives and mate selection, the one largest category of analysis for the content of character, in this study, is personality. With respect to personality factors, male and female characters by male and female authors score virtually the same. (The differences in their scores range between 0 and 0.2.)

DEVELOPING A PERSONALITY

When we speak of "human nature," we focus first of all on "human universals," on cognitive and behavioral features that everyone shares. We typically use personality, in contrast, to distinguish one person from another—for example, a friendly, careless extravert in contrast to a cold, conscientious introvert. The factors of personality can nonetheless themselves be conceived as stable, shared components of human nature. Each factor has a common substratum; individuals differ only in degree on each factor.

Current research into personality commonly distinguishes five broad factors (Buss 1996; Costa and McCrae 1997; MacDonald 1998; Nettle 2007; Smits and Boeck 2006). Extraversion signals assertive, exuberant activity in the social world versus a tendency to be quiet, withdrawn and disengaged. Agreeableness signals a pleasant, friendly disposition and a tendency to cooperate and compromise, versus a tendency to be self-centered and inconsiderate. Conscientiousness refers to an inclination toward purposeful planning, organization, persistence, and reliability, versus impulsivity, aimlessness, laziness, and undependability. Emotional Stability reflects a temperament that is calm and relatively free from negative feelings, versus a temperament marked by extreme emotional reactivity and persistent anxiety, anger, or depression. Openness to Experience describes a dimension of personality that distinguishes "open" (imaginative, intellectual, creative, complex) people from "closed" (down-to-earth, uncouth, conventional, simple) people.[8]

Personality gives us access to the deepest levels of personal identity. Strip away the now-standard triad of race, class, and sex, and what is left? More than has been taken away. Beneath ethnic and class identity, beneath even the two basic human morphs of male and female, there are elemental features of human nature, the bedrock of personal identity. The composition of that bedrock can be assessed with the five factors of personality: the biologically elemental interaction between an organism and its environment; the capacity of all higher organisms to feel pain and react against it; the disposition of all mammals for affiliative bonding; and the specifically human capacities for organizing behavior over time, carrying out plans, and generating imaginative culture. Since all these factors express themselves somewhat differently in different cultural contexts and in different situations for individual persons, evolutionary cultural critique should aim not just at identifying human universals in any given cultural context; it should aim at uncovering the interaction between elemental dispositions and the specific individual and cultural contexts in which those dispositions manifest themselves.

We predicted (1) that protagonists and their friends would, on average, score higher on the personality factor Agreeableness, a measure of warmth and affiliation; and (2) that protagonists would score higher than antagonists and minor characters on the personality factor Openness to Experience, a measure of intellectual vivacity.

Female protagonists score higher than any other set on Agreeableness, Conscientiousness, and Openness, and they score in the positive range on Stability (Figure 3). Male protagonists look like muted or moderated versions of the female protagonists. The personality profiles of male and female antagonists are similar to one another—both somewhat extraverted, highly disagreeable, and low in Stability and Openness. Female antagonists are somewhat more conscientious than male antagonists.

In the value structures implicit in the organization of characters in agonistic structure, Introversion, Agreeableness, Conscientiousness, Stability, and Openness are all positively valenced features. Agreeableness is the most strongly marked part of this array. Being agreeable is a trait that distinguishes good characters generally, but being conscientious and open to experience are more specifically characteristic of protagonists. With respect to personality, female protagonists are clearly the normative character set.

The value system embodied in agonistic structure links a volatile temperament with relatively weak self-discipline and a bad temper. Openness would be associated with the desire for education or culture and with the desire to build, discover, or create, and that whole complex of cognitive features is one of the two basic elements in Constructive Effort. As one would anticipate, then, Openness correlates with Constructive Effort ($r = .41$). The total profile for protagonists is that of quiet, steady people, curious and alert but not aggressive, friendly but not particularly outgoing. The antagonists, in contrast, are assertive, volatile, and unreliable, but also intellectually or imaginatively dull and conventional. The main

---

8. For commentaries on the cultural variability of the factors, see Saucier 2003; Saucier, Hampson, and Goldberg 2000; Saucier, Georgiades, Tsaousis, and Goldberg 2005; Zhou, Saucier, Gao, and Liu 2009.

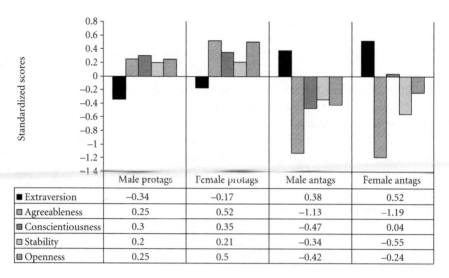

	Male protags	Female protags	Male antags	Female antags
■ Extraversion	−0.34	−0.17	0.38	0.52
▨ Agreeableness	0.25	0.52	−1.13	−1.19
▨ Conscientiousness	0.3	0.35	−0.47	0.04
▨ Stability	0.2	0.21	−0.34	−0.55
▨ Openness	0.25	0.5	−0.42	−0.24

FIGURE 3 Personality Factors in Protagonists and Antagonists.

antagonistic motive factor is Social Dominance, which correlates strongly and negatively with Agreeableness (r − -.54). Antagonists score in the extreme range both on Agreeableness (negatively) and on Social Dominance (positively).

BECOMING EMOTIONALLY INVOLVED

One of our chief working hypotheses is that, when readers respond to characters in novels, they respond in much the same way, emotionally, as they respond to people in everyday life. They like or dislike them, admire them or despise them, fear them, feel sorry for them, or are amused by them. In writing fabricated accounts of human behavior, novelists select and organize their material for the purpose of generating such responses, and readers willingly cooperate with this purpose. They participate vicariously in the experiences depicted and form personal opinions about the qualities of the characters. Authors and readers thus collaborate in producing a simulated experience of emotionally responsive evaluative judgment.

In building emotional responses into our research design, we sought to identify emotions that are universal and that are thus likely to be grounded in evolved, species-typical features of human psychology. Emotions at that conceptual level would be on the same level as the basic motives extrapolated from human life history. Over the past 40 years or so, psychologists have made substantial progress in identifying basic emotions. Much of this work was pioneered by Paul Ekman. The results from his decades of research are summarized in *Emotions Revealed* (2003)—a core text for this aspect of our study. By isolating emotions that can be universally or almost universally recognized from facial expressions, Ekman and other researchers ultimately produced a set of seven basic emotions: anger, fear, disgust, contempt, joy, sadness, and surprise.[9] Different researchers sometimes use slightly different terms, register different degrees of intensity in emotions (for instance,

9. For commentaries on the history of research into basic emotions, see Oatley 2004; Plutchik 2003.

anxiety, fear, terror, panic), organize the emotions in various patterns and combinations, or link them with self-awareness or social awareness to produce terms like embarrassment, shame, guilt, and envy (Haidt 2003; Lewis 2000; Panksepp 2000). Nevertheless, Ekman's core group of seven emotions has widespread support as a usable taxonomy of basic emotions (See Lewis and Haviland-Jones 2000; Plutchik 2003).

Our questionnaire contained a list of ten emotional responses. To produce this list, we started with the core of seven terms from Ekman and adapted them for registering graded responses specifically to persons or characters. We used four of the seven terms unaltered: anger, disgust, contempt, and sadness. We also retained fear but divided it into two distinct items: fear of a character and fear for a character. Ekman observes that the positive emotions have been less carefully observed and differentiated than the emotions that reflect emotional upset. The simple terms *joy* or *enjoyment* cover a wide spectrum of possible pleasurable or positive emotions, ranging from amusement to *schadenfreude* to bliss (Ekman 2003, 191). In adapting the term *joy* or *enjoyment,* we sought to register some qualitative differences and also devise terms appropriate to responses to a person. We chose three terms: *liking, admiration,* and *amusement.* Liking is an emotionally positive response to a person, but it does not contain a specific element of approval or disapproval. Admiration combines positive emotionality with a measure of approval or respect. By itself, *surprise,* like *joy,* seems more appropriate as a descriptor for a response to a situation than to a person. Consequently, we did not use the word *surprise* by itself. Instead, along with *admiration,* we used *amusement,* which combines the idea of surprise with an idea of positively valenced emotionality. Amusement extends emotional response to take in responses to comedy. (Sadness and fear take in responses to tragedy; and anger and contempt, mingled with amusement, take in responses to satire.)

We included one further term in our list of possible emotional responses: *indifference.* A number of researchers have included a term such as *interest* to indicate general attentiveness, the otherwise undifferentiated sense that something matters, that it is important and worthy of attention. Indifference can be regarded as the inverse of interest. Indifference provides a qualitatively neutral measure of emotional reaction to a character.

We predicted (1) that protagonists would receive high scores on the positive emotional responses of liking and admiration; (2) that antagonists would receive high scores on the negative emotions of anger, disgust, contempt, and fear-of the character; (3) that protagonists would score higher on sadness and fear-for the character than antagonists; and (4) that major characters (protagonists and antagonists) would score lower on indifference than minor characters.

Factor analysis produced three clearly defined emotional response factors: (1) Dislike, which includes anger, disgust, contempt, and fear of the character, and which also includes negative correlations with admiration and liking; (2) Sorrow, which includes sadness and fear for the character and a negative correlation with amusement; and (3) Interest, which consists chiefly in a negative correlation with indifference.

Male and female protagonists both score relatively low on Dislike and relatively high on Sorrow (Figure 4). Male and female antagonists score very high on Dislike—higher than any other set—low on Sorrow, and somewhat above average on Interest. Female protagonists score high on Interest, but male protagonists, contrary to our expectations, score below average on Interest. They score lower even than good minor males, though not lower than the other minor characters.

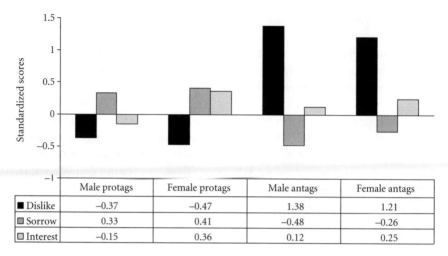

	Male protags	Female protags	Male antags	Female antags
■ Dislike	−0.37	−0.47	1.38	1.21
▨ Sorrow	0.33	0.41	−0.48	−0.26
▢ Interest	−0.15	0.36	0.12	0.25

FIGURE 4 Emotional Response Factors for Protagonists and Antagonists.

Once one has isolated the components of agonistic structure and deployed a model of reading that includes basic emotions as a register of evaluatively polarized response, most of the scores on emotional response factors are predictable. There is, however, one seemingly anomalous finding that emerges from the scores on emotional responses—the relatively low score received by male protagonists on Interest. This finding ran contrary to our expectation that protagonists, both male and female, would score lower on indifference than any other character set. We think this finding can be explained by the way agonistic polarization feeds into the psychology of cooperation. Male protagonists in our data set are relatively moderate characters. They are introverted and agreeable, and they do not seek to dominate others socially. They are pleasant and conscientious, and they are also curious and alert. They are attractive characters, partly because they are not assertive or aggressive characters. They excite little Dislike at least in part because they do not excite much competitive antagonism. They are not intent on acquiring wealth and power, and they are thoroughly domesticated within the forms of conventional propriety. They serve admirably to exemplify normative values of cooperative behavior, but in serving this function they seem to be diminished in some vital component of fascination. They lack power, and in lacking power, they seem also to lack some quality that excites intensity of interest in emotional response.

In these novels, the aggressive pursuit of Social Dominance—wealth, prestige, and power—is morally demonized. The desire for Social Dominance is overwhelmingly the single most distinctive motivational trait of both male and female antagonists. That motivational trait correlates with low scores on the affiliative personality factor of Agreeableness and high scores on the emotional response factor of Dislike. Despite this strongly valenced cluster of correlations, male and female antagonists score higher on interest (lower on indifference) than male protagonists. Readers dislike antagonists, but it is sometimes the case that antagonists are more exciting than protagonists, especially male protagonists.

The interest readers feel for antagonists might be a function of social vigilance—the need to track people who could pose a danger to us or to those we care about. However, the highest level of interest is felt for female protagonists, who produce very low levels of fear and anger in respondents. Interest can evidently be activated both by positive attraction and by aversive stimulus. Male protagonists possess many of the same features in motives and personality that make female protagonists attractive, but they are evidently lacking in some feature that excites interest specifically for males.

EMOTIONAL RESPONSE, THE SEX OF THE AUTHOR, AND VALENCE

In both the attributes of characters and the emotional responses of readers, differences of sex in characters are smaller than differences of valence—usually much smaller. Good characters (protagonists and their associates) and bad characters (antagonists and their associates) display wider divergences in scores than male and female characters.

Are male and female authors in agreement about what constitutes good and bad in characters? To answer this question, we isolated the most agonistically polarized factors and compared the direction of scores for good and bad characters by male and female authors. The most agonistically polarized factors are Agreeableness, Dislike, Social Dominance, Constructive Effort, Nurture, and a preference for Intrinsic Qualities in mates. On all these factors, the polarization of valence in male and female authors tends in the same direction. In novels by both male and female authors, good characters score higher than bad characters on Agreeableness, Constructive Effort, Nurture, and preferring Intrinsic Qualities in mates; good characters score lower than bad characters on Dominance and Dislike. Valence accounts for more variance among characters than sex, and male and female authors converge in producing the polarized structure of valence.

WHAT DO WE MAKE OF IT ALL?

Agonistic structure in the novels displays a systematic contrast between desirable and undesirable traits in characters. Protagonists exemplify traits that evoke admiration and liking in readers, and antagonists exemplify traits that evoke anger, fear, contempt, and disgust. Antagonists virtually personify Social Dominance—the self-interested pursuit of wealth, prestige, and power. In these novels, those ambitions are sharply segregated from prosocial and culturally acquisitive dispositions. Antagonists are not only selfish and unfriendly but also undisciplined, emotionally unstable, and intellectually dull. Protagonists, in contrast, display motive dispositions and personality traits that exemplify strong personal development and healthy social adjustment. Protagonists are agreeable, conscientious, emotionally stable, and open to experience. Protagonists clearly represent the apex of the positive values implicit in agonistic structure. Both male and female protagonists score high on the motive factor of Constructive Effort, a factor that combines prosocial and culturally acquisitive dispositions. Their introversion, in this context, seems part of their mildness. The extraversion of antagonists, in contrast, seen in the context of their other scores, seems to indicate aggressive self-assertion.

In the past 30 years or so, more criticism on the novel has been devoted to the issue of gender identity than to any other topic. The data in our study indicate that gender can be invested with a significance out of proportion to its true place in the structure of interpersonal relations in the novels and that it can be conceived in agonistically polarized ways out of keeping with the forms of social affiliation depicted in the novels. In this data set, differences between males and females are less prominent than differences between protagonists and antagonists. If polarized emotional responses were absent from the novels, or if those polarized responses co-varied with differences between males and females, the differences between male and female characters would have to be conceived agonistically, as a conflict (as it is, for instance, in Gilbert's and Gubar's *The Madwoman in the Attic* 1979). The differences between male and female characters in motives and personality could be conceived as competing value structures. From a Marxist perspective, that competition would be interpreted as essentially political and economic in character (as it is, for instance, in Nancy Armstrong's *Desire and Domestic Fiction* 1987). From a Darwinian perspective, it would ultimately be attributed to competing reproductive interests. The subordination of sex to agonistic role assignment, though, suggests that, in the novels, conflict between the sexes is subordinated to their shared and complementary interests. In the agonistic structure of plot and theme, male and female protagonists are allies. They cooperate in resisting the predatory threats of antagonists, and they join together to exemplify the values that elicit the readers' admiration and sympathy. Both male and female antagonists are massively preoccupied with material gain and social rank. That preoccupation stands in stark contrast to the more balanced and developed world of the protagonists—a world that includes sexual interest, romance, the care of family, friends, and the life of the mind. By isolating and stigmatizing dominance behavior, the novels affirm the shared values that bind its members into a community.

In *Hierarchy in the Forest: The Evolution of Egalitarian Behavior*, Christopher Boehm offers a cogent explanation for the way interacting impulses of dominance and affiliation have shaped the evolution of human political behavior. In an earlier phase of evolutionary social science, sociobiological theorists had repudiated the idea of "altruistic" behavior and had restricted prosocial dispositions to nepotism and to the exchange of reciprocal benefits. In contrast, Boehm argues that, at some point in their evolutionary history—at the latest 100,000 years ago—humans developed a special capacity, dependent on their symbolic and cultural capabilities, for enforcing altruistic or group-oriented norms. By enforcing these norms, humans succeed in controlling "free riders" or "cheaters," and they thus make it possible for genuinely altruistic genes to survive within a social group. Such altruistic dispositions, enforced by punishing defectors, would enable social groups to compete more successfully against other groups and would thus make "group selection" an effective force in subsequent human evolution. The selection for altruistic dispositions—and dispositions for enforcing altruistic cultural norms—would involve a process of gene-culture co-evolution that would snowball in its effect of altering human nature itself.[10]

10. On the social dynamics of dominance and cooperation, see Alexander 1989; Axelrod and Hamilton 1981; Bingham 1999; Darwin 1871; Eibl-Eibesfeldt 1998; Flinn, Geary, and Ward 2005; Richerson and Boyd 2005; Sober and Wilson 1998; Turchin 2006; D. Wilson 2002; D. Wilson 2007. On the now largely successful effort to resuscitate the idea of "group selection" as a component in "multi-level selection," see Boehm 1999; Eibl-Eibesfeldt 1998; Richerson and Boyd 2005; Sober and Wilson 1998; D. Wilson 2007; Wilson and Wilson 2007.

Taking into account not just the representation of characters but the emotional responses of readers, we can identify agonistic structure as a simulated experience of emotionally responsive social interaction. That experience has a clearly defined moral dimension. Agonistic structure precisely mirrors the kind of egalitarian social dynamic documented by Boehm in hunter-gatherers—our closest contemporary proxy to ancestral humans. As Boehm and others have argued, the dispositions that produce an egalitarian social dynamic are deeply embedded in the evolved and adapted character of human nature. Humans have an innate desire for power and an innate dislike of being dominated. Egalitarianism as a political strategy arises as a compromise between the desire to dominate and the dislike of being dominated. By pooling their power so as to exercise collective social coercion, individuals in groups can repress dominance behavior in other individuals. The result is autonomy for individuals. No one gets all the power he or she would like, but then, no one has to accept submission to other dominant individuals. Boehm describes in detail the pervasive collective tactics for repressing dominance within social groups organized at the levels of bands and tribes.

An egalitarian social dynamic is the most important basic structural feature that distinguishes human social organization from the social organization of chimpanzees. In chimpanzee society, social organization is regulated exclusively by dominance, that is, power. In human society, social organization is regulated by interactions between impulses of dominance and impulses for suppressing dominance. State societies with elaborate systems of hierarchy emerged only very recently in the evolutionary past, about 10,000 years ago, after the agricultural revolution made possible concentrations of resources and, therefore, of power. Before the advent of despotism, the egalitarian disposition for suppressing dominance had, at a minimum, 90,000 years in which to become entrenched in human nature—more than sufficient time for significant adaptive change to take place (Wade 2006). In highly stratified societies, dominance assumes a new ascendancy, but no human society dispenses with the need for communitarian association. It seems likely, then, that agonistic structure in fictional narratives emerged in tandem with specifically human adaptations for cooperation and specifically human adaptations for creating imaginative constructs that embody the ethos of the tribe.

As we have already observed, in non-literate cultures, social dynamics take place in face-to-face interactions, through the perpetual hubbub of dialogue, gossip, and the telling of tales. That kind of interaction is necessarily restricted to relatively small populations, to bands or tribes, usually not larger than 150 individuals (Dunbar 2004). In literate cultures, in contrast, social dynamics can take place vicariously through the shared imaginative experience of literature. In responding to characters, readers join the community of all readers responding in similar ways to the social dynamics depicted in the novels. Authors and readers thus collaborate in producing a virtual imaginative world. In this virtual world, readers affirm and reinforce cooperative dispositions on a large social scale. Agonistic structure extends an adaptive social process across social groups larger than the band or tribe. It is a medium both for gene-culture co-evolution and for natural selection at the level of social groups. It is, in other words, an adaptively functional feature of human nature.

References

Alexander, Richard D. 1989. Evolution of the human psyche. In *The human revolution: Behavioural and biological perspectives on the origins of modern humans*, ed. Paul Mellars, and Chris Stringer, 455–513. Princeton: Princeton University Press.

Andrews, Alice, and Joseph Carroll. 2010. *The Evolutionary Review: Art, Science, Culture* 1: 1–154.

Armstrong, Nancy. 1987. *Desire and domestic fiction: A political history of the novel.* New York: Oxford University Press.

Aronowitz, Stanley. 1996. The politics of the science wars. *Social Text* 14: 177–197.

Axelrod, Robert, and William D. Hamilton. 1981. The evolution of cooperation. *Science* 211: 1390–1396.

Baron-Cohen, Simon. 2004. *The essential difference: Male and female brains and the truth about autism.* New York: Basic Books.

Barrett, Louise, Robin Dunbar, and John Lycett. 2002. *Human evolutionary psychology.* Princeton, NJ: Princeton University Press.

Bingham, Paul M. 1999. Human uniqueness: A general theory. *The Quarterly Review of Biology* 74: 133–169.

Blum, Deborah. 1997. *Sex on the brain: The biological differences between men and women.* New York: Viking Adult.

Boehm, Christopher. 1999. *Hierarchy in the forest: The evolution of egalitarian behavior.* Cambridge, MA: Harvard University Press.

Boghossian, Paul. 2006. *Fear of knowledge: Against relativism and constructivism.* Oxford, UK: Oxford University Press.

Boyd, Brian. 2009. *On the origin of stories: Evolution, cognition, and fiction.* Cambridge, MA: Harvard University Press.

Boyd, Brian, Joseph Carroll, and Jonathan Gottschall, eds. 2010. *Evolution, literature, and film: A reader.* New York: Columbia University Press.

Brown, Donald. 1991. *Human universals.* Philadelphia: Temple University Press.

Brown, James Robert. 2001. *Who rules in science: An opinionated guide to the wars.* Cambridge, MA: Harvard University Press.

Buss, David M. 1995. Evolutionary psychology: A new paradigm for psychological science. *Psychological Inquiry* 6: 1–30.

Buss, David M. 1996. Social adaptation and five major factors of personality. In *The five-factor model of personality: Theoretical perspectives*, ed. Jerry S. Wiggins, 180–207. New York: Guilford.

Buss, David M. 2003. *The evolution of desire: Strategies of human mating.* 2nd ed. New York: Basic.

Buss, David M. ed. 2005. *The handbook of evolutionary psychology.* Hoboken, NJ: Wiley.

Buss, David M. 2007. *Evolutionary psychology: The new science of the mind.* 3rd ed. Boston: Allyn and Bacon.

Carroll, Joseph. 2004. *Literary Darwinism: Evolution, human nature, and literature.* New York: Routledge.

Carroll, Joseph. 2005. Literature and evolutionary psychology. In *The handbook of evolutionary psychology*, ed. David M. Buss, 931–952. Hoboken, NJ: Wiley.

Carroll, Joseph. 2008. Rejoinder to the responses. *Style* 42: 308–411.

Carroll, Joseph. 2008. An evolutionary paradigm for literary study. *Style* 42: 103–35.

Carroll, Joseph. 2010a. Intentional meaning in *Hamlet*: An evolutionary perspective. *Style* 44: 230–260.

Carroll, Joseph. 2010b. Three scenarios for literary Darwinism. *New Literary History* 41: 53–67.

Cooke, Brett. 2002. *Human nature in utopia: Zamyatin's we.* Evanston, IL: Northwestern University Press.

Costa, Paul T., Jr., and Robert R. McCrae. 1997. Personality trait structure as a human universal. *American Psychologist* 52: 509–516.

Damasio, Antonio R. 1994. *Descartes's error: Emotion, reason, and the human brain.* New York: Putnam's.

Darwin, Charles. 1871/1981. *The descent of man, and selection in relation to sex.* Eds. John Tyler Bonner, and Robert M. May. Princeton, NJ: Princeton University Press.

Davidson, Richard J., Klaus R. Scherer, and H. Hill Goldsmith. 2003. *Handbook of affective sciences.* Oxford, UK: Oxford University Press.

Dawson, Gowan. 2006. Literature and science under the microscope. *Journal of Victorian Culture* 11: 301–315.

Dissanayake, Ellen. 2000. *Art and intimacy: How the arts began.* Seattle: University of Washington Press.

Dunbar, Robin. 2004. *The human story: A brief history of mankind's evolution.* London: Faber.

Dunbar, Robin, and Louise Barrett, eds. 2007. *Oxford handbook of evolutionary psychology.* Oxford, UK: Oxford University Press.

Dutton, Denis. 2009. *The art instinct: Beauty, pleasure, and human evolution.* New York: Bloomsbury.

Eibl-Eibesfeldt, Irenäus. 1998. Us and the others: The familial roots of ethnonationalism. In *Ethnic conflict and indoctrination: Altruism and identity in evolutionary perspective,* ed. Irenäus Eibl-Eibesfeldt, and F. K. Salter, 21–53. New York: Berghahn.

Ekman, Paul. 2003. *Emotions revealed: Recognizing faces and feelings to improve communication and emotional life.* New York: Holt.

Feyerabend, Paul. 1987. *Farewell to reason.* London: Verso.

Flinn, Mark V., David C. Geary, and Carol V. Ward. 2005. Ecological dominance, social competition, and coalitionary arms races: Why humans evolved extraordinary intelligence. *Evolution and Human Behavior* 26: 10–46.

Fromm, Harold. 2009. *The nature of being human: From environmentalism to consciousness.* Baltimore, MD: Johns Hopkins University Press.

Gangestad, Steven W. 2007. Reproductive strategies and tactics. In *The Oxford handbook of evolutionary psychology,* eds Robin Dunbar, and Louise Barrett, 321–332. Oxford, UK: Oxford University Press.

Gangestad, Steven W., and Jeffry A. Simpson, eds. 2007. *The evolution of mind: Fundamental questions and controversies.* New York: Guilford.

Geary, David. 1998. *Male, female: The evolution of human sex differences.* Washington, D C: APA.

Gilbert, Sandra M, and Susan Gubar. 1979. *The madwoman in the attic: The woman writer and the nineteenth-century literary imagination.* New Haven, CT: Yale University Press.

Gottschall, Jonathan. 2008. *Literature, science, and a new humanities.* Houndmills: Palgrave MacMillan.

Gottschall, Jonathan. 2008. *The rape of Troy: Evolution, violence, and the world of Homer.* Cambridge, MA: Cambridge University Press.

Gottschall, Jonathan, and David Sloan Wilson, eds. 2005. *The literary animal: Evolution and the nature of narrative.* Evanston, IL: Northwestern University Press.

Gross, Alan G. 1990. *The rhetoric of science.* Cambridge, MA: Harvard University Press.

Gross, Paul R., and Norman Levitt. 1994. *Higher superstition: The academic left and its quarrels with science*. Baltimore, MD: Johns Hopkins University Press.

Gross, Paul R., Norman Levitt, and Martin Lewis, eds. 1997. *The flight from science and reason*. Baltimore, MD: Johns Hopkins University Press.

Haidt, Jonathan. 2003. The moral emotions. In *Handbook of affective sciences*, ed. Richard J. Davidson, Klaus B. Scherer, and H. Hill Goldsmith, 852–870. Oxford, UK: Oxford University Press.

Hill, Kim. 2007. Evolutionary biology, cognitive adaptations, and human culture. In *The evolution of mind: Fundamental questions and controversies*, eds. Steven W. Gangestad, and Jeffrey A. Simpson, 348–356. New York: Guilford.

Johnson, John A., Joseph Carroll, Jonathan Gottschall, and Daniel Kruger. 2008. Hierarchy in the library: Egalitarian dynamics in Victorian novels. *Evolutionary Psychology* 6: 715–738.

Johnson, John A., Joseph Carroll, Jonathan Gottschall, and Daniel Kruger. 2011. Portrayal of personality in Victorian novels reflects modern research findings but amplifies the significance of Agreeableness. *Journal of Research in Personality* 45: 50–58.

Kaplan, Hillard S., Kim Hill, Jane Lancaster, and A. Magdalena Hurtado. 2000. A theory of human life history evolution: Diet, intelligence, and longevity. *Evolutionary Anthropology* 9: 156–185.

Koertge, Noretta, ed. 1998. *A house built on sand: Exposing postmodern myths about science*. New York: Oxford University Press.

Kruger, Daniel, Maryanne Fisher, and Ian Jobling. 2003. Proper and dark heroes as dads and cads: Alternative mating strategies in British and Romantic literature. *Human Nature* 14: 305–317.

Latour, Bruno, and Steve Woolgar. 1979. *Laboratory life: The social construction of scientific facts*. Beverly Hills, CA: Sage.

Levine, George, ed. 1987. *One culture: Essays in science and literature*. Madison, WI: University of Wisconsin Press.

Lewis, Michael. 2000. Self-conscious emotions: Embarrassment, pride, shame, and guilt. In *Handbook of emotions, 2nd ed.*, ed. Michael Lewis, and Jeannette M. Haviland-Jones, 137–156. New York: Guilford.

Lewis, Michael, and Jeannette M. Haviland-Jones, eds. 2000. *Handbook of emotions. 2nd ed.* New York: Guilford.

Love, Glen A. 2003. *Practical ecocriticism: Literature, biology, and the environment*. Charlottesville, VA: University of Virginia Press.

Low, Bobbi S. 2000. *Why sex matters: A Darwinian look at human behavior*. Princeton, NJ: Princeton University Press.

MacDonald, Kevin B. 1998. Evolution, culture, and the five-factor model. *Journal of Cross-Cultural Psychology* 29: 119–149.

McEwan, Ian. 2005. Literature, science, and human nature. In *The literary animal: Evolution and the nature of narrative*, ed. Jonathan Gottschall, and David Sloan Wilson, 5–19. Evanston, IL: Northwestern University Press.

Miller, Geoffrey. 2000. *The mating mind: How sexual choice shaped the evolution of human nature*. New York: Doubleday.

Moir, Anne, and David Jessel. 1991. *Brain sex: The real difference between men and women*. New York: Carol Publishing Group.

Nettle, Daniel. 2007. *Personality: What makes you the way you are*. Oxford, UK: Oxford University Press.

Nordlund, Marcus. 2007. *Shakespeare and the nature of love: Literature, culture, evolution*. Evanston, IL: Northwestern University Press.

Oatley, Keith. 2004. *Emotions: A brief history*. Malden, MA: Blackwell.

Panksepp, Jaak. 1998. *Affective neuroscience: The foundations of human and animal emotions*. New York: Oxford University Press.

Panksepp, Jaak. 2000. Emotions as natural kinds within the mammalian brain. In *Handbook of emotions, 2nd ed.*, eds. Michael Lewis, and Jeannette M. Haviland-Jones, 137–156. New York: Guilford.

Paulhus, Delroy L., and Oliver P. John. 1998. Egoistic and moralistic biases in self-perception: The interplay of self-deceptive styles with basic traits and motives. *Journal of Personality* 66: 1025–1060.

Peterfreund, Stuart, ed. 1990. *Literature and science: Theory and practice*. Boston: Northeastern University Press.

Pinker, Steven. 1997. *How the mind works*. New York: Norton.

Plutchik, Robert. 2003. *Emotions and life: Perspectives from psychology, biology, and evolution*. Washington, DC: APA.

Richerson, Peter J., and Richard Boyd. 2005. *Not by genes alone: How culture transformed human evolution*. Chicago: University of Chicago Press.

Rorty, Richard. 1982. *Consequences of pragmatism*. Minneapolis, MN: University of Minneapolis Press.

Salmon, Catherine, and Donald Symons. 2004. Slash fiction and human mating psychology. *Journal of Sex Research* 41: 94–100.

Saucier, Gerard. 2003. An alternative multi-language structure for personality attributes. *European Journal of Personality* 17: 179–205.

Saucier, Gerard, and Lewis R. Goldberg. 2001. Lexical studies of indigenous personality factors: Premises, products, and prospects. *Journal of Personality* 69: 847–879.

Saucier, Gerard, Sarah E. Hampson, and Lewis R. Goldberg. 2000. Cross-language studies of lexical personality factors. In *Advances in personality psychology*, ed. Sarah E. Hampson, 1–36. Philadelphia, PA: Taylor and Francis.

Saucier, Gerard, Stelios Georgiades, Ionnas Tsaousis, and Lewis R. Goldberg. 2005. The factor structure of Greek personality adjectives. *Journal of Personality and Social Psychology* 88: 856–875.

Saunders, Judith P. 2009. *Reading Edith Wharton through a Darwinian lens: Evolutionary biological issues in her fiction*. Jefferson, NC: McFarland.

Scalise Sugiyama, Michelle. 2001. New science, old myth: An evolutionary critique of the Oedipal Paradigm. *Mosaic* 34: 121–136.

Scalise Sugiyama, Michelle. 2003. Cultural variation is part of human nature: Literary universals, context-sensitivity, and "Shakespeare in the Bush." *Human Nature* 14: 383–396.

Scalise Sugiyama, Michelle. 2005. Reverse-engineering narrative: Evidence of special design. In *The literary animal: Evolution and the nature of narrative*, eds. Jonathan Gottschall, and David Sloan Wilson, 177–196. Evanston, IL: Northwestern University Press.

Schmitt, David P. 2005. Fundamentals of human mating strategies. In *The handbook of evolutionary psychology*, ed. David M. Buss, 258–291. Hoboken, NJ: Wiley.

Smith, Barbara Herrnstein. 2006. *Scandalous knowledge: Science, truth, and the human*. Durham, NC: Duke University Press.

Smits, Dirk J. M., and P. D. Boeck. 2006. From BIS/BAS to the big five. *European Journal of Personality* 20: 255–270.

Sober, Elliott, and David S. Wilson. 1998. *Unto others: The evolution and psychology of unselfish behavior*. Cambridge, MA: Harvard University Press.

Sokal, Alan., and Jean Bricmont. 1998. *Fashionable nonsense: Postmodern intellectuals' abuse of science*. New York: Picador.

Symons, Donald. 1979. *The evolution of human sexuality*. Oxford, UK: Oxford University Press.

Tanaka, Jiro. 2010. What Is Copernican? A few common barriers to Darwinian thinking about the mind. *The Evolutionary Review: Art, Science, Culture* 1: 6–12 .

Thiessen, Del, and Yoko Umezawa. 1998. The sociobiology of everyday life: A new look at a very old novel. *Human Nature* 9: 293–320.

Tooby, John, and Leda Cosmides. 2001. Does beauty build adapted minds? Toward an evolutionary theory of aesthetics, fiction, and the arts. *SubStance* 30: 6–27.

Turchin, Peter. 2006. *War and peace and war: The rise and fall of empires*. New York: Pi Press.

Wade, Nicholas. 2006. *Before the dawn: Recovering the lost history of our sncestors*. New York: Penguin.

Weinberg, Steven. 2001. *Facing up: Science and its cultural adversaries*. Cambridge, MA: Harvard University Press.

Wilson, David Sloan. 2002. *Darwin's cathedral: Evolution, religion, and the nature of society*. Chicago: University of Chicago Press.

Wilson, David Sloan. 2007. *Evolution for everyone. How Darwin's theory can change the way we think about our lives*. New York: Delacorte.

Wilson, David Sloan, and Edward O. Wilson. 2007. Rethinking the theoretical foundation of sociobiology. *The Quarterly Review of Biology* 82: 327–348.

Wilson, Edward O. 1998. *Consilience: The unity of knowledge*. New York: Knopf.

Woolgar, Steve. 1988 *Science: The very idea*. Chichester, UK: Ellis Horwood.

Zhou, Xinyue, Gerard Saucier, Dingguo Gao, and Jing Liu. 2009. The factor structure of Chinese personality terms. *Journal of Personality* 77: 363–400.

22

LANGUAGE, COGNITION, AND LITERATURE

Barbara Dancygier

The explanatory power of evolutionary theory seems to present a welcome opportunity for some humanities disciplines to seek a new, interdisciplinary profile, at least partly relying on the sciences. Quite clearly, a makeover along these lines is tempting, and the explanatory potential of evolutionary theory seems to be almost limitless. After all, the evolution of our species must somehow account for all of our species-specific abilities. However, what remains puzzling is how to best build the bridge from science to the humanities (or to achieve vertical integration, the idea proposed in Wilson [1998] and Tooby and Cosmides [1992], and recently developed in Slingerland 2008). The preferred way (and also the natural way) is to connect one's discipline directly, in one leap, to evolutionary concerns. The subdiscipline of choice is typically the one that already makes claims about the role of evolution in the functioning of the human mind, evolutionary psychology. A number of literary scholars have chosen this route.[1]

In this chapter I will argue that directly integrating literary studies with evolutionary psychology causes evolutionary theory to lose much of its expected power to explain and convince. More specifically, I will show that evolutionary approaches to literature will be in jeopardy if they do not accept the seemingly unquestionable fact that literature cannot exist without language, and thus that the role of language calls for an explanation. Furthermore, the assumption that evolution affects literature directly results in a view of cognition that reduces it to its evolutionary roots, while disregarding how evolution supports the emergence of various cultural artifacts, including literature. While much of the evolutionary discussion of literature uses art as a starting point, it has little to say about the ways in which cognition makes it possible for visual arts or music to be linked to linguistic forms of art such as literature, but also to mixed modalities such as graffiti, video games, or virtual reality.[2] As a result of narrowing down the focus to "high art," the framework loses much of its evolutionary and cognitive appeal, as it treats human creativity in a rather narrow way, especially in its oversight of creativity prompted by language.

It is not unusual in literary studies to treat language as transparent, and thus irrelevant. However critical of structuralism some literary scholars are, they still accept, with

---

1. See e.g., Carroll 1995, 2005, and 2008; Gottschall 2008a, and b; Zunshine 2006; Boyd 2009.

2. For a discussion of the connection between evolution and art/literature, see Dutton 2009, Boyd 2009; also, for a variety of proposals linking art to cognition, see Turner 2006, especially Donald 2006 and Deacon 2006.

structuralists, that language is properly viewed as a set of forms, and as such is not an important player in the emergence of literary meaning, whether it resides in culturally or evolutionarily constructed concepts. When Orwell wrote in his essay *Why I Write* that "Good prose is like a windowpane," he meant that the authorial intention should not be visible in the text, and, even though assumed senses may vary, the "windowpane" metaphor seems to be tacitly accepted by many. However, it is brilliantly questioned in Magritte's painting, *Human condition*. It shows a window framed by heavy curtains and a view of green grass with a blue sky outside. A closer look reveals that only part of the view is indeed depicting reality outside the window. Much of it is actually a painting of the same view, almost imperceptibly merged with the window. One of the most striking ideas emerging from the painting is that we may not be aware of the degree to which our minds take representations, pictorial or mental, as actual reality.

The concept that helps us clearly distinguish the outside reality from the inner representation is that of construal: —an understanding of the situation being observed, as it is communicated to someone else. This concept is commonly used by cognitive linguists (e.g., Langacker 1990, 1991) to explain how the choice of words and forms portrays the mental construct the speaker attempts to communicate in order to render her understanding of what is observed. For example, Magritte's painting could be described as "a window overlooking a garden" or "a view of a green garden and a blue sky." The choice is a matter of construal, either foregrounding the content of the view or the means by which it is accessed. It is natural to disregard the means and reach directly for the content, which is how language falls by the wayside in literary studies and other humanities disciplines. Thus, when I tease my students by asking them to tell me what they see to their left (which is a wall-to-wall row of windows), they typically mention the trees outside, the rain, the passers-by, etc., and only occasionally the windows themselves, but they are only being introduced to the concept of construal and representation, and they do not purport to be experts in the psychology of window viewing. Literary critics, however, are experts at reading literature, and thus have no excuse.

Some of the methods of linking research on literature and language to evolutionary theory further reflect rather specific (though not spelled out) assumptions about the proper concerns of evolutionary study. Often the focus is on the "evolution of X" (language, literature, art, etc.), and the evidence for treating X is an adaptation or a by-product. The discussion then revolves around selective pressures or reproductive advantage. For the purposes of the humanities, the questions are interesting, but not central to the traditional concerns of disciplines deeply immersed in cultural concerns. For example, future answers (if at all possible to provide) might change the underlying assumptions of literary study, but they may do little to affect the core interests of most literary scholars. To put it simply, just knowing that literature is adaptive may not change the way in which most of the historicist or cultural research is done.

Another option is to study how our evolutionary concerns are reflected "in X"—for example, how the human evolutionary psychological profile is reflected in literature. This seems to be the preferred agenda of the so-called "literary Darwinists." Evolutionary concepts of mate selection or dominance are revealed as structuring the very plot and characterization, as well as some of the most respected critical concepts (such as "protagonist" or "antagonist"). The only worry is that concepts such as mate selection seem to have rather limited appeal, when much of contemporary literature is under scrutiny. However, Boyd's analysis of Dr. Seuss (2009) may suggest some areas of applicability.

Another option is to pose questions involving evolution, without reaching beyond the evolution of human ability. For example, much of the study about the evolution of language, especially within the Chomskyan paradigm, follows the assumption that language is a specialized module in the brain, and thus the discussion includes (failed) attempts to identify a "language gene" (such as FOXP2), or a construct distinguishing human language from animal communication (such as recursion, see Hauser, et al. 2002). The focus on the language module (or universal grammar) is often paired with a theoretical view of language that separates the theoretically described content of the module from unpredictable and messy daily performance. Given that the language "core" is described in terms accessible only to experts, the approach is often taken as an invitation to treat language as a transparent "windowpane." Thus, although the modular approach itself does not imply a rejection of the role of language in symbolic thought, literature, or art, it is often used as if it did. Interestingly, the paradigm seems to be changing. The hypothesis recently advanced by Bickerton (2009), previously an avid supporter of the Chomskyan view, avoids many of the earlier shortcomings. He proposes that language developed through a long series of proto-stages (rather than as a cognitive *deux ex machina*), in a feedback loop with a specific environmental niche, and in synchrony with cognition and other forms of creativity. It is too early to say how the hypothesis will be received, but at least the "universal grammar" approach has now been given more temporal and cognitive depth.[3]

Two approaches that promise the most explanatory hypotheses on the role of language in human development both see the emergence of language as correlated with the development of culture and cognition. Naturally, neither approach treats language as independent of its cultural and social role. Whereas Tomasello (1999, 2008) poses the question as the development of "communication," and sees it against his cognitively based theory of language acquisition, Deacon (1997, 2006) sees the development of language as the development of symbolic thought. In other words, in spite of important differences, these theories are, at least in principle, interested in how human culture participated in the emergence of highly specialized cognitive and linguistic skills. One thing is clear: in these approaches, language and cognition are inextricably connected. Of course, the discussion of whether thought precedes language (as in most work by Chomsky) or whether proto-language precedes thought (as Bickerton now argues) is important and informative, but the really interesting point of inquiry is the connection between the two, beyond simply stating the obvious fact that the words of language represent concepts or refer to real world objects as representatives of categories. An overt recognition of such links, regardless how they will be formulated, could be a more solid basis of literary inquiry than reaching back to the evolutionary profile of our hunter-gatherer ancestors.

There is now a large body of research on the roots of both language and cognition in embodiment (See Gallagher 2005; Pecher and Zwaan 2005a,b; Spivey 2007; Gibbs 2005;

---

3. The outlines presented so far simplify the picture and do not accurately represent the variety and depth of available research. However, they are needed as an explanation of the reasons why language is often not seen as a rightful participant in the literature/evolution/cognition debate.

Prinz 2004; Johnson 1987, 2007). The results clearly suggest that language supports mental simulation of processes that are still conceptualized at a level very close to the functioning of the human body. In view of this work, any attempt to separate language and cognition misses important aspects of both. What is more, it is not enough to talk about how our brain evolved to rely on both language and cognition, or where specific abilities are located in the brain. We also need a working model of how the mind does its job of supporting the on-line processes of conceptualization and communication. One answer is the theory of conceptual integration, or blending, originally proposed by Fauconnier and Turner (1994, 1996, 1998a,b, 2002), and now applied to a number of human abilities involving the processing and emergence of meaning.[4] The process known as "blending" is a mental operation that relies on conceptual packets called inputs, which are prompted by various forms of expression or behavior to selectively project structure into a new construct, known as the blend. Blending thus assumes that meaning, of whatever kind, must be constructed in the mind, and that it emerges through the dynamic process of dealing with available inputs, rather than being pulled out of some stable repertoire of forms and their senses. Unlike other theories of meaning, blending allows one to consider various language forms alongside or in conjunction with visual or aural prompts, and thus naturally crosses the modular barriers imposed by earlier theories. Moreover, blending is a natural ally of a model of the emergence of language and communication such as Tomasello's, because it already postulates mechanisms that yield both new forms and new meanings to satisfy emerging communicative needs. Thus, unlike other theories of language, it is prepared to respond to the changing environments, in which visual forms of communication either support or complement new uses of language (graphic novels, cartoons, film, etc.). Considering that one of the central goals of literary criticism is still, presumably, to explain how literature is read, blending would seem a helpful ally. Indeed, it is already used by a number of scholars (See Cook 2007, 2010; Dancygier 2005, 2006, 2007, 2008a,b,2011; Canning 2008; Sweetser 2006; Turner 1996, 2003).

The stress on communication and its embodied and mimetic roots also puts some standard views of evolutionary psychology in question. For example, cognitive scientists and linguists are now proposing a refreshed view of a module widely known as "the theory of mind" (also applied in the accounts of literary meaning, cf. Zunshine 2006).[5] It is argued that rather than attempting to attribute complete beliefs to others (which would be cognitively costly and inefficient), we participate in a communicative set-up that is by definition intersubjective. The postulated construct has been termed "the shared mind," in order to highlight natural understanding of language and behavior as a correlate of the ground against which the language exchange is set, and of the contributions of discourse participants.[6] In other words, rather than relying on perception of what happens around us and a specific set of theory-of-mind skills to store and process these experiences, we

---

4. Some of the broader discussions of blending can be found in Fauconnier and Turner 2002; Coulson 2001; Coulson and Oakley 2000, 2005; also consult the blending website at http://markturner.org/blending.html.

5. It is beyond the limits of this paper to discuss the research in any detail, but much can be found in Zlatev et al. 2008.

6. For a range of papers, see Zlatev et al. 2008.

rely instead on dynamically constructing the exchange in a way that coordinates the efforts of all its participants. Our minds (and our language skills) are thus not computational or representational in nature, but inherently intersubjective. From the evolutionary perspective, this hypothesis is interesting and potentially useful.

As Verhagen (2005, 2008), among others, has argued, linguistic constructions are often not only means of expressing the meanings the speaker wants to get across, but also of negotiating them while naturally including the positions communicated earlier as default. In this light, a hand or visual gesture indicating an opponent and an utterance that starts with "true" or "of course" will position the speaker as having said X, as assuming that the opponent would argue against X, and as refuting the criticism on the grounds explained later, all at once. The stress on intersubjectivity is thus a more economical view of communication, one which agrees with Tomasello's claims about language developing in the direction of constructions that best promote communicative patterns satisfying emerging needs. In other words, once language has appeared, it never stops changing, not only because of language contact and processes affecting grammar, such as grammaticalization or lexicalization, but also because it needs new constructions that serve the emerging communicative set-ups in which our intersubjective minds have to function. In conversation, in literature, and on the Internet, the goals of communication prompt new linguistic constructions. As this paper argues, constructions used in literary discourse have specific representational and communicative goals at their core.

In what follows I will look at literary texts as dynamic means of supporting intersubjective minds, in the context where communication is primarily in the written form. I will look at linguistic forms characteristic of early theater, through the emergence of the novel, all the way to contemporary texts, to show how linguistic constructions have been used to support not only the specific genres of literary production, but also enhanced access to other minds. Whereas early literary discourse tends to rely on forms that mimic a basic "someone said that X" mode rather closely, they gradually develop into forms that assume unobstructed access to fictional minds. Throughout the discussion, I will rely on frame theory and blending in order to show the ways in which the language of literature continues to adjust to new needs.

The primary question is the nature of the communicative "ground" in the context of a written text, especially a fictional one. In a conversational context, all participants are physically present, and they take turns making their contribution to the exchange. The "ground" may include parameters such as time and location, but also the record of the conversation and the knowledge shared by the participants. In a novel, there is an extended turn of the narrator, but the text itself constructs its ground independently of the parameters of the act of reading. At a minimum, the text needs to be assumed as communicating something. The presence of the communicator, although not physical, is built into the text itself in the form of first or third person narration, the distinction between narration and dialogue, and so on.

The distinction between true or fictional narration is, from the perspective of language, not an obstacle. Literary production has to be based in some reality, even a science-fiction reality, where various real bits are integrated into a brave new world. Also, our memory of past events is often not reliable enough to guarantee true narration. Additionally, older oral narratives, as described in Scalise Sugiyama (2005), do not have the report of

414 PART II CASE STUDIES

actual events as their primary goal. In other words, from the cognitive and evolutionary point of view (see also Boyd 2009, on the origin of stories), the main role of literary fiction is not directly relevant to the issue of truthfulness.[7] Finally, language offers many forms signaling the speaker's limited responsibility for the accuracy of what is said (whether because the speaker is quoting someone else's words or describing an imaginary scenario). To conclude, the "specificity" of literature does not seem to consist in its fictional character, but rather in its cognitive (and evolutionary) functions, and its linguistic form, which are designed to help fulfill those functions.

At the cognitive level, literary texts are deeply rooted in everyday understanding of the cultural significance of events, mainly through constructs referred to as "frames" (Fillmore 1985, 2006). The simplest example may be literature's reliance on social institutions such as family or marriage. While choosing a partner is a complex issue in every culture, it is not always reliant on the same frames. Clearly, there are cultures in which having a child out of wedlock would not cause a woman to become a social and family outcast. Thus a "marriage frame" may determine how the story is told and how the conflict is set up, but it may also determine how the story will be received. The cultural meaning of frames manifests itself in various contexts, but it is brought into the discourse through language forms.

Not all frames are as general as the "marriage frame." For example, I have argued elsewhere (Dancygier 2009) that proper names, rather than being simple pointers to unique referents, are in fact rich frames that determine their use in discourse. In the simplest case, the name "Everest" should typically refer to the mountain, but it is in fact commonly used to evoke its cultural frame alone (top achievement and high difficulty). Thus when Hillary Clinton's desire to be elected president was described as "her political Everest," what was being suggested was that in the area of politics the presidency would be her top achievement. What is more, such a use relies directly on the available frames of the "highest peak" and "highest achievement in climbing," and only then uses the conceptual metaphor STATUS IS UP to map height onto political hierarchy. It also supports the main characteristic of frames, that any aspect of the frame gives us access to its entire structure. To return to literature, proper names of characters from well-known texts (e.g., Hamlet, Romeo, Don Quixote) are often used to refer to the frames (e.g., an unsolvable dilemma, tragic love, or delusional pursuit of unrealistic goals), and not to the characters within the context of their texts. For example, "a postmodern Hamlet" may refer to the particular choices in acting and directing, "a contemporary Romeo" may describe today's unhappy lover, while "a political Don Quixote" could be a politician driven by delusions. Further analysis of how framing structures literary meaning would exceed the limits of this paper, but it should be clear that literature relies on frames both in how it is written and how it is read, and that frames are cognitive and linguistic correlates of its cultural specificity.

In a sense, the basic communicative set-up is also a frame we use to process various literary forms. The presence of a text evokes the presence of a communicator, and our access to the text frames us as addressees. We can thus naturally describe the reading experience in terms of communication, as in "author X or text Y describes, criticizes,

---

7. Also, the writer may intentionally try to blur the boundaries. For example, Poe's novel *The narrative of Arthur Gordon Pym of Nantucket* was first published as a true story.

says Z." Furthermore, the frame extends in interesting ways into the experience of drama. Theatre is ostensibly built on the assumption that the audience witnesses the events and conversations between characters while not being a participant, although this assumption is only accurate to a degree. However, some earlier forms of novelistic discourse clearly attempt to recreate a semblance of a "ground" where crucial events can occur, but also where characters can say what is on their mind. The addressee's access to characters' minds seems to be the problem that drives much of the development of literary genres, and the language constructions that emerge in the process. In what follows, I will attempt to trace some of these developments.

The very idea of a theatrical performance is striking in its similarity to the basic communicative set-up. Characters share a temporal and spatial frame in terms of the limits imposed by the stage, the duration of the play, and also in the represented story. They communicate with each other directly, so that anything relevant to the story can be attributed to a participant. Even when narration is required, it is delivered by a chorus or its equivalent, and thus communicated through a "mouthpiece." And yet, older theatrical forms (e.g., classical tragedy or Japanese nō) often rely on masks, rather than on the facial expressions of actors, as if assuming that the bodies of actors are best used as a medium which conveys words and takes the position of a discourse participant, rather than embodying the character in ways suggesting an emotional involvement.

Interestingly, the transition from early theater to early novel developed forms that attempted to preserve the "somebody said so" or "somebody saw them do it" set-up. For example, one of the first English novels, *Clarissa*, represents the so-called epistolary novel, where major characters "say" what they think and feel in letters. Zunshine (2006) sees *Clarissa* as a perfect exercise in our "theory-of-mind" skills, but we need to note that it is possible to interpret it this way because we are given access to characters' intimate exchanges, even if they are not always sincere. The text often hailed as "the first novel," *Don Quixote*, is closely preceded by another text in Spanish, *Celestina*, a bizarre narrative, basically a novel in dialogue. Characters take turns as if they were on stage, but their turns are sometimes several pages long. This blend of a novel and a play makes a huge effort to preserve the communicative authority of the story being told by someone, because various bits are directly attributed to specific participants. The idea that we cannot know what goes on in the story or in characters' minds unless they tell us themselves is preserved in a narrative form which paves the way for novelistic discourse.

Early English novels, by writers such as Sterne and Fielding, dispense with the theatricality, but their narrators create a very convincing illusion of telling the reader what happened in a personal tone. The formula, known as the "intrusive narrator," was quite common in Victorian novels, but not very popular in contemporary literature, with the exception of literature aimed at young readers.[8] It has a distinct flavor of irony, a direct result of the narrator's role as the story's teller, rather than a participant. The clash of viewpoints and the narrator's distance from the story are responsible for the disengaging

---

8. Interestingly, Tolkien uses "intrusive" narration in his novels for younger readers (*Farmer Giles, The Hobbit*), but not in *The Lord of the Rings*, where there is no room for humor and irony. Also, many children's stories use it to guide and amuse the young addressees, and also make the texts more natural for adults to read aloud.

effect resembling irony or humor. Intrusive narrators are communicators, engaging readers in a mock pretence of a "conversation," a formula that is still comfortably close to "real" communication. All these examples suggest that the language of the texts supports an emergence of discourse in which one participant in a written exchange (a narrator) can claim access to all the necessary facts of the story as well as the minds of the characters and report them to the reader reliably. The "ground" of such exchanges is the written narrative formula, in which, similarly to speech genres such as a lecture or sermon, one participant is granted an extended turn and all the authority.

However, with skill and imagination drama can naturally be used to tell a multidimensional story and represent the inner states of characters without them having to describe their thoughts directly. Shakespearean drama provides salient examples of how the essence of a dramatic story relies on a multimodal nature of theater and on specific language constructions. The richness of Shakespeare's skill in this respect calls for an extended study, but because space is limited I will focus here on a few selected examples.

First of all, Shakesperean characters often blend the roles of participants with that of a narrator. Many off-stage events in every play are reported by one character to another, often in detail and depth not warranted by their actual participation. This suggests a broader concept of narration on stage, where the ostensible addressee may be another character, but the actual addressee is the audience. This blend of dramatic roles is possible because of our natural assumption of communication being dependent not on just a unidirectional intention, but on the shared "ground" and joint attention. In a sense, anything said on the stage is ostensibly addressed to someone else on the stage, but tacitly used to engage the attention of the viewers, who are there, after all, to hear and see everything. The most salient example is the description of Ophelia's death, which, if observed by someone who could report it later on the stage, could have easily been prevented by the witness. But the role of the report is narration, not conversation, and thus the question does not arise.

Shakespeare's inventiveness is most visible in the way that he exploits the multimodal nature of the stage to give material presence to aspects of the story that provide access to the character's mental states, without their always going into lengthy soliloquies as statements of inner thoughts. Examples are numerous, from Othello's address to the candle whose flame metaphorically represents Desdemona's life, to Macbeth's witches, who give an account of his hidden wishes and desires, to ghosts and apparitions that narrate (and also embody) the story's past (Old Hamlet), or evoke emotional outbursts that reveal a sense of guilt and pain. Banquo's ghost is visible to Macbeth only, because it serves as a catalyst that allows Macbeth to display his fear and guilt to all present. However, the ghost is perhaps primarily visible to the audience, which needs to appreciate Macbeth's feelings in a way other characters do not. If Banquo's ghost were to tell a story, like Old Hamlet's ghost, he would have to be visible to all characters, because they, and not Macbeth, would need that knowledge. But Macbeth's feelings are the target here, not the story. These devices, remarkably less common in the production of Shakespeare's contemporaries, signal the transition from the "literature-of-the-story" to the "literature-of-the-mind."

Most remarkably, Shakespeare is a master of exploiting the materiality of the stage and matching it with linguistic constructions prompting very complex blends. Material objects, as discussed in Hutchins (2005), often serve as anchors for complex mental constructs and blends. In a contemporary context, a watch is an example of an object designed not only to measure time, but to give a tangible form to a rich conceptual understanding of the cyclical nature of time and its cultural consequences such as schedules, calendars, etc. On the other hand, objects vary significantly in their cultural salience and richness of framing. Thus an object such as a hair dryer has a very specific function and is relatively narrowly framed (beauty salon, hair styling), but an object such as a knife or a gun has a broad range of associations (danger, bodily harm, intent to kill, conflict, revenge, etc.). Moreover, a text may give more significance to the most innocuous objects by framing them within the story. Desdemona's handkerchief is an example of an object that acquires special meaning in the course of the play (it is used by another character to be framed as the proof of Desdemona's guilt). Objects can thus play a significant storytelling role, especially when they are newly framed within the story told in the play and used skillfully in combination with language use prompting increased joint attention.

Interesting examples of such language use can be found in *Romeo and Juliet*'s death scene. Romeo, fooled into thinking that his beloved is dead, drinks potent poison and dies, and then Juliet awakens from her drug-induced sleep and kills herself with Romeo's dagger. In the moment of death both are on the stage alone (not counting the dead surrounding them in the family tomb). How can their thoughts and feelings be expressed? Their faces are not visible to all the viewers clearly enough to rely on facial expressions. They have to talk. In the crucial moment of drinking the poison and plunging the knife in they both address their instruments of death and use the same linguistic form, one that is not common in colloquial discourse. Romeo addresses his poison vial with the words "Come, bitter conduct, come, unsavoury guide!," and a moment later Juliet says "O, happy dagger! This is thy sheath. There rust and let me die." In both cases, the characters have no addressees, but the audience needs an elaboration of the acts they are committing, and, perhaps most importantly, a sense of their emotional state as they take their lives. While it could be done through a monologue (Romeo speaks for a bit before he reaches the decision to die), the expressions quoted here are used just before their deaths. Quite clearly, the addresses to death weapons, in both cases, inform the audience of the characters intention to die in the next few moments.

From a linguistic point of view, the expressions are bizarre. First, we do not often talk to objects (unless they are misbehaving computers or cars), though if we do, it is usually to express exasperation or hope, so at least the objects share the role of expression of emotion. Second, it is unusual for adjectives like *bitter* (emotionally) or *happy* to describe objects like poison vials and daggers. Crucially, the contrast also shows the difference between Romeo's and Juliet's emotions. He dies in despair about her death, while she dies welcoming the end of their plight. The construction is in fact a complex deployment of frame evocation and blending, relying, also, on more basic aspects of materiality, embodiment, and joint attention.

Both the vial and the dagger evoke frames wherein there is a slot for a killer and for a victim, while the objects themselves are typically no more than instruments in the hands of killers. These frames are not available on the stage other than through the presence of these objects, and thus instruments of death become rightful participants in the discourse of the play and in the processes of meaning construction. The speakers (Romeo and then Juliet) using the instruments are profiled as both killers and victims, and thus the roles in the frame of discourse (an addressee and a speaker) are blended with the roles in the killing frame. Because of the specificity of theatrical discourse, in which the audience is the proper addressee, acts on stage need to be spoken about and identified clearly, to ensure joint attention even for those who have limited visual access to the stage. Thus, all the basic means of theatrical meaning construction (materiality/embodiment, visual access, joint attention, speech, and language constructions) are crucially involved in getting the meaning across.

A more detailed analysis of the blending processes responsible for such a combination of innovative linguistic constructions and the reliance on materiality and embodiment is beyond the scope of this paper, but there are general conclusions to be drawn here. First, language has evolved as a means of communication between humans, in the context of a shared "ground." The theater creates a situation where the ground is much more complex. The communication is indirect and subjected to the needs of telling a fictional story, so that either other characters or material objects serve as mediators.[9] Language has thus adjusted to new needs. At the same time, theatrical discourse relies very deeply on human cognition, and especially its oldest roots; embodiment and materiality. In a sense, human bodies and material objects are coopted to play a role in constructing representations of human mental states such as love, despair, resignation, and willingness to die, in ways reaching far beyong mimesis. All these paths of meaning construction are subordinated to the most general communicative goal of achieving joint attention, possibly the oldest and most central piece in the puzzle of the emergence of language.[10] It does not seem likely that a literary form such as theatrical discourse would emerge independently of all the cognitive and linguistic underpinnings it clearly relies on. But it is also not just an offshoot of stable mental and linguistic abilities already in place, because there is also a highly creative process of economically using language and constructing new paths of achieving joint attention. Finally, in Shakespearean drama the goal of representing emotional and mental states is clearly just becoming linguistically manageable, beyond the basic forms described above, wherein they have to be communicated by the person experiencing them.

As the observations here suggest, literary forms change through time, in the direction of better representing fictional minds. Specific narrative forms like Free Indirect Discourse[11] (which represent characters' thoughts and/or words without making it clear who the sayer or the thinker is and blend the narrator's voice with that of a character) seem to give immediate access to what a character may be thinking. Such forms appear quite late in the development of fiction (some narratologists find them in the texts written by Jane Austen). Later stages, such as modernism, are more and more adventurous in their attempts to reach directly into a character's "stream of consciousness." Access to

---

9. The links between embodiment and materiality on the one hand and the language of literature on the other can be observed in a much broader range of phenomena. For more discussion, see Dancygier (2011).

10. Joint attention has become one of the central concepts in the discussion of culture, language, and also literature (see Boyd 2009; Oakley 2009; Tomasello 2008).

11. Constructions representing speech and thought of characters are very complex and varied. For an excellent analysis of the types and their meanings, see Vandelanotte (2009).

minds becomes the central aspect of the narrative, and the story is overshadowed by it. Further developments include shifting viewpoints, fragmentation of the story, narrators changing without warning, narrators whose identity has to be guessed, split identities, and so on. Whatever the explanation for any specific narrative solution, the language of the narrative is evolving in ways that are motivated by increasing exposure to texts as representative of thoughts and other mental states. This new focus affects sentence structure, creative use of pronouns, misleading proper names, unrealistic choice of tense, disrupted structure of chapters (including one of Cela's novels which is one long sentence), and many more. Linguistically speaking, such changes cannot occur without cognitive support, such as increased openness to different viewpoints, understanding of non-standard discourse grounds, acceptance of discontinuity of thought, and so on. Although this fits the description of cognitive play used by Boyd, the rules of the game are being changed on the fly and still do not prevent successful processing. What is more, the "play" patterns solidify into some kind of "narrative intelligence" that yields enhanced reading skills, and a better concept of the mind (whether fictional or not).

At the same time, embodiment remains central to the construction of stories. Fictional bodies are changing almost as fast as the fictional minds. The list of examples is endless. Rushdie's main character, whose large nose and clogged nasal passages serve as a sort of "antenna" allowing him to communicate with other "midnight's children"; the heavy-bodied protagonist of *The Shipping News*, whose mind is equally weighed down until he finds his place and his love; the pair of lovers (one mute, the other blind) in *The Blind Assassin*, metaphorically unable to see the truth or to speak about it; Coetzee's *Slow Man*, unable to move, physically and metaphorically. Throughout, the bodily limitations of characters are naturally used to represent their mental dispositions. Even more interestingly, literary texts now commonly explore minds as brains. Recent novels have included patients suffering from autism, Tourette's syndrome, Capgras syndrome, Asperger's syndrome, de Clerambaut syndrome, Huntingdon's disease, and the like. Each is, in a different way, a story about the mind and the different ways in which the disorders help us understand who we are. Clearly, literature has moved on from mate selection and Oedipus complex to a more contemporary version of psychology and neuroscience, in its continued strive to understand humans and their minds.

To return to the main question, the relevance of language and cognition to literature and its evolutionary roots, it seems that the evolutionary program can only profit from a closer engagement with the issue of creativity and its cognitive underpinnings. Literature and other linguistic artifacts are intertwined with art, religion, and many other cultural products because they rely on abilities which allow humans to link conceptual structures across different domains and use all the expressive abilities (linguistic, visual, performative, musical, and so on) in creative conceptualization. Literature cannot be sufficiently explained through the minds of hunter-gatherers alone, because the abilities present in behaviourally modern human beings continue developing on the basis of new cognitive and cultural needs. The very emergence of literary forms (as written forms) out of oral storytelling[12] requires an extensive discussion of cognitive and linguistic abilities, even if it is not possible to attribute all such abilities to evolution. We need to be able to talk

---

12. Interestingly discussed in Boyd (2009).

about the cognitive underpinnings of such cultural changes in terms which are representative of the behavior of modern humans. Crucially, we need to be able to understand how the processes that lie at the bottom of these changes are capable of yielding new conceptualizations and giving new forms to the changing and varied viewpoints driving contemporary culture.

The processes of blending and framing have already been put in the centre of the discussion of the evolution of language. For example, Fauconnier and Turner (2008) argue that the emergence of language and other specifically human abilities should be viewed as the emergence of cognitive learning strategies and of double-scope blends.[13] As they point out, there will never be enough of "language" in the grammar and the vocabulary to allow us to deal with the vast scope of meanings, including new meanings, to be expressed. This requires reliance on conceptualization, representation, and blending. Deacon's theory, putting most of the weight on the slow emergence of language and mental ability as co-products of the same evolutionary processes, is an inspiration for a blending approach to language evolution and meshes well with it (see Deacon 2006). It has also been accepted by Bickerton (2009), whose focus until now has been on the emergence of grammar. Perhaps it is time for literary scholars interested in evolution and the mind to also start looking at language as the tool whereby new meanings can be expressed, and not a set of forms to be acknowledged and then put to one side. Without an understanding of how language and cognition are jointly responsible for the emergence of literature and other creative forms of expression, the evolutionary study of literature will not be able to account for new literary forms and themes, and will lack a solid foundation in its work towards the goal: the evolutionary explanation of one of the central manifestations of human creativity.

References

Barkow, Jerome, Leda Cosmides, and John Tooby, eds. 1992. *The adapted mind: Evolutionary psychology and the generation of culture.* New York: Oxford University Press.

Bickerton, Derek. 2009. *Adam's tongue: How humans made language, how language made humans.* New York: Hill and Wang.

Boyd, Brian. 2009. *On the origin of stories: Evolution, cognition, and fiction.* Cambridge, MA: Belknap Press of Harvard University Press.

Canning, Patricia. 2008. "The bodie and the letters both": "Blending" the rules of early modern religion. *Language and Literature* 17: 187–203.

Carroll. Joseph. 1995. *Evolution and literary theory.* Columbia, MO: University of Missouri Press.

Carroll. Joseph. 2005. *Literary Darwinism: Evolution, human nature, and literature.* Evanston, IL: Northwestern University Press.

Carroll. Joseph. 2008. Target essay: An evolutionary paradigm for literary study. *Style* 42(2/3), 3–138.

---

13. Blending theory identifies several levels of blending complexity. Double-scope blending can link more complex and more disparate conceptual structures, and involves the highest creativity skills.

Cook, Amy. 2007. Interplay: The method and potential of a cognitive scientific approach to theatre. *Theatre Journal* 59: 579–594.

Cook, Amy. 2010 *Shakespearean neuroplay:Reinvigorating the study of dramatic texts and performance through cognitive science.* New York: Palgrave Macmillan.

Coulson, Seana. 2001. *Semantic leaps: Frame shifting and conceptual blending in meaning construction.* Cambridge, UK: Cambridge University Press.

Coulson, Seana and Todd Oakley, eds. 2000. Conceptual blending (special issue). *Cognitive Linguistics* 11(3/4).

Coulson, Seana and Todd Oakley, eds. 2005. Conceptual blending (special issue). *Journal of Pragmatics* 37.

Dancygier, Barbara. 2005. Blending and narrative viewpoint: Jonathan Raban's travels through mental spaces. *Language and Literature* 14(2): 99–127.

Dancygier, Barbara. 2006. Preface: What can blending do for you? *Language and Literature* 15(1): 5–15.

Dancygier, Barbara. 2007. Narrative anchors and the processes of story construction: The Case of Margaret Atwood's *The blind assassin. Style* 41(2): 133–152.

Dancygier, Barbara. 2008a. "The text and the story: Levels of blending in fictional narratives." In *Mental spaces in discourse and interaction*, eds. Todd Oakley, and Anders Hougaard, 51–78. Amsterdam and Philadelphia: John Benjamins.

Dancygier, Barbara. 2008b. "Personal pronouns, blending, and narrative viewpoint." In *Language in the context of use: Cognitive and functional approaches to language and language learning*, eds. Andrea Tyler, Yiyoung Kim, and Mari Takada, 167–182. Berlin: Mouton de Gruyter.

Dancygier, Barbara. 2009. "Genitives and proper names in constructional blends." In *New directions in cognitive linguistics*, eds. Vyvyan Evans, and Stephanie Pourcel, 161–181. Amsterdam and Philadelphia: John Benjamins Publishing Company.

Dancygier, Barbara 2011. *The language of stories: A cognitive approach.* Cambridge, UK: Cambridge University Press.

Deacon, Terrence. 1997. *The symbolic species: The coevolution of language and the brain.* New York: W.W. Norton.

Deacon, Terrence. 2006. "The aesthetic faculty." In *The artful mind: Cognitive science and the riddle of human creativity*, ed. Mark Turner, 21–56. Oxford, UK: Oxford University Press.

Donald, Merlin. 2006. "Art and cognitive evolution." In *The artful mi, UKnd: Cognitive science and the riddle of human creativity*, ed. Mark Turner, 3–20. Oxford, UK: Oxford University Press.

Dutton, Denis. 2009. *The art instinct: Beauty, pleasure, and human evolution.* New York: Bloomsbury Press.

Fauconnier, Gilles and Mark Turner. 1994. Conceptual projection and middle spaces. San Diego: University of California, Department of Cognitive Science Technical Report 9401.

Fauconnier, Gilles and Mark Turner. 1996. "Blending as a central process of grammar." In *Conceptual structure, discoure, and language*, ed. Adele Goldberg, 113–130. Stanford: Center for the Study of Language and Information.

Fauconnier, Gilles and Mark Turner. 1998a. Conceptual integration networks. *Cognitive Science* 2(22): 133–187.

Fauconnier, Gilles and Mark Turner. 1998b. Principles of conceptual integration. In *Discourse and cognition: Bridging the gap*, ed. Jean-Pierre Koenig, 269–283. Stanford: Center for the Study of Language and Information.

Fauconnier, Gilles and Mark Turner. 2002. *The way we think: Conceptual blending and the mind's hidden complexities.* New York: Basic Books.

Fauconnier, Gilles and Mark Turner. 2008. "The origin of language as a product of the evolution of modern cognition." In *Origin and evolution of languages: Approaches, models, paradigms*, ed. Laks, Bernard, Serge Cleziou, Jean-Paul Demoule, and Pierre Encrevé. London: Equinox.

Fillmore, Charles J. 1985. Frames and the semantics of understanding. *Quaderni di Semantica* 6: 222–254.

Fillmore, Charles J. 2006. "Frame semantics." In *Cognitive linguistics: Basic readings*, ed. Dirk Geererts, 373–400. Berlin: Mouton de Gruyter.

Gallagher, Shaun. 2005. *How the body shapes the mind*. New York: Oxford University Press.

Gibbs, Raymond W., Jr. 2005. *Embodiment and cognitive science*. Cambridge, UK: Cambridge University Press.

Gottschall, Jonathan. 2008a. *The rape of Troy: Evolution, violence and the world of Homer*. Cambridge, UK: Cambridge University Press.

Gottschall, Jonathan. 2008b. *Literature, science, and a new humanities*. New York: Palgrave Macmillan.

Gottschall, Jonathan and David Sloan Wilson, eds. 2005. *The literary animal: Evolution and the nature of narrative*. Evanston, IL: Northwestern University Press.

Hauser, Mark, Noam Chomsky, and Tecumseh Fitch. 2002.The language faculty: Who has it, what is it, and how did it evolve? *Science* 298: 1569–1579.

Herman, David. 2002. *Story logic: Problems and possibilities of narrative*. Lincoln and London: University of Nebraska Press.

Herman, David. 2003. "Stories as a tool for thinking." In *Narrative theory and the cognitive sciences*, ed. David Herman, 163–193. Stanford: Center for the Study of Language and Information.

Herman, David, ed. 2003. *Narrative theory and the cognitive sciences*. Stanford: Center for the Study of Language and Information.

Hutchins, Edwin. 2005. Material anchors for conceptual blends. *Journal of Pragmatics* 37: 1555–1577.

Johnson, Mark. 1987. *The body in the mind: The bodily basis of meaning, imagination, and reason*. Chicago: Chicago University Press.

Johnson, Mark. 2007. *The meaning of the body: Aesthetics of human understanding*. Chicago: Chicago University Press.

Langacker, Ronald W. 1990. *Concept, image, symbol: The cognitive basis of grammar*. Berlin: Mouton de Gruyter.

Langacker, Ronald W. 1987/1991. *Foundations of cognitive grammar*, 2 vols. Stanford, CA: Stanford University Press.

Oakley, Todd. 2009. *From attention to meaning*. Bern, Germany: Peter Lang Publishing.

Oakley, Todd, and Anders Hougaard, eds. 2008. *Mental spaces in discourse and interaction*. Amsterdam and Philadelphia: John Benjamins.

Pecher, Diane, and Rolf A. Zwaan, eds. 2005. *Grounding cognition: The role of perception and action in memory, language, and thinking*. Cambridge, UK: Cambridge University Press.

Prinz, Jesse, J. 2004. *Gut reactions: A perceptual theory of emotion*. New York: Oxford University Press.

Scalise Sugiyama, Michelle. 2005. Reverse-engineering narrative: Evidence of special design. In *The literary animal: Evolution and the nature of narratives*, ed. Jonathan Gottschall, and David S. Wilson, 177–195. Evanston, IL: Northwestern University Press.

Slingerland, Edward. 2008. *What science offers the humanities: Integrating body and culture*. Cambridge, UK and New York: Cambridge University Press.

Spivey, Michael J. 2007. *The continuity of mind*. New York: Oxford University Press.

Sweetser, Eve. 2006. Whose rhyme is whose reason? Sound and sense in *Cyrano de Bergerac*. *Language and Literature* 15(1): 29–54.

Tomasello, Michael. 1999. *The cultural origins of human cognition*. Cambridge, MA: Harvard University Press.

Tomasello, Michael. 2008. *Origins of human communication*. Cambridge: MIT Press.

Tooby, John, and Leda Cosmides.1992. "The psychological foundations of culture." In *The adapted mind: Evolutionary psychology and the generation of culture*, ed. Barkow, Jerome H., Leda Cosmides, and John Tooby, 19–136. New York: Oxford University Press.

Turner, Mark. 1996. *The literary mind: The origins of thought and language*. New York: Oxford University Press.

Turner, Mark. 2003. "Double-scope stories." In *Narrative theory and the cognitive sciences*, ed. David Herman, 117–142. Stanford: Center for the Study of Language and Information.

Turner, Mark, ed. 2006. *The artful mind: Cognitive science and the riddle of human creativity*. Oxford, UK: Oxford University Press.

Vandelanotte, Lieven. 2009. *Speech and thought representation in English: A cognitive-functional approach*. Berlin: Mouton de Gruyter.

Verhagen, Arie. 2005. *Constructions of intersubjectivity: Discourse, syntax, and cognition*. Oxford, UK: Oxford University Press.

Verhagen, Arie. 2008. "Intersubjectivity and the architecture of the language system." In *The shared mind: Perspectives on intersubjectivity*, ed. Zlatev, Jordan, Timothy P. Racine, Chris Sinha, and Esa Itkonen. Amsterdam and Philadelphia: John Benjamins Publishing Company. 307–332.

Wilson, Edward O. 1998. *Consilience: The unity of knowledge*. New York: Alfred A. Knopf.

Zunshine, Lisa. 2006. *Why we read fiction: Theory of mind and the novel*. Columbus, OH: Ohio State University Press.

AFTERWORD
TWO POINTS ABOUT TWO CULTURES

Geoffrey Galt Harpham

When C. P. Snow gave the Rede Lecture in 1959, the gap between the "two cultures" seemed unbridgeable. The division involved not merely subject matter and methodology, but temperament, social attitudes, and politics. Much has changed in the last half century, and it is no longer the case that scientists and humanists regard each other with the disdain and indifference Snow describes. Indeed, very little of Snow's account remains true today. For one thing, few people now recognize what Snow called the "moral component right in the grain of science itself," or claim that scientists have "the future in their bones." The scientific establishment, which Snow characterized as "expansive...confident at the roots...certain that history is on its side, impatient, intolerant, creative rather than critical, good-natured and brash," is now largely dependent on (diminishing) government funding and can hardly afford the kind of pride in the manifest uselessness of its work that Snow noted among the scientists of his day. So difficult is it for a university researcher to obtain funding from sources other than the government or corporations that "blue skies" research of the kind on which Snow and his fellow scientists prided themselves does not get done at all.[1] And so difficult is it to sustain a research project on government funding that few scientists permit themselves to dream that their work may one day contribute to solving huge and intractable (and potentially politically controversial) problems such as the elimination of poverty. It is hard, in fact, to recognize in today's scientific community any of the characteristics that Snow attributes to scientific culture, other than a general rationality.

On the other side, the socially and intellectually complacent culture of "literary intellectuals" that Snow derides has simply vanished, and has been replaced by professors of the humanities disciplines, primarily literature. These professors do not labor, as Snow's literary intellectuals did, under the burden of the extreme right-wing politics of Yeats, Pound, Lawrence, Eliot, and Wyndham Lewis. Nor, as a rule, do they stand up for "traditional culture." In fact, for at least the last 30 years, humanists have been enthusiastically trashing the political right, and traditional culture has no harsher critics than professors of English. It is true that many humanists resist the notion that the final solution

1. See for example: http://arstechnica.com/science/news/2007/04/how-doubling-the-nihs-budget-created-a-funding-crisis.ars; and http://www.phds.org/the-big-picture/nih-funding-crisis/. In England, the situation is the same: s ee http://www.telegraph.co.uk/science/science-news/3325553/Pessimism-and-anger-over-science-funding-crisis.html.

to humanistic enigmas such as language, aesthetics, and ethics will be discovered in labs run by cognitive neuroscientists, evolutionary biologists, or primatologists. However, as a group, humanists are not socially complacent, ignorant of science, or politically conservative. Rather, they are, like their scientific counterparts: anxious, demoralized, conscious of losing ground, and detached from mainstream culture.

Yet, despite the massive transformations in the cultures he describes—changes that ought, it seems, to have rendered his analysis irrelevant—Snow remains pertinent. The division between science and the humanities (which predates Snow, of course: the Huxley-Arnold debate was a nineteenth century version of the war between Snow and his literary antagonist F. R. Leavis) remains a stubborn and even embarrassing feature of academic culture that many people believe engenders confusion and inhibits the advance of knowledge. Why is this? Have we been so convinced by Hume's fact-value distinction that we blindly reinstitute it wherever we can? Why can't we think our way out of this paper bag? Why has E. O. Wilson's consilience not become the watchword of the academy? If the division is not sustained by sound reasoning, as Wilson, along with many of the contributors to this volume confidently believe; if there are no divisions in nature corresponding to the current categories of knowledge; and if consilience would deliver all the goods its advocates promise, then why are we still awaiting the new dawn of "vertical integration"? If this baneful division serves us, and reflects on us, so poorly, why can't we simply do away with it? Why is a volume such as this still necessary?

I have two responses to these questions, each offered in a spirit of friendly non-partisan provocation. First, I would like to suggest that the division between science and the humanities is not as deep or radical as many believe, and second, that the consilience advocated by some represented in this volume would, if achieved, destroy both science and the humanities.

The first argument can only be sketched, but it is, in my opinion, indisputable. My own field of literary study, for example, is regarded by many as the most humanistic of the humanities, the field that represents the clearest opposition to the methodology of the sciences, but in the beginning, this was not the case. The hoary ancestor of today's blogging, Blackberrying, black-clad English professor is the Reverend Mr. Casaubon of George Eliot's *Middlemarch*, a black-clad antiquarian pedant convinced, absurdly, that his tedious labors had placed him in possession of "the key to all mythologies." Casaubon is a philologist. Invented at the end of the eighteenth century as a way of ascertaining the historical truth about Homer's text, philology rapidly developed methods of textual scholarship that remain impressive as feats of intellectual method and rigor. The primary object was to understand in a formal and historical sense the language of the text; but beyond this, philologists sought to recreate, from linguistic evidence, an account of the total culture from which the text emerged. Nor did they stop there. By developing methods for comparing languages, grouping languages into "families" with genealogies, and inferring long-lost "mother" languages from the known languages that descended from them, philology sought to recreate the aboriginal forms of human consciousness, which would provide the key to human nature, as well as to all mythologies. As early as the 1860s, one of the greatest, or at least most renowned philologists, Max Müller, was able to pronounce philology the "Queen of the Sciences," a claim that was not immediately challenged. Indeed, scholars in other fields that aspired to be sciences studied the methods of philology to learn what a science was. Darwin, for example, knew the work of Müller and other linguistic scholars, and found their linguistic genealogies so impressive that he included, as the sole illustration in *The Origin of Species*, a "Tree of Life" that was manifestly modeled on linguistic tree-diagrams. Darwin's most prominent German advocate, the polymath Ernest Haeckel, was persuaded that the key to understanding the evolution of the species was the study of language, and urged biologists to create taxonomies as rigorous as those of philology. There was, in short, a time when the scholarly study of language, literature, and culture was pursued as a science, and regarded by other scientists as a model for scientific method and rigor.

This situation, of course, did not last. As Gerald Graff showed in *Professing Literature: An Institutional History* (1987), modern literary studies were born out of the struggle of "generalists" to break away from the philological "scholars" who, by the beginning of the twentieth century, had degenerated into a disorderly combination of myopic pedantry on the one hand, and unembarrassed race-theory on the other. This struggle continued throughout the twentieth century, with a series of new theoretical approaches—New Criticism, psychoanalytic theory, Marxist theory, structuralism, poststructuralism, and deconstruction—promoting themselves as methodologies consistent with the research ethos characteristic of science, and promising to redeem the study of literature from its regressive belle-lettristic amateurism. In some ways, this internal struggle persists in English scholarship in the form of an ambivalent relationship to the concept of disciplinarity. Some among the professoriate insist on scholarship, professionalism, and certitude within a limited field, while others make a vitalist argument that the essence of literary study is interpretive judgment, the articulation of values, and charismatic teaching that awakens young minds and hearts. In "The Decline of the English Department,"[2] William M. Chace, past president of Wesleyan and Emory, and an English teacher of 40 years' standing, takes the latter position, citing and endorsing recurrent doubts about the viability of English as a scholarly pursuit. Chace offers, as a way out of what he sees as an "academic dead end," a return to "the aesthetic wellsprings of literature, the rock-solid fact…that it can indeed amuse, delight, and educate." In practice, Chace says, this means that English departments should surrender their claim to contributing to the research function of the university and prioritize courses in composition, the "sturdy lifeline" to university resources. For Chace and others of his persuasion, the study of literature is and ought to be no science.

If the formidably productive Joseph Carroll has his way, however, Chace will not prevail. A consilient literary study with evolutionary science at its core will become the vanguard discipline whose methods and discoveries will herald a general reconfiguration of knowledge. The essay that Carroll, along with Jonathan Gottschall, Daniel Kruger, and John Johnson contributed to this volume, gives something of the flavor of the Darwinian literary project, but not necessarily of its scope. Evolutionary literary studies now constitutes a well defined movement, with books, articles, conferences, special issues of journals, blogs, and every other accoutrement of a dynamic scientific undertaking. In a few years' time, the same might be said of a related but more recent movement to integrate cognitive science and literary study. Driven by younger scholars, this movement focuses on those aspects of the

---

2. William M. Chace, "The Decline of the English Department," *The American Scholar*, Autumn, 2009; online at: http://www.theamericanscholar.org/the-decline-of-the-english-department/.

literary experience that can be illuminated by the theory of mind developed by cognitive psychology.³ Other science-based approaches to narrative, metaphor, literary imagery, literary responsiveness, and to bioculture more generally, are also making strong claims to the future, with the result that literary study, which was for Snow the site of anti-scientific regression, is today the most promising site within the humanities of consilient rapprochement.

The larger point I want to make is that this approach to science by literary scholars is not an astonishing new development in the field, for literary study began as a science and only detached itself from science with immense difficulty and ambivalent results. Something similar can be said of philosophy in light of the recent interest in "experimental philosophy," in which philosophical concepts of, for example, normative ethics, are subjected to experimental testing of a kind more readily associated with social science. In a book that both announces and surveys this approach, Kwame Anthony Appiah argues that it should be taken very seriously. He points out that attempts by philosophers to distinguish moral from psychological components in a given ethical decision fail the common sense test, and that some kinds of problems are better served by an approach that does not make the attempt at all.⁴ To reassure philosophers who might be dismayed by the subjection of philosophy to social science, Appiah also contends that experimental philosophy, or "X-phi," merely continues philosophy's ancient preoccupation with empirical questions. This preoccupation has taken various forms, including the "linguistic turn" that dominated much of twentieth-century philosophy. This turn actually included within itself a science-humanities split: one branch—the branch on which Wittgenstein, Carnap, Frege, and Quine were perched—was manifestly empirical and logic based, focusing on the presumably hard and knowable facts of language; and the other, whose most prominent advocate was Richard Rorty, was militantly humanistic and dedicated to narrative and rhetoric.

As the example of philology has already suggested, language is the subject that most insistently and tantalizingly raises the prospect of the ultimate reconciliation of science and the humanities. At various times the object of theology (In the beginning was the Word), philosophy, history, literary studies, primatology, cognitive science, anthropology, and evolutionary psychology, language has seemed to be equally available to the scientific and humanistic perspectives. This is particularly evident in the work of Noam Chomsky. Even as he situates his linguistics in the general field of cognitive psychology, Chomsky has drawn attention to an altogether different disciplinary tree diagram that connects Descartes, Herder, and von Humboldt and himself. The most appealing and indeed compelling feature of this humanistic tradition, from Chomsky's perspective, is that it treats

---

3. For an indication of the interests and methods of one of the leaders of this movement, see Lisa Zunshine, *Why We Read Fiction: Theory of Mind and the Novel* (Columbus: Ohio State University Press, 2006), and *Strange Concepts and the Stories They Make Possible: Cognition, Culture, Narrative* (Baltimore: The Johns Hopkins University Press, 2008).

4. See Kwame Anthony Appiah, *Experiments in Ethics* (Cambridge: Harvard University Press, 2008). Also pertinent, with a claim to priority, are Joshua Knobe, *Experimental Philosophy* (New York: Oxford University Press, 2008), and Jesse Prinz, *The Emotional Construction of Morals* (New York: Oxford University Press, 2007).

language as a human endowment, a fact of human nature. The feature of language that most clearly reveals its "natural" rather than "cultural" status is, Chomsky says, the fact that it is not learned laboriously, one component at a time, but emerges with incredible rapidity and assurance, regardless of the linguistic environment the child is in. So far, we are firmly in the domain of cognitive science, but Chomsky does not stop there. Our capacity to produce and understand sentences we have never before encountered suggests to him that our linguistic nature—our human nature—is fundamentally "creative." From there it is but a short step to the commonsense proposal that our political systems should allow for the flourishing of human nature, hence "unarcho-syndicalism," Chomsky's own term for his political stance. So from the abrupt character of the emergence of language in childhood, Chomsky has extracted not only a program for a career's worth of research in general linguistics, but also a philosophy and a political viewpoint . Although he has often protested, disingenuously, that his linguistics and politics are entirely separate undertakings—that, in other words, his is not a consilient undertaking—they are plainly connected by strong and easily traced linkages.

In many scientific fields, researchers are undertaking their own versions of Chomsky's quest for the secret of the human essence. The surge in evolutionary theory has been immensely influential and productive in this respect, as has the development of imaging technologies capable of registering brain activity, including cognitive events once thought to be accessible only to humanistic reflection such as ethical judgments, linguistic understanding, and aesthetic responsiveness. For many years, the humanities have owned the task of understanding fundamental human capabilities, but no longer.

The integration of science and the humanities is an ongoing project that has been with us as long as these disciplines have existed. Integration is the original condition of inquiry, before the emergence of professional, sectoral, or departmental knowledge in a university setting. Each modern field contains within itself a dialectic between what are now considered practices of science, with their emphasis on testable evidence, their interest in pattern and regularity and method, their cognitive optimism (where ignorance was, there shall knowledge be), and their orientation toward prediction on the one hand, and, on the other hand, practices associated with the humanities, with their emphasis on reflection, their interest in local or particular instances, their cognitive pessimism (where certainty was, there doubt shall be), their tendency to plow the same row over and over, their indifference to utility, and their orientation toward the past . The consilience project is driven not only by the desire to advance knowledge by achieving a new synthesis, but also at a deeper level, by the throbbing presence within the fields of both humanistic and scientific forces. This double determination itself reflects a science-humanities convergence, for the one factor looks forward to a new dawn of clarity and the other looks backward to a prior complicating tension that had been eclipsed by the drive to knowledge.

If my first argument is that vertical integration is the original condition of knowledge, my second is that if the project of vertical integration were completed, the consequence would be the destruction of both science and the humanities. I am fortified in this paradoxical pair of convictions by the fact that they are both endorsed, in a sense, by Steven Pinker in this very volume. At the beginning of his essay, "The Humanities and Human Nature," Pinker states bluntly that the kind of knowledge represented by the humanities is essential to society and to human self-understanding; and at the end, he concedes that scientific approaches "are bound to consider only a fraction of the richness in a work of art or scholarship." The task of understanding a work of art requires, he says, with an admirable modesty, "expertise in the particulars of the work and the idiom, and not just generalities of psychology and biology." And throughout his essay, Pinker demonstrates a sympathetic understanding of works of art and humanistic scholarship, an understanding not always in evidence in the discourse of consilience. In his essay, in this volume on "Mind-Body Dualism and the Two Cultures," Edward Slingerland, seems to disqualify the claims to knowledge of that portion of humanities scholarship based on *Verstehen* or interpretive understanding because they are, in his view, based on a false and mystified way of knowing that is ultimately grounded in a mind-body distinction that few would defend on its own terms. Fact-based methods will, Slingerland says, invariably drive out interpretive non-methods because they are more persuasive and contribute to the accumulation of knowledge. Pinker makes no such case, and even suggests that evolutionary biologists could well have learned about "theory of mind" from fiction, which was engaging the subject in a sophisticated way *avant la lettre*.

Slingerland refers to the "special mode of understanding" claimed by the humanities, the "sympathetic understanding" of cultural products that can, according to humanists, only be grasped by mind to mind in an act Slingerland compares to "Vulcan mind-meld." I appreciate the pop-culture reference, which is virtually obligatory in humanistic scholarship, but the tone seems unnecessarily dismissive. Perhaps a more positive approach would be more productive. To meet Slingerland's challenge, let's take the most precious, impressionistic, and enchanted form of humanistic knowledge, literary knowledge. In a recent essay, the distinguished literary scholar Michael Wood notes that, within the field of knowledge, literary studies is distinctive.

> Literature…does not deal in information or announcement. Literature is embodiment, a mode of action; it works over time on the hearts and minds of its readers or hearers. Its result in us, when we are receptive or lucky, is the activation of personal knowledge: knowledge of others and ourselves; knowledge of stubborn, slippery, or forgotten facts; knowledge of old and new possibilities—a knowledge that is often so intimate and so immediate that it scarcely feels like knowledge at all because it feels like something we have always known[5]

I can only imagine the sneering response of some on the scientific side of the line to a passage such as this. But the knowledge Wood describes is not only valuable but essential. To imagine life without it—and Wood's essay is called "A World Without Literature?"—is, from my perspective, to imagine a profoundly impoverished, gray, savorless, and also terrifying and pathetic existence in which we are constantly in search of knowledge we do not have, knowledge that will overturn what we (think we) already know. A world without literature and the kind of knowledge literature provides, or "activates," would be a world without value, a world without a home. Of course, personal knowledge is slippery, inconstant, error-prone, and suspect in many ways. This is why scholarship and criticism are needed, to guide, stimulate, model, and inform this knowledge. But nobody, not even

5. Michael Wood, "A World Without Literature?" *Daedalus*, Winter (2009): 58–67, 62.

scientists, can do without personal knowledge. The history of science affords countless instances where a discovery is not simply mandated by the evidence, but comes at the end of a gradual process of realization undergone by a "receptive or lucky" scientist who eventually realizes something that he had "always known."

And so, the primary reason to resist the final or total integration of science and the humanities is not that it would finally put the serious scientific people in charge and force humanists to confess their crimes and ineptitudes, but that it would destroy both the humanities and the sciences. The real value of non-consilience is that it preserves the possibility within each mode of knowledge of another way of knowing altogether, a way that might not just differ but disconfirm the entire enterprise on which one has embarked. Robert Oppenheimer once wrote that both scientists and artists live "at the edge of mystery." He clearly meant this as a compliment to both groups, I think because he felt it was a good thing that the future should remain open and beckoning, beyond our grasp. A single way of understanding the world would represent not the edge, but the end of mystery. If knowledge were perfectly integrated, we would, in effect, be living not in a universe of expanding possibilities, but on a dying cinder with a finite future. The difference between science and the humanities does not stymie knowledge, but stimulates it, and stimulates it infinitely.

This statement calls out for an example, so I would like to close by referring to a set of experiments recently performed under the supervision of a British literary scholar, Philip Davis, which sought to explore with EEG and FMRI technology the possibility that "the shapes of mentality formed by literary language, in particular syntax, lock into, shift and modify established pathways of the brain."[6] Davis had subjects wired up, and then had them read passages from Shakespeare in which language is used in particularly creative ways, as when a word normally used as one part of speech is converted into another. For example, the noun *spaniel* is transformed into the verb *spanielled*, as when people follow a leader like a dog; or the adjective *mad* becomes *madded,* as in "driven mad." Noting that many believe that the nouns and verbs are processed in different sectors of the brain, Davis posits that such "functional shifts" force the brain out of its customary routines, forcing it to negotiate new pathways, "stretching the human mind towards new connections, making the language itself more alive to us, at a level of neural excitement never fully exorcised by subsequent conceptualization" (269). This excitement, a form of brain self-awareness, is measurable, Davis discovered, as a powerful surge on the EEG graph. "Consciousness," he concludes, "is called into being when simple automaticity is baulked." Davis concludes the essay on an exultant note. It has often been said that literature makes us more self-aware, stretches our horizons, and takes us out of our conventional ways of thinking, but he has discovered striking empirical verification for these clichés.

Davis also discovered a new way of thinking about literary language, as the purest form of consciousness itself, "the best model brain science has to work from, if it is to capture the spontaneous living complexity of the human brain, and not merely limit itself to subjects spotting the color red" (272). The last clause is a swipe at those scientific experiments in which super-sophisticated technology is deployed in the service of pointless or trivial questions that do not connect to any real human interest, or the kind of research

6. Philip Davis, "Syntax and Pathways," *Interdisciplinary Science Reviews* 2008 (33.4): 265–77, 265.

in which Snow's scientists took particular delight, regarding it as particularly pure. Davis's implication seems to be that scientific knowledge and technology are as dependent on imaginative and meaningful—humanistic— hypotheses and interpretations as humanists are on method, empiricism, and evidence. One can quarrel with Davis's experiments (which seem to me preliminary) and with the conclusions he draws from them (which seem to me adventuresome), but it is clear that he has been stimulated into productive humanistic thought by the possibility of empirical verification, even as he has maintained as a disciplinary prerogative the right to formulate the questions and interpret the data. I hope that neuroscientists read him and others like him and find themselves stimulated to develop even further the capacity to study the human mind in a way that will give us new ways of looking at the mystery of the human brain. The future lies not with the success of consilience alone, but also with its failure.

APPENDIX

"INTEGRATING SCIENCE AND THE HUMANITIES"

An Exploratory Workshop from the Peter Wall Institute for Advanced Studies at the University of British Columbia
Held at the University of British Columbia, September 26–28, 2008
http://www.sci-hum.pwias.ubc.ca/

Talks and Topics

Science and the Humanities in a Historical Perspective

Alan Richardson, "The Humanities as Vertically Challenged: A Short History"
Raymond Corbey, "Human Unicity: Primate Research as an Arena for Philosophical Controversies"
Edward Slingerland, "Moving from a Bi-versity to a True University: Prospects and Challenges"

What Is Vertical Integration and Why Should We Care?

Steven Pinker, "The Humanities and Human Nature"
Richard Shweder, "The Metaphysical Realities of the Unphysical Sciences; And Why Vertical Integration Seems So Unreal (and Unsavory) to Ontological Pluralists"
Stephen Stich, "We're All Connected: Science, Ethics and the Law"

Dualism and Our Concept of the Person

Emma Cohen, "Spirit Possession and Folk Dualism"
Rita Astuti, "The Emergence of Dualism in Madagascar: Ethnographic and Experimental Evidence"
Shaun Nichols, "The Folk Psychology of Consciousness"

An Integrated Approach to Ethics

Jesse Prinz, "Emotions and Moral Judgment: A Review of Competing Models"
Herbert Gintis, "Behavioral Ethics: Other-regarding Preferences and Character Virtues"
Dennis Krebs, "The Origin of Morality"

Why Do Humans Have Religion?

David Sloan Wilson, "Evolution and Religion: Toward a Convergence of Previous Disparate Views"
Robert McCauley, "The Importance of Being 'Ernest'"
Harvey Whitehouse, "Explaining Religion"
Ara Norenzayan, "The Coevolution of Religion and Prosociality"

What Is Culture? Cognitive and Evolutionary Approaches

Dan Sperber, "Naturalizing Culture: Two Challenges and One Solution"
Pascal Boyer, "Three Styles of Inquiry in the Study of Culture. Explaining the Current Dismal State of Cultural nthropology"
Bradd Shore, "Culture in General and in Particular: False Dichotomies in Culture Theory"
Darren Irwin, "Culture in Songbirds and Its Contribution Toward the Evolution of New Species"

Approaches to Literature

Brian Boyd, "Naturalistic Literary Theory and Naturalistic Literary Criticism"
Jonathan Gottschall, "Literature, Science, and a New Humanities"
Joseph Carroll, "Graphing Jane Austen—Using Human Nature in Empirical Literary Study"
Michelle Scalise Sugiyama, "Narrative Archaeology: The Oral Tradition as the Record of the Past"
Barbara Dancygier, "Fictional Minds and Storytelling: Blending and the Evolution of Literary Discourse"

List of Participants

Principal Investigators

Edward Slingerland, Asian Studies, University of British Columbia
Joseph Henrich, Psychology and Economics, University of British Columbia

Participants

Rita Astuti, London School of Economics and Political Science
Murat Aydede, Philosophy, University of British Columbia
Pascal Boyer, Psychology and Anthropology, Washington University
Brian Boyd, English, University of Auckland, New Zealand
Stefania Burk, Asian Studies, University of British Columbia
Joseph Carroll, English, University of Missouri, St. Louis
Emma Cohen, Anthropology, Oxford University
Mark Collard, Archaeology, Simon Fraser University
Raymond Corbey, Philosophy, Tilburg University, and Archaeology, Leiden University
Barbara Dancygier, English, University of British Columbia
Herbert Gintis, Economics, University of Massachusetts

Jonathan Gottschall, English, Washington and Jefferson
Steve Heine, Psychology, University of British Columbia
Leslie Heywood, English, State University of New York, Binghamton
Judy Illes, Neurology, University of British Columbia
Darren Irwin, Zoology, University of British Columbia
Dennis Krebs, Psychology, Simon Fraser University
Eric Margolis, Philosophy, University of British Columbia
Robert McCauley, Center for Mind, Brain, and Culture, Emory University
Anne Murphy, Asian Studies, University of British Columbia
Shaun Nichols, Philosophy, University of Arizona
Ara Norenzayan, Psychology, University of British Columbia
Sharalyn Orbaugh, Asian Studies, University of British Columbia
Steven Pinker, Psychology, Harvard University
Jesse Prinz, Philosophy, University of North Carolina, Chapel Hill
Alan Richardson, Philosophy, University of British Columbia
Richard Shweder, Committee on Human Development, University of Chicago
Bradd Shore, Anthropology, Emory University
Dan Sperber, Social and Cognitive Science, Directeur de Recherche au CNRS, Paris
Stephen Stich, Philosophy, Rutgers University
Michelle Scalise Sugiyama, English, University of Oregon
Eric Vatikiotis-Bateson, Linguistics, University of British Columbia
Harvey Whitehouse, Anthropology, Oxford University
David Sloan Wilson, Biological Studies, Binghamton University

INDEX